THE WASHINGTON ANCESTRY

The Washingtons in England
places to visit

Arms of
Selby Abbey

WILLIAM son of Bond
of Washington, Co. Durham

Agnes 1 = WALTER DE WASHINGTON = 2 Lady Julian de Ryal, heiress
seized of lands in Northumberland & Westmoreland in right of first wife, time of King John, Died 1264

ROBERT DE WASHINGTON = Amicia d and heiress of Hugh de Kernegard Lancashire.

Agnes, d and h. of Adam Derling (Agnes le Gentyl) = ROBERT DE WASHINGTON of Kernegard, 1318-19

JOHN DE WASHINGTON of Warton in Lonsdale, Lancs. d. 1386 = Alianora, d. and h. of John de Warton, Lancs.

Joanna = JOHN DE WASHINGTON of Warton wounded at Agincourt 1415

Margaret Lambertson widow = ROBERT DE WASHINGTON of WARTON living 1437-8

John Washington of Warton died 4th May, 1501-2

Robert d. 1517 (Sergeant at Arms to Henry VII and Henry VIII)

Washingtons of Warton, Lancs.

Elizabeth d. of Ralph Westfield of Westfield, Lancs. = ROBERT of TEWITFIELD WARTON

William de Washington held Manor of Washington from Bishop of Durham, at battle of Lewes, 1264 = Alicia, widow of John of Lexington

William de Washington given ½ manor of Helton Fleetham Westmoreland 1277-8

Robert de Washington of Washington d. 1327

Sir William de Washington Lord of Washington 1377-8 (1376 Arms=2 bars and in chief 3 mullets.)

Sir William (Arms Argent 2 bars gules 3 pierced mullets gules = Margaret d. and h. of John de Morville

Sir John Tempest of Studley, Yorks. = Eleanor

Dionysia = Sir William Mallory of Studley in right of wife

Elizabeth = Sir Richard Conyers of Norton Conyers, Justice of Common Pleas d. 1420

JOHN DE WASHINGTON born 1371, went to Durham College, Oxford
1398—Bursar
1407—Sacristan at Durham
1416—Prior
1426—Chairman of Benedictine Chapter retired May 1440
Died 9th April, 1451
ARMS IN STAINED GLASS OF SELBY ABBEY, YORKSHIRE

JOHN WASHINGTON of TEWITFIELD, WARTON = Margaret Kitson of Warton and London

Thomas Kitson Alderman of London

Katherine = Sir John Spencer

from whom are descended Earls Spencer and Sir Winston Churchill

Amée, d. of Robert Pargiter of Greatworth (Died 1564, Brass in Sulgrave Church and Porch added in memory) = LAWRENCE of Gray's Inn, Co. Middx. Mayor of Northampton 1532, 1545 Grant of Sulgrave 1538 died 1583-4 Arms 2 bars and in chief 3 mullets over door of Sulgrave Manor, Northants.

Elizabeth Light (1) of Redway Warcs. = ROBERT died 1619 = Anne Fisher (2) of Hanslope, Bucks.

Lawrence d. 1619 Barrister at law, Gray's Inn Registrar at High Court of Chancery Buried at Maidstone Church

9 other children

LAWRENCE 1568-1616 = Margaret Butler

① Sir William = Anne Villiers ½ sister of Duke of Buckingham

Earls of Dartmouth

④ Rev. LAWRENCE WASHINGTON Rector of Purleigh Essex 1633 Ejected in Civil War 1643 Died 1652 = Amphyllis Twigden of Tring d. 1655

Sir William of Packington, Leics.

(Col.) JOHN 1633-1677 emigrated 1657 from South Cave, Yorks. settled at Bridges Creek on Potomac River and was buried there = Anne Pope

Lawrence born at Tring emigrated to Virginia to join John 1666-7

(Capt.) LAWRENCE of Bridges Creek Virginia d. 1697 = Mildred, d. of Colonel Augustine Warner of Gloucester County

June, d. of Caleb Butler (1) Mar. 20.4.1715 died 24.11.1728 Buried in family vault at Bridges Creek = (Capt.) AUGUSTINE 2nd son b. 1694 buried at Bridges Creek 12.4.1743 = (2) Mary Ball, d. of Col. Ball of Leicester County Virginia

Lawrence = Anne, d. of William Fairfax of Belvoir, Virginia

GEORGE WASHINGTON
b. 1.2.1732 in Virginia
d. 14.12.1799

FIRST PRESIDENT OF THE UNITED STATES OF AMERICA

1776 DECLARATION of INDEPENDENCE

National Society
of the
Sons of the American Revolution

Our Patriots

Acclaim Press
— Your Next Great Book —
P.O. Box 238
Morley, MO 63767
(573) 472-9800
www.acclaimpress.com

Designer: M. Frene Melton
Cover Design: M. Frene Melton

Library of Congress Cataloging-in-Publication Data

National Society of the Sons of the American Revolution: our patriots / by the National Society of the Sons of American Revolution.
p. cm.
Includes index.
ISBN 1-935001-19-1 (alk. paper)
1. Sons of the American Revolution--History. 2. Sons of the American Revolution--Biography. 3. Sons of the American Revolution--Directories. 4. United States--History--Revolution, 1775-1783--Societies, etc. I. Sons of the American Revolution.

E202.4.A56 2009
369'.13--dc22

2009012793

First Printing: 2009
Printed in the United States of America
10 9 8 7 6 5 4 3 2 1

Contents

In Memory

This book is dedicated in memory of those of our number who died in service to this Nation. May our works and deeds be worthy of their great sacrifice.

President's Letter

Dear Compatriots:

Three years ago, we celebrated our 100th anniversary of the Congressional Act chartering the Sons of the American Revolution. In a joint resolution, the United States Congress commended the Sons of the American Revolution for its long and dedicated patriotic service to our nation. I know that each of you is proud of this record. The Sons of the American Revolution is a vibrant, growing organization dedicated to teaching the general public the principles of government founded by our forefathers.

We believe that the United States government—one of the people, by the people, and for the people—is our most prized possession. It is more valuable than our personal property and ranks equal with the value of our life itself. We affirm our belief in our Constitution and have pledged ourselves to defend, promote, honor, celebrate, improve and perpetuate our form of government.

Our patriot ancestors sacrificed all they had, and in some cases, their very lives to secure freedom and independence. Today, we have the opportunity to also act courageously. There are external challenges, of course, but we also face internal challenges, such as apathy, indifference, and complacency, which can contribute to the demise of the United States. We must stand up to these insidious challenges.

The "American Experiment" is unique in many important ways. We are not "just another country." Yet, the internal challenges we face to our nationhood are not unlike those that diminished all the great nations of the past. In order to maintain our precious liberty and continue a position of leadership, we must love the U.S.A. "first and foremost," and work to *educate the public* about the responsibilities of representative democracy.

Our State Societies and Chapters have worked successfully through the years to fulfill outreach education objectives. In particular, our youth programs have become more valuable as the history of our founding fades from the curricula of many schools. Now an Education Director has been added to the Headquarters staff to develop additional programs requiring a more centralized and mass media approach from the National Society.

This book is to be enjoyed as a celebration of our ancestors and their successes; but, keep in mind our obligation to these American heroes and future generations to now keep us a free nation.

David N. Appleby
President General 2008-2009

HISTORY
of the
NATIONAL SOCIETY OF THE SONS OF THE AMERICAN REVOLUTION

Gen. Charles O'Hara surrendering the British Army at Yorktown. Gen. Cornwallis was too ashamed to surrender in person and Gen. Washington decided to accept the surrender from an inferior officer (Oct. 17, 1781).

A Brief History *of the* National Society of the Sons of the American Revolution

by Stephen A. Leishman, Historian General 2008-2009

I would have you day by day fix your eyes upon the greatness of your country, until you are filled with the love of her; and when you are impressed by the spectacle of her glory, reflect that it has been acquired by men who knew their duty and had the courage to do it.
— Pericles

On the 100th anniversary of George Washington's inauguration as the first President of the United States, the "National Society of the Sons of the American Revolution" was founded at Fraunces Tavern in New York City. The date was April 30, 1889. The organization was an outgrowth of two previously established organizations: the "Society of the Sons of the Revolutionary Sires" and the "Sons of the Revolution."

The Society of the Sons of the Revolutionary Sires was founded in 1875 by James Lafayette Cogswell, DDS, in San Francisco, CA, as patriotic fever was running high with the approach of the Centennial Celebration. On July 4, 1876, The Society of the Sons of the Revolutionary Sires participated in a gala parade, with ten real sons attending.

On the east coast, John A. Stevens held a meeting at the New York Historical Society in January 1876 to organize a new society accepting Revolutionary War rank-and-file descendants. In 1883, an interested group of New York City men participated in the local celebration of the 100th anniversary of the evacuation of the city by the British. After the celebration, the group organized into a permanent society known as the Sons of the Revolution. In addition to New York, societies were formed in New Jersey, Massachusetts, Pennsylvania, and in a number of other states.

Steps were taken by the New York Society to form a national society to bind together the various new state societies. The Sons of the Revolution adopted a constitution providing that other state societies be auxiliary branches of the New York Society. In doing this it created a breach that finally resulting in the development of another organization, the Sons of the American Revolution.

On March 7, 1889, the ambitious New Jersey Society adopted a resolution to meet with the societies of other states to organize a National Society. William O. McDowell of Trenton, Josiah C. Pumpelly of Morristown and Major General William Stryker of Trenton were appointed to carry out the resolution. In April a call was sent out inviting delegates to meet at Fraunces Tavern in New York City, at 9 AM on April 30, 1889, to discuss all aspects to organize a national society. On that day, 20 delegates from 13 states, including the original California Society, were present in the famous 'long room' on the second floor for a two-day national convention. After some deliberations, the assembly decided to organize a national society with each state society a member, equal and independent, and the National Society of the Sons of the American Revolution was formed. The first national constitution would follow closely that of the New Jersey Society.

On the second day of this organizing convention General Officers were elected: the Honorable Lucius P. Deming of New Haven, Connecticut, as President General; LT James C. Cresap, USN, of the Maryland Society as Secretary General; James Otis of New York as Treasurer General, and L.L. Tarbell of Massachusetts as Registrar General. Vice President Generals were also elected for 26 states and for the Society in France.

In the course of the winter and spring, 15 new societies were organized. On January 17, 1890, the National Society was incorporated in the State of Connecticut. The first social meeting of the SAR was held at Delmonico's Restaurant in New York City on March 1, 1890, with 110 compatriots present from throughout the United States.

First Congress

The first SAR National Congress was held at the Galt House in Louisville, Kentucky, on May 30, 1890. A refined Constitution and other major issues were decided. Membership required lineal descent from a

Revolutionary Patriot. At this meeting, Compatriot William O. McDowell of the New Jersey Society received the special honor of a parchment certificate of membership, Number 1 in the National Society and Number 1 in the New Jersey Society. This certificate is, now framed, in the possession of the New Jersey Society.

At the third Annual Congress (1892) held in New York, General Horace Porter was elected President General for what became five consecutive terms. Horace Porter graduated from the United States Military Academy at West Point and served with the Union Forces in the Civil War. As a Captain, he was awarded the Medal of Honor for bravery in the Battle of Chickamauga, GA. Later in life, Horace Porter served as U.S. Ambassador to France. At his personal expense he conducted (1899-1905) a successful search for the body of John Paul Jones, who had died in Paris in 1792. He received the Grand Cross Legion of Honor from the French government in 1904.

During the term of President General Edward S. Barrett of the Massachusetts, the French Society was formed in September 16, 1897. In 1918 it became the custom, inaugurated by the French Society, of flying the American flag continuously over the grave of the Marquis de Lafayette in the Picpus Cemetery in Paris. During World War II, German forces respected the tradition and the American flag flew over Lafayette's grave every day. In May 1945 the French Society was reorganized and every year since has participated in a ceremony at the grave of Lafayette.

The original SAR organization was chartered in the State of Connecticut. A national charter was later secured from the United States Congress and signed by Compatriot President Theodore Roosevelt on June 9, 1906, constituting the National Society as a national organization, defining its duties and powers.

An early SAR resolution resulted in the United States Congress passing a law directing the War Department to collect and properly store Revolutionary War Records.

Patriot Graves Registration and Remembrance

The Massachusetts Society initiated a program to suitably mark the graves of Patriots. On October 19, 1894, Compatriot Nathan Appleton, an officer of the Massachusetts Society, placed the first grave marker, an SAR marker on the grave of Marquis General de Lafayette in Paris, France. Two years later, in 1896, a marker was also placed on Benjamin Franklin's grave in Philadelphia. The decade of 1900 to 1910 was a period when the SAR erected hundreds of tablets and monuments to commemorate the deeds and memories of Revolutionary War events and patriots. Many of these memorials were imposing tributes. Today, SAR members seek out Patriot graves to place the SAR marker. Other chapters and societies conduct wreath-laying ceremonies at Patriot graves.

Wreath laying and plaque dedication in the morning of July 4, 2007, to 32 known Patriots buried in Immanuel Episcopal Church on the Green Cemetery in historic New Castle, DE.

The SAR Colors

At the meeting of the 7th Congress (1896) in Richmond, VA, Compatriot Archie Lee Talbot of the Maine Society presented a resolution calling for a tricolor combination as the SAR Colors from the blue and white colors previously used. There was general feeling that the two color flag infringed upon the Colors of the Society of the Cincinnati. The proposal suggested using the complete colors of the Revolutionary Army – blue, buff and white. President General Horace Porter ruled the resolution out of order because it required a Bylaw change. At the 9th Congress (1898) in Morristown, NJ, Compatriot Talbot presented a Bylaw amendment. Congress approved the change to the present tricolors – blue, buff and white.

Our National Headquarters

For many years, the subject of a National Headquarters was discussed at Annual Congress – but no action was taken until 1927. The 38th Congress held in Richmond that year voted to purchase the Norman Williams Mansion and its valuable furnishings at 1227 Sixteenth Street, NW, Washington, DC, for $145,000. It began operating as the National Headquarters on October 1, 1927. The building was sold in 1958 to the National Educational Association and the headquarters moved to the General Patrick Hurley home of 8,000 square feet, located at 2412 Massachusetts Avenue, NW, Washington, DC. The new headquarters opened for business on September 1, 1958. At the February 1977 meeting of the Trustees the sale of the headquarters property to the Ivory Coast government for use as their embassy was authorized.

Temporary headquarters were rented in Alexandria, VA, from June 1977 to January 1979. On May 30, 1978 the 88th Congress met in Louisville, KY, and approved a National Headquarters Acquisition Commission with authority to acquire property for a new headquarters. After careful evaluation, four properties were visited and surveyed. The commission decided to purchase the 14,000 square feet Grand Lodge building located at 1000 South Fourth Street, in Louisville, KY. The actual purchase took place in December 1978 and SAR took possession on January 1, 1979. A special dedication ceremony was held at the National Trustees Meeting in February 1979, with President General Chunn presiding. In 1984, a 1,400 square foot extension was added to the southwest corner of the building to give an improved office arrangement and to provide space for new automation equipment. President General Arthur M. King gifted the $176,000 required for the project. The addition was dedicated at the 95th Annual Congress on June 1, 1985.

By the late 1990s, our Society's essential functions had outgrown the space available in the current building. The Society acquired property adjacent to our current location and began fund raising to build a new library on the property. By 2007 the Building Fund had accumulated over 3 million dollars, when a much better expansion opportunity was recognized. At the Spring 2008 Leadership Meeting, the trustees voted to purchase a building in the museum district of Louisville to be our new headquarters, library and to house the society's expanded outreach education initiatives – The Center for Advancing America's Heritage. The driving forces for this relocation to Louisville's cultural center were the elimination of inefficiencies in operating two separate buildings. The new location promises high foot traffic for our planned educational galleries, and should garner

Current National Headquarters of the SAR located at 1000 South Fourth Street, Louisville, KY.

Office of the President General at Headquarters in Louisville, KY.

significant financial support from the Louisville community.

To assist in the fund raising and financial management effort, the Society formed the SAR Foundation in 2002. Its nine-member Board of Directors is composed of qualified members who are elected by the Annual Congress. The sole purpose of the Foundation is to support the activities of the Sons of the American Revolution and to raise funds for the endowments and building funds.

When you visit the South Fourth Street headquarters you'll see a large, dramatic bust of George Washington displayed in the lobby. This generous gift from the Virginia Society was unveiled at the Spring 1999 Trustees Meeting in commemoration of the bicentennial of the death of George Washington. The late Paul M. Frantz, President of the Virginia Society, proposed making this gift to the National Society, and led the effort to raise the required funds. The original bust was rendered by Avard T. Fairbanks, Ph.D., (1897-1987) in 1975 for our nation's bicentennial. Standing 48 inches high, it is a colossal-size, bronze casting that captures the physical power and strength of Washington's character. It depicts Washington dressed in a jacket with a toll collar and a shirt with ruffled neck. Other bronze castings of this bust are displayed at George Washington University, the Scottish Rite Supreme Council in Washington, DC; the Washington State capitol building in Olympia, Utah State University, and aboard the USS *George Washington* (CVN-73), a gigantic aircraft carrier. Recently, another casting of this bust was made at the request of the Louisiana Society, and is prominently displayed in front of the Louisiana capitol in Baton Rouge.

The Pledge of the SAR

The Pledge of the Sons of the American Revolution, which we repeat at the beginning of each meeting, was written by Harold Putnam and Harold Marshall. It was first adopted by the California Society in 1939 and later adopted by the Trustees of the National Society at Washington, DC, in 1954. The pledge reads as follows:

> **"We descendants of the heroes of the American Revolution who, by their sacrifices, established the United States of America, reaffirm our faith in the principles of liberty and our Constitutional Republic, and solemnly pledge ourselves to defend them against every foe."**

At the 59th Congress in Jacksonville, FL, John W. Finger was elected President General. During this time, his wife, Carol Smith Allen Finger, served as the President General of the Daughters of the American Revolution. This was the only time that a husband and wife were to simultaneously head two national societies commemorating the American Revolution.

Bust of George Washington.

At the 66th Congress at held at the Hotel Sagamore, Lake George, NY, the position of Surgeon General was added to the General Officers.

Notable Compatriots

On September 8, 1971, at the Army and Navy Club in Washington, DC, President Donald Hays of the DC Society presented SAR Membership Certificate # 100,000 to Compatriot C. Tower French. Today, SAR membership rolls are approaching 200,000 Compatriots. Men from all walks of life have joined the SAR, including the following United States Presidents: Rutherford B. Hayes, Benjamin Harrison, William McKinley, Theodore Roosevelt, William Howard Taft, Warren G. Harding, Calvin Coolidge, Herbert Clark Hoover, Franklin Delano Roosevelt, Harry S. Truman, Dwight David Eisenhower, Lyndon Baines Johnson, Gerald R. Ford, James E. Carter, Jr., George Herbert Walker Bush, and George Walker Bush.

President Ulysses S. Grant was a member of our parent organization, the Sons of the Revolutionary War Sires, but died before the Sons of the American Revolution was founded. President Grant would have automatically transferred his membership to the SAR, hence his inclusion in the roster of 17 Compatriot Presidents of the United States.

From the 2008 Presidential election, candidate Senator John S. McCain, III is a member of the Arizona Society. President Barack H. Obama's application has been prepared and is awaiting his signature.

In addition to the U.S. Presidents, six known Medal of Honor recipients have been members of the SAR: Captain Ira Hobart Evans (Founder of the Texas Society) (Civil War); Captain Horace Porter (3rd President General) (Civil War); Lt. Colonel Theodore Roosevelt (26th U.S. President) (Spanish American War); Brigadier General Theodore Roosevelt, Jr., (WW II); General Douglas MacArthur, (WW II); and U.S. Navy Rear Admiral James B. Stockdale (Vietnam).

On June 14, 1946, Fleet Admiral (5 stars) William F. Halsey, II, became a member (National # 67259) of the New Jersey Society. His ancestor, Isaac Halsey, was a Member of the Committee of Safety and paymaster Infantry Troop, Essex County Light Horse. Admiral "Bull" Halsey's flagship, the USS *Missouri* was the site of the signing of the surrender documents by Japan in 1945.

Astronauts Alan B. Shepard, Jr., (National # 103332), a member of the New Hampshire Society, and Charles M. Duke, Jr., (National # 88302), a member of the South Carolina Society, walked on the moon. Numerous Senators and Congressmen have also been members.

In addition, SAR rosters have included such international compatriots as Sir Winston Churchill of England and King Juan Carlos I of Spain. On February 23, 2000, in an elegant room at Blair House, Juan Carlos I, King of Spain, was inducted into the Society by President General Howard Horne. The King was also awarded the Gold Good Citizenship Medal. The King is a direct descendant of Carlos III, who was the reigning monarch of Spain at the time of the American Revolution.

Youth Programs

Throughout the years, the SAR has conducted a number of youth programs and awarded its medals to recognize conspicuous public service and achievement of young adults of high school and college age. The emphasis in recent times has been to make these presentations at the local level in an effort to let the public know about our organization and goals. The programs include the JROTC/ROTC, the essay contest, the oration contest, and recognition of new Eagle Scouts. Each year the national winner in each of these youth activities is recognized at the Monday Youth Awards Luncheon at Congress.

Bronze Good Citizenship medals and JROTC medals are awarded by many chapters and societies in the high schools throughout the U.S. The Silver ROTC medals are awarded only to students in a college or university ROTC unit. The recipients for these awards are selected by the Commanding Officer of the ROTC unit for their high degree of merit with respect to leadership qualities, military bearing and general excellence. The Outstanding Cadet of the Nation receives a gold medallion on a neck ribbon, a gold frame for the ribbon bar and a gold star for wear on the ribbon bar, and a cash award.

The SAR essay contest was originally named in honor of SAR Compatriot President Calvin Coolidge, who won an SAR essay contest while a student at Amherst. In 1995, the contest was renamed the George S. and Stella M. Knight Essay Contest in honor of their generous gift to the SAR to support this youth activity. The contest is open to all high school sophomores, juniors and seniors. Each student must do original research and write an 800 to 1200-word essay in English. The topic of the essay shall deal with: an event, person, philosophy, or ideal associated with the American Revolution, the Declaration of Independence, or the framing of the United States Constitution. The contest is designed to give high school students an opportunity to explore events that shaped American History. A cash award is presented to the top three national winners.

Begun in 1945, the SAR oration contest is open to all students who are in their freshman, sophomore, junior or senior year of study. The contest is designed for students to explore the influence of the Revolutionary

War on present day America. Oration contests are conducted at the local and state levels. The Joseph S. Rumbaugh Oration Contest concludes with a national competition each year at Congress. Here the state winners compete against each other. The top six are chosen and the final competition is held Sunday evening in front of all Congress attendees.

The Arthur M. & Berdena King Eagle Scout Scholarship Contest is open to all Eagle Scouts who are currently registered in an active unit and have not reached their 19th birthday during the year of application. Eagle Scout contestants must be selected from chapter or society competitions. Each applicant is required to complete a two-page application, complete a four-generation ancestor chart, and write a 500-word essay. The top three national winners receive cash scholarships.

Tom and Betty Lawrence American History Teacher Award

Recently, the Tom and Betty Lawrence American History Teacher Award program was created to recognize extraordinary educators at private, public and parochial institutions for actively addressing the history of the American Revolutionary era in their classes. This program is to recognize those who teach our children in middle or high school. The teacher selected for this award receives a trip to Freedoms Foundation Summer Teacher Graduate Workshop at Valley Forge, Pennsylvania. This award, valued at $1,400.00, includes tuition, and expenses.

Recognition and Awards

The Sons of the American Revolution recognizes outstanding citizens for their service to our nation and community from all walks of life. Medals, citations and certificates may be awarded for good citizenship, heroism, academic achievement and exceptional professionalism to students, teachers, firefighters, police, medics, judges, elected officials, military personnel and writers. One award, The SAR Distinguished Patriotic Leadership Certificate, is available to companies and organizations that outwardly promote patriotism and Americanism in the community-at-large.

The SAR Color Guard

Compatriot members in colonial attire have performed civic services since the beginning of the National Society. In the 1980s, State Societies began forming Color Guard units wearing Continental

SAR Color Guard marches in annual Battle Days parade at Point Pleasant, WV.

uniforms. In 1989, President General James R. Westlake called for the formation of a National Color Guard. Today, we see SAR Color Guard units across the country participating in parades on patriotic occasions, naturalization ceremonies, wreath laying and other commemorative services, and at burials of SAR members.

Entering the Electronic Age

In 1985, an expenditure of $90,000 was approved to purchase a computer system for the National Society Headquarters to automate a variety of vital information. In the late 1980s, SAR employee Michael T. Scroggins allowed for his personal email account to be used for Headquarter's business. The sar.org domain was purchased in 1994 and the earliest website was up and running soon thereafter. Today, no fewer than seven districts have their own website, along with seven international societies, 50 US societies (40 states and the District of Columbia) and the ladies auxiliary. The SAR website has made thousands of people aware of our organization and its programs, significantly increased requests for information about SAR and its youth programs, and has made forms, the SAR Handbook, and pamphlets available without cost.

In 1995, Carroll Collins (MD Society) started the use of a 'list server', which allowed members to broadcast e-mail to other members so as to enable the discussion group via e-mail. This became known as SARtalk. SARtalk 'subscribers' are SAR members who have asked to be included in the e-mail discussion of SAR affairs.

George Washington Endowment Fund

At the Spring 1993 Trustees Meeting, the George Washington Endowment Fund was recommended by President General George H. Brandau and approved by President General Charles F. Printz. The purpose of the GWEF was to establish a continuing program for obtaining and distributing funds to support NSSAR committees and special projects. Individuals donating $1,000 or more are recognized as George Washington Fellows. The gifts may be paid in a lump sum amount or in installments of $200 or more annually over a five-year period. Membership as a GW Fellow is not limited to compatriots, but is open to all who support the ideals of SAR. Each person recognized as a Fellow receives a distinctive lapel pin and a certificate denoting his or her status. Today, there are more than 760 Fellows.

In 1999 the Howard F. Horne, Jr. Award was created. This award is presented to the State Society, which has recruited the most new George Washington Fellows as an annual percentage increase of total membership of the State Society within a given year. The first $500 cash award was made in 2000 to the Mississippi Society. By the end of the 2005, a sum of $812,962 was in the permanent endowment fund. Less than two years later, the GWEF reached the $1 million dollar mark. The GWEF was able to distribute $28,300 in support of unfunded and underfunded committees and for special projects in 2008.

George Washington Endowment Fund Lapel Pin.

In honor of Compatriot Walter Buchanan "Buck" Meek, the Walter Buchanan "Buck" Meek Award was created in 2007 to recognize the State Society that has recruited the most new George Washington Fellows during the year. Funding for this award comes from return on investment in the Walter Buchanan "Buck" Meek Endowment Fund. The first "Buck" Meek Award was presented in 2008 to the Georgia Society.

Education Outreach – Center for Advancing America's Heritage

The SAR began responding to changes in American popular culture in the 1990s. Higher education and other institutions including governments had largely stopped promoting Americanism in response to "political correctness" and the pernicious influence of multiculturalism. Consequently, if the United States is to remain a strong, united nation, organizations such as ours must take up the flag and promote assimilation and American unity. Our mission statements, "to inspire members and the community-at-large with a more profound reverence for the principles of government founded by our forefathers," and "to foster true patriotism," demand that we reach out and educate. Consequently in 1995, the National Society officially added a new function

In the lobby of our headquarters building, school children learn about the Liberty Bell from Colleen Wilson, the Center Director..

– that of "outreach education" – and our first Director of Education was added to the Headquarters staff. This position is charged with the responsibility to develop educational programs and content for the Center for Advancing America's Heritage.

Today, there is growing interest in the history of the American Revolution. It should be remembered that the strength and power of this nation rests not so much in the material resources as in the spirit of the people. It was this spirit, and a thirst for freedom, that inspired the creation of our Great Nation by our ancestors. The growth of the SAR has been steady and for the past 118 years the public spirited members have given generously of their time, labor, and means in promoting the objectives. The SAR is a story of a work in progress. Let us continue this enthusiasm into the 22nd Century for the benefit of America's future generations.

Before adjourning a meeting, the presiding officer may ask the members to rise and repeat in unison the SAR Recessional:

> **"Until we meet again, let us remember our obligations to our forefathers who gave us our Constitution, the Bill of Rights, an independent Supreme Court and a nation of free men."**

Sources:

Centennial History of the National Society of the Sons of the American Revolution 1889 – 1989, Turner Publishing Company, Paducah, KY. Copyright 1991 NSSAR Louisville, KY.

The History of the National Society of the Sons of the American Revolution, by John St. Paul, Jr., Historian General and Assisted by Stuart O. Landry. Published by the National Society of the Sons of the American Revolution, Louisville, KY. Originally published in 1962. Copyright in 1962 by Stuart O. Landry. Reprinted in 1982 with permission.

The Sons of the American Revolution, NSSAR History, Volume III, 1983-1999 An Historical Anthology, Edited by Robert F. Jackson, Historian General, and Garrett F. Jackson, Commander NSSAR Color Guard. Published by John Frederick Hopkins Lowewe, CASSAR. Published by the National Society of the Sons of the American Revolution, Louisville, KY. Copyright 2000 NSSAR Louisville, KY.

"King Carlos I of Spain Now A Compatriot," The SAR Magazine, Spring 2000, vol. XCIV, No.4. National Society Sons of the American Revolution. pp 4-5.

The SAR Handbook. Published by the National Society Sons of the American Revolution. October 2008 Edition.

George Washington's Seal Ring

President General Howard L. Hamilton (PG 1982-1983) describes this most valuable National Society possession.

The single most valuable property owned by the National Society of the Sons of the American Revolution is not its Headquarters building nor even it's Permanent Fund. It is a small circular object, about ⅞" in diameter, which rests in darkness, untouched for 364 days of the year, emerging for only one night when a new President General is installed. It shares its space in a thin safety-deposit box with the deed to the Headquarters Building, an insurance policy, some stock certificates, and an affidavit about its own origins. This precious possession is the Seal Ring owned and worn by General George Washington.

Figure 1. Washington's Crest on his Seal Ring.

The ring itself is of gold, with a thin band and delicate shank. It is a perfect size 10 on a modern mandrel. There is no maker's mark or any inscription whatsoever on the inside. On each outer surface, the metal of the shank is deeply incised to give in raised relief a stem, three leaves, and a three-part bud or flower at the top, too worn to identify. The annulus of the crown is oval, surrounding and holding in place the setting of light orange carnelian in which is incised the Washington crest (Figure 1); a shield with three stars at the top and two transverse bands beneath; surmounted by a crown containing a griffin; underlain by a ribbon bearing the Latin words, "Exitus acta probat." These words come from line 85 of the second Heroides of Ovid, and are translated literally as, "The outcome proves the deed." A common variation is, "The ends justifies the means."

A seal made by the Washington ring would now show the griffin facing left and the words of the motto read properly from left to right. The original Washington crest, done in colored glass, could be seen in a window of "what is now the buttery," at Sulgrave Manor, the Washington ancestral home in Northamptonshire, England.[2]

Unusual Box for Ring

Almost as interesting as the ring is its box, which is the original used by General Washington. It is made of varnished wood, possibly birch or fruitwood and measures 3-⅜" wide, 3-9/16" long, and 1-⅞" high. On its cover is a shield, ⅞" long and ¾" wide, inlaid of ivory – much crackled with age. A small brass knob at the front of the lower half controls the catch. (Figure 2).

Inside, the lid is lined with lavender silk, now brown and hanging in shreds. A pin holds a card loosely in place in the top pad, saying, "General Washington's Seal Ring. Statement and Affidavit under bottom pad." The bottom pad is covered with velvet, once lavender, but now faded to brown except around a center post where the ring rests snugly.

The affidavit is also in our lockbox and is preserved flat between two layers of plastic, because it is so fragile and cracked from being folded beneath the bottom pad. It gives the history and line of descent of the ring through the Washington family. Being typed, it is easily read (Figure 3).

Figure 2. Washington's Seal Ring inside its box.

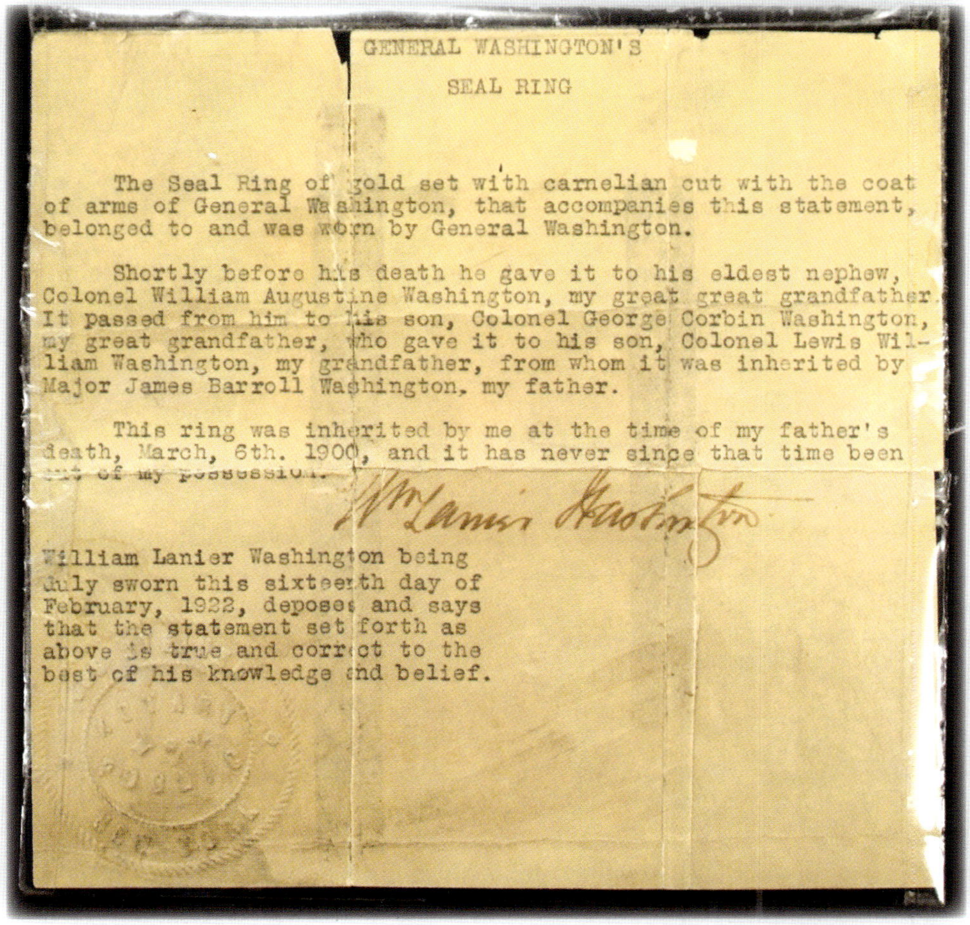
GENERAL WASHINGTON'S

SEAL RING

The Seal Ring of gold set with carnelian cut with the coat of arms of General Washington, that accompanies this statement, belonged to and was worn by General Washington.

Shortly before his death he gave it to his eldest nephew, Colonel William Augustine Washington, my great great grandfather. It passed from him to his son, Colonel George Corbin Washington, my great grandfather, who gave it to his son, Colonel Lewis William Washington, my grandfather, from whom it was inherited by Major James Barroll Washington, my father.

This ring was inherited by me at the time of my father's death, March, 6th. 1900, and it has never since that time been out of my possession.

Wm Lanier Washington

William Lanier Washington being duly sworn this sixteenth day of February, 1922, deposes and says that the statement set forth as above is true and correct to the best of his knowledge and belief.

Figure 3. Photo of Affidavit – General Washington's Seal Ring.

On the rare occasions that the ring is worn, it attracts the greatest of attention and excitement. People look at it with awe and almost reverence. Their greatest wish is to touch it. The ultimate thrill is to be allowed to slip it over the end of a finger and off again. Occasionally there is a skeptic who questions its authenticity despite the affidavit of William Lanier Washington and the great care given to the ring by the National Society since 1922 when it was presented to us. To these we can only give a very unscientific answer: when you put it on your finger and feel that comfortable fit from decades of wear, and see the inner glow of translucent orange radiance from the authentic Washington Seal Ring, you **know** it is real!

President Generals Wear Copies

The current and former President Generals are now permitted to purchase copies of the ring from a franchised jeweler. These are not replicas, for they are different purposely in several respects from the original. Sardonyx, a much darker and more opaque stone, is used for the Seal. There are variations in the gold work and in the carving of the seal. On my copy, the gold work is not as deeply sculptured. The oval Seal is smaller and darker. The griffin has a serpent's tongue and streamlined wings. There is no possibility of confusing the copy with the original.

The value of the Washington ring? Well, that cannot be expressed in terms of money. Who could place a price on such a rare and historic object? Besides, for security reasons, the National Society is not anxious for speculation or publicity on this subject. No amount of money could measure the mystique of this ring or the aura of grandeur, authority and dignity it bestows upon the office of President General.

Footnotes.

[1] Communication from Dr. and Mrs. Arthur F. Stocker. Compatriot Stocker is Chairman of the Department of Classics at the University of Virginia and Past-President of the Thomas Jefferson Chapter, VASAR, Charlottesville.

[2] Footnote from Vol. 1 of Washington Irving's Life of Washington.

Source.

Centennial History of the National Society of the Sons of the American Revolution 1889–1989, Turner Publishing Company, Paducah, KY. Copyright 1991 NSSAR Louisville, KY. Pages 111-112.

Photographs by Bob Gardner.

THE SAR LIBRARY

"When I go into my library, all history unfolds before me." — Alexander Smith

The need to establish a Library for the National Society of the Sons of the American Revolution was recognized by the National Founders, who specified provisions in the Constitution for the acquisition and preservation of Revolutionary War records, documents and artifacts. Between 1889 and 1926 the Society acquired 225 books, which were kept by the Secretary General or Registrar General.

On March 1, 1926 the Society established a Washington, DC (Registrar's General) office at 609 Hill Building on 17th and I Street, N.W. The Library's initial development depended upon the establishment of a Washington, DC Headquarters building in 1927. This office contained the "permanent records of the Society membership and genealogical records and reference library."

The 1927 Congress in Richmond, Virginia approved plans to purchase the Sixteenth Street Headquarters Building. With that came the creation of the first Library Committee. By 1933, the collection was expanded to 914 books. The collection continued to grow over the next few decades.

In 1978, the SAR purchased the current headquarters building in Louisville, Kentucky. Over the next year the second floor of the building was redesigned to accommodate a fully functional library. It officially opened its doors to the public on January 17, 1979 and included a professional staff. In 1988, a 544 square foot book vault was added to the floor space of the library and the collection grew to approximately 25,000 items. During this time the microfiche and microfilm holdings also grew.

Today, the library contains more than 50,000 books, periodicals, journals, microfilm, and microfiche. This includes 8,000 books on the American Revolution, 5,000 family genealogies in hard copy, 8,000 history books, 10,000 volumes of vital statistics, 15,000 rolls of microfilm, and 5,000 family genealogies on microfiche.

In addition to an on-line library search capability, the library computers permit instant access via the Internet to genealogy databases such as Ancestry and Heritage Quest Library Editions and Footnote.com.

The URL for the on-line library search is http://sar.library.net/.

In the early 1990s President General Arthur M. King paid for the construction of the George Washington Room within an original portion of the library as a repository for works about our first President. The room was designed to resemble Washington's study at Mount Vernon.

Libraries are not made; they grow. — *"Book Buying." Obiter Dicta.* Augustine Birrell (1850-1933)

The library serves many genealogy and Revolutionary War era researchers.

Library Collections

The SAR Library has grown in the past 30 years. Today, it has many outstanding collections. These include the George Washington Collection, the Lafayette Collection, the George Rogers Clark Collection, and the John Merz Collection.

The George Washington Collection

George Washington served as a Colonel in the French and Indian War. During the American Revolution he served as the Commanding General of the Continental Army. After the war, George Washington served his newly formed country as its First President (1789-1796).

This collection has been growing since the Society's founding in 1889. In the beginning books and papers were donated to the Society. Many of the books which the library had in 1987 had been obtained from Mr. C. Y. Thomas of Mission Hills, KS in 1980-1981 when Arthur King was President General. PG King encouraged C.Y. Thomas to will his collection to the National Society to form the nucleus of a special collection honoring George Washington. President General Richard Thompson continued to promote the concept of the George

Washington Collection by donating books and soliciting for financial assistance. Several George Washington titles were later given in memory of Richard Thompson. President General Arthur King continued his financial support through 1990 for developing the collection when adequate funds did not materialize as earlier envisioned.

In December 1990 the Society purchased the George Washington Collection belonging to Mr. George Washington Nordham, of Waldwick, NY. Interestingly, Mr. Nordham had been born on February 22 and had built his collection over a period of 35 years. During this time Mr. Nordham also authored nine books and several journal articles about George Washington. The purchase of this collection expanded the collection considerably.

The oldest printed document in the collection is the December 26, 1799 newspaper issue of the *Albany Gazette*. The newspaper contains a poem on the death of George Washington.

Today, the George Washington Collection has grown to a collection of over 84,000 manuscripts, books and journal articles.

In addition to these printed materials, the George Washington Room also contains the Morristown Manuscript Collection. This collection, held on sixty-nine rolls of microfilm, contains 17,500 documents. Over one-third of these documents are made up of manuscripts, journals, account books, letters, etc. relating to the Revolutionary War and George Washington. Another part of the Washington Room is the George Washington Papers Collection. These are held on 124 rolls of microfilm, which contain 64,786 documents dated from 1697 to 1799 relating to George Washington and his family.

George Washington Room in the Library.

The Lafayette Papers

The SAR Library is honored to house one of three collections of the Lafayette Papers in the United States. The other two locations are the Library of Congress in Washington, DC, and Cleveland State University in Cleveland, OH.

In the summer of 2000, President General Howard Horne led an SAR trip to France and took a remarkable gift from the SAR to the cemetery where Lafayette was buried. PG Horne presented two American flags, which had flown over the US Capitol in Washington, DC; one was immediately raised to replace a tattered American flag and the other was held in reserve. During his trip, PG Horne asked the Count de Chambrun, custodian of Lafayette's papers, for a copy of the microfilm reels containing the Marquis de Lafayette's papers. The microfilm reels were on deposit with the US Library of Congress and the Count de Chambrun promptly sent a letter to the Library of Congress authorizing it to provide the SAR a copy of the reels. PG Horne and his wife, Nancy, reimbursed the Library of Congress for the cost of producing the 64 reels of microfilm, and a major collection was secured for the SAR Library.

The Lafayette Papers Collection contain 25,000 documents including, among other things, correspondence between Lafayette and Washington, Thomas Jefferson, James Madison, Ben Franklin and others prominent in the American Revolution. The majority of the documents are in French, with much pertaining to American history in English. A 56-page compilation entitled "A Register of the Microfilm of His Paper in Chateau La Grange" describes the collection. The register is in French and the SAR has undertaken to have it translated into English. The documents may be briefly described as follows:

"Reels 1-45. Series: numbered 1457-1945, n.d. Correspondence and typed transcripts, notes, speeches, memoirs, writings, reports, minutes, legal documents and other matters. They are arranged according to the numerical classification scheme already established for the Lafayette archives. A table of contents describes the contents.

"Reels 46-52, miscellany, 1736-ca. 1990, n.d., Correspondence, typed transcripts, letterbooks, writings, notebooks, accounts, …etc., arranged alphabetically by topic.

"Reels 53-64, Jarnac-Lasteyrie Papers, 1745-1880, n.d. contain correspondence, typed transcripts, diplomatic communications and other official documents, military records, reports…and family papers, arranged alphabetically by name of individual and alphabetically by topic therein.

The George Rogers Clark Collection

George Rogers Clark was an American Revolutionary soldier and frontier leader who led the campaign against the British in the Northwest Territory. He succeeded in capturing the key British strongholds of Kaskaskia, Cahokia, and Vincennes, holding this territory and thereby saving the Illinois and Kentucky region for the colonies.

The George Rogers Clark Papers were filmed in 1991 from original documents at the Virginia State Library and Archives in Richmond. They pertain to the Illinois Regiment of the Virginia State Forces. The collection consists of 13 rolls of microfilm containing approximately 85,000 images of original documents (there is usually more than one document per frame). The documents are dated from January 1778 through November 1834 and are numbered, abstracted, and described by location in a 2080 page compilation. There is a six-volume printed index to the papers (also contained on two microfiche cards) along with abstracts held on seven microfiche cards. The index, completed in 1995, by SAR Librarian General Richard Eugene Wilson, has 97,579 entries for 20,110 documents filmed on the 13 reels.

The John Merz Collection

A collection of notebooks and resource material on the Hessian soldiers who fought during the Revolutionary War (not indexed at this time).

Friends of the SAR Library

The Friends of the SAR Library was organized to help the NSSAR Library raise funds to implement its Collection Development Plan and other goals and programs. The Collection Development Plan lists those books, microforms, etc. needed to fill in and expand the current collections. As specific items are acquired, the Collection Development Plan is updated.

The goal of the Friends of the SAR Library is to raise $250,000 for the Library Endowment Fund. Donations received for the Friends of the SAR Library are distributed as follows: 80% of the donation is deposited into the Library Endowment Fund (a permanent fund for the use of the Library only) and 20% of the donation goes directly to the Special Purpose Operating Fund. Only the income derived from the Endowment Fund is used to further the library programs of the NSSAR Library and to purchase materials and supplies that are not budgeted.

SAR Library Funding Programs

Interest from the Friends of the SAR Library Endowment have been used to purchase two personal computers for the Library reading room, a digital microfilm/fiche reader printer which allows the images to be saved to disk, emailed, or printed. The interest has been used to secure Ancestry and Heritage Quest Library Editions and Footnote.com licenses on the Library personal computers and on the Genealogy Staff's computers.

Membership in the Friends of the SAR Library

Membership in the Friends of the SAR Library is a donation of $25.00 or more. Membership is for a one-year period.

Benjamin Franklin Subscriber Plaque

A donation of $300 or more from an individual, a Chapter, State Society or non-SAR organization will qualify the donor's name or organization to be listed on the special plaque.

NSSAR Library Endowment Fund

Gifts of $500 or more from an individual, organization or estate are recorded on the Library Endowment Plaque.

Robert Morris Benefactor Plaque

One-time contributions of $2,000 or more by an individual or organization will have the donor's name listed on the special plaque with the date of contribution.

Future Library

In the very near future the SAR Headquarters and Library will move to a larger building on West Main Street in Louisville. The Library will increase its size and provide a location for up-to-date historical and genealogical research using today's technology.

"Whoever cares to learn will always find a teacher." — German Proverb

Sources:

"The NSSAR Library – A Real Gem," The SAR Magazine, Spring 1998, vol. XCII, No.4. National Society Sons of the American Revolution. pp 12-13.

The James A. Williams Revolutionary War Era Newspaper Collection

Compatriot James A. Williams was director of the Willmette, IL, Historical Museum from 1961 to 1981, and later Chairman of its Board. He had a great affection for early American newspapers and became a member of the Manuscript Society of America, whose membership is made up of individuals, libraries, and museums collating the history of American Newspapers and manuscripts. When the SAR moved to Louisville, KY, the SAR asked him to develop the SAR museum, and he served ably and well as director from 1981 until his retirement to Oregon in 1995. Upon his death, he willed a valuable collection of American Revolutionary War era newspapers to the SAR museum. This valuable research resource is part of the SAR museum collection.

A few of the newspapers are described below:

Boston Weekly News-Letter, Thursday, August 25, 1768 – news leading up to the Revolutionary War.

The London Chronicle, June 24, 1774. "Olive Branch" petition from the colonies to King George, III, signed by George Washington, Samuel Adams, Roger Sherman, Patrick Henry, and other members of the Continental Congress.

The Pennsylvania Gazette, June 29, 1774. General Gage arrives at Castle William under a discharge of cannon.

The Pennsylvania Gazette, June 28, 1775. Continental Congress appoints George Washington Commander-in-Chief of all Continental troops. An account of the battle of Bunker's Hill and the death of General Joseph Warren.

The Pennsylvania Gazette, November 12, 1775. Address by Governor William Franklin, illegitimate son of Benjamin Franklin, to the Assembly of New Jersey declaiming the actions of the colonists.

The London Gazette Extraordinary, Thursday, October 10, 1776. General Howe invades Long Island.

Dunlop's Pennsylvania Packet or the General Advertiser, Tuesday, July 22, 1777. Announces the opening of Princeton College by President John Witherspoon, a signer of the Declaration of Independence.

The Continental Journal and Weekly Advertiser, Thursday, August 7, 1777. Ft. Ticonderoga abandoned by the Americans.

The New Jersey Gazette, Wednesday, February 4, 1778. General Washington requires all persons residing within 70 miles of Valley Forge to thresh one-half of all their grain for use of his army or will be seized by the Quartermaster.

The Maryland Journal and Baltimore Advertiser, Tuesday, November 30, 1779. Examination of Joseph Galloway, Loyalist, before the House of Commons. Galloway served in the British Army when Washington crossed the Delaware.

New Hampshire Gazette and General Advertiser, Saturday, October 27, 1781. Benedict Arnold escapes to England. Surrender of Cornwallis at Yorktown.

The Salem Gazette, Tuesday, September 7, 1784. Notice of the ratification of the Treaty of Peace.

The Connecticut Gazette, Friday, April 30, 1790. Death of Benjamin Franklin.

Ulster County Gazette, Saturday, January 4, 1800. Death of George Washington.

Old Newspaper Tells of Death of George Washington

by Stephen A. Leishman, Historian General 2008-2009

Our SAR library houses many books on its shelves; but, in a very secure room that is an adjunct of the Library are several valuable historical collections that go largely unnoticed. There is the John H. Merz Collection on Hessian soldiers. Our library is one of three in the nation to have the complete collection of the Lafayette papers. The George Washington Collection is another. The oldest printed document in the collection within this collection is the December 26, 1799 edition of *The Albany Gazette.*

This New York newspaper was printed every Monday and Thursday by Charles R. and George Webster, at their store in the White-House at the Corner of State and Pearl-Streets. The cost of the paper was "Three Dollars per Annum." The paper consists of four pages with advertising on the front and back pages with the news found in the center two pages. Something else interesting too was that the words were spelled the American way versus the English way; e.g., honor instead of honour.

The George Washington Collection consists of thousands of such items as books, manuscripts and microfilms relating to the Patriot that have been accumulated since our Society was formed. A significant portion was selected for acquisition in the late 1980s by Librarian General Dick Wilson, with financing of those acquisitions provided by Former President General Arthur M. King. Everything is stored in the George Washington Room, an adjunct of the NSSAR Library in our headquarters building. Compatriot King funded construction of the room; it is an authentic replica of a portion of Washington's library at Mount Vernon.

The newspaper is important to us because of its date. When George Washington completed his second term as the first President of the United States in 1797, he was weary of the political infighting surrounding the presidency. He longed for retirement and the peace at his beloved Mount Vernon. Unfortunately, his solitude lasted less than three years as he died on December 14, 1799 at age 67. The newspaper was printed 12 days after the President's death and includes news items and tributes to George Washington. December 2008

The Albany Gazette.

[Vol. XVI.] THURSDAY, DECEMBER 26, 1799. [Numb. 1366.]

By CHARLES R. and GEORGE WEBSTER

Fondey and Winne, EARTHEN WARE, TEA BOARDS. The Highest Price in CASH paid for WHEAT, Pot and Pearl ASH, By WILLIAM JAMES. FOR SALE, William Bell, & Co. TEAS for Sale.

Fresh Durham Mustard, A few bbls. Pickled Shad. Just Received, Andrew Brown, & Co. Consignment, John Robison. DUDLEY WALSH.

G. W. & P. PORTER, Caldwell, Van Ingen, and Caldwell. WINES; Teas;

David Bedford, jun. Dry Goods, Groceries, Hard Ware and Crockery, CHEAP Grocery, Paint & Leather STORE. Mounsey & Nexon, HAVE FOR SALE, Jamaica Spirits, Salt, PAINTS,

FOR SALE, By Stewart & Townsend BAR IRON, GROCERIES, TO BE SOLD, By S. DEAN, 8 half pipes first proof WINES, TEAS, Sugar, DANIEL STEEL.

The Thursday, December 26, 1799 edition of The Albany Gazette.

marked the 209th anniversary of George Washington's death. Let's take a step back in history to read what was being written in the newspapers at the time of Washington's death.

In his last official duty in serving the General Washington as his private secretary, Colonel Tobias Lear, V, Esquire, writes to President John Adams residing in Philadelphia.

SIR,

It is with inexpressible grief, that I have to announce to you the death of the great and good General Washington. He died last evening between 10 and 11 o'clock, after a short illness of about twenty-four hours. His disorder was an inflammatory sore-throat which proceeded from a cold, of which his made but little complaint on Friday. On Saturday morning about 3 o'clock he became ill. Doctor Dick, attend him in the morning and Dr. Craik of Alexandria, and Dr. Brown, of Port Tobacco were soon after called in. Every medical assistance was offered, but without the desired effect. His last scene corresponded with the whole tenor of his life. Not a groan nor a complaint escaped him, in extreme distress. With perfect resignation and a full possession of his reason, he closed his well spent life.

I have the honor to be ----
Tobias Lear, Esquire
The President of the United States"

Soon thereafter, the President of the United States, John Adams, issues the following statement:

Gentlemen of the senate, and Gentlemen of the house of representatives.

"The letter herewith transmitted will inform you, that it has pleased Divine Providence to remove from this life, our excellent fellow citizen, *George Washington*, by the purity of his character and a long series of services to his country, rendered illustrious throughout the world. It remains for an affectionate and grateful people; in whose hearts he can never die, to pay suitable honor to his memory.

John Adams
Mount Vernon, December 15, 1799"

Congress of the United States

House of Representatives.
Thursday, December 19, 1799.

Mr. Marshall, with deep sorrow on his countenance, and in a low, pathetic tone of voice, rose and addressed the house as follows:

The melancholy event which was yesterday announced with doubt, has been rendered but too certain. Our Washington is no more – the hero, the sage, and the patriot of American – the man on whom in times of danger every eye was turned, and all hopes were placed, lives now only in his own great actions, and in the hearts of an affectionate and afflicted people...

Let us then, Mr. Speaker, pay the last tribute of respect and affection to our departed friend. Let the grand council of the nation display those sentiments which the nations feels.

For this purpose, I hold in my hand some resolutions which I will take the liberty to offer to the house.

"Resolved, That this house will wait on the President of the United States in condolence of this mournful event,

"Resolved, That the speaker's chair be shrouded with black, and that the members and officers of the house wear black during the session.

"Resolve, That a committee, in conjunction with one from the senate, be appointed to consider on the most suitable manner to paying honor to the memory of the man, first in war, first in peace, and first in the hearts of this country."

Resolved, That this house when it adjourn do adjourn to Monday.

These resolutions were unanimously agreed to. Sixteen members were appointed on the third resolution.

From Philadelphia we are informed as follows:

Philadelphia, Dec. 20

In consequence of the afflicting intelligence of the death of *George Washington*, Mrs. Adams' drawing room is deferred to Friday the 27th, when the Ladies are respectfully requested to wear white, trimmed with black ribbon, black gloves and fan, as token of respect to the memory of the late President of the United States: The Ladies of the officers of the general government will please to wear black."

And in Albany there is this short item.

NEW THEATER

In consequence of the melancholy event lately announced to the public, they are respectfully informed, that the entertainments of the Theater are suspended for the remainder of the week.

Dec 19. Wignell and Reinagle"

Washington was buried on Wednesday, December 18th, according to the rite of the Episcopal Church, with the Rev. Thomas David, Rector of Christ Church, Alexandria, officiating. Masonic rites were also performed by members of his lodge.

Following his death, the American army wore black armbands for 6 months, Napoleon ordered 10 days of mourning throughout France, and the British Navy lowered their flags to half mast.

Martha Washington died at Mount Vernon on May 22, 1802, slightly over two years after her husband.

Historian General Stephen A. Leishman and the Center Director Colleen Wilson look over the 1799 Albany Gazette.

History of West Main Street in the Museum District

(Present Fulton Conway & Co.), Louisville, Kentucky

by J. David Sympson, Historian General (2005 – 2008)

National Society SAR Prepares for the Future

On February 23, 2008, under the leadership of President General Bruce A. Wilcox, the General Officers, Vice President Generals, and the Trustees voted to take the first step pursuant to relocating our National Headquarters to 803-809 West Main Street in Louisville, Kentucky. The new location will provide the necessary space for National Headquarters, as well the future of our outreach education initiative – the Center for Advancing America's Heritage. This historic action required the purchase of the Kentucky Tobacco Company Warehouse and the attached Brandeis & Sanders building, which together are currently referred to as the Fulton Conway Building. The building is located in the West Main Street Preservation District Museum Row, named for the large number of museums located within the area. This article provides a history of the buildings at this new location.

A History of Main Street

The Early Years

The Falls of the Ohio River were a natural obstacle in its course from Pittsburgh to New Orleans, which prompted the founding and settlement of Louisville, Kentucky. Captain Thomas Hutchens made the first survey of the region in 1766. In 1773, Captain William C. Bullitt, under a commission from the College of William and Mary, spent most of the summer surveying, so land could be transferred by the end of the year. Ironically, Bullitt fought to drive Lord Dunmore out of Norfolk during the Battle of Great Bridge on December 9, 1775.

Not to be outdone, the surveyor of Fincastle County (the major portion of the present Commonwealth, which included the site of Louisville), Colonel William Preston, would not recognize Bullitt's survey as being official, and ordered the survey redone in 1774, even though Bullitt's survey was used under the original conveyance. Land claim disputes crowded the dockets of early Kentucky courts.

John Connolly, a staunch Tory for assistance to the Crown during the French and Indian War, received a deed for two thousand acres opposite the falls from Lord Dunmore. In 1774 the land was advertised; however, with the outbreak of the Revolutionary War, little more was accomplished until 1778, with the arrival of Lieutenant Colonel George Rogers Clark, who felt the Crown's land grants were very much out of fashion.

Soon after his arrival on May 27, Colonel Clark established a fort on seven-acre Corn Island, located in the Ohio River, starting at about the present 600 block of West Main Street. The small fort served as a base for the expeditions against British controlled Kaskaskia and Cahokia, both in present-day Illinois, as well as Fort Sackville, which later became the town of Vincennes, Indiana. The Corn Island fort was located on the margin of the most favorite hunting ground of numerous, hostile Indian tribes.

On April 24, 1779, lots were laid off on the Southside mainland along both sides of present-day Main Street (a block from the river's edge), from First to Twelfth Street. In 1779, Fort Nelson, a fort on shore, was constructed between Sixth and Eighth Streets on the north side of Main Street. The fort occupied about an acre of ground; present-day Seventh Street would have passed through its front gate. The fort was named for Virginia Continental Congressman, Thomas Nelson, Jr. The area was dotted with small ponds and stagnant water, giving Louisville the name, "Graveyard of the West." Severe epidemics occurred in 1817 and 1822, which led to the establishment of a Board of Health, in order to safeguard the inhabitants.

After receiving an act of incorporation from the Virginia Legislature in the summer of 1780, the city began two decades of slow, but steady, growth. In 1784 approximately two hundred houses were located along Main Street from First to Twelfth. By May of 1786, all of the riverfront lots had been auctioned off.

John James Audubon

John James Audubon was born in Saint Domingue (now Haiti). His mother died in his early infancy and he was raised by his stepmother, Mrs. Audubon, in Nantes, France, and took a lively interest in birds, nature, drawing and music. In 1803, at the age of 18, he was sent to America, in part to escape conscription into the Emperor Napoleon's army. He lived on the family-owned estate at Mill Grove, near Philadelphia, where he hunted, studied and drew birds, and met his wife, Lucy Bakewell. In September 1807, Audubon moved to Louisville to operate a mercantile store with his partner Ferdinand Rozier. On April 5, 1808, Audubon married

Lucy Bakewell and they returned to Louisville. They lived at the Indian Queen Hotel, located at Fifth and Main Streets, their home for more than two years. On June 12, 1809, the Audubon's first son, Victor Gifford, was born. While in Louisville, Audubon spent a great deal of his time in the woods, observing and drawing birds.

Louisville Flourishes

The city continued to prosper, and by 1813, Main was paved from Third to Sixth. By 1832, there were a total of 161 addresses of property along Main Street, between Fifth and Ninth Streets. This register contained a diverse list of entrepreneurs. However, in that same year, a disastrous February flood was responsible for destroying most of the frame buildings located along the river.

The scale of buildings began to change on Main Street during the 1850s. Hotels began appearing, and wholesale operations moved into the district. On Main, west of Eighth Street, there was a concentration of tobacco companies and warehouses. The decade of the 1860s saw Main Street increase as a wholesale center. During the Civil War, Louisville was supposedly a neutral city, and prospered as a supply depot, largely because of the network of connecting railroads. Immediately after the war, a strong economy supported new construction along the street. In 1864, the first streetcar ran on Main Street.

The Culture of Main Street

In an article entitled, *The Once and Future Main Street,* the author described Louisville's Main Street as it was in 1874. "Once Main Street was Louisville's commercial heart, the place where frock coated merchant princes, bankers, tobacco brokers, distillers, railroad executives, and manufacturers headed every morning after breakfast in their mansions on Walnut, Chestnut and Broadway. It was the destination of the less elegantly attired clerks (the office was an all male world in 1874), of shopkeepers, of the cooks and chambermaids and scullery maids who kept the Galt House and Louisville Hotel functioning smoothly, of the burley teamsters who filled Main Street with the rumble of their heavy wagons hauling goods between the riverfront and warehouses – the only Main Street sound that could match the deep throated whistle of arriving and departing steamboats at the wharf."

A business block was constructed by noted architect John Andrewarta (who also designed Louisville's City Hall) on North Main Street, between Eighth and Ninth, for Samuel Thorner of Cincinnati, according to information in The *Courier Journal* of March 10, 1873. This business block suffered a totally destructive fire on October 17, 1876, according to the *Louisville Commercial.*

Building of Kentucky Tobacco Co. Warehouse (Fulton Conway & Co.) – 803-807 West Main Street

In 1881, W. D. Depauw obtained an indenture with Samuel Thorner, owner of the parcel (Deed Book 237, page 492). Construction started soon after on a building in the style of Modified Renaissance Revival. A strong stylistic impression is created on the first story by ten cast iron columns, identical to the ones on the Fort Nelson building, adjacently located at the corner of Eighth and Main. Nine segmentally arched windows are separated on the second floor by ten wide brick pilasters. Above each window is a panel with a series of corbelled brick dentils which, taken together, constitute the only feature approaching an entablature in appearance.

The Kentucky Tobacco Co. Warehouse (KTCW) is located in the Cast Iron District of West Main Street. Cast iron was developed as a building material by Daniel Badger of New York and first used in Boston in 1842; James Bogardus is credited with the development of these cast iron units, generally imitating classical architecture. Cast iron was cheaper than stone or brick, and mass-produced units could be assembled quickly; consequently, there are some areas where whole streets were comprised of cast iron façades, resembling elaborate masonry buildings. The Soho district in New York City is the only place in the United States with more cast iron façades than Louisville's Main Street. Another area worth mentioning that has a similar concentration of cast iron façades is Portland, Oregon. Cast iron is light and strong, and its load-bearing capacity was such that it allowed taller structures to include wider expanses of glass. Almost coincidental to the expanded use of cast iron for local construction, a glass works in New Albany, Indiana, owned by John Ford and W.A. Depauw (note W. D. Depauw built KTCW), would soon develop the first successful American-made plate glass in 1870.

The cast iron used on Louisville's Main Street was probably manufactured in the Louisville foundries of Merz Architectural Iron Works or Sneed Iron Works. Both were leaders in the manufacturing of cast iron façades, and the Sneed foundry was located at Eighth and Market, the building where "Glassworks" is presently located. Louisville's network of railroads allowed its foundries to make cast iron available nationally.

The Kentucky Tobacco Co. Warehouse was built for the storage of tobacco hogsheads, which is a large wooden barrel used in America since colonial times to store and transport tobacco. By 1760 a standardized hogshead measured 48 inches long and 30 inches in diameter at the head. Fully packed with tobacco, it weighed about 1000 pounds. In all probability Main Street's earliest formation was actually as a tobacco road, where hogsheads of tobacco were rolled to the warehouses, thus packing down the primitive dirt road.

The warehouse was occupied in the early years by a variety of tobacco brokers. Soon after the start of the Twentieth Century, its use had switched to grocery and coffee storage. During the years surrounding the start of the Great Depression, it remained vacant. In 1936, A. J. Whitley purchased the building, and relocated Fulton Conway & Co., an automobile accessories business, from a location a few doors west on Main Street. His grandson, Whitley Courtenay, eventually purchased the business.

Tobacco Warehouses

West Main Street, from Eighth to Twelfth Streets, was lined with tobacco warehouses. The 1905 city directory lists 14 tobacco warehouses on West Main, from the KTCW at 805 W. Main to the United Dark Warehouse at 1116 W. Main, plus one at the corner of Ninth of Main, for a total of 15. While many of the tobacco warehouses were built prior to the approximate 1881 construction of KTCW, one might question the long-range planning of W. D. Depauw. The initial hogshead system of tobacco storage and sale had gradually given way in Virginia to the sale of loose-leaf tobacco by auction. In 1849 the Virginia Code recognized these methods, in lieu of the sale of hogsheads of the leaf, as provided in the 1730 Act. By 1865, the tobacco auction had completely replaced the earlier marketing techniques in Virginia (*Tobacco Institute, Virginia, 1971: 28-29*). While other states later followed suit, the tobacco industry conversion to the loose-leaf storing and selling procedures eliminated the necessity for an extremely heavy load supporting building such as the KTCW. This is probably the explanation for the building's not being restored to four floors after the Cyclone of 1890, and subsequently was only used for storage of tobacco for a little over 20 years.

Building of Brandeis & Sanders, a cotton warehouse (Fulton Conway & Co.) – 809 West Main Street

The earliest reference to the building appears in the *Louisville Commercial* account of the fire of 1876. The fire reached the rear portions of the structure, but the flames were quickly controlled and the damage was considered negligible. The building was originally a four-story structure of cast iron and stone facing. A somewhat open cast iron ground floor consisted of four attenuated pilasters supporting the cornice. The additional floors were adorned with Renaissance-inspired windows. While Kentucky was not a cotton growing state, the Brandeis & Sanders building is a testament to the importance of the Ohio River for transportation, and Louisville as a distribution point, for the southern cotton commodity trade.

Cyclone of March 27, 1890

On March 27, 1890, at 8:30 p.m., a class four cyclone hit Louisville. The storm entered from the southwest and swept over the West End including West Main Street. The storm is still listed in the top 25 cyclones (tornadoes) resulting in deaths in the United States, with 76 reported deaths in Louisville alone. The damage included the 800 block of West Main Street, and the Kentucky Tobacco Warehouse was "completely wrecked with the exception of a part of the front and back walls," according to an article in *Louisville Commercial* of March 29, 1890. The top two floors previously mentioned were never reconstructed. The Brandeis & Sanders building was "a heavy suffer with its warehouse completely wrecked," as reported in the *Louisville Commercial* article. It is evident the latter structure was reconstructed to its original height from Main Street photographs appearing in the *Courier-Journal*, April 25, 1921, edition.

National Society Sons of the American Revolution, 1st Congress, April 30, 1890

A little more than a month later from the evening of what became known as "That Awful Cyclone," the first NSSAR Congress was held in the Galt House Hotel, located at First and Main Streets, about eight blocks from the Kentucky Tobacco Warehouse and the Brandeis & Sanders building. The Galt House apparently suffered little or no damage.

The Great 1937 Flood

The Ohio River Flood of 1937 took place in late January and February, with damage stretching from Pittsburgh to Cairo, Illinois. Approximately a million people were left homeless, with 385 dead, and property losses reaching $500 million. By January 27, the water level reached 57 feet (normal is less than 13 feet) in the Louisville area, setting a new record; 70 percent of the city was under water at that time. Actually, since Main Street is situated on the top edge of the river bank, it was slightly higher than areas farther inland. Main Street at Fourth was above water. A. J. Whitley had just within the previous year moved the Fulton Conway business into its present location. Present owner, Whitley Courtenay, stated in an interview at the University of Louisville Oral History Center, that his grandfather said, "The water completely filled the basement, and a small amount entered a low point in the floor in the rear of the building, with Main Street remaining dry. We were forced to evacuate the premises during the flood, and upon returning it was discovered that the building had been entered, and parts were taken; however, a very complete list was left by a government agency for reimbursement."

1937 Fire, Brandeis & Sanders Building

Shortly after the flood receded, the Brandeis & Sanders Building caught fire, reducing the building to one floor, leaving the second floor with a false-front façade. A few years later, A. J. Whitley decided to buy the building from the insurance company and add it to his adjacent building, the Fulton Conway. While in the process of repairing the fire damage, it was discovered that a defective flue from the Fulton Conway boilers had caused the fire.

NSSAR Prepares for the Future

Soon the name on the building will reflect its new occupants: Headquarters of the Sons of the American Revolution. Within its walls will be the headquarters, an enlarged area for the genealogical and Revolutionary War era library, and our outreach education – the Center for Advancing America's Heritage. The Center will also include a Museum Store which will coordinate historical based items available to visitors with exhibits desplayed in the gallery. These items will also be available to our membership through the online catalog (http://store.sar.org). This will enhance the visitor's experience and provide lasting memories of their visit to the Center for Advancing America's Heritage.

Sources.

Kentucky Historic Resources Inventory JC-LC 40

National Register of Historic Places Inventory, 3/22/1974

West Main Street Preservation District Designation Report, 1/31/1977

The Encyclopedia of Louisville

Edited and picture added by Stephen A. Leishman, Historian General 2008-09.

Architectural renderings of the new SAR Center for Advancing America's Heritage on West Main Street, Louisville, KY. Courtesy of Architection.

Atrium.

Center for Advancing America's Heritage front.

NSSAR Genealogy Library.

Rooftop Terrace.

NSSAR Congressional Charter signed by Compatriot United States President Theodore Roosevelt on June 9, 1906.

(L to R) 4th Continental Artillery gunner in regulation uniform with artillery accoutrements, 4th Massachusetts Infantry soldier, Molly Pitcher, real name Mary McCauley, earned the title "Heroine of the Artillery Forces" and was made a noncommissioned officer for her bravery by George Washington.

English Six-Pound Bronze Revolutionary War Cannon

Bears the monogram 3 G.R., an English Crown, "L" in relief on top, and "W. Bowen, fecit, 1761" in relief around the breech. Cannons were used to provide protection during troop deployment and to make way for the advancement of troops by firing upon enemy formations. This approximately 600-pound cannon used round shot, grape, and case shot. On load from the Pennsylvania Society of the Sons of the American Revolution.

English Three-Pound Brass Revolutionary War Cannon

Inscribed "Surrendered by the convention of Saratoga Oct 17 1777." "I & P Verbruggen Fecerunt 1776" in relief around the breech. Each cannon, weighing approximately 200 pounds, was manned by two gunners, six soldiers and four artillery officers. Horses or oxen, with hired civilian drivers, transported the guns. On loan from the Pennsylvania Society of the Sons of the American Revolution.

Cap'n Sam's Long Rifle

"Free Born"

Gunsmith: Adam Haymaker, circa 1770
Reproduction Gunsmith: Peter Alexander, 2004

Adam Haymaker manufactured firearms in and around Winchester (Frederick County), Virginia from 1753 to 1804. It is believed this style 18th century southern rifle was carried into battle on October 7, 1780 at Kings Mountain, South Carolina by Captain Samuel Johnson, Wilkes/Surry County Militia, North Carolina.

President George Washington on a ceremonial barge on his way to New York City to be inaugurated in 1788.

Society of the Sons of the American Revolution

THIS · CERTIFIES · THAT

Rev. Samuel Goodale

IS A MEMBER OF THE

NEBRASKA

Society of the Sons of the American Revolution.

·Date of admission· August · 2 · 1895·

President General

Secretary General

Registrar General

State President

State Secretary

State Registrar

National No. 4633

State No. 33

The SAR Membership Certificate for Rev. Samuel Goodale.

A view of the South part of Lexington.

The Battle of Lexintgon, 1775.

A view of the town of Concord.

The Engagement at the North Bridge in Concord.

Replica of the Liberty Bell dedicated on February 20, 1982 at National Headquarters. This exact replica has visited 30 states and was viewed by 1,500,000 people while on tour under the direction of Compatriot Joseph B. Head and his wife, Leona May, during the years of 1976-1980.

Replica of John Trumball's "Signing of the Declaration of Independence" by Thomas Pelham Curtis.

The Story Behind the SAR Badge

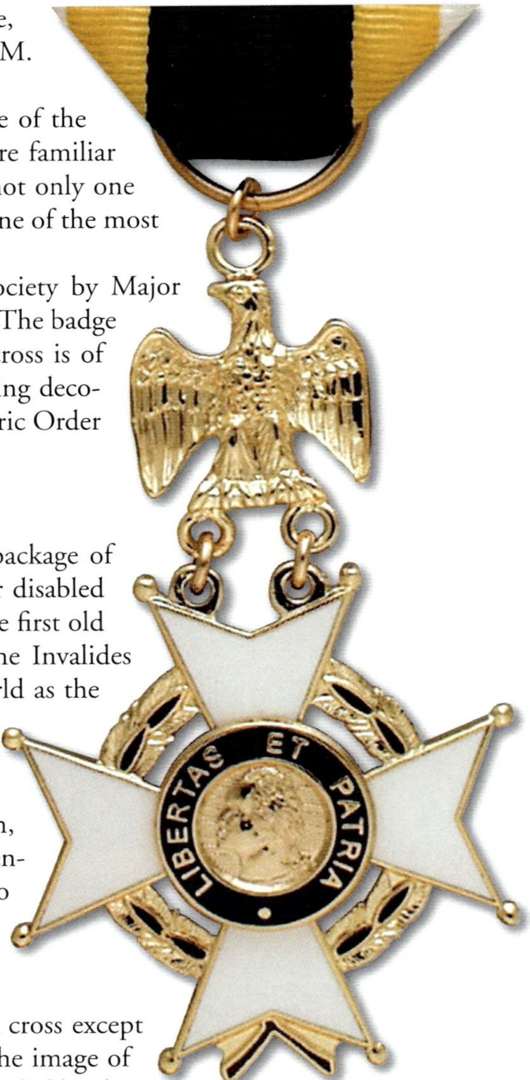

Our membership badge is steeped in historical significance, as related in this scholarly account by Compatriot Duane L. C. M. Galles.

Most Compatriots are familiar with the Membership Badge of the Society of the Sons of the American Revolution. Few perhaps are familiar with the history and significance that underlie it. The badge is not only one of the most beautiful of American Hereditary societies, it is also one of the most steeped with history and replete with significance.

The Badge was designed in the very early days of the Society by Major Goldsmith Bernard West, Vice-President of the Alabama Society. The badge consists of a cross of eight points suspended by an eagle. The cross is of white enamel and has four arms and eight points, each point being decorated with a gold head. Its source is the cross of the ancient chivalric Order of St. Louis, founded by Louis XIV in 1693.

Why the Order of St. Louis?

The royal and military Order of St. Louis was part of a package of war veterans' benefits decreed by the Sun King at that time. For disabled or needy war veterans, Louis founded the Hotel des Invalides, the first old soldiers' home of the modern era. Its chapel, the Church of the Invalides designed by Hardouin-Mansart, is today known around the world as the magnificent baroque interpretations of Michelangelo's St. Peter's and as the final resting place of Napoleon. To reward officers for distinguished service and merit Louis established the Order of St. Louis. The Order was named after his namesake and patron, Louis IX, saint crusader and king of France. It was also richly endowed so that a member received not only a decoration but also a pension. These varied depending on grade and seniority and ranged from 800 to 6,000 livres a year. In addition, a member was exempt from certain taxes.

The cross of the Order of St. Louis is identical to the SAR cross except in three details. The central medallion of the SAR badge bears the image of Washington rather than that of St. Louis; the medallion is surrounded by the SAR; motto "Libertas et Patria: (Liberty and Country) rather than the military order's motto "Bellicae Virtutis Praemium" (the Reward for Virtue is War); and the angles between the arms of the cross lack the French fleurs de lis. Instead, the SAR surrounds the cross with the Laurel wreath of republican victory.

French Aid Influential

Several reasons made the St. Louis cross an appropriate pattern for the SAR badge. The Grand Master of the Order of St. Louis, Louis XVI, lent the American rebels material and diplomatic aid, which was indispensable for the defeat of the British. Moreover, a great many of the French officers who fought for the Patriot cause were chevaliers of the Order. Beyond that the Order of St. Louis had had a significant presence in North America. During the French Colonial period something like 300 chevaliers of St. Louis saw service in North America. Hence, it was in recognition of the decisive aid of France and the significant presence of the Order in North America that the SAR chose the St. Louis cross as a pattern for its own.

But the adoption of the cross of St. Louis was appropriate for other reasons, too. The Order of St. Louis was the first order of military merit. Earlier orders, like the Order of St. John of Jerusalem and the Order of the Garter were crusading or chivalric orders. They were open to members of the nobility ready to undertake deeds of religion or chivalry. But those deeds were international in scope; all Christendom was to be the beneficiary of the knight's good deeds. By contrast, the Order of St. Louis was established to reward military service to one's own country and it was the first to do so. Since the SAR has as its purpose to remember and recognize the military service of their Revolutionary War ancestors to their country, the adoption of the St. Louis cross seemed most apropos.

Legion of Honour Influence

The laurel wreath is significant, for it is derived from another French order, the Legion of Honour. Instituted by Napoleon shortly after his advent to power, the Legion of Honour was intended to fill a vacuum left by the disappearance of the old royal orders during the Revolution. Napoleon, like Louis XIV before him, recognized the importance of rewarding faithful public service and recognizing merit. Hence, he instituted the Legion of Honour, which to this day remains one of the most prestigious orders of merit in the world. Napoleon's order however differed from the old royal orders. Those either presupposed or conferred nobility. They were inextricably linked to the caste system. But with the Legion of Honour came a new basis for reward – personal merit rather than birth. Thus, it will not be surprising that the SAR badge is consciously modeled on that of the Legion of Honour. The laurel wreath is borrowed from the Legion of Honour. Even the size of the badge is designed to be exactly that of the Legion of Honour. But the badge refuses to follow the Legion of Honour in all respects. Unlike the Legion of Honour cross which as five arms, the SAR cross resolutely retains the four arms of eh cross of Christ. This is as if to declare that the excesses of deism and atheism of the French Revolution are to be eschewed by an American Patriotic society; American is a nation under God.

Eagle Denotes Patriotism

Distinctly American also is the eagle which suspends the cross. Badges of European orders had used a trophy (a war helmet), a wreath, or a gold loop. These symbolized their chivalric purpose. But the purpose of the SAR was not chivalry, but patriotism. Hence, the SAR appropriately adopted the eagle which the Cincinnati had previous selected for their badge. The SAR was conceived as a society of the Cincinnati, open to all sons of Revolutionary sires without regard to primogeniture. The choice produced a uniquely American badge.

Bibliography.

National Society of the Sons of the American Revolution, *Historical Notes* (New York, 1890) pp. 39-40.

Aegidus Fauteux, *Les Chevaliers de Saint Louis en Canada* (Montreal, 1940)

H. Gourdon de Genouillac, *Nouveau Dictionnaire des orders de chevalerie* (Paris, 1891)

Hanson, *An Accurate Historical Account of All the Orders of Knighthood at Present Existing in Europe* (London, n.d.)

Paul Hieronymussen, *Orders and Decorations of Europe* (New York, 1967)

When this article was first printed Compatriot Galles was Vice-President of the Minnesota Society. He also served as President of the Minneapolis Chapter. He holds a Bachelor of Arts Degree from George Washington University, Master of Arts from the University of Minnesota and Doctor of Jurisprudence from the William Mitchell College of Law. He has also studied at the University of Edinburgh and the University of Toronto.

Source.

Centennial History of the National Society of the Sons of the American Revolution 1889 – 1989, Turner Publishing Company, Paducah, KY. Copyright 1991 NSSAR Louisville, KY. Page 110.

THE NATIONAL SOCIETY AWARDS

The awarding of medals and awards is always given very careful and serious deliberation in order to determine that the proposed recipient who qualifies is deserving, and the occasion for presentation is appropriate. It is essential that the integrity of NSSAR medals and awards be maintained.

There are a number of medals and awards presented each year. Listed below are four: the prestigious Minuteman Award for members only, the Gold Good Citizenship Medal which is awarded to both members and non-members, The Distinguished Patriot Award is presented to individuals and The Distinguished Patriot Leadership Award is presented to companies and organizations.

Minuteman Award

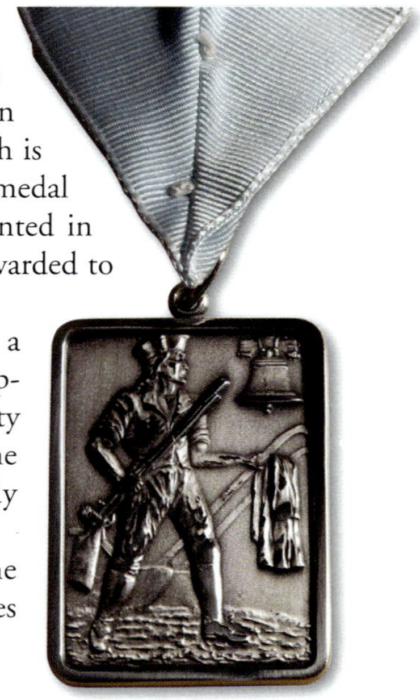

The Minuteman Award is the highest award presented to a member by the National Society. It is presented for distinguished service rendered to the SAR on the national level. Members are selected by the Minuteman Committee, which is appointed by the President General from previous recipients of the medal. The medal is presented by the President General at an Annual Congress. It is not presented in absentia. It was authorized in 1952 and beginning in 1968 the medal is not awarded to more than six recipients per year.

The medal is rectangular in shape, struck in sterling silver. It depicts a Minuteman holding a rifle with a plow in the background. The Liberty Bell appears on it also. On the reverse is inscribed "Highest Award of the National Society Sons of the American Revolution. Presented to (National Number, Year)." The medal is worn suspended from a neck ribbon of light blue silk. It is awarded only to individual members on a one-time basis.

Listed below is a complete list of those compatriots who have received the Minuteman Award. The list is divided into year groups and compatriots names are listed in alphabetical order in each year group.

1952

John H. Babb	IL Society
Wheaton H. Brewer	CA Society
Arthur de la Houssaye	LA Society
Ray O. Edwards	FL Society
H. Ragland Eubank	VA Society
A. Herbert Foreman	VA Society
William Rea Furlong	DC Society
John R. Gobble	ID Society
Wallace C. Hall	MI Society
Douglass G. High	OH Society
Milton M. Lory	IA Society
H. Lewis Mathewson	CA Society
Arthur M. McCrillis	RI Society
Mason E. Mitchell	AR Society
Allen L. Oliver	MO Society
Benjamin H. Powell, III	TX Society
Harold L. Putnam	CA Society
Louis F. Ridgway	OH Society
George S. Robertson	MD Society
Howard C. Rowley	CA Society
Aaron M. Sargent	CA Society
Harry E. Sherwin	NH Society
Clarence E. Shriner	OH Society
Lewis A. Smith	WA Society
Harry K. Torrey	ME Society
Edgar Williamson, Jr.	NJ Society

1953

Clarence A. Cook	IN Society
John W. Finger	NY Society
Edward M. Hall	OH Society
Folks Hanford	GA Society
Messmore Kendall	NY Society
S. Denmead Kolb	MD Society
James Francis Miller	KY Society
Sterling F. Mutz	NE Society
Randolph F. Sellers	OH Society
Robert H. Smith	AL Society
Loren E. Souers	OH Society
James D. Watson	GA Society
Oliver B. Wight	MD Society

1954

William S. Bennet	NY Society
Howard E. Coe	CT Society
Charles E. J. Gilbert	TX Society
Stanley S. Gillam	MN Society
J. B. Ladd	MN Society
Robert H. McNeill	DC Society
Herschel S. Murphy	NJ Society
Charles P. Summerall	SC Society

1955

William T. Carpenter	AL Society
Eugene P. Carver	MA Society
Redmond S. Cole	OK Society
Charles Burke Elder	IL Society
John A. Fritchey	PA Society
Edwin B. Graham	PA Society
Stuart O. Landry	LA Society
Gardner Osborn	NY Society
Crawford S. Rogers	VA Society
Walter A. Wentworth	NY Society

1956

Arthur F. Cole	NJ Society
Charles A. Jones	OH Society
John E. King	IL Society
Charles Ostrom	CA Society

1957

Cyril E. Cain	MS Society
Stanton T. Lawrence	NJ Society
Warren M. Taylor	OH Society

1958

William F. Bulkley	UT Society
John E. Dickinson	WI Society
Jean A. Hibbard	WA Society
F. W. Huntington	TX Society
Augustus M. Roan	GA Society
Mott R. Sawyers	MN Society
Samuel Hubbard Scott	OH Society
George E. Tarbox, Jr.	CO Society

1959

John G. Ballord	MN Society
Franklin Blackstone	PA Society
Robert P. Gordon	AL Society
Albert W. Hawkes	NJ Society
Stephen C. Luce, Jr.	MA Society
T. Earl Pardoe	UT Society
Arthur G. Trimble	PA Society
Robert P. Waters	VA Society

1960

James G. Cecil	IN Society
Horace Y. Kitchell	MS Society
Edward W. Milligan	CO Society
Reginald H. Runge	NY Society

1961

Calvin C. Bolles	CT Society
Frank L. Lowmaster	MI Society
Harold I. Meyer	IL Society
John J. St. Paul, Jr.	LA Society

1962

Charles A. Anderson	OH Society
Ross K. Cook	NJ Society
Samuel K. Houston	OH Society
John F. Lanier	FL Society
Chester R. Martin	RI Society

Augustin G. Rudd — NY Society
Robert S. W. Walker — DC Society

1963
Harry T. Burn — TN Society
George A. Davis — ME Society
J. Boyd Davis — OH Society
Austin R. Drew — FL Society
Louis J. Heizmann — PA Society
Jedediah H. Hills — TX Society
William Y. Pryor — NJ Society
Donald G. Snider — LA Society
Stuart H. Tucker — RI Society

1964
Harry F. Morse — CT Society
William F. Turrentine — KS Society

1965
Donald C. Little — KS Society
W. Giles Parker — MD Society
Herbert C. Roberts — FL Society
Robert L. Sonfield — TX Society
Lynn D. Sprankle — DE Society
Walter G. Sterling — TX Society

1966
Marion H. Crawmer — MI Society
George D. Deyo — NJ Society
Allen R. Foster — DC Society
Horace R. McDowell — NM Society
Lee Young Smith — IL Society
William E. Springer — AZ Society
Earle L. Whittington — TN Society
Edwin A. Williams — CO Society
John C. Wroe — MA Society

1967
Herman R. Carson — IN Society
James B. Gardiner — NY Society
Floyd G. Hoenstine — PA Society
A. Jackson Lawrence — OK Society
Walter R. Martin — RI Society
Kenneth G. Smith — PA Society
Hugh M. Wilkinson — LA Society

1968
Neil A. Cameron — MI Society
Eugene C. McGuire — OH Society
Ryall S. Morgan — AL Society
Grahame T. Smallwood — DC Society
Warren S. Woodward — NY Society

1969
S. Neil Arrington — NJ Society
J. Merle Brallier — PA Society
Thomas McEwan — IL Society
Martin I. Stutler — WV Society
Chester A. Walworth — WV Society

1970
Donald W. Baldwin — VA Society
Fred M. Davis — VA Society
Guy L. V. Emerson — CO Society
Robert D. Savage — PA Society
O. M. Wilson, Jr. — TN Society

1971
Roy V. Barnes, Sr. — MI Society
Calvin C. Bolles — CT Society
James A. DeWeerd — IN Society
Donald R. Fraser — MS Society
Robert G. Luckey — NM Society
Harry S. Schanck — NY Society

1972
John H. Bell, DDS — PA Society
Marshall E. Miller — IN Society

1973
Darall G. Hawk — OK Society
Joseph B. Head — MN Society
Vincent Van Inwegen — NJ Society

1974
W. Clark Erwin — SC Society
Carl K. Hoffmann — FL Society
Ralph M. Pabst — AZ Society
Willis G. Tetrick — WV Society

1975
M. Graham Clark — MO Society
Thomas T. Currie — TX Society
Lynn S. Gordon — MI Society
Joseph X. Harris — MD Society
Donald E. Lathrop — PA Society

1976
Neill F. Amsler, Jr. — TX Society
Leslie A. Bryan — IL Society
Richard E. Crane — NJ Society
Webb W. Wilder — RI Society

1977
Jack K. Carmichael — IN Society
Benjamin P. Garrison — OK Society
Fred T. Leathers — PA Society
Harold E. Wilmoth — MD Society

1978
Wilson King Barnes — MD Society
Ronald O. Baymiller — WI Society
Robert Warburton Miller — CA Society
Matthew B. Sellers — FL Society

1979
Carl Francis Bessent — MD Society
Calvin Ellsworth Chunn — CA Society
Arthur Mansfield King — KS Society
Gradie R. Rowntree — KY Society
Richard Thompson, Jr. — FL Society

1980
Alexander Hamilton — ME Society
James B. Hoge — OR Society
Frank W. Kinnamon — DE Society
Winston C. Williams — WI Society
Albert C. Wirth — NC Society

1981
Tullius Brady — MS Society
Clovis H. Brakebill — TX Society
Carleton E. Fisher — FL Society
Cecil W. Grange — IL Society
Howard L. Hamilton — VA Society
John R. Naisby — NJ Society

1982
Augustus di Zerega — KS Society
O. D. Fontenot — LA Society
Warren G. Hayes, Jr. — PA Society
G. Arthur Luther — IA Society
John C. Mowbray — NV Society

1983
Richard F. Boddie — NC Society
P. Harry Byerly — DC Society
James G. McGrew — CO Society
Joseph W. McLark — CA Society
Asa E. Phillips, Jr. — MA Society
Richard E. Willson — IL Society

1984
Samuel J. Holt — OH Society
A. Peter N. McArthur — WI Society
John L. McConnell — AL Society
Benjamin Hume Morris — KY Society
Oliver Rollin Smith — UT Society

1985
John Hallberg Jones — MN Society
Judson P. Mason — VA Society
Albert A. Remington, III — RI Society
Gordon P. Tierney — IL Society
Harry L. Walen — MA Society
William B. Worthy — SC Society

1986
C. Norman Flanders — AZ Society
Royce N. Kent — NZ Society
Charles W. Overton — AR Society
Charles F. Printz — WV Society
James A. Williams — IL Society

1987
Timothy R. Bennett — DC Society
Robert Eugene Burt — KS Society
Nolan W. Carson — OH Society
Wendell R. Lovering — NY Society
John L. Ruby — MI Society
J. King B. E. Seegar, Jr. — MD Society

1988
James R. Calhoun — NM Society
James J. Hamm — IL Society
George S. Knight — VA Society
Stewart B. McCarty, Jr. — DC Society
William H. Roddis — WI Society
Robert B. Vance, Sr. — GA Society

1989
Raymond M. Henshaw — CT Society
Burton L. Showers — IL Society
Charles A. Vencill — CA Society
Robert G. Webb — OH Society
James R. Westlake — GA Society
Claude L. Withers — KS Society

1990
Wilson King Barnes, Jr. — MD Society
George H. Brandau — TX Society
William C. Gist, Jr. — KY Society
James G. Harrison — MS Society
Donald J. Pennell — MI Society
Homer E. Wright — GA Society

1991
Duane L. C. M. Gallas — MN Society
Edward S. Hoyt — FL Society
Luther C. Leavitt, Jr. — OH Society
Conrad P. Mook — VA Society
Carl A. Nissen, Jr. — FL Society
Kenneth J. Petro — IN Society

1992
Lee Walace Derrer — SC Society
William R. Eddleman — TX Society
Richard Edward Friberg — FL Society
William Harry Lees — IA Society
Lee Duncan Stokes — KY Society
Paul Howard Walker — MA Society

1993
Philip W. Bernstorf — KS Society
Thomas J. Bond, Jr. — DC Society
McCarthy DeMere — TN Society
Grant Vansice Harrison — VA Society
William M. Melone — AZ Society
Charles B. Schweizer — IL Society

1994
Billy E. Hightower — TX Society
Hardwick Johnson, Jr. — GA Society
Chester E. May — OH Society
Donald N. Moran — CA Society
George Nelson Sells — NM Society
James A. Shelby — MO Society

1995
William T. Algood — SC Society
Bruce B. Butler — LA Society
Lester R. Dunham — NJ Society
Horace R. Jordan — AL Society
Barrett L. McKown — MD Society
Vance E. Senter — WA Society

1996
Delbert M. Fowler — TX Society
Reon G. Hillegass, Jr. — VA Society
Howard F. Horne, Jr. — DE Society

Fred O. Jeffries, Jr.	WY Society
Richard F. Locke, Jr.	CA Society
John F. Newell	AZ Society

1997

Larry L. Blackett	MI Society
David J. Gray	MA Society
Lawrence L. Loker	MO Society
Larry D. McClanahan	TN Society
Russell D. Page	IL Society
Richard G. Sauner	VA Society

1998

Herrick H. Kesler	KS Society
Marshall Lignian	PA Society
George W. Orton	AZ Society
Duane T. Sargisson	MA Society
Bert E. Sells	OH Society
Raymond Zimmerman	MD Society

1999

Charles W. Britton	OK Society
Peter Arrott Dixon	DC Society
Stanley A. Evans	TN Society
Lester A. Foster	MD Society
Robert F. Galer	GA Society
D. Gene Patterson	PA Society

2000

Thomas N. Clark	NC Society
Paul M. Franyz	VA Society
Edward S. Gray	MO Society
Carl H. Lamb	CA Society
Clarence E. Monroe	MI Society
William R. Ward	UT Society

2001

B. Rice Aston	TX Society
John A. Horner	OH Society
Robert F. Jackson	CA Society
Ralph D. Nelson	DE Society
W. Ramsey Richardson	VA Society
O. Lee Swart	AL Society

2002

Jack Jones Early	KY Society
John C. Haughton	TX Society
Ronald J. Horton	SC Society
Raymond G. Musgrave	WV Society
William B. Neal	DE Society

2003

Charles F. Bragg	IN Society
Edward O. Cailleteau	LA Society
T. Fisher Craft	GA Society
Roland G. Downing	DE Society
P. Rod Hildreth	AL Society
Bruce A. Wilcox	VA Society

2004

Richard S. Austin	VA Society
Robert W. Coker	TX Society
Edgar E. Grover	KS Society

2005

M. Joseph Hill	IL Society
Garrett F. Jackson	CA Society
Andrew M. Johnson	DC Society
Henry N. McCarl	MA Society
Travis E. Spears	CA Society
J. David Sympson	KY Society

2006

David N. Appleby	MO Society
Edward F. Butler, Sr.	MX Society
Larry T. Guzy	GA Society
Charles R. Lampman	CA Society
J. Phillip London	DC Society
Nathan E. White, Jr.	TX Society

2007

Walter F. Baker	NM Society
William T. Cox	AR Society
Floyd L. Jernigan	KY Society
J. Michael Jones	AZ Society
James A. McCafferty	MD Society
Douglas T. Stansberry	GA Society

2008

I. Barnett Ellis	KS Society
Stephen A. Leishman	DE Society
Larry J. Magerkurth	CA Society
Larry R. Perkins	OH Society
George E. Thurman	GA Society
John R. Wallace	AL Society

Minuteman Class of 2008. Front l to r: John R. Wallace (AL Society), I. Barnett Ellis (KS Society), George E. Thurmond (GA Society). Standing: Stephen A. Leishman (DE Society), Larry R. Perkins (OH Society) and Larry J. Magerkurth (CA Society).

Gold Good Citizenship Award

The Gold Good Citizenship Medal is awarded for outstanding and unusual patriotic achievement and service of national importance. It may be presented only once to any individual. This medal was authorized in 1954.

The medal is presented to persons of prominence on a national level in the areas of government (including military service), religion, education, business and the professions, and other appropriate fields of endeavor.

Former President Generals may be awarded this medal, but the request should be processed as any other. Other SAR members may receive the medal if they meet the requirements established for all applicants.

Each state society is limited to awarding two Gold Good Citizenship Medals in any calendar year.

The Gold Good Citizenship Medal may be presented posthumously if the recipient died between the time the award was approved by the Medals and Awards Committee and Executive Committee and the date it was to have been presented.

The medal is gold filled, and may be presented by the National Society, a state society or chapter with the approval of its state society. A certificate is presented with the medal.

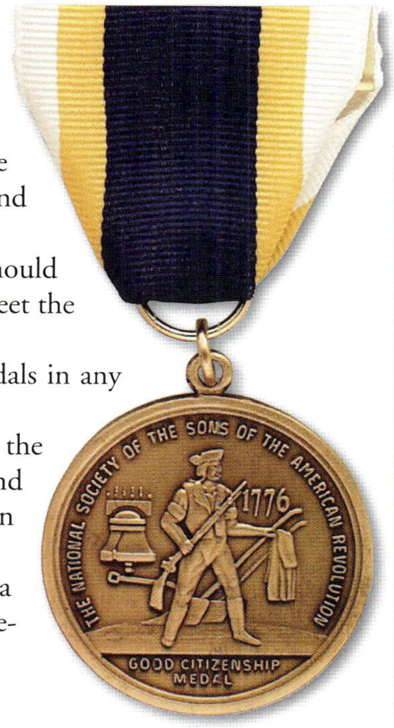

Below is an alphabetical listing of recipients.

A
Abercrombie, J. S.
Abshire, David M. Dr.
Akaka, Abraham A. Reverend
Aldisert, Ruggero J. Hon.
Alessandro, Victor Dr.
Allee, A. Y. Mr.
Allio, Joseph H. Mr.
Allott, Gordon Senator
Allyn, Stanley C.
Ambrose, Stephen
Ames, Glenn C., Maj. Gen. USA
Amilee, Meill F.
Amsler, Neile
Anderson, Charles A., MD, PG 1962-1963
Armstrong, Neil A., Test Pilot & Astronaut
Aston, B. Rice, PG 2002-2003
Atkins, Catherine Priest
Avery, William H.

B
Baker III, James Addison
Baker, Delmar
Baker, Lynn F. Dr.
Barnes, Wilson King, PG 1977-1978
Barridge, Homer D.
Barry, Desmond A.
Bartlett, Steve, US Representative
Bass, Joseph Mrs.
Baymiller, Ronald O.
Beals, Walter Burgess, Judge
Beeson, Cecil Everett, Sr.
Bell Telephone Co., New Jersey
Bell, John C. Judge
Benjamin, A.
Bennett, Charles E., US Representative
Bennett, Paul W.
Benson, Ezra Taft
Bentsen, Lloyd, US Senator
Berl, William, Jr., Brig Gen DE National Guard
Bernsdorf, Betty James Mrs.
Bessent, Carl F., PG 1984-1985
Biden, Joseph R., Jr., US Senator
Blair, Tony
Blough, Roger Miles
Bockstruck, Lloyd
Boden, Harry Clark Mrs. (Marguerite O.)
Boden, Henry Black
Bodine, William W., Jr.
Boggs, James Caleb, US Senator
Bolack, Thomas F.
Bond, Christopher Samuel
Boomer, Walter E., General, USMC
Booth, Edin C.
Bowen, Otis R., MD
Boyer, Robert W.
Bradbury, Norris E.
Brady, Tullis
Brakebill, Clovis H., PG 1986-1987
Brandau, George H., MD, PG 1991-1992
Branigan, Roger D., Governor
Breidster, Waldemar Fritz, Maj. Gen. USA
Briens, John A.
Brockel, Harry C.
Brown, A. Paul
Brown, Roderick Dew
Brownfield, Albert Ray
Broyhill, Joel T., US Representative
Brumbaugh, John D. PhD
Bryant, Anita Ms.
Brzezinski, Zbigniew, National Security Advisor
Bullis, Harold Edmond, Colonel
Burgoyne, Bruce
Burn, Harry T., PG 1964-1965
Burn, Larry T., PG 1964-1965
Bush, George H. W., 41st President of the US
Bush, George W., 43rd President of the US
Butler, James B.
Butler, Rosalie L. Ms.
Buxton, Charles B.
Byrd, Harry F., Jr., US Senator
Byrd, Joe III

C
Calhoun, James R., Col., PG 1990-1991
Cann, Ruth Miller Mrs.
Cantrell, Russell S.
Carlos I, Juan, King of Spain
Carmichael, Jack Kemper
Carper, Thomas R., Governor & US Senator
Carr, J. Wilfred
Carroll, Winchell S.
Carson, Nolan W., PG 1987-1988
Carter, James E., 40th President of the US
Carvel, Elbert S., Governor
Carver, Eugene P., Jr., PG 1956-1957
Case, James Royal, Colonel
Cassett, George Col.
Michael Newbold Castle, Governor & US Representative
Cathy, S. Truett
Chaney, Clarence R.
Cheeks, Thomas M.
Cheney, Donald Alexander
Cheney, Richard B., Vice President of the US
Chiles, Lawton
Christensen, A. Sherman
Chunn, Calvin E., PhD, PG 1978-1980
Clark, Edward A.
Clark, M. Graham, EdD, PG 1974-1975
Clark, Randolph Lee Dr.
Clark, Thomas D. Dr
Clarke, Owen F. Col.
Clarke, Philip C.
Claudel, M. Henri
Clyburn, Van, Concert Pianist
Coe, Howard E., PG 1965-1965
Coe, Howard E. Mrs.
Coleman, James P., Judge
Coleman, Philip N.
Collier, Everett Dulton
Colmer, William Meyers, US Representative
Conable, Barber B. Hon.
Conner, S. Grant
Cooch, Edward W. Jr.
Cooley, Denton MD, Pioneer Heart Surgeon
Corns, David Wayne
Crail, Joe
Crane, Richard E.
Crawmer, Marion, PG 1973-1974
Crownover Jr. , Arthur
Currie, Thomas
Curry, John Costen

D
Dall, Curtis B. Col.
Daly, Adrien J. Mrs.
Daly, Edward J.
Daniel, Marion Price, Governor & US Senator
Daniel, W. C. 'Dan'
Davidson, T. W. Judge
Davis, Eva Whitaker Mrs.
Davis, Raymond G., Maj. Gen. USMC
de Chambrun, Jean Pierre, Marquis
de la Houssaye, Arthur A., PG 1953-1954
Deal, Edson Hart
Dempsey, Jack
Denham, Richared Lane
Dent, Frederick B.
Deweerd, James A. Reverend.
Disney, Walt
Dobler, Walter
Dodd, Lamar
Dole, Robert J., US Senator
Doolittle, Jimmy, General USA
Downing, Roland G., PhD., PG 2005-2006
Drouilhet, Adrien
du Pont, Pierre S. IV, Governor & US Representative
Dudley, Alice E. Miss

Dudley, Ambrose
Dudley, Guilford
Dufour, Charles L.
Duke,Charles M., Jr.,, Colonel USAF
Astronaut
Dunn, Bernard J. Lt.
Dunn, Sr., John S.
Dyer, Frank G. Mrs.

E

Eagleton, Thomas F., US Senator
Eaker, Ira C., Lt. Gen. USAF
Early, P. J., Admiral
Eaton, Hubert Dr.
Eisenhower, Milton S., University President
Elsten, Dorothy F. Ms.
Emerson, Guy E. V.
Emmons, John
Evans, M. Stanton
Everett, Frank E., Jr.
Everett, W. Hume

F

Fabian, Harold
Falk, Richard S.
Feld, Irvin
Fellus, Bonner, General
Felmly, Lloyd Dr.
Ferguson, John P. Col.
Fleck, Anne D. D., Ms., PG NSDAR 1986-1989
Fluck, Henry K., Maj. Gen. USA
Fly, Claude L.
Flynn, Paul B.
Foglietta, Thomas M., Judge
Fortson, Ben W.
Fox, Bartholomew, Reverend
Frank, Anton J., Rt. Reverend Msgr.
Frank, Philip E.
Fulton, Robert Harrison

G

Galanti, Paul, Lt. Cdr.
Gallegly, Joseph S.
Gardiner, James, PG 1969-1970
Garn, Jacob E., US Senator
Garrison, Denzil D.
Garrison, Homer, Jr.
George, Walter F., US Senator
Giarrussa, Joseph I.
Gibble, John R.
Gill, Norman N.
Gilliam, Alfred E.
Gist, William C., Jr. DMD PG 1995-1996
Goar, Everett Logan Dr.
Godwin, Mills E., Governor
Goebel, Edmond J., Rt. Reverend. Msgr.
Goldwater, Barry, US Senator
Grant, Robert A., Judge
Grant, Ulysses S., III, General USA
Grede, William J.
Greer, Dewitt C.
Grimsley, James A., Maj. Gen. USA
Guiliani, Rudolph, Mayor New York City

H

Hackerman, Norman Dr.
Hahn, George A. Dr.
Halbousy, Michel T.
Haley, J. Evett
Hall, Glendon C.
Hames, James C., General
Hamilton, Howard L., PhD, PG 1982-1983
Hammond, Stanton Dr.
Hannan, Philip N., Archbishop
Hansen, Robert N., Judge
Harman, Ernest N., Major General
Harper, Henry Holmes
Harris, Frederick Brown Dr.
Hart Sr. , Joseph N.
Hatch, Orrin G., US Senator
Hawkins, William S.
Hayes, Warren G., Jr., PG 1983-1984
Head, David
Head, Joseph B.
Heatherton, Ray
Hebert, F. Edward, US Representative
Helmick, Robert Hanna
Helms, Jesse, US Senator
Herndon, Richard T.
Herring, Robert R.
Herrmann, Daniel L., Esquire
Hershey, Lewis B., General USA
Herster Jr. , Andrew L.
Heston, Charlton
Higgins, Frank Hon.
Higgins, Walter H., Major General
Hightower, Cato
Hild, Jack R. Dr.
Hill Jr. , Joe M.
Hill, Jim Dan, Maj. Gen. TX NG, Educator, Author
Hillegass, Reon G., Jr., PG 1996-1997
Hitch, Oliver M.
Hodges, Luther Gov.
Hoffman, Julius J., Judge
Hoffmann, Carl K., PG 1997-1998
Holiday Jr. , Harry
Horne, Howard F., Jr. PhD, PG 1999-2000
Hosmer, Merritt D.
Hottenbacher, Helen Miss
Houghton, Amory, Jr.
Howell Jr. , Hugh H.
Humphrey, Walter R.
Hunt, Haroldson L.
Hunter, Marshall E.
Hurlbert, Max Kent

I

Ingraham, Joe Mc., Judge
Ingram, T. Robert, Reverend
Isaacson, H. Harding, Colonel

J

Jani, Robert F.
Jessie, Howard G., Lt. Col.
Johnson, Sam, US Representative
Johnson, Walter S.
Jones, Charles A., PG 1959-1960
Jones, Russell R.

K

Kean, John Mrs.
Kearn, G. V.
Keating, Frank, Governor
Keeler, W. W.
Kellett, Howard P., Reverend
Kelso, William
Kemper, Charles Kell Mrs. PG NSDAR 1995-1998
Kenneday, Harry S., Bishop
Kennedy, Marshall H., General
Kennon, Robert Floyd, Governor
Kidd, Frank Dr.
King, Arthur M., PG 1981-1982
King, Stafford
Kitchell, Horace Y., PG 1961-1962
Knott, James R.
Knott, Walter
Knowland, William F., US Senator
Knowles, Warren P., Governor
Knowlton, William A., General USA
Koey, Howard W.
Kraissl, Cornelius J.
Krulak, Victor H., Lt. Gen. USMC

L

Laingen, Bruce,, Ambassador
Lane, Thomas A., General
Lanier, John F.
Latting, Patience, Mayor
Lausche, Frank J., US Senator
Layton, John D.
Lee, J. Bracken
Leist, George Amos
Lemaistre, Charles Aubrey
Lemnitzer, Lyman L., General USA
Lent, Norman F., State Senator
Leonard, D. P.
Leonard, Lewis K.
LePage, W. Lawrence Dr.
Letters, Anne Miss
Lewis III, Robert Fulton
Lewis Jr. , Fulton
Linthicum, T. G.
Livingston, James E., Maj. Gen. USMC
Lockwood, Robert Lee
Lodge, John Davis, Judge
Longley, Ralph L. Mrs.
Longstreth, Thacher
Lory, Milton M., PG 1954-1955
Lott, Trent, US Senator

M

Mack, Connie, US Senator
Mack, William P., Vice Admiral
Manley, Dixon
Manning, Reg
Manship, Charles P., Jr.
Markley, Howard, General
Marsh Jr. , John O.
Martin Jr., Wade C.
Martin, Jen. Edward
Martin, Walter P., PG 1970-1971
Marvil, James E. Dr.
Mason, Ed
Matchett, Henry J., General USA
Mathias, Charles M., US Senator
Mathnson, H. Lewis
McArthur, A. Peter N.
McArthur, Jean Mrs.
McCain III, John Sidney, US Senator
McCain, William Dr.
McCarl, Henry N., PG 2004-2005
McCarty, Stewart Boone, Colonel, PG 1994-1995
McClanahan, Larry D., PG 2001-2002
McClellan, John L., US Senator
McClure, Charles Boone
McCollough, David
McComb, John Alex
McConnell, John P., General USAF
McCord, James I., Reverend
McDonald, Larry P. Dr.
McDonald, Roger
McFarland, Kenneth Dr.
McGuffie, Anne Mrs.
McGuire, Eugene C., PG 1971-1972
McKee, Kinnard R., Rear Admiral
McKenrick, Ivan, Jr., Judge
McNally, James B. M., Judge
Mead, David
Meadows, James E.
Mecom Sr. , John W.
Meier, Lewis
Meyner, Robert B. Gov.
Michaelian, Edwin C.
Michaelian, Edwin C.
Middleton, Troy Houston, Lt. Gen. USA
Miller, Robert Warburton Dr.
Miller, Ward Ira Dr.
Milligan, Fred J.
Mischer, Halter M.
Mishoe, Luna I. Dr.
Mitchell, James P.
Mohammed V,, King of Morocco
Mollenhoff, Clark R.
Monroe, J. Blanc
Montgomery, G. V. “Sonny”, US Representative
Moore III, William Henson
Moore, Fred W.
Moore, Weaver
Moorer, Thomas H., Admiral
Morcan, Cecil
Morgan, Ryall S., PG 1972-1973
Morris, Albert T.
Morris, Benjamin H., Col., PG 1985-1986
Morris, Florence Pearl
Morrow, Wright
Moshovic, Alex
Mott, Hugh B., Adjutant General State of TN
Mowbray, John Cade
Moyle, James D.
Moyse, Hermann, Sr.
Mundt, Karl E., US Senator
Murphy, Herschel S., PG 1960-1961
Musgrave Jr. , C. E.

Musgrave, Raymond G., PG 2002-2003
Myers, Richard B., General USAF

N
Neely, Frank Henry
Neese, Harold A.
Neilan, Edwin P.
Newby, George E.
Newman, Guy D. Dr.
Nichols, Murvin C.
Nickerson, Herman Jr., Lt. Gen. USMC
Niebell, Eleanor Mrs.
Northen, Mary Moody Ms.
Nunn, Charles Edgar
Nunn, Sam, US Senator

O
Ochsner, Alton, MD
O'Conner, Sandra Day, Supreme Court Justice
Ohonesion, Victor, Lt. Colonel
Ore, Val

P
Pabst, Ralph H.
Page, Russell D., PG 1998-1999
Pagenstecher, William
Parnell, Donald J.
Patton, George S., Maj. Gen. USA
Patty, Kenneth C.
Pearson, Willard, Lt. Gen.USA
Pell, John H. G.
Peoples, C. E. Dr.
Perot, H. Ross
Perry, Christopher
Perry, Marcella D. Mrs.
Peterman, Ivan H.
Philbrick, Herbert
Phillips Sr. , Edwin Keith
Phillips, Asa
Phillips, James Clayton
Piazza, Marguerite
Pickett, Louis Loening
Piggins, Edward S., Judge
Pipes, C. S.
Plumley, H. Ladd
Powell, Colin Luther, General USA
Powers, Eugene E.
Powers, Frederick S. Dr.
Powers, Peter Reverend.
Prickett, Louise L.
Printz, Charles F., Sr., PG 1988-1989
Pryor, Samuel

Q
Quayle, James Danforth, Vice President of the US
Quinn, Michael C.

R
Rader, Paul C. Dr.
Rahsam, John William, Colonel
Ransom, Harry Dr.
Rarick, John Rep.
Rathbone, M. J.
Rawlings, John H.
Ray, Frank Earl
Raynor, John R., Rt. Reverend
Reagan, Ronald, Governor
Reed, Howard E., Brig. Gen.
Rees, James C., IV
Reid, Allan Himes
Reid, Ogden R.
Reinhold, Paul B.
Rhodes, James A., Governor
Rich, Richard H.
Richardson, Elliott L.
Rickord, Milton A., Lt. Gen
Rickover, Hyman, Vice Admiral
Robbins, Howard A.
Roberts, Arch Major
Roberts, Ralph S. Dr.
Robertson, Clifford Parker, III
Robertson, W. W., US Senator
Rockefeller, Winthrop, Governor
Rogers, Joe M.
Rogers, Scobey, Jr.
Romney, George Wilcken, Businessman & Politician
Romulo, Carlos F., General
Roth, Willliam V., US Senator
Rowny, Edward L., Lt. Gen. USA & Ambassador
Rudder, Earl
Rumaggi, Louis Col.
Rundles, J. Clinton
Russell, J. Clarkson
Ryder, James

S
Sahloff, Willard H.
Saied, James G.
Saltonstall, Leverett, US Senator
Sanders, Joe W.
SAR Riverside, Southern California Chapter 1974
Savage, Robert D., LtCol, PG 1975-1976
Saylor, John Rep.
Schaefer, William Donald, Mayor of Baltimore
Schmidt, Rodney H. C.
Schriver, Bernard Adolph, General, USAF
Schwarzkopf, H. Norman, General USA
Scott, James L. P.
Scott, Robert Lee, Brig. Gen. USA, Flying Ace, Author "God is My Co-Pilot"
Seaman, Jonathan C., Lt. Gen. USA
Seimes, Elizabeth N. Mrs., PG NSSAR 1968-1971
Sellers, Matthew B., PG 1976-1977
Shepard, Alan, Rear Admiral & Astronaut
Shivers, Allan, Governor
Shoemaker, W. Joseph
Shofstall, Nelson P.
Short, Herman
Shotts, Bryan M., Lt. Gen. USAF
Simon, Paul, US Senator
Singlaub, John Kirk, Maj. Gen. USA
Sisney, Sherleen Mrs.
Skelton, Isaac Newton, IV
Skifton, Clifford R. Dr.
Skutnik III, Martin Leonard'
Sloane, Douglas
Smith, Dwight L.
Smith, Howard W., US Representative
Smith, Jerry
Smith, Kenneth G., Sr., PG 1966-1967
Smith, Len Young, PG 1967-1968
Smoot, Dan
Snarr, Douglas T.
Solomon, Gerald B. H., US Representative
Sondermann, Fred A., Professor
Sonfield, Robert L., PG 1963-1964
Sopkin, Henry
Spanogle, Robert W.
Squires, J. Duane Dr.
Stackpole, Edward J., Lt. Gen. USA
Stackpole, Robert J.
Staggs, Ralph E.
Stahl, Elmer Ware
Stallworth, Hugh W.
Stein Jr. , Charles Francis
Sterling, Walter G., PG 1968-1969
Stewart, Harvy E. Col.
Strampf, Edward F.
Stuebben, Lawsrence J., Reverend
Suttie, Col.
Swan, Harry Kels
Sweet, Richard E.
Swope, Guy J.

T
Tarbox, George E., Jr., PG 1957-1958
Tarr, James L.
Taylor, Clarence Wilson
Taylor, Helen Marie Ms.
Taylor, Henry J.
Taylor, Rep. Gene
Terry, Charles L., Governor
Thomas, Julian Baldwin
Thompson Jr. , Meldrin
Thompson, Parker C. Col.
Thompson, Richard H., Jr., PG 1981-1982
Thompson, Robert F.
Thurmond, Strom, US Senator
Toole Jr. , Wycliffe D., Rear Admiral
Tower, John, US Senator
Trexler, Duke C.
Tribbett, Sherman W., Governor
Tritico, Frank E.
Trudeau, Arthur G., Lt. Gen. USA
Truly, Richard H.
Truman, Harry S., 33rd President of the US
Tuck, W. M., Governor
Tunnell Jr. , James M.
Turnage, Thomas K.

U
Urban, Matt, Lt. Col.

V
Van Antwerp, Lee Douglas
Van Brunt, Bergen
Van Diver, Frank Dr.
Van Dusen, Francis L., Judge
Van Fleet, James A., General USA
Van Zandt, James E., US Representative
Vance, Robert B., Sr., Colonel, PG 1993-1994
Vanderbilt, Arthur T., Judge
Verheden, Jack Clyde
Vinson, Carl, US Representative
Voultsos, De Periclea, Count

W
Waggoner, Joe D., Jr.
Walker, Paul H., PG 1992-1993
Walker, Robert S. W.
Wallace, Dewitt
Wallace, Lila Acheson
Walters, Vernon A., Lt. Gen. USA & Ambassador
Walworth, C. A.
Warner, John William, US Senator
Watson, Wade W.
Watts, Clyde I., General
Wayne, John
Weeks, Raymond
Weggandt, Carl Victor Judge
Weinberger, Casper W.
Weisser, Edward O.
Weitz, Paul S. Cmdr
Wentworth, Walter A., PG 1958-1959
Werlein, Erwing Judge
Werlein, Presley E. Judge
West, Gordon Judge
Westlake, James R., PG 1989-1990
Westmoreland, William C., General USA
White, Nathan E., PG 2006-2007
White, Thomas, Jr., Major General
Whitman, George P., Sr., Judge
Whittington, Earl L.
Wilbur, Gen.
Wilcox, Bruce A., PG 2007-2008
Wilkinson, Eugene P., Admiral
Williams, Edwin A.
Williams, John J., US Senator
Williams, W. Walter
Williams, Winston C.
Williamson, Edgar, Jr., PG 1955-1956
Willits, Leon M.
Willliams, G. Mennon
Wilson, Samuel U., Lt. Gen. USA
Wise, Paul E.
Witcher, Robert Campbell,, Rt. Reverend
Woodward, Warren S.
Worchester, Morrill
Worrilow, George M.
Wright, John M., Jr., Lt. Gen. USA
Wright, Leslie Stephen PhD, University President
WTIC & WTIC (TV),

Y
Yahnke, E. E.
Yochim, Eldred M. Mrs., PG NSDAR 1989-1992

Z
Zaun, Allan A., Reverend
Zumwalt, Elmo, Admiral

The Distinguished Patriot Award

The Distinguished Patriot Award, authorized in 1987, is presented only once during the tenure of a President General to an American citizen for outstanding patriotism to his country. It is a framed, engrossed certificate. It is presented at the discretion of the incumbent President General and does not require other approval.

The following individuals have been presented with this award.

Bob Hope, (Leslie Townes Hope, Entertainer), 1986
Ronald W. Reagan, (40th President of the US), 1989
Carl F. Bessent, (President General 1984-1985), 1989
William Westmoreland, (General, US Army), 1992
Martha Raye (prepared but never presented)
Phyllis S. Schlafly, (American Conservative – Political Activist), 1998
George W. Bush, (43rd President of the US), 2005
J. Phillip London, (Chairman of the Board/Director, CACI International), 2006
Tom Bock, (National Commander, American Legion), 2006
Paul Morin, (National Commander, American Legion), 2007
Jack Kamrath, (Co-Founder & President, American Heritage Education Foundation), 2008
Martin (Marty) Conatser, (National Commander, American Legion), 2008
Lynne V. Cheney, PhD, (Historian, Author, Chair of the National Endowment for the Humanities), 2008
Frank W. Buckles, 2009
Philip W. Blake, 2009

The Distinguished Patriot Leadership Award

The Distinguished Patriotic Leadership Award is presented by the President General or his designee to a business, organization, or group for outstanding patriotism. It is a framed, engrossed certificate. It is presented at the discretion of the incumbent President General with approval of the Executive Committee. The award was authorized in 2005.

Organizations to which this award has been presented include:

San Diego Padres, 2005
Nick Snider (Founder of the National Museum of Patriotism, Atlanta, GA), 2006
American Village (Montevallo, AL), 2007
The History Channel, 2007
Grace Foundation for the Preservation of Americana (Cave Creek, AZ), 2008
Freedoms Foundation at Valley Forge, 2009

Minnesota Society Stephen Taylor Award

CALL FOR PAPERS

Minnesota Society Stephen Taylor Award

This award is presented to the compatriot who by research and writings has made a significant contribution to the preservation of the history of the American Revolution era, and its patriots.

All entries are due to NSSAR Headquarters, 1000 South Fourth Street, Louisville, KY 40203-3208 by May 1st.

The winner is determined by the National Society Historian General. The award is presented each year at Congress.

The award is named in honor of **Stephen Taylor**, the only Revolutionary War veteran buried in Minnesota. Stephen Taylor was born on March 23, 1957 and died on June 2, 1857. He is buried in Woodlawn Cemetery, Winona, MN. Stephen Taylor was part of the First Massachusetts Regiment of the continental Army under General George Washington.

**"A courageous member of Ethan Allen's band of 88,
who took part in the surprise attack on the British at Ft. Ticonderoga."**

Nine Compatriot Medal of Honor Recipients

The Medal of Honor is the highest military decoration awarded by the United States government. It is generally presented by the President of the United States in the name of Congress and thus is often called the Congressional Medal of Honor. There are seven known compatriot recipients who have received the nation's highest military award. Their names are listed in alphabetical order.

Major Ira Hobart Evans – Civil War

Ira Hobart Evans was born in Piermont, New Hampshire on April 11, 1844. Following the death of his father in 1852, his mother moved the family to her hometown of Berlin, Vermont, where the young Evans attended school and later graduated from the Barre Academy. With the Civil War and a call to arms sounding across the country, Evans enlisted as a private in Company B, 10th Vermont Volunteer Infantry on July 1862. He would later be promoted to Captain and eventually Brevet Major. Major Evans received the Congressional Medal of Honor for heroism while serving with Company B, 116th US Colored Troops, at the Battle of Hatcher's Run, Virginia. According to the citation, on April 6, 1865 "Evans voluntarily passed between the lines under heavy fire from the enemy and obtained important information." Following the assassination of President Lincoln, Evans was selected to march in the Honor Guard for the fallen Commander in Chief.

At the conclusion of the Civil War, Evans was transferred to Texas as part of the Federal Forces to help oversee Reconstruction and served as the Provost Marshall of Brownsville. In 1867, he was discharged from active duty in New Orleans. Liking Texas, he returned to the area and soon entered politics. He was elected to the Texas House of Representatives and became the Speaker of the Texas House of Representatives at the age of 25. In addition to being a legislator he was a businessman, religious leader and a philanthropist.

Evans was an early member of the Vermont Society, Sons of the American Revolution (SAR) with a national number of 2751. On December 8, 1896 he founded the Texas Society of the Sons of the American Revolution and transferred his membership to that new society. He held Texas Society membership number 1, and served as the group's first President. Compatriot Evans is the only known Medal of Honor winner to serve as a Society President.

Ira Hobart Evans died in San Diego, California on April 19, 1922 of a heart ailment. His body was returned to Berlin, Vermont, to be buried with members of his family in the Berlin Corner Cemetery.

Captain Horace Porter – Civil War

Horace Porter was born in Huntingdon, PA on April 15, 1837, the son of David R. Porter, a wealthy ironmater who later served as Governor of Pennsylvania, and grandson of Andrew Porter (1743-1813), an officer in the Continental Army during the War of Independence. Horace Porter studied for a year (1854) at the Lawrence scientific school of Harvard University, and then entered the United States Military Academy (West Point). He graduated in 1860, third in his class.

He served in the Union army in the American Civil War, reaching the rank of brigadier general. He received the Medal of Honor at the Battle of Chickamauga (September 18–20, 1863). The battle took place approximately three to four miles downstream on the Tennessee River from Chattanooga. On September 20, 1863, Horace Porter was serving as a Captain in the Ordnance Department. His citation reads "While acting as a volunteer aide, at a critical moment when the lines were broken, rallied enough fugitives to hold the ground under heavy fire long enough to effect the escape of wagon trains and batteries." In the last year of the war, he served as a personal aide to the General-in-Chief Ulysses S. Grant.

From 1869 to 1873, Porter served as Grant's personal secretary in the White House. Horace Porter resigned from the army in December 1873 and became vice president of the Pullman Palace Car Company. He also served in other business enterprises.

In 1893 at the third Congress in New York City, Horace Porter was elected President General of the Sons of the American Revolution. He was re-elected four times and is the only man to serve in this position for five years.

Porter was president of the Union League Club of New York from 1893 to 1897. In that capacity, he was a major force in the construction of Grant's Tomb.

From March 1897 to May 1905 he was US Ambassador to France. At his personal expense he conducted (1899-1905) a successful search for the body of John Paul Jones, who had died in Paris in 1792. He received the Grand Cross Legion of Honor from the French government in 1904. For this he received on May 9, 1906 a unanimous vote of thanks of both Houses of Congress, and the privileges of the floor for life. In 1907 he was a member of the American delegation to the Hague Peace Conference.

General Porter became well-known as a public speaker, and delivered orations at the dedication of General Grant's tomb in New York, at the centennial of the founding of West Point, and at the re-interment of the body of John Paul Jones at Annapolis. (John Paul Jones was later re-interred in the crypt under the chapel of the US Naval Academy in Annapolis, MD.)

Horace Porter's National number is 4069 and his New York Society number is 69. He died May 25, 1921. He is buried in the Old First Methodist Churchyard, West Long Branch, NJ. Horace Porter was also a prolific author. Three of his publications include *West Point Life* (1866) and *Campaigning with Grant* (1897), and *Letter of John Paul Jones* (1905). Compatriot Porter is the only known Medal of Honor winner to serve as a President General.

Lt. Colonel Theodore Roosevelt – Spanish-American War

Theodore Roosevelt was born at 28 East 20th Street in New York City on October 27, 1858. He graduated Phi Beta Kappa and *magna cum laude* from Harvard in 1880, and entered Columbia Law School. Finding the law boring Roosevelt researched and wrote his first major book, *The Naval War of 1812* (1882), which is still considered the only comprehensive history on the subject. In 1881 Roosevelt was elected as a New York Assemblyman, left law school, and began new career in public life.

In 1884 his first wife and his mother died on the same day. Roosevelt spent much of the next two years on his ranch in the Badlands of Dakota Territory. There he mastered his sorrow as he lived in the saddle, driving cattle, hunting big game. On a visit to London, he married Edith Carow in December 1886. One of their children was Theodore Roosevelt, Jr.

During the Spanish-American War, Roosevelt was a lieutenant colonel of the Rough Rider Regiment, in which he led a charge at the battle of San Juan on July 1, 1898. He was one of the most conspicuous heroes of the war. For his bravery he was recommended for the Medal of Honor but was not awarded the medal for another 103 years. President William Clinton presented the Medal posthumously at White House on January 16, 2001.

After the war, Roosevelt in 1898 was elected Governor of New York State and served with distinction. He was the 25th Vice President before becoming the 26th President in 1901 upon the assassination of President William McKinley. Inaugurated at the age of 42, Roosevelt became the youngest President and served two terms. He was also the first American to win a Nobel Prize in any category, having been awarded the Nobel Peace Prize in 1906 for his mediation of the Russo-Japanese War.

The National Society of the Sons of the American Revolution was chartered by an Act of the United States Congress on June 6, l906. The charter was signed by Compatriot President Theodore Roosevelt, who was a member of the SAR. Theodore Roosevelt's National number is 12000 from the State of New York.

Theodore Roosevelt died June 6, 1919 at Sagamore Hill, Oyster Bay, NY, and is buried in a nearby cemetery.

Brigadier General Theodore Roosevelt, Jr. – World War II

Theodore Roosevelt, Jr., universally known as "Teddy," was the son of President Theodore Roosevelt. He was born September 13, 1887 at the family estate in Oyster Bay, NY. Teddy was graduated from Harvard University in 1908 and entered the business world in the steel and carpet industries before becoming a branch manager of an investment bank.

After service as an officer (rising to the rank of lieutenant colonel in World War I), he began his political career in the New York State Assembly. He later was to serve as Assistant Secretary of the Navy, Governor of Puerto Rico (1929–32), and Governor General of the Philippines (1932–33). He resigned that position and returned to the US when his cousin, Franklin D. Roosevelt, was elected President. He later served as chairman of the board of the American Express Company and as vice president at Doubleday. Theodore Roosevelt, Jr.'s, National number is 23876 from the State of New York.

He returned to active duty in April 1941 and was placed in command of the 26th Infantry Regiment, 1st Infantry Division, the same group he fought with in World War I. Late in 1941, he was promoted to the rank of brigadier general. Throughout World War II, Teddy suffered from heart trouble and arthritis problems which caused him to walk with a cane. Teddy saw action in northern Africa, Sicily, and Italy. In 1944 General Eisenhower assigned Teddy to England to help lead the Normandy invasion on June 6, 1944. On D-Day, Teddy led the first wave of the US 4th Infantry Division's landing at Utah Beach. BG Roosevelt's Medal of Honor Citation reads in part "He repeatedly led groups from the beach, over the seawall and established them inland. His valor, courage, and presence in the very front of the attack and his complete unconcern at being under heavy fire inspired the troops to heights of enthusiasm and self-sacrifice. Although the enemy had the beach under constant direct fire, Brig. Gen. Roosevelt moved from one locality to another, rallying men around him, directed and personally led them against the enemy. Under his seasoned, precise, calm, and unfaltering leadership, assault troops reduced beach strong points and rapidly moved inland with minimum casualties. He thus contributed substantially to the successful establishment of the beachhead in France."

One month after the landing at Utah Beach, he died of a heart attack in France. He is buried at the American cemetery in Normandy, next to his brother, Quentin, an air corps pilot.

General of the Army Douglas MacArthur – World War II

Douglas MacArthur was born January 26, 1880 in the Little Rock Arsenal, Little Rock, Arkansas. He was the son of Lieutenant General Arthur MacArthur, Jr., also recipient of the Medal of Honor during the Civil War in the Battle of Missionary Ridge in November, 1863.

Douglas MacArthur was graduated from the US Military Academy (West Point) in 1903 as valedictorian of his 93-man class. During his life General MacArthur took part in three major wars (World War I, World War II, Korean War) and rose to the rank of General of the Army, one of only five people to hold that rank in US history. He served his country for over 60 years. General MacArthur's National number is 65843 from the State of New York.

General MacArthur was awarded the Medal of Honor for his actions early in World War II in the Philippines and on the Bataan Peninsula. The Citation accompanying the award reads "For conspicuous leadership in preparing the Philippine Islands to resist conquest, for gallantry and intrepidity above and beyond the call of duty in action against invading Japanese forces, and for the heroic conduct of defensive and offensive operations on the Bataan Peninsula. He mobilized, trained, and led an army that has received world acclaim for its gallant defense against a tremendous superiority of enemy forces in men and arms. His utter disregard of personal danger under heavy fire and aerial bombardment, his calm judgment in each crisis, inspired his troops, galvanized the spirit of resistance of the Filipino people, and confirmed the faith of the American people in their Armed Forces."

General of the Army Douglas MacArthur died on April 6, 1964. The General along with his wife are buried in Norfolk, Virginia.

Captain James B. Stockdale – Vietnam

James Bond Stockdale was born December 23, 1923, in Abingdon, Illinois. He was graduated from the US Naval Academy in 1946. Upon graduation he earned his pilot's wings at Pensacola, Florida. In 1954 he reported to the Test Pilot School at Patuxent River, Maryland.

In August of 1964, while serving as squadron commander, Stockdale was one of the US pilots flying overhead during the Gulf of Tonkin Incident. On a mission over North Vietnam on September 9, 1965, Stockdale's A-4E Skyhawk was disabled by anti-aircraft fire and he was forced to eject. Stockdale parachuted into a small village, where he was severely beaten and taken into custody. He was held as a prisoner of war in the Hoa Lo prison for the next seven years where he was tortured many times but he refused to capitulate. Stockdale was released as a prisoner of war on February 12, 1973. His citation reads, in part, for "his valiant leadership and extraordinary courage in a hostile environment," James Bond Stockdale received the Medal of Honor in 1976 from President Gerald Ford.

After his retirement, he became the president of The Citadel in South Carolina in 1979. He left The Citadel to become a fellow of the Hoover Institution at Stanford University in 1981. During the following two decades, Stockdale wrote a number of books both on his experiences during the Vietnam War and afterwards, and on philosophy. His best known work is *In Love and War: the Story of a Family's Ordeal and Sacrifice During the Vietnam War*, co-written with his wife Sybil and published in 1984. It was later made into an NBC television movie of the same name.

Stockdale came to know H. Ross Perot through his wife's work in establishing an organization to represent the families of Vietnam POWs. Ross Perot asked Stockdale to accept the nominated as the Vice-President on the ticket for the Reform Party in March 1992.

Stockdale retired to California, as he slowly succumbed to Alzheimer's disease. He died on July 5, 2005. Stockdale's funeral service was held at the Naval Academy Chapel and he was buried at the United States Naval Academy Cemetery, Annapolis, MD.

In September 2008, the Navy accepted delivery of the guided missile ship (DDG-106) named for him. Compatriot Stockdale, National number 110583, was a life member from the Illinois Society.

David Sloane Stanley – Civil War

David Stanley was born in Cedar Valley, Ohio on June 1, 1828. He served in the U.S. Volunteers, entering service at Congress, Wayne County, Ohio, and achieved the rank of Major General. He was awarded for actions taken at Franklin, Tennessee on November 30, 1864, when "at a critical moment rode to the front of one of his brigades, reestablished its lines, and gallantly led it in a successful assault."

Robert Hugo Dunlap – World War II

Robert Dunlap was born in Abingdon, Illinois on October 19, 1920. He served in the U.S. Marine Corps Reserves, Company C, 1st Battalion, 26th Marines, 5th Marine Division, achieving the rank of Captain. He was awarded the Medal of Honor for actions taken on Iwo Jima, Volcano Islands, on February 20-21, 1945. His citation reads:

"...Defying uninterrupted blasts of Japanese artillery, mortar, rifle and machinegun fire, Capt. Dunlap led his troops in a determined advance form low ground uphill toward the steep cliffs from which the enemy poured a devastating rain of shrapnel and bullets, steadily inching forward until the tremendous volume of enemy fire from the caves located high to his front temporarily halted his progress. Determined not to yield, he crawled alone approximately 200 yards forward to his front lines, took observation at the base of the cliff 50 yards from the Japanese lines, located the enemy gun positions and returned to his own lines where he relayed the vital information to supporting artillery and naval gunfire units. Persistently disregarding his own personal safety, he then placed himself in an exposed vantage point to direct more accurately the supporting fire and, working without respite for 2 days and 2 nights under constant enemy fire, skillfully directed a smashing bombardment against the almost impregnable Japanese positions despite numerous obstacles and heavy marine casualties.

"A brilliant leader, Capt. Dunlap inspired his men to heroic efforts during this critical phase of the battle and by his cool decision, indomitable fighting spirit, and daring tactics in the face of fanatic opposition greatly accelerated the final decisive defeat of Japanese countermeasures in his sector and materially furthered the continued advance of his company."

Major Joseph J. Foss – World War II

Joseph Foss was born in Sioux Falls, South Dakota on April 17, 1915. He served in the U.S. Marine Corps Reserve, Marine Fighting Squadron 121, 1st Marine Aircraft Wing, earning the rank of Captain. He was awarded the Medal of Honor for outstanding heroism and courage for his action at Guadalcanal, Solomon Islands. His citation reads:

"...Engaging in almost daily combat with the enemy from October 9 to November 19, 1942, Captain Foss personally shot down twenty-three Japanese planes and damaged others so severely that their destruction was extremely probably. In addition, during this period, he successfully led a large number of escort missions, skillfully covering reconnaissance, bombing and photographic planes as well as surface craft.

"On January 15, 1943, he added three more enemy planes to his already brilliant successes for a record of aerial combat achievement unsurpassed in this war. Boldly searching out an approaching enemy force on January 25, Captain Foss led his eight F4F Marine planes and four Army P-38s into action and, undaunted by tremendously superior numbers, intercepted and struck with such force that four Japanese fighters were shot down and the bombers were turned back without releasing a single bomb. His remarkable flying skill, inspiring leadership and indomitable fighting spirit were distinctive factors in the defense of strategic American positions on Guadalcanal."

Source:

United States of America's Congressional Medal of Honor Recipients and Their Official Citations, Fifth Edition, Highland House II, Columbia Heights, MN, Copyrighted 2006.

Compatriot Presidents of the United States

The Sons of the American Revolution is proud of its compatriot Presidents of the United States. We honor these Compatriots who used their position as President to build a better America. Each remembered the founding of this great nation and the role of his Revolutionary War ancestor in making American the beacon of liberty and justice of all.

Six Presidents were real sons of Revolutionary War Patriots. These included John Quincy Adams, Martin Van Buren, William Henry Harrison, John Tyler, IV, Zachary Taylor, and Franklin Pierce.

Five Presidents were grandsons of Revolutionary War Patriots. These included: James Knox Polk, Millard Fillmore, Abraham Lincoln, Chester A. Arthur, and Grover Cleveland.

President James A. Garfield was the great grandson of a Revolutionary War Patriot. President Richard M. Nixon was the great great grandson of a Patriot.

As of the date of this article (before the 2008 elections) there have been 16 Presidents of the United States who were also Compatriots. The Winter 2001 issue of *The SAR Magazine* featured the Presidents with details of their backgrounds, including information about their Revolutionary War ancestors. When President George W. Bush became President and a member of the Society the magazine carried a major news story that included a photo of him receiving his Membership Certificate.

President Ulysses S. Grant was a member of our parent organization, the Sons of the Revolutionary War Sires. General Grant died before the Sons of the American Revolution was founded. President Grant would have automatically transferred his membership to the SAR, hence his inclusion in the roster of Compatriot Presidents of the United States.

Presidential candidate Senator John S. McCain, III, is a member of the Arizona Society. President Barack H. Obama's application has been completed and awaits his signature.

Rutherford Birchard Hayes – 19th President of the United States

Rutherford B. Hayes served for one term from 1877 to 1881 as the 19th President. He was born in Delaware, OH, on October 4, 1822 and graduated from Harvard Law School. At the outbreak of the Civil War he enlisted in the Union Army, was wounded five times and rose to the rank of Major General. He served in the House of Representatives and served as Governor of Ohio for three terms. The nation was still suffering from the pangs of the Civil War when he became President. One of his first actions was to withdraw Federal troops from the Southern States. Compatriot Hayes enjoyed being President but disliked politics and chose not to run for a second term.

President Hayes was very proud of his ancestry, especially his Revolutionary War ancestors. He became an early member of the SAR. President Hayes died in Fremont, OH, on January 1883.

Benjamin Harrison – 23rd President of the United States

Benjamin Harrison served for one term from 1889 to 1893 as the 23rd President. He was born on August 20, 1833, at his grandfather's farm near North Bend, OH. He was the grandson of William Henry Harrison, 9th President of the US, and great grandson of Benjamin Harrison, Signer of the Declaration of Independence. Benjamin Harrison's term as President came between the two terms of Grover Cleveland.

The New Jersey Society SAR was organized on March 7, 1889 in Newark, NJ, and many patriotic men answered the recruiting bugle. The first public activity of the new Society was on April 29, 1889, at Elizabeth, NJ, when President Harrison visited Elizabeth on his journey to New York City for the Centennial ceremonies of George Washington's Inauguration as the first President. At a reception by NJ Governor Green at his home the individual members of the new Society were presented to the President. Later the Society members served as an Honor Escort for the President from the Governor's residence to the wharf where he boarded a barge for New York City.

President Harrison's wife, Caroline Scott Harrison, was elected as the first President General of the Daughters of the American Revolution. Caroline Harrison and Rutherford B. Hayes's wife, Lucy Webb Hayes, were cousins. President Harrison died in Indianapolis, IN, on March 13, 1901 at the age of 67. He is buried in Indianapolis, IN.

Harrison has had numerous institutions named in his honor: The Benjamin Harrison Law School in Indianapolis, a 1942 United States Liberty ship named the SS *Benjamin Harrison*, and a US Army post, Fort Benjamin Harrison, in Indianapolis.

William McKinley, Jr. – 25th President of the United States

William McKinley was twice elected and served from 1897 to 1901 as the 25th President. He was born in Niles, OH, on January 29, 1843, attended Allegheny College in Pennsylvania, and volunteered for the Union Army in the Civil War. He distinguished himself in action, rising to the rank of major. William McKinley was the last veteran of the Civil War to be elected President. He later was graduated from the Albany Law School.

McKinley served in the House of Representatives, later was elected Governor of Ohio, and became a national figure. In 1896 he was nominated at the Republican National Convention and elected President by a large plurality.

President McKinley died in Buffalo, NY, on September 14, 1901 at the age of 58, of wounds received in an assassination attempt eight days after being shot. Vice President Theodore Roosevelt succeeded President McKinley. McKinley is buried in Canton, OH.

Theodore Roosevelt – 26th President of the United States

Theodore Roosevelt became our 26th President of the US with the death of President William McKinley in 1901. At the age of 42 years, he was the youngest man to become President. Theodore Roosevelt was born in New York City on October 27, 1858. He graduated from Harvard and attended law school. In the War with Spain led a daring charge up San Juan Hill and later received the Medal of Honor. In 1905 President Roosevelt was awarded the Nobel Peace Prize for negotiating the peace treaty between Russia and Japan.

Theodore Roosevelt joined the SAR on April 10, 1898, while Governor of New York. His Revolutionary War ancestor was Jacobus Roosevelt who served as a Captain in the New York Militia and who died in 1777. Jacobus Roosevelt's son, Jacobus I. Roosevelt, served as a Commissary for the entire war.

President Roosevelt died at Oyster Bay, NY on January 16, 1919 at the age of 60. He is buried in Youngs Memorial Cemetery in Oyster Bay, NY.

Bust of Theodore Roosevelt.

William Howard Taft – 27th President of the United States

William Howard Taft served one term as our 27th President of the US. He was born in Cincinnati, OH, on September 15, 1857. William H. Taft graduated from Yale and the University of Cincinnati Law School. He became the 5th US Solicitor General in 1890. In 1901 he became the first Civil Governor of the Philippines. In 1904 President Roosevelt nominated him to be Secretary of War. In 1906 he became the first Provisional Governor of Cuba. Three years later in 1909 William H. Taft became President Taft.

After leaving the White House, Taft became a law professor at Yale. In 1921 President Harding appointed Compatriot Taft Chief Justice of the Supreme Court. He died one month after his retirement from the US Supreme Court on March 8, 1930 in Washington, DC at the age of 72. He is buried in Arlington National Cemetery, VA.

Warren Gamaliel Harding – 29th President of the United States

Warren G. Harding was born near Blooming Grove, OH, on November 2, 1865. He was graduated from Ohio Central College and went into newspaper work. Soon he entered politics and because a state senator in 1899. Four years later he was elected Lieutenant Governor of Ohio. In 1910 he ran for Governor but lost. In 1914 he was elected to the United States Senate, becoming Ohio's first senator elected by popular vote. He served in the Senate from 1915 until his inauguration as President on March 4, 1921, becoming the first sitting Senator to be elected President of the United States.

Warren Harding joined the Ohio Society on July 2, 1920. He was a descendant of Abraham Harding, Jr., who resided in Walhill, NY, at the outbreak of the Revolutionary War. Abraham Harding, Jr., served as a Lieutenant in the New York Militia. President Harding was invited to attend the 34th SAR National Congress to be held in Nashville, TN.

President Harding was the sixth President to die while in office. While traveling on a "Voyage of Understanding" he was in San Francisco, CA, and died on August 2, 1923 at the age of 57. He is buried in Marion, OH.

(John) Calvin Coolidge, Jr. – 30th President of the United States

Following the death of President Harding, Vice President Calvin Coolidge was sworn in by his father, a Justice of the Peace, in Plymouth Notch, VT. He was the sixth Vice President to become the Chief Executive on the death of a President. Calvin Coolidge was born on July 4, 1872 in Plymouth, VT. He was later elected to a full term as President. Although named John Calvin Coolidge he dropped the John as he preferred a single name.

Coolidge graduated with honors from Amherst College in 1895. In his senior year he wrote an essay on "The Principles Fought for in the American Revolution: and was awarded a Gold Medal by the National Society.

Calvin Coolidge joined the SAR in 1921 while serving as Vice President. His Revolutionary ancestor was John Coolidge, who at the age of 19 answered the call on April 1775, joined the Massachusetts Militia as a private. He fought at the Battle of Bunker Hill and was discharged in 1778.

The 39th SAR Annual Congress was held in Washington, DC. Many of the delegates and their ladies marched from the Mayflower Hotel to the White House to be received by Compatriot President Coolidge. The President briefly spoke to the group and greeted many personally.

After the presidency, Coolidge served as chairman of the Railroad Commission, as honorary president of the Foundation of the Blind, as a director of New York Life Insurance Company, and as a trustee of Amherst College. President Coolidge died suddenly of a heart attack at his home in Northampton, MA, on January 5, 1933, at age 60. He is buried in Notch Cemetery, Plymouth Notch, VT.

Herbert Clark Hoover – 31st President of the United States

Herbert C. Hoover served one term as our 31st President from 1929 to 1933. Herbert Hoover was born in West Branch, IA, on August 10, 1874. He was orphaned at an early age and lived with an uncle in Oregon. In 1891, Hoover graduated from Stanford University. He pursued mining engineering in many parts of the world – Australia, Africa, and China. While in China he directed food relief operations for victims of the Boxer Rebellion.

When World War I began, Hoover was a wealthy mining engineer. He was appointed Chairman of the American Relief Commission, then Chairman of the Commission for Belgium Relief, and then US Food Administrator. He was recognized as a great humanitarian and an excellent administrator.

Herbert Hoover's Revolutionary War ancestor was Jacobus Wynne, a private in the first Regiment, Ulster County Militia, New York Troops. Another ancestor was Isaac Sherman, Lieutenant in the Second Regiment of the New York Line. On November 1, 1928, President Hoover accepted an invitation to join the Pennsylvania Society of the SAR. He visited the SAR National Headquarters on 16th Street to be inducted into membership.

Hoover served in both President Harding's cabinet and President Coolidge's cabinet. When Coolidge chose not to run for re-election, Herbert Hoover was elected President. Hoover worked conscientiously at being a good President and is wrongly judged because of the Great Depression. In 1929 the stock market crashed and the economy collapsed. There was widespread unemployment. Hoover was defeated by Franklin D. Roosevelt.

At the conclusion of World War II President Truman appointed Hoover as Coordinator of the European Food Program. Later, he was appointed Chairman of the Commission to Reorganize the Executive Branch.

Hoover died in New York City on October 20, 1964, at the age of 90. 31 years and seven months after leaving office. President Hoover is buried at the Herbert Hoover Presidential Library and Museum in West Branch, Iowa.

Franklin Delano Roosevelt – 32nd President of the United States

Franklin Delano Roosevelt was elected to four terms as our Chief Executive – longer than any other President (1935 - 1945). He was born at Hyde Park, NY, on January 30, 1882. He was President during the Great Depression and most of World War II.

Roosevelt's Revolutionary War ancestor was Isaac Roosevelt who served as a private in the 6th Regiment, Dutchess County Militia, New York Troops.

On June 14, 1931, Franklin D. Roosevelt, then Governor of New York, attended the SAR Flag Day ceremonies and "Descendants Day" on the village green adjoining St. Paul's Episcopal Church in the quaint village of Eastchester, NY. Many members along with the Color Guard of the New York Chapter of the Empire State Society attended. Theodore Roosevelt's and Franklin D. Roosevelt's ancestor was an original pew holder and vestryman of the church. The church's bell, prayer book, Bible, and chalice had been secretly buried during the Revolutionary War. The bell hangs in the belfry today, and the books and chalice are displayed on special occasions.

On April 20, 1933, President General Frederick W. Millspaugh and General Fries called at the White House to inform the President that his SAR Membership had been approved. Two of President Roosevelt's sons joined the SAR: Colonel James Roosevelt and Congressman Franklin D. Roosevelt, Jr.

One month prior to the surrender of Germany, and less than three months after being elected to his fourth term, President Roosevelt died of a cerebral hemorrhage at Warm Springs, GA, on April 12, 1945, at the age of 63. Roosevelt is buried at the family home at Hyde Park, NY.

Harry S. Truman – 33rd President of the United States

As Vice President, Harry S. Truman became the 33rd President from 1945 to 1954 succeeding Franklin D. Roosevelt. Truman was born in Lamar, MO, on May 8, 1884. He was working on the family farm at the outbreak of World War I when his National Guard unit was called to active duty. He saw action in France and was discharged as a Captain.

After the war, Truman operated a clothing store in Kansas City, MO, which failed. He then entered politics and was elected county judge. In 1934 he was a US Senator from Missouri. He served effectively in the Senate until he was selected as the Vice President Candidate for President Roosevelt's fourth term.

Upon completing his second term in office in 1953, President Truman returned to Independence, MO, and wrote his memoirs.

Harry Truman's Revolutionary War ancestor was Lieutenant James Holmes of the 2nd Regiment of the Virginia Militia, who served from 1777 to 1781.

At Truman's home in Independence, MO, President General Lee Young Smith presented the former President with his membership certificate, the SAR Membership Insignia Badge, and the SAR Gold Good Citizenship Medal.

President Truman died in Kansas City, MO, on December 26, 1972 at the age of 88. He is buried at the Truman Library in Independence, MO.

Dwight David Eisenhower – 34th President of the United States

Dwight David Eisenhower served two terms as the 34th President from 1953 to 1961. He was born in Dennison, TX, on October 14, 1890. He graduated in the upper half of his class from the US Military Academy at West Point in 1915.

Eisenhower served a career in the US Army culminating as Supreme Commander of all Allied Forces and led the Normandy invasion in 1944. He was President of Columbia University in 1948. He returned to active duty in 1950 as Commander of NATO troops.

Eisenhower's Revolutionary Ancestor was John Peter Eisenhower who furnished supplies to the Continental Army troops during the winter of 1777-1778 at Valley Forge. Another ancestor was John Matter, a Pennsylvania Militia soldier who fought at the Battle of Long Island. Thanks to work of the Empire State Society, the General's application for membership was approved in 1945. President Eisenhower's son, John Doud Eisenhower, and his brother Dr. Milton Stover Eisenhower, joined the SAR.

Eisenhower was the Republican Party candidate and was elected President. He began his first term in 1952 and was re-elected for a second term. When his term of office was completed, he retired to his farm in Gettysburg, PA.

General of the Army Eisenhower retired as a five-star general. Today, we are sometimes reminded by commemorative on the signs denoting Interstate Highways as part of the Eisenhower Interstate System, which display five silver stars on a light blue background.

President Eisenhower died in Washington, DC, on March 28, 1969, at the age of 78. He is buried at the Eisenhower Library in Abilene, KS.

Lyndon Baines Johnson – 36th President of the United States

Lyndon Baines Johnson served as the 37th Vice President of the United States and became the 36th President of the United States (1963 to 1969) following the assassination of President John F. Kennedy. He was born in Stonewall, TX, on August 27, 1908. He graduated from Southwest Texas State Teachers College in 1930. With the assistance of his wife, Ladybird Johnson, he developed an extensive enterprise in farming and broadcasting. In 1937 he entered politics being elected to the first of four terms in the US House of Representatives.

Johnson was the first Congressman to enter active duty when the US entered World War II. He was discharged as a Lieutenant Commander after four years in the Navy.

In 1948 Johnson was elected to the first of two terms as a US Senator. In 1955 he became the youngest Majority Leader in history. When President Kennedy ran for office he asked Johnson to be his Vice President. After completing Kennedy's second term, Johnson was elected President in his own right in a landslide victory in the 1964 Presidential election.

Compatriot Johnson's Revolutionary War ancestor was John Johnson who served as a soldier in the Georgia State Militia.

President Johnson died of a heart attack on his ranch in Stonewall, TX, on January 22, 1973 at the age of 64. Johnson is buried in the family cemetery now part of the Lyndon B. Johnson National Park in Stonewall, TX.

Lyndon B. Johnson Presidential Library is located in Austin, TX.

Gerald Rudolph Ford – 38th President of the United States

Gerald R. Ford was elected to the US House of Representatives in 1950 and served as a Congressman for 25 years. He was leader of the House Republicans for eight years. On October 12, 1973 he was nominated for 40th Vice President by President Richard M. Nixon when Vice President Spiro Agnew resigned. He was the first person appointed to the office of vice-president under the terms of the 25th Amendment. Less than a year later on August 9 1974, Ford became President upon Richard Nixon's resignation. Ford was the fifth President never to have been elected to that position, and the only one never to have won any national election.

Gerald Ford was born in Omaha, NE, on July 14, 1913. He was a football star at the University of Michigan where he received his Bachelor degree. He graduated from Yale Law School in 1938. He served as a Naval Officer for four years in World War II and was discharged as a Lieutenant Commander.

President Ford's Revolutionary War ancestor was Ezra Chase who served as a Minuteman in the Massachusetts Militia.

In 1975 President General Graham Clark visited the Oval Office in the White House to present the President with his Membership Certificate (National # 105000), the SAR Membership Badge. In 1989, the SAR Centennial Year, the former President Gerald R. Ford was presented the SAR Gold Good Citizenship Medal.

President Ford died at Rancho Mirage on December 28, 2006. He was also the longest-lived president in US history, living until the age of 93. He is buried at the Gerald Ford Museum and Presidential Library in Grand Rapids, MI.

James (Jimmy) Earl Carter, Jr. – 39th President of the United States

James Earl "Jimmy" Carter Jr. served one term as the 39th President from 1977 to 1981. He was born in Plains, GA, on October 1, 1924. He attended Georgia Tech and Georgia Southwestern State University before receiving an appointment to the United States Naval Academy where he received a Bachelor of Science degree in physics in 1946 and is the only graduate of the Naval Academy to become President. Carter finished a high 59th out of his Academy class of 820. Jimmy Carter served on surface warfare ships and qualified for diesel-electric submarines. He is the only U.S. President to qualify in submarines.

Upon the death of his father in 1953, Jimmy Carter resigned his commission and returned home to take over and expand his family business in Plains. Carter served two terms in the Georgia Senate and as the 76th Governor of Georgia, from 1971 to 1975. As Governor he campaigned and won the election to become the 39th President of the US.

President Carter received the Nobel Peace Prize in 2002 for his work "to find peaceful solutions to international conflicts, to advance democracy and human rights, and to promote economic and social development" through The Carter Center. He was the third US President to be awarded the Prize. The two previous Presidents were Theodore Roosevelt and Woodrow Wilson.

President Carter's Revolutionary War ancestor was Perry Scott, who served as a private in Capt. Allen McLane's Company of the Delaware Militia.

President Carter is a member of the Georgia Society. He was presented his Membership Certificate (National # 134672) in 1990. In 1996, President Carter was presented the SAR Gold Good Citizenship Medal.

The Jimmy Carter Library and Museum is located in Atlanta, GA. It houses President Jimmy Carter's papers and other material relating to his administration and his life. The library also hosts special exhibits such as a showing of the United States Bill of Rights and Carter's Nobel Peace Prize.

George Herbert Walker Bush – 41st President of the United States

George H. W. Bush served two terms as the 41st President from 1989 to 1993. He was born in Milton, MA on June 12, 1924. His family moved to Greenwich, CT, shortly after his birth. George Bush was 18 when the Japanese attacked Pearl Harbor. He joined the Navy and became a naval aviator and was commissioned an Ensign. He served until the end of the war and then attended Yale University. Upon graduation in 1948 he moved to Texas and entered the oil business. He soon entered politics.

Bush held a number of political positions prior to his presidency, including member of the US House of Representatives, US Ambassador to the United Nations under President Nixon, Chief of US Liaison Office to the People's Republic of China, Director of the CIA, and Vice President of the United States in the administration of Ronald Reagan.

President Bush's Revolutionary War ancestor was Col. Samuel Herrick, who served with distinction as commander of the Vermont Ranger Militia.

President Bush is a member of the Texas Society and a life member of the Paul Carrington Chapter of Austin, TX. He was presented his Membership Certificate (National # 155305) in his Houston, TX, office on May 1, 2001. Texas Society, Nathan White, Jr., inducted the former president as a Compatriot. President General Bruce Butler pinned the SAR rosette on President Bush. Secretary General B. Rice Aston and several other members of the Paul Carrington Chapter were also present.

The George Bush Presidential Library and Museum is located on a ninety-acre site on the west campus of Texas A&M University in College Station, TX. The library contains the papers and memorabilia from his days in public service as well as those of James Danforth "Dan" Quayle former Indiana Senator and the 44th-fourth Vice President of the United.

George Walker Bush – 43rd President of the United States

George W. Bush, son of President George H. W. Bush served as the 43rd President from January 2001 to 2009. He was born in New Haven, CT, on July 6, 1946. He is a graduate of Yale University and the Harvard Business School. Before becoming our president, George W. Bush served as Governor of Texas.

President Bush's Revolutionary War ancestor was Col. Samuel Herrick, who served with distinction as commander of the Vermont Ranger Militia.

In July 1988 George W. Bush received his membership certificate and lapel rosette while he was Governor of Texas. He is a member of the Patrick Henry Chapter of the Texas Society.

Sources:

Centennial History of the National Society of the Sons of the American Revolution 1889 – 1989, Turner Publishing Company, Paducah, KY. Copyright 1991 NSSAR Louisville, KY.

The History of the National Society of the Sons of the American Revolution, by John St. Paul, Jr., Historian General and Assisted by Stuart O. Landry. Published by the National Society of the Sons of the American Revolution, Louisville, KY. Originally published in 1962. Copyright in 1962 by Stuart O. Landry. Reprinted in 1982 with permission.

The Sons of the American Revolution, NSSAR History, Volume III, 1983-1999 An Historical Anthology, Edited by Robert F. Jackson, Historian General, and Garrett F. Jackson, Commander NSSAR Color Guard. Published by John Frederick Hopkins Lowewe, CASSAR. Published by the National Society of the Sons of the American Revolution, Louisville, KY. Copyright 2000 NSSAR Louisville, KY.

United States of America's Congressional Medal of Honor Recipients and Their Official Citations, Fifth Edition, Highland House II, Columbia Heights, MN, Copyrighted 2006.

"Former U.S. President Bush Receives SAR Membership," The SAR Magazine, Summer 2001, Vol. XCVI, No.1. National Society Sons of the American Revolution. Page 13.

"Texas Compatriot Bush Elected U.S. President," The SAR Magazine, Winter 2001, vol. XCV, No.3. National Society Sons of the American Revolution. pp. 4-7.

The Sons of the American Revolution, NSSAR History Membership Directory - 2006, Copyright 2006. The National Society of the Sons of the American Revolution, Louisville, KY.

SAR Leadership

President General David N. Appleby

David N. Appleby is a member in good standing with the Missouri Society. David N. Appleby was elected President General of the National Society, Sons of the American Revolution, on July 8, 2008 to serve a one-year term.

Secretary General Edward F. Butler

Edward F. Butler is a member of the Texas Society. He is responsible for the maintenance of records of the activities of the executive committee, trustees, and national congresses; headquarters staff operations; compiling officer and committee reports for distribution at meetings; meeting registration. He was elected to a one-year term on July 8, 2008.

Treasurer General J. Philip London

Jack London is a member of the District of Colombia Society. He is responsible for the maintenance of financial records; advice and action on financial issues; headquarters merchandise operation; and dues. He was appointed to fill an unexpired term until July 2009.

Chancellor General James K. Say

James K. Say is a member of the IL Society. The Chancellor General shall be an attorney at law. He is responsible to provide advice and action on legal issues relating to the national society. He was elected to a one-year term on July 8, 2008.

Genealogist General Joseph W. Dooley

Joseph W. Dooley is a member of the Virginia Society. He is responsible for guidance on genealogical problems related to applications for membership and supplemental applications. He was elected to a one-year term on July 8, 2008.

Registrar General J. David Sympson

J. David Sympson is a member of the Kentucky Society. He is responsible for the maintenance of membership records. He was elected to a one-year term on July 8, 2008.

Historian General Stephen A. Leishman

Stephen A. Leishman is a member of the Delaware Society. He is responsible for securing and interpreting of the records required for documenting the history of the national society. He was elected to a one-year term on July 8, 2008.

Librarian General Richard D. Brockway

Richard D. Brockway is a member of the West Virginia Society. He is responsible for providing guidance for maintaining the national headquarters library and museum. He was re-elected to a one-year term on July 8, 2008.

Surgeon General Charles R. Treadway, MD

Dr. Treadway is a member of the Tennessee Society. He provides advice and assistance for maintaining the health of our members. He was elected to a one-year term on July 8, 2008.

Chaplain General Reverend David A. Hockensmith

Rev. David Hockensmith is a member of the Vermont Society. He is responsible for providing advice and assistance for ministering to the spiritual needs of our members. He was elected to a one-year term on July 8, 2008.

PRESIDENT GENERALS AND CONGRESSES OF THE SAR

The President General, in addition to his general duties, shall maintain a general supervision over the business and affairs of the Society, he shall appoint all committees, unless otherwise provided for in the Constitution or in these Bylaws, he shall be *ex-officio* Chairman of the Board of Trustees and the Executive Committee and a member of all Standing Committees as set forth in Bylaw No 18, Section 1 The President General shall have the authority to fill any vacancy which may occur for good cause in any General Office, on the Executive Committee, or in the Chairmanship of any Committee, subject to the approval of the Board of Trustees at its next meeting (The SAR Bylaw No 4 - The President General)

The following shows a list of the years, Congress number, the names of the men elected to this high office, and the Society of which they were a member.

Year & No. of Congress		Place of Congress	President General Elected	Society
1889		New York (Fraunces Tavern)	Lucius P Deming	Connecticut
1890	1st	Louisville, KU	Dr William S Webb	New York & Vermont
1891	2nd	Hartford, CT	Dr William S Webb	New York & Vermont
1892	3rd	New York City	General Horace Porter	New York
1893	4th	Chicago, IL	General Horace Porter	New York
1894	5th	Washington, DC	General Horace Porter	New York
1895	6th	Boston, MA	General Horace Porter	New York
1896	7th	Richmond, VA	General Horace Porter	New York
1897	8th	Cleveland, OH	Edward S Barrett	Massachusetts
1898	9th	Morristown, NJ	Edward S Barrett	Massachusetts
1899	10th	Detroit, MI	Franklin Murphy	New Jersey
1900	11th	New York City, NY	Joseph C Breckinridge	Kentucky & DC
1901	12th	Pittsburgh, PA	Walter S Logan	New York
1902	13th	Washington, DC	Gov Edwin Warfield	Maryland
1903	14th	New Haven, CT	Gen Edwin S Greeley	Connecticut
1904	15th	St. Louis, MO	James D Hancock	Pennsylvania
1905	16th	Philadelphia, PA	Francis H Appleton	Massachusetts
1906	17th	Boston, MA	Cornelius C Pugsley	New York
1907	18th	Denver, CO	Nelson A McClary	Illinois
1908	19th	Buffalo, NY	Henry Stockbridge	Maryland
1909	20th	Baltimore, OR	Morris B Beardsley	Connecticut
1910	21st	Toledo, OH	William A Marble	New York
1911	22nd	Louisville, KY	Dr Moses G Parker	Massachusetts
1912	23rd	Boston, MA	James M Richardson	Ohio
1913	24th	Chicago, IL	Rogers Clark Ballard Thruston	Kentucky
1914	25th	Syracuse, NY	Rogers Clark Ballard Thruston	Kentucky
1915	26th	Portland, OR	Newell B Woodworth	New York & San Francisco
1916	27th	Newark, NJ	Elmer M Wentworth	Iowa
1917	28th	Nashville, TN	Elmer M Wentworth	Iowa
1918	29th	Rochester, NY	Louis Annin Ames	New York
1919	30th	Detroit, MI	Chancellor L Jenks	Illinois
1920	31st	Hartford, CT	J Henry Preston	Maryland
1921	32nd	Buffalo, NY	Wallace McCamant	Oregon
1922	33rd	Springfield, MA	Washington Irving Lincoln Adams	New Jersey
1923	34th	Nashville, TN	Arthur Preston Sumner	Rhode Island
1924	35th	Salt Lake City, UT	Marvin Harrison Lewis	Kentucky
1925	36th	Swampscott, MA	Judge Harvey Foote Remington	New York
1926	37th	Philadelphia, PA	Wilbert H Barrett	Michigan
1927	38th	Richmond, VA	Ernest E Rogers	Connecticut
1928	39th	Washington, DC	Ganson Depew	New York
1929	40th	Springfield, IL	Howard Rowley	California
1930	41st	Asbury Park, NJ	Judge Josiah A Van Orsdel	DC
1931	42nd	Charlotte, NC	Benjamin Newhall Johnson	Massachusetts
			(Died in office) – Judge Van Orsdel *(appointed by ExComDC)*	
1932	43rd	Washington, DC	Frederick W Millspaugh	Tennessee
1933	44th	Cincinnati, OH	Arthur M McGrillis	Rhode Island
1934	45th	Baltimore, MD	Arthur M McGrillis	Rhode Island
1935	46th	Louisville, KY	Henry F Baker	Maryland
1936	47th	Portland, ME	Messmore Kendall	New York
1937	48th	Buffalo, NY	Messmore Kendall	New York
1938	49th	Dallas, TX	Messmore Kendall	New York
1939	50th	New London, CT	Messmore Kendall	New York

1940	51st	Washington, DC	Loren E Souers	Ohio
1941	52nd	Columbus, OH	G Ridgely Sappington	Maryland
1942	53rd	Williamsburg, VA	Sterling Fahn Mutz	Nebraska
1943	54th	New York City, NY	Smith Lewis Multer	New Jersey
1944	55th	Harrisburg, PA	Smith Lewis Multer	New Jersey
1945		*No Meeting on Account of the War*		
1946	56th	Trenton, NJ	Allen L Oliver	Missouri
1947	57th	Huntington, WV	A Herbert Foreman	Virginia
1948	58th	Minneapolis, MN	Charles B Shaler	Pennsylvania
			(Died in office) – Ben H Powell *(appointed by ExCom Texas)*	
1949	59th	Jacksonville, FL	John Whelchel Finger	New York
1950	60th	Atlantic City, NJ	Wallace C Hall	Michigan
1951	61st	San Francisco, CA	Wallace C Hall	Michigan
1952	62nd	Houston, TX	Ray O Edwards	Florida
1953	63rd	Cincinnati, OH	Arthur A de la Houssaye	Louisiana
1954	64th	Williamsburg, VA	Milton M Lory	Iowa
1955	65th	Chicago, IL	Edgar Williamson, Jr	New Jersey
1956	66th	Lake George, NY	Eugene P Carver, Jr	Massachusetts
1957	67th	Salt Lake City, UT	George E Tarbox, Jr	Colorado
1958	68th	Biloxi, MS	Walter A Wentworth	New York
1959	69th	Pittsburgh, PA	Charles A Jones	Ohio
1960	70th	Memphis, TN	Dr Herschel S Murphy	New Jersey
1961	71st	Clearwater, FL	Horace Y Kitchell	Mississippi
1962	72nd	Philadelphia, PA	Charles A Anderson, MD	Ohio
1963	73rd	Lexington, KY	Robert L Sonfield	Texas
1964	74th	Detroit, MI	Harry T Burn	Tennessee
1965	75th	Albuquerque, NM	Howard E Coe	Connecticut
1966	76th	Groton, CT	Kenneth G Smith, Sr	Pennsylvania
1967	77th	Columbus, OH	Len Young Smith	Illinois
1968	78th	Williamsburg, VA	Walter G Sterling	Texas
1969	79th	Salt Lake City, UT	James B Gardiner	New York
1970	80th	Houston, TX	Walter P Martin	Rhode Island
1971	81st	Atlantic City, NJ	Eugene C McGuire	Ohio
1972	82nd	Indianapolis, IN	Ryall S Morgan	Alabama
1973	83rd	Palm Beach, FL	Marion Crawmer	Michigan
1974	84th	Baltimore, MD	M Graham Clark, EdD	Missouri
1975	85th	Boston, MA	Robert D Savage, Lt Col USA Ret	Pennsylvania
1976	86th	Philadelphia, PA	Matthew B Sellers	Florida
1977	87th	Milwaukee, WI	Wilson King Barnes	Maryland
1978	88th	Louisville, KY	Calvin Ellsworth Chunn, PhD	California
1979	89th	San Diego, CA	Calvin Ellsworth Chunn, PhD	California
1980	90th	Dallas, TX	Arthur Mansfield King	Kansas
1981	91st	Oklahoma City, OK	Richard H Thompson, Jr	Florida
1982	92nd	Portland, OR	Howard L Hamilton, PhD	Virginia
1983	93rd	Atlanta, GA	Warren G Hayes, Jr	Pennsylvania
1984	94th	Cincinnati, OH	Carl F Bessent	Maryland
1985	95th	Louisville, KY	Col Benjamin H Morris	Kentucky
1986	96th	Tampa, FL	Clovis H Brakebill	Texas
1987	97th	Valley Forge, PA	Nolan W Carson	Ohio
1988	98th	Tyson's Corner, VA	Charles F Printz, Sr	West Virginia
1989	99th	San Francisco, CA	James R Westlake	Georgia
1990	100th	Louisville, KY	Col James R Calhoun	New Mexico
1991	101st	Kansas City, KS	George H Brandau, MD	Texas
1992	102nd	Norfolk, VA	Paul H Walker	Massachusetts
1993	103rd	Phoenix, AZ	Col Robert B Vance, Sr	Georgia
1994	104th	New Orleans, LA	Col Stewart Boone McCarty, Jr	DC
1995	105th	Louisville, KY	William C Gist, Jr DMD	Kentucky
1996	106th	San Antonio, TX	Reon G Hillegass, Jr	Virginia
1997	107th	Baltimore, MD	Carl K Hoffmann	Florida
1998	108th	Orlando, FL	Russell D Page	Illinois
1999	109th	San Diego, CA	Howard F Horne, Jr, PhD	Delaware
2000	110th	Boston, MA	Bruce B Butler, DDS	Louisiana
			(Died in office) – Howard F Horne, Jr, PhD *(appointed by ExCom Delaware)*	
2001	111th	Louisville, KY	Larry D McClanahan	Tennessee
2002	112th	Nashville, TN	B Rice Aston	Texas
2003	113th	Chicago, IL	Raymond G Musgrave	West Virginia
2004	114th	Pittsburgh, PA	Henry N McCarl, PhD	Massachusetts
2005	115th	Louisville, KY	Roland G Downing, PhD	Delaware
2006	116th	Dallas, TX	Nathan E White	Texas
2007	117th	Williamsburg, VA	Bruce A Wilcox	Virginia
2008	118th	Sacramento, CA	David N Appleby	Missouri
2009	119th	Atlanta, GA	In planning	
2010	120th	Cleveland, OH	In planning	
2011	121st	Winston-Salem, NC	In planning	
2012	122nd	Phoenix, AZ	In planning	
2013	123rd	Kansas City, MO	In planning	

SAR Districts

The SAR organization is made up of 15 districts (two of which are located outside the US). Each District is headed by a Vice President General (VPG). These districts are then divided into Societies (usually a State) and a State is divided into chapters. Our Bylaws say there shall be one Vice-President General elected from each districts and that the President General shall appoint a Vice-President General for an International District.

Each VPG is to promote the interest and activities that further the objectives of the National Society among the State Societies in his district. He should visit each of the State Societies in his district at least once annually. Each VPG should endeavor to visit the various chapters in his district during his term of office and encourage the enrollment of new members and formation of new chapters where needed.

Each VPG shall provide a written report on the activities of his district at the Spring and Fall meetings of the Trustees as well as to the delegates Annual Congress of the National Society. A copy of this report is to be available for all members by the National Society. A copy of the report shall also be placed in the archives of the National Society for future reference.

The 15 districts are listed below with their respective Vice President General.

New England	Maine, New Hampshire, Vermont, Massachusetts, Rhode Island, and Connecticut. VPG Hans E. Jackson
North Atlantic	New York and New Jersey VPG John A. Moller
Mid-Atlantic	Delaware, Maryland, The District of Columbia, Pennsylvania, and Virginia VPG Gareth H. Bonds
South Atlantic	North Carolina, South Carolina, Georgia, and Florida. VPG Lindsey C. Brock
Southern	Alabama, Tennessee, Mississippi, and Louisiana VPG Andrew M. Jones
Central	Ohio, Indiana, West Virginia, and Kentucky VPG Stephen C. Emery
Great Lakes	Michigan, Illinois, and Wisconsin VPG Russell M. Buhr
North Central	Minnesota, The Dakota Society, Iowa, and Nebraska VPG William H. Lees
South Central	Missouri, Kansas, Arkansas, Oklahoma, and Texas VPG Robert L. Grover
Rocky Mountain	Arizona, Colorado, and New Mexico VPG Norman H. Kronvall
Inter-Mountain Pacific	Idaho, Montana, Utah, and Wyoming VPG Benjamin D. Horne
Western	California, Nevada, and Hawaii VPG Elvin L. Spray
Pacific	Washington, Oregon, and Alaska VPG Melvin M. Scott
Europe	United Kingdom, France, Switzerland, Germany, and the remainder of the Continent of Europe VPG Jacques de Trentinan
International	All territory outside of the other districts VPG Gerald R. McCoy

SAR Societies and Chapters

The following is a list of SAR Societies and the chapters within those societies. Each society and chapter is lead by a society or chapter president. Some societies are small in geographic area and do not have any chapters such as the District of Columbia Society. The states of North and South Dakota are large in geographic area but sparsely populated so are listed together as the Dakota Society. Below is a list of Societies with active chapters as of October 2008.

Society Name	City Where Meetings and/or Area Covered
Alaska Society SAR	
Society only	
Alabama Society SAR	
Birmingham	Birmingham Metro Area
Black Warrior River	Tuscaloosa, Tuscaloosa County & surrounding area
Cahaba Coosa	Columbiana, Shelby County area
Cheaha	Annison, Calhoun County & surrounding area
Cullman	Cullman, Cullman County & surrounding area
Etowah	Gasden & surrounding area
Gen. Galvez	Mobile, Spanish Fort, Daphne & surrounding area
Gen. John Archer Elmore	Prattville, Autauga County & surrounding area
Gen. Richard Montgomery	Montgomery, Montgomery Co. & surrounding area
John Henry Lentz	Athens, Limestone County & surrounding area
Little River	Fort Payne, DeKalb County & surrounding area
Richard Henry Lee	Auburn, Opelika & surrounding area
Tennessee Valley	Huntsville, Madison County & surrounding area
Tri-State	Dothan & surrounding tri-state (AL, GA, FL) area
Warrior River	Jasper, Walker County & surrounding area
Wiregrass	Enterprise/Geneva & surrounding area
Arkansas Society SAR	
Abraham Van Buren	Clinton
Bayou Bartholomew	Pine Bluff
Chickasawba	Blytheville
Count Pulaski	Little Rock
Crowley Ridge	Jonesboro
Desoto Trail	Hot Springs
Ecore Fabre	Camden
Gen. Lafayette	Northwest Arkansas
Jordan Milam	Harrison
Southwest Trail	Texarkana
Arizona Society SAR	
Barry M. Goldwater	Phoenix, Scottsdale, Paradise Valley & Fountain Hills
Colorado River	Kingman, Bullhead City & Lake Havasu City
Palo Verde	East Valley Communities
Phoenix	Phoenix, Scottsdale & Paradise Valley
Prescott	Prescott & surrounding area
Saguaro	Sun Cities, Glendale, Litchfield Park, Peoria & Youngtown
Tucson	Tucson & southern Arizona
California Society SAR	
Butte	Butte County area
Central Coast	San Luis Obispo, Northern Santa Barbara, & Southern Monterey counties
Coachella Valley	Eastern Riverside County
Delta	Modesto
Gen George Patton	Western Los Angeles & Ventura counties
General George Washington	Chico
Gold Country	Placer County
Harbor	Long Beach area
Kern	Kern County
Monterey Bay	Monterey Bay
Mother Lode	El Dorado County
Orange County	Fullerton
Redding	Redding
Redlands	Inland Empire & High Desert
Redwood Empire	Sonoma County
Riverside	Riverside
Sacramento	Sacramento
San Diego	San Diego
San Francisco	San Francisco
Santa Barbara	Santa Barbara
Silicon Valley	Cupertino
Sons of Liberty	Northern Los Angeles County
South Coast	South Orange County
Thomas Jefferson	San Francisco/East Bay Area
Colorado Society SAR	
Grand Mesa	Western Slope
Longs Peak	Northern Front Range
Mount Evans	Central Front Range
Pikes Peak	Southern Front Range Colorado to Pueblo
Connecticut Society SAR	
Capt Matthew Mead Branch #11	Greenwich
Capt Nathan Hale Branch #6	New London
Captain John Couch Branch #2	Meriden
Col Jeremiah Wadsworth Branch #7	Hartford
Colonel Elisha Sheldon Branch #8	Salisbury
Gen David Humphreys Branch #1	New Haven
Gen Gold Selleck Silliman Branch #3	Bridgeport
Gen Israel Putnam Branch #4	Vernon
Gov Oliver Wolcott, Sr. Branch #10	Torrington
Gov Samuel Huntington Branch #12	Norwich
Rev Ebenezer Baldwin Branch #9	Newtown
Roger Sherman Branch #5	Mid-Fairfield County
Dakota Society SAR	
Society only	
DC Society SAR	
Society only	
Delaware Society SAR	
Caesar Rodney	Kent County, Dover
Major Peter Jaquett	New Castle Country, Wilmington
Major Robert Kirkwood	New Castle Country, Newark
Florida Society SAR	
Aaron Snowden	Milton, Santa Rosa County
Brevard	Cocoa Beach, Brevard County
Caloosa	Ft. Myers, Lee County
Central Florida	Orlando, Orange County
Charlotte	Charlotte County
Clearwater	Clearwater, Pinellas County
Daytona-Ormond	Daytona, Volusia County
Deland	Deland, Volusia County
Major John Devane	Hillsborough County
Emerald Coast	Okaloosa County
Flagler	Palm Coast, Flagler County
Ft Lauderdale	Ft Lauderdale, Broward County
Gainesville	Gainesville, Alachua County
Jacksonville	Jacksonville, Duval County
Lake Sumter	Leesburg, Lee & Sumter counties
Lakeland	Lakeland, Polk County
Miami	Miami, Dade County
Naples	Naples, Collier County
Ocala	Ocala, Marion County
Palm Beach	Palm Beach County
Panama City	Panama City, Bay County
Pensacola	Pensacola, Escambia County
Saramana	Sarasota, Sarasota & Manatee counties

Chapter	Location
St Augustine	St Augustine, St. Johns
St Lucie River	St. Lucie County
St Petersburg	St Petersburg, Pinellas County
Tallahassee	Tallahassee, Leon County
Tampa	Hillsborough County
Treasure Coast	Indian River County
William Dunaway	Greenwood, Jackson
Withlacoochee	Inverness, Citrus & Hernando counties

France Society SAR

Society Only

Georgia Society SAR

Chapter	Location
Abraham Baldwin	Albany, Dougherty County
Altamaha	Jesup, Wayne County
Athens	Athens, Clarke, Madison, Oconee, Jackson, Barrow & Oglethorpe counties
Atlanta	Atlanta, (south) Fulton County
Blue Ridge Mountains	Blairsville, Union County
Button Gwinnett	Lawrenceville, Gwinnett County
Capt John Collins	Marietta, Cobb County
Casimir Pulaski	Carrollton, Carroll County
Cherokee	Canton, Cherokee County
Coweta Falls	Columbus, Muscogee County
Dalton	Dalton, Whitfield County
Edward Telfair	Savannah, Chatham County
George Walton	Conyers, Newton County
Joel Early	Bainbridge, Decatur County
John Milledge	Milledgeville, Baldwin County
Joseph Habersham	Cornelia, Habersham County
LaGrange	LaGrange, Troup County
Lyman Hall	Gainesville, Hall County
Marquis De Lafayette	Fayetteville, Fayette County
Marshes Of Glynn	Brunswick, Glynn County
Mill Creek	Statesboro, Bulloch County
Ocmulgee	Macon/Warner Robins, Bibb County
Patrick Carr Rangers	Waynesboro, Burke County
Piedmont	Alpharetta/Roswell, (north) Fulton County
Rome	Rome, Floyd County
Samuel Butts	Jackson, Butts County
Samuel Elbert	Elberton, Elbert County
Sons of Liberty	Hiram, Paulding County
Valdosta	Valdosta, Lowndes County
William Few	Augusta, Richmond County
William Miller	Waycross, Ware County

Germany Society SAR

Society only

Hawaii Society SAR

Society only

Iowa Society SAR

Chapter	Location
Central Iowa	Des Moines

Idaho Society SAR

Chapter	Location
Old Fort Boise	Boise

Illinois Society SAR

Chapter	Location
American Bicentennial	Northwest part of Cook County
Capt Elijah Smith	Cass, Morgan & Scott counties
Ewington	Eastern part of Fayette & Effingham counties
Fox Valley	DeKalb, DuPage, Kane, Kendall & Will counties
Ft Dearborn	City of Chicago & metro area
Gen George Rogers Clark	Madison County
Gen Joseph Bartholomew	McLean, Woodford & Livingston counties
Kishwaukee	Boone, Winnebago, & Ogle, counties
Lake Defiance	McHenry & Lake counties
Lewis & Clark	St. Clair, Monroe, Randolph & Clinton counties
Long Knife	Southern part of Illinois
Othniel Looker	Jasper, Crawford & Lawrence counties
Piankeshaw	Champaign, Vermillion & Douglas counties
Salt Creek	Chicago & western Cook County
Springfield	Menard & Sangamon counties
Stephen Decatur	DeWitt, Macon & Piatt counties
Capt. Zeally Moss	Bureau, Henry, Knox, Marshall, Peoria, Putnam, Stark & Tazewell counties

Indiana Society SAR

Chapter	Location
Alexander Hamilton	Fishers
Alexis Coquillard	South Bend
Anthony Halberstadt	Fort Wayne
Benjamin Franklin	Franklin
Clarence A Cook	Indianapolis
Continental	Muncie
Daniel Guthrie	Bedford
David Benton	Brownstown
Duneland	Valparaiso
Gen Thomas Posey	Mount Vernon
George Rogers Clark	Vincennes
John Hay	Salem
John Martin	Rockville
Ohio Valley	Evansville
Seth Jewel	Auburn
Simon Kenton	Rensselar
Thaddeus Kosciuszko	Warsaw
William Henry Harrison	Lafayette
William Knight	Greencastle

Kansas Society SAR

Chapter	Location
Bennington	Salina
Charles Robinson	Lawrence
Delaware Crossing	Shawnee Mission
Fort Hays	Hays
Fort Scott	Fort Scott
Henry Leavenworth	Leavenworth
Konza Prairie	Manhattan/Junction City
Monticello	NW Johnson County
Sons Of The Plains	Hutchinson
Thomas Jefferson	Topeka
Washington	Wichita

Kentucky Society SAR

Chapter	Location
Big Sandy	Prestonsburg
Capt Charles Gatliff	Williamsburg
Capt James Campen	Paducah
Capt John Metcalfe	Madisonville
Capt John Scott	Georgetown
Capt William Arnold	Williamstown
Charles Duncan	Bowling Green
George Mason	Maysville
Gov. Isaac Shelby	Shelbyville
James Early	Corbin
John Manire	Hopkinsville
John Weaver	Scottsville
Lafayette	Lexington
Louisville-Thurston	Louisville
Lt. Robert Moseley	Owensboro

Louisiana Society SAR

Chapter	Location
Attakapas	Lafayette
Benjamin Tennille	Monroe
Enemund Meuillion	Alexandria
Galvez	Shreveport
Gen Philemon Thomas	Baton Rouge
George Washington	New Orleans
Oliver Pollock	Lake Charles
Pierre Georges Rousseau	Slidell

Massachusetts Society SAR

Chapter	Location
Boston/Old Colony/Plymouth	Boston
Cape Cod	Harwich
Col William Henshaw	Worcester
Fairbanks	Halifax, NS
Gen Benjamin Lincoln	Plymouth County
George Washington/Berkshire/ Seth Pomeroy	West Springfield
Old Essex/Old Suffolk	Manchester-By-The-Sea, Essex County
Old Middlesex/Minuteman	Concord
Robert Treat Paine	Taunton

Maryland Society SAR

Chapter	Location
Capt John Smoot	Somerset, Worchester, Wicomico, & Dorchester counties
Charles Carroll of Carrollton	Howard County
Col Aquila Hall	Harford County
Col Henry Hollingsworth	Cecil County
Col John Eager Howard	Baltimore City
Col Nicholas R Moore	Baltimore County
Col Tench Tilghman	Caroline, Kent, Queen Anne & Talbot counties
Gen William Smallwood	Montgomery County
John Hanson	Prince George County
John Paul Jones	Anne Arundel County
Little Meadows	Allegany & Garrett counties
Sgt Lawrence Everhart	Frederick County
Thomas Stone	Calvert, Charles, & St. Mary's counties
Westminster	Carroll County

Maine Society SAR

Society only

Mexico Society SAR
Society only

Michigan Society SAR
Detroit Metropolitan ... Detroit Metro Area
Northern Michigan ... Traverse City
Oaks ... Bloomfield Hills
Paul Emery ... Flint
River Raisin ... Adrian
Sauk Trail ... Battle Creek
West Michigan ... Grand Rapids

Minnesota Society SAR
Minneapolis ... Minneapolis
St Paul ... St Paul

Missouri Society SAR
Alexander Majors ... Kansas City
Allen Laws Oliver ... Cape Girardeau
Cpl Braxton C Pollard ... Kirksville
Christopher Casey ... Jefferson City
Fernando De Leybe ... St. Charles
Harry S Truman ... Independence
Independence Patriots ... Independence
Joseph Morgan ... Platte City
M. Graham Clark ... Columbia
Martin Warren ... Warrensburg
Ozark Mountain ... Springfield
Sgt Ariel Nims ... Joplin
Spirit of 76 ... Harrisonville
Spirit Of St Louis ... St. Louis
William C. Corum ... Liberty
Lewis & Clark Expedition ... Chillicothe

Mississippi Society SAR
Capt William Hillhouse ... Columbus
Central Mississippi ... Jackson
Daniel Mackie ... Oxford - Inactive
David Murphree ... Bruce
Desoto Patriots ... Southaven
Dr Joseph Warren ... Vicksburg
Greenwood ... Greenwood
Gulf Coast ... Gulfport-Biloxi
Isaac Carter ... Hattiesburg
Jacob Horger ... Laurel
John Wheat ... Picayune
Nathaniel Greene ... Greenville
Patrick Boggan ... Meridian
South Central ... Brookhaven
Thadeuz Kosciuszko ... Kosciuzko
William Gray ... Booneville/Tupelo

Nebraska Society SAR
Lincoln ... Lincoln
Omaha ... Omaha

New Hampshire Society SAR
Society only

New Jersey Society SAR
Abraham Clark ... Roselle
Capt Abraham Godwin ... Passaic & Bergen counties
Col John Rosenkrans ... Warren & Sussex counties
Col Richard Somers ... Atlantic Cumberland & Cape May counties
Princeton-Cranbury ... Hunterdon, Mercer & parts of Somerset, Middlesex & Monmouth counties
Elizabethtown ... Any NJ Compatriots
First Mountain ... Essex, Bergen & Hudson counties
Jockey Hollow ... Morris, Hunterton & Somerset counties
Monmouth ... Monmouth county
Pinelands ... Ocean & Burlington counties
Raritan Valley ... Middlesex county
South Jersey ... Burlington, Camden, Gloucester, Salem, & Cumberland counties
West Fields ... Union, Middlesex & Somerset counties

New Mexico Society SAR
Albuquerque ... Albuquerque
Las Cruces ... Las Cruces
Santa Fe ... Santa Fe

Nevada Society SAR
Northern Nevada ... Reno & surrounding area
Signers ... Las Vegas & surrounding area

Empire State (New York) Society SAR
Binghamton ... Binghamton - Central Region
Buffalo ... Buffalo - Western Region
Chautauqua ... Jamestown - Western Region
Columbia-Mid Hudson Valley ... Columbia - Capitol Region
Finger Lakes ... Ithaca - Western Region
First New York Continental ... New York City - Metropolitan Region
Long Island ... Long Island - Metropolitan Region
New York ... New York City - Metropolitan Region
Newtown Battle ... Painted Post - Elmira - Western Region
Oriskany Battle ... Rome - Utica - Central Region
Rochester ... Rochester - Western Region
Saratoga Battle ... Saratoga - Albany - Capital Region
Schoharie- Leatherstocking ... Schoharie - Capital Region
Stone Arabia Battle ... Capital Region
Stony Point ... Stony Point - Metropolitan Region
Syracuse ... Syracuse - Central Region
Valcour Battle ... Capital Region
Walloomsac Battle ... Capital Region
Westchester-Putnam ... Westchester - Putnam - Metropolitan Region

North Caroliina Society SAR
Alamance Battleground ... Burlington
Bethabara ... Winston-Salem
Blue Ridge ... Asheville
Catawba Valley ... Conover
Colson's Mill ... Albemarle
Gen. Francis Nash ... Durham
General George Washington ... Washington
Halifax Reserves ... Halifax
Le Marquis de Lafayette ... Fayetteville
Lower Cape Fear ... Wilmington
Lt. Col. Felix Walker ... Enka
Lt. Col. John Phifer ... Concord
Mecklenburg ... Charlotte
Nathanael Greene ... Greensboro
New Bern ... New Bern
Northern Albemarle ... Hertford
Raleigh ... Raleigh
Salisbury ... Salisbury
Silas McDowell ... Franklin
Yadkin Valley ... Elkin

Ohio Society SAR
Arthur St Clair ... Chillicothe
Benjamin Franklin ... Columbus
Bill Of Rights ... Bowling Green - Maumee - Perrysburg
Camp Charlotte ... Circleville
Centennial ... Lima
Cincinnati ... Cincinnati
Constitution ... Mansfield
Ebenezer Zane ... St. Clairsville
Ethan Allen ... Warren
Ewing ... Athens - Pomeroy
Firelands Bicentennial ... Lorain
General Henry Knox ... Mt. Vernon
George Rogers Clark ... Springfield
John Hancock ... Findlay
John Stark ... Canton
Lafayette ... Akron
Marietta ... Marietta
Nathan Hale ... Youngstown
Northeastern Ohio ... Ashtabula County
Northwest Territory ... Bryan
Richard Montgomery ... Dayton
Rufus Putnam ... Zanesville
Samuel Huntington ... Painesville
Western Reserve Society ... Cleveland

Oklahoma Society SAR
Bartlesville ... Bartlesville
Norman ... Norman
Oklahoma City ... Oklahoma City
Tulsa ... Tulsa

Oregon Society SAR
Central Coast ... Florence
Eugene ... Eugene
Lewis and Clark ... Beaverton
Republic ... Salem
Southern Oregon ... Medford

Pennsylvania Society SAR
Centre County ... State College
Christopher Gist ... Butler
Conococheague ... Chambersburg
Continental Congress ... York
Erie ... Erie
Fort Halifax ... Halifax
Fort Jackson ... Waynesburg
Frontier Patriots ... Altoona
Gen Anthony Wayne ... Beaver Falls
Gen Arthur St Clair ... Greensburg

Gen James Potter ... Coudersport
George Washington ... Washington
Gov Joseph Hiester ... Reading
Harris Ferry ... Harrisburg
New Castle ... New Castle
Northeast ... Scranton – Wilkes Barre
Philadelphia-Continental ... Philadelphia
Pittsburgh ... Pittsburgh
Somerset Cambria ... Somerset
Tiadaghton ... Williamsport
Valley Forge ... Allentown – Bethlehem – Easton
Washington Crossing ... Washington Crossing
Washingtonburg ... Carlisle
William Maclay ... Sunbury

Rhode Island Society SAR

John Peck Rathbun ... East Greenwich
Gen. Lippitt & Col. Olney ... Providence
Washington County ... Westerly

South Carolina Society SAR

Battle Of Eutaw Springs ... Orangeburg
Cambridge ... Greenwood
Col Joseph Kershaw ... Camden
Col Lemuel Benton ... Myrtle Beach
Col Robert Anderson ... Greenville
Col Thomas Taylor ... Columbia
Col William Bratton ... Rockhill
Daniel Morgan ... Spartanburg
Dr George Mosse ... Hilton Head Island
Gen Andrew Pickens ... Clemson
Gen Francis Marion ... Bennettsville
General James Williams ... Clinton
Gov Paul Hamilton ... Beaufort
Henry Laurens ... Aiken
Major General William Moultrie ... Charleston
Matthew Singleton ... Sumter

Switzerland Society SAR

Society only

Tennessee Society SAR

Andrew Crockett ... Franklin/Williamson County area
Andrew Jackson ... Nashville/Davidson County area
Col. Benjamin Cleveland ... Cleveland/Bradley County area
Christopher Strong ... Charlotte/Dickson County area
General Joseph Martin ... Ruttledge/Grainger County area
Hiwassee ... McMinn/Meigs/Monroe County areas
Isaac Shelby ... Memphis/Shelby County area
Jackson Purchase ... Union City/Obion County area
James Madison ... Jackson/Madison County area
John Sevier ... Chattanooga, Hamilton & Marion County areas
Kings Mountain ... Johnson City/Washington County area
Lt. W.P. Quarles ... Cookeville/Putnam County area
Stephen Holston ... Knoxville/Knox/Blount County areas
Stones River ... Murfreesboro/Rutherford County area
Sumner ... Gallatin/Sumner County area
Tombigbee ... Columbia/Maury County area
Valentine Sevier ... Clarksville/Montgomery County area
Watauga ... Elizabethton/Carter/Johnson County areas

Texas Society SAR

Aaron Burleson ... Smithville
Alexander Hodge ... Sugar Land
Ambassador Fletcher Warren ... Greenville
Arlington ... Arlington
Athens ... Athens
Bernardo De Galvez ... Galveston
Big Country ... Abilene
Bluebonnet ... Fredericksburg
Boerne ... Boerne
Brazos Valley ... Granbury
Capt John McAdams ... Huntsville
Capt William Barron ... Tyler
Col Turner R Sharp ... El Paso
Corpus Christi ... Corpus Christi
Cradle Of Texas ... Lake Jackson
Dallas ... Dallas
Daniel Wood ... San Angelo
Denton ... Denton
East Fork-Trinity ... Garland
East Texas ... Longview
Edmund Terrill ... Sherman
Fredonia ... Nacogdoches
Freedom ... Conroe
Heart Of Texas ... Salado
Hill Country ... Kerrville
Independence ... College Station
Laredo ... Laredo
Leon River Valley ... Hamilton
Liberty ... South Padre Island
Live Oak ... George West
Lt Nathan Gann ... Lufkin
Major K. M. Van Zandt ... Fort Worth
Major White ... Baytown
McKinney ... McKinney
Mesquite ... Mesquite
North Central Texas ... Wichita Falls
Panhandle Plains ... Amarillo
Patrick Henry ... Austin
Paul Carrington ... Houston
Paul Revere ... Beaumont - Longview
Permian Basin ... Midland
Piney Woods ... Kingwood
Plano ... Plano
Red River Valley ... Paris
Robert Rankin ... Katy
San Antonio ... San Antonio
Texas Tech ... Lubbock
Victoria ... Victoria
William Hightower ... New Braunfels

UK Society SAR

Society only

Utah Society SAR

Society only

Virginia Society SAR

Clinch Mountain Militia ... Tazewell area
Col Fielding Lewis ... Eastern Piedmont area
Col George Waller ... Martinsville area
Col James Wood Jr. ... Northwest Virginia
Colonel William Grayson ... Prince William County area
Culpeper Minute Men ... Central Piedmont area
Dan River ... Danville area
Fairfax Resolves ... Fairfax County
Fincastle Resolutions ... Roanoke Valley area
Fort Harrison ... Harrisonburg area
Gen Daniel Morgan ... Staunton area
Gen William Campbell ... Abingdon area
George Mason ... Arlington County
George Washington ... Alexandria
James Monroe ... Upper Northern Neck
Lt David Cox ... Galax/Independence
Martin Station ... Cumberland Gap
New River Valley ... New River Valley area
Norfolk ... Norfolk/Virginia Beach area
Overmountain Men ... Gate City area
Patrick Henry ... Lynchburg area
Richard Henry Lee ... Lower Northern Neck
Richmond ... Richmond/Petersburg
Rockbridge Volunteers ... Lexington/Staunton
Sgt Major John Champe ... Leesburg
Thomas Jefferson ... Charlottesville
Thomas Nelson Jr ... Newport News/Hampton
Williamsburg ... Williamsburg/Yorktown

Vermont Society SAR

Society only

Washington Society SAR

Alexander Hamilton ... Tacoma Junction
Cascade Centennial ... Redmond
Seattle ... Seattle
Spokane ... Spokane

Wisconsin Society SAR

Capt Hendrick Aupaumut ... Green Bay Fox River Valley
Elisha Raymond ... Sturtevant
Morgan-Kosciuszko ...
Nathaniel Ames ... Dane County
Stephen Tainter ...

West Virginia Society SAR

Capt James Neal ... Parkersburg
Capt Ralph Stewart ... Oceana
Daniel Boone ... Charleston
Gen Adam Stephen ... Martinsburg
Gen Andrew Lewis ... Huntington
George Rogers Clark ... Clarksburg
Greenbrier Valley ... Lewisburg
Pt Pleasant ... Pt Pleasant

Wyoming Society SAR

Society only

Organization Dates of State Societies

The membership of the National Society is organized in state societies, and in most states there are local chapters. The various state societies were organized as follows:

Alabama	Feb. 10, 1889	Missouri	April 23, 1889
Alaska	Oct. 21, 1953	Nebraska	April 6, 1890
Arizona	June 13, 1896	Nevada	Feb. 19, 1910
Arkansas	Feb. 11, 1890	New Hampshire	April 24, 1889
California +	Oct. 22, 1875	New Jersey	March 7, 1889
Colorado	July 4, 1896	New Mexico	Dec. 5, 1908
Connecticut	April 2, 1889	New York	Feb. 11, 1890
Delaware	Jan. 29, 1889	North Carolina	March 31, 1911
D.C.	July 25, 1890	North Dakota *	Feb. 4, 1911
Florida	March 14, 1896	Ohio	April 22, 1889
France	Sept. 16, 1897	Oklahoma	Feb. 22, 1905
Georgia	March 15, 1921	Oregon	June 6, 1891
Germany	July 2, 2001	Pennsylvania	Nov. 23, 1893
Hawaii	June 17, 1895	Rhode Island	Feb. 1, 1890
Idaho	April 8, 1909	South Carolina	April 18, 1889
Indiana	Jan. 15, 1890	South Dakota *	April 24, 1899
Iowa	Sept. 5, 1893	Switzerland	June 1, 1973
Kansas	March 31, 1892	Tennessee	Dec. 2, 1889
Kentucky	April 8, 1889	Texas	Dec. 8, 1896
Louisiana	May 15, 1890	United Kingdom	Feb. 20, 1982
Maine	March 14, 1891	Utah	Jan. 27, 1895
Maryland	April 20, 1889	Vermont	April 2, 1889
Massachusetts	April 19, 1889	Virginia	July 7, 1890
Mexico	Feb. 17, 2002	Washington	June 17, 1895
Michigan	Jan. 18, 1890	West Virginia	Feb. 22, 1911
Minnesota	Dec. 26, 1889	Wisconsin	Jan. 14, 1890
Mississippi	May 10, 1909	Wyoming	March 28, 1908

+ CASSAR was founded as an independent society prior to founding of the SAR.

* At the request of the two state societies, North Dakota and South Dakota Societies have been combined into one Dakota Society, effective October 18, 1980.

Compatriot Stories

of the

National Society of the Sons of the American Revolution

General von Steuben drilling the troops at Valley Forge (1777-78).

Colonial Heroes: The Battle of Point Pleasant

by Lois T. Allen

"From 1764 there were ten years of peace in Augusta County, Virginia. No war, or rumors of war, disturbed the inhabitants." The last wrathful incursion by Indians in the valley had occurred about 1766.

But these sanguine days did not last. The early part of 1774 brought belligerent action from Indian tribes. Alarmed at the settlement of whites moving toward Kentucky led to war-like activity. Single and isolated murders, and the slaying of an entire family of a noted Indian chief, raised the height of retaliations on both sides.

Logan, a son of the Cayuga chief, had been friendly to the settlers until his family was murdered by a party of marauding white men. Then he turned into a "fiend incarnate." He proceeded to form tribe alliances to get revenge against his former friends.

The government at Williamsburg found it necessary to initiate protection of the Western Virginians. Lord Dunsmore, the Governor, ordered Brigadier General Andrew Lewis to raise a regiment of some 400 Augusta men. They were to be commanded by Colonel Charles Lewis, his brother.

Two more Augustan brothers, Lt. Hugh Allen and James Allen, were employed to scout out a route to a point where the Kanawa River meets with Ohio. This place of heavy forests and meadows was called Point Pleasant. When the Allen party returned to Staunton, Virginia, a plan of action was completed. Large numbers of cattle were herded, for wagons could not be deployed over the rough 160-mile route. In addition, they drove 400 packhorses, carrying 54,000 lbs. of flour to feed the men. The company under Gen. Lewis' command was now about 1,100. On Sept. 11th, the party began its march over the mountains. They forged ahead, averaging over eight miles a day. In 19 days the rugged territory was scaled.

Logan, the Indian chief who had vowed revenge for the murder of his family, was a tribal leader at Point Pleasant. Cornstalk, another chief, aided in the fray. He was heard to exhort the Indians by loudly shouting through the trees, "Be Strong! Be Strong!"

The loss of Virginians in the action was 70 killed and 70 wounded. The bodies of 20 Indians were found in the woods, and another eight died of wounds. Traditionally, Indians were known for carrying fallen comrades with them as they ran from battle, so how many others were killed is not known. The Indians were completely routed.

Col. Charles Lewis fell in battle, as did the scout of the expedition, Lt. Hugh Allen. Hugh's brother, James, stood sorrowfully as his kinsman was buried, side by side with his commander.

Today, a memorial obelisk marks the burial site of those lost at Point Pleasant. A DAR marker tells the tale of the heroes that fought in what is sometimes called, "The First Battle of the War of Revolution." Names of all the Augusta combatants lost in the battle are inscribed on the four sides of the monument.

Bibliography

"Chronicles of the Scotch-Irish Settlement in Virginia, Vol. I," by Lyman Chalkley.

"Seedtime on the Cumberland," by Harriett Simpson Arnow.

"Annals of Augusta County, Virginia, 1726-1871," by Joseph A. Wadell.

Who Held the Lanterns in Paul Revere's Ride?

The *Untold* Story of the Signal Lanterns at Christ Church, Boston[1]

by Marston Watson

For over a century, we have held the words of *Paul Revere's Ride*, a poem written by Henry Wadsworth Longfellow, to be the true story of what happened on that fateful night in 1775. In fact, his second verse really sets the stage for the subject of this article.

> He said to his friend, "If the British march
> By land or sea from the town to-night,
> Hang a lantern aloft in the belfry arch
> Of the North Church tower as a signal light, ...

Longfellow's words would come to roost, when twelve years after its publication, a controversy would brew, involving the **Rev. John Lee Watson, D.D.**,[2] whose letter on "Paul Revere's Signal: The True Story of the Signal Lanterns in Christ Church, Boston" was published July 20, 1876 in the *Boston Daily Advertiser*, and **William W. Weildon**, who responded later in 1878 with his *History of Paul Revere's Signal Lanterns*.

The war of words between Watson and Weildon pitted one man against the other as to who really carried the signal lanterns at Christ Church (Old North Church) on the night of April 18, 1775. Nowhere in Longfellow's poem is the identity of Revere's "friend" revealed. Nowhere in Revere's own writings does he name his friend although he mentions other friends, even though the planning and execution of this event were held in absolute secrecy.

The Rev. Dr. Watson offered his conclusion in 1876 that his uncle, Captain John Pulling, was the "friend" chosen by Paul Revere to provide the signal. Two years later, William Weildon wrote his paper in support of his position that the sexton, Robert Newman, carried the lanterns at the Old North Church. Rev. Watson wrote a second letter in March 1879 to the *Boston Daily Advertiser*, in which he referred to testimonials from a number of people, including Capt. Pulling's second wife Sarah who died a widow in 1843 at age 97.

Paul Revere's own narrative [with additional clarification] provides the primary evidence of what happened on the evening of April 18, 1775. "On Tuesday evening, it was observed [by Richard Devens][3] that a number of soldiers were marching toward Boston Common. About ten o'clock, Dr. [Joseph] Warren sent, in great haste, for me [at Revere's home in North Square], and begged that I would immediately set off for Lexington, where were [John] Hancock and [Samuel] Adams, and acquaint them of the movements, and that it was thought they were the objects. On the Sunday before, I agreed with a Colonel [William] Conant, and some other gentlemen," – in Charlestown, - "that, if the British went out by *water*, we should show *two* lanterns in the North Church steeple, and if by *land*, *one*, as a signal; for we were apprehensive it would be difficult to cross over Charles River. I left Dr. Warren, called upon a friend [possibly his trusted friend Pulling] and desired him to make the signal. I then went home, took my boots and surtout [heavy winter cloak], went to the north part of the town, where I had kept a boat. Two friends [Joshua Bentley and Thomas Richardson] rowed me across Charles River, a little to the eastward where the [British] Somerset Man of War lay." Revere stated further, "When I got into town [Charlestown], I met Col. Conant and several others. They said they had seen our signals [but *not* Revere who already knew what was happening]."

With Revere's own narrative in mind, all other accounts of Revere's meeting at the Newman home prior to his departure, as well as the description of an interrogation of Newman by the British must be considered speculative without actual proof. No records have been found regarding specific details of conversations that took place between Newman and his friends at his home or at Christ Church, nor of his supposed interrogation by the British afterwards. However, Newman and Pulling descendants and some historians generally agree that Robert Newman, Capt. John Pulling and John Bernard were at the Old North Church together when the lanterns were hung. Who climbed the stairs and who stayed below is the historical equivalent of the $64,000 question.

There are some known facts that cannot be disputed. Paul Revere was born 31 Dec. 1734 O.S. (or 1 Jan. 1734/35 N.S.), Capt. John Pulling 18 Feb. 1736/37 and Robert Newman 20 Mar. 1751/52. Revere and Pulling attended the North Grammar School, likely together. Newman attended the same school for less than four months, nearly twenty years later, but not as a purported "classmate of Revere," as he was only five years old when Revere married in 1757. Furthermore, Pulling and Revere served on the Committee of Safety together, but not Newman. Pulling and Revere were members of the Sons of Liberty together, but not Newman. Pulling was an undisguised participant in the Boston Tea Party, along with other Sons of Liberty patriots. However, the three men were members of the Masonic Order, and there is no doubt that Revere knew Robert Newman and perhaps one or two of his older brothers as well.

The Rev. Dr. Watson wrote a second letter in March 1879 to the *Boston Daily Advertiser*, in response to comments he received from his first letter. He agreed with other accounts that Robert Newman had indeed denied to the British authorities that he had made the signal, as "*he told the truth*." He reiterated his earlier statements that "the only *wise precautions* that the sexton could have taken were to tell the truth, deny that he had made the signals, and tell them that *he had given the keys to Mr. Pulling*." Watson concluded in his letter "It appears, however, that the British authorities were fully satisfied that he was not *the man who made the signals*, and accordingly *they set him at liberty*, and *at once began their search for* John Pulling."

This last statement by Watson is suggested by family tradition that Capt. John Pulling did indeed flee Boston in haste for Nantucket Island [i.e. Nantasket?] with his wife and children. Purportedly, his possessions were confiscated and house destroyed, which was not the case with Newman's home and possessions. Apparently, Pulling and his family continued to hide on the island until the Siege of Boston by the British was lifted in 1776.

The editor of the *Transcript* may have had the last word, when he published his response on September 23, 1899. Obviously not wanting to continue this controversy in the newspaper any longer, he stated finally, "One correspondent suggests that it seems likely that both of the men had a hand in the affair, and both should share in the glory, which would certainly be a most gratifying conclusion to the general public." It appears that **David Hackett Fischer, Ph.D.** of Wayland, Massachusetts and author of *Albion's Seed* would agree.

Dr. Fischer observed, that, "there needs to be a generous allowance for family tradition, as well as a respect for the best and most probable fit in the evidence." Perhaps it is time for the stewards of this significant event at the Old North Church to allow for this "happy ending" when presenting the story of the signal lanterns to the public.

Footnotes

[1]This is a condensed version of the article that was published in the *SAR Magazine* (Winter, 2003, 4-8).

[2]The Reverend John Lee Watson, D.D. is the 2nd great-grandfather of author Marston Watson.

[3]Richard Devens is the 5th great-grandfather of author Marston Watson.

Letter of Captain John Chester Addressed To Rev. Joseph Fish, of Stonington, Connecticut

Submitted by David W. Chester

Camp at Cambridge
July 22d, 1775

Rev. and Much Respected Sir,

Your favor of the 4th instant I received the day before the Fast, and should have answered it by the bearer, Mr. Niles, had I not been that day on fatigue duty. The day after Fast Mr. Niles set off for home, from Roxbury. I want words to espress my gratitude and reasons for our animation and support in the glorious struggle for freedom, and your tender expressions of friendship for my family, as well as your anxious concern for my own personal safety.

I shall endeavor, as far as my time and business will permit, to give you, sir, the particulars of the battle of Charlestown. Though, as to the greater part of account published, I may not be able to mend it.

In the latter part of the day before the battle, our adjutant informed me that orders were issued from head-quarters that 1800 province men, and 200 Connecticut men, parade themselves (****) clock, with provisions for twenty-four hours, blankets (***) there wait for further orders. About nine O'(clock t)hey were ordered to march to Bunker Hill, a nu(mbe)r of wagons accompanying them with intrenching tools, &c. Just about twelve o'clock at night they began intrenching, and went with great vigor till daybreak and were then discovered by the regulars, who were heard from the ships and Cops Hill, which was kept up with little or no cessation till afternoon. But finding our people paid little regard to their cannon, and knowing the great importance of the post, they landed, (I believe it was about two o'clock," and formed in three or four solid columns, and advanced into a line for battle, and marched on very regularly, rank and file. They were very near Mystic River, and, by their movements, had determined to outflank our men, and surround them and the fort. But our officers in command, soon perceiving their intention, ordered a large party of men (chiefly Connecticut) to leave the fort, and march down and oppose the enemy's right wing. This they did; and had time to form somewhat regularly behind a fence half of stone and two rayles of wood. Here nature had formed something of a breastwork, or else there had been a ditch many years agone. They grounded arms, and went to a neighboring parallel fence, and brought rayles and made a slight fortification against musquet-ball. Here they received the enemy to very tolerable advantage. Our officers ordered their men not to fire till the word was given. Lieut. Dana tells me he was the first man that fired, and that he did it singly, and with a vewi to draw the enemy's fire, and he obtained his end fully, without any damage to our party. Our men then returned the fire well-directed, and to very good effect, and so disconcerted the enemy that they partly broke(e and re)treated. Many of our men wee for pursuing, (but by) the prudence of the officers they were prevented lea(ving s) o advantageous a post. The enemy again rallied and ad(vanc)ed, and in the same manner were repulsed a second, and some say, a third time. But at last they stood their ground, and the action was warm, till the enemy carried the fort which was on their left wing, and soon there was a retreat of the whole of the provincials. I am told that a gentleman on Chelsea side saw the whole engagement, and that he said it lasted thirty-five minutes with the musquetry, and that our first fringes swept down the enemy most amazingly. The men that went to intrenching over night were in the warmest of the battle, and, by all accounts, they fought most manfully. They had got hardened to the noise of cannon; but those that came up as recruits were evidently most terribly frightened, many of them, and did not march up with that true courage that their cause ought to have inspired them with. And to this cause, I conceive, was owing our retreat. Five hundred men more, that might easily have been there, if they were in any tolerable order and spirits, might have sent the enemy from whence they came, or to their long homes.

I wish it was in my power to give you a satisfactory reason "why our intrenchments were not supported with fresh recruits from Cambridge, and why that important pass over Charlestown Neck was not guarded against annoyance form Mystic River, as well as the other side from the fire of the ships and floating batteries, and our retreat secured," &c. &c. Possibly the whole attempt was rather premature, and not thoroughly well planned. If we might again attempt it, we should undoubtedly, have contrived and executed much better. Perhaps it may be better, however, to prepare ourselves well for some future attempt, than to lament the unfortunate success of the last, which we cannot now possibly mend.

As to my own concern in it, with that of my company, would inform, that one subaltern, one sergeant, and thirty privates, were draughted out over night to intrench. They tarried, and fought till the retreat. Just after dinner, on Saturday, 17th ult., I was walking out from my lodgings, quite calm and composed, and all at once the drums beat to arms, and bells rang, and a great noise in Cambridge. Capt. Putnam came by on full gallop. What is the matter? say I. Have you not heard? No. Why the regulars are landing at Charlestown, says he; and father says you must all meet, and march immediately to Bunker Hill and oppose the enemy. I waited not, but ran, and got my arms and ammunition, and hasted to my company, (who were in the church for barracks,) and found them nearly ready to march. We soon marched, with our frocks and trowsers on over our other clothes, (for our company is in uniform wholly blue, turned up with red,) for we were loath to expose ourselves by our dress, and down we marched. I imagined we arrived at the hill near the close of the battle. When we arrived there was not a company with us in any kind of order, although, when we first set out, perhaps three regiments were y our side, and near us; but here they were scattered, some behind rocks and hay-cocks, and thirty men, perhaps, behind an appletree, and frequently twenty men round a wounded man, retreating, when not ore than three or four could touch him to advantage. Others were retreating, seemingly without any excuse, and some said they had left the fort with leave of the officers, because they had been all night and day on fatigue, without sleep, victuals, or drink; and some said they had no officers to head them, which, indeed, seemed to be the case. At last I met with a considerable company, who were going off rank and file. I called to the officer that led them, and asked why he retreated? He made me no answer. I halted my men, and told him if he went on it should be at his peril. He still seemed regardless of me. I then ordered my men to make ready. They immediately cocked, and declared if I ordered they would fire. Upon that they stopped short, tried to excuse themselves; but I could not tarry to hear him, but ordered him forward, and he complied.

We were then very soon in the heat of the action. Before we reached the summit of Bunker Hill, and while were going over the Neck, we were in imminent danger from the cannon-shot, which buzzed around us like hail. The musquetry began before we passed the Neck; and when we were on top of the hill, and during our descent to the foot of it on the south, the small as well as cannon shot were incessantly whistling by us. We joined our army on the right of the centre, just by a poor stone fence, two or three feet high, and very thin, so that the bullets came through. Here we lost our regularity, as every company had done before us, and fought as they did, every man loading and firing as fast as he could. As near as I could guess, we fought standing about six minutes, my officers and men think****

Editor's Note: this letter is in the possession of the Wethersfield Historical Society, and is quoted in almost every serious book I have read on the Battle of Bunker Hill. Capt. John Chester was a 5th generation American whose great-great-grandfather Leonard Chester, Armiger, along with 10 Adventurers founded Wethersfield as the first English settlement in Connecticut during the hard winter of 1634. Later generations of Chester's became wealthy landowners & Planters along the fertile Connecticut River Valley.

Capt. John Chester was the 4th generation of Chester's to command the Wethersfield Militia Company, formerly known as the Broad Street Train Band, following his father Col. John Chester Sr (1703-1771), his grandfather, Judge and Major John Chester (1656-1711) and his great-grandfather Capt. John Chester (1635-1698).

The Wethersfield Company of 100 mounted soldiers was one of the few companies during the Siege of Boston that arrived on horse in fully tailored uniforms, "wholly blue turned up in red" and with full military provisions per man. In recognition of their Company's battle history (spanning most of New England's Indian Wars) and the social status of their officers, the Company avoided the miserable conditions of the Militia groups encamped around Boston and were quartered in Christ Church in Cambridge common per orders of General Ward.

It is interesting to learn that Capt. Chester, a Connecticut man, was willing to order his men to shoot retreating Massachusetts militia if they did not return to the front and the fact that his men acknowledged they would be willing to comply with his order. Fortunately this incident was resolved by the Massachusetts militia in question changing the direction of their march!

Robert Ayers, A Soldier of the Revolution, 1765-1833

by William D. Rockwell

Near dawn, on the morning of July 27, 1777, during General Burgoyne's invasion of New York, a courier left the safety of the British camp at Sandy Hill, a tiny hamlet 60 miles north of Albany, and headed south toward enemy lines. By following strict instructions as to the route to take, he avoided capture by the rear guard of the American army that was preparing to abandon Fort Edward, an old dilapidated military post on the Hudson River. A few hours later he arrived safely at his destination, a log cabin near the fort, the home of Sarah McNeil. There he delivered a message to Jane McCrea, Mrs. McNeil's houseguest.

The note was from Lt. David Jones, Jane's fiancé, a Fort Edward Loyalist who had fled to Canada and was now approaching Fort Edward with Burgoyne's victorious army. Jane, the sister of Colonel John McCrea of the American Militia, had agreed, by previous correspondence, to hide from her brother at the McNeil home, avoid evacuation with the retreating Americans, and be reunited with Jones.

The message however, contained a change of plans. Lt. Jones, certain that the recent British victories had won the war, requested that Jane go immediately to Burgoyne's camp where they would be married. A band of Indians, sent by Jones, would see her safely through to American lines.

Later that day, dressed for her wedding, Jane was killed and scalped by her escorts on the way to the British camp. Within days, news of her death at the hands of "Burgoyne's Indians" spread throughout the colonies. It didn't matter whose side she was on; her murder became a call to arms for thousands of colonial farmers. Outraged, and in fear for the safety of their families, they flocked to the American army and helped defeat Burgoyne at the Battle of Saratoga.

Robert Ayers, a 12-year-old indentured servant, was the messenger to Jane McCrea. Born on April 12, 1765 in Stillwater, NY, he was an orphan living with a Loyalist family near Fort Edward in 1777. After Burgoyne's defeat, the family fled to Canada, leaving Robert Ayers behind.

On April 1, 1782 at the age of 16 and apprenticed to Col. Dickinson's tannery in Stillwater, he ran away and joined the American army. He signed up for two years, as a land bounty soldier, to defend the frontiers of New York State. Young Ayers was assigned to Col. Marinus Willett's regiment of New York State Troops. For most of his service, he guarded the farmers of Ballston Spa and the Mohawk Valley against Tory and Indian attacks from bases in Canada.

In February 1783, while stationed at Fort Herkimer, an outpost on the Mohawk River 80 miles west of Albany, Robert Ayers was part of a rare winter campaign. Just weeks before peace with England was declared, Gen. Washington, fearful the British would retain Fort Ontario at Oswego, New York (a threat to the Mohawk Valley in future wars) secretly requested Col. Willett, a hero of Fort Stanwix, to conduct a surprise attack on the British stronghold. To provide sufficient manpower, the New York State troops were augmented by Col. Jeremiah Olney's Rhode Island regiment of African American troops garrisoned at Saratoga. On Feb. 9, 1783 Willett and his 500 raiders, with high expectations of fame and glory, left Herkimer and headed west.

They traveled half of the 90-mile trek on horse-drawn sleighs and the rest on foot. Although exhausted and cold, the raiders were still in high spirits when they arrived at Oswego near midnight on February 13th.

With just four miles to go, their scout, Captain John, an Oneida Indian, led the way. In a few hours, under the cover of darkness, they would reach their objective, fix bayonets, scale Ontario's walls and take the fort by storm!

Unfortunately, it was not to be! The storming of Fort Ontario never took place. By what some soldiers would call treachery and Willett would rule a mistake, Captain John had gotten them lost.

At daylight, after wandering for many hours through a half frozen swamp, the raiders sighted the fort, three quarters of a mile away. Discovery by the enemy was imminent. Gen. Washington had warned Willett to abandon the effort and save his men if surprise was lost. Col. Willett obeyed his commander. He turned his tired, half-starved, frostbitten army around and began to long, dreary trip home. The last campaign of the Revolution was over! Fort Ontario at Oswego would remain in British hands until 1796. Robert Ayers was discharged as a non-commissioned officer on Jan. 6, 1784 and went home to Stillwater.

Soon after his return to Stillwater, he began calling on a young lady named Sarah Ashton, the daughter of gentleman farmer John Ashton. Young Ayer's courting of Sarah got off to a rocky start however, when her father took a disliking to him. Ashton believed Ayers was "not of Sarah's class."

Not welcome in the Ashton home, Robert courted Sarah at the home of her married sister, Elizabeth. When Ayers asked for permission to marry Sarah, John Ashton, believing his refusal would not matter, agreed, but bitterly assured Ayers that he would not get one farthing (1/4 of a cent) as a dowry.

On March 1, 1785 Sarah Ashton and Robert Ayers exchange vows before the Reverend Robert Campbell at the First Congregation Church of Stillwater.

As it turned out, Robert Ayers would not need John Ashton's money. In November of 1785, Ayers was awarded 500 acres of land by the State of New York for his service as a land bounty soldier. The land grant was traded by the newlyweds for acreage in Ballston Spa, Saratoga County, NY. There they built a farm and prospered. Eventually they acquired over 700 acres on the road to Saratoga Springs. John Ashton, impressed with Ayers' success, eventually became reconciled with his son-in-law. Ashton left Ayers land in his will.

In December of 1832, Robert Ayers was granted a soldier's pension of $70.88 a year. He died on April 30, 1833 at the age of 68. He and his wife, Sarah, are buried on a grassy knoll surrounded by stately pines in the old section of The Ballston Spa Village Cemetery. His grave is honored with markers from the DAR and SAR.

Peter Trautman (1738/40–1809), Mahantonga Valley Pioneer and Patriot

by Steve E. Troutman as editor for Gary Schreckengast, educator from Lancaster, PA

Since the war started in 1775, the Mahantonga Valley of central Pennsylvania had been largely untouched by the conflict. Although a few of its more adventurous members had gone off to enlist in the Continental Line, most stayed home and in the local militias. Pennsylvania Germans wished merely to live their own life and be left alone. When others tried to impose their will upon them, however, they would fight back with a vengeance.

With the entry of the French into the war in 1778, the British chose to more heavily arm their Indian allies in the West and lead them in raids toward "rebel settlements" that dotted the frontier to draw the Continentals away from the coast. For example, during the summer, Forts Jenkins, 40-Fort, and Wilkes-Barre, PA were razed by Indians of the four allied Iroquois-speaking tribes, the Onondaga, Seneca, Mohawk and Cayuaga (the Oneidas and Tuscarawas sided with the rebels), and the Queen's Rangers, led by Canadian Colonel William Butler. Today it is known as the infamous "Wyoming Massacre."

Fort Augusta (present day Sunbury, PA) was defended by some 100 Continentals commanded by Col. Thomas Hartley, including Capt. Hawkins Boone. With the increase of enemy activity from the north, Hartley believed that to stay on the defensive with such a paltry force was a farce. He therefore resolved to take the war to the enemy and on Sept. 18, 1778 called the Northumberland County Militia to must at Fort Muncy. Although militia Col. Brady's muster was not copious, Hartley proceeded up the West Branch of the Susquehanna to the mouth of the Lycoming (present Williamsport) with 200 men, then north to Towanda to the North Branch of the Susquehanna to the old Munsee town of Sheshequin (in present Bradford County). From there he pressed on to the Onondaga town of Tioga (present Athens), but found it abandoned.

While at Tioga, Hartley learned that some 500 Indians and Queen's Rangers under William Butler — those responsible for the Wyoming Massacre — were several miles north up the Chemung River at a place called "Newtown." But being outnumbered, Hartley decided to withdraw in canoes to return to Fort Augusta. Near old Wyalusing, his rear guard commanded by Hawkins Boone and John Brady of Northumberland County, was struck by the Onondagas and a running fight proceeded along the river. In all, four Americans were killed and ten wounded.

On October 5, Hartley's expedition returned to Fort Augusta and it was the first major offensive against the British-allied Onondagas since the war began. Covering some 300 miles by land and water, Hartley's force showed the value of offensive action.

In March 1779, Washington resolved to remove the Onondaga threat once and for all by forming the "Army of the West" under Maj. Gen. John Sullivan. Sullivan's army would assemble at Wilkes-Barre from April-July and march up the North Branch as Hartley had done, destroying Iroquois settlements as far north as possible. Sullivan's army was impressive.

As Sullivan assembled his forces, Butler did not sit still and decided to launch a spoiling attack into Northumberland County in hopes of drawing Sullivan away. The Seneca Chief Cornplanter and Capt. John McDonell of the Queen's Rangers led a few hundred of Butler's forces from Towanda and Tioga to present-day Williamsport and the West Branch, where they raided/burned several settlements and were headed to the fortified settlements of Freeland, Rice, Boone, and Schwartz. "They were," according to historian Roger Schwartz, "also looking for plunder...because their own people were starving."

In order to reinforce Fort Augusta and push the invaders back, Northumberland County once again called up its militia. As such, Peter Trautman was enrolled in Capt. Weaver's Militia, of the 5th and 6th Class commanded by Lieutenant Colonel Peter Hosterman of the 3rd Battalion, Northumberland County Militia (consisting mostly of Mahantongo Valley Germans) from April-July 1779. Peter Trautman's Revolutionary War service record is preserved in the National Archives, Washington DC. This record commencing April 5, 1779 states that he received payment of 16 lira for service of one month, five days. During this time the "Great Runaway" of 1778 and 1779 occurred. Many Susquehanna River Valley settlers abandoned their homes and for several years the area was sparsely populated, as the threat of the Indian attack loomed over the valley. No doubt, the militia guarded and defended the Mahanoy Creek water gap in the Line Mountain. This mountain pass is one of the few places where English and Indian invaders could enter the valley from the north. The local area south of the gap called "Mahanoy" became a mustering place for the local patriots.

On July 27, 1779, news reached the valley that some 300 raiders were approaching Fort Freeland, about 20 miles north of Fort Augusta. "Fort Freeland," actually a fortified homestead, was garrisoned by 32 Northumberland County militiamen. On July 28, the militiamen, wholly surprised and outnumbered by Cornplanter's Indians, agreed to surrender if they and their families' lives would be spared as prisoners of Fort Niagara.

While the surrender terms at Fort Freeland were being finalized, the commander of Fort Augusta had ordered the intrepid Capt. Hawkins Boone and a company of militia to reinforce Freeland. As Boone's force approached the farm, however, Cornplanter's Indians ambushed it. In the ensuing struggle, the local militia lost 40 men killed, including their commander, Boone. With the battle won but resistance growing, McDonell and Cornplanter ordered the retreat with prisoners in hand. Needless to say, not a single enemy soldier ever set foot in the Mahantongo Valley. The militia were relieved from duty on August 9, 1779.

Peter Trautman is recorded as a resident of the valley prior to 1776, and having made an improvement by 1780, PA Archives land record D-52-154, (west of the Village of Hebe). The improvement as noted, indicates clearing of land or establishment of a dwelling.

The Salt Works of Dover Township, New Jersey

by Joel D. Monteith

Article previously appeared in SAR Magazine, Fall 1990, Vol. LXXXV, No. 2

The small coastal state of New Jersey, one of the oldest in the colonies, bore its share of suffering during the Revolutionary

War against Great Britain. Stories and legends are numerous. The scenes of conflicts, small and large, dot nearly every area of the state. Edwin Salter's classic, *History of Monmouth and Ocean Counties*, published in 1890, states that "no other state suffered more." The Battles of Trenton and Monmouth are famous. Others, such as described herein, are more localized but yet do not diminish in any way the service of our heroic patriot ancestors. One could well surmise that if these small, almost daily conflicts were not waged, perhaps no larger ones would have even taken place.

One particular area, the scene of numerous bloody encounters, is the subject of this article. Located within present-day Ocean County, the Township of Dover — bounded by the Toms River on the south, Kettle Creek on the north and Barnegat Bay, with the now closed, ancient Cranberry Inlet to the Atlantic, on the east — contained a well-known patriot hotbed. The very nature of the area — with Barnegat Bay, first described by Henry Hudson's voyage in the ship, *Half-Moon*, in the year 1609 — attracts attention. At the time of the conflict, this area was contained within historic Monmouth County in Old Dover Township, created by special act in the year 1767. The bay area held a bounty of fish, clams and crabs. Ducks and geese by the thousands furnished game meat. Along the bay were salt works, bogs and boat builders. Trade vessels came and went often to distant ports. Timber was also an important export. Through the inlet, privateers sailed forth to capture unwary British ships, bringing them into the Port of Toms River for disposal.

Salt Works Important in War

The all-important, large salt works at Shelter Cove — located on the west side of the bay, just north of the mouth of the Toms River — was known to be a source of imitation to the British. These works, built by the Pennsylvania Council of Safety, had been in operation since about 1776. They were located on a site formerly owned by John Tilton almost opposite to Cranberry Inlet. A large part of the salt used by the colonies for food preservation and in the making of gunpowder, was produced here. One account tells us that these works were the largest along the entire colonial shore.

The structure for the boiling and refining of the salt was said to be 169 feet long. The huge iron and brick stove inside was reported to be at least 50 feet long. The site itself was a natural one, located on low meadows which were flowed by the incoming saltwater of the Atlantic by tidal action through the inlet (which was tragically closed in a tremendous storm in the year 1812). The incoming waters were trapped in long, shallow ditches by mean of gates and dams. As the water evaporated, a brine would be left behind. This was scooped up into large, iron kettles and in turn boiled down until thick salt remained. After boiling, the salt was placed in wicker baskets, which allowed any excess brine to seep out, leaving pure salt product in the basket. Other accounts also recite that as the works were improved, pumps were placed on platforms over the bay waters to pump salt water into large tanks from which the water descended directly into the boiling kettles. This type of salt was the only kind produced in the colonies. The importance of this to the colonial war effort cannot be stressed enough.

The settlement of Kettle Creek, now within the town of Silverton about three miles northerly from Shelter Cove, produced many patriots, most of whom served at one time or another in the all-important militia. This area was settled early in our nation's history. A record found in the East Jersey Proprietors Office, dated May 11, 1690, grants 400 acres to George Willcox (Wilcox), late of Scotland. It is described as: "Begins at the South cape of Fishing Creek, otherways called Kettle Creek, on the North point of the homock, where the Indians have planted a little corn...." A Road Return for this area was recorded dated in 1755. A later inscription in 1767 called for a fence "3/4 of a mile long." Various deeds recited that there were several mills in operation on the Kettle Creek prior to 1750. Many of the militia rolls give the names of Applegate, Tilton, Irons and Clayton as patriots: all are prominent and common to this area. The service records of these families have enabled many to enter the SAR or DAR.

One of the prime functions of the militia of this region was the defense of the Shelter Cover salt works. It is known that the British launched at least three attacks on the works. Against this background, the writer would be remiss not to pause here to insert the record of his Patriot ancestor, Jacob Tilton.

He was born in 1752, the son of John and Ann (Applegate) Tilton near Cassville, New Jersey at an area called Goshen. The family later moved to the Kettle Creek area, where Jacob married Charity Hagerman. He subsequently enlisted in the militia; official records show he first held the rank of Sergeant in the Monmouth County militia, under the command of Captain John Cook in 1775. By 1777, he was promoted to Captain in the First Regiment, under Cols. Asher Holmes and Samuel Breese. War records tell us that he guarded the salt works and had engagements with both the refugees and British. In late fall of 1777 Captain Tilton was on duty when it was first attacked by the Tory New Jersey Royal Volunteers, under the command of Col. John Morris. This attack was defeated.

British Attack Again

Enraged, the British assembled a mixed force of about 150 men under the command of a Major Robertson to mount a second attack. This force was ferried by British ships through the Cranberry Inlet late in March 1778.

The small militia force under Captain Tilton was overrun and the works virtually destroyed. In fact, by the end of May 1778 all the colonial salt works along the Monmouth coast from Toms River north to Squan Inlet had been wiped out.

Nevertheless, the vital works at Shelter Cover were rebuilt by 1779 through the efforts of a Mr. Savage under authorization and support of the Pennsylvania Council. The works were reportedly sold in December 1779 to a John Thompson of Burlington, New Jersey. War records state that Captain Tilton continued to serve at the works through 1779 and 1780. In 1780 he was a co-signer of the Monmouth County Articles of Depredation (Retaliation). Apparently the British had again tried to destory the works and may have partially succeeded; very little is known about them past 1780.

The Port of Toms River was likewise vital to the patriots. From it the salt produced at Shelter Cove and other bay area works was shipped. It was a hub of activity and a sore spot to the British. All the militiamen were therefore required to serve a monthly tour at the small fort, which overlooked the port and village. This monthly force usually consisted of about 25 men and officers. Various accounts tell us that Captain Tilton indeed served at the fort and had the unfortunate duty of being there on Sunday, March 24, 1782. The British mounted a major attack on the fort early that day before reinforcements could arrive.

Despite pitched fighting, the fort was overrun and the port razed by fire. One account, quoting a British record, states that two captains, a major, a lieutenant, and six others died. Wm. S. Horner's book, *This Old Monmouth of Ours*, relates that the British force captured 16 men, but five escaped and six were killed. It is also interesting to note that of the militia present, at least eight can be identified as members of the original 1775 Monmouth Militia, under then Captain John Cook. Unfortunately, John Cook, who was now a major, died that Sunday at the fort.

Captain Tilton Escapes

An excerpt from a letter dated January 12, 1873 from Kenneth Tilton (son of Captain Tilton) to Col. Henry R. Tilton states that his father was indeed at the fort when it was attacked. We are not told how Captain Tilton escaped this vicious attack; it may have been just a sheer stroke of luck. We do know that Captain Joshua Huddy, who was also on duty at the fort, was tracked from house to house in the village. He was subsequently captured and later inhumanely executed. His story is well-known and will not be retold here, but it does indicate the depth of the Tory and British hatred and frustration against the patriots of this locale.

Captain Jacob Tilton did escape and survived the conflict. He raised a family of eight and apparently prospered, since in 1798 he filed a cattle estray. One son, Kenneth, served in the War of 1812 again against the British, who obviously bore a deep grudge against the upstarts in America. One can only imagine the feeling of Captain Tilton at that time. His health remained good, even to 1827 when he conveyed land to his son-in-law, Miles Clayton. A written note, affixed to Captain Tilton's service records, indicates he died in 1833 at the age of 81.

He may have been exceptionally fortunate to have served almost seven years in the great conflict of revolution and live to a ripe, old age. History reminds us, however, that he was only one among many exceptional men who endured the hardships, fought the battles and suffered as few have — before or since — to secure for themselves and their posterity this precious Land of Liberty.

Sources

SAR Records

War Records at the New Jersey State Library.

Sketch of Captain Jacob Tilton, by Katherine Wallace Kitts, 1928.

Registrars Office, East Jersey Proprietors Records.

Vol. 5, Stillwell's *Historical Miscellaney*.

Personal documents of James Wilbur Clayton on Capt. Tilton.

History of Monmouth and Ocean Counties, by Edwin Salter.

This Old Monmouth of Ours, by Wm. S. Horner.

Letter from Joshua King Regarding Capture of Major John Andre, Sept. 23, 1780

Originally appeared in The History of Ridgefield, CT by Daniel W. Toller, Danbury, CT (T. Donovan), 1878.
Submitted by Richard Edwards III

Dear Sir:

Yours of the 9th is before me. I have noted the contents and am sorry to express the indignation I feel at the idea of being obliged to translate a foreign language to obtain a true history of any part of our revolution. The facts, so far as I am acquainted with them, I will state to the best of my ability or recollection. Paulding, Williams and Van Wort I never saw before or since that event. I know nothing about them. The time and place where they stopped Major Andre seem to justify the character you have drawn of them. The truth is, to the imprudence of the man, and not the patriotism of any one, is to be ascribed the capture of Major Andre. I was the first and only Officer then at Esquire Gilbert's in South Salem. He was brought up by an adjutant and four men belonging to the Connecticut militia, under the command of Lieut Col Jamison from the lines near Tarrytown, a character under the disguised name of John Anderson. He looked somewhat like a reduced gentleman. His small clothes were nankin, with long white top boots, in part his undress military suit. His coat purple, with gold lace, worn somewhat threadbear, with small brimmed tarnished beaver on his head. He wore his hair in a quieu with long, black band, and his clothes somewhat dirty. In this garb I took charge of him. After breakfast my Barber came in to dress me — after which I requested him to undergo the same operation, which he did.

When his ribbon was taken form his hair, I observed it full of powder. This circumstance, with others that occurred, induced me that I had no ordinary person in charge.

He requested permission to take a bed, whilst his shirt and small clothes could be washed. I told him that was needless, for a change was at his service — which he accepted.

We were close pent up in a bed-room with a guard at the door and window. there was a spacious yard before the door which he desired he might be permitted to walk in with me. I accordingly disposed of my guard in such a manner as to prevent escape. While walking together, he observed, he must make a confidant of somebody, and he know not a more proper person than myself, as I had appeared to befriend a stranger in distress. After selling the point between ourselves, he told me who he was and gave me a short account of himself from the time he was taken at St. John's in 1775 to that time. He requested pen and ink and wrote immediately to Gen Washington[1], declaring who he was. About midnight the express returned with orders from Gen Washington[1] to Col Sheldon to send Major Andre immediately to Headquarters.

I started with him and before I got to North Salem meeting house met another express with a letter directed to the Officer who had Major Andre in charge, and which letter directed a circuitous route to Headquarters for fear of re-capture, and gave an account of Arnold's desertion, &c. — with directions to forward the letter to Col. Sheldon. I did so, and before I got to the end of my journey I was joined by Capt. Hoodgers first and after, by Major Talmage and Captain Rogers. Having given you this clue, I proceed with the major's own story. He said, he came up the North river in the Sloop of war Vulture for the purpose of seeing

Capt. Joshua King, Col. Elisha Sheldon's 2nd Regt., Continental Light Dragoons, 1779-1783, South Salem Headquarters.

a person by flag of truce. That was not however accomplished. Of course he had to come ashore in a skiff, and after he had done his business, the wind was so high, the Dutchman who took him ashore dare not venture to return him on board. The night following the Militia had lined the shore, so that no attempt would be made with safety, consequently he was furnished, after changing his clothes, with a continental horse and General Arnold's pass, and was to take a route by Peekskill, Crumpound, Pinesbridge, Sing Sing, Tarrytown, &c. to New York.

Nothing occurred to disturb him on his route until he arrived at the last place, except at Crumpound. He told me, his hair stood erect and his heart was in his mouth on meeting Col Samuel B. Webb of our army plump in the face. An acquaintance of his said that Col Stoddert knew him and he thought that he was gone but they kept moving along and soon passed each other. He then thought himself past all danger and while ruminating on his good luck and hairbreadth escapes he was assailed by three bushmen near Tarrytown, who ordered him to stand. He said to them, "I hope you gentlemen belong to the lower party." We do," says one. "So do I," says he, "and by the token of this ring and key you will let me pass." "I am a British officer on business of importance and must not be detained." One of them took his watch from him and then ordered him to dismount. The moment that was done, he said he found he was mistaken, he must shift his tone. He says, "I am happy gentlemen to find I am mistaken" — "you belong to the upper party and so do I, and to convince you of it, here is Gen[l] Arnold's pass," handing it to them. "Damn Arnold's pass," said they. "You said you were a British officer. Where is your money?" "Gentlemen I have none about me," he replied. "You a British Officer with a gold watch and no money! Let us search him." They did so, but found none. Says one, "He has got his money in his boots; lets have them off and see." They took off his boots and there they found his papers, but no money. They then examined his saddle, but found none. He said he saw they had such a thirst for money, eh would put them in the way to get it, if they would be directed by him. He asked them to name their sum to deliver him to King'sbridge. They answered him in this way, "If we deliver you to King'sbridge we shall be sent to the sugar-house and you will save your money." He says, "If you will not trust my honor, two of you may stay with me and one shall go with the letter I will write, name your sum" – the sum was agreed upon, but I cannot say whether it was 500 or 1000 guineas but the latter, I think, was the sum. They held a consultation a considerable time and finally they told him if he wrote, a party would be sent out and take them and then they should all be prisoners. They said "they had concluded to take him to the commanding Officer on the lines." They did so and retained the watch until Gen[l] Washington sent for them to Tappen, when the watch was restored to Major Andre. Thus, you see, had money been at command, after the imprudent confession of Major Andre, or any security given that the British would have put confidence in, he might have passed on to Sir Henry Clinton's Headquarters with all his papers and Arnold's pass into the bargain. I do not recollect to have seen a true statement of this business in any history that has fallen into my hands. If my memory serves me, Arnold solicited and obtained, the command of West Point in consequence of his being an invalid and the reason why his negociation was not completed by flag of truce, I will state what General Washington told the French embassador, Lucerne. He stated on his route to Hartford, that he dine with Gen[l] Arnold at Haverstraw at Joshua Smith's, where Arnold and Andre met. Gen[l] Arnold shewed him a letter from Gen[l] Robinson direct to Gen[l] Israel Putnam or Officer commanding West Point requesting an interview by flag on business of the first importance to the United States. Gen[l] Arnold asked Gen[l] Washington if he should go and hear what he had to say. Gen[l] Washington replied that it would be very improper for the Commander in chief of a post to meet anybody himself — he could send a trusty hand if he thought proper. But, he added, I had no more suspicion of Arnold than I had of myself. This accounts for Major Andre's failure to negociate by flag and his subsequent movements. I have thus complied with your request, giving you such fact, viz, what I had from the mouth of Major Andre and what I heard Gen[l] Washington tell the French minister soon after the execution of Andre[1].

Footnote

[1]Teller, 82-85

Lochry's Defeat

by Charles G. Edwards

One of the few Revolutionary War engagements to take place on Indiana soil and the only one in Dearborn County, this battle pitted patriots against marauding Indians. The battle took place near this spot on August 24, 1781.

Frontier defense in Western Pennsylvania was little help against the frequent ravaging Indian attacks. The Indian base of operations was at the garrison at Detroit. As long as this British fort existed, Indian attacks would continue. Yet any attack against Detroit was a hazardous venture because the 400 miles of wilderness separating it from the American frontier in Pennsylvania was guarded by fortified settlements of the eight most war-minded Indian nations. However, an attack on the British- and Indian-occupied Detroit garrison was the only means of achieving safety for American pioneers.

Clark Heads to Detroit

In June 1781, Pennsylvania's Westmoreland County voted to furnish part of its militia at the recommendation of Col. Archibald Lochry. Clark then assembled his own 400 volunteers at Wheeling, and waited for Lochry's forces to join him. Many of Clark's recruits, however, considered the expedition hopeless, so they deserted. To prevent further thinning of the ranks, Clark headed out toward Detroit along the Ohio River in August, having left limited provisions and boats, as well as instructions for Lochry to overtake him.

As it turned out, Clark left Wheeling the day before Lochry's party arrived, so he did not know that Lochry's real needs were additional boats to transport men and horses, as well as ammunition. Lochry sent Capt. Shannon, along with seven men, to overtake Clark and inform him of their situation. Unfortunately, Shannon and most of his men were captured by the Indians, who found the letter to Clark disclosing Lochry's lack of supplies and the fact that Clark and Lochry's forces were not coming down the river together as had been supposed by the Indians and their British leaders.

Lochry Attacked

On Aug. 24, 1781, Lochry's boats approached a level spot at the mouth of what is now known as Loughrey Creek (later named for him, but misspelled), the dividing line between Ohio and Dearborn Counties, Indiana (near Aurora). This was about ten miles below the Great Miami River. They killed buffalo to feed the hungry men and while they were cooking it, about 100 Indians led by that famous Indian Mohawk chieftain Joseph Brant, together with the renegade George Girty, burst from the woods with guns blazing. Many of Lochry's men were killed or wounded. A fleet of Indian canoes shot out from the Kentucky shore, completely cutting off escape for Lochry's men. After a few minutes of returning fire, Lochry realized he was trapped and surrendered.

Only one American account by a participant has come down, the diary of Capt. Isaac Anderson. He states that when the attack began, the soldiers took to the boats and tried to cross the river, but the Indians in canoes prevented this and forced the surrender.

The men found themselves prisoners of Joseph Brant and the renegade George Girty, along with a large band of Iroquois, Shawnees and Wyandots. The fierce Shawnees could not be controlled and it was not time before they began killing their prisoners. While Col. Lochry sat on a log, a Shawnee warrior sunk a tomahawk into his skull, tearing off the scalp before he was dead. It was only with great difficulty that Brant prevented the massacre of the men assigned to the Mohawks and Wyandots.

Internment Camp

Thirty-nine of Col. Lochry's force were killed, most of them after their surrender. The prisoners, to the number of 64 by the British report, were marched up the Ohio River about eight miles where they encamped for the night. The next day the march continued up the Great Miami River about another eight miles, where a campsite was chosen. Today this is

This marker notes the site of the internment camp for Col. Lochry's expedition, near present day Cleves, Hamilton County, OH, Aug. 25, 2001. Pictured are members of the Cincinnati Chapter SAR Color Guard, Ross Amos, Brian Schilling and Paul Wilke; Society of Tennessee Long Hunters, Randall Bales and Earl Bay; and, in front, are Charles Edwards and Harry Sjolin.

a quiet, beautiful spot about 150 yards west of the junction of the East Miami River and Jordan Roads, about three miles east of Cleves, Hamilton County, Ohio. This spot became the internment camp between August 26 and Sept. 16, 1781, while 100 British soldiers (Butler's Rangers) and more than 300 additional Indians, under the command of Capt. Thompson and Alexander McKee, joined Brant's force.

Prisoners Taken to Canada

They were then taken to Detroit, where they were sold to the British for ten gallons of rum each. Then they were taken to Niagara and from there to Montreal, where several escaped. The remainders were released by the British in 1783.

On Aug. 25, 2001, a dedication ceremony was held to dedicate a marker, which was installed at the Internment Camp site on East Miami River Road near Cleves, Hamilton County, Ohio. The marker was erected by the Cincinnati Chapter, Sons of the American Revolution, spearheaded by myself.

Roster of Patriots Killed

Allison, William – Sergeant; Bailey, John – Private; Barrickman, Peter – Private; Black, James – Sergeant; Brooks, Josias – Private; Burns, John – Private; Burris, Ebenezer – Sergeant; Butcher, George – Private; Cahill, Daniel – Ensign; Cain, William – Private; Campbell, William – Captain; Corn, John – Private; Crawford, Joseph – Private; Dellinger, David – Private; Dougan, Robert – Private; Erskin, Archibald – Private; Erwin, Adam – Private; Evans, Samuel – Sergeant; Forsyth, John – Sergeant; Gallagher, Hugh - Sergeant; Gibson, John – Private; Hardin, Zenas – Private; Hudson, William – Private; Lamb, Mathew – Private; Lochry, Archibald – Colonel; Maxwell, Alexander – Ensign; McKinley, John – Private; McRight, James – Private; Mechlin, Peter – Private; Milligan, John – Private; Patton, Isaac – Corporal; Peters, Jonas – Private; Pershing, John – Private; Ralph, Ephraim – Ensign; Row, John – Private; Smith, John – Private; Stewart, John – Private; Stratton, John – Private; Young, John – Private

---

(20 years research consulting 56 sources with complete documentation by Charles G. Edwards, Historian, Ohio Society, SAR)

John Fry and The Battle of Blue Licks

by Matthew Stephen Lee

The saga of the Fry Family in this country begins with the arrival of Heinrich, or Henry Fry, in 1680, as the first German immigrant in Pennsylvania and progenitor of the family. Fry Family members have used the spellings Fry, Frey and Frye interchangeably throughout history. Heinrich Fry married Anna Catherine Levering in the Friends Meeting House in Germantown, Pennsylvania in a ceremony performed by Daniel Pastorious on April 26, 1692. The Frys became prosperous land owners and nine children were born to this union. Benjamin, the youngest, migrated to Frederick County, Virginia and established Fry Fort on Cedar Creek. The fort, built over the creek to insure a water supply in the event of Indian siege, is still in existence today. Benjamin and his wife, Christian, also had nine children. Son, Jacob, served as a patriot in the American Revolution and was the father of John Fry, for whom this tribute is given.

In a pleasant little park just north of Liberty, Casey County, Kentucky, this handsome marker was erected by the Kentucky State Historical Society as a memorial to John Fry.

John Fry was born in 1754 to Jacob and Molly Fry of Frederick County, Virginia. He married the beautiful Catherine Spears, daughter of the well-to-do planter, George Spears and his wife, Christeenah of the Shenandoah Valley of Virginia. George Spears was also a Revolutionary War soldier and fought at Brandywine.

John Fry served in the Rockingham Militia during the Revolutionary War and engaged in the Battle of Point Pleasant in 1774. He received land grants signed by Governor Benjamin Harrison from his service in the Revolution into the new western country of Kentucky. Sometime in 1780, John, Catherine and daughter, Leah, born November 11, 1778 in Rockingham County, Virginia and other adventurers crossed over the mountains to the Cumberland Gap on the Wilderness Road. John, Catherine and Leah entered land on Carpenter's Creek on a Treasury Warrant. Here they established residence on Fry's Creek, in the vicinity of Carpenter's Station, in Lincoln County, Kentucky.

The Battle of Blue Licks

Vicious Indian attacks were rampant in Kentucky in the 1780s and almost all able-bodied men were automatically members of the Militia. The men of Carpenter's Station took turns in service in the Militia so that the station would not be undermanned any more than could be helped. Living behind log walls in fear and on constant alert was quite a difficult situation for the young Kentuckians. Therefore, when a large war party of Indians with the infamous renegade, Simon Girty, laid siege to Bryan Station, not far from present-day Lexington, Kentucky, in the summer of 1782, George Rogers Clark called up the Kentucky Militia to give battle and end the Indian problem once and for all.

So, on August 18, 1782, 182 men gathered, 130 of which were from Lincoln County, with the rest from Fayette County. They were commanded by Colonel Stephen Trigg. Among the men were Daniel Boone, his son, Israel, and John Fry from Carpenter's Station. On August 19, the two opposing groups met at the bloody, tragic Battle of Blue Licks, where the Kentucky Militia walked into an ambush and where 60 Kentuckians died before the rest fled. The battle itself last only a few minutes, "The rest was a panic-stricken rush on foot for the river, more than a mile away. The Wyandots first used their rifles, but then dropped them and leaped ahead with knives and plied their tomahawks or tripped up the fleeing men to stab them as they fell." After the attack, the Indians scalped and horribly mutilated all the bodies of the dead. Israel Boone was killed and also Colonel Trigg. Carpenter's Station was fortunate to lose only one man, but that man was young John Fry, husband of Catherine Spears. It had been his turn to serve.

After the battle, Daniel Boone was quoted, "So valiantly did our small party fight that, to the memory of those who unfortunately fell in the battle enough honor cannot be paid." Robert Patterson added, "The men who fought the Battle of Blue Licks were as well qualified from experience to face the Indians as any body of men that were ever collected."

The monument at the Blue Licks Battlefield lists John Fry as buried there with the rest of the slain. On the 225th anniversary of the Battle of Blue Licks, I visited the National Park, viewed the handsome monument erected to the fallen by the Sons of the American Revolution and visited the mass gravesite marked by the Daughters of the American Revolution.

Historians now consider that the Battle of Point Pleasant was in reality the opening battle of the Revolution. Blue Licks is considered the last major battle, so, John Fry has the distinction, possibly unmatched, of having served at the very beginning and at the very end of the Revolutionary War. On October 19, 1782, John Fry, Jr. was born to widow, Catherine Spears Fry, following the death of his father.

The Rattlesnake Flag of Westmoreland County, Pennsylvania

by Charles G. Edwards

The materials for the Rattlesnake Flag were known to be crimson silk and gold thread. It also contained a canton in the upper right hand corner, which was known as the Union Jack. It had the red cross of St. George for England, the white cross of St. Andrew for Scotland, and of Ireland, St. Patrick in blue. It's interesting that the rattlesnake is on the wrong side. That could have been to show their dissatisfaction with the British rule at the time. But because they did keep it there, it shows that they still considered themselves subjects of the king.

The rattlesnake had 13 rattles, very prominently displayed to the left above a coiled rattlesnake. Below the snake are prominently lettered words, the warning, "DON'T TREAD ON ME." This beautifully-made flag was carried by John Proctor's Battalion. It had the letters "J.P." for John Proctor and "I.B.W.C.P." for Independent or 1st Brigade Westmoreland County Pennsylvania or Provincials.

Lt. Samuel Craig, Sr. (Color Bearer) and his three sons (Brig. Gen. Alexander, John and Samuel Jr.) were with the army of Gen. George Washington when it crossed the Delaware River to fight at Trenton and Princeton, New Jersey. Samuel Craig Sr. carried the Rattlesnake Flag of Westmoreland County, Pennsylvania throughout these battles.

****

In 1775, a study was made of the symbolic use of the rattlesnake, as follows: "The rattlesnake's eye is brighter than that of any other animal and has no eyelids; therefore, ever vigilant, and never begins and attack but when once attacked, never surrenders. The weapons with which nature has furnished her she conceals in the roof of her mouth so that, to those who are not familiar with her, she appears to be a most defenseless animal, and even when those weapons are shown and extended for her defense, they appear weak but their wounds, although small, are fatal. She never attacks until she has given notice and cautions against treading on her. This was a strong picture of the temper and conduct of America — vigilant, courageous and ready to defend herself when provoked.

The rattlesnake has 13 rattles, the exact number of colonies united in America. This is the only part of the rattlesnake that increases in numbers, just as new states were added to the union. The rattles are distinct and independent of each other, and yet united together, so as never to be separated except by breaking them to pieces, just like the colonies in America.

The rattlesnake is solitary, and associates with her kind only when it is necessary for her preservation. Therefore, those who consider the liberty and blessing which America affords and once come over to her, never leave but spend their lives with her. The rattlesnake strongly resembles America in this — beautiful in youth and her beauty increases with age.

These were the qualities of the hardy pioneers of America who engaged in a mighty struggle for independence. And so it was with the colonies: distinct and independent of each other and yet firmly united. Singly and alone no one of them could withstand an assault of the mother country, but joined together and in unison, they could and did strike terror to those who would take away their liberties. The American Colonies did indeed give notice: "Don't Tread Upon Me."

Charles Edwards (left) and John Simmons (right) holding "The Rattlesnake Flag of Westmoreland County, Pennsylvania."

****

The original Rattlesnake Flag of Westmoreland County, Pennsylvania is displayed in the William Penn Memorial Museum in Harrisburg, Pennsylvania. It measures 76 inches by 70 inches. It originally read, "DON'T TREAD UPON ME" but the letters "UP" flaked off during the years.

The Rattlesnake Flag was proposed in the meeting of May 16, 1775 at Hanna's Town, Pennsylvania, where a group of local men drew up the "Hanna's Town Resolves," a letter of protest to King George III of England written before the Declaration of Independence. It was made with great care and handcrafted by Elizabeth Craig, daughter of Samuel Craig, Sr. (the Color Bearer). Elizabeth was 18 years of age at the time. It is the oldest banner representing what is now the United States.

It was brought home by Elizabeth's brother, General Alexander Craig, and handed down to his daughter, Margaret Craig, and then to Jane Maria Craig, great-granddaughter of Gen. Alexander Craig.

When Jane Maria Craig moved to New Alexandria from the Craig farm, she brought the flag, wrapped in newspaper, with her. During the Civil War, when John Hunt Morgan threatened to raid this section, she hid the flag, determined that in any event, this highly-prized relic should not be lost. She willed the flag to the state. It found its way to the attic, where it gathered dust until discovered in 1913 by Mrs. Gertrude Seanor, who bought the home of Jane Maria Craig. Gertrude took it to her parents, William C. and Mary L. Steele who, having realized its great importance, had Gertrude take the flag to James Cook, where he displayed it in his drug store. It was then taken to Harrisburg, Pennsylvania for safe keeping by J.C. Gibson and William Cunningham.

Note: Samuel Craig, Sr. (Color Bearer) is the 5th Great-Grandfather of Charles G. Edwards and father of Samuel Craig, Jr., who was with Lochry's ill-fated expedition in 1781.

Colonel Timothy Matlack
Penman of the Declaration of Independence

by Gerald Starr, David Starr and Logan Starr

Timothy Matlack, Jr. was a merchant, brewer, soldier and statesman. He was born in Haddonfield, Camden, New Jersey, on March 28, 1736. He is the descendant of one of the first families of New Jersey, William Matlack, who arrived on the ship "Kent" at Raccoon Creek, New Jersey, on the 14th of August 1677 from Cropwell Bishop, Nottinghamshire, England and Mary Hancock, his future wife, who arrived on the ship "Paradise" in 1682 from Brayles, Warwickshire, England.

Matlack was a servant four years to Daniel Wills, Commissioner for the West Jersey land. After completing his indenture contract, William Matlack received a 100-acre grant on the north branch of the Pensauken Creek. William Matlack and Mary Hancock were married on Nov. 14, 1682 in Evesham Township, New Jersey. They had nine children. Timothy Matlack, Sr., their seventh born, bought a tract of land in 1714 in Waterford Township, Gloucester County, New Jersey, and took up the family tradition of farming. He later sold his farm in 1726 and bought lots in the family tradition of farming. He later sold his farm in 1726 and bought lots in Haddonfield, built a house and store to pursue the mercantile business on Kings Highway.

These two portraits of Timothy Matlack, Jr. were painted by Charles Willson Peale. The painting of Matlack in his later years was completed in 1826, when the patriot was 86-years-old. Note the liberty cap he is wearing, which signified his belief in the rights of the common man.

Timothy Matlack, Jr., was born at the site of the Gloucester Historical Society, the Old Tavern House, which is located in Haddonfield, New Jersey. The original foundation of the house where Timothy was born is still visible in the basement of the structure. He was educated by the Friends Schools in Haddonfield, New Jersey and Philadelphia, Pennsylvania. His father sold his property in February 1745, moved to Philadelphia and settled on Market Street above the post office in 1746. He continued with the mercantile business and engaged in the brewery business.

It is believed that Timothy, Jr. was in the hardware store business in 1762 on Market Street, also dealing in bottled beer in 1770 on Fourth Street, Philadelphia. On Oct. 5, 1758, he married Ellen Yarnall at Arch Street Meeting House. In 1765, Timothy Matlack was disowned by the Quakers for "frequenting company in such manner as to neglect business, whereby he contracted debts, failed and was unable to satisfy the claims of his creditors and negligent in attending religious meetings." He also loved horse racing and was fond of cock fighting.

When the Battle of Lexington broke out on April 19, 1775, Timothy entered into the war for liberty with his heart and soul. Timothy Matlack is quoted in saying, "I am going to fight for my property and my liberty." On May 15, 1775 in the minutes of the Continental Congress, the following entry appears: "Agreed that the Secretary, Charles Thomson, be allowed to employ Timothy Matlack as a clerk under he having first taken an oath or affirmation to keep secret the transactions of the Congress that may be entrusted to him or come to his knowledge."

Timothy prepared the Commission for George Washington as Commander in Chief on May 20, 1775. He was a member of the Pennsylvania Constitutional Convention of July 15th through September 28th, 1776. He penned the Declaration of Independence on Parchment and was on the Declaration of Rights with Judge Bryan and James Cannon during the 25th session, and at the same time Col. Timothy Matlack and James Cannon were appointed to the committee responsible for writing an essay for the frame government. Timothy Matlack served in the Fifth Rifle Battalion, known as the "Shirt Battalion" of Philadelphia Associate's. As Colonel, he commanded the troops that destroyed the bridges across the Rancocas and Pensauken creeks near Dunk's Ferry near the Battle of Trenton in December 1776, and served throughout the campaign that ended at the Battle of Princeton in January 1777. He was a member of the Pennsylvania Council of Safety on July 24, 1776. On the 7th of August 1776 the Council resolved that Matlack raise the camp and on the 8th of August he, Dr. Rittenhouse, Owen Biddle and others appointed a committee "to fix on a plan of fortification at Billingsport and employ engineers and workmen to carry the same into execution."

He was chosen Secretary of the Supreme Executive Council of Pennsylvania on March 6, 1777 and served until the end of the war. He was appointed keeper of the Great Seal of Pennsylvania. He was made storekeeper of military stores on February 20, 1778.

In 1778, Timothy Matlack's son, Mordecai, was killed at sea on board the frigate *Randolph* during a fight with the British frigate *Yarmouth*. Colonel Matlack presided at the court martial of Benedict Arnold in Morristown, New Jersey on December 3, 1779. He helped found the Society of Free Quakers in 1781 and designed the Free Quaker Meeting House at Fifth and Arch Streets in Philadelphia, Pennsylvania. He was on the board of trustees of the University of the State of Pennsylvania 1779-1785. He was elected to the Second Continental Congress in 1780-81. Matlack was a director of the Bank of North America in 1781-85; elected to the American Philosophical Society, serving as secretary from 1781-83. He became master of the rolls of Pennsylvania from 1800-09. He was appointed Prothonotary of the United States district court at Philadelphia, Pennsylvania on March 14, 1817 and elected to the Philadelphia Board of Alderman from 1813-18.

Timothy Matlack died on April 14, 1829 at his son-in-law, Guy Byran's home, in Holmesburg, Pennsylvania; interment was in the Free Quaker Burial Ground, Philadelphia, Pennsylvania, and re-interment was in 1905, Bakewell Cemetery, Montgomery County in Audubon (Fatlands) on the Schuylkill River near Valley Forge, Pennsylvania.

References

Colonel Timothy Matlack, Patriot and Soldier by Dr. A.M. Stackhouse, 1910

Asa Matlack, Family Historian

Dictionary of American Biography

The Right to Bear Arms in the First State Bills of Rights: Pennsylvania, South Carolina, Vermont and Massachusetts by Stephen P. Halbrook.

U. of Pennsylvania Archives, painting by Charles Willson Peale, about 1790.

The Carpenters
Founders of Carpenter's Station, Kentucky

by Matthew Stephen Lee

I would like to thank my mother, Anna Marie Carpenter Lee, DAR Regent and Colonial Dames XVII Century President, for her devoted study and tireless research on our ancestors.

The saga of the Carpenter family begins with the progenitor, George Carpenter, Sr. immigrating from Switzerland to this country in 1740. George married twice; his first wife's name is unknown. His second wife was Ann Schulteli. Two sons were born to the first wife: George, Jr. and John. Four sons were born to the second wife: Conrad, Henry, Adam and William. There were five daughters in all: Anna, Barbary, Elisabeth, Margaret, and Solema, as stated in the Adam Carpenter Family Bible. The Carpenter family settled in Virginia's Shenandoah Valley near McGaheysville, Stonewall District, Peaked Mountain area. This is in the vicinity of the southern tip of Massanutten Mountain. This section was originally in Orange County, Virginia. In 1738, it was placed in Augusta County, and in 1777, it was made a part of Rockingham County, as it is today. George Carpenter was a physician, well-to-do planter and also a surveyor, acquainted with another surveyor of the time, George Washington. The Carpenters were educated well above the standards of the day, with all members able to speak, read and write English, their second language, as well as German, George's native language, girls included.

The Shenandoah Valley contributed heavily in manpower to the Revolutionary War, and the Carpenters participated. George Carpenter Sr. served as a private in Captain Thomas Hamilton's Company of the First Virginia Regiment commanded by Colonel George Gibson. He enlisted for three years and his name is borne on those roles from September 14, 1777 until November 1777. From December 1777, he served at Valley Forge under General George Washington as a member of General Peter Muhlenburg's Brigade. He survived the brutal months of December, January and February at Valley Forge, but died while in service in March 1778. John Carpenter, second son of George Carpenter, served three years as Sargeant of the Virginia State Line and also served in the 12th Regiment of the Virginia Continental Army. He fought in the battles of Brandywine and Yorktown, and his warrant for Kentucky land was signed by Patrick Henry. Adam Carpenter, full brother to Conrad, half-brother of John and George Jr., served Captain Robert Barnett's Virginia Company during the Revolutionary War. George Carpenter, Jr. also served and furnished supplies to the cause of American independence.

Sometime during the war years, the idea of moving into a new land seized many of the colonists and the young veterans. For men who served in the Revolutionary War, the land was there for the taking, since both Virginia and North Carolina set aside land for payment to veterans, the amount depending on rank and length of service. So, Adam, Conrad, John, George Sr., and George Jr. were entitled in their own right to free land and through inheritance, to the rights of their deceased father. Many Revolutionary War veterans sold their land grants. The Carpenters did not, or if they did, they sold to one another. Lists are incomplete, but the Kentucky Land Office records that Conrad Carpenter by Treasury Warrant took up 1755 acres of land in Lincoln County and John Carpenter under seven warrants took up about 2,870 acres. Bearing in mind that Adam, George Sr. and George Jr. were also entitled to land warrants, we are then speaking of a large area. So sometime in 1779, a group was ready to leave for the western country over the mountains, along with household possessions, farming equipment, horses, cattle, sheep, hogs, fruit tree stock, etc. The entourage would travel south to Cumberland Gap, then northwest along the old Indian trails, on a route called the Wilderness Road. It is difficult to contemplate the problems of transporting equipment to the new land. From Cumberland Gap into Kentucky, there was no wagon road, so all of the Carpenter equipment had to be carried on pack animals. The known members of the group were: Conrad Carpenter; Adam Carpenter; John Carpenter with his wife, the former Elisabeth Spears; and John Fry, also a Revolutionary War Veteran, with his wife, Catherine Spears and their daughter, Leah. Catherine Spears Frye and Elisabeth Spears Carpenter were sisters. Undoubtedly, there were also other families who made the trek.

Carpenter's Station

In 1780, Carpenter's Station was established on the waters of Hanging Fork near present-day Hustonville, Kentucky. The land they chose lies at a high point in south-central Kentucky, covering the head waters of both the Green and Kentucky Rivers draining to the north and west into the Ohio River, and also within reach of the Cumberland River, which runs south into Tennessee. This land lies in the northern foothills of the Cumberland Mountains and is often referred to as 'The Knobs Region' because of the densely-wooded hills which rise abruptly and steeply out of the rolling terrain. Carpenter's Station, rectangular in shape, was built on a low hill with knobs visible in almost every direction. A station is defined as a walled settlement unmanned by military personnel.

The Kentucky Historical Society placed this memorial marker on the site of Carpenter's Station in 1969.

Carpenter's Station was among the very first permanent stations to be built in Kentucky, following Daniel Boone at Boonesborough, James Harrod at Harrodsburg, and Benjamin Logan's Fort at St. Asaph, near the present city of Stanford, Kentucky. The station was located on a trace, an ancient trail, leading from the Kentucky River to the Green River territory.

Another Revolutionary Father Gone
A Tribute to Jacob Pyeatt

Written by John Buchanan and originally published as an obituary in the "Banner & Advocate," Thursday, November 7, 1844.
Submitted by Charles Buchanan-Boardman

Died, near Cane Hill, in Washington Co., Arkansas, on the 16th of August last, Mr. Jacob Pyeatt, in the 84th year of his age. The deceased was born in the state of North Carolina, and in early life entered in the service of his country, served through one tour of enlistment, and was engaged in the second when peace was declared. He lived long to enjoy the blessings of that liberty for which, in youth, he periled his life. The rich boon of freedom purchased by the heroes of '76 causes the history of their departure to be read with deep emotion and sympathy by the sons of American freedom. But father Pyeatt was a Christian; his religious history, although briefly given, will be peculiarly interesting to the church in which he long lived a worthy member. He professed religion under the ministry of the venerable McGready, in the revival of 1800 in the State of Kentucky, joined the Cumberland Presbyterian

Church at its first organization, emigrated to Arkansas in 1811, and was one of the members constituting the first Cumberland Presbyterian Church ever organized in the then territory of Arkansas. Although often deprived of a preached gospel and the benefits of the ordinances of the church, and surrounded with the wickedness so common in the first settlement of a new country, yet he always stood firm to this profession, honoring the cause of his divine Master. I was intimately acquainted with his father P. for sixteen of the last years of his life. I never heard ought said against his character as a man or a Christian, by any friend or acquaintance. As to foes, I think I can safely say in truth, he had none in the entire circle of his acquaintance. He was a warm and liberal supporter of the gospel, particularly of the circuit rider, as almost everyone traveling through the church where he lived can testify. From his own hand have I received liberal contributions, every year since I have been laboring in the ministry. His seat was never vacant in the church, in time of public worship, unless prevented by some unavoidable providence and when at preaching, he always seated himself near the minister, often looking him in the face, saying, as plain as visage could speak, "O Lord, help thy servant to preach and bless his labors this day!" He spent much of his time in reading the Bible, and was particularly fond of reading McGready's sermons, having heard many of them, as they fell from the lips of the living speakers. Being present at the burial, and while gazing upon the pale corpse until closed forever from human vision, I could but say in my heart, farewell, father Pyeatt, until the morning of the resurrection! The ministers of God will have you no more by their side, in the church upon earth. No more will your tears and groans mingle with the penitent suppliants; nor your faltering voice, trembling, lisp the praises of Emmanuel. No, thy immortal spirit is gone to happier scenes! Instead of being seated near an earthly pulpit to listen to a work of the dust, feebly pleading his Maker's cause, methinks thou art seated near the throne of God, listening to the heavenly voice of the blessed Jesus. Instead of mingling thy tears and groans or faltering voice in prayer and praise with the church militant, thou art surrounded in triumph with the Angelic choir and redeemed throng, singing with high and melodious accents the immortal notes of LIFE, LIFE, ETERNAL LIFE! GLORY TO GOD IN THE HIGHEST! Being suddenly and violently attacked, while at a camp meeting, with the disease which carried him off, and every effort to procure relief having failed, his pious son said to him, "Father, nothing will relieve y ou; you will have to die." With a smiling countenance he looked his son in the face, saying, "Son, I am not afraid to die; for 84 years I have been trying to serve God. I am ready and willing to go, whenever he calls for me." Yes, he truly decided to depart and be with Christ. He lived some six or seven days after the first attack, suffering intensely, but bore it with Christian fortitude. He lost the power of speech, but retained his reason until the last, frequently giving evidence to surrounding friends of his happy state of mind. He has left children, grandchildren, great-grandchildren, and many other relatives and friends to mourn their loss — But blessed be God; we sorrow not as those who have no hope. — John Buchanan"

My Recent Genealogy Journey

by Howard Peters, originally appeared in "The Forge," newsletter of the Silicon Valley Chapter of SAR, 2003

Always be open to finding a benefit in adversity. Our Patriot ancestors, I am certain, never foresaw the benefits we still enjoy 225 years later — they were in the middle of the Revolution. They also didn't foresee that their continental currency would not be worth anything, they would have to start over, and a new government would be needed in a few years with the Constitution.

In May of 2000, I fell cleaning my garage in Menlo Park and badly broke my right wrist. I am left-handed (and therefore, in my right mind) so I was still able to write as a chemical patent attorney in Peters Verny Jones and Schmitt LLP (my law firm) in Palo Alto. It took four hours of surgery, two metal plates, seven screws, two days on morphine in the Stanford Hospital to repair the shattered bones and for me to be on the mend. As one wag commented from the East Coast by email, "I'm sure your surgeon enjoyed the fact that he finally had the chance to screw a lawyer." Since 9/11, I set off the airport X-ray machines and have to be wanded and searched. In addition to a twice week physical therapy at a clinic, I was advised to exercise my fingers by playing the piano – but I don't play. The alternative was to use the computer keyboard, so I really got hooked on the genealogy internet sites.

Forty years ago in my small home town of Beech Creek (Clinton/Centre County), Pennsylvania, I did some talking with some older relatives and took some notes. So I had learned the names of some of my ancestors. My father had been orphaned early, so we didn't have documents or know much about any family history. I had two purposes for checking into the family tree. For one, I was looking for the rich relative. (I have since learned that things were so tough in my family that I was the rich relative.) Second, I had become engaged to Sally Brown from the big city of Pittsburgh, who has been my wife for 38+ years (and I have had no time off for good behavior).

We were sitting on her front porch in the summer of 1962, when I remarked about her father's name on the mailbox, "Elmer E. Brown." I said, "I hope to God your father's middle name isn't 'Ellsworth.'" After she turned white and asked, "Why?," I replied that my grandfather, my father and my brother were all Elmer Ellsworth Peter(s). Her father was, indeed, Elmer Ellsworth Brown. Also, we both had an Uncle Bill and she had an Uncle Howard. She had an Aunt Emma. Coincidently, my grandmother and sister were named Emma. I had an Aunt Bertha and her mother's middle name was Bertha. This was truly bizarre. Was I going to marry a distant cousin? Marrying cousins in not unusual in German families. Cousins might do this rather than to marry outside the German line. Ultimately, I could find no family connection and we concluded it was just old-generation German names. As an aside, when we sent out the wedding announcements, every newspaper called back, asking, "Is there a mistake here? The father of the groom, the father of the bride and the best man are all named "Elmer E." We replied, "There was a mistake, but not in the names."

The internet genealogy sites and information I found in two years are amazing. I found I have distant cousins all over the country who had been working on various branches of the family tree for years. After I made some connections, it was of interest for me to learn how to document some of these family connections. SAR will not accept internet sources as primary genealogy sources. Some books were available and particularly useful was the Commemorative Biographical Record of Centre (where Penn State University is located) and Clinton County, Pennsylvania, published in 1898. Bill Clark and Don Miller of the local Silicon Valley SAR Chapter were particularly helpful and patient with their guidance.

A Centre Co. genealogist was able to obtain for me some certified copies of recorded wills and letters of administration for distant family members. See for example his will at http://www.geocities.com/Heartland/Hills/5807/docs.html. An SAR search for record copies uncovered a 1955 SAR-approved application for a 9th generation ancestor of mine, Johann (John) Christian Nestlerode in Lancaster County, PA who was listed in the Penna Archives as member of a local RW militia. Again Bill Clark and Don Miller were instrumental in putting all the family links together and the SAR application was finalized and submitted. It was approved in April 2001.

What I have learned in my searches is that in my mostly German line all my ancestors back to 1800 (six generations) rest in a single cemetery in Blanchard, Centre County, PA, just across the street from the same Christian (Disciple) Church where I was baptized many years ago. The 7th and 8th generations rest in an overgrown family cemetery only two miles further on the old family farm. Christian Nestlerode, the son of Patriot John Nestlerode, is reported in Howard Nestlerode's SAR approved application in 1955 to have been a teamster (driving a team) for the Continental Army in Lancaster Co. PA in 1776 at age 14. He was also listed in the DAR records and in Penna Archives as being enlisted in a different Lancaster Co. militia. These German families were also known for not getting along with each other. But then I learned he was not yet established as a patriot in the SAR records. After the RW, he migrated to Centre County, taking up farming, etc., and died having 18 children with two wives – the second wife was his niece. There are probably 10,000 Nestlerode descendants around the U.S. These were big farming families.

On Sept. 14, 2001, three days after 9/11, we flew for a family wedding from San Francisco Airport to Pittsburgh on one of the first flights of US Airways. Later that weekend I visited four cemeteries and was able to find the gravesites five miles from where I was born for Christian and Margaret (Bott) Nestlerode in the overgrown family cemetery. (I never knew this when I grew up there.) His mountain stone marker is faded, but readable, and someone has placed a DAR medallion and flag there. With the help of Dwayne Meyer of the local SAR chapter, I was able to submit a supplemental application to SAR for the son Christian Nestlerode and learned in October 2002 that it had been accepted.

Cracking the Code on Recruiting New Members, Researching Their Ancestry, and Submitting Their Applications

by Larry P. Cornwell

As my chapter's registrar, I struggled for the first six years of this decade to recruit, research ancestry, and submit only 26 new members. In 2007 I submitted over 60 new applications. Why the difference? I've cracked the code!

For years, I labored the old-fashioned way, plying free internet sites such as Genforum and surname boards at Ancestry.com. I submitted queries, wondering if anyone were reading them or would answer them. I used the U.S. Postal Service to send for documents at county courthouses, again wondering if I would get anything in return. And, I used a 20-year-old electric word processor to type an application, with an ink eraser close at hand. I lost 90% of my prospects because of the built-in time delays and not being able to find all the necessary documentation. Sound familiar? Is this how you or your chapter registrar is struggling to get new members?

I found three keys to crack the code on effectively recruiting new members, quickly researching their ancestry, and efficiently preparing their applications.

First, rather than just wearing my Revolutionary War uniform to perform color guard duties, I found out how enormously popular I could become by making myself available as a luncheon of after-dinner speaker, in uniform, of course. You know how your chapter is always looking for speakers at your own meetings? Every other group is also looking for them. Also, members of your chapter belong to other organizations. have them spread the word that you are available to speak. Just in September and October, I've been invited to speak at two Sons of Confederate Veterans meetings, two historical societies, two church men's breakfasts, the American Legion, and my own chapter to showcase one of my speeches. I've developed three talks: The American Revolutionary War Soldier, Finding Your Revolutionary War Soldiers on the Internet, and The Christian Faith of Our Forefathers. Talk about what you know! Talk about the SAR. have packets of SAR brochures and a sheet for sign-ups. Military groups, heritage groups, and genealogical groups all have members who think they have a patriot ancestor back there "somewhere," and they see you as a way to lock in their suspicions.

Second, because I was soon getting inundated with prospective members wanting to join, I knew I had to become more efficient in tracking these prospects' ancestry. I bit the bullet and paid for a subscription to Ancestry.com. Here's the track to follow: click on "family trees," fill in the blanks, and the search engine will look through something like 40 million names in genealogies that have been submitted. Many ancestries are surprisingly complete and accurate. Print off each generation's page, which will be full of the very names, dates and locations you are looking for. Then, use this information to go after the census records (found under "historical records" on the home page). Census records can be used to prove each generation's relationship to the next one. Start with the parent or grandparent of the applicant, usually the 1930 census, and work backwards. Try the applicant's surname line first, so you won't have to go after marriage records.

Exploit the DAR and SAR indexes available on line or on a compact disk. After you've found an ancestor who was the right age to be in the Revolution in the "family trees" section of Ancestry.com, check the DAR members-only web site to see if any DAR member has already claimed this individual as a patriot ancestor. Also, use the SAR Patriot Index compact disk (available at www.sar.org, click on "for members," then "SAR merchandise," then "books and other materials"), and check it for the same information. Take note on the patriot's unit and state of service.

Third, whether or not you find success with DAR and SAR indexes, invest in a subscription to www.footnote.com, which has over four million Revolutionary War records on line. You will quickly learn to use its search engine to find muster rolls, payrolls and pension files. Sometimes, genealogies will be found in these pension files. Often times, you won't even have to send off for DAR papers or use a member's SAR number as documentation. If your prospective member is sitting with you as you find, download and print the records, I guarantee that he will be astonished and deeply gratified to get his own copy of all this documentation on the spot.

Time for a war story: A 68-year-old came to my home at 3 p.m. one day, having only a copy of his birth certificate and his maternal grandparent's names. He thought his grandparents were from South Carolina, but he didn't know for sure. He knew nothing else of his ancestry. By 5 p.m., I had found his line back to a patriot ancestor, downloaded and printed all the necessary documentation, and prepared his application using one of the electronic forms (available by going to www.sar.org, clicking on "membership," and clicking on "application programs"). I drove to his recruiter's house and had the recruiter sign as co-sponsor by 6 p.m. The application was in the mail to the state registrar that evening. Of course, they don't all work out this easily.

After only eight months of work, I have submitted 14 applications to start a new chapter in a town 12 miles away, and am working with 20 other prospects there. Our state will charter that chapter in February. We inducted 26 new members at our chapter meeting in September, and we will be inducting 26 more by the end of the year. I actually don't know how to turn off the supply line of applicants, nor would I want to. I will train at least one, and perhaps more, chapter members to help with the load, using the above keys.

Knowing the cost per member under the Family Plan, it's pretty easy to sell the applicant on bringing in his sons, grandsons, and perhaps his brothers and nephews. And with an electronic application form, it's easy to bump down generations to add a child on a new application.

Perhaps your chapter or a member would be willing to purchase the on-line subscriptions and SAR Patriot Index for you. If not, dig into your own pockets, and become so much more efficient at processing new applications that you will wish you had all these new techniques sooner.

I'm convinced that the SAR could become as large as the DAR by using our computers to the fullest. You just have to be willing to put out the few bucks to subscribe to a couple of web sites and use the modern tools available. Happy recruting!

Memorial to Revolutionary War Veterans

by George E. Livingston

From 2000-2004, the Ebenezer Zane Chapter, Ohio Society, Sons of the American Revolution, conducted research to locate and identify the gravesites of Revolutionary War Veterans buried in the Upper Ohio Valley. This search covered the counties of East-central Ohio and the Northern Panhandle of West Virginia. By "rough" estimate, there may have been as many as 2,500 Revolutionary War veterans buried in this area. The chapter was able to locate documentation on 970 of these men, and another 250 or so probably, but without sufficient proof of service. The others who may have been buried here remain unknown.

SAR members from Pennsylvania, Ohio and West Virginia at the dedication ceremony of the Revolutionary War Monument, May 21, 2005. Photos courtesy of the Ebenezer Zane Chapter, OHSSAR.

As a result of this research, early in 2004 the membership of the Ebenezer Zane Chapter approved a motion to raise money for a monument dedicated to the Revolutionary War veterans buried in the Upper Ohio Valley. This memorial was to be of black Pennsylvania Granite at a cost of $4,346 and placed at the Brooke/Hancock Veterans Memorial Park in Brooke County, at the south entrance to Weirton, West Virginia.

From March until mid-September of that year funding was secured from grants and private donations in the amount of $4,450 for this monument. It was ordered from Rock of Ages Memorials, Inc. in September 2004 and placed on site on November 10th of that year.

On Saturday, May 21, 2005, the Ebenezer Zane Chapter held a monument dedication ceremony with over 70 people attending, including SAR members from Pennsylvania, Ohio and West Virginia, many of whom took part and spoke at the ceremony. Ebenezer Zane Chapter President, Randall Crumpler, acted as MC for this event. Members of the DAR from Ohio and West Virginia were also in attendance. A combined SAR Color Guard posted the colors and fired a three-volley musket salute. Taps was played by Compatriot Norman Moran and a Bagpipe rendition of Amazing Grace was performed by Patrick Coughlan of the Wheeling Celtic Society.

After the ceremony, a reception was held at the First Christian Church in Weirton for SAR and DAR members and others who rendered support for this project.

Revolutionary War Monument, Brooke/Hancock Veterans Park, Weirton, WV.

President Hoover poses with members of Sons of the American Revolution, Oct. 25, 1929. Photo by National Photo Company, courtesy of the Library of Congress Photographs and Prints Division, Call No. LC-F8-43242, Reproduction No. LC-DIG-npcc-17987.

Compatriot and Patriot Biographies

of the

National Society of the Sons of the American Revolution

Washington's ragged Army at Valley Forge (1777-78).

ABBOTT, CHAD – Born and resides in Bloomington, IN. He is a pastor at Lockobee Methodist Church in Indianapolis, IN. He serves on the Indianapolis Church Board.

Chad is married to Shannon Norman and they have one son.

Johnathon McNeil was born in 1700 in Scotland. He served as a soldier in Simon Kenton's Company of Lincoln County Militia, under the command of George Rogers Clark. His occupation was a farmer, hunter and blacksmith. Jonathan is buried in Bloomington, IN.

AIKEN, SCOTT – Lieutenant Colonel Scott Aiken is the Deputy for Recruiting Operations for the First Marine Corps District in Garden City, NY.

Lieutenant Colonel Aiken graduated from McGavock High School and Vanderbilt University. He has also received two Masters Degrees, one in Public Administration and one in Military Arts and Science.

Scott Aiken

Lieutenant Colonel Aiken was commissioned into the United States Marine Corps in 1985. He has attended several military schools, most recently the United States Army Command and General Staff College at Fort Leavenworth, KS in 2000.

Previous assignments include various infantry units from the platoon to division level, two Marine Barracks, and recruiting duty.

Since Sept. 11, 2001, he has deployed twice in support of the War on Terrorism. On short notice he deployed to the U.S. Naval Base, Guantanamo Bay, Cuba for three months as the Operations Officer of Joint Task Force 160. During this time, JTF-160 prepared the Base for the reception and detention of Al-Qaida and Taliban terrorists in support of Operation Enduring Freedom. He was also deployed to the east Africa as part of Combined Joint Task Force Horn of Africa for over seven months as the Current Operations Officer. During this time, the Combined Joint Task Force Horn of Africa participated in combating terrorism operations in support of Operation Enduring Freedom.

He is the co-author of the soon-to-be released book, *Donelson and Hermitage Tennessee, A Suburban History.*

He is a member of the Lower Cape Fear Chapter of the Sons of the American Revolution located in Wilmington, NC.

He has been selected to take command of an infantry battalion in the Second Marine Division in the Autumn of 2004.

George Settle, born about 1732 in Virginia. Served in the PS VA Regiment. George was married to M. Mary Morgan. He died 1820 and is buried in Kentucky.

James Garrison was born March 11, 1747 in Pennsylvania. He was at Private in the NC Regiment. He was married to M. Ester Roberts. James died March 4, 1841 and is buried in Illinois.

John Cosby was born in Virginia. He married M. Jemima Yancey, who was also born in Virginia. John died in 1840 and is buried in Barren County, KY.

AKINS, BILLY JOE – Billy Joe Akins was born Nov. 27, 1927, in Hills County, TX to Earl Akins and Grace Glover Akins. He grew up in West, graduating from West High School in 1944. He served in WWII in the U.S. Army Medical Corps as a medical technician, being discharged in 1947. He graduated from Hill Junior College, now Hill College, and earned a BBA degree at Baylor University class of 1950. He married Martha Louise Amos on July 21, 1950 at Mart, McLennan, County, TX.

He was a businessman, owner of Bill Akins Pontiac, Inc., Centralia National Leasing Company and a National Car Rental Franchise in Centralia, IL, for several years before retiring and moving to Waco in 1980. In Centralia, he was active in community affairs, President of Centralia Shrine Club, a member of Rotary Club and was active in Centralia United Methodist Church. He was an airplane pilot with an instrument rating and enjoyed flying and promoting aviation in Centralia. Starting a second career in Waco, he was a real estate broker and a member of the Waco Board of Realtors, Texas State Association of Realtors and the National Association of Realtors. In 1988 he accepted a job as Realty Specialist at the Department of Housing and Urban Development (HOD) in Oklahoma City, retiring in 1993 and moving back to Waco. His office was on the seventh floor of the Alfred P. Murrah Building, the building that was bombed in 1995.

In Waco he is a member of Austin Avenue United Methodist Pathfinders Class and has served on the Board of Trustees. He is a member of Waco Masonic Lodge #92, 32nd Degree Mason Scottish Rite Bodies of Waco and Karem Shrine, Charter Member and Past Commander of Karem Legion of Honor, Past Patron of McLennan Chapter #639 Order of the Eastern Star, a member of Baylor Alumni Association, Baylor Heritage Club and is active in the National Society of the Sons of the American Revolution Waco Chapter #32. He has enjoyed flying, hunting, traveling, family activities and is a devoted husband, father and grandfather. He and his wife, Martha, have a son, Douglas Dale Akins and his wife Linda Claire Heid Akins, a daughter, Beverly Gayle Akins Mullen and her husband Kenneth Carl Mullen; two grandsons, Daniel Douglas Akins, Anthony Tristan Akins, two granddaughters, Laura Anne Mullen, and Sarah Lynn Mullen.

William Akins Sr., Patriot Ancestor of Billy Joe Akins was born in Maryland on June 27, 1756.

He served as a Private for four years in the North Carolina militia and one year as a First Lieutenant in the South Carolina militia. In 1783, William married Elizabeth Jane McCorkle. She was born in 1764 in York County, PA. William died in March 1840 in Alabama. He is buried in Carmel Presbyterian Church Cemetery in Cherokee County, AL.

ALBERT, STEVEN JOHN – Born Jan. 8, 1950 in San Diego, CA, while his father was serving in the U.S. Navy. Steven's military service consisted of two enlisted terms in Vietnam, starting in 1968. He served in the 25th Inf. Div. in Cu Chi and the 8th PsyOp, Co. B, located in Pleiku. In Pleiku he began a different job of distributing propaganda with the 4th PsyOp group. He walked, rode on trucks, flew in helicopters, rode on tanks, flew in airplanes of all sizes and shapes, and even got to fly some of the aircraft himself. He traveled throughout the Central Highlands, winning the hearts and minds of the enemy--very cool for a kid just 19 years old.

Steven Albert in Army in Pleiku Viet Nam in 1968.

Steven's wife, Jean, is the Registrar for the National Society Daughters of the American Revolution. They live in the mountains of Arizona. Steven has one daughter, Jennifer, and two grandsons, Ryan Albert and Jacob Albert.

Steven Albert being inducted into SAR on Jan. 17, 2009 by John Thorne, President of the Prescot Chapter.

Steven descends from his mother's line to his ancestors, **Benjamin and Nicholas Dudley Hill**. Benjamin Hill was baptized Sept. 7, 1727, probably in New Hampshire. His son, Nicholas, who was born Mar. 1, 1759 in Epping, NH, served with his father in the Revolution and was at his father's side when he died at Fort Ticonderoga, Sep. 17, 1776, of a non-battle related illness.

Benjamin was one of the founding fathers, a "Pioneer," of Northwood, Rockingham Co., NH.

ALBRIGHT, JAMES – Born Aug. 14, 1941 in Racine, WI; he joined the Ohio SAR on May 7, 2008. He served in the U.S. Army Corps of Engineers, 1st Lieutenant. As a civilian, his last job was as National Sales Manager for Clayton Industries, retiring on Sept. 30, 2006.

He served as Chair, Board of Trustees and Founding Trustees, Leadership Institute of Yellow Springs. James is married to Jan E. Albright, and they have two children and two grandchildren.

Ludwig Albright was born Nov. 11, 1731 in what is now Germany. A wheelright by trade, he died on Nov. 16, 1810 and is buried in Orange County, NC.

ALLEGRETTI, EDWARD PHILIP – Born Jan. 31, 1962 in San Jose, CA. Edward joined the SAR Oct. 10, 1984 in California. His military service was as a Colonel on the staff of the Governor of Kentucky. He is the proprietor of Pendorff Manor Farm and Stables, and is a retired County Commissioner.

Vice-president of Silicon Valley, CA chapter 1986-87 and 1988-89. Vice-president Laurel, MS Chapter 2006 and 2007; President in 2008. He received the Silver R.O.T.C. Medal in 1981. Member and past chapter president of: Sons of Confederate Veterans, Military Order of the Stars and Bars, California Pioneers.

Edward is married to Connie and they have two children. They reside in Ellisville, MS.

Another ancestor, **Charles Ripley**, born 1733 in Windham, CT, Private in Elkderkin's Co., Conn. Troops was also a farmer and 2nd Lt. 9th Co., 4th Reg. Conn. Troops in the French and Indian Wars.

The Rev. Boyce Eidson was born 1752 in Bedford County, VA. He was a member of the Virginia Militia.

His civilian occupations were planter, Methodist minister and a constable. He died in 1816 and is buried in Bedford County, VA.

ALLEN, DENNIS K. – Born Aug. 23, 1938 in Corpus Christi, TX. He joined the SAR, South Carolina Soc., on Mar. 28, 2008. Dennis retired from the U.S. Navy with the rank of Captain, and later worked as an executive director for the BellSouth Corp., retiring Aug. 1, 1996. He is married to Judith Shotts Allen, with two children and four grandchildren.

Dennis Allen

Thomas Stovall, born c. 1710 in Henrico Co., VA, furnished guns to the Virginia Militia during the war. He died in 1798 and is buried in Halifax Co., VA.

ALMONY, GUY E. JR. – Guy was born July 4, 1997 in Baltimore, MD. He is a CAR-DAR-SAR Liaison Chairman. He has received the SAR Silver CAR Medal, and Bronze Good Citizenship Medal. Guy is presently a student. He also belongs to the Children of the American Revolution and they War of 1812 Society in Maryland. He resides in Essex, MD.

David Wiley was born in 1747 in PA. He served with the 8th Battalion, York Co., PA, and attained the rank of Major. His civilian occupation was as a farmer. David died Oct. 17, 1817 and is buried at Centre Presbyterian Church, York County, PA.

ALTER, WARREN M. – Born May 7, 1954 at Aurora, CO. He has held the office of President AZSSAR 2005-2006; National Trustee, AZ 2006-2007; Chairman Public Service and Heroism Committee 2006-2008. Warren has also served on the following committees: Public Service and Heroism Committee, Eagle Scout Committee, GWEF Board of Directors.

He has been awarded the Law Enforcement Commendation Medal 2006 and AZSSAR Meritorious Service Medal 2008.

Warren and wife Nancy L. Alter have two children. He is employed at Pima County Sheriff's Department - Bureau Chief. The Alters live in Tucson, AZ.

Jacob (Johan) Alter was born in Germany in 1742. He served as a Private with the 2nd Pennsylvania, 7th Infantry. His civilian occupation was as a Shoe Maker and Mill Operator. Jacob died April 18, 195 and is buried at the Alter Farm, near Buffalo Church, Washington County, PA.

ALTIC, STEPHEN – Born in Dayton, OH in 1954, Stephen Altic graduated from Northwestern University and Ohio University. He is in private medical practice in Columbus, OH and has been an SAR member since 1985. He is also a member of the Descendants of Washington's Army at Valley Forge and the First Families of Ohio. Dr. Altic is currently at work writing a regimental history of the Western Sharp Shooters, a Civil War regiment whose roster included two grandsons of his Revolutionary War ancestor Amos Spencer.

Seventeen year old **Amos Spencer** enlisted in the 11th Virginia Regiment commanded by Col. Daniel Morgan in November 1776 at Cedar Run, Prince William County, VA. He was born May 8, 1759. His regiment later combined with the 15th Virginia, and then was renumbered the 7th Virginia Regiment of Foot.

Grave of Amos Spencer, Old Stronton Cemetery, Miami County, OH.

Private Amos Spencer spent the winter of 1777-1778 with Washington's army at Valley Forge. He fought at the battles of Monmouth Court House, Germantown, the storming of Stony Point, and was injured at the battle of Brandywine. After having served three years, he mustered out in November 1779.

Amos Spencer came to Ohio in the early 1800s with his family and was occupied as a farmer and weaver, settling in Miami County. He is buried in the Old Staunton Cemetery, Staunton Township, Miami County, OH, where he died in 1847.

ANDERSON, JOHN J. – John was born Apr. 2, 1961 in New Rochelle, NY. He is the chapter historian for his SAR unit, and serves on the Eagle Scout Committee. John is retired from the U.S. Navy Reserves, LCDR, in 2001, and serves in the U.S. Coast Guard Auxiliary. He has five children.

George Christie was born Oct. 10, 1731 in Londonderry, NH. He served in Poor's 2nd NH Regiment as a captain. He died Apr. 22, 1790 and is buried in New Boston Cemetery, New Boston, NH.

ANDRIANO-MOORE, RICHARD NORVEL – Born May 25, 1932 in Petaluma, CA. Richard retired as a Commander U.S. Navy, having served at sea and ashore for over 25 years of active service. He received the Defense Meritorious Service Medal for service within the Office of the Secretary of Defense and retired as Chief of Staff NRRC, Treasure Island, San Francisco, CA on August 29, 1985.

Richard Norvel Andriano-Moore

He has served as the California and San Francisco Chapter President, and has been awarded the Patriot Medal, Silver Distinguished Service Medal, Meritorious Service Medal (with two oak leaf clusters), and the Silver and Bronze Good Citizenship Medals. He is a Gentleman of the Council for the California Society of Colonial Wars, and is a former Commander of the California Commandery of the Loyal Legion of the U.S.

Richard has received the Scoutmaster Award of Merit, and was Senior Society President of the Coast Range Society, CAR 1987-1980. He was awarded a Papal Knighthood in the Order of Saint Syvester (KSS) by his Holiness Pope Benedict XVI, in 2008. Since retiring Richard has been a high school teacher and is married to Janice (Cartee) and has two children, a daughter Erika and a son Stephen.

Jonathan Weed, born Feb. 5, 1755 in Danbury, CT, served as a Private and later as a Corporal from Berkshire Co., MA marching from Lanesborough, MA at various times between 1777 and 1780. He died on March 13, 1839 and is buried in the Old Lanesborough Cemetery near Pistfield, MA; along with his father, Benjamin, also a Revolutionary War Soldier from Lanesborough, MA.

James Ould, born before 1750 in North Ashford, CT. He married Sarah Kingsley on 21 March 1754. James served as a Private in the Connecticut Militia and was on the list of men who marched from Ashford to the Lexington Alarm of April 1775 for the relief of Boston. He died about 1808, probably in Huron Co., OH.

Timothy Olds, born March 6, 1763 in North Ashford, CT. Timothy served as a Private in the Connecticut Militia. He died in July of 1819 in Huron Co., OH. The inventory for his estate was paid for by one barrel of whiskey according to his record of probate.

Caleb Mead, born October 28, 1716 in Greenwich, CT. Caleb served as a Captain and Company Commander, 9th Regiment, 4th Brigade, Connecticut Militia and died in January of 1798. His gravestone is located in the Family Cemetery, North St., Greenwich, CT.

ANDRIANO-MOORE, STEPHEN ALBERT – Born Jan. 26, 1978 at the Presidio of San Francisco, CA. Stephen is a former member of the Coast Range Society of the Children of the American Revolution. Along with this sister Erika, Stephen joined the Redwood Empire Chapter, California Society, Sons of the American Revolution on November 7, 2007.

Stephen Albert Andriano-Moore

An Eagle Scout, he earned his BA degree from San Francisco State U. and a Master's Degree from Stockholm University in Sweden. He is currently a Doctoral Candidate at The University of Nottingham in the UK. He was awarded the SAR Bronze Good Citizenship Medal while a member of the CAR and has received the accolade of a Knight Bachelor. While attending Santa Rosa Junior College, where he was an honor Student, he worked as a sales representative for his uncle Randy at Larsen's Racing Products, Inc. in Petaluma, CA. While in California, Steve enjoys restoring his 1963 Nova and is an avid sports fisherman.

Home of Jonathan Weed on Silver Street, Lanesborough, MA.

Jonathan Weed, born Feb. 5, 1755 in Danbury, CT, served as a Private and later Corporal in the Berkshire Regiment from Lanesboroughi, MA between 1777 and 1780. He lived on Silver Street in Lanesborough where he died March 13, 1839.

APPERSON, JACK A. – Born Dec. 21, 1934 in Fredericksburg, VA. He joined the Virginia Society SAR on Jan. 25, 2008 (Nat. #170928, State #7113 Fielding Lewis). He holds a BS from United States Military Academy, West Point, NY, MS from Univ. of Alabama, AA from Texarkana Community College, and graduated from Army War College, Carlisle, PA.

His service in the U.S. Army is as follows: 1957-58, 82nd Abn. Div., Ft. Bragg, NC, Platoon Leader; 1958-59, 6th Arm. Cav. Regt., Ft. Knox, KY, Company Exec. Officer; 1959-60, Army Missile Command, Redstone Arsenal, AL, Project Officer; 1963-64, 546th Ordnance Co., Kaiserslautern, Ger., Comd. Ofc.; 1964-66, 66th Maintenance Batt., Kaiserslautern, Ger., Battalion Exec. Officer, CM; 1967-69, Dept. of Ordnance, USMA, West Point, NY, Asst. Professor, CM; 1969-70, 801st Main. Batt., 101st Abn. Div., RVN, Comd. Ofc., 2BS, 2AM, CM; 1970-72, OPO, DA, Wash. DC, Chief of Ordnance Comp. Grade Assignments, MSM; 1973-74, 701st Main. Batt., 1st Inf. Div., Ft. Riley, KS, Comd. Ofc., MSM; 1974-76, ODCSLOG DA/OCSA, Wash., DC, Action Off, Chief of War Reserves; 1976-77, OASA (I&L), Washington, DC, Executive to ASA (I&L), LM; 1977-79, Red River Army Depot, Texarkana, TX, Depot Commander, MSM; 1979-81, Army Missile Comd., Redstone Arsenal, AL, Deputy Comd. General; 1981-82, Depot System Command, Chambersburg, PA, Comd. General, DSM.

Jack Apperson

BG Apperson later served as the Group President, Day & Zimmerman, Inc., retiring in July 1995. He is a member of the Huguenot Society, Who's Who In America, and the US Army Ordnance Hall of Fame. He has three children and six grandchildren.

Peter Apperson was born Dec. 29, 1759 in New Kent County, VA. He was a private in Col. Gibson's Virginia Regt., Capt Kemp's Co. A farmer, he died on Jul. 21, 1834 and is buried in Orange County, VA.

ARMITAGE, JIM RODGERS – Born in Tampa, FL on Nov. 29, 1945. He enlisted in the military in 1963 and retired with 20 years active service in 1983 at Fort Eustis, VA. He married Kristin McKenzie in 1966; they have two children and two grandsons.

Jim earned a B.A. degree from Saint Leo College and an M.P.A. degree from Golden Gate University. He was employed by the Florida Dept. of Labor from 1985 to 2005, and again retired with 20 years civil service.

Jim Armitage

Jim joined the SAR in 1982. He served as Chapter president of the Major John DeVane Chapter from 1994-98adn, as West Central Region Vice President of the FLSSAR from 2002-04. He has been awarded the War Service Medal, Patriot Medal, Meritorious Service Medal, Bronze Good Citizenship Medal, and others. He is a member of several veterans, historical and fraternal organizations, including the American Legion, VFW, MOAA, SCV, MOSB, BPOE, USCG Auxiliary, Masons, Scottish Rite, York Rite, Sojourners, OES, and Shriners. He always enjoys wearing his reproduction Revolutionary War Continental Army uniform to schools and civic organizations, and speaking on George Washington and the Revolutionary War.

My patriot ancestor is my 6th great-grandfather, **Major John DeVane** (1834-1808), who was born in New Hanover County, NC. John was a member of the Provincial Congress, which met at Halifax, NC on April 4, 1776; he was elected a member of the Council of Safety, Oct. 15, 1776 for New Hanover County. John was elected Major of the 2nd Brigade of the 1st NC Militia. Major DeVane participated in the Battle of Moore's Creek and the Battle of Guilford C.H., NC. He was elected as a representative to the 2nd Assembly of the House of Commons in 1778. He owned a large plantation and was involved in the manufacture of naval stores, cotton production, grain stores, and gun repair. He is buried at Saint James Episcopal Church in Wilmington, NC.

ARNOLD, DOUGLAS J. – Born Jan. 17, 1973 and joined the SAR on March 13, 2003. Douglas is employed at Sam's Club, Bloomington, IN.

John McCabe was born ca. 1735 in Shelbyville, DE; d. Jan. 20, 1800, Sussex County, DE. He was a Private and Corporal in the Delaware Continental Regiment, Captain Enoch Anderson's Company, commanded by Colonel David Hall. He was among the first to enlist in January, 1777, when the Regiment was reorganized under Colonel Hall. He served throughout the war and was one of the relative few remaining members when the Delaware's returned from their distinguished service in the South in January, 1783. A review of the various muster rolls certainly indicate that he was present for many of the war's major engagements. He was wounded during the Siege of Ninety Six.

ARNOLD, JAMES CLAUDE – Born Sept. 26, 1946 in Indianapolis, IN. He served in the U.S. Navy; PO3 from May 1964 to February 1968, and SFC from May 1968 to September 1984, retiring in 1984. He joined the SAR in November, 2002.

James C. Arnold

SAR offices held and committees on: Vice President Daniel Guthrie Chapter INSSAR 2003/4-2004/5; President Daniel Guthrie Chapter INSSAR 2005/6-2006/7; Secretary 2007-Current; INSSAR District Director South Central Indiana 2006-Current; INSSAR Partners in Patriotism Chairman 2005-Current; Daniel Guthrie Chapter Fresh Fruit for V A Hospital Chairman.

SAR awards include: Meritorious Service Medal Chapter Level; War Service Medal w/ Vietnam and Korea Bars; Good Citizenship Medal Bronze; Color Guard Medal Bronze; NSSAR Charter Centennial Medal and Life Membership Pin.

James and Rosaio I. had two children, one deceased. James married second to Song Cha (deceased). He is presently employed at Sam's Club, Bloomington, IN and lives in Ellettsville, IN.

Other organizations: Life member Veterans of Foreign Wars Post 1405, Spencer, IN; life member Veterans of Foreign Wars National Children's Home; life member AMVET Post 2000, Bloomington, IN; Member American Legion Post 18,

Bloomington, IN; Monroe County Veterans Honor Guard for Military Funerals; Owen County Veterans Honor Guard for Military Funerals; Blue Lodge #95, Spencer IN; Ancient Accepted Scottish Rite of Freemasonry 32nd Degree, Valley of Terre Haute, IN and A.A.O.N.M.S. Zorah Temple, Terre Haute, IN.

James C. Arnold

Sgt. John Lewis, born June 23, 1748 in Loudoun County, VA, d. Feb. 17, 1835 in Rush County, IN. John volunteered at the age of about 28 as a minuteman as a Private in Captain George West's Company, July 1775-January 1777.

He moved west of the Allegheny Mountains to Washington County, PA and in 1777 he was drafted and served one month at Fort Wheeling under Captain Mason and Colonel Abraham Shepherd. Again in 1777 he was drafted for six months and served as a Drummer under Captain Isaac Pierces' Company of "Woods Rangers" under Major Henry Taylor, defending the frontier settlements from the Indians. In 1780 he was drafted again for one month as a First Sergeant in Captain Bates Company under Colonel Campbell, and was stationed at Fort Laurens in the Tuscarawes-Muskingurn Valley (now Ohio).

ATKINSON, HAROLD O'HANLON – Harold was born July 31, 1934 in San Antonio, TX. He became a member of the SAR, San Antonio Chapter in December 2005.

His military service was with the U.S. Army 1957-1959 as Specialist 4.

Harold retired in October 2004 after serving as the Assistant United States Attorney in the Western District of Texas. Harold is married to Jeanette Ludwig Atkinson. They have two children and three grandchildren.

Although Harold has not joined any Civil War groups, he has ancestors who fought both for the Union and the Confederacy.

His memberships include Sons of the Republic of Texas; San Antonio Art League; San Antonio Opera League; Federal Bar Association; State Bar of Texas; and the San Antonio Bar Association.

Joseph Clyde served as a Minuteman in New Hampshire. He fought in the Battle of Lexington.

AUGUR, CHARLES ALFRED – Born June 3, 1952 in Tampa, FL. He joined the SAR on April 19, 2005 in South Carolina. John worked for Navis Global as a Senior Mechanical Engineer. He is a member of the Sons of Union Veterans of the Civil War and the Civil Air Patrol. Charles is married to Rosemary Vernon Augur.

John Augur was born June 11, 1748 in North Branford, CT and died Jan. 8, 1827. A farmer, he responded to the Lexington Alarm and is buried at North Branford Cemtery, CT.

AURAND, CHARLES H. – Born Sept. 6, 1932 in Battle Creek, MI. He serviced in the U.S. Air Force as a Captain. He joined the SAR on March 31, 1999. He has been the Arizona State President, Chapter President, Secretary/Treasurer, Chaplain, and will be Tours Committee Chairman, 2012 National Conference.

Charles and Donna M. have five children. He was the Dean at College of Creative Arts, No. AZ. Univ. and retired in June 1994. Dr. Aurand lives in Tucson, AZ.

He has been the President of Flagstaff, AZ Kiwanis as well as President AZ Alliance Arts Education.

Henry Aurand, born 1747 in Germany, and **Johannes Aurand**, born 1725 in Ebersbach, Germany, both served as Rangers/Penn. Frontier in Capt. Forster's Company. Both were businessmen in civilian life, died in 1819 and buried at Union County, PA.

BAKER, BERNARD – Born Jan. 21, 1961, Norfolk, VA. He served in the U.S. Air Force from 1984 to 1987 and Virginia Air National Guard 1987 to 1989. Bernard and Belinda have no children. They reside in Danville, VA.

He is the city editor for the Danville Register & Bee. His civic affiliations include Disabled Americans Veterans; Morotock Lodge AF&AM 210; and American Legion Post 1097.

Thomas Hollandsworth/Hollingsworth was born 1740 in Pennsylvania. He was a Private in Henry County Virginia Militia Patriot. He participated in the battle at Guilford Courthouse. His civilian occupation was as a Gristmill owner. Thomas died in 1820 and is buried at Blackberry Creek, Henry County (private cemetery).

BAKER, SILAS K. JR. – Born May 19, 1934 and served in the U.S. Air Force, as a Captain in SAC. He joined the SAR on March 16, 1962.

Silas and wife, Frances M., have two children and five grandchildren. Kurtis Silas and Barry Kenneth Baker, sons, are both members of the SAR. Silas was the Launch Director for Lockheed Martin and retired in 1999. The Baker's reside in Rockledge, FL.

Other civic organizations: Space Florida Board Member and Bravard County School Board elected member.

Silas Baker Sr. was born Jan. 19, 1747 or 1748 in Littleton MA. He was a Private in the Militia, Company MA. Silas took part in the New York Campaign, 1776. He was a farmer in civilian life, died July 30, 1825 and is buried at Phillipston, MA.

BARHAM, RICHARD W. – Born on April 29, 1923 in Toccoa, GA. He joined the SAR in Dec. 1997 in TX. He has served as the Registrar for the Patrick Henry Chapter in Austin, TX.

Richard W. Barham, Oct. 1990.

Richard served as a First Lt. in the US Army Air Corps, later Company Cmdr. for the Inf. Training Reg. He later worked as a US Foreign Service Officer, and a Senior Political Advisor for Exxon Corp, retiring in May 1985. He is a member of the Chancellor's Council, University of Texas/Austin. He was a member of Who's Who in America, 1964-93; Royal Order of the Phoenix, Kingdom of Greece, 1964; and Phi Beta Kappa, 1950.

He is married to Elaine Barham; they have five children and eight grandchildren.

Hartwell Barham was born 1759, in Southhampton Co. V. He served in the Virginia Regt. as a Private under Cols. Mason and Morgan, and fought at Brandywine, Monmouth and Germantown, 1776-79. A farmer, he died in 1841 and is buried in Stokes Co., NC.

BARNHOUSER, JOHN A. JR. – Born Oct. 23, 1997 in Baltimore, MD. He serves as a CAR-DAR-SAR Liaison, and received the Bronze Good Citizenship Award. He is an active member of Children of the American Revolution and a Jr. member of SAR; supplemental for Johann Nicholas Fry of the German Regiment.

William Blackiston Rasin was born 1760 in Kent Co., MD. Capt. Rasin served in the 1st and 5th Regt. of the Maryland Line Co., and fought at Camden, Eutaw and Cowpens. A farmer, he died in 1810 and is buried in Worton, Kent Co., MD.

BARON, PETER THOMAS JR. – Peter comes from a long line of Patriots. Peter was born May 21, 1974 at MCB Quantico. His father, a career Marine, married a Virginian while at OCS. Peter has proven family lines to the Sons of the American Revolution, Sons of the Revolution, Daughters of the American Revolution, Sons of Confederate Veterans, and the Jamestowne Society. He has five supplementals to the SAR and four to the Jamestowne Society. He is a life member of the Northern Neck Historical Society (VA) and the Northumberland County Historical Society (VA). Peter has a great love of the history of the Northern Neck and visits as often as possible. His family has lived there since before 1660. Peter graduated from the Texas Academy of Mathematic and Science and from Texas A&M University. Peter is currently an Engineer with the San Antonio Fire Department and a proud member of Texas Society SAR Color Guard.

Peter T. Baron, Texas Color Guard.

Sergeant John Cralle gave all for the cause. John was a large landowner in Northumberland County, VA at the outset of the Revolution. He left his family and enlisted in Captain Thomas Gaskins Co, 5th VA Regiment of Foot under command of Colonel Parker. He served from February of 1776 until his death in service, Feb. 1, 1778. John fought in the Chesapeake Campaign. He crossed the Delaware with General Washington in the Battle of Trenton. He fought in the Battles of Princeton, Defense of Philadelphia, Brandywine and Germantown. John died during the horrible winter of 1777 at Valley Forge. John's son, **Samuel Cralle**, served as a 2nd Lieutenant in the Northumberland County Militia and was at Yorktown for the surrender of Cornwallis.

Peter T. Baron at grave of patriot Christopher Denman, Westfield, Essex County, NJ.

BARR, JAMES HOUSTON III – Born Louisville, KY 1941, son of James Houston Jr. and Elizabeth Hamilton Pope Barr. Lt. Commander, USNR, 1967-81, Lt. Colonel, USAR, 1981-91. University of Virginia, 1960-63, University of Tennessee Law, 1963-64, University of Louisville Law, 1964-66. Law clerk, Kentucky Court of Appeals (Set.), 1966-67. Assistant Attorney General for Kentucky, 1967-71, 1979-82. Assistant U.S. Attorney, Louisville, 1971-79, 1983-. First Assistant U.S. Attorney, 1978-79. Assistant District Counsel, U.S. Army Corps of Engineers, Louisville, 198283.

James Houston Barr, III

Married Sarah Jane Todd (div.). One child, Lynn Jamison (b.1971). Married Cindy Ann Jeffries. Sons, Worden Pope Washington (b.1999), Augustine Washington Jeffries Barr (b.2001). Member Kentucky Bar Association, Federal Bar Association (president Louisville Chapter, 1975-76, Younger Federal Lawyer Award, 1975), Society Colonial Wars, SAR (chancellor Louisville Thruston Chapter, 2008-), Washington Family Society, Louisville Boat Club (president 2004-05), Filson Historical Society, Delta Upsilon. Author: *Lt. Colonel Nathaniel Pope, c1610-60, Ancestor of Washington and Governors, History of his Descendants.*

Ensign Benjamin Pope, born May 10, 1740, Westmoreland County, VA. A third cousin of General George Washington. Served in Captain James Patton's militia, Louisville. Died June 12, 1616, Bullitt County, KY.

BATEMAN, JACOB L. III – Born Oct. 28, 1952 in Montgomery, AL. He joined the Alabama Society SAR in Aug. 2003 and is a member of the Revolutionary War Soldiers Graves Marking Committee. He worked as a genealogist, retiring in 1999 for health reasons. He is a member of Camp 2002 Sons of Confederate Veterans, and Chapter 199 Commander in the Military Order of the Stars & Bars.

James Oates, born Dec. 25, 1757 in Dobbs Co., NC, served with the 4th Regt. NC Infantry, a Private in Armstrong's company. He later served as Justice of the Peace in Sampson Co., NC. He died Mar. 25, 1815 and is buried in Sampson County.

BAUMANN, DOUGLAS NELSON JR. – Born Jul. 12, 1952 in Rahway, NJ. Doug is employed as a business analyst for Merrill Lynch, and is an Asst. Scoutmaster for Boy Scouts of America. He is married to Louise Ann Hawrusik and they have three children.

John Nelson was born 1748 in Yorktown, VA. He was a major in the Virginia Cavalry, and served in the Northern Virginia Campaign, 1780-81. John died Feb. 18, 1827 and is buried at Oak Hill, VA.

BELAIR, BRIAN V. – Born June 18, 1969 in Jacksonville, FL. He joined the SAR on Oct. 2, 2001. Brian is employed at Pneumatic Controls and resides in Annville, PA.

Major Michael Forrer was born May 8, 1732 in Berks County, PA. He was a Major with the 6th Battalion, Berks County. He was engaged in battles at South Amboy, NJ and Flying Camp. Michael died Nov. 15, 1798 and is buried at Reith Cemetery, Berks County, PA.

BENNETT, MICHAEL JAMES – Born Nov. 23, 1947 in Pittsburgh, PA. He joined the Michigan SAR on Jan. 26, 2009. He was a manager for Ford Motor Company, retiring on Mar. 1, 2007. He is married to Marilyn Sue Bennett, and they have two children and five grandchildren.

Michael Bennett

William Bennett was born Apr. 19, 1742 in France. He was an ensign in Joshua Wingate's 2nd NJ Regt., Simon Marston's Co. He fought at the battles of Bunker Hill and Yorktown. A farmer, he died on Sept. 13, 1828 and is buried at Rose Hill Cemetery in Mason, OH.

BENZ, JOHN E. – Born May 18, 1944 in Houston, TX. He is the 2009 Chancellor, George Washington Chapter, Louisiana Society SAR, and has been awarded the War Service Medal. John served in the U.S. Navy Reserve, active duty from 1965-67, and is an attorney at law.

John is a member of the Louisiana Bar Assoc., Jefferson Bar Assoc., South Shore Yacht Club, and New Orleans Yacht Club. He was an Eagle Scout (1959) and worked for 12 years (1967-79) in law enforcement with the Jefferson Parish Sheriff's Office.

He is married to Cynthia Crocker, and they have three children and four grandchildren.

Thomas Leslie (Lesly) was born Apr. 15, 1760 in Carrickfergus, Antrim, Ireland. He was a private in the South Carolina Militia (1776-78), and fought at the Battle of Cowpens, Siege of 96 (SC) and in various skirmishes in and around South Carolina, Georgia and North Carolina. A farmer, Thomas was born Feb. 22, 1839 in McMinn County, TN.

BERGER, LEWIS C. – Born Dec. 9, 1927 at Germantown, Philadelphia County, PA. In 2003 he joined the SAR. In 2007 he was on the "Board of Members" and is Vice President, Mt. Evans Chapter in 2008. Lewis was in the Navy during WWII, Pacific with the rank of AM 3/C.

Lewis and Patricia Hain have six children, ten grandchildren and five great-great grandchildren. He was the manager of Truck Tire Sales for General Tire. Lewis retired in Denver in 1986 and now resides in Wheat Ridge, CO.

Lewis is a member of the Kiwanis, Knights of Columbus, American Legion and Veterans of Foreign Wars.

Andrew Moore, was born Dec. 1, 1733 at Glen, Chester County, PA. He was a Private in 3rd Battalion – Lancaster Co. Militia, serving in Capt. McQueen's Company. He likely was with "Gen. Sullivan's" Exp. – 1779. In civilian life, Andrew was a farmer and Congressman – State of Pennsylvania. He died May 1, 1801 and is buried at Harrisburg, Sadsbury Township, Chester County, PA.

BERRY, DANIEL P. – Born March 25, 1959; currently resides in Staunton, VA. Daniel joined the SAR Feb. 25, 2008.

He was a Sgt. in the U.S. Air Force with the 3/7 TAC. He now is a Maintenance Technician at McKee Feeds.

John Ralston was born 1735 in North Hampton, PA. He was a Lt. Col. And served as Paymaster, NC Militia and Paymaster, PA Militia. In civilian life, he was a member of Provincial Congress Auditor of Depreciated Accounts. John died in 1795 and is buried close to Allentown, Weaverville, PA.

BETHARD, ALVIN YOUNG – Born Aug. 14, 1947 at Shreveport, LA, is the son of Alvin Jones and Bertha Mae Young Bethard. He is a member of Attakapas Chapter, SAR, a veteran of the Vietnam War and a librarian.

Alvin Y. Bethard

Victor Richard, my fourth great-grandfather was born c1747 in Acadie, Canada. to Alexandre and Marie Thibodeau Richard. His family was among those expelled from Canada by the British in the 1750's. After living in Baltimore, MD for several years, they moved to Saint Landry Parish, LA, where Victor married Marie Magdalene Brasseux, daughter of Mathien and Anne Pitre Brasseux. c1773. She was born in Acadie, c1749. They had eight children, Jean Baptiste Victor Richard being my third great-grandfather.

Victor is on the rolls of the Opelousas Company, Louisiana Militia for 1770, 1776, 1777, 1785 and 1788 as a fuselier (musketeer). This unit was part of the Army of Don Bernardo de Galvez, which fought against the British in Louisiana and Florida during the American Revolution.

Victor was a prominent planter and landowner in the Prairie Bellevue section of southern Saint Landry Parish, where he died Sept. 1, 1808. His widow died Nov. 6, 1809. Both are interred in Saint Landry Catholic Cemetery, Opelousas, LA.

BILES, DR. GEORGE EMERY – Born Nov. 5, 1934, at Las Cruces, NM. He was held the following SAR offices: President, Pittsburgh, PA Chapter, PASSAR; President, Las Cruces, NM Chapter, NMSSAR. He has served on PASSAR Americanism, Permanent Trust, National Congress Committees, Chapter Genealogist. George received War Service (Vietnam) Award, Meritorious Service Medals, Color Guard Medal, and Martha Washington Medal.

George and Janet G. Frame have two children and seven grandchildren. He was Professor of Management, American University, Washington, D.C.; Dean, Business School, Robert Morris University, Pittsburgh and retired in 1995. George is also a member of Rotary, U. S. Naval Academy Alumni Association.

John Emery was born Jan. 1, 1742 in New Jersey. John was a Private with the Fifth Pennsylvania Regiment. In civilian life John was supposedly a carpenter. He died May 12, 1814 and is buried at Plaingrove Cemetery, Slippery Rock, PA.

BINGHAM, RICHARD W. – Born May 13, 1941 in Washington, DC. He joined the Massachusetts Society SAR on June 15, 2000. He serves as the state chapter vice president, Asst. Sec. Alt. National Trustee Chapter (Cape Cod), Sec., VP and President. He has received the War Service Medal, two Bronze Oak Leaves Cluster, Silver Good Citizenship Medal, Bronze CAR Medal of Appreciation.

Richard W. Bingham, USMC, 1961, Parris Island, SC.

Richard served as a L/CPL in the USMC, Co. B, 1st Bn 8th MAR. He later served as Asst. Vice President for Manhattan Savings Bank, retiring in Dec. 1990. He is a member of the Massachusetts Society of Mayflower Descendents, and the Sr. Soc. President Cotton Tufts Society, CAR. He has five children and one grandchild.

Elisha William Bingham was born July 13, 1740 in Windham, CT. He served as a Corporal in Hobart's Colonial Regt. under Capt. J. Handee, and in the New Hampshire Militia. A farmer, he served as town clerk for Enfield, NH and made a census of men able to bear arms. He died Dec. 21, 1821 and is buried at Wheatland Baptist Meeting House Cemetery in Wheatland, NY.

BLACKMON, WILLIE E. BONEY – Lt. Col in the U.S. Air Force Reserves. Blackmon was a Judge Advocate with the Strategic Air Command and served with the 55th Strategic Reconnaissance Wing at Offutt AFB, Nebraska, and the 12th Air Division as the Deputy State Judge Advocate at Ellsworth AFB, South Dakota. He was the Staff Judge Advocate with the now retired 147th Fighter Wing, Texas Air National Guard, on Sept. 11, 2001. On that day in history the fighter jets of the 147th ruled the skies over the Gulf Coast and escorted Air Force One during a critical time of national security. Col. Blackmon has served as an Individual Mobilization Augmentee with the 64th Flying Training Wing at Randolph AFB, Texas. He will retire May 30, 2009 with 28 years of commissioned service. He is the recipient of numerous military awards and decorations. Col. Blackmon is a distinguished graduate of Texas A&M University. He retired as a municipal judge in 2004, and is married to Dr. Gaye Lang, a native of New Orleans, LA.

Willie E. Boney Blackmon

Amand Broussard was born in 1754. He and his older brother, Claude Broussard, served as fusiliers with the Militia Company of Attakapas under Spanish Governor of Louisiana, General Don Bernardo de Galvez. He died in 1818 in Fausse Point, near New Iberia, Louisiana. Interred St. Martin de Tours Catholic Church.

Pierre Zepherin Broussard was born in 1752. He was the first cousin of Amand Broussard and served as a sergeant with the Militia Company of Attakapas under Spanish Governor of Louisiana, Gen. Don Bernardo de Galvez. Sgt. Broussard's commanding officers with the Attakapas Militia were Capt. Augustin Grevenber and Lt. Sorrel. He died in 1828 in St. Martinville, LA.

Jean Francois Clement DeCuir (Francois) was born in 1747. He served with the Pointe Coupee Militia under Spanish Governor of Louisiana, Gen. Don Bernardo de Galvez. He died at St. Martinville, Louisiana and is interred at St. Martin de Tours Catholic Church. Several of his brothers also served the cause in aid of American Independence: **Pierre DeCuir**, **Joseph DeCuir** and **Jean Paul DeCuir**.

BLACKWELL, JAMES SCOTT – Born June 1, 1960 at Plymouth, MA and presently resides there. James was in the U.S. Army, Mass. Army National Guard 1978-2006 Staff Sergeant and is an Iraq War Veteran. He joined the SAR on Jan. 23, 2007.

James and Pia M. have three children and two grandchildren. He is a Field Engineer at International Power. In addition to SAR, James also belongs to Mayflower Society, Sons of Union Veterans, Sons of Confederate Veterans, VFW Post 1822, American Legion Post 40, DAV, Amvets, 3rd Inf. Div. Society.

James Scott Blackwell

Gravestone of Jonathan Thrasher.

Jonathan Thrasher was born June 14, 1761 at Middleboro, MA. He was a private with Bailey's 2nd Massachusetts Regiment, Capt. Dunham's Company. Private Thrasher was engaged in battles at Saratoga, Valley Forge, Monmouth Court House, and West Point. He died in 1837 and is buried at the Pioneer Cemetery, Sandy Creek, NY

BLAND, CAROLD WELDON – Born April 11, 1923, he resides in Kirksville, MO. He has held the office of President/Exoficio Secretary of the Cpl. Braxton C. Pollard Chapter. Carold has received the War Service Award and Meritorious Service Award. He also belongs to 12th Armored Division Association, Disabled American Veterans Post 48, Veterans of Foreign Wars Post 2508, American Legion Post 20.

Carold was drafted into the U.S. Army in January 1943 He was a radio operator and gunner of a Stewart M5-A1 light tank during WWII as forward reconnaissance for the 92nd Cavalry Reconnaissance Squadron (mechanized), 12th Armored "Hellcat" Division, commanded by Major

Carold W. Bland receiving Meritorous Service Award from Bob Comer, President of MOSSAR, April 26, 2008.

General Roderick R. Allen. The Hellcats fought across France, Germany and Austria, including the liberation of Nazi concentration camps near Landsburg, Germany with the 7th Army commanded by Lt. General Alexander M. Patch.

As one of the first American Divisions to be commanded by a foreign general, he fought under the command of French General de Lattre de Tassingny, 18t French Army, driving the Nazis out of the Colmar pocket which was their last stronghold in France. Later, his Division was attached to General George S. Patton's 3rd Army, and was known as the "Mystery Division," spearheading the rush to the Rhine.

Carold and Doris have four living children and 13 grandchildren. He retired in 1985 as Claims Supervisor, Casualty Insurance.

Exekiel Billingston Sr. was born March 22, 1759 at Newark, NJ. He was a Private and in the last battle at Eutah Springs. He died Sept. 28, 1848 and is buried at Marshall County, TN.

BOOKS, DANNY L. – Born Aug. 18, 1939 in Cincinnati, OH and resides in Mount Orab, OH. Danny and spouse Donna J. have four children and nine grandchildren. He was a baker from childhood to 33 years of age, then New Carhauler for 27 years, retiring Aug. 28, 1999. Through his maternal grandmother Viola Dutton they have records to the year 160.

Ephraim Dutton was born Aug. 30, 1753 in Lunenburg, MA. He was a Private with the 7th Regiment of Col. Alden in Maryland, Captain William H. Ballard's Company. He took part in battles at Lexington on April 19, 1775, Cherry Valley, was captured at Cherry Valley by Indians taken to New York, married an Indian Maid, Escaped October, 1779, left her behind. In April 1780, discharged at West Point. Ephraim was a carpenter and cabinate maker. Built the first frame house in Ludlow, VT in 1790. He died July 2, 1840 and is buried at Ludlow, VT.

BOOTH, DUANE – Born June 11, 1942 at Glen Falls, NY. Duane joined the SAR in March, 1994 and has held the office of Regional Society V-P; Asst. State Secretary; DB Manager; Past State Manager; Past State Treasurer; Past Chapter President; Chapter Treasurer and Chapter Registrar (5). He has received the Patriot's Medal; Meritorious Service (Society and two Chapters); Florence Kendall (2007); and National Society-Life Member.

Duane's wife Carol Ann is deceased and they had no children. He retired in December 1996, having been in the Teacher's Retirement System and an Investment Transaction Specialist. Duane also belongs to the Society of Mayflower Descendants; SUVCW – Col. George Willard Camp.

John Weir was born ca. 1741 near Boston, MA. He was a Sergeant with the 16th, Albany County, NY, Militia. He was engaged in the battle at Bennington. In civilian life, he was a farmer who died March 5, 1826 and is buried at Turnpike, Cambridge, NY.

Nicholas Mosher was born March 9, 1728 at Riverton, RI. He served in the 12th Regiment of Foot with Col. Douty's Company as an Adjutant. He died May 25, 1819 and is buried at Day District, Sharon, VT.

Asa Coon was born March 12, 1856 at Hopkinton, RI. He was a Private with the 2nd Company (George Thurston Jr.). Asa was a minister who died Oct. 22, 1801 and is buried at Seventh Day Baptist, Berlin, NY.

Elisah Coon was born ca. 1724-1727 at Westerly, RI. He took the Oath of Allegiance. He died before May 4, 1778 and is buried at Hopkinton, RI.

Elisha Stillman was born April 25, 1722 at Westerly, RI. He also took the Oath of Allegiance. He died July 26, 1796 and is buried at Hopkinton, RI.

William Potter was born Jan. 2, 1715 at Dartmouth, MA. He was a Surveyor of Highways. He died before Dec. 7, 1801 and is buried at Richmond, RI.

Ebenezer Hartwell was born 1746. He was a Private with the 5th Regiment Dutchess County, NY. He died April 2, 1813 and is buried at Old Castleton, Castleton, VT.

Samuel Bangs was baptized Sept. 23, 1722 at Harwich, MA. He was a Private with the 4th Regiment Ulster County, NY. He died March 1, 1787 and is buried at Sears, Brewster, NY.

BORDNER, LARRY RICHARD – Larry graduated from Western Illinois University in 1973 and began his career at Caterpillar INC, Peoria, IL. Larry travels to Caterpillar Dealers throughout the World to improve their Sales and Rental Processes and Software Skills.

Larry R. Bordner

Larry Richard Bordner (National No. 102624) originally used his father's ancestors for membership. His father, Lawrence Inman Bordner, was descended from John Bordner and also Josiah Bearce, and Lawrence is now deceased on April 21, 2004. Larry is now adding approved patriot ancestors on his mother's side, via her DAR lineages.

One of these new ones for SAR is **Jedediah Turner** who served during the American Revolution in the colony of Connecticut, where he was a Private in Capt. Fitch's Co. of Independent Volunteers, 3/1/1762 to 3/1/1783. Also **Thomas Turner** with the same service. This was a Patriot Father and Son who answered the call together.

BOWLES, DAVID ALTON – Joined SAR Nov. 21, 1994 in San Antonio, TX. He is 2008 President-Elect of the San Antonio Chapter, Knight Essay Chair, and recipient of the Chapter Service medal in 2007 with oak leaf cluster in 2008.

David founded dabow-inc®, a credit card processing company, in 1990. Honored as Business Leader of the Year (1994) by the Greater San Antonio Chamber of Commerce and appointed to the White House Conference on Small Business (1995) by Congressman Lamar Smith, he has served on the San Antonio Crime Prevention Commission and was the first civilian member of the San Antonio Police Review Board. An active member of the Alamo Chapter of the Sons of the Republic of Texas, the Alamo Executives Association, and numerous historical and genealogical societies, he serves on the board of the One Hundred Club of San Antonio.

David Bowles

Bowles based his award-winning novel series, The Westward Sagas, on the true story of his Patriot ancestor, Adam Mitchell 1745-1802. *Spring House: Book 1,* tells of the Battle of Guilford Courthouse, which was fought on the Mitchell farm, now the site of the Guilford Courthouse National Military Park in Greensboro, NC, the first Revolutionary battlefield preserved by the Federal Government.

Adam Mitchell was born in Chester County, PA, circa 1745 and died in 1802 in Jonesboro, TN. He served in the militia in Thomas Blair's Company and as Captain of the Guard at the Guilford County Courthouse. His distillery supplied whisky for the Colonial Army's soldiers and his farm corn and fodder for their horses.

On March 15, 1781 Adam was a local militiaman on the front line of General Greene's defense of Guilford County Courthouse, just south of his property and less than a mile from where his mother Margaret, wife Elizabeth, and six children had taken refuge in a spring house on the Mitchell Farm.

The local militiamen were fighting to protect their families and property from the British, but they were no match for the well-trained Hessian soldiers. Adam was captured and imprisoned. His mother negotiated his release.

The battle ended in Adam Mitchell's cornfield, which became a mass burial ground for casualties on both sides. His mother and wife cared for the wounded; his oldest son Robert buried the dead.

The family never farmed the land again knowing that gallant fighting men lay under its soil. Today the farm is The Guilford Courthouse National Military Park.

BOYD, THOMAS WILLIAM – Born June 28, 1943 in Bethlehem, Lehigh Co., PA, he joined the New Jersey SAR in Oct. 2008. He graduated from William & Mary College with a BA degree in 1965, and served in the U.S. Army, 1/Lt., 536th HEM Co., Vietnam. In civilian life he worked for Conrail as Manager of Costing, retiring in Feb. 1999.

He is married to Linda J. DeVane Boyd with one child, Kelly.

Johann Simon Driesbach, Jr. was born Feb. 18, 1730 in Witgenstein, Germany. He served in the Northampton Co., Pennsylvania Militia. Johann was a farmer, a member of the Council of Censors, and the House of Representatives (1793). He died on Dec. 17, 1806 and is buried in Zion's Stone Church Graveyard, Kreidersville, Northampton Co., PA.

BOYD, WALTER L. – Born Nov. 8, 1925 at Eureka, Navarro County, TX. His parents were John Carlisle Boyd and Bertha Jane Wilkinson. Walter graduated from Mildred High School in Navarro County, TX in 1943.

Walter served in the U.S. Army Infantry from 1944 to 1946 as a Private First Class in the 96th Infantry. In 1947 he served as a Military Policeman in Company "B" 384 Military Police Battalion at Wels, Austria, reaching the rank of Staff Sergeant. He was awarded the Purple Heart and Combat Infantry Badge for action on Okinawa.

On May 13, 1947 Walter married Brownilee Parker at Kerens, Navarro County, TX, her birthplace. To them were born three sons, Parker Lewis, Mark Alan and Brett Carlisle Boyd. All three sons are also members of the Waco, TX SAR Chapter #32.

About 1950, Walter attended Central City Commercial College at Waco, TX studying accounting. Walter was an accountant and co-owner of Clark Concrete Company in Waco, TX from 1947 to 1987.

Other organizations that Walter has been involved in are the Jamestowne Society - John Clay Company, Austin, Texas. He served as Registrar for one term. Walter is also a member of the Sons of the Republic of Texas, George B. Erath Chapter, Waco, TX. He served as Secretary-Treasurer for 12 years.

Mack Wilkinson, was born in Chesterfield County, VA. He was a farmer and landowner. He served in the 3rd Virginia Continental Line, having enlisted on Feb. 10, 1778. He was discharged on Feb. 28, 1779. He was on the payroll at West Point. His engagement area was New York. On Aug. 27, 1779 at Chesterfield, VA, Mack Wilkinson married Mary Jackson. He died in 1802 at Chesterfield, VA.

BOYER, DENNIS ERROLL – Born Aug. 18, 1939 in East St. Louis, IL. He has served as SAR Trustee; Past President, Arkansas Society; and Past President, Gen. Lafayette Chapter, Arkansas Society; and also served on the Patriotic Education Committee. He has received the Patriot Medal and the Meritorious Service Medal.

Dennis Boyer

Dennis served in the US Army Reserve, and worked as a Psychological Examiner for Arkansas Rehabilitation Service, retiring on Oct. 1, 2004. He has served as Past Chair, Arkansas Board of Examiners in Psychology, and was Charter President, Arkansas Assn. of Psychological Examiners. He is married to Jean and has five children, ten grandchildren and four great-grandchildren.

Caleb Wallace

Caleb Wallace was born 1742 in Charlotte Co., VA. He was a member of the Committee of Safety, Charlotte Co., VA, and a Representative, District of KY, VA House of Representatives. He served as a Presbyterian Minister and a Justice for the original KY Court of Appeals. He died in 1814 and is buried in Versailles Cemetery, Versailles, KY.

BOYER, HAROLD A. – Born March 25, 1908 in Philadelphia, PA, joined the SAR in the 1960's. He currently resides in Plymouth, MA. Harold is about the oldest member in Massachusetts. He founded the Drum Corp.

Harold A. Boyer enacting Alexander Scammell, Revolutionary Soldier.

Harold served in the US Coast Guard Band. He and wife Ellen C (deceased) had four children and 17 grandchildren.

Harold was recognized by the Governor of Pennsylvania for painting 52 hydrants in Plymouth, MA to represent a Revolutionary Soldier.

The Concord Parade Celebration, April 19, 2008.

Harold was a musician (drummer) for the first 30 years, then contractor painting and interior decorator. He retired in 1999. He is a past President of Old Colony Cub of Plymouth, MA 195, the oldest in the county.

In 1776 and 1777, two of his ancestors were soldiers in the American Army, namely **Lt. Col. Jacob Boyer** and **Lt. Peter Boyer**.

BOYER, THOMAS E. – Born Oct. 21, 1929 in Paterson, NJ; presently residing in Sacramento, CA. Thomas was a S/SGT with the 1009th Special Weapons Squadron, USAF.

Thomas E. Boyer

Thomas married Esther Mae Berkley and they had three children and have three grandchildren. He was the manager, Florin County Water District and retired Jan. 31, 1992.

Other organizations: Florin Water District Board of Directors 1959-1979, Manager 1979-1992; American Legion, Sacramento German Genealogy Society; Palatines to America; Society German Genealogy Eastern Europe (SGGEE).

Henry Bartholomew Sr. was born Aug. 16 1728 in Zwei Brucken, Germany and died Sept. 7, 1807 and is buried at Zion Stone Church Cemetery, Kreidersville, Northampton County, PA. On May 14, 1778, listed on Rev. War Muster Roll, Pvt. 5th class.

Henry Bartholomew Jr. was born Sept. 23, 1758 at Allen Township, Northampton County, PA, died Feb. 23, 1829. He is buried at Zion Stone Church Cemetery, Kreidersville, Northampton County, PA.

Both were listed on the General Muster Roll of the 4th Battalion of Northampton County, PA Militia, Second Co. Capt. George Edelman in 1778. On May 14, 1778, both listed on Rev. War Muster Roll, Pvt. 6th class. Between 1781-1783, Henry Jr. was listed with 8th Co. 3rd Batt. Northampton Co. Militia, Pvt. 6 class.

BOYNTON, STANLEY G. – Born May 13, 1951 in Gardiner, Maine. He joined the Maine Society SAR on Nov. 18, 2008. Stanley worked for the Augusta Water District as a maintenance supervisor for 27-1/2 years, retiring on Dec. 29, 2006. He is also a member of Bethlehem Lodge #35 A.F. & A M. in Augusta, Maine. Stanley is married to Martina Bingel of Bad Hersfeld, Germany; they have five children and four grandchildren.

Stanley G. Boynton

Solomon Tracy, Sr. was born Mar. 4, 1750 at Old Falmouth, York, Maine. He served in the Revolutionary War as a private in Capt. Francis Shaw's company. He enlisted on Sept. 11, 1775 and served three months, three weeks and six days. His company was stationed at Gouldsborough No. 4, Narraguagus and Pleasant River to defend the coastline. After his military service, he settled in Durham, where he lived a number of years.

Solomon died in Rome, Maine.

BRADY, HAROLD JUDSON – Born Apr. 23, 1925 in Arkansas City, KS. He served in the US Navy. He was educated as a petroleum engineer at the University of Oklahoma, and migrated to Texas to work in the oil field, living in West Texas, finally settling in South Texas in the 1950's. He is married to Gloria and they have three children and seven grandchildren.

James Brady was born in 1743 in Cumberland Co., PA. He was a Private in the Cumberland Co. Regt., 5th & 6th Company, and fought in both the Revolutionary War and the Indian Wars. A farmer, he died in 1818 and is buried in Gilgal Cemetery, East Mahoning Township, Indiana County, PA.

BRAGG, DANFORD E. JR. – Born May 8, 1967 Welch, McDowell County, WV to Danford and Sylvia Acord Bragg. Grew up in Oceana and graduated Oceana High School. Has been active in sports most of his life. Is coach and referee for Little League and school sports baseball and Basketball.

Danford E. Bragg, Jr.

Between my parents I have seven Revolutionary War Patriots.

He and wife Barbara Short Bragg have one son Danford Bragg III and one daughter Taylor Ann Bragg. They have two grandchildren, Tatum Elizabeth and Rome Elijah Bragg. They live in Oceana, WV where he has been a coal miner for 20 years as a Heavy Equipment operator and EMT coal miner.

He is on the Board of Directors Oceana little league, safety officer, and also fields and grounds Committee member; also Umpire Committee Member.

He coaches for Oceana Biddy Buddy Basketball, Little league T-Ball and Girls Softball as well as umpires for The Babe Ruth Senior League baseball. He loves to hunt and fish with his father.

Ralph Stewart, born June 17, 1746, Augusta County, VA to James Stewart and Ann Lafferty. He died Nov. 17, 1835, Logan County, WV. Married first Mary Elliott, approximately 1867, Augusta, VA. She was born before 1750, died approximately 1787. Married second Mary Clay, June 25, 1788, Montgomery County, VA, daughter of Mitchell Clay and Phoebe Belcher; born 1762 Bedford County, Virginia, died April 25, 1851 Wyoming County, WV had 13 children.

Gravestone of Ralph Stewart.

Captain Ralph Stewart, soldier of the Revolutionary War (pension 3 23949, W6168), commissioned Captain 1773 by Lord Dunmore as Governor of Virginia. Served as a ranger, fought at Point Pleasant under General Andrew Lewis the "Battle of Point Pleasant," fought against the Native Americans led by Chief Cornstalk, in 1774.

During one of these engagements he received a saber wound in the right arm inflicted by English General "Butcher Tarleton" himself. When Cornwallis surrendered at the siege of Yorktown General George Washington, Captain Stewart was one of the guards that kept Cornwallis a prisoner of war.

BRAGG, DANFORD EARL SR. – Born March 17, 1939 in Oceana, WV to Lloyd and Rita Elkins Bragg. He was raised on a portion of the land grant received by 4th Great Grandfather; John Cooke Sr., who received this grant in 1810 when Wyoming County, WV was Giles County, VA. He has four NSSAR supplementals for Revolutionary War patriots.

Danford E. Bragg, Sr.

Entered United States Air Force in 1956 and served at Lackland Air Force base in San Antonio, TX. Then Malstrom Air Force Base in Great Falls, MT.

Graduated from heavy equipment school in Cherry Hill, NY in 1976. Married to Sylvia Acord, on Jan. 24, 1961 in Oceana, WV. They have two children Danford E. Bragg Jr., Danice Lilly Bragg.

He served 11 years in the Army National Guard and attained the rank of Staff Sergeant. Had to leave the military when disabled due to black lung from the coal mines where he was a heavy equipment operator. Spent 24 years in the great coal mines of West Virginia.

He is Vice President of NSSAA Capt. Ralph Stewart Chapter, Oceana, WV.

John Cooke Sr. born 1752 in London, England was among several young people, also included was Nellie Pemberton, that were kidnapped later to be sold as bonded servants, 4th Sunday in May, 1766.

Gravestone of John Cooke, 8th Virginia Regt.

John and Nellie were bought by the same planter in Virginia. John completed his term and worked for a while to pay Nellie's term. They married and settled in the Shenandoah Valley.

John fought the "Battle of Point Pleasant" against the Indians led by Chief Cornstalk. Was a member of Captain Thomas Buford's Bedford County Riflemen, marching with General Andrew Lewis on Oct. 10, 1774 Pt. Pleasant, VA (now WV).

In January 1777, enlisted in the Revolutionary War, given rank Private.

Served under Captain Jonathan Langdon, Abraham Hite, and George Waite in Colonel James Wood's regiment, the 8th Virginia Continentals.

Battle of Monmouth, NJ, later with Gen. "Mad" Anthony Wayne in the storming of Stony Point on the Hudson River, discharged Dec. 29, 1779.

John Cooke was the first man in 1799, along with wife Nellie and his four sons, to settle in present day Wyoming County, WV.

BRANNAN, DEE ARLIN – Dee Arlin Brannan was born Feb. 14, 1924 in a house behind the courthouse in Fort Sumner, NM. My father was living out land at Dunlap, NM.

In 1928 my father bought a ranch 15 Miles NW of Melrose, NM where I spent my schooling and graduated in 1941. I attended New Mexico A&M for one year and married Jeane Simmons in Floydada, TX, Feb. 20, 1944 when I was 20 years old. I have four children, 10 grandchildren, and eight great grandchildren.

I was drafted and ended up an Naval Aviation Electrician after attending school in Jacksonville, FL and then going to Corpus Christi Naval Air Station. After discharge I started to the University of New Mexico where I graduated and became Assistant Supt. of Utilities for them. I then worked for Pritchard & Abbott doing evaluation for advalorem taxes & investment banking. I then went to work for Reynolds Metals as a Maintenance Engineer and finally became Facility Planning Engineer before going to Peru as Electrical Superintendent for Southern Peru Copper mine, mill & smelter. I then became a Resident Mining Engineer for Brown & Root until retirement. After retirement I started donating work for the building & rebuilding of churches and church related projects and finished in February 2008. I was given the bronze good conduct medal from SAR and am the chaplain. **Arden Evans** is my compatriot. Written in 2008 after I was 84 years old and have been married for 64 of them. We now reside at New Braunfels, TX.

BRISTOL, DONALD C. – Born Aug. 21, 1937 in Ogdensburg, NY, NSSAR member #167127. Donald worked for the North Georgia Health District, GA Dept. of Human Resources, District Director of Environmental Health, retiring on Aug. 1, 2002. He is a member of the Georgia Environmental Health Assoc. and the Georgia Public Health Assoc. He was first married to Waneta Taylor, and second to Betty Faith, with three children and seven grandchildren.

Samuel Bristol was born Jan. 9, 1757 in Newtown, CT. During the war he was a private serving in militias from Vermont, mainly on scouting missions and fortification repairs. Some officers he served under include Col. Brush, Col. Ira Allen, Col. John Williams, Capt. Eben Wallace, Capt. Johnathan Allen, Capt. Richard Hurd, and Capt. Samuel Bradley. In civilian life he was a farmer.

Samuel died Aug. 2, 1834. His gravesite is unknown, but place of death is listed as DePeyster, NY.

BROCKWAY, RICHARD D. – Born Jun. 29, 1941 in Hartford, CT, he joined the WV SAR in Sept. 1990. He is currently the Librarian General (2007-09), Vice President General (2005-06), Trustee (2002-04), State President (2000-02), Comm. Chm. Hospitality/Music, Comm. Chm. Master of Ceremonies. He has been awarded the Distinguished Service Medal,

Patriot Medal, Liberty Medal, Silver and Bronze Color Guard, Bronze Good Citizenship Medal, Meritorious Service Medals (chapter, state and national).

Richard D. Brockway in Colonial Uniform, NH Militia.

Richard worked for the U.S. Forest Service and the Postal Service, retiring in Oct. 1992. He is a member of Lions Clubs Int. (over 40 years, District Governor 1979-80), the Greenbrier Historical Society, and the Washington, NH Historical Society.

He is married to Norma Lee (Simmons) Brockway; they have two children, Richard W. and Amy L., and four grandchildren, Cassia, Ella, Alex and Allyson.

Town Common, Washington, NH. L-R: Congregational Church, School House, Town Hall (Metting House).

Captain Jonathan Brockway was born May 28, 1738 in Lyme, CT, and commanded a company in Col. Chase's Regt. In 1777 he twice commanded companies in an effort to retake Fort Ticonderoga from the British. A sea captain and entrepreneur, he died in Oct. 1829 and is buried in E. Washington Cemetery in Bradford, CT.

BRONNER, HERBERT BENJAMIN – Herbert was born and raised in Virginia's Northern Neck. He is married to Hilda Alice Dameron Bronner, DAR. Herbert is a Deacon at Jerusalem Baptist Church. His love of God and devotion to family is a trait passed on to his five children and 13 grandchildren. Herbert served in the Army Air Corps from 1945 to 1947. He still farms the property he was born on and the entire family enjoys a visit to Totuskey Creek. Herbert is descended of three SAR lines from Westfield, Essex County, NJ.

Jonathan Cory; Revolutionary Patriot of Westfield, Essex County, NJ. Born Jan. 22, 1732 in Westfield. Jonathan was brought to life by stories told by his granddaughter Abby. Jonathan served the cause by providing wood, feed, carts, and horses to Washington's Army in New Jersey. He died June 20, 1793. His son, Benjamin, married Susan Denman. Susan's Father served in the Essex County Militia. Her Grandfather, **Isaac Hendricks**, provided supplies to the Army. All three are buried at Westfield Presbyterian Cemetery with stones.

BROOKEY, BRIAN R. – Born 1990 in Oklahoma, joined SAR in 2007 and lives in Tulsa, OK. Brian is a high school student at Jenks High. He is a member of Children of the American Revolution, member of Choctaw Nation of Oklahoma, Jr. member of Oklahoma Society of Mayflower Descendants.

Thomas Cunningham was born in Dublin, Ireland. He served 13 months in Captain James Booth's Company of Virginia Militia as a Private, in an expedition against the Indians, as well as one month after the surrender of Cornwallis, when he guarded prisoners at Winchester Barracks. His wife Phebe Tucker (born 1761, England, died 1845, West Virginia) is also recognized by DAR. She was an Indian captive of the Delaware Tribe for three years (all four of her children were murdered in her capture). After she was freed by Simon Girty, she and Thomas raised a family in Ritchie, WV.

Thomas died June 2, 1826 and is buried at Freed, WV.

BROOKEY, ROBERT L. – Born 1957 in California and lives in Tulsa, OK. SAR Office held was Tulsa Chapter Registrar.

Robert and spouse Lauren have two children. It is a design engineer at Team Oil Tools. He is a member of the Oklahoma Society of Mayflower Descendants, member of Choctaw Tribe of Oklahoma and a member of Founder and Patriots.

Lawrence Shunpuker/Shinpock, aka **Lorenz Schoenbacher**, was born before July 1752 in Neutal, Hungary. He was a Hessian soldier of the Rall Grenardier Regiment. He deserted on Apri l25, 1779 from his post as a sentry on the Savannah River. He joined Lt. Col. Hampton's Regiment between April 1781 and January 1782 and attained the rank of Private. Due to his service in Burns Troop, W. Hampton's Regiment and Sumters Brigade, he was paid 94 pounds sterling. He was also given land in South Caroline for his service. He died after 1800 and is buried in Montgomery County, NC.

BROOKS, KENNETH WAYNE – Born Oct. 31, 1933 at Muskogee, OK. Served in the US Army, 1st Armored Div., 1953-55, and later worked as a senior editor for McGraw-Hill, Inc. retiring in Oct. 1989. He is treasurer for the Nowata City-County Library. He is married to Janet Simpson, and they have one child.

Kenneth Wayne Brooks

Thomas Brooks was born ca. 1745 and died on Oct. 4, 1795, buried in Fauquier, VA. He was a rancher who supplied beef to the Continental Army.

BROWN, BOBBY CALVIN – Born Aug. 5, 1931 in Kuttawa, Lyon County, KY. He joined the North Carolina SAR on Jun. 11, 2008. He served in the U.S. Navy (MU2), and later was Manager, Health/Safety Dept., Superamerica Div., Ashland, Inc., retiring on Oct. 1, 1993.

Bobby Brown

He was married to Opal Orr (now deceased), and they have two children. He is also a member of the Kentucky Historical Society and National Genealogical Society.

John Lockhart was born 1759 in Virginia. He was a private in the 3rd SC Continental Regt., Capt. William Caldwell's Company, and in the South Carolina Militia under Capt. John McClure and Lt. John Steele. He fought at Purrysburg, Stone Ferry and Savannah (3rd SC Regt.), and Congarees and Hanging Rock (SC Militia). A farmer, he died Aug. 4, 1843 and is buried in Warren County, TN.

BROWN, CARL WOOD – Carl is descended from Peter Hockenberry through his son, Joan, and grandson Casper Hockenberry. He lives in Jacksonville, FL and is currently President of the Jacksonville Chapter, Sons of the American Revolution. Carl is married to the former Susan Miller, DAR, and they have two daughters, Victoria Moulder and Palmer Lamb, and five grandchildren.

Peter Hatchenburg was born in or near Hatchenburg, Germany, a few miles from Bonn, about 1718. Upon arrival in America the name Hatchenburg was anglicized by many family members to Hockenberry.

Peter, his first wife and five children landed in New Jersey about 1750 and went to the western edge of settlement in Pennsylvania, which was the Susquehanna River. They settled just beyond the river in what is now Fannett Township, Franklin Co., PA, and north of Chambersburg, PA. After a period of time Peter and his oldest sons owned large tracts of land, three mills and a number of homes. During the Revolutionary War, Peter and four of his sons: Henry, John, James and Jeremiah fought several tours of duty.

Peter Hockenberry was enrolled as a Private, First Class, First Company, First Battalion, Cumberland County Militia in which capacity he served a tour of active duty in Captain Thomas Askey's Company of the First Class, under Order of Council, dated July 20, 1777.

BROWN, GERALD L. – Born Mar. 8, 1940 in Athens, Clarke Co., GA. He joined the SAR in 2003, with dual state memberships in the Virginia Society and Georgia Society. He served in the U.S. military from 1961-95: USMC (E2), Infantry; USN (04), Medical Officer; and U.S. Public Health Service (USPHS) (06), Scientist. He received the Commendation Citation (USN) and Commendation Medal (USPHS). He is presently a staff psychiatrist for the Veterans Administration.

He was previously married to Margaret Stadler and is now married to Sima Peyman. He has seven children and 12 grandchilden.

Gerald Brown

William Rucker II, aka "Long Nose," was born Sept. 28, 1744 in Orange, VA. He was a private in Col. Finney's VA Troops, Capt. Beall's Company, and had also fought under Capt. Slaughter/Col. Slaughter and Capt. Phinks Co. His pension was granted on Jan. 18, 1833 while he was living in Elbert, GA. He died Feb. 26, 1835 and is buried in the Rucker Family Cemetery, Ruckersville, Elbert Co., GA.

BROWN, LON D. – Lon, the son of Dale and Josephine Parrish Brown was born and raised outside of Kalispell, MT. After graduating from high school, he attended Gonzaga University in Spokane, WA, receiving his degree in History and Political Science. A member of the Portage Chapter of the Montana Society, he joined through the service of his fifth great grandfather, William Parker.

William Parker, born on Oct. 6, 1760 at Wallingford, New Haven Co., CT, enlisted in Capt. Bunnell's Co., 5th Battalion (Wadsworth Brigade), of the Connecticut Line of the Continental Army on Feb. 16, 1777. He served as a private (drummer) until his discharge on Feb. 17, 1780 near Springfield, NJ. On March 26, 1789, William married Ruth Smith at Stockbridge, Berkshire Co., MA and by 1800 they had relocated to Lexington, Greene Co., NY. William joined the Lexington Congregational Society and the local militia, achieving the rank of major. On Oct. 31, 1818 William applied for and subsequently granted a pension for his war service. He died on Oct. 5, 1827 and was buried in the Jewett Heights Cemetery along with his wife. Mr. Brown descends through their daughter, Dolly Parker, the wife of George Cross.

BROWNING, DANA W. – Born Feb. 26, 1932 to Noah W. Browning and Dora J. (Kirk) Browning at Sarah Ann, Logan County, WV. He graduated from Logan HS in May 1950 and enlisted in the USAF. He served 22 years in the USAF, being stationed at several AF bases in the US and Puerto Rico. While stationed at Amarillo, TX, he married Frances N. Veazey on April 12, 1952. Dana graduated from the University of Texas at Austin in 1957, and retired from the USAF in 1973. He taught AFJROTC 21 years and retired in 1994.

Their son Keith was born June 3, 1953 and married Kathy in 1978. They have two children: Ashley and Christine. Their daughter Brenda was born Dec. 14, 1958 and married Randy in 1977. They have three children: Reed, Danica and Eliza.

Dana and Frances are members of First Baptist Church, and are very active in Sunday School and church. He is a descendent of Patriot Enos Browning, born in 1751 in Culpepper, VA, and Patriot George Hardwick, born Aug. 1759 in Amherst County, VA.

Enos Browning was born in 1751 in Culpepper Co., VA and died in Washington Co., VA in 1815. He married Jane (Jeannie) Trim in Caswell Co., NC. Jane was born in 1750 in Culpepper Co. and died in Logan Co., WV in Sept. 1842. Enos served in the Revolutionary War as a private and was involved in the Battle at Kings Mountain. He was with the North Carolina Line for a period, then with the Virginia Continental Line for two years. In 1779 he was granted land for his military service. His wife, Jane, applied for his military pension (W9753) after his death. Among his children were: Edmond, Francis, John James, Henry, and Jacob.

George Hardwick joined the Army under George Washington in April 1777. He was in the Battle of Germantown. After visiting his family in VA, he rejoined Capt. Nathaniel Rice at Prince Edward Courthouse, VA. From there he marched directly to Old James Town on the river. He was in the Battle of Monmouth, which was fought in the summer of 1778. Other battles were Blue Licks and Brandywine. He then volunteered under Captain Charles Gwatkins and marched to Boonsboro in the month of April 1780. Col. Boone and Col. Callaway were at the fort, along with about 35 officers and men. In the month of May 1781, he went back to VA and substituted for three months for David Wadeton under Capt. Jacob Moon at New London. He then marched to where Lynchburg is now and crossed the James River, then on to York, joining the American Line of Washington on the 12th of September. He witnessed the surrender of Cornwallis, but was not in the storm of Pigeon Hill. He was later discharged and drew a government pension.

BROWNING, NOAL L. – Born June 5, 1935 to Noah W. Browning and Dora J. (Kirk) Browning in Sarah Ann, Logan County, WV. He graduated from Logan HS in 1953 and married his wife, Kay Francis Browning on July 2, 1955. They moved to Ft. Lauderdale, FL in 1959, where he worked as a cabinet maker. Their daughter Kimberly was born in 1961. In July of that year they moved to Boynton Beach, FL, where he was foreman for a cabinet company. They then moved to Stuart, FL in March 1963, where they opened they own cabinet business. Their son, Noal Kirk, was born in 1969. They moved to Venice, FL in Jan. 2002, where they now live.

Noal and Kay Browning

Kimberly married Scott Wesley Albert and they have children Kaiya Kay and Tyson Wesley Albert.

Noal and Kay are of the Baptist faith and very active in their local church. Noal is a descendant of Patriot Enos Browning, born 1751 in Culpepper, VA and Patriot George Harwick, born August 1759 in Amherst Co., VA.

Enos Browning was born in 1751 in Culpepper Co., VA and died in Washington Co., VA in 1815. He married Jane (Jeannie) Trim in Caswell Co., NC. Jane was born in 1750 in Culpepper Co. and died in Logan Co., WV in Sept. 1842. Enos served in the Revolutionary War as a private and was involved in the Battle at Kings Mountain. He was with the North Carolina Line for a period, then with the Virginia Continental Line for two years. In 1779 he was granted land for his military service. His wife, Jane, applied for his military pension (W9753) after his death. Among his children were: Edmond, Francis, John James, Henry, and Jacob.

George Hardwick joined the Army under George Washington in April 1777. He was in the Battle of Germantown. After visiting his family in VA, he rejoined Capt. Nathaniel Rice at Prince Edward Courthouse, VA. From there he marched directly to Old James Town on the river. He was in the Battle of Monmouth, which was fought in the summer of 1778. Other battles were Blue Licks and Brandywine. He then volunteered under Captain Charles Gwatkins and marched to Boonsboro in the month of April 1780. Col. Boone and Col. Callaway were at the fort, along with about 35 officers and men. In the month of May 1781, he went back to VA and substituted for three months for David Wadeton under Capt. Jacob Moon at New London. He then marched to where Lynchburg is now and crossed the James River, then on to York, joining the American Line of Washington on the 12th of September. He witnessed the surrender of Cornwallis, but was not in the storm of Pigeon Hill. He was later discharged and drew a government pension.

BROWNING, WILLIAM – Born Sept. 15, 1942 to Noah N. Browning and Dora J. (Kirk) Browning in Barnabus, Logan County, WV. He graduated from Logan County HS in 1960. He moved to Ft. Lauderdale, FL right after graduation and worked in a cabinet shop. In July 1961 he moved to Boyton Beach, FL with the same cabinet company. He married Connie L. (Therber) Browning on July 13, 1961. In March 1963 they moved to Stuart, FL and worked for his brother, Noah Browning in his cabinet company. They moved to Macon, GA in 1988, where they still live. In 1991 he went to work for network television, working for ABC, CBS, NBC and ESPN doing football games. In 1994, while covering the Alabama-Ole Miss football game in AL, he was struck by lightning and now has vertigo.

They have three children: Mark William Browning, born in 1966; Melissa Lou Browning, born in 1969; and Michael Wayne Browning, born in 1973. Mark is married to Dora. Melissa is married to Brian Edwards. Michael is not married.

They have four grandchildren. Mark has Brett Daniel and Taylor Michelle. Melissa has Shelby Nicole and Summer Elaine.

In 2003, William rebuilt a working gristmill as well as the water source, the dam. He joined SAR in 2002; National number is 167983 and GA number is 4458. He is a descendant of Patriot Enos Browning, born in 1751 in Culpepper, VA, and Patriot George Hardwick, born in August 1759 in Amherst County, VA.

Enos Browning was born in 1751 in Culpepper Co., VA and died in Washington Co., VA in

1815. He married Jane (Jeannie) Trim in Caswell Co., NC. Jane was born in 1750 in Culpepper Co. and died in Logan Co., WV in Sept. 1842. Enos served in the Revolutionary War as a private and was involved in the Battle at Kings Mountain. He was with the North Carolina Line for a period, then with the Virginia Continental Line for two years. In 1779 he was granted land for his military service. His wife, Jane, applied for his military pension (W9753) after his death. Among his children were: Edmond, Francis, John James, Henry, and Jacob.

George Hardwick joined the Army under George Washington in April 1777. He was in the Battle of Germantown. After visiting his family in VA, he rejoined Capt. Nathaniel Rice at Prince Edward Courthouse, VA. From there he marched directly to Old James Town on the river. He was in the Battle of Monmouth, which was fought in the summer of 1778. Other battles were Blue Licks and Brandywine. He then volunteered under Captain Charles Gwatkins and marched to Boonsboro in the month of April 1780. Col. Boone and Col. Callaway were at the fort, along with about 35 officers and men. In the month of May 1781, he went back to VA and substituted for three months for David Wadeton under Capt. Jacob Moon at New London. He then marched to where Lynchburg is now and crossed the James River, then on to York, joining the American Line of Washington on the 12th of September. He witnessed the surrender of Cornwallis, but was not in the storm of Pigeon Hill. He was later discharged and drew a government pension.

BUCHANAN-BOARDMAN, CHARLES EDWARD – AAS, CAPA, a Bachelor; born in rural Las Vegas, Clark, Nevada on February 14, 1981; the son of Patricia Danielle Boardman, A.B. and Sgt. Larry Wayne Tarin (USAF Vietnam); Educated at the College of Southern Nevada (AAS Business Administration- Human Resource Management), University of Maryland (Accounting Major); Member of S1, George's Society of New York; Member of the Sons of the American Revolution; Member of the Sons of Confederate Veterans; Member of the White Lion Society; Member of the Heraldry Society; Member of the American College of Heraldry; Member of the American Institute of Professional Bookkeepers; Armiger according to the laws of the United States of America; Armorial Bearings Registered with The State Herald of South Africa, Registered under Government Notice No. 134 of 17th February 2006 (H4/3/4/798), Certification 3589 Dated July 7; Further Registration with the Westphalian Heraldry Society in Germany, 21st October 2003; American College of Heraldry in the United States of America, 18th April 2003 Number 2316; and the Commission on Heraldry for The New England Historical and Genealogical Society on 15th November 2003 in the United States of America.

Charles Edward Sean Buchanan-Boardman with medals, St. Georges Society, SAR, SCV.

Arms: Azure, within a Bordure barry of nine, Argent and Gules, a Lion rampant guardant Argent holding in the dexter forepaw a quill Or feathered Argent and in the sinister forepaw an open book, the pages Proper fore edges and clasps Or, the lower clasp joined to a gold chain reflexed over the shoulder of the lion and terminating in a Bezant pierced trefoilwise, the pages inscribed in Black Letter SAPIENS QUI ASSIDUUS.

Crest: Out of a Coronet pallisady Or a demi Lion Azure grasping between its paws a closed book Gules fore edge and clasps Or the lower clasp joined to a gold chain reflexed over the shoulder of the Lion and terminating with a Bezant pierced trefoilwise.

Charles Buchanan-Boardman Armorial Bearings

Lineage: (9th) Capt. Jacob Pyeatt (US Army, American Revolution) and Margaret Finely (8th) Peter Pyeatt and Mary Miller (7th) Pvt. Jessie Henry Pyeatt (Confederate Army, Civil War) and Jane Isabelle Buchanan (6th) Shadrach Nelson West and Mary Elizabeth Pyeatt (5th) Charles Cannon Conway and Ida Esmer West (4th) Marcellus Candler Boardman and Bonnie Leota Conway (3rd) Col. Charles Robert Boardman, BS (USAR) and Mary Darlene Head (2nd) Sgt. Larry Wayne Tarin (USAF) and Patricia Danielle Boardman, AB (1st) Charles Edward Sean Buchanan-Boardman.

Captain Jacob Pyeatt (US Army, American Revolution) born in Guilford, NC in 1760; the Son of John Pyeatt and Martha Jane Blair; military service: served in the American Revolution in Virginia under Colonel George Rogers Clark; married Margaret Finley in Guilford, NC on March 8, 1791; in March of 1812 led first group of Protestants into Arkansas with brother James and established Pyeattstown which today is part of the golf course of the Maumelle Country Club; in 1812 the first Protestant service ever said on Arkansas soil was said in the house of his brother James by the Reverend John Carnahan; founding member of the Cumberland Presbyterian Church; died August 16, 1844 in Washington, AR; buried in the Old Cane Hill Cemetery in Cane Hill, AR.

BURKHART, RONALD ERNEST – Born Jul. 9, 1940 in Indianapolis, IN. He joined the SAR in Feb. 2008 and is President, Daniel Guthrie Chapter, Bedford, Indiana. A member of the Indiana State SAR Color Guard, he has received the War Service Medal with Vietnam devise and Purple Heart pin.

He enlisted in the U.S. Marine Corps on Feb. 9, 1960 and served 28 years, during which time he served over 15 accumulative years as a private through first sergeant (1stSgt) in various infantry units of the 3rd, 5th, 7th, and 9th Marine Regiments, which included a tour as a tactics instructor at the Infantry Training Regiment for marines being assigned to Vietnam. 1962-65, he served on Department of State Duty at embassies in Sudan and Kenya. 1967-68, he served as a platoon sergeant/commander with 3rd Battalion, 9th Marine Regiment in Vietnam. 1968-70, he was a Drill Instructor at San Diego. 1973-75, he was the leader of the marine guards at the U.S. Embassy in Indonesia. 1975-77, he completed embassy duty by serving as instructor as the Marine Security Guard School. 1977-81, he served as a CoGySgt of "B" Company, 1st Battalion, 3rd Marines, 1st Marine Brigade; Operations Chief for the battalion; 1stSgt of the newly activated Weapons Co. in the same battalion; and ending his tour as 1stSgt of Headquarters Company, 3rd Marines, 1st Marine Brigade. 1981-84, he was 1stSgt of the I&I Staff, South Bend, Indiana, where he was promoted to Sergeant Major (SgtMaj). 1984-88, he was SgtMaj of two battalions at Camp Pendleton, California, during which time he was assigned as a member of the senior enlisted promotion board at Headquarters, U.S. Marine Corps. His last tour of duty was Inspector SgtMaj of 1st Force Service Support Group, Camp Pendleton, where he retired Feb. 1988.

Ronald Ernest Burkhart

Military awards include the Purple Heart with gold star; Meritorious Service Medal; Navy Achievement Medal with combat V and gold star; as well as other metals, ribbons, commendations, and letters.

He is a part-time lecturer, Indiana University, Kelley School of Business, and served as vice president of the Monroe County Historical Society, Indiana.

He is married to Ngoc Thi "Kathy" Nguyen, with four children and seven grandchildren.

Maj. John Meason was born Feb. 22, 1753 in Frederick Co. (now Berkeley Co.), WV. He married Hannah Frost, daughter of William and Hannah Frost. John served as a major in the 3rd Battalion of Westmoreland County Militia of Pennsylvania under LtCol Nehemiah Stokely during the Revolutionary War.

In 1784 he was a Justice of Common Court of Pleas in Fayette County, PA. About 1804 he was Justice of the Peace in Justice District No. 1 in Fayette County.

He died Aug. 1, 1805 and is buried on Green Lick Run farm in Bullskin Twp., Fayette County, PA.

BURKLAND, GERALD JAMES – Born April 27, 1945, Detroit, MI. He has served as MISSAR State President 2005-07; National Trustee 2007/09; and as National Chairman, NSSAR Revolutionary Graves. He received the

Silver Good Citizenship, Distinguished Service Award, and Bronze Good Citizenship.

He married Carol Ann Derk and they have two children and three grandchildren and currently reside in Millington, MI. He recently was reunited with his daughter, Rebecca Marie Burkland-Cottrell after 40 years. Gerald was in manufacturing of Military Goods, 1965-1969. He is the President of Landview Development Inc.

Civic organizations include: Masonic Lodge 470, Millington, MI; History Channel Club; Life Member Mayflower Society; Michigan Archeology Society and Member Ferguson Clan.

Isaac Livermore was born June 11, 1752 in Spencer, MA. Patriot Regiment: Col. Dike's Regiment Patriot Company: Capt. Ezekiel Knowlton's Co. Patriot Rank: Private Patriot Battles: Concord Bridge, Battle of Bunker Hill Patriot Battles: Patriot Occupation: Farmer Patriot death date: 1838 Patriot burial place: Castle Creek, NY, Baptist Cemetery, name is on bronze plaque.

BURLESON, BILLY REX – Born on Nov. 29, 1929, to Evel Merle and Blanche Moseley Burlseson (their only child) at Rt. 2, Abbott, Hill County. He grew up in rural Hill and McLennan Counties.

In April 1948, he met his future wife, Lillian Purvis Burleson, one Sunday morning after church services. This country boy and the city girl were introduced by their mothers, who had known each other in their younger years, but had recently renewed friendship at church. After 2-1/2 years of courtship, they married on Nov. 11, 1950.

In 1996, Bill and Lillian were certified by the Texas State Genealogical Society as descendants of early settlers who were in Texas before 1846, and were presented with Texas First Families Certificates.

He volunteered for the US. Air Force in August 1950, served to October 1953, being discharged as a Staff/Sgt. This was during the Korean police action.

From Oct. 23, 1953 to Dec. 1, 1991, he embraced the occupation of an insurance claim representative .... the last 28 years with the State Farm Insurance Companies.

In August 1988 he was accepted into the SAR membership. In January 1989, he was elected 1st Vice President. In 1994 he was elected President of Chapter #32 for two years, whereas he followed up by being registrar and secretary/treasurer for 10 years. He has been active in promoting the American Heritage program and working with presentation of ROTC medals and certificates in addition to working with the essay programs. He is currently the secretary/treasurer of the Sons of the Republic of Texas chapter.

He served as President of the Waco Claims Association in 1966-67. President of the Harris Creek Country Estates Home Owners Association in 1994-95. After retirement he worked with writing to read computer program for the Midway ISD.

He served as a Bible Class teacher for High School and Middle School classes, served in the benevolence committee, insurance committee, visitation work and recently spear-headed an outreach program of the House to House/Heart to Heart mail out for the Hewitt Church of Christ where he is an active member.

The Burleson's have been blessed with two children, Patricia Burleson Duran and husband, Joe Duran of Temple and Pamela Burleson Logan of Hewitt. They have six grandchildren and eight great-grandchildren. He is the Patriarch of the Burleson family in his role as husband, father, grandfather and great-grandfather.

His dad was born Nov. 16, 1894 near Jewitt, Leon County, TX ... died Jan. 7, 1976, buried at Oakwood in Waco. His mother was born Aug. 31, 1900 near Aquilla, Hill County, TX, died Sept. 12, 1980 ... buried at Oakwood in Waco. They married Feb. 9, 1928 in Waco, TX.

David Burleson was born in 1755 at Luneburg County, VA. He was a private in James Farris' Battalion, Colonel Wade's Regiment, NC. He married Ursula Weatherford in 1773. He died Aug. 13, 1832, buried Rutherford, TN. Ursula died Feb. 27, 1836, Rutherford County, TN.

BURNETT, JOHN ALBERT, Ph.D. – Born Nov. 1, 1961 at Waycross, GA. He has been President of the Nevada State Society 2007; President of the Northern Chapter (Reno, NV) 2008. John received a Membership Certificate Sept. 8, 1987 at Jacksonville, FL. National Number 129889.

John married Katherine Dana Miller on May 7, 1993. They have two children; John Edward Burnett and Amy Katherine Burnett, both members of the CAR. They reside in Renova, NV. His occupation has been with University of Nevada, Reno (UNR). Director of Equal Opportunity/Affirmative Action.

He is a Life Member of the Baker County, FL Historical Society; member of Florida State Genealogical Society and a member of Lambda Chi Alpha Fraternity.

John's supplemental Revolutionary ancestors are: **John Anderson**, **Edward Carter**, **Henry Dyess** and **John Henry Stonecypher**.

Lewis Roberts was born circa 1755 in South Carolina. He was a Private in the South Carolina Militia under Colonel Winn. In civilian life, Lewis was a farmer. He died circa 1820 and is buried in Wayne County, GA.

BURNS, EDWARD A. JR. – Born April 24, 1938 in Brockton, MA. He is the Registrar of the Long Island Chapter.

Edward and Patricia A. have three children and six grandchildren. They reside in Fresh Meadows, NY. He was the CFO Bank of Montreal (USA) and retired February 1, 2002.

Edward A. Burns, Jr.

Edwardalso belongs to General Society of Mayflower Descendants and Alden Kindred of America.

Samuel Brett was born Aug. 22, 1714 at Bridgewater, MA. He served in Colonel John Bailey's Regiment (Minutemen), later the 2nd Massachusetts Regiment. Bailey's Regiment was part of General John Thomas' Brigade. Thomas' Brigade was part of Major General Artemas Ward's Division of the Continental Army of 1775. Samuel was also in Captain Josiah Hayden's Company.

As a private, he was at the April 19, 1775 Alarm at Lexington, MA, in the Battle at North Bridge. On Dec. 6, 1776, in the Battle at Newport, RI, Alarm at Newport, RI as a corporal. On July 22, 1780, as a sergeant, in the Battle at Newport, RI. On Sept. 1, 1786 at Taunton, MA, a 2nd Lieutenant at Shay's Rebellion Gathering.

Samuel was a farmer in civilian life. He died March 7, 1807 and is buried at North End or Ashland Cemetery, Bridgewater, MA.

BUROW, RICHARD W. – Born Aug. 16, 1939 in Danville, IL and resides in Kingsport, TN.

Richard married Suzanne Porter and they have 2 children and 2 grandchildren. He retired Feb. 28, 1999 as a principal mechanical engineer with the EastmanChemical Company.

Richard W. Burow

Other organizations include: First Families of Massachusetts; Boy Scouts of America 50 years service; Eagle Scout; Scoutmaster; Scouters Key; Silver Beaver; Sertoma Club 40 years perfect attendance; American Society of Mechanical Engineers Section and Region Officer; Dediced Service Award; Appalachian Trial Conservancy Life Member; Masonic Fraternity Past Master; Masonic York Rite Past Officer; Masonic Scottish Rite KCCH; York Rite Sovereign College Past Grand Governor TN Order of the Purple Cross, Jericho Shrine Templer and Kingsport Bicycle Club Past President.

Oliver Whitney gravestone, Twenty Mile Stream Cemetery, Cavendish, VT.

Oliver Whitney, born was born April 15, 1744 at Natick, MA. He was a Private with the Natick Company. Oliver was farmer, died Dec. 29, 1813 and is buried at Twenty Mile Stream Cemetery, Cavendish, VT.

BURT, ROBERT E. – Born June 5, 1926 in Bussey (Marion County) IA. Joined Jan. 1, 1978 Delaware Crossing Chapter, Overland Park, KS. Dual membership Kansas and Florida.

Past President-Delaware Crossing Chapter,

past president Kansas Society Sons of the American Revolution, and their Trustee, Genealogist General, Founder of the Arthur M. and Berdena King Eagle Scout Scholarship program and chairman for 12 years. Awards – Minuteman, Patriot, Five memberships plaques plus the Liberty medal with three palms, Syracuse Award (six new chapters in Kansas), Stephen Taylor award (Bates Genealogy), Silver and Bronze Good Citizenship Medals, Meritorious Service Award with two palms, George Washington Fellow, Life Member in KS and NSSAR, Boy Scouts of American/Sons of the American Revolution Robert E. Burt Volunteer Scouting A ward, Awarded the Daughters of the American Revolution Medal of Honor in Kansas, a Kentucky Colonel.

My deceased first wife Mary and I had five children: Kenneth, Roberta, Carl, Rodney, Lori; married Gertrude (Trudy) Welshans and she had three children: Wayne, Charles and Martha Ann. Together we have 19 grandchildren, 22 great grandchildren.

Past Treasurer Mayflower Society of Kansas and Governor of the Elder William Brewster Colony Miami, FL and now Governor of the State of Florida Mayflower Society (James Chilton was my passenger.) Member of the Descendants of Washington Army at Valley Forge (William Waller my Patriot); Member Platte Woods United Methodist Church, past President Key Largo Village and past president of the Federation of home owners associations in Key Largo.

Mary and I have published five family history books, Bates, Hauenstein, Burt, Sloggett and Bruere.

James Bruere (a French Huguenot) was born Feb. 9, 1750 in Allentown, NJ; married Sarah Horsful (Welcome Society of Pennsylvania). James was a Captain in Colonel Forhan's Company, 2nd Regiment, Monmouth County Militia. He was appointed the President of the Regional Court Martial.

James was a farmer owner and operator (apples and grain). He died July 7, 1807 and is buried in the Colonial Section of the Allentown Presbyterian Church Cemetery, Allentown, Monmouth County, NJ.

BUSHNELL, DR. EARLE SCOTT – Born May 30, 1942 in Utica, NY; he joined the Florida SAR on Mar. 3, 2008 and has served as the North Central Regional V.P., Veterans Committee, and Webmaster. Scott served in the U.S. Navy, Vietnam, 1967-68 (including the TET Offensive), and retired as a consultant on Oct. 3, 2003. He is a member of the VFW, American Legion, Masons, National Eagle Scout Association, Orland Veterans Advisory Council. He is married to Myra J. Bushnell and they have three children and 15 grandchildren.

Handley Bushnell was born in 1731 in Saybrook, CT. He served in the Colonial Wars and Poughkeepsie, NY, and was the Purchasing Agent for Commissaries of Towns of Saybrook, New London, Lyme and Killingsworth. He died Jan. 1, 1811.

BUTLER, EDWARD F. SR. – Edward is a native of Memphis, TN, who currently resides in San Antonio, TX. He is the son of Oliver John Butler, Sr. and Arlene Lovelace. He obtained his B.A. degree in political science from the University of Mississippi in 1958, where he was a "regional scholar." He was a Ford Foundation Scholar at Vanderbilt University School of Law, where he received a J.D. degree with honors in 1961. He practiced law in Memphis, TN from 1961-1984, during which time he also maintained an office in Houston, TX, from 1972-1976.

In Memphis he served as a special judge in the City Court, General Sessions Court, Juvenile Court and Probate Court. He was also the Chief Judge for the West Tennessee District of the Tennessee Medical Malpractice Review Board.

Edward F. Butler, Sr.

In early 1985 he practiced for a few months with his brother, Oliver, in Brownsville, TX, after which he entered into private practice on South Padre Island, TX. There he served as president of the South Padre Island Merchants' Assn., the Port Isabel-South Padre - Laguna Vista Chamber of Commerce, and the Laguna Madre Area Republican Club. From 1987-1988 he served as the presiding municipal court judge of South Padre Island. Judge Butler was board certified as a Civil Trial Advocate by the National Board of Trial Advocacy, and was also board certified as a Civil Trial Lawyer by the Texas Board of Legal Specialization.

In 1991 he was appointed as a United States Federal Administrative Law Judge. He worked in the Office of Hearings and Appeals of the Social Security Administration in Dallas, TX. Due to injuries to his neck and back received in a work connected accident, he retired in 1997.

His first international travel occurred in July, 1961, when he spent a few days in Mexico City. Since then he has traveled to over 165 countries. He is married to Robin Melissa Butler, a registered nurse. Ed has two sons, Edward F. "Rhett" Butler II, and Jeffrey Darrell Butler (both perpetual life members of the SAR), and two step daughters Melissa Crum and Melanie Little Morris, and three grandchildren.

Since retirement he has been very active in the National Society of the Sons of the American Revolution, which he joined in 1986. He is a perpetual life member. He served as chapter president of the San Antonio, TX SAR chapter, and as Genealogist and Vice President of the Texas SAR Society. Judge Butler founded the Mexico Society of the SAR, and served as its charter president and trustee. He also founded two chapters in Texas: Laredo and Boerne. He has served two terms as NSSAR Vice President General; two terms as Genealogist General; and as Chancellor General, Treasurer General, and Secretary General. He has also served as legal counsel, treasurer and secretary of the SAR Foundation.

At press time he was a non opposed candidate for President General. He served as National Trustee for five years. In 2006 he was presented the coveted "Minuteman Award," the highest honor that can be bestowed upon a member by the National Society, SAR.

Judge Butler retired in 1990 from the US Navy Reserve as a Commander, after 35 years in the reserve. He was an adjunct Professor of Political Science at the University of Memphis, Shelby State Community College in Memphis, and the University of Texas in Brownsville. He acted as a Professor of Law at the Reynaldo G. Garza School of Law of the University of Texas at Edinburg.

Judge Butler is the author of two law books, four family history books and three books about his travels around the world. He is a biographee in *Who's Who in American Law*; *Who's Who in the South and Southwest*; and *Who's Who in Practicing Attorneys*.

He has also served as Governor of the Texas Society of Colonial Wars; President of the Texas Society of the War of 1812; and as Vice President General and Judge Advocate General of the national society; President of the Texas Sons of the Revolution, and currently is serving as Deputy Grand Prior of the Sovereign Military Order of the Temple of Jerusalem, commonly known as the Knights Templar.

Frederick Hambright was born May 17, 1727 in Neunstetten, Germany. At age 11, he came to America with his family aboard the ship, *St. Andrew*, arriving in Philadelphia, PA on Oct. 17, 1738. Abt. 1755 he moved to Virginia and later married Sarah Hardin. By 1760 they had moved to North Carolina.

He served with Capt. Samuel Cobrin's Co. during the Spanish Alarm at Wilmington, NC in 1747-48. During the French and Indian War in the 1750s, he served as a private with Capt. Samuel Colburn's company in Anson Co., NC. By 1771 he was the Captain commanding the Tryon Co., NC Militia. In 1776 he served as a Captain against the Indians on the western frontiers, serving with Gen. Rutherford's successful campaign against the Cherokees in the fall of that year. In 1777 he was appointed Major of the NC Militia. In 1779 he was promoted to Lt. Col., serving in Lillington's Brigade in the Battle to relieve Charleston.

In 1780, he was second in command of the Lincoln Co. Volunteers during the Battle at King's Mountain. During the battle, he assumed command on the death of the commander, and he was wounded in the leg but refused to dismount, leading his men to victory.

Frederick and Sara Hambright had 12 children, six of whom lived to adulthood. She died before 1780. In 1781 he married Mary Dover, and they had 10 children, nine of whom lived to adulthood. He died on May 9, 1817 in York Co., SC, and is buried in the old Shiloh Presbyterian Cemetery, one mile east of Grover, NC.

BYERS, JOHN RAOUL III – Born Nov. 24, 1931 in Rochester, NY, he joined the Empire (NY) Society SAR on Jul. 11, 2008. He received a B.A. from Cornell University in 1954 and an MBA from New York University in 1960. John served in the U.S. Army, SP 4, Army Security Agency (ASA) from 1954-56.

John was the V.P. for Gill & Duffus, Inc. and served for 20 years as an international cocoa merchant. He retired in 1994. He served as General Manager for the Garth Woods Conservancy on the Bronx River Parkway, Inc. (1997-2004); was a member of *Who's Who in America* (2001-06); authored the book, "Calaboose, The Life and Times of a Frontier Lawman, 1835-1858," Jay Street Publishers, NY, 2002; is an Eagle Scout; and was President of the Cocoa Merchants Assoc. of America, Inc, (1973-74).

John Byers (left) receiving NSSAR Membership Certificate from Ken Stevens, President of Westchester-Putnam Chapter, Dec. 13, 2008.

He is married to Sharon Lynne Schlag and they have two sons, James J. and John W., and two grandsons, Andrew J. and John Ryan.

Nathan Harwood was born Feb. 22, 1737 in Uxbridge, MA, and served as a lieutenant and later captain in Col. Ezra May's Regt., Capt. Bannister's Company. He participated in the battles of Stillwater, Saratoga and Bennington. In civilian life he was a physician in Windsor, MA. Nathan died Feb. 3, 1790 and is buried in Shaw Cemetery, Windsor, MA.

BYRD, ABRAHAM RUDDELL III, MD. – Born Aug. 1, 1943 in Tucson, AZ. He served as President, Tucson Chapter, AZSSAR 2006-07, and Historian, AZSSAR 2006-present. He is on the Medical Committee and the Chorus. He has a private medical practice in Tucson (Sonora Family Practice), Board Certified in Family Medicine and Fellow of the Academy. He is also a Merit Badge Counselor, Boy Scouts of America, and a living history volunteer for Presidio\'soldado. He is married to Gayle Reay and they have one child.

Amos Byrd was born ca. 1737-38, serving as a Capt. in the NC Militia. He was one of the "Overmountain Men," although it is not known if he was at the Battle of Kings Mountain. A weaver, frontiersman and farmer, he died June 6, 1818 and is buried on the Byrd or Penny Farm, Cape Girardeau County, MO.

CAMP, EUGENE CARTER – He joined the Alabama SAR on Oct. 17, 2008. A pilot, he won a gold medal at the Community Challenge Pentathalon in Montgomery, AL. A graduate of Auburn University, he was a JROTC Officer and served on the Color Guard. He is an inventor and actor, and is the CEO of Camp and Associates.

Thomas Camp, born 1747 in Halifax, VA, was raised with the family "old Virginia pattern hospitality." He married Nancy Ann Tarpley in Richmond, VA in 1769. He refused to be impressed into the British Army and to burn his neighbor's homes. So, he helped the Patriots fight at King's Mountain, where his brother, Nathaniel, claimed to have shot British Major Ferguson dead on the left flank that morning. The Camp brothers fought at Cowpens, Dan River, VA, and probably finally at Yorktown. Brother Stephen, at age ten, was severely wounded. Their father gave

Attackers charging up the hillside and becoming overwhelmed.at King's Mountain.

them each "five Shillings starlin" in his 1798 will. Thomas died in NC in 1811 and is buried in Walton Co., GA.

CAMPBELL, BENJAMIN CARTER – Born Nov. 11, 1973 in Lake Charles, Calcasieu, Louisiana. He joined the Louisiana Chapter SAR on Nov. 4, 2008. He served in the Army National Guard, FSC 527 EN BN, SSG, E-6, and is a veteran of Operation Enduring Freedom, Afghanistan. He currently does sheetmetal work Ductwork, Inc.

He is a member of Sons of Confederate Veterans, Military Order of the Stars and Bars, and American Legion.

John Milford I was born 1760 in Antrim, Antrim Co., Ireland. He entered the service while residing near Ninety Six, under a Capt. Logan and General Pickens. He served as a guard at Ninety Six jail and was on an expedition into Georgia. During 1780, he was under Gen. Greene. In 1781, he was at Cowan's Ford when Lord Cornwallis crossed the river. During 1781 and 1783, he was under Capt. John Calhoun. A farmer, he died in 1837 and is buried at Antreville, Anderson Co., SC.

CAMPBELL, MARION SANDERS JR. – Born June 16, 1933 at Rock Hill, SC. He presently resides in Plano, TX. He was in the US. Army as a Master Sergeant in the 30th and 51st Infantry Divisions for 10 years.

Marion has held SAR offices as Chapter President, 1st VP, Secretary and Sgt.-at-Arms. He has received the Bronze and Silver Good Citizenship, Meritorious w/cluster; Liberty, Veterans; Chapter and TXSSAR Service and War medals and has received several Certificates of Appreciation. Marion also produced a Pictorial Directory of his chapter.

Marion Sanders Campbell Jr.

Marion received his MBA and spent 45 years in the telephone and communications industry. He retired from Motorola in 1993 as are manager of 35 states. He was elected Fellow of The Radio Club of American and was awarded five Colonel Commissions from six Southern State Governors.

He married Nancy Parker and they have four children, seven grandchildren and five great-grandchildren.

Marion also belongs to American Radio Relay League; Quarter Century Wireless Association, Independent Telephone Pioneers Association; is a 32-degree Mason and Shriner.

John Campbell was born in Scotland in 1740. He came to America on board the Ship *Lord Dunluce* and landed in Charleston, SC. Sometime after his arrival he was awarded 300-Acres of land by King George, 3rd. He later served as an Aide-de-Camp to Capt. John Buchanan with the South Carolina Regulars of the 3rd Regiment. He and Capt. Buchanan were captured during the Battle of Charleston and was a Prisoner of War at Haddrell's Point, near Sullivan's Island, SC. They were later exchanged for a large supply of Tobacco for Lord Cornwallis. He spent the remainder of his life farming. It is believed that he is buried in the Harmony Baptist Churches Cemetery but not confirmed.

CAPLES, ROBERT M. – Born March 10, 1952 in Baltimore, MD. He presently lives in Rowson, MD.

Robert joined SAR on Nov. 10, 1975 and has served as Chapter Manager and received a Bronze Good Citizenship Medal on June 9, 1984 and Jan. 11, 1997.

He became disabled from 1998 after working at Social Security Headquarters of Maryland.

Robert Lemon Caples Jr. was born circa 1717 at Baltimore County, MD. In March 1778 he took the Oath of Fidelity recording him as supporting the Revolutionary War but was unable to bear arms due to health and age. He was 61 years old at that time. The oath is recorded in Baltimore County, page 308, Hall of Records, Annapolis, MD.

Robert was married twice; first to Anne Cox and they had three children, second to Ailcy (Aliese) Cole and they had nine children.

Robert was a farmer and died between Feb. 7, 1801 and March 21, 1801. He is believed to be buried on 395-3/4 acre parcel of land in Baltimore County, MD known as Caples Habitation Property.

CARLSON, JOHN "JC" – John was born March 24, 1943 in Holland, MI. He was in the USN – *USS Wainwright* (DLG-28), FTM 1.

JC and wife Nancy have three children and eight grandchildren. They reside in Holland, MI.

JC was Power Plant Maint. Supervisor Electrical Electronics, and retired in 1998.

He belongs to Michigan Trust Fund, founder *USS Wainwright* Veterans Association. He is a 2 x Vietnam Veteran Operation and Rolling Thunder.

Hains Daniel French joined the Whitcomb's Rangers; he was a scout and spy in Vermont and Canada. He was at Chatgaugay; Four

Corners, NY; War of 1812 and a Major with 31st Infantry Regt.

His civilian occupation was a court clerk and farmer. He died in 1814 and burial place is unknown.

CARVIN, JOSEPH FRANKLIN – Born Oct. 19, 1914, Edinburgh, IN. Veteran WWII, drafted into Army, July 3, 1941, Fort Harrison IN. Basic training Camp Lee, VA; Military Police Carlisle, PA. After Pearl Harbor attack, sent to Fort McDowell, CA, from there to Fort Shafter, HI. Assigned to the 5th Medal Supply Depot, there until discharged Oct. 19, 1945. Was Maintenance Technician for Medical and Dental Equipment on the Islands. Reached the rank of S/Sgt.

Joseph F. Carvin

Married Mildred Alice Hart November 1944 while on leave to the States. Received the following Awards: Good Conduct; Asiatic-Pacific Theater; American Defense; WWII Victory Medals; Meritorious Unit Emblem and Foreign Service Bar.

He belong to the following organizations, several Masonic Bodies, American Legion Post #443, Columbus, OH; Sons of Union Veterans of the Civil War and First Families of Ohio.

During my years in the Sons of the American Revolution I served as President of the Benjamin Franklin Chapter Ohio Society SAR; OhSSAR Central District Chairman; Chapter Registrar; Chapter Flag Chairman; State Historian. Awards received.: Patriot Medal; War Service Medal; Meritorious Service Medal; Three Liberty Medals and four Appreciation Certificates and the State Hub Scott Award.

John Hawkins, born on Maryland's Eastern Shore, was a private in Queen Anne's County Maryland's Minute-Men which was formed by Captain James Kent by order Council of Safety to repress Lord Dunmores' invasion and check the Tories on Virginia's Eastern Shore. They left George Hanson's Tavern February 1776 for Hampton Court House, VA, reaching there Feb. 14 and accomplishing their mission.

Later he was a Lieutenant in the Upper Battalion of Maryland's Eastern Shore that was sent to New York and became engaged in the battle of Harlem Heights in September. Drove the enemy from their lines with bayonets (the first American troops to use bayonets), took part in two more New York battles. March 1777 he was a Captain in the 5th Regiment of General Smallwood's 1st Maryland Brigade.

After the War he settled in Abbieville County, SC. Died there 1799, place of burial unknown. He was married to Elizabeth Jones, dau. of Joseph Jones.

Four other Patriots were **Thomas Little** of Seawall's North Carolina's Militia, **William Vaughan**, **Samuel Vaughan** and **Richard W. Gregory**, who furnished Beef and fodder.

CASH, JIMMY HADEN – Born Feb. 12, 1949 at Forest Cottage, Cumberland County, KY and resides at Shepherdsville, KY.

Jimmy and wife Madonna Rinkel have two children and six grandchildren. He is employed by US Postal Service.

Jimmy Haden Cash

Jimmy also is a Volunteer fireman and has belonged to the Boy Scouts of American for 30 years.

Shadrack Claywell was born Nov. 7, 1760 in Poccnoke City, Worchester County, MD. He lived in Bedford County, VA, until 1806 when he moved to Cumberland County, KY, where he lived until his death in 1838 on Bear Creek.

In 1778 Shadrack served 18 months as a militia private from Bedford County, VA, under Captain Robert Adams and was stationed principally on New River at Chissel's Mines. At the end of 18 months, he was discharged.

In 1780, he again served three months as a militiaman from Bedford County, VA, under Captain Thomas Leftwich and marched to Hillsborough, NC. At the end of his tour in June 1780, he enlisted in the regular service on Continental Establishment in the south for 12 months. He was in the battle of Guilford, NC, in the spring of 1781 commanded by Colonel William Washington. Shadrack was a part of the Virginia and Delaware Patriots under the command of Captain Robert Kirkwood and Lieutenant Colonel William Washington, veterans of Cowpens, who helped support the flanks. Shadrack was also at the skirmish at the Shallow Ford of the Yadkin about 20 miles from Salisbury, NC.

Shadrack returned to Bedford County, VA and lived there until 1806 when he moved to Cumberland County, KY.

On Feb. 4, 1833, Shadrack Claywell Senior, age 73, declares in 1778, he served 18 months as a militia private from Bedford County, VA. He applied for a pension for his time spent in the American Revolution. On June 16, 1836, J. J. Crittenden writes from Washington, D.C., that Shadrack Claywell was stricken from the list of Revolutionary pensioners upon a charge of his having joined the enemy during the war. Upon the trial of the indictments against the King in the Circuit Court of the United States, during the past year Claywell was a witness and this charge became incidentally a subject of investigation. The result was a clear conviction on Crittenden's part that Shadrack was guiltless of the charge. While in service, he was taken prisoner by the British and during his captivity, he became infected with smallpox's and being very badly afflicted with it. He was lodged in some exposed out house and was otherwise cruelly neglected. In the condition, to save his life, he agreed to join the British upon their importuning him to do so and promising him he would be taken care of and receive better treatment. Not long after that, about the time of his recovery, peace was made and he was carried off by the British to Canada. It was several years before Shadrack made his way back to the United States. It does not appear that Shadrack, in fact, ever served the British. He stated on oath he did not.

On Feb. 11, 1833, Cumberland County, KY, George Richardson of said county, aged near 75, declares he knows Shadrack Claywell Senior, served the second tour mentioned in his declaration from Bedford County, VA, and the year as an enlisted private, having often seen him in service in the fall of 1780 and the spring of 1781. He saw him in the regiment commanded by Colonel White.

Shadrack Claywell of Cumberland County, KY, private of cavalry in the company of Captain Adams in the regiment of Colonel White in the Virginia militia for 18 months, was placed on the Kentucky pension roll at $70 per annum under the Act of 1832. Certificate 13885 was issued July 9, 1833.

Shadrack continued to live in Cumberland County, KY and moved to another farm, when received a land grant for 175 acres on Illwill Creek, on Oct. 9, 1806. On June 28, 1813, Shadrack bought 200 acres on Bear Creek. He built a log cabin around 1813, where he and eight members of his family lived. He lived on this farm for the rest of his life. He, his wife, and other family members are believed to be buried in the Claywell graveyard on this farm.

In 1969 the log cabin was moved and reconstructed in the Burkesville Community Park, Cumberland County, KY. The cabin was a typical dogtrot house that was popular in the Cumberland's in the early 1800s.

CHAMBERLAIN, TOBY LEE – Born July 22, 1942 in Eldorado, KS. He joined the Illinois Society SAR on Apr. 4, 2008. He served in the US Marine Corps, Marine Air Group 36 and HQ USMC, Corporal.

Toby worked for 35 years with the Dept. of Defense, 11 years as a Senior Watch Officer at the Naval Intelligence Command, and 24 years with the Army Recruiting Command. He is a member of the Moultrie County (Illinois) Historical Society, and is a "Find A Grave" volunteer.

He has been married to Sue (Selby) for 42 years. Two daughters: Stephanie Chamberlain and Tracy (Chamberlain) Turk. Four grandchildren: Graham Turk, William Turk, Lleyton Turk, and Erin Turk. Stephanie and Tracy are DAR members. Graham, William, Lleyton and Erin are CAR members.

John Kennedy was a Private in the Virginia Militia. He was taken prisoner by the British of Guilford Courthouse (NC) and put on the prison ship Jersey, where he died of starvation on Jun. 26, 1781. He was married to Esther Stilly, who is listed as a Patriot by the DAR for providing supplies to the Continental Army. They had seven children, several of whom were instrumental in settling Kentucky after the Revolutionary War.

CHAMBERS, ROBERT ALLEN – Born May 3, 1948 in Seattle, King Co., WA. He served in the U.S. Navy from 1968-70. He is a member of Vietnam Veterans of America, Disabled Veterans of America, American Legion, and SAR. Robert is also active in ham radio and politics. His wife, Patricia Lou Chambers, is active in DAR. They have two children.

Daniel Poorman was born Aug. 31, 1744 in Lancaster, PA. He was a private in Col. James Johnson's Cumberland County Militia, Capt. Conrad Snider's Company. He died about 1841 in Indiana.

CHAPIN, JOHN NETTLETON JR. – Born Dec. 26, 1933 in St. Louis, MO. He joined the SAR on Dec. 9, 2008. Chapin served the U.S. Army 531st AAA Msl Bn (NIKE) as Fire Control Officer, Ellsworth AFB, Rapid City, SD (1956-58). Upon discharge, completed his MBA (1960) Olin School of Business, Washington University in St. Louis; joined IBM, relocating to Chicago in 1966.

John N. Chapin

Following 19 years in the computer industry, he joined Coopers & Lyband (1979) starting Litigation & Claims Services in the Midwest, reaching partner mandatory retirement age (1996); now retired senior consulting partner, PricewaterhouseCoopers LLP; a Forensic Economist; president, CHAPIN Associates Ltd.; chairs arbitration panels for FINRA.

Chapin was honored by Sigma Chi Fraternity as a Significant Sig (2001) and awarded the Order of Constantine (2005). Fewer than 90 of the 300,000 initiates have been so designated. He was National Chairman (1994-96) and Fellow of the Institute of Management Consultants USA, Inc.

Chapin and his wife of 53 years, Meryl, live in Northfield, IL, where he is a Village Trustee; president, Fox Meadow Community Association. They have two daughters, Carolyn Strandberg of Scottsdale, AZ; Sharon Crist of Lewes, DE; four grandchildren.

A gun, originally the property of Phineas Chapin, carried by him in 1776 at the defense of Dorchester Heights, near Boston, under Gen. George Washington, and again at the Battle of New York the following summer, hangs in Chapin's study. The original flintlock has been changed to a percussion one.

Phineas Chapin was born Decl 15, 1755 in Somers, CT. He was a private in Col. S.B. Webb's 9th Regt., Capt. Whiting's Company. He died Jan. 21, 1849 and is buried in Newport, NH.

CHASE, CHARLES A. – Born Oct. 11, 1933 in Hillsboro, IL. He joined the Texas Society SAR on Jan. 16, 1997, and has served as Hill Country Chapter President, TXSSAR Flag Committee, and TXSSAR Awards and Medals Committee. He has received the Meritorious Service Medal (2), the Silver Good Citizenship Medal; and the Bronze Good Citizenship Medal (2).

Charles served in the US Army as a Federal Sr. Exec. Service Level 5, and the Deputy Asst. Secretary of the Army. He retired on April 30, 1994. He is a member of the Assoc. of the United States Army, the American Society of Military Comptrollers - Life Member, and the National Rifle Assoc.

Charles A. "Chuck" Chase

He is married to Kathleen P. Chase, and they have six children and 13 grandchildren.

William Brown, Jr. was born Jan. 26, 1753 in Orange Co., NC. He was a private in the 9th Regt. NC Militia. He died in 1839 in Orange Co., NC.

Other Patriot Ancestors for Charles Chase include: **William Brown, Sr.**, NC; **William Cabe,** NC; and **Barnaby Cabe,** NC.

CHESTER, DAVID WILLIAM – Born April 3, 1956 in Milwaukee, WI, currently resides in Sherborn, MA. He was in the US Navy, attaining the rank of Lieutenant, SW Face Ware Officer (1979-1983).

David and wife Kimberly Bell have four children. David has spent 25 years in high tech sales and is a private investor.

4th and 5th great-grandsons David William Chester (back) and Ben Chapman Chester (front) prior to Memorial Day Parade 2007, Sherborn, MA.

Other organizations: Councilar, Mass. Society of the Order of Founders; Patriots of American; Member society of the Descendants of the Founders of Hartford; member Order of Americans of Armorial Ancestry; is a Volunteer Firefighter Sherborn Fire and Rescue and is a baseball parent/coach.

Col. John Chester, born Jan. 18, 1748 or 1749 in Wethersfield, CT. He was with Wadsworth's Conn. Brigade as the Battalion Colonel. He served at Bunker Hill, Siege of Boston, Long Island; Harlem Heights; White Plains; Princeton, Trenton.

Portrait of Col. John Chester currently hanging in the Morris-Jumel Mansion north of Manhattan.

In civilian life he was a Judge of Hartford County, on the Governor's Council, appointed Supervisor of US Revenue for District of Connecticut by Pres. Washington. He represented the 5th generation of the Chester family living in Colonial America at the outbreak of the American Revolution. He died Nov. 4, 1809 and is buried at Wethersfield, CT.

CHRISMAN, THOMAS ALLEN – Born in Akron, Ohio on 01 Nov 1950; joined SAR on 01 Nov 2007.

Thomas Allen Chrisman

Tom earned 2 degrees from Emory University in Atlanta, GA, and has worked in the healthcare industry since 1975 as a manufacturer's representative specializing in lasers, microsurgical optical systems, and related healthcare products.

His wife, Joyce Waller Chrisman, a retired educator, is an active member in NSDAR, Society of the War of 1812, and Dames of the Court of Honor. They have 2 daughters, Kathryn and Elizabeth, also members of NSDAR.

He also writes articles for The Hite Family Association Newsletter, is a speaker for Americans for a Fair Tax, and teaches martial arts holding a 2nd degree black belt in Okinawan Karate and Chinese Ta'i Chi Ch'uan.

Gravestone of Jacob Chrisman II

Tom Chrisman is a descendent of **Jacob Chrisman II**, the son of Jacob Chrisman, Sr, and Magdalena Hite, born in 1730 at Pennypacker Mills near Philadelphia, Pennsylvania. In 1731, Jacob's family and others, led by grandfather, Jost Hite, migrated to Virginia and were among the first settlers in the Shenandoah Valley. At the onset of the American Revolution, Jacob, having served in the Virginia Militia in the 1750's and too old for service supported his

Gravestone of Robert Fulton

friend George Washington by providing livestock and horses.

Tom is also a descendent of **Robert Fulton**, born c 1752 in Ireland, who served as a ranger on the western frontier of Pennsylvania towards the end of the Revolution; and, **Cornelius Van Ausdalen** who served in the Virginia militia.

CHRISTIAN, DR. ALLEN L. – Born April 20, 1939. He is a member of TXSSAR, joining on Nov. 4, 2002 (#159346) and a National Life Member since Oct. 17, 2005. He is dual member of the Dallas Chapter (Chapter Service Medal) and the East Fork Trinity Chapter, TXSSAR.

Dr. Christian was a Professor Emeritus, Mathematics, at Eastfield College of the Dallas County Community College District, retiring after 44 years in May 2008. He is a member of Sons of Confederate Veterans (Life Member), Descendents of Confederate Veterans, Military Order of the Stars and Bars, Society of the War of 1812, First Families of Tennessee, and Sons of the Revolution.

He is married to Jane Ellen Christian, and they have two children and two grandchildren.

Private James Hays was a soldier in Capt. John Bailey's company of regulars. He served under Col. George Rogers Clark in his Illinois Regt. With Col. George Rogers Clark, he participated in the founding of the state of KY. Private Hays was a citizen of Albemarle County, VA, where he founded the township of NY in Albemarle County. James was a surveyor and Tavern keeper.

CHRISTIAN, CARROL R. – Born Feb. 23, 1954 in Russell, KS. He has served as Vice President and is current President of the Fort Hays, KS.

Carrol married Linda K. Ramsey and has one stepson. They currently reside in Russell, KS. He graduated from KS Law Enforcement Training Center in 1978. He served as a police officer at Russell, KS (1977-1988) and Salina, KS (1990-1991). Became a Special Investigator for State of Kansas Dept. of SRS, presently Senior Special Investigator. He also served as Reserve Sheriff's Deputy for Finney County, KS. Carrol is also an Adjunct Instructor at Fort Hays State University, and Associate Faculty Instructor at Barton County Community College. In 1996 he was selected to Security Team Program and served as an Olympic Security Officer for the 1996 Olympic Games and in 2002 served in Salt Lake City for the Winter Olympics.

He belongs to the General Society Sons of the Revolution, Sons of the Union Veterans of the Civil War Civic: Society of the Descendants of Washington's Army at Valley Forge.

Valentine Christian was born May 10, 1756 at Hunterdon County, NJ. He was with the New Jersey Continental Line, 3rd Battalion with Col. Elias Drayton as a Private. He also served as a Private with the New Jersey Militia and as a Teamster at Valley Forge under the command of Arthur Henry, Wagonmaster.

Valentine was a farmer and died Dec. 14, 1844. He is buried at Columbia County, PA.

John Sherbondy/Jean Sherbondie/Cherpantier/Sharbonda/Sherbuny/Scherbondy was born in 1735 at Sherbondyville, France. He served as a Private with the 1st Company, 4th Battalion of the Pennsylvania Militia 8th Class.

John was a farmer and millwright. He died after 1798 and is buried in Pennsylvania.

CHRISTIAN, CHARLES L. – Born July 20, 1932 in Portland OR and presently lives in Santa Rosa, CA. Charles joined SAR in 1978 and has been Chapter President and Chaplain. and received the Korea War Medal and Meritorious Service Medal.

Charles served as a Sgt. in USAF A.A.C.S. He and wife Mary Lou have three children and four grandchildren.

He also was employed by the CIA US State Department as Communications Officer, retiring in June 1986.

Charles also belongs to the Sons of Union Veterans, American Legion and A.A.C.S. Alumni Association.

Benjamon O. Tallman was born Sept. 15, 1741 at Portsmouth, RI. He served as a Colonel in the 1st RI Militia.

He was a master ship builder who died June 10, 1836.

CHRISTIAN, DAVID S. – Born Apr. 28, 1934 in Barnes, Warren County, PA; he served in the U.S. Navy and received SAR's Military Service Medal. His civilian employment was Monsanto, Data Processing, Radio Shack Sales, retiring in Sept. 1991. He is a member of the American Legion, VFW, Military Order of World Wars, AMVETS, Reserve Officer's Assoc., Naval Reserve Assoc., Naval Institute, Military Officers Association of America, Forty and Eight Association, Korean War Veterans Association, Fleet Reserve Association, St. Louis Genealogical Society, and Western Pennsylvania Genealogical Society.

He is married to Bonnie Jill, with four children and four grandchildren.

Nicholas Shanafelt was born Mar. 11, 1758 in Center Co., PA. He served in the war as a private, and died Apr. 30, 1826 in Hains Twp., Center County, PA.

CHRISTOU, REV. CHRISTOS JR. – Born Aug. 3, 1966 in Baltimore, MD. SAR duties include: State President, National Essay Committee Chairman, National Trustee, and Secretary. Has served on the following committees: Essay, Orations, Patriot Index, Americanism, and Newsletter. He has received the Patriots Medal, Distinguished Service Medal, Meritorious Service Medal, Silver CAR, Silver Good Citizenship, and Bronze Good Citizenship.

Rev. Christou works as an IT Manager and QA Manager. He is a member of the War of 1812 Society, Order of Crown of Charlemagne, Sons of Confederate Veterans and Children of the American Revolution. He has 18 approved supplementals and is active in all levels of SAR.

He has two children and three grandchildren.

Alexander Anderson was born 1762 in Augusta Co., VA. Private Anderson served with Capt. John McKitrick's company. A farmer, he died Dec. 25, 1825 and is buried in Shutterle Cemetery in Augusta Co., VA.

CHURCHILL, DAVID L. – Born June 12, 1930 at Bloomfield, NJ. He served as a 1st Lt., USAF, Aug. 24, 1952 to Oct. 8, 1956; Capt. (Ret.), USAF Reserve. He attended USAFIT Russian Language School at Syracuse University from Oct. 1952-Oct. 1953 and was a Russian Language Intelligence Officer assigned to NSA, Oct. 1953-Oct. 1956. He later worked as a marketing manager for Union Carbide's Linde Division and successor companies, retiring on Aug. 31, 1991. He is married to Janet F. Churchill, and they have two children and three grandchildren.

Freegift Patchin was born Feb. 20, 1758 in Wilton, CT. He was a Fifer for Col. Phillip Burr Bradley's Regt. of Capt. Elijah Abel's Company. He participated in the Battle of Long Island and served in the Connecticut Line from June-Dec. 1776. He also served in the New York State Militia until begin captured by an Indian war party in April 1780. A farmer and millwright, he died Aug. 31, 1831 and is buried in the Patchin family cemetery in North Blenheim, NY.

CLAGGETT, STEVEN FOREST – Born May 27, 1947 in Richmond Heights, MO. He joined the SAR in 2008 and is currently serving as the historian for the Spirit of St. Louis Chapter.

Steve received a Bachelor of Science and Masters of Science degrees in Industrial Engineering from the University of Missouri in Columbia. He earned his Professional Engineering license in 1974. During his career he was held in a variety of technical and management positions in industry and government, including Bendix Corp., Missouri State Courts Administrator's Office, and the Regional Justice Information Service in St. Louis, finally serving as General Manager. The last 20 years he was employed at Ajilon Consulting, retiring in 2006 as President of the U.S. Division.

Since retirement, Steve has been active in the Franklin County Genealogical Society, serving as Corresponding Secretary and Treasurer, as well as the Washington Historical Society. He has published books for sale by these organizations, the last of which was the "Medal of Honor Winners of Franklin County."

Steve has been married 40 years to the former Gale Delbruegge. He also has two children and two grandchildren who live in the Baltimore metropolitan area. His patriot is Dr. Samuel Claggett.

Dr. Samuel Claggett was born 1756 in Croom, MD. At 17, he apprenticed to his grandfather, Dr. Gustavus Brown of Port Tobacco, MD.

In 1777, he joined the Continental Army in Maryland as Surgeon's Mate, and served until Feb. 1780, when he resigned and went to France. During his first enlistment he served in many hospitals including Valley Forge and Bethlehem. Upon returning, he reentered the Army until the end of the War.

Dr. Claggett settled in Virginia after the War and married Amey Jane Remy, bearing ten children. He died 26 March, 1821 at his home in Fauquier Co., VA.

CLARK, DAVID PAUL – Born Mar. 8, 1962 in Boulder, CO, is the President and CEO of DavidClarkCause, LLC. He is married to Kristen Elizabeth Fox and they have one daughter.

Abraham Clark was born Feb. 15, 1725 in Elizabethtown, NJ. He helped raise supplies for

Gen. Washington's army throughout the Revolution, and served in the United States Congress for two terms from 1791 until his death in 1794. Abraham signed the Declaration of Independence for New Jersey. He died on Sept. 15, 1794 and is buried at the Rahway Cemetery in Rahway, NJ.

CLINE, WILLIAM OTHO (BILL) – Born Jun. 7, 1960 in Rutherfordton, NC; joined SAR Jan. 15, 2008.

Plant Pathologist, NC State University. Master of Science, Plant Pathology, 1986. NCSU research assistant, small fruit diseases: blueberry, strawberry and grape. 1987 relocated, Wilmington, NC. Indentified blueberry diseases, east and west coasts of North America, Chile, Argentina, and Spain. Past President, Plant Pathology Society NC; member, committee chairman, American Phytopathological Society; chairman, Vaccinium Working Group, International Society Horticultural Science; author, publications and periodicals.

Bill Cline

North Carolina Society Children of the American Revolution, state board member; C.A.R. liaison, NSSAR Lower Cape Fear Chapter, Wilmington, NC.

1985, married Angela Chatham, of Rutherfordton; daughter Emily Cline, a NCSCAR state officer. Wife's patriot ancestor: John Flack, died 1792 Rutherfordton, NC, and descendant of Squire Boone, 1696-1765 buried Rowan County, NC.

His patriot ancestors:

Martin Elliott, born 1752 Virginia, resided Charlotte County, VA; Private, Virginia Light Dragoons, 2nd Troop, 1st Regiment, commanded by John Watts, Continental Troops. January 20, 1780, married Anne Finch (b. VA 1761, d. NC 1825), 12 children. April 14, 1806 purchased farmland, Rutherford County, NC where he is buried, (current Cleveland County) Hwy 74 Bypass, Hwy 226, Dover Road, Shelby, NC; died March 4, 1832.

Martin Roberts, born 1758 in Virginia, enlisted Chesterfield Courthouse, VA, 1776-78, private under Capt. Ralph Faulkner, 5th Virginia Regiment Continental Line. Battles: Trenton, Princeton, Germantown. Forage Master, Quartermaster's Dept. (Aug. 5, 1780-Aug. 1, 1782).

May 10, 1787, Fast Landing, Kent County, DE, married Elizabeth Durboro, daughter of Daniel Durboro. 1797 moved to Rutherford County, NC, purchased farmland (current Cleveland County); 1825 applied for pension at Rutherford County Courthouse. Died 1834; they are buried at Quinn-Roberts-Borders Cemetery in Shelby, NC, near his father, pioneer Morris Roberts III. Patriot Joshua Roberts was his brother.

CLOKE, PAUL LEROY – Born Orono, ME, after high school attended Harvard University, thanks partly to his placing within the top ten in the Sixth Annual Science Talent Search. He graduated Magna Cum Laude in 1951 and proceeded to earn a Ph.D. at MIT in 1954.

For the next three years he worked for the Anaconda Copper Mining Company in Butte, MT. In 1959 he joined the geology faculty at the University of Michigan. His research work there focused largely on investigations of the origin of hydrothermal ore deposits.

Paul L. Cloke

After 26 years he transferred to Battelle Memorial Institute in Columbus, OH to pursue geochemical studies and manage work on the disposal site in the panhandle of TX, which was terminated in 1987. All subsequent HTRW disposal activities were directed toward a site at Yucca Mountain, NV. While working on that project, he put together for the first time a computer model for the chemical degradation of an entire waste package. He presented some aspects of this model at an international meeting in Germany in 2007.

He enjoyed playing in amateur symphony orchestras, skiing, swimming. He serves on the color guard for the Prescott, AZ Chapter of SAR. He is married to Edith Annie Cloke with two children and three grandchildren.

John Poland was born in 1754, Monmouth County, NJ and enlisted Nov. 1, 1775 in the New Jersey Continental Line and reenlisted on March 22, 1778 for the war. Participated in the battles of Crosswicks Bridge, NJ, Monmouth, NJ, campaign against the Six Nations (Indians), Newtown and Chemung, Virginia Campaign, siege and battle of Yorktown, and was present at the surrender of Lord Cornwallis on Oct. 19, 1781. Discharged Nov. 3, 1783 and received two badges of merit for six years honorable service during the Revolutionary War. He died Jan. 19, 1823 in Monmouth Co., NJ.

COLE, ALVIN BENNETT JR. – A twelfth generation descendant, Alvin was born in 1977 in Baltimore, MD, the only child of Janet Cora (Ward) Cole and Alvin Bennett Cole Sr. After attending Carroll County schools he graduated from The University of Maryland Baltimore County. Alvin works as a contractor for the U. S. Army. He enjoy outdoor activities and have begun collecting JEEPS.

Alvin Bennett Cole, Jr.

His mother's father - Prescott Glenwood Ward - served in WWII as a Captain in the U S Army Air Corps in the Pacific Theater. He was an avid hunter.

He and his father are members of The General William Smallwood Chapter of the Maryland Society; they also belong to The Order of The First Families of Maryland.

For the biography of **Captain James Stewart** refer to the Patriot biography under Alvin Bennett Cole Sr.

Many ancestors served in conflicts before during and subsequent to the Revolutionary War. Some names in his lineage are: Arnold, Ashford, Bailey, Demid, Garrettson, Gilbert, Harkins, Jackson, Kimble, Moulton, Neville, Numbers, Osborn, Preston, Reduto, Scogans, Weston, White, Wilkinson, Wood, and Wicholl (Mitchell).

COLE, DR. ALVIN BENNETT SR. – Born in 1932 in Baltimore, the only child of Jessie Lynn (Wilkinson) Cole and Harry Taylor Cole who was a merchant; Alvin's father served in WWI. Alvin attended the Baltimore City College and then after premedical courses entered and graduated from the National University of Health Sciences in Lombard, IL. In 1976 he married Janet Cora Ward and they have only one child, Alvin Bennett Cole Jr. Alvin practiced as a chiropractor in Gaithersburg, MD and retired in 2003.

His lineage dates from before 1638 with the ancestor Robert Stewart and at least one son - David, born 1616 - having come from Scotland. The Cole ancestors date from before 1785 in Frederick Co., VA. It appears that all other known ancestors came from England and Ireland.

Dr. Alvin Bennett Cole, Sr.

Patriot **James Stewart** the great, great, grandson of Robert Stewart was born 1746/7 and died in 1781 in Harford Co., MD. He married Elizabeth Garrettson, they had children. Elizabeth born 1747 and died in 1810 (Record St. George's Parish Reg. and was buried at Spesutia Cemetery).

James took the "Oath of Allegiance" in Harford Co. in 1778 listed in the Mordacai Amos Returns. He was Captain of Volunteers, Co. No. 9 mentioned on page 115 in Preston's *History of Harford Co. MD.*

Also noted in Capt. Stewart's company were - James Talbot 1st Lieutenant, James Ware 2nd Lieutenant, Jesse Pritchard Ensign and 65 privates mentioned in Brumbaugh's Maryland Records - 1928.

COLLETTE, CLARENCE A. – Born Nov. 25, 1929 in Los Angeles, CA; he joined the Arizona SAR on Oct. 8, 2008. Clarence served in the USMC Reserve in June 1948 and was discharged two days before the Korean War began. In Jan. 1951 he was drafted into the U.S. Army and served in Korea during the War for ten months. He was in the Infantry, 5th Regimental Combat Team (5th Inf. Regt.) attached to the 24th Infantry Division. After discharge, he joined the National Guard. He was a M/Sgt., Infantry, and became a 1st Sgt. for 2-1/2 years.

Clarence A. Collette

Clarence has been a member of the Masonic Lodge, F. & A.M. for 57 years, VFW, DAV, and the Sons of Union Veterans of the Civil War, the Descendants of Mexican War Veterans, and the Korean War Veterans Association. He was an analyst for Pacific Telephone, retiring on Feb. 17, 1982 after 33 years. He is married to Jean Marilyn Collette and they have two children and four grandchildren.

Abel Butterfield was born Feb. 1, 1742 in Dunstable, MA. During the War, he was a private with Col. Thomas Gardner's Regiment, Capt. Isaac Hall's Company. Col. Thomas Gardner's Regiment assembled on the alarm of April 19, 1775. Private Abel Butterfield served five days. Col. Gardner's 37th Regt. returned from Prospect Hill on Oct. 6, 1775. Capt. Isaac Hall's Company marched from Medford ot occupy Dorchester Heights in March 1776 by order of Gen. George Washington, serving four days.

A farmer, he died in Oct. 1793 in Medford, MA. The cemetery and location are unknown.

COLLIER, FARRIS GLEN – Born Dec. 31, 1928 in Mesquite, TX. Joined SAR in June of 1985 and has held offices of President, Vice President, Treasurer, Secretary and Registrar. He has received the Good Citizenship Medal, Liberty Medal and 20 year service pin.

Farris was Active US Naval Air Reserve from 15 June 1947 to May 1959. He was Aviation Machinist's Mate, ADE3.

Farris G. Collier

Farris married Edna Renee Nelson and they have one daughter and two grandchildren. He was with Equifax Services, Inc. for 46 years; retiring in March 1989; but continued part-time until July 1992.

He also belongs to Sons of the Republic of Texas, Sons of Confederate Veterans, Descendants of Mexican War Veterans, Society of Colonial Wars in Texas, Mesquite Historical and Genealogical Society, and on advisory board of Mesquite Public Library.

He has nine proven ancestors in SAR and three proven ancestors in Sons of the Republic of Texas.

Thomas King was born March 14, 1754 near Middletown, Lancaster County, PA. He was a private in Morrow's Pennsylvania Regiment.

Volunteered, August 1776, Paxton Township, PA under Capt. James Crouch. Was marched to Amboy, NJ, joined Flying Camp under Capt. James Morrow and Col. Thomas Morrow. They joined Washington's Army and marched to Ft. Lee. Was with Washington's Army in New Jersey when repulsed by the British back into Pennsylvania above Philadelphia. In 1777 moved with his family to what would become Sullivan Co., TN. In August 1778, volunteered under Capt. John Duncan and went to Glade Hollow Fort in Virginia to guard against the Shawnee Indians. Later, same year volunteered under Capt. James Colvan, went to three forks on New River to disperse a body of Tories. In 1779 volunteered under General Sullivan and Major Clark, went to Logan's Station in Kentucky, from there to Hazard's Station and then to Lickin River, where they built a fort that was taken the following spring by the British and Indians. In 1780 he volunteered under Capt. Andrew Cowan, Col. Arthur Campbell, marched to Chotee, against the Cherokee Indians. In 1781 he substituted for William King, his brother, was under command of Capt. Thomas Wallace, Lt. Bleecher, and Col. Isaac Shelby, went to Santee Swamps in South Carolina, where they joined General Francis Marion's Army. In 1888 his great grandson, Elisha Sterling Price King, after interviewing last living sibling of Thomas King, wrote that he was with the militia and fought under General Morgan at the Cowpens in 1781 which essentially ended his military service.

Thomas King gravestone, New Bethel Presbyterian Church Cemetery, Piney Flats, TN.

Thomas was a farmer in civilian life and died June 18, 1847, buried at New Bethel Presbyterian Cemetery, Piney Flats, Sullivan County, TN.

CONGER, BUEL MILTON – Born of the "Greatest Generation" in 1925 in Memphis, MI. He was the son of Charles Austin Conger and Myrtle Burnell. He had many fond memories of his childhood. His memories included his great grandfather Burnell, who taught him to whistle. He remembers the stories of Jacob Burnell telling of the "War between the States."

Buel's patriot ancestor was **Joseph Conger** [1758] Sangerfield, Oneida County, NY, born in Fairfield, CT. In the fall of 1775 enlisted, Connecticut Militia of Captain Gaylor Hubbell's Company and spent the winter in New York where he was discharged. In April 1776 he again enlisted at New Fairfield for six months and was discharged. In 1777 he was drafted in the Connecticut State Militia, after war moved to New York.

Buel Conger served in US Army during the World War II. He returned from California to marry his wife (of 62 years) Margaret, together, raised their nine children, two nephews and niece in Port Huron. They watched their 24 grandchildren grow and mature. Buel was second generation Detroit Edison Co., where he worked for 40 years as a lineman. http://www.congfoo.com/gen/buel_milton_conger.html.

CONGER, JOSEPH CHARLES – Born in Mt. Clemens, MI, son of Buel Conger and Margaret Rumenapp was admitted to Ferris State University, School of Pharmacy and received a Bachelors of Science in Pharmacy in 1970. He married Mary Weiss of Frankenmuth, MI and has two sons Austin and Thomas.

Joseph interned for Hurley Medical Center in Flint, MI. He worked in retail pharmacy for 10 years and then purchased Consultant Pharmacy, in Flint, MI. Mr. Conger is a member of Kappa Psi Pharmaceutical Fraternity, American Society of Consultant Pharmacists, Michigan Pharmacist Association, past president of the Genesee County Pharmacist Association, where he was Pharmacist of the Year in 1982. He was given a national honor when presented the US Pharmacist for Community Service Award presented by G.D. Searle as Pharmacist of the Year in 1995. He served on a number of boards and committees in the community. Mr. Conger is a member of National Ski Patrol System serving as Senior Ski Patroller for 30 years. He is member of Sons of the American Revolution (SAR) and Sons of Union Veterans of the Civil War (SDVCW). He enjoys sailing, skiing, genealogy and travel.

Joseph Conger (1758-1842) is his patriot ancestor. Joseph died in 1842 and is buried at Steckton Cemetery, Sangerfield, NY. http://www.congfoo com/gen/joseph_conger.html.

CONLEY, PATRICK ROLLYSON – Born in Akron, OH on Jan. 10, 1944. He was the youngest of 12 children of Millard Fillmore Conley and Pruna Eunice Rollyson.

Patrick volunteered and served in the U.S. Army from 1962 through 1984. He served in Germany, Vietnam, Japan, Korea and many U.S. bases. He worked as a cook, baker, hospital food service supervisor, and instructor. He received two awards of the Army Commendation Medal and attained the rank of Master Sergeant.

Patrick left the Army in 1984 to begin a second career with the federal government, retiring in 2002 with a total of 37 years of combined federal service. He is a member of Disabled American Veterans, Veterans of Foreign Wars, Sons of the American Revolution, and Sons of Union Veterans. Fam-

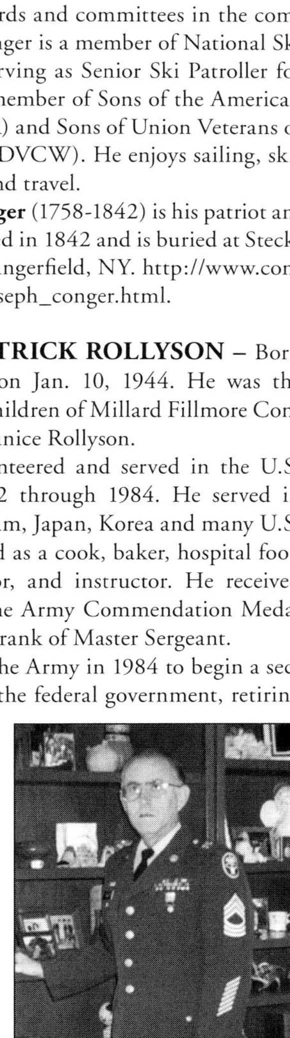

Patrick Conley

ily members or ancestors have served in all major conflicts from The French and Indian War through the Vietnam Conflict. Patrick's direct ancestor, Thomas Holcombe, was a founding father of Windsor, CT in 1635.

Patrick presently lives in the San Antonio, TX area, where he attended college and majored in residential construction. He has been married to the former Laura Louise Eldridge for over 40 years and has two daughters, Denise Irene and Darcy Marie, both born in Japan, and three grandchildren.

Timothy Holcomb was born Feb. 25, 1756 in Simsbury, CT. He entered the service by voluntary enlistment as a private in May 1776 for a term of one year in a company commanded by Capt. Noah Phillips. He marched to Middletown, CT and sailed to New York. Timothy remained there a few weeks and then crossed the Hudson River into New Jersey. He then went back over the Hudson a little above Kings Bridge into New York until about the first of Dec. 1776. Timothy was sent back into the country with some sick soldiers and taken sick himself, and came home sometime in Dec. 1776. In Aug. 1779, Timothy volunteered again and marched to New Haven at the time the enemy plundered that town. He remained there about eight weeks and came home and served about eight more weeks.

In April 1780 he was drafted and marched to Litchfield, CT and guarded military stores for two months, and returned home in June. Timothy stated that he knew "Generals Washington, Putnam and Spencer."

At the end of the war he went to Virginia, where he received grants of land and died sometime after 1840.

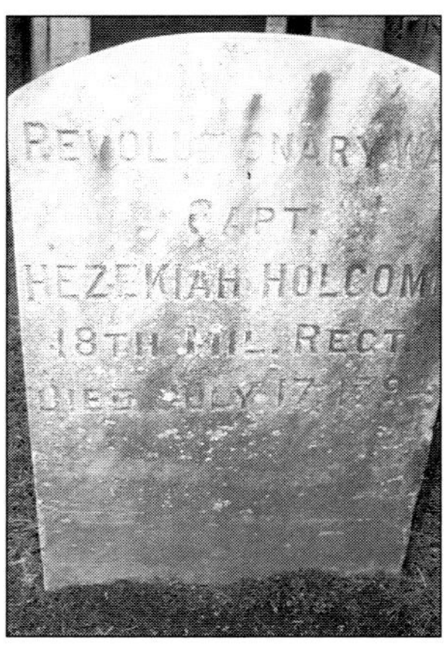

Gravestone of Hezekiah Holcomb.

Timothy Holcomb's father, **Hezekiah Holcomb**, was born Jan. 3, 1726 in Simsbury, CT and lived near the crossing Salmon Brook. He served on the school committee in Dec. 1765 and was a deputy from Simsbury, later named Granby. He also served as a church moderator in East Granby in 1778.

Hezekiah was a captain with the 18th Connecticut Regt. He commanded the 11th CT Regt. for duty in New York, arriving there Aug. 26, 1776 and discharged Sept. 25, 1776. Hezekiah died Jul. 17, 1794 and he and his wife are buried in St. Andrews Cemetery, Scotland, Bloomfield, CT.

CONNELLEY, DONALD GENE – Born Dec. 15, 1925 at Indianapolis, IN and resides in Arizona. He has been State of Arizona Assistant Secretary and Secretary/Treasurer of Tucson, AZ Chapter. Awards/Accomplishments: George Washington Fellow. He served as a Yeoman 3 Class in the Navy, USSLST 755.

Donald married Helen E. Rothweiler and has 4 stepchildren and 10 step-grandchildren. He was employed by VA Department of Veterans Affairs/Chief Medical Administration Service and retired in January 1981.

Donald G. Connelley

James Grimes was born in 1754 in County of Down, Northern Ireland. He was private and sergeant in Captain George Houston's Company, Colonel Benjamin Harrison's Virginia Regiment. He served in battles of Burnt Chimney and Williamsburg (pension claim S17455). James was a farmer in civilian life. He died Nov. 11, 1833 and is buried at The Old Washington Cemetery, Washington Township, Ripley County, IN.

Grave of James Grimes, Old Washington Cemetery, Washington Twp., Ripley County, IA.

Joseph McDoniel (McDonald) was born in 1760 in Frederick County, MD. He was a private in Captain Thomas Norton's Company, Captain George Enslow's Company and Clarke's Company, Colonel Ashman's Pennsylvania Regiment and North Carolina Regiment. Joseph was also a farmer. He died June 15, 1841 and is buried at The Old Washington Cemetery, Washington Township, Ripley County, IN.

Grave of Joseph McDonald, Old Washington Cemetery, Washington Twp., Ripley County, IA.

CONNELLEY, LAWRENCE MICHAEL – Born Sept. 21, 1938 in Fort Worth, TX, Mike Connelley joined the Fort Worth, TX Chapter of SAR in Dec. 2008. He and his wife, Sarah, are natives of Fort Worth and currently reside in Aledo, TX.

Mike graduated from Arlington State College, Arlington, TX in 1962 and obtained an ROTC commission as a Second Lieutenant in the Artillery; he served two years in military service before returning to civilian life in 1964. He married in Fort Worth, TX and in Nov. 1965 was appointed a Special Agent with the FBI.

Mike's FBI service took him to Minnesota, South Dakota and Illinois before returning to Texas in 1973; he served in the Fort Worth, TX FBI office until retiring in Sept. 1988. Upon retirement, Mike began a security consulting/investigative business that has taken him around the country.

Mike and his wife, Sarah, have two children: Todd Connelley, who resides in Dallas, TX, and Melissa Thomas, who resides in Arlington Heights, IL. He has four grandchildren, Beck and Van Connelley of Dallas, and Tatum and Tripp Thomas of Arlington Heights, IL.

Mike is descended from Revolutionary War Patriot, **Edward Rippy**, who served as a private in the North Carolina Militia from 1780 to 1782. He was taken prisoner by the British, and held as a prisoner on board a ship for six months before being released. Edward Rippy remained in North Carolina and South Carolina, died Dec. 1853 and is buried in Buffalo Baptist Church Cemetery in Cherokee, SC.

COOK, ERIK WINSTON – Born Nov. 12, 1967 at Beckley, WV and resides at Matheny, WV. He is a member of the Captain Ralph Stewart Chapter, West Virginia's newest chapter, Oceana, Wyoming County, WV.

Erik married Tracey Morgan and they have one child. Erik is a welder and machinist.

The patriots in Erik's family are: **Capt. Ralph Stewart; Pvt. John Cooke; Lt. Daniel Shumate; James Pinnell; William Brooks; James Ellison; Mitchell Clay; Jacob Albert** (all Virginia) and **Jacob Acker** (Pennsylvania).

COOK, IRA JR. – Born June 7, 1940 at Matheny, WV. He is a member and President of the Captain Ralph Stewart Chapter, West Virginia's newest chapter, Oceana, Wyoming County, WV.

Ira married Lillian Marie Aker and they have two children and three grandchildren. Ira was Secondary Schools Administrator in Wyoming County, WV and retired in June 1992.

Battle Day, Point Pleasant, WV, Oct. 7, 2007. Left to right: Lt. Jason Cook; Ira Cook, Jr., President Capt Ralph Stewart Chapter; John Sauer, President WVSAR; Paul Blankenship, Sec./Treas. Capt Ralph Stewart Chapter.

He also belongs to Logan County, Boone County and Wyoming County Genealogical Societies.

The patriots in Ira's family are: **Capt. Ralph Stewart; Pvt. John Cooke; Lt. Daniel Shumate; James Pinnell; William Brooks; James Ellison; Mitchell Clay; Jacob Albert** (all Virginians).

COOK, JASON BRADY – Born Sept. 30, 1971 at Beckley, WV; resides at Lonetree, CO. Jason is a member of Captain Ralph Stewart, the newest West Virginia Chapter.

Jason and Marla Buob Cook have two children. He is a Harley-Davidson technician.

Jason has the following Revolutionary War

patriots – **Capt. Ralph Stewart; Pvt. John Cooke; Lt. Daniel Shumate; James Pinnell; William Brooks; James Ellison; Mitchell Clay; Jacob Albert and Jacob Acker.**

COOK, DR. JOHN THOMAS – Born Nov. 6, 1930 in Sarasota, FL; joined the TN SAR on Aug. 14, 2008. He served in the U.S. Navy (Seabees), M.C.B. #4, Petty Officer, 2nd Class, and was a Minister in the United Methodist Church, retiring on Jun. 6, 1996. He is married to Sandra Hooper Cook and they have three children and five grandchildren.

Anthony Mullins was born about 1750 in Genoa, Italy. He was a well-known family worker in vineyards of Leghorn, Italy. An Italian businessman who had traded with U.S. founding fathers, including Benjamin Franklin and Thomas Jefferson, recruited Antonio to go to the colonies to work. He liquidated his Italian assets and moved to Virginia, taking vine cuttings, olive trees, and silkworm eggs to start his new life.

Antonio worked at and near Monticello. He had Albemarle Co. Court assignments to keep the road from Monticello to the next district repaired and useable. Thomas Jefferson and Antonio were members of the crew from 1783-85.

Painting by renowned military artist Don Troiani of 3rd Continental Light Dragoon, circa 1780.

He joined the 3rd Regt. of the Light Dragoons in Feb. 1777, as Private Anthony Mullins, having changed his name to qualify for Revolutionary Services as a citizen of the colony. He was discharged in Aug. 1783, and returned to his residence adjoining Monticello, VA. He first bought land in Virginia. Later, after a fire, he sold his land to James Monroe and moved to Lincoln Co., TN.

He married Polley Clark. They had ten children. He and Sarah "Sally" Rambols had eight children. Anthony Mullins died Nov. 3, 1836 at the age of 85.

COOK, KYLE C. – Born Apr. 28, 1937 in Norvell, WV, he joined the WV (General Andrew Lewis Chapter) SAR on Dec. 9, 2008. Kyle served in the U.S. Army (SP5) and was Manager, Business Services for AT&T in West Virginia and Western Pennsylvania, retiring on Jan. 1, 1990 after 33 years.

He has been a member and Past President of the Huntington Kiwanis Club for the past 40 years, and Past Chairman of the Huntington Salvation Army Advisory Board (life member of both organizations). He is married to Jo Ann Cook and they have one daughter, Cheryl L. Cook, M.D.

John Cooke was born about 1752 in London, England. During the Revolution he served as a Private with the Eighth Virginia Continentals. He fought in the Battle of Monmouth, NJ and Stony Point on the Hudson, and also served with Gen. Andrew Lewis in 1774 during the Battle of Point Pleasant. He received a land grant for his service in what is today Oceana, WV. A farmer in civilian life, he died on Nov. 21, 1832 and is buried at Delilah Chapel Cemetery in Oceana, WV.

CORNELL, DUANE FRANKLIN – Born Sept. 14, 1951 in Jefferson County, Louisville, KY. He presently lives in Venice, FL.

Duane and Carole A. have three sons and one grandchild. Duane worked in real estate and as a land developed. He retired in 2007.

He also belongs to St. George's Society, New York; Society of Colonial Wars; Florida, New York and OFPA, Indian V Bench and Bar, PFA, FFK, Sarasota County Historical Commission; Cornell Club of New York; Venice Yacht Club; ESU of Palm Beach; Samuel Victor Constant Fellow. He a Former Deputy Gov. Gen. Society Colonial Wars, KY; Honorary State Governor OFPA, Kentucky.

Solomon Cornell was born ca. 1750 in Dutchess County, NY. He served in the 7th Regiment, Dutchess County (NY) Regiment as a private. In civilian life he was a farmer. He died in August of 1812 and is buried at Bullitt County, KY.

Edward Tyler was born Jan. 18, 1719 in Prince George County, MD. Provided Patriotic Service. He was a farmer and owner of largest plantation in Jefferson County, KY (Blackacre, now a historical park) in Louisville, KY. He died May 20, 1802 and is buried at Blackacre, Louisville, Jefferson County, KY.

CORNWELL, COL. LARRY PATRICK – Retired, twice served as the General Richard Montgomery Chapter president in Montgomery, AL, was the Alabama Society President, and is the Alabama Society Trustee. He serves on the National Genealogy, Membership, and Veterans Committees. He wears the War Service Medal (Vietnam), Patriot Medal, Meritorious Service Medal (state and chapter), Law Enforcement Medal, Liberty Medal with oak leaf clusters, Bronze Good Citizenship Medal, Bronze Color Guard Medal, Silver Color Guard Medal, and the Silver Council of State Presidents Medal. Wife Leanne Chambers, daughter Patricia, son Brian, grandson William Miller.

Leanne and Larry Cornwell

Revolutionary War Patriots - **James Banks**, Private, Pennsylvania; **Philip Barger**, Soldier, Militia, Virginia; **Alexander Beatty**, Private, Pennsylvania Militia; **John Beatty**, Lieutenant, Pennsylvania Militia; **Francis Brandon**, Private, 13th Virginia Regiment; **Jeremiah Bryant**, Soldier, 2nd Virginia Continental Regiment; **Caleb Brokaw**, Private, New Jersey Militia; **Isaac Brokaw**, Soldier, New Jersey Militia; **John Bush**, Soldier, New Jersey Militia; **Catherine Clemans**, Public Service, Virginia; **Charles Cornwell**, Public Service, Virginia; **James Elder**, Signed Petition, Pennsylvania; **John Ewing**, Private, Pennsylvania Militia; **John Gunckel**, Soldier, Pennsylvania Militia; **Adam Haymaker**, Private, Pennsylvania Militia; **John Daniel Helm**, Public Service, Virginia; **Philip Lorentz Houtz**, Private, Pennsylvania Militia; **Jacob Houtz,** Private, Pennsylvania Militia; **Drury Jackson,** Private, 8th Virginia Regiment, Brandywine, Germantown, Valley Forge; **Abraham Jenkins**, Soldier, Virginia; **Robert Kerr**, Private, Pennsylvania Militia; **Adam Lambert**, Public Service, Pennsylvania; **John George Overmier**, Captain, Pennsylvania Militia; **Anna Barbara Vogt Overmier**, Public Service, Pennsylvania; **Peter Stryker**, Troop, Light-Horse, New Jersey Militia; **Jacob Van Fossen**, Ensign, Pennsylvania Militia, Brandywine, Monmouth; **Simon Van Nortwick**, Private, New Jersey State Troops; **Peter Whitmer Sr.**, Matross, Pennsylvania Continental Line; **Peter Whitmer Jr.**, Private, Pennsylvania Militia.

COTELL, ROBERT D. – Born April 7, 1919 and presently resides in Wellesley, MA.

Robert was with the US Army, Sig. C. in WWII and a Capt. Retired Reserve.

He married Irene M. Brown and they have four children and three grandchildren. Robert retired in 1989 as a staff member from the Mitre Corp., Bedford, MA.

Robert is a member of the Mayflower Society.

Peter Cotelle was born in 1750 in France. He attained the rank of Private in the 9th Massachusetts Regiment, Col. Jackson's Company. Peter served at West Point, NY.

Peter was a tinker and owned a grocery store at Hissing Springs, Barnstable, MA. He died May 25, 1810 and is buried Barnstable, MA.

COUNIHAN, MICHAEL ALAN JR. – Born Feb. 21, 1989 in Myrtle Beach, SC. Michael was accepted by the District of Columbia SAR on Oct 8, 2008 at the age of 19.

Michael is currently an undergraduate student at Georgetown University, School of Foreign Service, majoring in International Political Economy, and a member of the Hoya Battalion of Army ROTC. Upon graduation, he will receive a commission as a Second Lieutenant in the US Army.

Michael is descended from his mother, whose ancestor is Samuel Elisha Britt.

Samuel Elisha Britt, born Oct. 1760, Johnston County, NC, was a patriot soldier in the North Carolina forces. During the Revolutionary War, he resided in Wilmington District, NC, and received the North Carolina Certificate for Services Rendered. He was married to Dorcas Baggett and was the father of 12 children. Samuel died Mar. 18, 1848 in Lumberton, NC.

COVINGTON, L. CHARLES – Born Aug. 24, 1932 in Savannah, GA. He joined the Georgia SAR on Feb. 13, 2007, and has served as Chapter Treasurer for the Captain John Collins Chapter. He is a member of the Huguenot Society of South Carolina, and Beta Gamma Sigma International Honor Society.

Charles Covington

Charles was a pilot in the U.S. Air Force, attaining the rank of Captain. He was worked for the Kimberly-Clark Corp. (Director Administration), retiring on Jan. 31, 1991.

He is married to Shirley L. Covington, with two children and three grandchildren.

John Mark Verdier I was born Aug. 24, 1759 in Beaufort County, SC, the son of Andre' (Andrew) Verdier, a Huguenot immigrant of French-Swiss decent, and Rebecah Verdier (nee Howard). He married Elizabeth Grayson of Beaufort County on Dec. 1, 1785. They had four children.

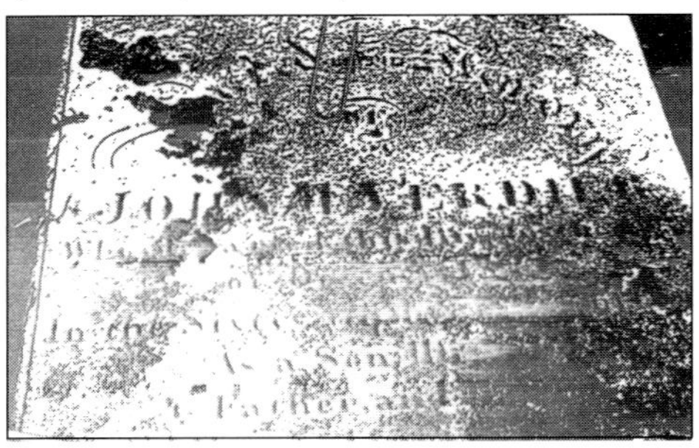

Photo of the grave of Patrion John Mark Verdier, buried in Charlestown, SC in the churchyard of St. John's Lutheran Church.

He served in Beaufort as Deputy Paymaster for the State Militia during the Revolution, serving under Paymaster General Daniel DeSaussure. His father served as Justice of the Peace during this time and was himself a land owner and manager of a store and plantation.

John Mark was both a planter and well-known merchant in Beaufort County. The tabby store where John Mark conducted business still stands. Also, he was very active in the church, St. Helena's Episcopal Church, serving in a number of capacities.

Today, in Beaufort, the John Mark Verdier House Museum on Bay Street, built circa 1801-1805, provides a glimpse of the rich history and architecture of that era.

John Mark died Oct. 17, 1827 and is buried at St. John's Lutheran Churchyard, Charleston, SC.

COWAN, ALTON E. – Born Aug. 5, 1943 in Norfolk, VA. He joined the Northern Albermarle Chapter, North Carolina SAR on Sept. 1, 2008. Alton served in the U.S. Army/Armor, and later worked in U.S. Navy Civil Service as a Civil Engineering Technician, retiring on Jun. 1, 2005.

He is the past president of the Williamsburg Scottish Festival, past commander of Patrick Henry Post 76, Scottish American Military Society (8 years), past vice president of the Scottish Society of Tidewater Virginia, FSA Scot (Fellow in the Society of Antiquities, Scotland), member of Ocean View Masonic Lodge #335, and member of the Sons of Confederate Veterans.

John White was born ca. 1752 in North Carolina. He was a private in the 10th North Carolina State Troops, Shepherd's Brigade, Captain Baker's Company. He served for three years. A farmer, his date of death and final resting place are unknown.

COWAN, CAIN K. – Born Sept. 13, 1963 in Norfolk, VA. He joined the Northern Albermarle Chapter, North Carolina SAR on Sept. 1, 2008. He is an office manager for United Parcel Service (UPS). Cain is a member of the Scottish Society of Tidewater and Sons of Confederate Veterans.

John White was born ca. 1752 in North Carolina. He was a private in the 10th North Carolina State Troops, Shepherd's Brigade, Captain Baker's Company. He served for three years. A farmer, his date of death and final resting place are unknown.

COX, DAVID COLLINS – Born June 19, 1951 in Darby, PA. He joined the PA SAR in 1992, and served as the Washingtonburg Chapter Secretary/Treasurer from 1995-96. David works as a computer analyst for the State of PA. He is married to Rosemary Dolores Donlevy Cox, with two children, and is a soccer coach, and is an Eagle Scout.

Amos Munroe was born May 31, 1747 in Billerica, MA. He served in Col. Shay's Company as a Private. A farmer, he died on Aug. 29, 1820 and is buried in Spencer, MA.

COX, CAPTAIN JOSEPH FREDERIC, USNR (RET) – Born in Portland, ME, May 17, 1919. Graduated from Yale University with honors in 1941. Joined the PA SAR on Feb. 28, 1989. Has served as the Washingtonburg Chapter Secretary/Treasurer, 1992-94; President, 1995-96; Secretary/Treasurer, 1997-99; and Treasurer, 2000-06. Received the War Service Medal.

Cox served as a Captain with the US Naval Reserve, receiving the Bronze Star Medal w/ V Device. He later worked for Penn Mutual Life Insurance Co. as a Computer Supervisor, retiring on Sept. 30, 1983. He is also a member of the Appalachian Mountain Club, Delaware Chapter President for three years; the Military Order of World Wars; and the St. Andrew's Society of Philadelphia. He is married to Katherine Mary Collins Cox, with one child and two grandchildren.

Capt. Joseph Frederic Cox

Amos Munroe was born May 31, 1747 in Billerica, MA. He served in Col. Shay's Company as a Private. A farmer, he died on Aug. 29, 1820 and is buried in Spencer, MA.

Daniel Cocker was born Mar. 1, 1725 in Barnstable Co., MA. He was a Capt. in the 2nd Co., 1st Barnstable Co. Regt., Massachusetts Militia. He died Nov. 12, 1788 and is buried in Barnstable Co., MA.

COX, KEVIN COLLINS – Born Aug. 9, 1979 in Harrisburg, PA and is a member of the PA SAR Society. He works for the State of PA in Computer Systems, and is married to Dana Agnew Cox.

Amos Munroe was born May 31, 1747 in Billerica, MA. He served in Col. Shay's Company as a Private. A farmer, he died on Aug. 29, 1820 and is buried in Spencer, MA.

COX, MICHAEL DAVID – Born Dec. 13, 1983 in Harrisburg, PA. He joined the PA Society SAR in 2001, and is a Project Manager for the Whiting-Turner Contracting Co. in Baltimore, MD.

Amos Munroe was born May 31, 1747 in Billerica, MA. He served in Col. Shay's Company as a Private. A farmer, he died on Aug. 29, 1820 and is buried in Spencer, MA.

COX, SHAWN ALAN – Shawn was born on Oct. 7, 1972 to John David and Rose Marie (Havens) Cox in Washington Court House, OH. Shawn is an Eagle Scout and a Kentucky Colonel. He is a member of the National Eagle Scout Association; the Ohio Genealogical Society; the First Families of Ohio; the Settlers and Builders of Ohio; the Society of Civil War Families of Ohio; the Sons of Union Veterans of the Civil War (PCC of Henry Casey Camp No. 92); and the Society of the War of 1812.

Shawn Alan Cox

Shawn became a member of the Arthur St. Clair Chapter, Ohio Society, SAR on June 14, 2006 and is descended from Anthony Sims Davenport.

Anthony Sims Davenport was born near Piscataway, MD on May 19, 1758. Anthony was a resident of Berkeley County, VA when he entered the Revolutionary War as a Corporal in Capt. John Lyle's company of Colonel George Scott's Virginia Militia in the Fall of 1778. He served three months and went on General McIntosh's expedition against the Indians and helped to build Forts McIntosh and Laurens. In the Fall of 1781, he again served three months as a Sergeant in Capt. James Eaton's Virginia company and guarded the British prisoners at Winchester, VA. He resided in Virginia until 1798 when he moved to what is now Pickaway County, OH. Anthony died on June 19, 1835 and is buried in Spring Bank Cemetery in Ross County, OH.

COXON, THOMAS C. – Born Sept. 6, 1963 in Casa Grande, AZ.

Thomas and Leslie A. have three children. He works with investments and they reside in San Francisco, CA. He also belongs to the Thomas Rogers Society.

Additional remarks: This first time filing was made possible by Rose Haria-Mitcham of DAR. Special thank you to her as well as those of the San Francisco Chapter of the SAR. And thank you to my parents, Franklin and Mary Coxon, for this opportunity. May I have the strength to share the values from our Founding Fathers in raising our children.

Silas Richmond was born ca. 1710 in Middleboro, MA. Patriot Service by: 1) Oath of Allegiance; 2) supplying Army; 3) reviewing recruits; and 4) taking up arms to assist Danbury, CT. Silas died Feb. 21, 1784 and is buried at New Milford, CT.

COZBY, WARREN REYNOLDS – Born in Kansas City, MO to Warren Abram Cozby and Mary Frances Atteberry Cozby on July 27, 1917. His parents came to Texas in October 1920, and moved to Ranger, TX in February 1922.

Warren graduated from Ranger HS in 1934 and Ranger Junior College in 1936. He joined the CCC in 1937. He was in Albuquerque when Dec. 7, 1941 hit.

He returned to Ranger and was selected for pilot training, Class of 43-E. Commissioned in April 1943 and trained in B-24s and later, B-47s. He was sent to Europe by boat.

After three missions, his crew was assigned to a "Pathfinder" unit. On his fifth mission as a B-47 copilot, his aircraft was shot down and he became a prisoner of war at Stalag Luft I, Germany until freed by the Russians.

Upon release from service, he returned to Ranger and married Lilian Ashcraft. He graduated from Southern Methodist U. in 1948 and was employed by General Adjustment Bureau, moving to El Paso, TX. He later applied to the Air Force, was selected for active duty and sent to Denver, CO for training and then to Honolulu, HI. Assigned as Munitions Officer, and later the Quarterly Property Officer at Hickam AFB and Wheeler AFB.

He served five years at Lake Charles, LA, one year at Dharan, Saudi Arabia, four years at Mountain Home AFB, ID, and four years at James Connally AFB, Waco, TX, where he retired with 20 years active service.

He worked as an insurance salesman for Prudential, a Quality Control Inspector for A.O. Smith in Waco and a teacher's aide at Texas State Tech. School.

Warren and Lilian have seven children.

Isaiah Warren was born 1749, and died Sept. 11, 1848, Sampson Co., NC. He served as a private in the Revolution.

CRAFT, COL. DONALD E. – Born April 13, 1928 in Detroit, MI. Retired from the US Army in April 1976. He served with 75USA MAC and attained the rank of Colonel.

Donald and wife Bernice have five children and seven grandchildren. They presently reside in Florence, KY.

He is a life member MOAA, life member ROA, life member MENSA, 33rd degree Scottish Rite member, life member Royal Order Scotland, El Hasa Shrine, Royal Order Jesters, Nero's '76 and National Sojourners.

Archeloys Craft was born Dec. 25, 1749 in North Carolina. He was at the battle of Hanging Rock – Eutaw Springs. A farmer, he died in 1853 and is buried at Millstone, Letcher County, KY. His brother, Ezekiel Craft, was also born in North Carolina.

CRITCHETT, DAVID LOREN – Born in 1935 at Cleveland, OH. Parents were Daniel Critchett and Helene Baker. They moved to Atlanta, GA when he was age 6, residing there until age 18. Received a BBA from the U. of Michigan in 1957 and an M.B.A. in 1960. Married Jacqueline Snyder of DeKalb, IL in 1959. Her parents were Kenneth Snyder and Dorothy Porath. They have two children-John David and Cathie Snyder. Employed by the Northern Trust Company and Goldman Sachs and Company-Investment Bankers in Chicago. Later employed by the General Electric Company in New York. Moved to Ann Arbor, MI in 1961 becoming Senior Vice-President, Treasurer, Chief Financial Officer and Chief Investment Officer of National Bank and Trust Company. Then thru a merger an Estate and Trust Officer of Bank One (now J.P. Morgan Chase and Company). Retired 1998. Graduate of the Stonier Graduate School of Banking at Rutgers, NJ; the A.B.A. Investment School at Dallas, TX; On faculty of the U. of Michigan Graduate School of Banking (3 years) and the Graduate School of Banking at the U. of Wisconsin (4 yrs.). Listed in "*Who's, Who in the Midwest.*" Currently, President of the Huron Valley Chapter of the Michigan Society of the Sons of the American Revolution. This chapter was officially sanctioned on October 4, 2008.

David Loren Critchett

Benjamin Critchett, born in 1725 at Brentwood, NP. Parents were Thomas Critchett and Mary Roberts. They moved to W. Chester (now Candia), NH when he was age 10. About 1772, he married Miriam Harvey of Nottingham, NH. Her parents were Jonathan Harvey and Susanne George. They lived in Deering, NH until 1776, then moved to Perrystown (now Sutton), NH. In February, 1777 Benjamin enlisted in Capt. Isaac Farwell's Company of Col. Joseph Cilley's 1st New Hampshire Regiment as a private until 1780. He re-enlisted in Capt. Moody Dustin's Company becoming a lieutenant in 1781, and served until April, 1783. He was discharged at Windsor, NH after serving over six years. During the war, he fought in the battle of White Plains, Ticonderoga, King's Bridge, and was at Saratoga for the surrender of Burgoyne. After the war, he returned to Perrystown and farmed there until 1790. He then moved to Fisherfield (now Newbury, NH). While in Perrystown they had two sons, Matthew Harvey (1783) and Jonathan (1785). When in Sutton, they had another son. In 1800, they moved to Unity, NH, and then in 1801 to Canandaigua, NY, where he lived until 1810. Then in 1811, he, Miriam, and their two oldest sons and their families moved to Granville, OH, as very early pioneers, where he was a cooper. He lived there until 1822, when he died. His wife died there in 1825.

CRITCHETT, JOHN DAVID, Ph.D. – Born in 1960 at Chicago, IL. Parents were David Critchett and Jacqueline Snyder. Resided in Ann Arbor, MI. Graduate of Duke University-B.A. (1983); University of Michigan Graduate School of Business-M.B.A. (1985); University of Kentucky School of Business-PhD (1997). Married Beth Anne Campbell (1987).They have a daughter-Lauren Michele. Employed at Arthur Young (C.P.A.'s) in Detroit. On the faculty of: University of Toledo (Ohio); Now Associate Professor of Accounting and Finance at Madonna University in Livonia, MI. Previously Chair of Undergraduate Business Studies there. Taught graduate courses on several occasions in mainland China. Listed in "*Who's Who Among American Teachers,*" and also holds a Michigan C.P.A. Certificate. Currently is the State Treasurer of the Michigan Society of Sons of the American Revolution.

Joohn David Critchett

Benjamin Critchett, born in 1725 at Brentwood, NP. Parents were Thomas Critchett and Mary Roberts. They moved to W. Chester (now Candia), NH when he was age 10. About 1772, he married Miriam Harvey of Nottingham, NH. Her parents were Jonathan Harvey and Susanne George. They lived in Deering, NH until 1776, then moved to Perrystown {now Sutton), NH. In February, 1777 Benjamin enlisted in Capt. Isaac Farwell's Company of Col. Joseph Cilley's 1st New Hampshire Regiment as a private until 1780. He re-enlisted in Capt. Moody Dustin's Company becoming a lieutenant in 1781, and served until April 1783. He was discharged at Windsor, NH after serving over six years. During the war, he fought in the battle of White Plains, Ticonderoga, King's Bridge, and was at Saratoga for the surrender of Burgoyne. After the war, he returned to Perrystown and farmed there until 1790. He then moved to Fisherfield (now Newbury, NH). While in Perrystown they had two sons, Matthew Harvey (1783) and Jonathan (1785). When in Sutton, they had another son. In 1800, they moved to Unity, NH, and then in 1801 to Canandaigua, NY, where he lived until 1810 Then in 1811, he, Miriam, and their two oldest sons and their families moved to Granville, OH, as very early pioneers, where he was a cooper. He lived there until 1822, when he died. His wife died there in 1825.

CROUCH, MARVIN – Born Dec. 24, 1922 in Granby, MO, he joined the California SAR

Rita and Marvin Crouch

in Apr. 2008. He was a private in the Army Air Corps, and later served as a manufacturing representative (President), retiring in 1963. A member of the American Legion, he is married to Rita C. Crouch, with two children and three grandchildren.

Wiliam Crouch was born in Goochland Co., VA on Nov. 15, 1762, and served in the Virginia Militia. A farmer, he died May 18, 1832 in Goochland County.

CROWELL, JOHN W. – Born May 12, 1940 in Hartford, CT. John has been in SAR as historian, treasurer, programs and Eagle Scout Awards. He was served in the US Navy/internship LT during Vietnam and received the Vietnam Medal.

John and Karen (Holly) have one child and two grandchildren. He was a self-employed dentist who retired in March, 2005. John also belongs to the Masons, Boy Scouts, Church Choir and American Dental Association. He is an Eagle Scout.

John Crowel was born in 1748 at King's Hill, Walden, NY. He served as an Ensign in Ulster County Militia with John Conkling's Fourth Regiment. In his civilian life, he was a weaver and farmer. He died May 11, 1824 and is buried at Berea Cemetery, Orange County, NY.

CULLEY, JOHN HENRY III – Born Aug. 14, 1947 in Buna Vista, TX; he served in the United States Air Force Reserve as a Judge Advocate from 1972 to 1997 and received two Meritorious Service Medals and an Air Force Commendation Medal. Lieutenant Colonel Culley (retired) served with the 327th Air Division (PACAF), 22nd Bomb Wing (SAC), 90th Missile Wing (Space Command) and various Air Training Command Units including the Technical Training Centers at Chanute AFB and Lowry AFB. He also has a doctorate in American History and resides in Morrison, CO with his son, Matthew John-Lawrence Culley. He has served as President of the Mount Evans Chapter of the S.A.R.

Lt. Col. John H. Culley III

Sergeant Thomas Smith's pension file (No. 30707) affidavit states that he was born in Albemarle County, VA, July 23, 1752 old style. In March 1776 he enlisted in the Albemarle County minute service in the company commanded by Captain Nicholas Lewis that was part of the 4th Regiment commanded by Colonel Charles Lewis. The company was ordered to build a fort in North Carolina and then was sent to New Castle where Thomas Smith became ill in July 1776.

Thomas Smith entered the Albemarle County Militia company commanded by Captain William Grayson on Jan. 15, 1781. After marching to Hampton he was ordered to the HalfWay House between York and Hampton under Colonel James Barnett. Smith's unit was then ordered to York to block a British force where he was commanded by Colonel Charles Dabney who praised Smith's company in a letter to Governor Thomas Jefferson dated March 23, 1781. On March 15, 1781 he was granted leave in an order signed by Major Mordecai Throckmorton to get his sick brother William (pension file no. 4806) home. Thomas Smith rejoined Captain William Grayson's militia company on May 15, 1781 and was sent to Albemarle Glebe for two weeks where quartermaster Captain Charles Russell appointed him Supply Sergeant to fill the place with stores. As indicated by Russell's receipt book and a document signed by Joseph Yarbrough in Sergeant Smith's pension file, Russell then ordered Sergeant Smith to take 80 to 90 men to Irvings Store to guard British prisoners and move stores across the James River. During June 1781 he moved these supplies to New Glasgow by wagon. In July 1781 Colonel Hugh Rose ordered Sergeant Smith to return to the Albemarle militia unit under Lieutenant Beckam where he remained subject to orders until he again became ill. He was sick when he heard Cornwallis had surrendered. He moved from Virginia to Clark County, KY on Dec. 14, 1794 where he died on July 25, 1838. He was buried on the plantation of his son-in-law, Nathaniel Ragland.

CUNNINGHAM, JOHN H. J. III – John was born Jan. 16, 1931 in Vienna, WV. He has held the offices of Joel Early Chapter Secretary/ Treasurer and Chapter Chaplain.

John served in the US Navy Submarine Service from 1948-1952. He and wife Helen Larayne Stinson have five children and 13 grandchildren.

John has been an electrical engineer, systems analyst and project manager in industry and for US Government and a minister. He is presently semi-retired.

He also belongs to General Society of the War of 1812; Order of the First Families of Maryland; United States Submarine Veterans; Decatur County Historical Society; is a practicing genealogist; author of two family genealogies and wrist a genealogy column for the local newspaper. In the past has been a teacher in Christian High School and Bible Institute; and a part-time pastor in churches.

Amos C. Reed was born in 1737 in New Jersey. He was a Corporal with Capt. Jonathan Phillips' Company in the 2nd New Jersey Regiment. He served in battles at Short Hills, Brandywine, Germantown and Springfield; and wintered at Valley Forge from 1777 to 1778.

Amos was a shoemaker and died Jan. 7, 1834. He is buried at Belmont County, OH.

DAVIS, JOHN WARREN – A real estate broker, consultant; b. York, PA, Feb. 14, 1946; s. Frank Asbury Jr. and Lillian Margaret (Billings) D. BA in Polit. Sci., Drake U., Des Moines, 1968; AA in Real Estate, San Diego City, CA, 1976; MS in Acquisition and Contract Mgmt., West Coast U., LA, 1987; postgrad., Walden U., 1992-; grad. in Overseas Procurement, Kellogg Brown and Root Procurement Acad., Houston, 2005. Cert. profl. contract mgr. NCMA. Real estate sales staff, 1972-79; clk. GS 3 Naval Ocean Sys. Ctr., 1979-80; contract intern, contract adminstr. Office of Naval Rsch., 1980-84; contract specialist, warranted ordering officer Gen. Svc. 1102-11 Naval Weapons Sta., 1984-86; contract specialist Gen. Svc. 1102-12 Navy Space Sys. Activity, 1986-88; procurement analyst Gen. Svc. 102-12 COMNAVAIRPAC, 1988-98; def. contract mgr. Def. Contract Mgmt. Command, 1998-2000; sr. v.p. Azan Corp. Group, San Diego, 2001-03; subcontract adminstr. Kellogg, Brown & Root, Houston, 2005-06; contractor cons., 2006-. Del. San Diego State U. to the Nat. Acad. Conf. for Contract Mgmt. Educators, 1991, 92, 93; profl. cons. Computer Applications, Inc., 1992; memo tech. program com., chairperson for electronic data interchange Soc. of Logistics Engrs., 1995; memo Golden Hill planning com. City of San Diego; adj. prof. San Diego State U., chmn. curriculum rev. com. for acquisition. Author, Paperless Contracting, The ED! Revolution, 1995, contbr. articles to profl. pubis. Mem. Golden Hill planning com. City of San Diego. With US Army, 1968-72, Vietnam. Decorated Army Commendation Medal, War medal SAR. Fellow Nat. Contract Mgmt. Assn. (life; cert. profl. contract mgr.); memo ABA (mem. sub-com. pub. law sector, sub-com. on intellectual property), SAR (nat., Calif. and San Diego chpts.), VFW (life), Am. Arbitration Assn. (nat. panel mem.), Soc. Govt. Meeting Planners (v.p. San Diego chpt.), Soc. Logistics Engrs., San Diego Athletic Club, San Diego Writers and Editors Guild, Author's Guild (life, past pres.), Black Tie Club Internat. Episcopalian. Avocations: swimming, travel.

John W. Davis at the Taj Mahal, Nov. 2005.

Pierby Bayly was a Private in the Virginia Continental Line during the Revolutionary War.

DAVIS, ROBERT D. – Born Nov. 7, 1939 in Sandy Hook, KY and joined the KY SAR on Aug. 5, 2004. He served with the 123rd Wing of the Kentucky Air National Guard, and worked for Ashland Inc. SuperAmerica, as Regional Vice President, retiring in Nov. 2004. He is

Robert Davis

married to Betty Hancock Davis, and they have four children, 12 grandchildren.

Ambrose Jones was born Aug. 10, 1756 in VA. He was a Corporal with Nathaniel Gist's 16th Regt., Capt. Thomas Bell's Co. Jones was at Valley Force in the winter of 1778, and participated in the Siege of Charleston, 1780. A Baptist minister, he died June 12, 1833 and is buried at the South Fork Cemetery, Malone, Morgan Co., KY.

DAVIS, WILLIAM FRANK SR. – William (SAR #539), son of Ishmael Davis (b. 1793) of Maryland, was born Jan. 12, 1840 in a log house at Rock House Prairie, Buchanan Co., IL, and died abt. Feb. 25, 1919. His grandfather was Wollom Davis of Maryland. As a boy, Frank attended a log schoolhouse, and later completed schooling at Plattsburg College.

During the Civil War, he enlisted in Co. E of the 1st Missouri Confederates Cavalry, under the command of Col. Elijah Gates and attached to the command of Gen. Sterling Price. He served in both Missouri and Arkansas, and was also in Mississippi. He was discharged in 1863 due to disability.

In January 1865, he married Virginia Byrd Asbury, who died Feb. 20, 1898. Their children were: John Marshall, William True Davis, Mrs. W.H. Seymour, Frank A. Davis, Mrs. O.C. Gebhart, and Clara.

Frank was a farmer, worked in the mercantile business, served as sheriff and county collector for Clinton Co., and also worked in the livestock commission business. He was a member of the St. Joseph Police Commission, the Charity Lodge of the Masonic Order, and was one of the trustees of the Francis Street Methodist Church.

He is buried at Mount Mora Cemetery, St. Joseph, MO.

Pierce Bayly served in the Virginia Continental Line with the rank of Private.

DEERING, DONALD ARTHUR – Born January 10, 1944 Bowman, North Dakota; joined SAR July 21, 2008. Military service: 82nd Airborne Division, 82nd Military Police 1962-1965.

Donald Arthur Deering

Civilian employment: Chief of Police Maryland National Capital Park Police 1966-1997; Chief of Law Enforcement Federal Office of Child Enforcement, US Dept Health & Human Services 1997-2000; Security Chief Administration for Children & Families, Health & Human Services 2001-2005; Acting Director Division of Security & Emergency Services, Health & Human Services 2006-2009.

Affiliations: Lifetime member 82nd Airborne Association; Fellow Brookings Institution, Washington, DC; Former Legislative Chair Maryland State Lodge Fraternal Order of Police; Former staff member Congressional Sub-Committee, Oversight of Criminal Justice Policy & Drug Policy.

Married Elizabeth Ann Gardner Deering; two children from first marriage, Kirsten Deering Asuncion and Justin Glenn Deering; three grandchildren. Maternal grandfather, Glenn Howe, is a direct descendant of his Patriot.

Timothy Howe, Sr. born October 6, 1742, Marlborough, Massachusetts; served as 1st Lieutenant under Captain Hewitt in the defense of Forty Fort July 3, 1778 with the 24th Regiment at the Wyoming Massacre, PA, one of 56 men to survive. Fathered 14 children; **Timothy Jr.** also a Patriot. Died 1764 in Stillwater, NY.

DEERING, JUSTIN GLENN – Born June 8, 1976 in Cheverly, Maryland; joined SAR July 21, 2008.

Justin Glenn Deering

Graduate: Culinary Institute of America, Hyde Park, New York.

Culinary Career: Tre Vigne, St. Helena, CA; Fifth Floor, Hotel Palomar, San Francisco, CA; Redwood Park, San Francisco, CA; Jeanty at Jacks, San Francisco, CA; Boulevard, San Francisco, CA; Conduit, San Francisco, CA where he is part owner and Executive Chef.

Maternal great-grandfather, Glenn Howe, whom he is named after, is a direct descendant of his Patriot and ancestor Timothy Howe, Sr.

Timothy Howe, Sr. born October 6, 1742, Marlborough, Massachusetts; served as 1st Lieutenant under Captain Hewitt in the defense of Forty Fort July 3, 1778 with the 24th Regiment at the Wyoming Massacre, PA, one of 56 men to survive. Fathered 14 children; **Timothy Jr.** is also a Patriot. Died 1764 in Stillwater, NY.

DENSLOW BROTHERS – Three Denslow brothers grew up learning the daily discipline of dairy and potato farming on their parent's, Otis and Margaret (Peacock) Denslow's, Central Michigan farm (west of Weidman, MI).

Left to right: Stuart Denslow, Dean Denslow, Gary Denslow.

STUART OTIS DENSLOW – Oldest of four children, attended Weidman and Fancher Elementary Schools (Mt. Pleasant, MI) graduating from Weidman High School. Stuart graduated from Michigan State University with a B.S. Degree and was commissioned into the U. S. Army serving two years as an officer with the electronics and engineering dept. of the U. S. Army Air Defense Center, Ft. Bliss, El Paso, TX. Upon completion of his military service, he completed both Master of Science and Ph.D. Degrees at Michigan State University in East Lansing, MI.

His career path led him from director of city planning for the City of Jackson, MI and chosen by the Jackson Jaycees as the "outstanding young man of 1966;" to director of an 8-county planning post in Rochester, NY; planning and management with an architectural firm in Anchorage, AK city manager and VP of Sheldon Jackson College in scenic historic Sitka, AK; with retirement in Tulsa, OK area.

Stuart enjoys visiting historic sites; keen interest in community development serving nine yrs. with the Sitka Economic Development Association and six yrs. on the Sitka Planning commission; various leadership roles in the United Methodist Church and SAR Chapters; stalwart Rotarian for 40 yrs. He is a charter member of the American Planning Assoc. and life member of the National Society of the Sons of the American Colonists.

DEAN EDWIN DENSLOW – Third of four children, attended Weidman, MI Elementary School graduating from Barryton, MI High School. For the next three yrs., he attended Garrett Theological Seminary graduating with a Bachelor of Science Degree from Ferris State University, Big Rapids, MI and a Master of Science Degree from Central Michigan University, Mt. Pleasant, MI; concluding with many post graduate courses completed at Michigan State University, University of Michigan and Western Michigan University.

His winning smile and integrity made him a successful leader in public service for forty plus years with the State of Michigan Family Independence Agency retiring in 2005. Additionally, Dean served twelve church parishes in the Central Michigan United Methodist Church Conference retiring in November 2002. Dean serves as a Sunday school teacher in the Mt. Pleasant, MI United Methodist Church; trustee, and many boards and committees of the church conference. Additionally, he is a member of the local Rotary Club, Lions Club, Chamber of Commerce and Masonic Lodge. His grandchildren are the light of his life; he shows his family unconditional love and the importance of faith. An avid outdoorsman, he enjoys hunting, fishing, photography, leisure-time reading and traveling.

GARY THAN DENSLOW – The youngest of four children, attended Weidman Elementary School and graduated as co-valedictorian with his future wife, Lorma Spangler, from Barryton High School, Barryton, MI. He graduated with high honors with a Bachelor of Science Degree from Michigan State University; and with a Doctor of Medicine Degree from the University of Kentucky, Lexington, KY. His internship was conducted at the University of Iowa Hospitals and Clinics with a fellowship in Pediatric Ophthalmology, Boston Children's Hospital Medical Center, Boston, MA. He is proud to be a veteran of the Vietnam War serving as a captain and physician. Gary's residency was in the Ophthalmology Department at the University of

Kentucky Medical Center, Lexington, KY.

In 1979, he established a private practice known as Pediatric Eye Associates in Tulsa, OK. His company is known for service to people in the Tulsa Metropolitan Community. Gary is active in and a leader in the First United Methodist Church serving in various boards and committees; Chairman of section on Ophthalmology of the American Academy of Pediatrics; gardening, reading and helping those in need. He is a member of the American Association of Pediatric Ophthalmology and Strabismus and numerous other medical associations. Gary is known for his pragmatic view of life and sharp wit.

Furthermore, the brothers' sister, Carolyn Margaret Denslow Baker, second born, is a member of the Sophie deMarsac Campau DAR Chapter in Grand Rapids, MI, also based on the American Revolutionary War Service of their 4th great grandfather, Charles Denslow.

MARK STUART DENSLOW – Son of Stuart O. Denslow, born in Lansing, MI; attended elementary schools in Jackson, MI and Penfield, NY; and graduated from Harley School in Rochester, NY. He graduated with a Bachelor of Science Degree in geology from Dickinson College, Carlisle, PA. Mark was awarded the Sloan Fellowship for Research and honored as the "Outstanding Mineral Economics Graduate Student of the Year" graduating with a Master of Science Degree from Colorado School of Mines in Golden, Colorado.

Mark Stuart Denslow

He established and owns Agilenet Company in Oxford, CT. Mark is active in and serving as a leader in the local and district Boy Scout committees and boards; member of the Oxford Congregational United Church of Christ; and member of the General David Humphreys Branch No. 1 SAR Chapter, New Haven, CT. An enthusiastic outdoorsman, he enjoys biking, hiking, skiing, jogging, and canoeing with his family and reading technical manuals.

Charles Denslow, was born 1739 in the New Haven Colony later known as Hamden, CT to William and unknown wife Denslow. He was the 4th child and third born son. Evidence suggests young Charles joined his dad, William, and older brothers, William and John, in a move to Stamford, CT prior to 1756.

A descriptive list of men raised to serve in the Berkshire County in 1779 to serve in the Continental Army provides a physical description of Charles Denslow as follows: age, 40 years; height of 5 ft. 5 inches; and of dark complexion; engaged for the Town of Lanes borough, Massachusetts and delivered to Ensign Clark.

In 1756, the French Forces at Crown Point, NY erected Ticonderoga Fort (about 25 miles south of Crown Point). May 15, 1756, England declared war against France to determine which country was going to be in control of the North American Colonial Territory. In July 1756, the British assembled their offensive against the French. There were more than 3,000 regular soldiers in New York and the militia establishment increased the number to about 10,000 men who were scattered along the road from Albany to Lake George, NY.

Seventeen-year-old Charles Denslow and his older brothers, William and John served side-by-side in the same Militia Regiment from Stamford, CT in an ill planned assault on Fort Ticonderoga. The following year he enlisted again as a private in the Sixth Company, again with Capt. Waterbury, 3rd, in a Regiment commanded by Colonel Phineas Lyman. Col. Lyman was appointed as second in command under William Johnson, much to the pleasure of the New England troops.

The training gained during four campaigns of the French and Indian War made him a veteran for the opening scene of the American Revolution. Thus, Charles became a soldier in both the French and Indian and American Revolutionary Wars.

Charles enlisted Dec. 16, 1776 and again saw military service at Ticonderoga, NY, serving first as a private in Captain David Wheeler's Company, Colonel Benjamin Simond's detachment from Berkshire County, MA Militia. He was discharged the following March 11, 1777 with having served 96 days at Ticonderoga. Charles reenlisted June 30, 1777 in again Capt. David Wheeler's Company, Colonel John Brown's militia detachment.

Charles was one of 550 Americans at Fort Ann known as the gateway to the north on July 8, 1777 who resisted the British in a two-hour skirmish. The advance British units began moving south and encountered significant resistance at Fort Ann on July 8th. Papers show his discharge dated July 25, 1777 having served 26 days at Fort Ann. However, his name is listed on the Oriskany Battlefield Monument, Oriskany, (Mohawk Valley in Saratoga County and known as the "breadbasket of the main supplier of food" for George Washington's army), NY. This battle engagement occurred 12 days after his supposedly discharge date. The names on the Oriskany Battlefield Monument are those of revolutionaries who fought in that particular battle.

Charles again served in 1779 as he is listed as engaged to serve in the Continental Army for the Town of Lanesborough, MA.

Apparently, Charles moved his family westward in New York State, probably following the military road after seeing service in the Continental Army. In 1788, his son, Jeremiah, is born in Cherry Valley, NY (Otsego County). The birth places of his last two children are not known but probably between Cherry Valley and Albany, NY. Charles died between 1789-1790 (last child, Ruth, born in 1790) and his wife, Martha Alcott Denslow, remarried prior to 1793.

DEYOUNG, THYS J. – Born Dec. 31, 1960, Hamilton, OH. He joined the District of Columbia SAR on Jan. 30, 2008 and is on the chapter's Board of Managers. He is a contracting officer for the U.S. Office of Personnel Management.

James Theophilus Lewis Sr. was the son of Nathaniel Lewis and Elvira Helton. James was born Aug. 9, 1736 in Wales, United Kingdom, and died Sept. 1, 1825 in Cutshin, Leslie County, KY. He married first Elvira Griffin before 1771 in Perry County, KY. He married second Winnetrey Henson between 1774-1780 in Wilkes County, NC. James Theophilus Lewis Sr. is buried in the John Lewis Cemetery, Leslie County, KY. He served in the North Carolina Militia during the Revolutionary War and brought his family to Kentucky in 1810.

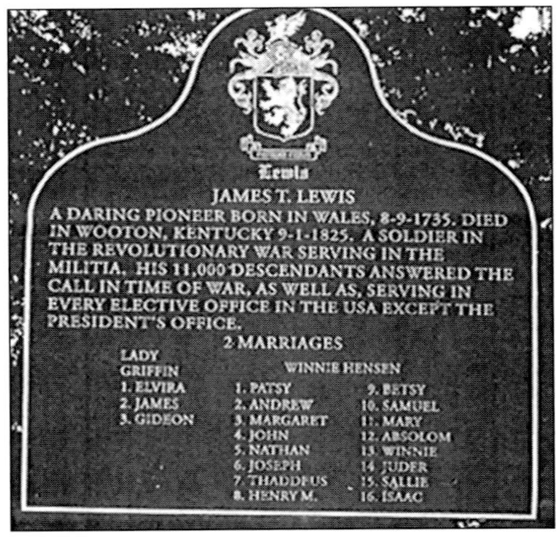

Marker for James T. Lewis

Foot marker for James T. Lewis

DICKEY, NORMAN – Born Apr. 12, 1955 in Jefferson County, IL. He joined the Illinois SAR in Dec. 2008. He is an engineer. His wife, Rita (Stark) Dickey is active in DAR with eight patriots. They have two children. Both son and daughter were married in 2008. Daughter Janet is in DAR and has 18 approved supplementals, 12 from Norman's side.

Capt. George Dickey was the son of James Dickey, an Irish immigrant. George was born in Pennsylvania but lived in North Carolina. George married Martha Johnston. His brother Anthony married her sister Sarah. While George was leading a group of men on May 12, 1780, they were attacked by Cherokee Indians. George and two others, including Elias McFadden, were killed. Three were killed and two wounded of the group of seven men. The next day Anthony, leading 70 men, gathered the bones and buried them in a sheet, in a sinkhole on the hill by Hooper Creek, where they were killed. Anthony then led a three-day raid on Indian villages, and the men killed all they could find. The area was part of Old Tyron/Rutherford County, NC, but now is somewhere in Polk County, NC.

George's children include George, Moses, Martha, Robert and possibly James. George's service was proven by Anthony's Revolutionary War pension application record. Their brother David was also a Rev. soldier with a pension. David married Mary, the widow of Elias McFadden. Anthony reported his younger brother Moses was also a soldier, and was taken prisoner and put aboard a

British prison ship. Thus, James Dickey had four sons who were soldiers in the Revolutionary War.

Frederick Mayberry Sr. (1722-1801), an immigrant from Germany, gave beef to the militia in Bedford Co., VA, and spent nine days driving the beef to the Army location. His sons, George and Frederick, were in the militia.

Frederick Mayberry Jr. (1756-1842) was in the Bedford County Militia. In 1781 he joined and served almost six months under Captains Dooley and Downey. After the war he moved to Kentucky, then to Hamilton Co., IL. Mayberry Township of Hamilton County, IL is named for him. He married and had a large family.

DONALDSON, MICHAEL B. – Born Jun. 21, 1940 in Seattle, WA. Joined the Gascade Centennial Chapter SAR on Apr. 11, 2006 and has been the treasurer since 2006. Michael was a business owner, retiring in Nov. 2001. He is married to Carol J. Donaldson and they have four children and four grandchildren.

Abraham Donaldson was born between 1729-33 in Elizabethtown, NJ. He served as Director of Militia (for New Paltz, NY?). A land owner and farmer, he died in 1805/06 in New Paltz, NY.

Michael Donaldson

DORCY, DARYL BIRNIE – Born Jan. 1, 1945, Orange, CA. Graduated University of California, Berkeley 1967, BS. Worked for the Texas State legislature and governmental agencies 25 years including eight years with the Speaker of the House of Representatives. Presently, National Director, State Government Affairs for Abbott laboratories, Inc. in Chicago, IL. Married Diana Lynn Hunter, Ph.D. Daughter, Nicole Hunter Dorcy born 1997 is a member of the National Society of the Children of the American Revolution. Daryl is also a member of Society of the War of 1812.

Daryl B. Dorcy

Nathaniel Holmes Downs, was born Nov. 1, 1763, Boston, MA. Served as a marine in the Navy of the State of Massachusetts Bay from Jan. 26, 1780 to Aug. 17, 1780 aboard the Ship *Protector* including a battle with the Admiral Duff, an English 32 gun ship. Was captured May 5, 1781 by the British war ships *Roebuck* and *Media*, sent to New York and confined in the Jersey Prison Ship. Sent to Ireland, and condemned to the military prison near Plymouth Feb. 6, 1782. Nathaniel was exchanged in July 1782, and after six weeks arrived at Marble Head. Discharged Aug. 14, 1782. He died Jan. 27, 1838 and is buried at Bangor, ME.

DOWNS, FREDERICK S. JR. – Born May 1, 1942 in Framingham, MA. He held the office of President of Daniel Morgan Chapter. Frederick was in the US Navy, GMG3, *USS Myrles C. Fox.*

He and wife Carol Ann have two children and five grandchildren. Frederick was a TFC, Connecticut State Police and retired in May 1989.

He also belongs to the American Legion and is on the Board of Directors, Salvation Army.

Samual Smith was born in 1762 in Stratford, CT. He as a Sgt. Major in Capt. Well's Company, 2nd Co. 4th Regiment. In civilian life he was a farmer. Samual died May 13, 1845 and is buried at Southbury, CT.

DUER, RICHARD CONLEY – Born 1935 in Eugene, OR. He joined the 1725 Republic Chapter SAR in Nov. 2008 and is also a member of the Masonic Lodge. He worked as a Lobbyist, United States Chamber of Commerce, Washington, DC, retiring on Sept. 1, 2008. He is married to Lorna L. Duer, and they have three children and six grandchildren.

John Duer was born Jan. 19, 1748 in Cranbury, NJ. He served as a private in the Sussex County, New Jersey Militia. A farmer, he died Apr. 3, 1831 and is buried at Covenanter Cemetery, Jackson, Trumbull, OH.

DUNNELLS, ROBERT EDGAR – Capt. Dunnells, CEC, USN (RET) was born Dec. 7, 1925 at Sanford, ME. He received the Legion of Merit w/Combat V and retired in 1974.

Robert married Corinne Jean Buckley in Yokosuka, Japan. They have three children and four grandchildren.

In civilian life, Robert was a Consultant and Treasurer, DGA International Inc.; Consultant and Treasurer, General Technology Applications, Inc.; President, Dunnells Associates, Inc. and retired in 1999.

Robert E. Dunnells

Robert has been SAR Chapter Vice President in 2005; President 2006-2007 and served on VASSAR Committee Public Safety 2006-2007. He has received the Virginia Society Medal w/oak leaf cluster; Meritorious Service Medal; Bronze 2007 Congress Appreciation Medal.

Patriot ancestors are: **Nathanial Treadwell**, Ipswich, MA, born Dec. 20, 1752; member of Capt. Wade's Company. **Capt. Cutting Cilley,** Nottingham, NH, born 1728, New Hampshire Militia; **John B. Davis,** Berwick, ME, born 1750, member of Capt. Phillip Hubbard's Company and **Caleb Nason,** Berwick, ME, born Nov. 16, 1760, member of Capt. Esaias Preble's Company.

DUPREE, JOHN THOMAS – John was born Aug. 2, 1967 in Weslaco, TX to John Kyle and Lois DuPree. John's dad had a passion for history and politics; two passions that he quickly passed on to his son. The old man (as John affectionately referred to him) who was a veteran of World War II entertained young John with stories of his time in the Army Air Corps along with John's namesake, John Thomas Munk. John's mother Lois also shared stories about her brother, Melvin Bourne, who earned a Purple Heart during the Battle of the Bulge while serving in the 3rd Army under Gen. Patton during the war.

John's passion for the history of the American Revolution began in high school when he was first exposed to the writings of the Revolutionary period in high school English class. John quickly became intoxicated with the words of Thomas Jefferson, Patrick Henry and Thomas Paine. In his college years, wile most of his peers kept posters of rock stars on their walls, pictures of Jefferson and Monticello adorned the walls of his room.

John T. DuPree

John joined the San Antonio Chapter of the SAR in 2006 after proving his lineage to Mathias Clark, who was a 1st Lieutenant in the 1st Div. of New York from June 28, 1775 to Jan. 1776.

John graduated in 1991 with a BBA in Accounting from University of Texas Pan American. In 1999, he graduated from the Sam Houston State University with an MBA. Today, John is a CPA and an Audit Manager with Carneiro Chumney & Co. in San Antonio. He is married to his wife of 13 years, Karen. Their daughter, Aimee, is ten and is a member of Children of the American Revolution.

Mathias DeClerk (Mathew Clark) was born in Tappan, NY on Oct. 24, 1739, on what is the north end of New York City today. The records of the Reformed Dutch Church of Albany, NY recorded a marriage between Mathias and Immetje Page on Jan. 2, 1774. Many immigrants changed their names to more common ones and it seems plausible that the DeClerks changes theirs to Mathew and Emma Clark around the time of their wedding. Emma was born in 1752 and died on Sept. 12, 1813 at age 72. Mathew died a year later on Dec. 14, 1814, age 72. Mathew and Emma spent their lives in the New York area and together had nine children, five girls and four boys. Mathew served in the War of the Revolution as 1st Lt. in the 1st Div of NY, from June 28, 1775 to Jan. 1776.

Mathew's service was not the only impact that the Clark's had on the Revolution. Mathew's ancestor, **Daniel DeClerk**, immigrated to New York in 1684. In 1700 he built an imposing house using brick brought from Holland as ship ballast. That house served as Washington's headquarters four times during the Revolutionary War. It was at the house built by Daniel DeClerk that Washing-

ton met the British Commander Sir Guy Carelton in 1783. Today, the house still stands and is a National Historic Site. In addition to building the house that would later serve as Washington's headquarters, Daniel was a Captain of the Militia, a Justice of the Peace, and in 1689 was a member of the New York Committee of Safety.

EBARB, THOMAS – Born Oct. 21, 1957 at Shreveport, La. Parents Thomas and Rosie Ebarb. Graduated May 1976, Zwolle High School. Join the US Army June 1976, as a light weapons Specialist 11B/11C. Last active duty Infantry AIT at Tiger Land Fort Polk, LA. Switched to the Signal Corps's as a radio repairman June 1979. Tours: Germany, Camp Cassey, Korea and Saudi Arabia. Retired SFC (E-7) after 22.5 years active duty November 1998. Awards: Meritorious Service Medal, Army Commendation, Army Achievement, Good Conduct, National Defense Service Ribbon, Southwest Asia Service Ribbon with bronze star, Noncommissioned Officers Ribbon Numeral 3, Army Service Ribbon, Overseas Ribbon, Driver and Mechanic Badge, Bronze German Army Marksmanship and Proficiency Badges. Civilian employment: Communications/Electronics Tec. for Lockheed Martin Germany. Transferred to Lockheed Martin Ft. Polk, LA, September 2002 as a Photo Optic Tec. III. Children are Micheli M. and Thomas Marcel. Became a member of SAR, August 2006. A member of the Awards and Scholarship committee. SAR award: SW Asia War Service Medal. Organizational memberships include American Legion Post No. 387 New Llano, LA. Knights of Columbus Leesville, LA. Sheriffs Honorary Membership and Louisiana Historical and Genealogical Association.

Thomas Ebarb

Don Antonio Gil Y'Barbo, was born 1729 at Los Adaes, LA, Province of Spanish Texas at that time. Parents: Matheo Antonio and Juana Y'Barbo. His father, Lt. Y'Barbo, was a soldier sent by the Spanish Crown from the Province of Andalusia, Spain. As a child, Antonio had a good command of the Spanish language and an education that combined with a remarkably sound judgment that marked him as a future leader. Gil Y'Barbo served as Lieutenant Governor, Judge and Commander of the militia in Nacogdoches, TX. Y'Barbo participated in the first cattle drive in Texas, which was to provide cattle, horses, mules, bulls and feed to General Galvez in New Orleans. The cattle were used to feed the troops and to provision George Washington's Continental Army at Valley Forge. Gen. Galvez and his troops removed the British threat from the Gulf of Mexico, Mississippi and Ohio Rivers. Therefore contributing greatly to the American Revolution. Gil Y'Barbo died in 1809 and was buried in the Old Spanish Cemetery in Nacogdoches, TX. That burial place, the corner of North-South and East-West main streets now under the Nacogdoches County courthouse. Don Antonio Gil Y'Barbo is known as Father of Nacogdoches, TX.

Statue of Don Antonio Gil Y'Barbo, the Father of Nacogdoches.

ECHERD, JOHN C. – Cdr. John Echerd was born Jan. 6, 1926 at Statesville, Iredell County, NC. John has held offices of President John Sevier Chapter and President TNSSAR, Trustee Tennessee. He has served on the committees of Membership, Historic Sites, Revolutionary War Graves, Writers and Speakers Bureau. Award received: Meritorious Service, Patriot, Liberty, Distinguished Service (Tennessee), War Service.

John served the Navy WWII, Reserve (1943-1986) with the rank of Commander.

John married Kathryn A. Sylar and they have 3 children and 4 grandchildren. He was employed at Chief Personnel Services Staff, Office of Power TVA and retired Jan. 1, 1988. He has also been V. Chairman, National Management Assn. and President Kiwanis, Ooltewah, TN.

Peter Little, was born Sept. 13, 1752 in Rowan County, NC. He was a soldier, with North Carolina Troops as a private. Peter was at the battle of Cowpens. He died March 14, 1822, and is buried at St. John's Lutheran Church, Conover, Carawba County, NC.

James Stevenson, was born May 27, 1746 in Rowan County, NC. He served as a private with the North Carolina Regiment. He was at the following battles: Ramsour's Mill, Col. Locke's Command; King's Mountain, Col. Cleveland's Command; and at Guilford Courthouse-Siege of Yorktown. James was a farmer-blacksmith. He died Sept. 3, 1828, and buried at Stevenson Cemetery - Vashti Community - Alexander County, NC.

Martin Echerd, born Aug. 22, 1759 in Rowan County, NC, was a solder for North Carolina. He died Nov. 29, 1830 and is buried at St. John's Lutheran Church, Conover, Catawba County, NC.

Adam Echert, was born in 1735 in Germany. Adam provided service to North Carolina and signed an Oath of Allegiance. Adam died in 1803 and is buried at St. John's Lutheran Church, Conover, Catawba County, NC.

Joseph Starnes was born April 3, 1755 at Smiths River, VA. He served with the Virginia Line as a private. Joseph was at Kings Mountain - served with Col. W. Campbell - wounded. He died 1844 and is buried at Bethlehem Baptist Church, Rt. 127, Alexander County, NC.

Theobold Hunsucker was born Jan. 24, 1744 at Alsace, France. He was a patriot who provided support to Militia of North Carolina. Theobold died March 12, 1822 and is also buried at St. John's Lutheran Cemetery, Conover, Catawba County, NC.

Johannes Hunsucker was born in 1720 in Northampton County, PA. He was a Member of the General Committee of Northampton Co., PA, and provided support to Pennsylvania. Johannes died in 1751 and is buried at Heidelburg Union Church - Lehigh Co., PA.

Samuel Oxford was born about 1730 in Virginia. He was a soldier with the North Carolina Troops. In civilian life, he operated a ferry on the Catawba River. Samuel died about 1810 and is buried in a cemetery under water of Hickory Lake behind Oxford Dam, Alexander County, NC.

James Barnes was born about 1722 in Pennsylvania. He was a private with a North Carolina Regiment. He died after 1822.

EDMONDS, BRUCE SCOTT – Born Sept. 29, 1964 in Philadelphia, PA, he joined the PA Society SAR on Nov. 26, 2002 and is a member of the Philadelphia-Continental Chapter Color Guard. Edmonds graduated from Peirce College of Philadelphia with a degree in computer science in 1984. He is employed by SEI, Inc. in Oaks, PA as a computer programmer. He is also a member of the Society of the War of 1812, Sons & Daughters of the Pilgrims, and Sons of the American Colonists.

Bruce Scott Edmonds

He is married to Patricia Gorman-Edmonds and they have two children.

Dr. Thomas Stewart was born about 1727, probably in VA. A doctor and large-scale farmer, he provided patriotic service to Continental troops, supplying food, animals and wagons. He died in 1810 and is buried in Dinwiddie Co., VA.

EDWARDS, CHARLES G. – Born Feb. 2, 1930 in Kittanning, PA. Charles has been Historian, OH Society 2005; President, Cincinnati Chapter 1986; proposed and started the New Historic Sites and Buildings Committee in 1985 and was appointed as 1st Chairman; OHSSAR Publicity 1987; Cincinnati Chapter Revolutionary War Graves 1986.

He has received the Patriot Medal; Meritorious Service Medal 3 times; War Service Medal

– Korea; Bronze Good Citizenship Medal; Silver Good Citizenship Medal; 25 Year Membership Service Award; Four Supplementals and had two feature articles in *Common Patriot* magazine. He was the editor of *OHSSAR Bulletin* in 1988 and editor of Cincinnati Chapter newsletter in 1986.

Charles Edwards

Charles served in the US Air Force from 1948 to 1952, attaining the rank of Sergeant. He and wife Mary have two children and three grandchildren. Charles worked as sales correspondent for National Underwriter Co, and retired in 1994.

He also belongs to American Legion, Sons of Union Veterans of the Civil War, Clan MacThomas Soc., Society of Indiana Pioneers, Sons of Indian Wars, Claedonian Soc.; Westmoreland Co., PA Historical Society; Society of Sons and Daughter os the Pilgrims; Armstrong Co., PA Genealogy Club; Derry Area, PA Historical Society, First Families of Western Pennsylvania and Boone Society.

Joseph Thom was born in 1748 in Aberdeenshire, Scotland and removed to Ireland with his parents at an early age. He grew to manhood in Ireland and emigrated to America at the age of 25, in company with a brother. They landed in New York late in 1773, then moved to Jacobs Creek, near New Alexandria, Westmoreland County, PA. He was a farmer and a member of the Presbyterian Church.

Gravestone of Joseph Thom, Morling Cemetery, Saluda Twp, Jefferson County, IN.

Upon the outbreak of the Revolutionary War he joined the army. The only official record located of his military service is that of militia duty in Captain White's company of the Fifth Battalion of the Pennsylvania Militia in 1782. A letter written by a descendant states that he was present at the Battle of Brandywine and that he was detailed, with others, to guard a certain ford, and that he was placed in charge of a squad of men and sent to perform some important mission and while on this duty they captured a British officer in full uniform.

Joseph Thom died Nov. 23, 1829 in Jefferson County, IN, at the age of 81 years. He is buried in Marling Cemetery, Saluda Township, Jefferson County, IN.

John Bowser was born in 1740 in York County, PA and died Sept. 1, 1813 in Hopewell Township, Bedford County, PA. He was buried in Hopewell Township, Bedford County, PA (cemetery unknown). His parents were Mathias Bowser Jr. and Anna Elizabeth Edelman Bowser.

John Bowser married Mary Helm about 1767 in Hopewell Township, Bedford County, PA. They were the parents of 12 children, five girls and seven boys.

John Bowser was a Private in the Revolutionary War, Fifth Battalion, York County, PA Associates Militia, Paradise Township under Captain Peter Ford and on Aug. 8, 1781 was in Captain William Heffer's Third Company. He was also a Frontier Ranger in Northumberland Company, PA.

John Bowser bought land on Yellow Creek, Hopewell Township, Bedford County, PA on April 5, 1797 from Joseph Haines for the sum of twenty-six pounds ten shillings. Here on these fertile acres John Bowser and Mary, his wife, lived until his death in 1813.

Peter Miller Sr. was born in 1741 in Culpepper County, VA, the son of Daniel Miller and Sarah (Unknown). Peter died 13 April 1815 in Loudoun County, VA.

Peter Miller Sr. married Catharine Shular between 1776-1780. They were the parents of 12 children, three girls and nine boys.

He enlisted in the Revolutionary War from Loudoun County, VA and served as a Private in Captain Burgess Ball's Company, Fifth Virginia Regiment.

Peter Miller Sr. was in the Revolutionary War only a short time when he was wounded in the leg and was discharged.

Benjamin Boone II was born Aug. 13, 1741 in Morlottan, Berks County, PA to Benjamin Boone I and Susannah Likens Boone.

Benjamin Boone II married Eve Loeffer on Oct. 1, 1771 in St. Gabriel's Episcopal Church, Morlottan, Berks County, Exeter Township, PA. They were the parents of ten children, eight girls and two boys.

Benjamin Boone II was a Private in the Revolutionary War from the state of North Carolina.

He died Sept. 25, 1824 in Columbia County, PA and is buried in Hidlay Cemetery, North Center Township, Columbia County, PA.

Capt. John Craig was my 4th great-granduncle. He was born April 27, 1753 in Belvidere, Warren County, NJ to Samuel Sr. and Elizabeth McDonald Craig. Capt. John Craig married Martha Clark in 1780 in Westmoreland County, PA and they had five children.

Gravestone of John Craig, Freeport, Armstrong County, PA.

Captain Craig was five feet, seven inches tall and a remarkably active man until an advanced age. He died on March 3, 1850 at his home near Freeport at the age of 96 years and buried in the Old Freeport Cemetery. His wife Martha preceded him in death by 25 years.

Sometime prior to the establishment of permanent peace by Wayne's victory in and treaty with the Indians, a blockhouse was erected by John Craig (1792), called Craig's Fort or Craig's Blockhouse on the Allegheny River about 120 rods above the mouth of Buffalo Creek, at what is now Freeport, Armstrong County, PA. Its Commander was Captain John Craig, whose command consisted of 40 men, whose business it was to watch the Indians from the Red Bank Creek to the Kiskiminetas River.

EDWARDS, RICHARD H. III – Richard was born Sept. 5, 1929 in Boston, MA. He was a US Navy Seaman 1st Class, USSLSMR 522.

Richard and wife Shirley have two children. He was a retail buyer, toy sore owner and department manager until he retired in 1991.

Richard H. Edwards, III

Richard is a heritage member Sheldon's Light Horse, 2nd Regiment and also belongs to Lebanon Historical Society and New Haven Historical Society.

Joshua King was born Nov. 24, 1758 at Braintree, MA. He was a Captain in Troop 6 of Sheldon's Light Horse Regiment.

General King was a soldier of the Revolution and entered the service from Bridgewater, MA, serving in Massachusetts and Rhode Island from 1775 to 1779.

Pvt. Joshua King (fifer), Capt. Josiah Hayden's Co., Col. Bailey's Regiment of Minutemen which marched on the alarm of April 19, 1775-1776.

Enlisted as Private in Continental Army at Camp Roxbury, March 30, 1777. Promoted to sergeant in Capt. Nathaniel Cushings Co., Col. Joseph Vose's 14th Regiment. In charge of protecting military stores in Boston area.

Secret expedition to Rhode Island Oct. 1, 1777 to protest the town of Newport and Providence from the British. In the fall of 1778 promoted to Sergeant-Major, forage master, served in Providence. Reported discharged March 1, 1779

Enlist as Coronet in Sheldon's Light Dragoon-Continental Army at Wethersfield, CT on Nov. 16, 1779 and promoted to Lieutenant Nov. 20, 1779. In 1780 Major Andre was captured and King's association with him continued until Andre's death on Oct. 2, 1780.

In 1781, promoted to

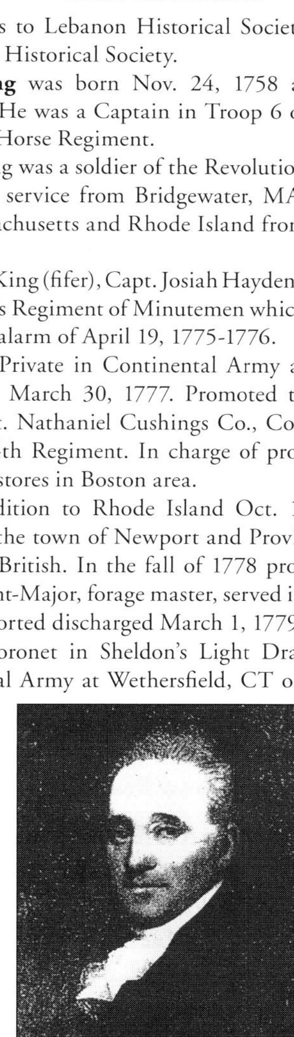

Lieutenant Joshua King

Captain; sent to South Carolina on detached duty; wounded at Eutaw Springs, Sept. 8, 1781. Present at surrender at Yorktown, VA, Oct. 19, 1781; promoted to Quartermaster and Lt. Col. On Sept. 13, 1782; in 1784 Lt. Col to General in State Militia.

In civilian life, Joshua was a merchant, banker, delegate to Constitutional Convention of Connecticut, State Legislator. He died Aug. 13, 1839 and is buried at Titicus Cemetery, Ridgefield, CT.

Samuel Fletcher was born Sept. 30, 1744 in Grafton, MA. He served a year in the French and Indian War, married a daughter of Col. John Hazeltine, and was at the Bunker Hill fight as a sergeant. He was made captain of militia, was at the siege of Ticonderoga and the Bennington fight in 1777. Later promoted to major and continued in the service until after the surrender of Buroyne. He was afterwards a brigadier and major general in the Vermont Militia before servicing as a councilor, sheriff and judge in later years. He died Sept. 16, 1814 and is buried in West Townshend, VT.

General Samuel Fletcher homestead.

John Hazeltine was born in Bradford (Rowley), MA in 1702 and was instrumental in the settlement of the town of Townshend and represented the town in most of the meetings held when the new state of Vermont was struggling to be accepted by the Union. He was chairman of the convention at Westminster, Oct. 19, 1774, which resolved to "assist the people of Boston in defense of their liberties to the utmost of our abilities." In May 1775 he was appointed a delegate from Cumberland County to the Provincial Congress and Convention of New York, and was the person to whom bonds with security were given by sundry of the persons who were arrested for participation in the Westminster massacre. He died in 1778.

EDWARDS, WENDELL E. – Dr. Edwards was born Aug. 25, 1937 in Waco, TX. He grew up on a cotton and dairy farm seven miles north of Waco. He received his BBA and MBA degrees in Accounting from Texas A and M University, College Station, and a Ph.D. in Accounting from the University of North Texas. Wendell served three years of active duty with the USAF - two years as a Hospital Squadron Commander and one year as Hospital Business Offices.

Dr. Wendell E. Edwards, Amb. Fletcher Warren Chapter, TXSSAR.

He retired from the Accounting Faculty at Texas A and M University-Commerce after 38 years and served as the Department Head for 22 years. He was awarded Professor Emeritus of Accounting. He has been a CPA for 43 years and is a past Trustee of the Accounting Education Foundation of the TSCPA's and Chair of the Scholarship Committee.

He has been a member of TXSSAR for 10 years and has served as President of the Ambassador Fletcher Warren Chapter for nine years. He served as Chairman of the TXSSAR Audit Committee, Secretary and Vice-President of Council of Chapter Presidents, and elected State Chaplain of TXSSAR in 2007. He is an active member of the TXSSAR Color Guard.

Dr. Wendell E. Edwards at Veterans Vigil held at Texas A&M University.

He is married to Linda Yeats Edwards and has two daughters, Kathryn Myers and Karen Raumaker, and five grandchildren.

Robert Edwards was born in 1759 in Orange County, NC to Edward and Agnes Edwards. He died in 1831 in Wilson County, TN and is buried seven miles south of Lebanon, TN.

Robert Edwards was a Soldier of the revolutionary war with the rank of an Orderly Sergeant in the company Commanded by Capt. William Lytle and regiment commanded by Col. Thaxton and General Lincoln. He was in the battle at Stono where he was wounded and at another time captured by Cornwallis' army. Robert was also a volunteer soldier with the rank of Orderly Sergeant in three other campaigns in the years 1780-1781 under General Butler, Col. Mebane, Fannin, Capt. Joseph Ross and one other tour as light infantry or horseman principally against the Tories in South Carolina and North Carolina.

Nancy Quesenberry and Robert Edwards were married shortly after peace was declared in 1781. Robert Edwards served in the North Carolina Constitutional Ratification Convention. They had 11 children and were property owners in both North Carolina and Tennessee. Around 1801 Robert received a land grant in Wilson County, TN. He served in the Tennessee legislature as a Representative of Wilson County during the Legislative Sessions of 1807-1819.

EGGER, FRANK NORRIS – Born Jan. 3, 1941 in Amory, MS to Houston Burdine Egger and Frances Rebecca Dansby, DAR member.

Frank graduated from Amory High School in 1958, served in the military from 1958-1967 attaining rank of Sgt. and Warrant Officer. Frank has three children. Frank was an investigator with various Federal Agencies. He retired from Metropolitan Life Ins. Co.

Frank Norris Egger

He has served as President of Lions Club, AARP, Jaycees, Adjutant/Chaplain American Legion, Quartermaster/Chaplain of Sons of Confederate Veterans, currently Secretary of SAR John Wheat Chapter, is a reenactor at battle activities, and Chamber of Commerce member.

Francis Meriwether, a student at William and Mary College where he was studying medicine, intended to complete his education in Edinburgh, Scotland, but the war between England and France prevented this. During the Revolutionary War, he served as a civil servant, Virginia Troops, gifting all his time to caring for the sick and wounded. As a medical office for the Virginia Militia, he served with distinguished honor and was given a County Grant of Land in Georgia for his services with the Virginia Troops.

President Thomas Jefferson called the Lewis family one of the most distinguished in Virginia. Two of Jefferson's siblings married into a line of the Lewis family and Nicholas Lewis, Meriwether's uncle managed Jefferson's affairs while Jefferson was minister to France. Robert Lewis, a British Army Colonel and grandfather of Meriwether Lewis, was given 33,033 acres in Albemarie County, Va. on a grant from the King. The Lewis and Meriwether families intermarried 11 times in the 18th century, choosing cousins, a common practice.

Meriwether Lewis learned to read and write by the age of 13 and at 18 was running a plantation. In December, 1880 Lewis was promoted to Captain in the Army, met Captain William Clark. Rest is History. Proud to be a descendent of above.

ELLINGSON, JOHN C. – Born June 18, 1921 in Mankato, MN, now living in Spokane, WA. He served in the US Army Air Force from July 1942 to January 1946, as a Private.

John has been Chapter President, Secretary and Historian; WASSAR president; National Trustee, National Vice President and served on National Committees – History, Newsletter, Genealogy and Revolutionary War Graves. He has received the Distinguished Service Medal, Patriot Medal, Meritorious Service Medal and Liberty Medal.

John C. Ellingson

John has two children and one grandchild. He was president of Inland Audio Visual Co. from 1953 until his retirement in June 1986.

John also belongs to the American Legion, 40 et 8, Lions, Sons of Norway, VASA, Moose, Westerners, and EWGS.

David Thurston was born March 20, 1762 in Rahway, NJ. He was a private in Capt. John Craig's Company, Seeley's New Jersey Regiment. David serviced as a scout and reported Cornwallis' progress going to Yorktown.

In civilian life, David was farmer. He died Oct. 22, 1843 and is buried at Ewing Cemetery, East Mead Township, Crawford County, PA.

EMBREY, DAVID HARVEY – Born Jan. 21, 1953 in Washington, D.C., he is a member of the MDSSAR where he served as Field Musician Cmdr. and Charles Carroll Chapter President, and serves on the Eagle Scout Committee and Americanism Poster Contest Committee. He has received the Bronze Color Guard Medal.

David works for the Bethesda Service Center, serving as a Service Manager, Maryland Safety Inspector. He is an Asst. Scoutmaster with Boy Scouts of America, and is a fifer with the MDSSAR Color Guard. He is married to Vicki Lynn Embrey with two children.

John Eskridge Sr. was born about 1743 in Westmoreland, VA. He was a 2nd Lt./Ensign in Captain Die's Company, and was a messenger to Commander of Richmond Co., VA and Ensign of Captain Die's Co. John was a landowner in Virginia; his grandfather was Col. George Eskridge, guardian to Mary Ball.

He died about 1830 in Virginia.

EMBREY, JEREMY DAVID – Born May 13, 1986 in Silver Spring, Montgomery Co., MD, he is a student at Duquesne University of the Holy Spirit in Pittsburgh, PA and a member of Boy Scouts of America.

Rueben Kemp was born in 1754 in Billerica, Middlesex, MA. He served in Col. John Stark's New Hampshire Regt., Col. Bedel's and Wait's New Hampshire Regt., Capt. Wilkens' Co. and Capt. Benjamin's Co. He fought at the Battle of Bunker Hill. His civilian occupation was blacksmith.

ENGLISH, KENNETH LEE – Born June 23, 1923 in Guthrie, OK, he joined the Oklahoma City Chapter SAR on Dec. 9, 2008. He served with E Troop, 94th Recon, 14th Armored Div. (Corporal), and was later self-employed, retiring on Mar. 31, 1981. He is a member of the VFW and American Legion. Kenneth is married to Bea English, with three children and ten grandchildren.

Stephen English was born 1726 in Hanover County, VA, and participated in the Battle of Point Pleasant, Oct. 10, 1774, the first battle of the Revolution. He died Feb. 1783 and is buried in Beford Co., VA.

ERICKSON, DR. (COL.) RICHARD J. – Born in Alexandria, VA. He received his BA (international relations and speech; minor in history) with honors and his MA (government) from The Florida State Univ. In 1970, he graduated from The Univ. of Michigan School of Law, JD cum laude, and in 1971 from The Univ. of Virginia, PhD (foreign affairs). In 1994, he received an LLM (international law) with distinction from The Georgetown Univ. Law Center.

Richard J. Erickson

From June 1995 until Nov. 2001, Dr. Erickson served as Senior Attorney-Advisor (International) and Deputy Chief, International and Operations Law Div., HQ USAF. He retired from the AF in 1993, rank of colonel. Active duty achievements were serving as a US Expert to the 1972 Geneva Conf. on the Development of International Humanitarian Law Applicable to Armed Conflict; Editor-in-Chief, The Air Force Law Review; faculty member (international law), the AF law school; Chief, International Law Div., HQ USAF Europe; senior Defense Dept. attorney in Greece and legal advisor to the Joint US Military Aid Group (Greece); Deputy Legal Advisor, HQ US Central CMD; and policy-advisor and negotiator in the Office of the Asst. Secretary of Defense for International Security Affairs.

In August 2001, he received the Dept. of the AF Outstanding Civilian Career Service Award. Military awards include the Defense Superior Service Medal, Legion of Merit, Defense Meritorious Service Medal, Air Force Meritorious Service Medal (w/3 oak leaf clusters), and National Defense Service Medal (w/1 oak leaf cluster). He has numerous professional and civic society affiliations.

Erickson is married to the former Joan Kathryn Harmony of New London, OH, and they have a daughter, Karen, who is married to Dr. Crispin Michael, MD. They have two grandchildren. Dr. and Mrs. Erickson live in Montgomery, AL.

Capt. William Sumpter was born Oct. 29, 1731, in Hanover Co., VA, the second of six children born to William and Elizabeth. William married Judith Randall abt. 1754 in Albemarle Co., VA, and they had eight children. The family moved to Burke Co., NC before the war. After the death of Judith in 1788, he married a second time and had 11 more children.

During the war for independence, he served as Captain of a company of Burke Co. troops under Col. James Rickard, and was engaged in minor skirmishes with the Torres and Indians during the entire period of the war. William owned more than 400 acres of land on the Brumley Branch of Lower Creek in Burke Co. (now Caldwell Co.). He died on Oct. 23, 1820.

ESSEX, MATTHEW T. – (SAR member 169483, State Society 8218) Born June 10, 1964 in Burbank, CA, presently living in Laguna Niguel, CA. Matthew joined the SAR in July 2007 and is a Life Member.

Matthew is married to the former Christine M. Dausch. He is employed as territory sales manager with A – Z Bus Sales, Inc.

He graduated from University of Texas in 1988, earning his B.A.

Matthew T. Essex

Isaac Pier was born March 3, 1759 in Fairfield, NJ. He was a private in the 2nd Essex Militia. Isaac was in battles at Long Island, White Plains and Fort Washington.

He was a farmer and died Jan. 31, 1846. He is buried in New Jersey.

EVANS, STANLY A. SR. – Born Jun. 7, 1939 at Boynton, FL and joined SAR on Feb. 9, 1988, Stan is the Former Vice President General (1996-97), Former State President, FLSSAR (1994); and Former National Trustee (1995). He has received the Minuteman Medal, Patriot Medal, Meritorious Service Medal (3), Florence Kendall Medal, and Silver Good Citizenship Medal, and organized six new chapters. He is also a member of the Soc. of the Cincinnati, Sovereign Military Order of Temple of Jerusalem, Order of Crown of Charlemagne, Masonic Order (Past Master, 1991, Past District Deputy Grand Master, 1996), KCCH, Scottish Rite, York Rite, and Shriners.

Stan was a Chief Petty Officer with the U.S. Navy, and also served in the Army National Guard. He retired as Test Engineer/Manager on Mar. 1, 2004. He is married to Marguerite (Maggie) Wilson Evans, with four children and six grandchildren.

Ambrose Cobb was born 1729 in Bruton Parish, York Co., PA, and provided aid to the military during the Revolution. He died about 1797 and is buried in Lincoln Co., NC.

FAITH, ROBERT DAWSON – Born Sept. 21, 1951 in Atlanta, GA at the old Piedmont Hospital location where the old Fulton County Municipal Stadium used to stand. Bob, as a State Financial Auditor for the State of Georgia, retired after 34 years of public service. He is a Certified Public Accountant.

Organizational memberships include a lifetime membership in the Boy Scouts of America National Eagle Scout Assoc., the Georgia Society of Certified Public Accountants, a founding member of the Cherokee Running Club and the Etowah River Run.

Bob is married to Elaine Nikas Faith of Atlanta, GA. They have two children, Micky and Sandy, and one grandchild. Bob is descended from his mother's father's side of the family.

Oliver Willard was born Oct. 13, 1741 in Harvard, MA. Private Oliver served in Capt. Deliverance Davis' Company of the militia. Col. Asa Whetcomb's Regt. He marched in response to the alarm of Apr. 19, 1775 and Apr. 20, 1775. He left his place of rendezvous on Apr. 27, 1775. Oliver's civilian occupations included farming and becoming the founder and Mayor of a small town in Vermont. Oliver died in May 1813 in Rockingham, VT.

FANCHER, CHRISTOPHER PATRICK – Born Dec. 19, 1980 in Marshall, Harrison Co.,

TX to proud parents Patrick A. and Margaret Sue Stark Fancher.

Christopher Patrick Fancher

Christopher was in the top 10% of his class and graduated from Marshall HS. He was very successful as a football and track star. As quarterback, he scored touchdowns of 25 and 94 yards on his first two varsity plays. He was a member of the Academic All-State Team. In track he ran the 1600 meter relay, and his team qualified for regional his junior and senior years. Chris attended East Texas Baptist University, being the first football player to commit to their new program.

After college, Chris began working for Weatherford, an oil related industry. Soon he was promoted to district engineer. Chris is a member of TXSSAR Captain William Barron's Chapter 25, Tyler, TX. His NSSAR membership is by decent from John Wright III. He is an associate member of the Winthrop Society, a member of First Families of Tennessee, and the National Society of Washington Family Descendants. Other eligibilities include: First Families of Alabama and Sons of the Republic of Texas.

On Jan. 3, 2004, Chris married Amanda Wynne (b. Nov. 30, 1980). Amanda graduated 10th in her class of 440 from Marshall HS. She excelled in choir. Amanda attended Baylor University and majored in nursing. Amanda now works at Marshall Regional Medical Center. Christopher and his family attend Cypress Valley Bible Church.

John Wright III is the ancestor that qualifies Christopher for NSSAR membership. Based upon the research of Charles Arthur Hoppin, John Wright III was born in about 1731 on his grandfather's 1000-acre estate of Leesylvania, between Powell's Run and Neapsco Creek, near the Potomic River in Prince William County. According to Hoppin's findings, John Wright III is the great, great grandson of Col. John Washington of Westmoreland County, and the second cousin, one generation removed from President George Washington. He married Ann Williams, daughter of Honour Williams. John and Ann moved to Surry County, NC in about 1774, where they accumulated large land holdings. Of their 18 children, Rosanna was Christopher's line of descent to John.

John Wright III served in Smith's Co. 4th North Carolina Regt. in the American Revolutionary War. The regiment was formed by order of the Provincial Congress at Halifax, NC, April 4, 1776, Col. Thomas Polk, commander. John enlisted in 1777. Tradition is that John became ill from exposure and was omitted from some duty with the regiment in Sept. 1777. John likely fought in the Battle of Brandywine, Sept. 11, 1777, in which North Carolina regiments were known to have fought. The Records of North Carolina tend to show that John Wright was a member of the 4th regiment at the roster of 1783.

John Wright III died in 1789 of a severe cold. He's probably buried at Flat Rock Baptist Church, where Elder William Martin Brittain served as pastor, and met and married Rosanna Wright before they moved westward in 1824 and became Citizen's of the Republic of Texas.

FANCHER, LAYTON STARK – Born to happy parents Christopher Patrick and Amanda Lynn Wynne Fancher on Jan. 26, 2007 at Marshall Regional Medical Center in Marshall of Harrison Co., TX. His first name, Layton, was taken from his maternal grandmother's surname, while his middle name, Stark, was taken from his paternal grandmother's surname. Fancher, of course, is his father's surname.

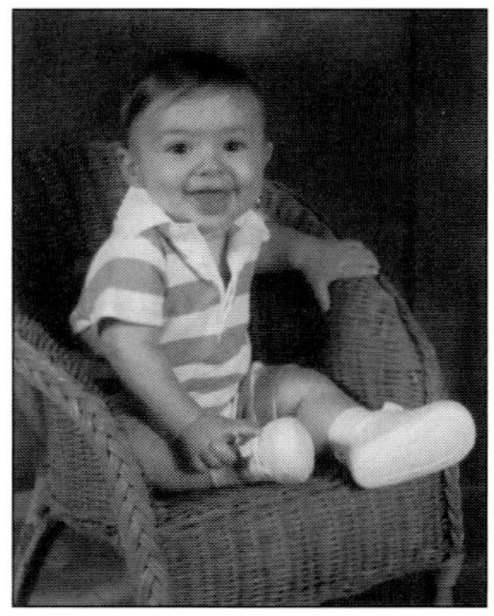
Layton Stark Fancher

Layton was 19 inches long when he was born. He weighed 8 lbs. and 1 oz., and after his 20 months he has developed a million dollar smile, which he shows often. Layton's birthday coincides with his great, great grandfather, Jerry F. Fancher's death, which occurred by drowning on Jan. 26, 1927 in the Sabine River at Burr Ferry, LA.

Layton is a junior member of Capt. William Barron's Chapter 25 TXSSAR, Tyler, TX, and is eligible for NSSAR by virtue of his descent from John Wright III. In addition to SAR membership, Layton is also an associate member of the Winthrop Society, a member of First Families of Tennessee, and the National Society of Washington Family Descendants. Other eligibilities include First Families of Alabama and Sons of The Republic of Texas.

Layton's parents and grandparents are extremely pleased to have such a pleasant and special addition to the family. They all attend Cypress Valley Bible Church.

John Wright III is the ancestor that qualifies Layton for NSSAR membership. Based upon the research of Charles Arthur Hoppin, John Wright III was born in about 1731 on his grandfather's 1000-acre estate of Leesylvania, between Powell's Run and Neapsco Creek, near the Potomic River in Prince William County. According to Hoppin's findings, John Wright III is the great, great grandson of Col. John Washington of Westmoreland County, and the second cousin, one generation removed from President George Washington. He married Ann Williams, daughter of Honour Williams. John and Ann moved to Surry County, NC in about 1774, where they accumulated large land holdings. Of their 18 children, Rosanna was Christopher's line of descent to John.

John Wright III served in Smith's Co. 4th North Carolina Regt. in the American Revolutionary War. The regiment was formed by order of the Provincial Congress at Halifax, NC, April 4, 1776, Col. Thomas Polk, commander. John enlisted in 1777. Tradition is that John became ill from exposure and was omitted from some duty with the regiment in Sept. 1777. John likely fought in the Battle of Brandywine, Sept. 11, 1777, in which North Carolina regiments were known to have fought. The Records of North Carolina tend to show that John Wright was a member of the 4th regiment at the roster of 1783.

John Wright III died in 1789 of a severe cold. He's probably buried at Flat Rock Baptist Church, where Elder William Martin Brittain served as pastor, and met and married Rosanna Wright before they moved westward in 1824 and became Citizen's of the Republic of Texas.

FANCHER, PATRICK ANTHONY – Born Apr. 2, 1949, Jasper, TX. He graduated from Burkeville HS in 1967. He attended South Texas Junior College in Houston, and Lamar University in Beaumont, before graduating from East Texas Baptist College in Marshall, TX. After graduating, he met and married on June 15, 1974, Margaret Sue Stark, b. Jul. 2, 1956 in Hearne, TX. She was the daughter of Dotson Damon Stark and Ollie Sue Merryman Stark of Hearne. Since marriage, the Fanchers have lived in Marshall, TX.

Patrick Anthony Fancher

Mr. Fancher worked as a teacher and counselor for Marshall Public Schools until retiring in 2004. He came out of retirement to become the manager of Children's Services for the Marshall Public Library. Mrs. Fancher was very successful in her work as a secretary and bookkeeper after graduating from Hearne Independent School District. The Fanchers had one child, Christopher Patrick Fancer, b. Dec. 19, 1980. The family attends Cypress Valley Baptist Church.

In addition to being a member of TXSSAR, Capt. William Barron's Chapter 25, Tyler, TX, Patrick is an associate member of the Winthrop Society, and a member of the First Families of Tennessee, and the National Society of Washington Family Descendants. Other eligibilities include First Families of Alabama and Sons of the Republic of Texas.

John Wright III is the ancestor that qualifies Mr. Fancher for NSSAR membership. Based upon the research of Charles Arthur Hoppin, John Wright III was born in about 1731 on his grandfather's 1000-acre estate of Leesylvania, between Powell's Run and Neapsco Creek, near the Potomic River in Prince William County. According to Hoppin's findings, John Wright III is the great, great grandson of Col. John Washington of Westmoreland County, and the second cousin, one generation removed from President George Washington. He married Ann Williams, daughter of Honour Williams. John and Ann moved to Surry County, NC in about 1774, where they accumulated large land holdings. Of their 18 children, Rosanna was Christopher's line of descent to John.

John Wright III served in Smith's Co. 4th North Carolina Regt. in the American Revolutionary War. The regiment was formed by order of the Provincial Congress at Halifax, NC, April 4, 1776, Col. Thomas Polk, commander. John enlisted in 1777. Tradition is that John became ill from exposure and was omitted from some duty with the regiment in Sept. 1777. John likely fought in the Battle of Brandywine, Sept. 11, 1777, in which North Carolina regiments were known to have fought. The Records of North Carolina tend to show that John Wright was a member of the 4th regiment at the roster of 1783.

John Wright III died in 1789 of a severe cold. He's probably buried at Flat Rock Baptist Church, where Elder William Martin Brittain served as pastor, and met and married Rosanna Wright before they moved westward in 1824 and became Citizen's of the Republic of Texas.

FAST, WILLIAM CLAYTON – Born Dec. 5, 1929 in Haviland, Paulding Co., OH, he joined the Ohio SAR on Dec. 5, 2008. He served in the U.S. Army, Oppama Ordnance Shop, 8187th AU-Corporal, and later was a public school teacher and guidance counselor, retiring in 1981. He is a member of the Van Wert County and Paulding County, OH Historical Society. Bill married Gloria M. Mohr and has three children and eight grandchildren.

John Jacob Fast was born ca. 1758 in Pennsylvania. He served in the Patriotic Service Regt., and died in 1827. He is buried at Fast Cemetery in Fairfield Co., OH.

FAZZINI, P. A. – Joined SAR in 2006, no. 165755, Ohio Society 8847. He works as a part time clerk.

P. A. Fazzini

P. A. belongs to the Ancient and Honorable Artillery Company of Boston; Veteran Corps of Artillery – State of New York; Society of the Cincinnati (Mass); Society of the War of 1812/Ohio Soc. War of 1812; Sons of Union Veterans of Civil War; Sons of Confederate Veterans (Ohio Branch); Sons of Sherman's March to the Sea; Former member of Sons of Spanish American War; Sons of Italy and Cub Scouts.

Joseph Crane was born in 1741 in Westfield, NJ. He was a 2nd Lt. in Capt. Dodd's Company, 2nd Regiment Essex Co. Troop.

Joseph died of wounds after the assault on Fort Delaney, Saltersville, Newark Bay, NJ. He died June 8, 1778 and is buried in Presbyterian Church Yard, New Providence, NJ.

FILES, MAJOR CHESTER A. JR. – Born in Providence, RI on Dec. 21, 1923. He is a member of the Rhode Island Society, NSSAR (No. 102275). He served in the RI Army National Guard, Field Artillery, from July 1943 to March 29, 1946 (S/Sgt) and Sept. 1950 to July 1952 (1st Lt). He later served as a title examiner for Commonwealth Land Title Insurance Co., retiring in June 1995.

He is a member of Providence Marine Corps of Artillery and the Society of Mayflower Descendants.

Nicholas Mathewson was born Oct. 14, 1752 in Warwick, RI. He served in the Kentfish Guards and fought at the Battle of Lexington. He died October 18, 1822 in Cranston, RI and is buried at Potter Cemetery.

FINCH, JAMES CONRAD – Born May 23, 1944 in Kenton, OH. Finch joined the SAR on Apr. 11, 2008 at the age of 64. Finch joined the SAR under the Revolutionary War patriot **Joshua Finch**. Joshua Finch is the 3rd Great Grandfather to James Finch. Joshua Finch, who assisted in establishing American Independence while acting in the capacity of Corporal in Massachusetts in Capt. George King's Co., Col. Benjamin Simon's Regt. Dec. 16, 1776 – Mar. 24, 1777, 98 days; roll endorsed "marched to Ticonderoga in Dec. 1776"; also, Quartermaster Sergeant, Capt. King's Co., Col. Benjamin Simon's detachment of Berkshire Co. Militia; muster roll dated Ticonderoga, Feb. 25, 1777; reported sick in camp.

James C. Finch

Corp. Joshua Finch was born on Nov. 3, 1748 and deceased Feb. 19, 1841. He is buried in Joy, NY.

James C. Finch's military service consisted of being a member of the 37th Division Band and the 122nd Army Band of the Ohio Army National Guard. He also joined the Sons of Union Veterans of the Civil War in 2008. He also has been working on his family lineage for the last two years.

He belongs to the Amvets Post 1994, Kenton, OH, and also belongs to the American Legion Post 259, Forest, OH. He is also a bugler for the VFW 1182, Forest, OH, and also for the Kenton Amvets Post 1994 in Kenton.

He has been a member of the Civil Air Patrol (US Air Force Auxiliary) for 26 years. He has served as a flight instructor and a check pilot for the C.A.P.

James has found a 3rd cousin, Doris Lewis Ward (DAR member), of Denver, CO, as a lineage to the above-named Revolutionary War patriot, Joshua Finch.

James Conrad Finch has a 14-year-old daughter, Jillan Suzanne Finch.

FINLEY, JOHN C. III – Born in 1949, son of John C. Finley, Jr. and LaVerne Kenneweg Finley, is an eighth generation descendant of Josiah Nicholson and now resides in Ashdown, near the original R.H. Scott plantation.

He is a graduate of Ouachita Baptist University and the University of Arkansas School of Law. His father began practicing law in Ashdown in 1938, and served as State Representative, deputy prosecuting attorney and served in the Counter Intelligence Corps in Europe during World War II. They formed a partnership for the practice of law in 1974, which continued until his father's death in 1994.

John C. Finley, III and father.

Judge Finley currently serves as District Judge for Little River County, and was state president of the Arkansas District Judges Council in 2007. He has served in the House of Delegates, and on the Board of Governors of the Arkansas Bar Assoc., and is a past president of Southwest Arkansas Bar Assoc. He is President of the Little River County Historical Society since 2002, a Rotarian, church organist, and past president of the Southwest Trails Chapter of the SAR in Texarkana, USA. He served as Chairman of the History Book Committee that published the first history of Ashdown, AR in 2006.

George Nicholson was born in Virginia, the son of William and Alice Nicholson. The general region of Norfolk, Surry, Isle of Wright and Princess Anne Counties of Virginia was the locale of Nicholson's ancestors. He moved from VA to NC after his father's death about 1729, where his sons were mentioned in the deeds of Halifax, Edgecombe and Nash Counties. His son, Josiah, was born in 1750. Four of his sons were involved in the American Revolution, including **Josiah Nicholson**, of NC, who served from 1771 as a lieutenant.

At the council meeting in Kingston, July 30, 1779, it was "Resolved, that the Governor appoints...Josiah Nicholson second Major of Currituck Regiment of militia."

Josiah's daughter, Sarah, born Aug. 17, 1792, married Judge Robert Hamilton Scott. The family moved to Clarke Co., AL about 1818, where Josiah died in 1833. The Scotts then moved to AR in 1834 and established their plantation at Pine Prarie.

FIRSE, JOHN A. – USAF (retired), joined the Lewis and Clark Chapter of the Illinois Society, SAR on May 5, 2005. Jack was appointed Illinois Historical Sites Chairman 2006-2010 and was elected President of the Lewis and Clark Chapter ILSSAR from 2008-2010. His wife Shirley was elected Illinois Ladies Auxiliary President from 2007-2009.

Shirley and John Firse.

John was born in Cleveland, OH in 1937. In 1958 he married the former Shirley Grund of Brimfield, OH. They have three daughters: Cheryl McElroy; Karen Pinkston; Jill Firse and five grandchildren: Angela and John McElroy, Trevor, Tyler and Abby Pinkston. He has a BS from Florida State University and an MBA from Southern Illinois University.

During his Air Force career he was a combat Search and Rescue pilot flying HH-3E "Jolly Green Giant" helicopters into North Vietnam where he rescued eight pilots. His Air Force decorations include: The Air Force Cross; Silver Star; 3 Distinguished Flying Crosses and 7 Air Medals. He was also awarded a Distinguished Flying Cross and an Air Medal for rescues while on Exchange Duty with the Coast Guard. As Director of the SARSAT /COSPAS US Mission Control Center, he joined with NASA; Canada; France and the Soviet Union to develop a system of satellites to detect, identify and pinpoint Emergency radio signals from ships aircraft and persons in distress. In its 25 years of operation through 2007, over 22,000 lives have been saved worldwide.

Jack and Shirley reside in Belleville, IL where they are adjunct Faculty at Southwestern Illinois College and are active in the Shiloh United Methodist Church where they serve as group leaders and Jack is a Trustee. Jack's winter hobby is woodworking, but when the weather warms up he and Shirley share a love of "Trailer Sailing" and have sailed the Great Lakes, the Gulf of Mexico, and many places in between.

Moses Porter, son of Experience and Abigail Porter, was born at Mansfield, CT, Sept. 30, 1738, He married Sarah Kilham, May 12, 1765, at Preston, CT. They had seven children: Abigail; Sarah; Elijah; Joseph; Solomon; Moses and Hervey.

In the spring of 1775, Moses enlisted in the Connecticut Militia, and was given the rank of Sergeant. He went to Lexington under the command of Col Putnam, but they arrived after the battle. His Regiment then marched to Boston and fought in the battles of Bunker's and Breed's Hill.

In June of 1776, he joined Wadsworth's Brigade to reinforce George Washington in Long Island during the battle of White Plains. They were caught in the retreat of Sept. 15th, when the city was abandoned. They continued on to New Jersey where they defeated a force of 1500 British-Hessians and reoccupied Trenton.

In the spring of 1777, he joined Capt. Eben Lathrop's Company of "Mounted MinuteMen" or "Rangers." In July 1777, they advanced to Bennington, VT to engage the British. It was there that he was given a battlefield commission as Second Lieutenant by the Governor of Connecticut, Jonathon Trumbull. Lt. Porter commanded a Company under General Stark.

Following the engagement at Bennington, they marched under Col Morgan to Saratoga, NY to join General Gates at the Battle of Bemis Heights. They were assigned to General Poor's Continental Brigade in Benedict Arnold's Division and fought in battles with the enemy on Sept. 19th and Oct. 9th.

He finished his service as Adjutant and aide to General Arnold until after the surrender of Burgoyne. After returning home, he received a promotion to Major and was discharged from the army. In 1780, he took up residence at Pawlet, VT, where he served as a selectman and Deacon in the Congregational Church. He died Feb. 11, 1803, at the age of 64. He is buried in the "Old Cemetery" at Pawlet.

FITE, HOWARD EDWARD – Born Jun. 28, 1935 in Wyandotte, Wayne Co., MI, he joined the Michigan SAR on Nov. 8, 2008. He was the first new charter member of the Huron Valley Chapter and is the 2nd Vice President of this chapter in Ann Arbor, MI.

Howard served in the USMC, H&S Co., 2nd Bat., 3rd MAR Regt., 3rd MAR Div., FIMF. He later worked as a salesman, retiring in June 1997. He is a member of SAR, Society of the War of 1812, Sons of Confederate Veterans, Sons of Union Veterans, and the Marine Corps League. He is married to Patricia Lynn (Butler) Fite, and they have two children.

Michael Ripple was born Oct. 15, 1751 in New Hampton Co., PA and married Sarah Elizabeth ---, born 1755 in New Hampton Co. PA. During his first enlistment, he was a private with the 1st Pennsylvania Continental Regt., Co. E., serving for six months and fighting at Long Island, Brooklyn Heights, Manhattan Island, and Harlem Heights, NY.

In his second enlistment he was a Lightguard Hourse Man with Gen. Washington's Life Guard Dragoons. He served at Trenton, NJ, Brandywine, Germantown, PA, Morristown, NJ. Anywhere Gen. Washington was, his guards where there also.

In his third enlistment (2 years) he served with Gen. Kasimir Pulaski (IL) Dragoons, Independent Legion. He served at DE; Egg Harbor, NJ; MD; Yorktown, VA; NC; Charlestown, SC; and Savannah, GA.

He died on Jun. 4, 1833 and is buried in Edgar Co., IL.

FITTS, WILLIAM CALVERT – Served in the US Navy, *USS Newport (LST 1179)* as Quartermaster.

William has been married to Nadine Marie (Ptak) Fitts for 27 years. He and Nadine have three wonderful sons, William, Christopher Michael and Sean Matthew. He states, "My family has been an inspiration in shaping me into the man I have become and I thank them for that."

"I earn my living as a Union Steamfitter/Pipewelder and I have traveled to many places in the US to practice my craft and it has been a rewarding occupation." Family genealogy and history are his favorite hobbies and both provide him with endless satisfaction.

He belongs to the following organizations: AF and AM of Utica Lodge #47; Ziyara Shriners A.A.O.N.M.S. of Utica, NY; Chapter No. 57 Royal Arch Masons of Utica, NY; Commandery No. 3 Knights Templar of Utica, NY; Council NO. 12 Cryptic Masons, ROTICA, Vernon, NY; American Legion, Post No. 229, Utica, NY; Vietnam Veterans of America, Life Member, Chapter NO922, Baytown, TX; Guild of Colonial Artisans and Tradesmen 1607-1783, General No. 178; The Order of Founders and Patriots of America, General No. 5780/New Hampshire State Society No.. 40; Sons of the Revolution, National No. 40540/New York State Society No. 10439; Order of the Crown of Charlemagne in the United States of America, National Life Member No. 2293; The Military Order of the World Wars; The Order of the Merovingian Dynasty, Life Member No. 112; Order of Descendants of Colonial Physicians and Chirurgiens, National No. 448; Sons of Union Veterans of the Civil War, Camp Homer Searle No. 114, Bridgewater, NY; Baronial Order of the Magna Charta; General Society of Colonial Wars, New Hampshire Society; Ancient and Honorable Artillery Company of Massachusetts; General Society of the War of 1812, New York State Society (pending) Society of the Descendants of the Colonial Clergy (pending); Charlton, MA, Historical Society, Life Member; Washington County, NY Historical Society, Member; New England Historic and Genealogical Society, Member.

John Fitts or Fits was born June 16, 1747 at Sutton, Wocester County, MA. He served as a private with Captain Samuel Curtis's South Co. of Charlton Minutemen, which marched on the Alarm of April 19, 1775; service, 14 Days, Roll dated Camp at Roxbury, Mass., *Mass. Soldiers and Sailors in the Revolution*, Vol. 5, pg. 739; also Mass. Archives. He also served as a private with Colonel Cushing's Regiment Captain Alijah Lamb's Company, enlisted Aug. 15, 1777 discharged Nov. 29, 1777; service 3 mos. 24 days, travel included, with Northern Army. *Mass. Soldiers and Sailors in the Rev.*, Vol. 5, pg. 742; also National Archives. Military experience: Minuteman from Charlton, Mass. who marched on Alarm April 19, 1775 "Patriots Day," to reinforce engagements at Lexington/Concord Mass.; and reinforcement for General Gate's at the Battle of Saratoga, NY.

Gravestone of John Fitts, Bath Path Cemetery.

Gravestone of John Fitts, Bath Path Cemetery, with family on either side.

John died May 11, 1838 at age 89, at Charlton, Mass., and is buried at Bay Path Cemetery, Charlton, MA.

FLETCHER, DR. CHARLES ROBERTS – He was born Nov. 23, 1939 as the only child of Charles Simmons Fletcher Jr. and Lucile Hester Roberts Fletcher in Birmingham, AL. He attended public schools in Jefferson County, AL;

was awarded a National Merit Scholarship to Rice University, Houston, TX where he studied Physics. He received his PhD from the University of Illinois in 1967. He performed Geo-Physics research in lunar science at the Johnson Space Center. He then worked at Halliburton during research in oil well bore-hole Geo-Physics. He is the author of numerous scientific publications. He retired in 1992.

Charles Roberts Fletcher

Francis Nash was born in 1742 at Templeton Manor, Prince Edward County, VA. He moved to Hillsboro, NC around 1763, where he became a successful lawyer and public official. In 1775, he was commissioned as a lieutenant colonel in the 1st North Carolina regiment, quickly rising to the rank of Brigadier General. General Nash joined General Washington's staff in the defense of Philadelphia as commander of the 1st North Carolina Regiment. Francis fought in the battle of Brandywine. He later was mortally wounded by cannon fire in the battle of Germantown on Oct. 4, 1777. He is buried at the Towanencin Mennonite Meetinghouse Cemetery in Pennsylvania.

FLOWERS, NELSON J. – Born Aug. 7, 1965 in Phoenix, AZ (Maricopa County), Nelson was a Sgt. in the U.S. Army National Guard, Reserves and R.O.T.C. Cadet (1983-93), honorable discharge. He has worked with the Tuthill Corporation for the past 15 years. Nelson is married to Heather J. Canino.

Valentine Flowers was born Jul, 1765 in Buckingham, VA. He served in the Virginia Militia and was at the Battle of Yorktown, present at the siege and surrender of Cornwallis. He died April 1838 and is buried at Forsee Cemetery in McEwen, Humphreys, TN.

FLOYD, WILLIAM MONTGOMERY – Seventh in succession from General William Floyd, is a member of the Tampa, Florida chapter. Mr. Floyd has been in business his entire life, and is a graduate from the University of South Florida, Manager of the Year from a billion dollar corporation, Southeastern Salesperson of the Year, two time Pinnacle Club winner, and three time Distinguished Performance Award winner in both sales and sales management. His personal interests include being a USA Triathlon Certified Coach, Level II, USA Cycling Certified Coach, TEAM in Training National Certified Coach, National Age Grouper in triathlon, Ironman, and recipient of the prestigious Mentorship Program from U.S.A. Triathlon, and has assisted the staff coaches at the U.S. Olympic Training Center in Colorado Springs, CO.

Mr. Floyd has a song and daughter, Patrick and Leslie, and four sisters and a brother, several of whom have been affiliated with the Sons of the American Revolution and the Daughters of the American Revolution.

General William Floyd from the state of NY, with his home in Westernville, helped to lead the Continental Army during the American Revolution. A tall man of 6'4", and always carrying his cane, he was seen as a man of dignity and commanded respect.

General William Floyd

The General was a man of wealth and owned an additional home in Long Island, NY. General Floyd's home in Westernville is a registered National Historic Home.

His strength and leadership was exhibited by well thought out plans and his decisiveness.

General Floyd represented the state of NY during the signing of the Declaration of Independence, as his name appears on the second row from the right, top name on the row. Later, approximately 1790, five copies of the Declaration of Independence were distributed to the remaining survivors of the 1776 signing, of which General Floyd was a proud recipient. The original copy is still in the possession of the Floyd family, along with his desk, and other items of interest to the family.

FOLEY, JAMES D. JR. – Born Feb. 24, 1954 in Chelsea, MA. He joined the Tennessee SAR on Dec. 9, 2008. James served in the Massachusetts Army National Guard, Troop B, 26th Armored Cavalry 26th Division, and is a supervisor for Penske Truck Leasing. He is a member of SCV Brandy Rifles, Co. E, Culpepper, VA, Out of Time Teachers Living History of Revolution and Civil War, the American Society of Military Insignia Collectors (ASMIC), and the US Army Armor Society. He married first Beverly Funk, and is presently married to Gail Paquim. He has two children and two grandchildren.

Moses Foley Sr. was born 1757 in Prince William, VA and was a private in the Montgomery County, VA Militia, Capt. Edwards' Company. He also was in the cavalry under Gen. Greene. In 1793, he was a member of the first court of Grayson County, VA, and on Sept. 23, 1793 served a warrant to truly officiate the office of a minister of the gospel and solemnize the rites of matrimony. He started churches throughout southwest Virginia, and in 1815 moved to Barbourville, Knox County, KY, and settled on the Cumberland River and was the Pastor of several churches until his death in 1823. He is buried at Foley Family Cemetery in Barbourville.

FOLGER, HARRY P. III – Born Jan. 17, 1940 in Neptune, NJ and raised in the Boston area of MA, he is the son of a Methodist minister. He graduated from Northeastern University with a BS in Business Administration and passed the CPA Exam. For the past 26 years he has worked as the Dir. of Data Processing and Accounting at Woodruff Energy in Bridgeton, NJ.

He joined the NJ Society SAR on March 20, 1987 and is a former Vice President General for the North Atlantic District, Past NJ State President, Past President of the South Jersey Chapter, and Vice President of the Col. Richard Somers Chapter. He has received the Patriot Medal, Meritorious Service Medal (State & Chapter) Bronze Good Citizenship Medal, and Council of State Presidents Medal.

Harry P. Folger, III

He is a member of 15 Hereditary Societies and 8 Historical Societies, including: Past Governor, Society of Mayflower Descendants in NJ; Counsel Member, Pennsylvania Society Founders & Patriots of America; Past President, New Jersey Society of the War of 1812; Asst. Governor General, General Society of Mayflower Descendents; and Honorary Governor General, Descendants of Founders of New Jersey. His Revolutionary War Patriots include:

Jeremiah Smith was a member of the 3rd Battalion, Gloucester County, NJ Militia, achieving the rank of 2nd Maj.

Owen Folger, Nantucket, MA.

John Brisbane, Captain, Pennsylvania Line.

Henry Reeves, Private, Cumberland County, NJ Militia.

Thomas Marshall, Private, Gloucester County, NJ Militia.

FOLMAR, DAVID STUART – Born Aug. 10, 1934 in Fairhope/Baldwin, AL. He served in the US Army Armored Division-Tank Corp 1952 to 1956 in Germany.

He was employed at Union Glazier from 1957 to 1995 when he retired in Texas. David married Virginia Augusta Manasco and they have four children and six grandchildren. His wife is a member of DAR under patriot name Manasco and their sons also belong to SAR.

David Stuart Folmar

David also is a member of American Legion International.

Jacob Fulmer Jr. was born in 1762 in the Dutch Fork, Lexington District, SC. He was a private the in John Adam Summer Company with Beard's Regiment of Militia. In the summer 1779 was under John A. Summer in Beard's regiment, stationed at Ancrum on the Congaree River. The same summer under Henry Summer, scouted in the Enoree River settlements and in Ninety Six District, under command of Colonel Glenn. In 1780 was in Henry Summer's company and joined the army of General Greene, who took the British fort at Granby, then marched to Ninety Six to attack the British there under Cruger. In 1781, marched under Colonel Beard, rendezvoused at Kaigler's Mills and at Williamson's

Branch. The forces joined under General Greene, joined the enemy at Battle at Eutaw Springs. 1782, Stationed at Dreher's Mills on Saluda River.

Jacob was a farmer in civilian life. He died Jan. 23, 1839 and is buried at Leesville, SC.

FOLMAR, SHELBY CARTER II – Born July 22, 1960 in Birmingham, AL. He is a member of the Saguaro Chapter AZSSAR (National #171784, State #2338). He served in the US Navy, EN1 (E-6), Engineman First Class and worked as a AC Technician, Management, Diesel Tech, retiring Dec. 31, 1997. He is also a member of the American Legion.

Folmar is married to Donna Marie and they have two children, Shelby Carter Folmar III and Kimberly Gayle Folmar, and one granddaughter, Lauren Elyse Rodriguez.

Jacob Fulmer Jr. was born about 1760 in Lexington, SC. He served with General Pickens Regt., a Private, war #w7343. He fought in the battles of Eutaw Springs, Musgrove's Mill, King's Mountain, and Cowpens. A landowner and farmer, he died Jan. 23, 1839 and is buried in Leesville, SC.

FOLMAR, STEPHEN LEE – Born in Birmingham, AL and resides in Sealy, TX. Stephen is an insurance adjuster.

He married Donna Lynn Boothe and they have 5 children and six grandchildren. Stephen's father and brother are in the SAR under Patriot Jacob Fulmer Jr.

Jeremiah Manasco was born in 1745 in Wales. He served as a Captain in the Revolutionary Army. See information in I, pp. 276-8. In civilian life, Jeremiah was a farmer. He died Jan. 15, 1815 and is buried at Manasco Cemetery, Walker County, AL.

FOSDYCK, JAMES C. – Born Sept. 28, 1948 at Amarillo in the Texas Panhandle. James and his parents moved to CA in 1953.

James attended local California elementary, intermediate and high schools. After a stint in the military, he earned as Associate of Arts degree in the Administration of Justice.

James served in the US Army as a member of the 3rd Infantry Regt. --*The Old Guard*, the official escort to the President -- in Washington, DC, where he participated in the funeral of former President Dwight D. Eisenhower and the Inauguration of President Richard M. Nixon. James attained the rank of sergeant and was awarded several medals including the Expert Infantryman Badge, Good Conduct Medal, National Defense Medal and Army Meritorious Unit Citation.

James joined the Los Angeles County Sheriff's Dept. in 1970. He served the citizens of Los Angeles County for more than 35 1/2 years while policing the communities of Southcentral Los Angeles, Carson, East Los Angeles, Norwalk, LaMirada, and Santa Fe Springs.

James earned numerous honors during his law enforcement career; *Letter of Commendation for Life Saving, Commendable Restraint Commendation* for his non-lethal actions when confronted by a crazed armed suspect, *Sheriff's Award, Meritorious Service Award* and two *Distinguished Service Awards*. James retired from law enforcement Jan. 20, 2004.

Sergeant James Fosdyck

James is the Junior Reserve Officers' Training Corp Award Chairman for the Orange County, California SAR Chapter. James' SAR awards include the Military Service Medal and Law Enforcement Commendation Medal.

James and his wife Un Hui Yi travel extensively. They have visited all 50 of our United States, Asia, central Europe and the Mediterranean. They have a son, a daughter, a son-in-law and two grandchildren. James' family is the primary focus of his life.

James' interest in his family history began in 1976. James wrote and published *History of the Fosdick – Fosdyck Family* in 1998. He is a member of the General Society of Mayflower Descendants, William Brewster Society, Sons of Union Veterans of the Civil War and Sons of Confederate Veterans of the Civil War.

Headstones of Charles Sullivan and his son Hewlett Sullivan at Lebanon Methodist Church and Cemetery; Dunklin Township, Greenville County, SC.

One of James' patriot ancestors was his 5th great-grandfather **Charles Sullivan**. Charles was born Apr. 2, 1728 at Brunswick County, VA. Charles was a private in the Rangers, serving with Gen. Francis Marion in SC and GA. After the surrender of Charleston, Charles, his two sons **Moses** and **Hewlett**, with assistance of a kinsman, Capt. George Martin, organized the Sullivan Scouts, which cleared the SC and GA countryside of Tories and hung many of them at an old fort on Reedy River to the rear of the present Baptist Church known as "Prospect."

Moses Sullivan headstone.

Charles died Nov. 3, 1808 at Greenville County, SC. He is buried at the Old Sullivan Cemetery, also known as The Grove Cemetery, which is located not far from the Lebanon Methodist Church and Cemetery in Dunklin Township, Greenville County, SC. Charles' grave is marked by the SAR as a Revolutionary War soldier.

Another of James' patriot ancestors was his 5th great-grandfather **Samuel Fosdick III**. Samuel was born Mar. 11, 1710 at New London, CT. Samuel was a private in the Third and Fourth New York Line Regiments. It appears Samuel saw limited service near his home in Nassau County, NY.

A blacksmith and farmer, Samuel resided in CT, MA and NY. He married twice: (1) Deborah Shadbolt and (2) Mary Moore Wright.

Samuel died on the farm of his brother Silas near Nine Partners, Dutchess County, NY in 1792 at age 82. In accordance with the custom of the community, Samuel was probably buried on Silas' farm, perhaps with a fieldstone or rough headstone. If so, the memorial was long ago plowed under and the site of the grave forgotten.

FREEMAN, LESLIE B. – Born June 24, 1931 in Alpine Junction, NY. He grew up in Freeville, NY and graduated from Ithaca High School, Ithaca, NY in June 1949. After high school, he enlisted in the US Air Force and became a control tower operator. After a medical discharge in 1953, he enrolled at the Milwaukee School of Engineering, majoring in electronics.

Leslie B. Freeman

Leslie spent 35 years in the aerospace industry, working on such projects as the F3 and F4 Navy fighter, the F101 Air Force fighter and the Mercury space capsule, among others. He has taught English and technical report writing in Tokyo, Japan, owned an A&W restaurant franchise in the South Pacific, living in Tahiti, worked for Litton Industries in Australia, General Electric in the Fast Breeder Nuclear Reactor Division in Sunnydale, CA, Cleveland, OH and Germany. He also worked for Stanford Linear Accelerator as a consultant and Lockheed Missiles and Space Company. He retired in Dec. 31, 1984.

He joined the SAR on June 2, 1988 and has served as Chapter President, State President (Oregon), National Trustee, and Vice President General - Pacific District. He has been awarded the War Service Medal (Korea), Patriot Medal, Meritorious Service Medal, Silver Good Citizenship (2), SAR Centennial, and Fire Safety Commendation.

His patriot ancestor is **Samuel Wheeler**, who was born 1758 in England. He came to America with General John Burgoyne and the British Army, but deserted and joined the Albany County, NY Militia, a private. A surveyor, he died in 1808 and is buried at the Baptist Church Cemetery in Brisben, NY.

FREUDENTHAL, GLENN DANIEL – Born April 6, 19423 in Nashville, TN and married Bettye Reneau on June 2, 1962. Bettye is a member of Col. Jethro Sumner Chapter DAR. They have two children and two grandchildren.

Glenn Daniel Freudenthal

He joined the US Navy during the Vietnam Conflict and was attached to VA-216 Attack Squadron aboard the USS Coral Sea between 1966 and 1970. He graduated from Nashville State Technical and worked as a Tool Design Engineer until retiring April 2008. Glenn joined the Sumner Chapter of the Tennessee SAR Dec. 2007.

Glenn is descended from his ancestor, **William Amos Reynolds**, who was born Sept. 11, 1763 in Wake County, NC and enlisted as a substitute school boy. He served as a private in a NC horse company under Capt. Lewis Bledsoe until joining forces with Gen. Butler's regiment and was commanded by Col. William Moore. Following the war, William returned to Wake County and married his wife, Catherine Dickson in 1781. They settled in Dickson County, TN by way of Hawkins County and Powell's Valley. They lived on his land grant located on both sides of the Leatherwood Fork of Yellow Creek. William died on Oct. 29, 1834 and is buried in Dickson County.

FULLER, ROBERT RICHARDS – Robert is from Henrietta, NY, member of Rochester Chapter SAR, under Empire State Society SAR. First joined Rochester Chapter in 1977, after one year or two, did not renew membership. Rejoined in the year of 2003 and is now serving as board officer with Rochester Chapter. Has received two awards: Bronze Medal Good Citizenship and Robert E. Burt Boy Scout Volunteer Medal Award.

Robert Richards Fuller

Robert's wife is Barbara Menge Fuller, married for 29 years. Presently employed by Pittsford Wegmans as full-time and Christmas Tree Shops as part time. Retired from Monro Muffler Brake in July, 2003.

Was Scoutmaster for seven years and has been involved in various organizations in Rochester, NY. Was Warden and Vestry Member of Ephphatha Episcopal Church of the Deaf; President and Secretary of Rochester Civic Association of the Deaf; Vice President, Secretary and Board Member of National Technical Institute for the Deaf Alumni Chapter of Rochester, NY; Board Member of Rochester Tel-Com Association of the Deaf; was member of Rochester Fraternal Society for the Deaf, under National Fraternal Society for the Deaf; Score Keeper and Secretary for Deaf Connection Bowling League for seven years; Membership Director for World Recreation Association of the Deaf - USA for seven years; Membership Director and Treasurer for Rochester Recreation Association of the Deaf.

Jonathan Allen, son of Jonathan and Amy (Beecher) Alling, was born on June 28, 1753 in New Haven, CT. His death date was June 3, 1836 in Smithboro, Tioga County, NY. Buried in old cemetery in Smithboro, NY, off Bridge Street, south of State Route 17C.

Tombstone and burial site of Jonathan Allen.

First enlisted for one year in the month of April, 1776 in the City of New Haven, CT, company commanded by Capt. Jeremiah Parmerlee, under the regiment by Col. Samuel Elmer. Re-enlisted in 1777, during the war, in a company by Capt. Jeremiah Parmerlee (Parmerlee was later killed, replaced by Capt. James Duncan), under the regiment commanded by Col. Moses Hazen. Served in Fort Stanwix, Rome, NY during the month of April, 1777. He was involved in the battles of Brandywine and Germantown, PA. He stayed in the army until the disbanding of the army in June, 1783 at Pompton, Morris County, NJ. After the war, Jonathan Allen was farmer and had applied for war pension during the years of 1818 and 1820.

His first wife was Hannah Bradley, daughter of Jabez and Esther (Beach) Bradley. They had four children: Mary, Chloe, Randolph and a unnamed daughter (died in birth). Second wife was Lucy _____, had one daughter, Hannah. Third wife was Hannah Case, had two daughters, Olive and Abigail. Hannah Case is buried next to Jonathan Allen.

GAGE, FLOYD HIGLEY – Floyd was born July 26, 1926, Canandaigua, Ontario County, NY, the son of Floyd Byron and Laura Higley Gage. He grew up on his parent's farm in the Town of Gorham and attended the Reed Comers district no. 8 school. He went to the Gorham Central School for high school and graduated in 1944.

Floyd Higley Gage

He worked with his father and grandfather Anson Gage on their farms and in 1947/48 he attended Coyne Electrical School in Chicago.

He married Gladys Elizabeth Mallaber, Aug. 20, 1949 in Webster, NY. They bought a house on one acre in 1950 near Reed Corners and sold it in 1952 when they bought a nearby farm of 49 acres. He drove school bus for three years for the Gorham School. They now had four children, Kathleen, Alan, Joan and Karen. In 1958 he started working for a small Electric, Plumbing and Heating company in Gorham.

In 1968 they sold the property of now 190 acres and moved to a new house in Fort Lauderdale, FL. He worked as an electrician and in 1970 joined the I.B.E.W. Local 728 and worked as a union electrician until he retired in 1989.

They bought a 2 acre lot on Turner Road, Canandaigua, NY, in 1974. Floyd drew up the plans for a house and started building it himself in 1979, working on it on vacation each year until it was finished. They sold the Florida house and moved to the new one in 1985.

They now spend six months in New York and six months in a Lantana, FL house they bought in 1997. They enjoy gardening, dancing and doing genealogy.

Samuel Gage was a Private, Capt. John Albee s (1st Mendon) Co. of Minutemen, which marched on the alarm of April 19, 1775, to Roxbury; service, nine days; also, Corporal, Capt. David Batcheller's co., 3rd Worcester Co. Regt. commanded by Lieut. Col Nathan Tyler; entered service Dec. 8, 1776; service, 1 mo. 15 days; company marched to Providence on the alarm of Dec. 8, 1776; roll dated Northbridge.

Gravestone of Corporal Samuel Gage, North Bush Cemeterh, North Bush, NY.

Source: *Massachusetts Soldiers and Sailors of the Revolutionary War*; published by the Secretary of the Commonwealth; Wright & Potter Printing Co., State Printers, Boston; 1899; page 221.

Samuel Gage was born in Mendon, Worcester County, MA, Dec. 8, 1749. He married Lydia Fish at Uxbridge, MA, June 8, 1769. Before 1790 the family emigrated to Pittstown, Rensselaer County, NY. The 1790 census of Pittstown shows Samuel Gage's family of 13. They emigrated to North Bush, now Caroga Township, Fulton County, NY, and were in the 1800 census in the then Montgomery County. They built a log home near a clear spring there. He lived and farmed there until he died in 1820. Lydia had died sometime before Samuel had died.

GALER, LT. COL. ROBERT F. – Born July 19, 1918, now resides in Columbus, GA. Has been VPG, So. Atlantic Dist.; VPG, Int'l. Dist.; President, Georgia Society. He has served as Chair, Rev. War. Graves (10 years); Minuteman; Hist. Sites and Cel. and Membership.

He served as a US Army Lt. Col. during WWII and the Korean Conflict. He retired in 1983. He served over 20 years active military and 20 years as Federal Civil Servant.

Robert married Mary Jane Perkins and they have three children and two grandchildren. He also served as Chairman, Race Relations Advisory Commission; on the Board, Historic Linwood Cemetery Foundation.

John Armington, born 1735 in Rehoboth, MA served in the Massachusetts Militia. He was at the Alarm at Lexington and Concord, MA. He was a farmer until his death in 1818. He is buried at Passumpsic Cemetery, St. Johnsbury, VT.

Stephen England, born 1758. Served in the 4th and 38th Regt. Massachusetts and at Valley Forge, PA. His civilian occupation was as a tavern owner. He died in 1810 and is buried at Plain Cemetery, Fairfax, VT.

GALLAGHER, MICHAEL RYAN – Born in 1983 in Wilmington, DE. He joined SAR in 2001.

Michael has served as Robert Kirkwood Historian, 2002-present; Assoc. Registrar 2008-present; JROTC (Christiana and Glasgow High Schools, 2000); also co-presenter Newark 2007; Scout Chair May 2001-present; Presented Eagle Scout Certificates, 2002-present.

He has received awards for extraction of information on strength and movement of Delaware Continentals (2002-2006), Robert E. Burt Boy Scout Volunteer Award (2001 and 2008).

Michael also belongs to Boy Scouts of America, Alpha Phi Omega, Castor Assn. of America; and a former member of Sons of Union Veterans of the Civil War.

Christopher/Christophel/Christoffel Rex (aka **Stophel or Stoffel**) was born about 1754 in Washington Township, Lehigh, PA. He served with 5th Co. 3rd Battalion, Northhampton Co., PA 1778, was a private under Conrad Reader/Ritter/Reder; 6th battalion under Capt. Conrad Reders. Christopher was a Sergeant in Adam Deal's Co. Northampton Co. 1781-1783 under Reder. Also with the 6th Reg't. Northampton Co., PA under Col. Henry Geiger. He was at Brandywine and Germantown, according to bio of his company.

Christopher was a cobbler until his death Before May 9, 1823. It is believed he is buried on his farm in Heidelberg Township, Lehigh County, PA.

Bernard Jacob Rex was born April 5, 1724 at 8031 Germantown Avenue, Philadelphia, PA. Jacob, as he was known, was a private, member of the 4th Class, 6th Co. (Capt. Matthias Brabst) in 3rd Battalion Northampton Co., PA militia under Col. Michael Bobst. Jacob was a grist mill owner. He died April 11, 802 and is buried at Heidelberg Union Church, Germansville, Lehigh County, PA.

GARDNER, ALLEN LESLIE – Born February 9, 1951 in Washington, DC; joined SAR July 21, 2008.

Employed by United States Federal Government, State Department, Foreign Service.

Married: Suzanne Barbara Phillips, April 9, 1981 in Rockville, Maryland. Two children, Laura Gardner Nishikawa and Michael Gardner.

Descended from Patriot **Benjamin Gardner** through paternal great-great grandmother, Susan Ann Gardner.

Benjamin Gardner, born November 9, 1746, North Kingston, Rhode Island. Enlisted and served as Private, Ensign and Sergeant with Exeter Alarm Company, guarding the shores of Narragansett Bay against British. Served under Capts Hoxsie, Harrington, Clark and Alsberry & Colonel Dyer. Served spring 1776 to August 1780. Married Tabitha Browning, 8 children. Died September 5, 1832, Slocum, RI. Received pension S21765.

Allen Leslie Gardner

GARDNER, IRA HENRY – Born May 14, 1916 in Scranton, PA; joined SAR July 21, 2008.

Inducted into the Army at age 24, February 6, 1941 in Newark. Trained at Fort Hancock, New Jersey. Date of separation: December 5, 1945. T/4 Radio Mechanic with AS-Pac Theater Service w/3 Brass Stars, Victory Medal American Theater Service Medal, Good Conduct Medal, Philippines Liberation Ribbon w/Brass Star, American Defense Service Medal.

Ira Henry Gardner

Married: Margaret Godfrey McLaughlin Dodds, September 13, 1944 in Chicago, IL. Married 65 years. Two children: Allen L. Gardner and Elizabeth A. Gardner Deering. Four grandchildren; 3 great-grandchildren.

Worked for DC Transit, Washington, DC; first as a streetcar operator and then as bus operator for 33 years, retiring 1979.

Descended from Patriot **Benjamin Gardner** through paternal great-grandmother, Susan Ann Gardner.

Benjamin Gardner, born November 9, 1746, North Kingston, Rhode Island. Enlisted and served as Private, Ensign and Sergeant with Exeter Alarm Company, guarding shores of Narragansett Bay against British. Served under Capts Hoxsie, Harrington, Clark and Alsberry and Colonel Dyer. Served spring 1776 to August 1780. Married Tabitha Browning, 8 children. Died September 5, 1832, Slocum, RI. Received pension S21765.

GASKINS, JAMES STEPHEN – Born Jan. 26, 1974, Kingsville, TX, is presently a Sergeant for State of Florida Highway Patrol. He joined the SAR Dec. 5, 2007 in Florida.

James and Alexandra Camille Perry Gaskins have two children. James is also a member of the Sons of Confederate Veterans.

Hezekiah Wade was born April 13, 1754 at Frederick County, MD. Hezekiah first entered the Revolutionary War effort in April 1776 at Monongahalia County, VA as a Private and Indian Spy, serving variously under Captains Owen Davy, John Minor, John Lucas and James Cochran, for a period of at least 32 months. References: (A) Pension No. W6387 Service Record, National Archives Trust Fund Board; (B) District of Columbia Pension Roll of 1835; (C) "*The Wade Family*" published 8/15/1927, By Franklin Marion Brand of Morgantown, West Virginia Chapter XX ppg 308-314.

Hezekiah was a farmer until his death Nov. 23, 1834. He is buried at Fish Creek Settlement, Tyler County, (West) Virginia.

GASKINS, CDR. JAMES YOST, USN (RET.) – Born Oct. 30, 1947, Portsmouth, VA and resides in Jacksonville, FL.

James' military service includes: US Navy; Naval Air Station Kingsville, TX, HSL-36, HSL-30; HSL-36; Commander Helicopter Sea Control Wing Three, Air War College, Administrative Support Unit Bahrain, Training Air Wing Five, *USS W.S. Sims, USS Vreeland, USS Iowa*, retiring Sept. 1, 1994 from the US Navy.

He married Donna Sheri Gantt and they have two children and three grandchildren. James also worked for the State of Florida, Department of Juvenile Justice.

James belongs to the Sons of Confederate Veterans and is a Master Mason.

Hezekiah Wade was born April 13, 1754 at Frederick County, MD. Hezekiah first entered the Revolutionary War effort in April 1776 at Monongahalia County, VA as a Private and Indian Spy, serving variously under Captains Owen Davy, John Minor, John Lucas and James Cochran, for a period of at least 32 months. References: (A) Pension No. W6387 Service Record, National Archives Trust Fund Board; (B) District of Columbia Pension Roll of 1835; (C) "*The Wade Family*" published 8/15/1927, By Franklin Marion Brand of Morgantown, West Virginia Chapter XX ppg 308-314.

Hezekiah was a farmer until his death Nov. 23, 1834. He is buried at Fish Creek Settlement, Tyler County, (West) Virginia.

GASKINS, JOSEPH LEE – Born Sept. 14, 1976 in Portsmouth, VA. is presently a Trooper with the North Carolina State Highway Patrol. He also joined the SAR Dec. 5, 2007 in Florida.

Joseph and Jaymee Marie Hill Gaskins have one child. Joseph is a member of the Sons of Confederate Veterans.

Hezekiah Wade was born April 13, 1754 at Frederick County, MD. Hezekiah first entered the Revolutionary War effort in April 1776 at Monongahalia County, VA as a Private and Indian Spy, serving variously under Captains Owen Davy, John Minor, John Lucas and James Cochran, for a period of at least 32 months. References: (A) Pension No. W6387 Service Record, National Archives Trust Fund Board; (B) District of Columbia Pension Roll of 1835; (C) "*The Wade Family*" published 8/15/1927, By Franklin Marion Brand of Morgantown, West Virginia Chapter XX ppg 308-314.

Hezekiah was a farmer until his death Nov. 23, 1834. He is buried at Fish Creek Settlement, Tyler County, (West) Virginia.

GEISHERT, PHILIP L. – Born Apr. 6, 1944 in Rockford, IL. A graduate of the University of Illinois, he was commissioned in the U.S. Army in 1967. He first served in Minnesota with a follow-on tour in Vietnam. Upon his return to the United States in 1971, he married Marie Stanley, his wife of 38 years. In 1972, he was assigned to Germany where he held various Army Air Defense positions. They returned to the United States in 1976 and served four years at Fort Bragg, NC. In 1980, he served a year in Korea, returning to Fort Bliss, TX as the Deputy Director of Tactics at the U.S. Army Air Defense School. His final assignment was at the U.S. Army Recruiting Support Command, Alexandria, VA. He retired at the rank of Lieutenant Colonel in 1987.

In 1992, he became manager of the Washington Sailing Marina, a National Park Service facility in Alexandria, VA. Retiring from that position in 2004, he and Marie moved to Jacksonville, FL.

Philip has served as a member of the Military District of Washington Retiree Council; and a member of the board for the Leukemia Cup Regatta, a fund-raising arm of the Leukemia Society of America. He is a life member of the Military Officers' Association of America.

Philip became a member of the NSSAR, Florida Society, Jacksonville Chapter on Jul. 1, 2008 by descent from **Abraham Stoner** through the Wiles-Snively-Stoner branch of the family. Abraham, born in 1745 in Coventry, Chester, PA, was the son of German immigrants and the last born of 16 children. Abraham married Mary Ann Miller in 1765 and together they raised nine children of their own. In 1780, he served as a private in the Cumberland County, Pennsylvania Militia under the commands of Captain Daniel Clapsaddler and Colonel James Johnston. Abraham's brother, David, served in the same unit from 1780-81. Abraham died on Sept. 25, 1824 and is buried in the Stoner Graveyard near Welty Mill, southeast of Waynesboro, PA.

GIBSON, HARRY LEE – Born Dec. 18, 1932 in Shirley, Washington County, MO. He served in the US Army from Sept. 1953-July 1955, and later worked as a professor at Colorado State University in Fort Collins, CO, from 1966 to January 1990. He then worked as Director of Master of Business Program at Hong Kong Baptist University.

He is married to Anita Sue Gremore Gibson, and they have six children and 12 grandchildren.

Thomas Johnson was born about 1754, probably in Cumberland, PA. He served with the 1st Battalion, Cumberland County Militia under Capt. Alexander Peeples. A private, he also served under 1st Lt. Daniel Smith, 8th Batt., Jan. 1778, and Capt. John J. Company, 8th Batt. A farmer and land owner, he died in 1821 and is buried in Monroe County, WV.

GILBERT, JOE DELBERT – Born Joe Delbert Poole on Jul. 28, 1939 in Shannon, Floyd City, GA. He joined the SAR in Nov. 2008. Joe attended schools in Shannon, Plainsville, Calhoun, Oostanala, Tifton, and LaGrange, GA. Joe attended Massey College in Atlanta, GA also.

Joe joined the US Coast Guard at age 17 in 1957, serving in Cape May, NJ, New York, NY. He served aboard the US Coast Guard Cutter *Campbell* and Port Security in Philadelphia, PA. Joe and wife Virginia Helen Stuart (Jenny) live near Columbus, Georgia in Alabama.

Joe has three children, Kimberly Ann Titlton, Coleen Michele Brown, and Jason Patrick Gilbert, and five grandchildren, Michael Andrew Tilton, Jesse Allen Tilton, Ashley Nicole Brown, Ryan Patrick Gilbert, and David Wyatt Gilbert.

Joe worked with Alabama Kraft Paper Co. also known as Mead Paper Co., and then Mead Westvaco Paper Co. for 35 years before retiring in 2002.

He has three patriot grandfathers and one patriot grandmother who served in the American Revolutionary War. **Joseph** and Mary McCool Babb, husband and wife, have been proven patriots of the Revolution. **Mary McCool Babb** furnished supplies to the South Carolina Militia. A housewife, she died Jan. 3, 1816 and is buried at Babb-Kellett Cemetery in lower Laurens County, SC.

GRAHAM, STANLEY JAMES – Born Aug. 10, 1916 in Rock Springs, WY, joined SAR Aug. 21, 2006. Stanley enlisted into the Army in April 1941. He was with the 115th Cavalry Regt., honorably discharged at Fort Douglass, UT on Jan. 13, 1946 as Staff Sergeant. On Apr. 2, 1947 he married LaVeda May McIlvain (Apr. 2, 1925-Aug. 17, 2001). They have six children, 12 grandchildren and seven great-grandchildren. Five children are in SAR or DAR; six grandchildren are in SAR, DAR or CAR. Stanley worked for Mountain Fuel Oilfield Company and retired A-foreman after 34 years. Finding that he missed work, he worked for Cessna Aircraft, several oilfield companies, and then retired a second time with Bloomfield School District at age 83. He enjoys reading and braiding. He is a 4th great-grandnephew of George Washington.

Stanley James Graham

Fielding Lewis Sr. was born Jul. 7, 1725; died Dec. 7, 1781. He married Betty Washington, sister of George Washington on May 7, 1750. They had 14 children. Fielding was Colonel and County Lieutenant of the Spotsylvania Militia, elected to the House of Burgess. Fielding was the Chairman of the Virginia Committee of Safety in Spotsylvania Co., and established, at great personal expense, manufactory for arms and ammunition required by American forces. He was in charge of defense at Rappahannock, joint commissioner and financial supporter of Fredericksburg arsenal. Fielding died before seeing the end of the Revolution. His wife and children had to leave their home, Kenmore, and depend on help from friends, because they had put their fortune into the Revolution.

Colonel Fielding Lewis of Kenmore

GREEN, CHARLES E. – Born Nov. 25, 1933 in Haralson Co., GA. Following graduation from high school, 1951 in Anniston, AL, he worked in the Florida Everglades before joining the U.S. Navy. Following his resignation from military service, he attended the University of Alabama and graduated in 1962 with a degree in electrical engineering. He worked for Sperry Rand, designing electronic tubes for use in controlling missiles, and later worked for St. Regis Paper as a Corporate Engineer. He retired in 1998, after 32 years in the paper industry.

He joined the Georgia SAR Society in 2008, and also holds memberships in the Military Order of Stars and Bars and Sons of Confederate Veterans. He and his wife, Betty, are the parents of three children.

Jacob Greene was born in 1769 in Rutherford Co., NC and served with the South Carolina troops during the Revolutionary War. He died 1840-50 in St. Clair Co., AL.

John Taylor Duke Sr. was born in 1710 at Martins Brandon Parish, Prince George Co, VA. While his specific rank is unknown, the fact that he received three 287-1/2 acre bounty grants totaling 862.5 acres in Washington Co., GA indicate he was definitely an officer above the rank of captain.

GREENWOOD, DR. GORDON E. – Born Aug. 21, 1935 in Jasonville, IN and lives in Gainesville, FL. He has served as Reg. VP – No. Cent. Reg.; Chairman Rumbaugh and DAR Liaison committees; member of Amer. Heritage and membership P and R committee; and president of Gainesville chapter. He has received the Meritorious Service Award.

Gordon and Priscilla Normandy Greenwood have seven children and four grandchildren. Gordon served as Professor Emeritus, University of Florida and retired Jan. 1, 2001.

He also belongs to Order of Crown at Charlemagne; Baronial Order of Magna Charta; Descendants of Knights of the Bath. Gordon has 14 additional patriots: **Samuel Dyer**, **George Griffith**, **Conrad** and **Johann Heninger**, **George Hikes**, **Peter Hitt**, **Diana Allen** and **John James**, **Edward Jones**, **Abraham Kellor**, **John Netherton**, **Jacob Oldweiler**, **Lawrence Ross** and **Leonard Young**.

Philip Greenwood was born Nov. 28, 1755 in Frederick County, MD. He attained the rank of Private with Capt. Valentine Creigher's Company, Maryland Flying Camp and Militia. In 1776 he was at the battle at Trenton and in 1777 at Germantown where he was "slightly wounded" by grape shot passing by and grazing the left side of his head. Being "swift of foot" he ran away to Gen. Sullivan's lines when a British soldier tried to capture him. He received a military pension after the war.

After the war, he was a pioneer and blacksmith. Philip died Sept. 5, 1842 and is buried at Dutch Bethel Cemetery, Arney, Owen County, IN.

GREGORY, JAMES R. – Born March 31, 1948 in Hanford, CA, James joined SAR in November, 2007.

James was married first to Marjorie Wolf and second to Margaret Frazee. He has one child.

James was an agronomist with Verdegaal Brothers, Inc.

He was a Peace Corps Volunteer, Western Samoa 70-71, Hanford Breakfast Lions Club and is a Kings County Planning Commissioner.

Stephen Lewis was born August, 1749 in Stratford, CT, where he also died at the age of 90, in July 1839. He was the fourth generation Lewis to reside in Stratford, CT. He enlisted in 1775 as a private in Captain Ichabod Lewis's company. In the summer of 1776, he was a private and belonged to Captain Nathaniel Wheeler Militia Company in Stratford when the Company was ordered to go to the City of New York.

He was in Captain Abraham Brinsmade's company in 1777. He was stationed at Sasco Mill in the Town of Hanford on Long Island Sound, where he performed one month's service as a private. He turned out in 1779 when Tryon invaded the colony, and was at the burning of Fairfield. He was at both Danbury and Hanford for one week when they were burnt. In 1779 he belonged to the Militia which was commanded by Captain Stiles Judson of Stratford when he was drafted to help guard at a place called the Ferry in Stratford under the command of Lieut. John Whiting. He was placed on the pension roll as a veteran at the age of 84.

GRIFFETH, DAVID DWIGHT – Born Oct. 24, 1958, Athens, GA, he joined the Georgia SAR Society on Jun. 18, 2008. He is a mail carrier for the U.S. Postal Service, and also is a member of the Sons of Confederate Veterans and Military Order of the Stars and Bars. He has two children.

John Griffith was born 1744 in North Carolina. He was a private in the 1st North Carolina Regt., James Reed's Company, and was wounded-in-action at King's Mountain. A farmer, he died on Sept. 12, 1809 and is buried in Oglethorpe County, GA.

GRIMES, HUGH RUSSELL – Born July 11, 1931, at Carthage, MS. Joined SAR in January 2007, Marquis de Lafayette Chapter in Georgia.

Hugh was a Corporal with 1st Marine Division, UMSC.

Hugh and Betty S. Grimes have four children and 11 grandchildren. He was self-employed air conditioning contractor and retired in 1985. He is also a lifetime member of SCV and VFW.

Elizabeth Whitehead Grimes, and her husband Hugh Grimes, moved from Bertie County, NC to Duplin County, NC, where they settled on land in the Wolfscrape District in about 1752. Elizabeth, mother of James, Joseph and Sampson, is listed in *Women Patriots of the American Revolution: a biographical dictionary* by Charles E. Claghorn, and on the payroll voucher list from July 1783 to 19th of March 1784 for the Comptrollers Office as receiving pay vouchers for supplying provisions for the army. Elizabeth was one of the few women who was listed as a patriot. She died in Duplin County after 1784.

Hugh Grimes, son Hugh Grimes, Jr., and grandson, James Grimes at the graves of Elizabeth W. Grimes and James Grimes.

James Grimes Sr. born about November 1747 in Bertie County, NC, moved with his family to Duplin County, and died there in about 1831. James married Sarah Winders of Duplin County on Feb. 19, 1777. They were the parents of eight sons and four daughters. James served as a Private in the Duplin Co., NC militia. He received a land grant in Duplin County on Oct. 20, 1778 for his Oath of Allegiance and was plantation owner and wheelwright.

GRINGRICH, JACOB E. SR. – Born Feb. 13, 1925 in Dauphin County, PA. Jacob joined Harris Ferry Chapter, PA in May of 2001.

Jacob and wife Gloria Mae Nye Gringrich have five children and 12 grandchildren. He is the owner of Gringrich's Fruit Farm in Annville, PA.

Major Michael Forrer was born May 8, 1732 in Berks County, PA. He attained the rank of Major in 6th Battalion, Berks County. Michael was in battles at South Amboy, NJ and Flying Camp.

In civilian life, Michael was a farmer and Berks County Commissioner. He died Nov. 15, 1798 and is buried at Reeth Cemetery, Berks County, PA.

GROUT, GARY ROLAND – Born Nov. 26, 1933 at Redford, MI; served in the US Navy from 1951 to 1959, AA(0019), placed on inactive reserve in 1953 due to health.

Gary is married to Arline Ann Blount, who is a member of DAR. They were married 53 years and have three children, three grandchildren and one great-grandchild. Arline passed away on April 20, 2005.

Gary R. Grout

Gary was employed at Dearborn Lithograph, Livonia, MI, General Manager from 1993 to 2005 and in graphic arts with other firms. He retired in April 2005.

Gary is the author and producer of a historical video about Steamer Tashmoo and Harsens Island.

He also belongs to Sons of Union Veterans of Civil War, General Society War of 1812 and Algonac Clay Historical Society.

Abel Grout was born Feb. 19, 1758 at Petersham, MA. He enlisted at Templeton, MA on Aug. 15, 1775 in Col. Doolittle's Regiment and Capt. Fletcher's Company. He served for 4-1/2 months. The following September Abel went to war as a substitute for one Thomas Johnson in Col. Dana's Regiment and Capt. Boynton's Company and served in Tarrytown, NY. On Dec. 13, 1776 he again went to war as a substitute for Joel Grout and Abner Ward for the term of three months in Col. Sparhawk's Regiment and served in the State of New Jersey. Abel served for several other short periods at various places until the war ended. He served in "the place of Joel Grout his father" who was drafted in July of 1778. "Knew I Gen. Washington, Gen. Lee, Gen. Sullivan, Gen. Green, Gen. Ward, Col. Nims, Poor, Rand, Stark in New Jersey. Gen. Warner commanded the Brigade." From a deposition in the record made by John Mahan: "General Arnold left and went off to the enemy while we was there at West Point"(pension Record WS 18403). Abel, in his pension record, states that from Templeton he moved to Brattleboro, VT in 1781 where he remained until 1806 when he removed to Stratton, VT where he was living at the time he applied for his pension on 30 July 1832, age 74. Abel was a farmer and blacksmith. He died Jan. 1, 1841 and is buried at District #2 Cemetery, Stratton, VT.

Abel Grout gravesite.

GROVER, ROBERT L. – Joined SAR March 19, 1979, is life member of NSSAR, Missouri, Kansas. He is Past President (1999-2000) and National Trustee of the Missouri Society. Missouri Color Guard Commander.

South Central District Vice President General elect 2008-2009, past Color Guard Commander holds array of awards ranging from the Patriot Medal, State Medal of Distinguished Service, Meritorious Service Medal (4), Silver Good Citizenship Medal, Bronze Good Citizenship Medal (4), War Service Medal, Liberty Medal (4), Bronze, Silver and Gold Color Guard Medals, SAR Centennial Medal, George Wash-

Robert Grover

ington Bicentennial Medal. George Washington Fellow, C.A.A.H contributor.

Has served on Americanism, Carl Bessent Communication, Color Guard, Council of State Presidents, Historic Sites and Celebrations, Magazine Advisory, Membership and Reinstatement, Newsletters and Periodicals, Nominating, Patriotic Education form committees totaling 55 years.

Robert and Carolyn S. have four children and 11 grandchildren. He was employed at Ford Motor Co. - Utility Upgrader until retiring July 1, 1997.

Robert also belongs to Sons of Revolution, Sons and Daughters of the Pilgrims, War of 1812 in Minnesota, and Sons of Union Veterans.

John Grover was born Dec. 6, 1712, at Killingly, Windham Co., CT. He served as a Captain in Col. Webster's Regiment of Militia, Charlotte Co., NY. John died Sept. 17, 1806, Galpin Hill Cemetery, Fleming, Cayuga Co., NY.

GROW, GARRAN CHARLES – Born in Rapid City, SD, July 6, 1938; graduated from Parsons College, Fairfield, IA in May 1960; received a commission in the Marine Corps on Dec. 10, 1960 and designated a Naval aviator on May 22, 1962. He flew helicopters at the Marine Corps Air Station New River in Jacksonville, NC until his discharge in May 1965.

Garran C. Grow

In Nov. 1966, he accepted a direct commission in the U.S. Coast Guard to continue his flying career, retiring July 1, 1992 at the rank of Captain with over 32 years of active service and more than 4,000 hours flight time. While in flight school, he met and married the former Sallie Madison Baylor of Charles Town, WV. They have two daughter and two granddaughters. They currently reside in Mobile, AL.

Garran is a descendent of patriot **John Grow**, born May 9, 1750 in Pomfret, CT and married to Deborah Davison. On June 1, 1776, when he was 26 years old, married with three children, John enlisted in Captain Asa Bacon's company of Col. John Chester's Connecticut Regt. He fought in the battle of Long Island on Aug. 27, 1776, and was discharged after six months and 8 days for disability.

GRUGAN, GARRY ALAN – Born May 24, 1972 in West Chester, PA, Mr. Grugan is the son of Larry A. Grugan and Kathleen A. Doan. He is a graduate of the University of Iowa and Illinois Central College. Mr. Grugan is employed as a Fire Fighter/Paramedic for the City of East Peoria, IL. He is the Genealogist for the Illinois Society as well as Vice-President and charter member of the Captain Zeally Moss Chapter. Mr. Grugan is a member of the International Association of Fire Fighters and Associated Fire Fighters of Illinois Honor Guard. He is married to the former Amy S. Zircher and has four children: Emily, James (deceased), Maggie and Samuel.

Garry Alan Grugan

Patriot **Charles Grogan** arrived in Philadelphia from Northern Ireland in 1773 and settled in Lancaster County, PA. He served as Private, Pennsylvania Militia, Capt. John Rutherford's Co., Col. Robert Elder's Fourth Battalion in 1777 and was on the march to Philadelphia. Also, in 1778 with Capt. Andrew Stewart's Company of the 7th Class, Fourth Battalion, Lancaster County Militia and in 1779 as a Private with the "Paxtang Volunteers." Charles froze to death in Buffalo Valley, PA in the winter of 1790-1 and the surname of his children became Grugan.

HALL, ROBERT KEITH – Born March 21, 1954 at Fort Worth, TX. Inducted in Plano Chapter #37 SAR in July 2006. He has served as Plano Chapter President, 2008; Plano Chapter Historian, 2007-08; TXSSAR Color Guard, rank of Lieutenant in Nov. 2007; Chapter Color Guard Commander, 2009; Chapter C.A.R. Liaison, 2009. Served on the State Archive Committee, 2008-09. Dual member McKinney Chapter #63 and Denton Chapter #23.

Robert K. Hall

Robert and wife Patricia have one daughter, Cindy. He has a bachelor's degree in business from Wayland Baptist University. Robert worked as a supervisor at Texas Instruments in the Semiconductor Division as a Diffusion area Supervisor in Lubbock, Texas and Houston, TX for 25 years until he being placed on disability in 2004.

He also is a life member of the Sons of the Republic of Texas, Dallas Chapter and Sons of Confederate Veterans Camp 1588.

1st Sergeant Moses Allen born 1754 in Shenandoah Valley, VA, enlisted in Apr. 1776 at Fauquier Court House, VA. Fought with the 3rd Continental Virginia Regiment at the Battles of Brandywine, Germantown, Monmouth Courthouse, and The Siege of Charleston, where he was captured and spent 13 months on a British prison ship in Charlestown Bay until being traded for a British sergeant. After returning to Virginia, he was discharged for poor health in Mar. 1782. His War Record shows he served at Valley Forge from Feb.-Jun. 1778. After the war, Moses Allen married Martha Atwood on Feb. 13, 1783 and had six children. They moved to Lebanon, TN around 1820. Moses died Sept. 22, 1845 and Martha died Dec. 14, 1837.

HALSEY, HOBERT S. JR. – Born April 11, 1945 in Elkton, MD; joined SAR Maryland Society on Jan 23, 1992; has served as Chapter Treasurer, Vice President and President, and is the Head of the American Flag Certificate Program for the chapter. He worked as a fork lift driver for the Chrysler Corp, retiring July 31, 2001.

Hobert S. Halsey, Jr.

Hobert is a 32nd degree Master Mason with the York Rite Knights Templar, life member of the Honorable Artillery Co., Order of the Founders and Patriots of American Society of the War of 1812, Sons of Union Veterans, Sons of Confederate Veterans, and Royal Society of St. George.

He is married to Carol, and they have four children and four grandchildren.

Gravestone of William Halsey.

His patriot is **William Halsey Jr.**, born Mar. 23, 1760 in Columbia, NJ. He served with the Continental Line of New Jersey as a private, and fought at the battles of Brandywine, Bunker Hill, Ash Swamp, and Cowpens. He was a farmer. Williams died Feb. 21, 1832 and is buried in Piney Creek, Alleghany Co., NC.

Other patriots of Hobert are **Elijah Cole**, 1st Lt, Cecil Co., MD, and **John Vail** of Cecil Co., MD.

HARLEY, JAMES E. – Born in Orangeburg, SC, he joined the Thomas Taylor Chapter SAR on Nov. 5, 2007. He is a digital technician for AT&T, and is a member of Sons of Confederate Veterans, Friends of the Hunley, and the Camp Point Lookout Foundation. He is married to Misty Dawn Shotts Harley, and they have one child.

Joseph Harley III was born 1748 in Barnwell, SC and was a lieutenant in McCoy's South Carolina Militia. A plantation owner, he died in 1807 and is buried at Lower Three Runs Baptist Church in Barnwell, SC.

HARRIS, CHARLES DAVID – Born May 18, 1961 in Zwolle, LA; joined SAR Jun. 26, 2008. David's parents were missionaries to Africa. He lived in Ethiopia and Kenya from age 9 until 20 years old. When he came back to America, he went to college and worked as a pipe fitter. On Nov. 21, 1987, he married Zadeea Jean Graham in Arlington, TX; they have one son. In 1990 they moved to Bloomfield, NM. David began working for Flint Energy as a welder. He worked for Flint for 18 years. In 2008 he became Project Manager for MVCI Energy Services. David loves the outdoors, hunting, fishing, hiking, and playing guitar.

Charles David Harris

Moses Ball Sr. was born May 2, 1717 in Fairfax County, VA; died Sept. 3, 1792 in Fairfax Co. and buried in the Ball-Calvin Cemetery, Arlington Co., VA. He married Nancy Ann Brashear on Jun. 27, 1745. Civil Service Virginia, and signed the Fairfax Resolve. Moses was a neighbor to George Washington and a possible cousin through Mary Ball Washington, George's mother. Moses and George together surveyed the boundary between their properties in 1785.

HARRIS, LTC JOE E. JR. (RET.) – Joe was born Oct. 25, 1949 at Elkin, NC and joined SAR in 1997. He is a Past State President, North Carolina Society, 2005-2007.

Joe served in the Infantry, USA. He and wife Gail have three children - all males.

Joe is Executive Director, NSSAR.

During **Samuel Johnson's** lifetime, he repeatedly said that the gunshot wound to his body would have been fatal had it not been that for three days before the battle he had not eaten. Constantly on the move as they tracked the Loyalists to Kings Mountain, they did not stop and eat or rest. They consumed tack and water on the move. This deprivation resulted in the empty condition of his bowels and was therefore attributed to his escape from death and helped in a speedy recovery.

Samuel Johnson was married to Mary Hamon in Wilkes County June 25, 1782. Soon after their marriage they settled on the headwaters of the Roaring River in what is now Traphill, Wilkes County, NC. They lived out their lives there and are buried on the old home place, in what is now called the Old Newt Johnson Cemetery. Samuel Johnson was 77 years old at his death. The Johnsons produced nine children. The youngest, Rachel Walker Johnson, is my great-great-great Grandmother.

Various affidavits and testimonies on file in the Revolutionary War Pension files state, "Captain Johnson was known as a brave man, and most effective officer and soldier during the Revolutionary War. He was highly esteemed by the citizens of the country and entitled to distinguished consideration for his service."

HARRIS, STANLEY JOHN DAVID – Born Jul. 15, 1988 in Arlington, TX, joined SAR Nov. 13, 2006. David, a member of National Honor Society and graduated top 10 percent from Bloomfield High School, Bloomfield, NM, was a member of JROTC for four years, receiving the rank of Captain and was on Staff. He received the ROTC Scottish Rite Medal, NSSAR Medal and NSDAR Good Citizenship Medal. David was Organizing President for the Young Patriots Society NSCAR and was State President for New Mexico Children of the American Revolution in 2007. He has been attending San Juan College in Farmington, NM, and is a music major. He is an accomplished guitar player, enjoys old rock and roll, blues and classical music. He will be attending Texas Tech in Lubbock, TX in the fall of 2009. Besides David's love for music, he is an avid history buff. His expertise is Middle Ages warfare. David is proud of his heritage and family history. He is a 6th great-grand-nephew of George Washington.

Stanley John David Harris

Fielding Lewis Sr. was born Jul. 7, 1725; died Dec. 7, 1781. He married Betty Washington, sister of George Washington on May 7, 1750. They had 14 children. Fielding was Colonel and County Lieutenant of the Spotsylvania Militia, elected to the House of Burgess. Fielding was the Chairman of the Virginia Committee of Safety in Spotsylvania Co., and established, at great personal expense, manufactory for arms and ammunition required by American forces. He was in charge of defense at Rappahannock, joint commissioner and financial supporter of Fredericksburg arsenal. Fielding died before seeing the end of the Revolution. His wife and children had to leave their home, Kenmore, and depend on help from friends, because they had put their fortune into the Revolution.

Colonel Fielding Lewis of Kenmore

HARROP, DANIEL S. – Dr. Daniel S. Harrop 3rd, son of Dr. Daniel S. Harrop Jr. and Dorothy Jane Hickey, was born June 15, 1954, in Warwick, RI. He received a B. A. in Biology in 1976 and an M.D. in 1979, both from Brown University, and an M.B.A. from the Edinburgh Business School in Scotland. Professionally, he is a Clinical Assistant Professor of Psychiatry at the Warren Alpert Medical School of Brown University, where his area of teaching and research is in group therapy practice. He was formerly on the faculty at Harvard Medical School. Board-certified in adult and geriatric psychiatry, he is a past president of the Rhode Island Psychiatric Society, a member of the Medical Education Committee of the RI Medical Society, and a member of the Committee on Medical Quality of the American Psychiatric Association. He is President of the Brown Club of RI, President of the RI Catholic Medical Society, and Governor of the RI Branch of the Sons and Daughters of the Pilgrims. He is also a Grand Trustee of the Sigma Chi Fraternity and serves as a state officer in the Knights of Columbus and the Ancient Order of Hibernians. He currently serves as the Surgeon of the RI Branch of the SAR.

Jacob Rittenhouse, son of Garret Rittenhouse and Mary Bartleson, was born in Cresheim, Philadelphia Co., PA on Sept. 18, 1756. He enlisted in the American Revolution from Heidleberg, now in Lehigh Co., PA. He was a descendent of William Rittenhouse, who built the first paper mill in America, in Germantown, PA, and second cousin of David Rittenhouse, the first Director of the U.S. Mint and a Professor of Astronomy at the University of Pennsylvania. Jacob served about two years (1776-1777) as a private and drummer in the Pennsylvania Line under Captains Rader, Stahler, and Teal, and Colonels Geyer and Miller. He was listed as a communicant at the Heidelberg Union Church in Heidelberg, Northampton (now Lehigh), PA, in 1776. He was pensioned on Cert. No. 18.555, paid at Penna. Agency. He was among the pioneers that settled Sugarloaf Township Luzerne Co., PA. In 1808, he bought a gristmill in Sugarloaf from his cousin William Rittenhouse. He married Catherine Marie Salome Arner, daughter of Felix and Marian Aner (or Arner), immigrants from Switzerland, at Whitehall, Northampton, PA, on March 20, 1781. They had six children who lived to adulthood. He died on March 8, 1847 at Sugarloaf Twp., Luzerne Co, PA, at age 91.

HASBROUCK, THEODORE L. JR. – WWII Veteran and award-winning advertising executive for over 50 years, was born Dec. 2, 1924, in Centralia, IL to Theodore L. Hasbrouck Sr. and Lenna Marie Norton. He grew up in Peoria and Bloomington, IL and White Bear Lake, MN, and lived most of his adult life in Richardson and Mesquite, TX, having moved to the Dallas area in the 1940's to work in advertising.

During WWII he briefly attended the U.S. Merchant Marine Academy at Kings Point, NY and was transferred to San Mateo, CA, to complete his training before being immediately shipped out due to the war. Hasbrouck served in WWII as a Merchant Marine in the Pacific, participating at the Battle of Leyte gulf, in the Liberation of the Philippines and other key engagements. He was twice wounded while off-loading supplies for troops fighting on the beaches.

Ted Hasbrouck

After the war, he was active in the Merchant Marine Veteran's Association and assisted veterans in many ways. When confined to a wheelchair in 2004 after breaking a hip, he began trying to give others joy at the veteran's home in Bonham, TX-drawing and painting for veterans, families, and their children. In 2005, he began giving presentations and drawing cartoons for those in the Alzheimer's Unit to lift their spirits. For his efforts he received an award from the George Blakey Chapter, NSDAR, and the Volunteer Pin from the Texas State Veteran's Home. He helped design award-winning Christmas floats and enjoyed participating in Veteran's Day activities at the local high school.

As a child he was a gifted artist and attended the Chicago Art Institute. After the war, he went to work as an illustrator for Disney Studios. Several of his painting of WWII and post-war aircraft now hang in the Pentagon in Washington, D. C. His artistic and creative talents turned into a 50 year career in advertising and public relations-later becoming President of his own firm, BWA Advertising in Dallas, TX. His work was recognized with local and national awards including the Dallas Press Club Katy Award and the Cleo Award. He was known for creating big events and generating free publicity for clients.

Ted was a founding member of St. Paul the Apostle Catholic Church in Richardson, TX, and helped with publicity and fundraising. He was married first to Beverly Ann Murphy on Nov. 25, 1950 of South Bend, IN, and after she passed away on Nov. 29, 1979, he was married for the second time to Claudene Norris of Oklahoma in 1985, and lived in Mesquite, TX until her death in 2004.

"Texas Ted" Hasbrouck

Ted Hasbrouck, affectionately known as "Texas Ted" passed away June 18, 2007, after a lengthy illness. He is survived by his children Colleen Ann Hahn, and husband Earl, of Richboro, PA, Patricia Marie Martin, and husband Jim, of Richardson, TX, and Theodore Louis III, and wife Carol of South Charleston, SC, and grandchildren Christopher Michael Hahn, Jennifer Hahn, and Amy Colleen Hahn; and his step-children Cynthia Norris, and her daughter Ashley B. Norris, and Kimberly Norris Rainwater.

Hasbrouck was a member of the Dallas Chapter, National Society Sons of the American Revolution and the Texas Chapter, National Society Sons of Founders and Patriots of America.

Ted was descended from a long line of American founders and patriots including 16 Revolutionary War heroes. His ancestors Abraham Hasbrouck and Jean Hasbrouck were two of the original Patentees in the State of New York.

Joseph Hasbrouck Jr. was born Sept. 8, 1754 at Marbletown, Ulster County, NY. He was a Lieutenant in Capt. John Hasbrouck's Company, Ulster County Militia. Joseph died May 17, 1828 and is buried at Stoneridge, Ulster County, NY.

HATCHER, THOMAS C. – Thomas C. Hatcher, Ph. D, of 65 River Road, PO Box 369, War, WV (24892), (Telephone: 304875-2841) was born Aug. 6, 1939 in Iaeger, WV. Graduating from West Virginia University (B.S., M.A.) and The Ohio State University (Ph.D.), he was employed throughout his career as teacher, as Professor of Education at WVU, and as Secretary General of the Council of International Programs, an international exchange program for professionals, retiring in 1999, but continuing to serve as Mayor of the City of War, WV, from 1997-2009. He is a Co-Founder of the Clinch Mountain Militia (Tazewell County, VA) of VASSAR of SAR and has served as President, Registrar, and is the current Secretary. Active in community affairs, he has held leadership positions throughout his life in educational associations, in senior citizen groups, in historical and genealogical societies, in development organizations, in Kiwanis International, in his church, and has been active in fostering interests in citizenship, patriotism, community service, and religious commitment. He has been married and has three children and three grandchildren.

Thomas C. Hatcher

Lt. Rees Bowen, ca 1750- 1780, Lieutenant and Commander of a Virginia Regiment under Col. William Campbell, is one of his Revolutionary War ancestors. Lt. Bowen was killed at the Battle of King's Mountain and is buried there in an unmarked grave. Captain James Moore of the Virginia Militia, who also served under Col. William Campbell, is another ancestor. He is buried in Tazewell County, VA.

HAYES, WILLIAM CHARLES JR. – Born March 1938 in East St. Louis, IL. SAR membership registered on May 23, 2008 under National Number 171742 and Illinois Society 7970.

Memberships include - Life member of the Masons, Scottish Rite and Ainad Shriners (Past President of Ainad's Provost Guard and Uniformed Units). Life member of American Legion Post 365, Collinsville, IL. Endowment member of the NRA Life member of the St. Clair Co., IL Genealogical Society. Member of Erie Co., PA and Chautauqua Co., NY Genealogical Societies. Member of the Clan Morrison Society of North America.

William C. Hayes, Jr., 1960.

Retired May 31,2002 from the Federal Reserve Bank of St. Louis, Facilities Management Department, Chief Engineer with 21 years of service.

Military - Served on active duty in the U.S. Navy for ten years aboard submarines. Qualified in submarines aboard the *U.S.S. Sea Poacher SS 406* in 1956. After completion of Nuclear Power School, William was assigned in 1960 to the Gold Commissioning Crew ("Plank Owner") on the *U.S S. Abraham Lincoln SSB(N) 602* and made seven three-month patrols in the North Atlantic. Final duty on the *Lincoln* was IC1 (SS), LPO of the Nuclear Reactor Operator/Technician gang. Joined the Illinois Army National Guard in 1976, awards included the Army Commendation Medal. Retired in 1987 as the BN S2 intelligence MSG with 21 years total military service.

William married Patricia A (Rushing) Hayes and has six children (William, Pamela, Ronald, Steven, Donald and Judith) by former marriages and lives with Pat and her daughter, Christy in Collinsville, IL.

Joseph Barbee, born Feb. 7, 1761 in Orange County, NC. Joseph completed three tours of three months as a Dragoon in the North Carolina Line, commanded by Col. John Taylor and Capt. M. Patterson. Joseph died Oct. 3, 1826 in Christian County, KY. Joseph's wife, Sally (Trice), was granted a widow's pension (W 23522) while living in Marion Co., IL.

HAZEL, DAVID JOHN – Born Aug. 17, 1955 in Osaka, Japan. Joined the Virginia Society Fielding Lewis Chapter in 2006 (National number 167325) and was Secretary in 2008.

David and Laura Wilkinson Hazel have no children. David is self-employed.

Bennett Hazel was born about 1765 in St. Mary's County, MD. He served with the St. Mary's County Militia. After service, he was a farmer and died before May 29, 1813. He is buried in St. Mary's County, MD.

HELLUMS, LAWRENCE ALAN – Lives in Oxford MS. He also belongs to the Calhoun County (MS) Historical and Genealogical Society, Skipwith Historical Society, SCV, MOS and B.

Jonathan Clark was born May 20, 1759 in Campbell County, VA.

Jonathan was a Lieutenant in Capt. James Shepherd's Co., North Carolina Militia. Jonathan was in numerous skirmishes against Tories in the Yadkin River area of North Carolina. In civilian life, he was a farmer. He died March 12, 1851 and is buried in Clark Cemetery, Christian County, KY.

HENDERSON, STANLEY GEORGE – Born Oct. 31, 1935, Vancouver, Victoria Island, British Columbia, Canada. He became a naturalized citizen in January 1989. Offices held: CASSAR State Genealogist, 2007-08, 2008-09; CASSAR State President, 2004-05; Gen. Geo. Washington Chapter-CASSAR, Chapter President, 2000, 2001 and 2002.

He received the Florence Kendall Award in 2003 and the Carl F. Bessent Award in 2004. Has also received Distinguished Service Medal; Patriot Medal; Liberty Medal with several oak leaf clusters; War Service Medal; Bronze Good Citizenship Medal; Meritorious Service Medal; Bronze Color Guard Medal and State Color Guard Medal.

From 1952-58, Stanley served with US Army 82nd Airborne Division; 1959-62, US Army Reserves and 1962-65, US Army 11th Armored Cavalry.

Stanley G. Henderson with wife, Linda.

Stanley and Linda L. Henderson have three children and three grandchildren. Stanley was Vice President/ Director of Security, Sacramento Savings and Loan until retirement in 1992.

He also belongs to Phi Kappa Tau National Fraternity, American Philatelic Society, American Legion, Sons of the Revolution, Financial Crime Investigators Assoc.

Cornelius Linderman was born May 15, 1786 in Montgomery, NY. He served as a private in Capt. John Graham's Company, New York Militia. Cornelius was at the Battle of White Plains. He died Feb. 8, 1848.

Additional patriots for Stanley are: **Jacob Linderman**, **Jacob Brouwer**, **Coenradt Esselstyne**, **Nathan Hallet Sr.**, **Johann Michael Lampman**, and **Johan Christian Young**.

HENDRICKSON, SIR BENJAMIN S. III – Born Jan. 23, 1931 in Springlake, NJ; he joined the Arkansas Society SAR in 2002 and has served as Secretary/Registrar, State Finance Committee. SAR awards include the War Medal w/ Korean & Vietnam Bars (2003), Law Enforcement Commendation Medal (2003-04), Medal of Appreciation w/ Oak Leaf (2004), Good Citizenship Medal w/ Silver & Bronze Oak Leaves (2005-06), Meritorious Service Medal w/ 2 Silver Oak Leaves (2004-05), Service to Veterans Medal (2006), and the Distinguished Service Medal (2008).

He is a retired Lt. Col. USAF/CAP (July 1984), retired Psychotherapist/Hpnotherapist, and retired from the Arkansas Police Dept. in 2005. He is a member of over 28 professional, hereditary and civil associations. He has three children and three grandchildren.

His patriot ancestor is **Daniel Hendrickson**, who was born on Long Island, NY or in the Netherlands, date unknown. He fought with the District 6, 3rd Regt. Light Horse Company, attaining the rank of Colonel, and was at the battle of Sandy Hook. He worked as a sheriff and land surveyor.

He is buried in Middletown, Monmouth County, New Jersey.

HENDRIX, KENNETH DEAN – National number 111477; born March 1, 1933 in Harrisburg, PA. Kenneth joined the SAR on July 28, 1976.

SAR Awards: National – A Century of Commitment Medal with 3 Oak Leaf Clusters, 1989; New Jersey Society – The Patriot Medal – April 20, 1989; Elizabethtown Chapter No. 1 – Distinguished Service Medal.

Kenneth D. Hendrix

Kenneth's military service was in Yugoslavia for six weeks under General Water's command teaching ordnance logistics. His last post was at Seneca ordnance depot, unit 9374, Romulus, NY.

Kenneth's civilian employment consisted of 40 years as principal engineer and engineering manager of a major gas and electric utility.

Organizational membership included the Springfield, NJ Historical Society as member and former president.

Civilian awards received from Lehigh University were: The Alumni Award 2005; Senior Alumni Council Meritorious Service Award - March 2008; the Robert A. Harrier Reunion Award for Exemplary Service Supporting Reunions - May 2008.

Kenneth's wife, Dorothy M. Hendrix, nee Lapham, is deceased. They have a son, Brian, a daughter, Valerie Yacik and five grandchildren, Alina and Danika Yacik and Christopher, Creighton and Caroline Hendrix.

Hans Peter Menges, born June 10, 1731, was a Private, with Capt. Reinhart Botts 1st Company, 3rd Battalion, York County Militia. He came to America on the ship *Sarah and Mary* and took the oath of allegiance on Oct. 26, 1764.

Joshua Cromwell, born Dec. 8, 1744, was commissioned an ensign in the Anne Arundel County Battalion on Feb. 22, 1776 and 2nd Lieutenant in the 7th Battalion, Anne Arundel County Militia on April 11, 1776. He was born on Dec. 8, 1774 and died in 1793.

HENRY, JAMES RUSSELL – Born Feb. 14, 1940 in Athens, GA. Rev. Henry served in the Army, Reserves (inactive) as 1st Lt.

James and Nancy Ann Sinclair Henry have one child and one grandchild. He served as an Episcopal Priest, retiring February of 1998. He was also a mental health counselor, retiring in September of 2006.

James Russell Henry

James served churches in Georgia and Virginia; has Doctor of Ministry Degree from Virginia Theological Seminary and Med. Degree in Counseling.

He belongs to Association for the Preservation of Virginia Antiquities; W.A.R. Godwin Society, Colonial Williamsburg Foundation.

Andrew Barry was born 1746 in Pennsylvania. He served as Captain in the S. C. Partisan Rangers under Col. John Thomas' Spartanburg Regt.

Andrew was wounded at the battle at Musgrove's Mill, South Carolina and was at the Battle of Cowpens, South Carolina.

In civilian life, Andrew was a blacksmith and farmer. He died June 17, 1811 and is buried at the family cemetery, Moore, SC.

HEPLER, J. JEFFREY – Associate of Arts Degree 1985 from Lynn University, Boca Raton, FL; Docent, Historic Odessa Foundation; retired Flight Officer, DuPont Flight Operations; Airline Transport Pilot Rating.

J. Jeffrey Helper

Memberships include Sons of the Revolution and Forefather Member of The Swedish Colonial Society (having proven descent from Peter Jochimsson progenitor of the Yocum family), a native of Schlesvig-Holstein, Germany who arrived on the Delaware River/Valley on a crowded ship with Governor Johan Printz in 1643.

Jonas Yocom served as a Private 1st Class in PA Militia, Philadelphia Co. under Capt. Nathaniel Child, 1777-1780 and Capt. Jacob Witz (1781, PA Archives Series 6, Vol. 1, pp 796-7). Note: Jonas Yocom (b. 1744 d. 1823) and his two brothers John Yocom (b. 1752 d. 1818) and Peter Yocom were veterans of the Revolutionary War. Peter Yocom (b. 1750 d. 1836) served in the Pennsylvania line and received a Rev. War Pension (File No. S22616).

Daniel Maurer served as a Private 1st Class in PA Militia, Berks Co. under Capt. Valentine Houpt's Co. 1780-1782. Note: Daniel Maurer also served in Capt. Michael Shafor's Co. of PA Militia in Northampton Co. in 1785. PA State Archives listing of service from 1780-1782 (PA Archives Ser. 6, Vol. 3, pp 782-784).

Casper Hepler served as a Private 1st Class in PA Militia, Northampton Co. under Capt. Kooken and Lt. Col. Balliet, 5th Co. 1st & 2nd Batt. 1778-1782 (PA Archives 5th Series Vol. 8 pp 17, 48, 55 and 104).

Frederick Sowers (Sauers or Sours) enlisted into the Army of the United States as a Private in the fall of 1779 under Command Capt. Benjamin Roberts' Company of the Regt. Virginia Line commanded by Major (later Colonel) Slaughter's battalion for the western service and not long thereafter marched to the Falls of the Ohio River and joined General George Rogers Clark's Illinois regiment and served two years.

During his two-year enlistment he was stationed at Fort Nelson at the Falls of the Ohio River. Fort Nelson is present day Louisville, KY. It protected the center of Kentucky from Indians. Frederick's wife Ann Mary Roddolph and others have heard him speak of skirmishes with the Indians and knows that he came home when the War was over (she thinks in 1781).

On Oct. 11, 1781 he received the sum of $1,950 for his term of service. The Draft reads as follows:

"October the 11, 1781 Fort Nelson the Falls of Ohio

Sid please pay Unto Frederick Sowers the sum of Nineteen hundred & fifty Dollars for value received

By S-e Silas Bollar his
Silas X Bollar
To the pay M- of Colonel mark
Crocketts Regiment"

Frederick was discharged in the autumn of 1781 and returned to Shenandoah County. He married Ann Mary Roddolph on March 12, 1783 (recorded by Jacob Snider).

Frederick died on August 11 or 12, 1832 in Shenandoah County, which became (Page County) near the town of Luray, VA. On account of the military service of Frederick Sowers, Ann Mary Sowers was allowed pension on her application executed Oct. 24, 1836, at which time she was living in Page County, VA, and she then stated she was 70 years old. She was a resident of that county in 1843 when she stated she was 81 years of age. Ann Mary Rudolph-Sowers died in Page County Aug. 14, 1847. She was the last Revolutionary War pensioner in Page County, VA.

Source: Pension claim, W. 6144 based on Revolutionary war service of Frederick Sowers. Mary Sowers received a widow's pension of $80.00 per annum. *George Rogers Clark and His Men Military Records, 1778-1784* by Harding, pp 82 and 86 lists Private Frederick Sowers.

Captain George Printz (Prince) was a Captain during the Revolutionary War. On Oct. 11, 1780 he was promoted to Captain, in the Shenandoah County Militia signed by Governor of Virginia: Thomas Jefferson.

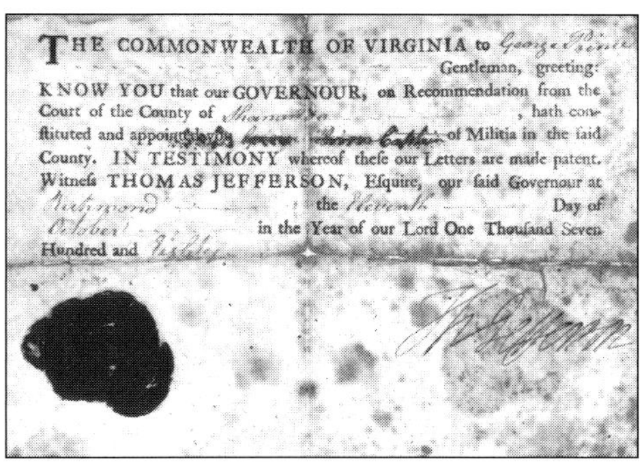

THE COMMONWEALTH OF VIRGINIA to George Prince Gentleman, greeting:
KNOW YOU that our GOVERNOUR, on Recommendation from the Court of the County of Shenando, hath constituted and appointed you Captain of Militia in the said County. IN TESTIMONY whereof these our Letters are made patent. Witness THOMAS JEFFERSON, Esquire, our said Governour at Richmond the Eleventh Day of October in the Year of our Lord One Thousand Seven Hundred and Eighty.

"The Commonwealth of Virginia to George Prince. Gentleman, greeting: Know You that our Governour, on Recommendation from the Court of the County of Shenando, hath constituted and appointed you George Prince Captain of Militia in the said County. In Testimony whereof these our Letters are made patent. Witness Thomas Jefferson, Esquire, our said Governour at Richmond the Eleventh day of October, in the Year of Our Lord One Thousand Seven Hundred and Eighty."

George Printz's name also appears on a list of General Nelson's Corps of Virginia Light Dragoons (List dated Baltimore, July 29, 1778. Source: National Archives of The United States. Microfilm Publication M881 Roll 1087).

Captain George Printz, was an aide to General George Washington. He was in command of a militia that served at the battle of York. Captain Printz, was one of the officers that was present at the surrender of General Cornwallis at Yorktown in 1781.

George Printz was granted 160 acres of land, for his services in The Revolutionary War. The 160 acres of land was located near Canton, OH. It was secured to him by letters of patent dated July 18, 1812, signed by President James Madison.

On Captain George Printz tombstone is inscribed, "Aide to General Washington." At the Valley Forge Memorial Bell Tower dedicated by the NSDAR, Captain George Printz name is inscribed on a brass plate.

HEYER, JOHN HENRY – Born Rochester, NY, May 4, 1946; admitted to bar, 1973, Colorado; 1976, New York; 1979, Pennsylvania; 1982, U.S. Supreme Court; 2003, Law Society of England and Wales.

Education: University of Colorado (B.A., 1969); University of (J.D., 1972).

Author: *Environmental Regulation of Oil and Gas Drilling Operations* 6 Eastern Mineral Law Institute, 1985; *Liability Risks of Free Gas Clauses*, 8 Eastern Mineral Law Institute, 1987; *New York Oil and Gas Statutes*, 1 Volume, 1986. Co-Author: *Real Estate Tax Sales and Mineral Titles*, 11 Eastern Mineral Law Institute, 1990.

Assistant District Attorney, Cattaraugus County, 1978-1981. Director, 1982-; Secretary, 1987; Vice-President, 1988-; Chairman, Legislative Committee, 1988-, Independent Oil and Gas Association of New York.

Member: Erie County, Cattaraugus County Secretary-Treasurer, 1997; Vice President, 1998, President, 1999) and New York-State Member, Sections. on: Real Property Law, 1982-) Bar Associations; Energy and Mineral Foundation (Trustee-at-Large, 1984-; Reporter, Case Update, 1985- 1995); Selden Society.

John and wife Alenka M. have four children and four grandchildren.

John Hyer was born Oct. 29, 1752 in Freehold, NJ. He was a private in Capt. Van Cleef's and Carhart's Companies, Col. Holmes' Regt., Monmouth County Militia.

In civilian life, John was a farmer and weaver. He died June 24, 1832 and is buried at Old Red Meeting House Yard in Holmdel, NJ.

HIGGINS, ROBERT CHARLES – Born Feb. 9, 1938 in Newark, NJ; member of Jockey Hollow Chapter (#6940) since Feb. 26, 2001 (Nat. #155413). He served for six years in the New Jersey Army National Guard, 50th Armored Div., 5th Recon, SGT-E5, and worked for 20 years in the New Jersey State Police, retired Mar. 1, 1989 and formed the Skylands Detective Agency (Private Detective).

Sgt. Robert C. Higgins, NJ State Police.

He is a member of the Former Troopers Assoc. of New Jersey and the New Jersey Licensed Private Investigators Assoc.

His patriot ancestor is **Ebenezer Phillips III**, born Feb. 23, 1752 in Grafton, MA. He was a minute man (Sgt.) serving with Col. Jon Ward's Regt. in Capt. L. Drury's Co., and was engaged in the Battle of Bunker Hill, MA. He died June 5, 1834 in Grafton, MA.

HIGGINSON, JERRY ALDEN JR. – Born July 21, 1957 in Mt. Vernon, IL. He joined SAR on Sept. 24, 2007 and has served as the Treasurer and President of the San Antonio Chapter, Texas Society. He has received the Bronze Chapter Service Medal and the Bronze Good Citizenship Medal. Professionally, he is the President/CEO of Greater Randolph Area Services. He is also a member of the Mayflower Society and Alden Kindred of America.

He is married to Leah, with two children.

His patriot ancestor is **Elisha Alden**, born Nov. 15, 1745 in Stafford, CT. He was a Lt. in the militia. Elisha died Mar. 3, 1826 and is buried at Stafford Cemetery in Stafford, CT.

HILL, MARVIN JOSEPH – Joined SAR in 1987. His Illinois State Society service includes President of the General George Rogers Clark Chapter, State Treasurer, and State President. his national offices includes Great Lakes District Vice President General, National Trustee for six years and alternate Trustee for two years. He has served on 12 committees including being elected a member of the George Washington Endowment Fund Board for a four-year term. He was Chairman of the George Washington Endowment Fund Distribution Committee for five years. He became a Minute Man in 2005.

Dr. Katherine Hill-Miller, Genevieve Bytner Hill, and Marvin Joseph Hill.

Joe carried the Illinois flag while wearing his Color Guard uniform when he escorted Russ and June Page as they were presented to SAR members just prior to Russ' inauguration as President General in 1998. Joe has been presented many State and National awards.

Joe has been married for 60 years to Genevieve Bytner Hill. They have one daughter, Dr. Katherine Hill-Miller; one grandson, Christopher Miller; and son-in-law Frederic Alling Miller. Joe is a retired Chemical Engineer and an Illinois Licensed Professional Engineer.

William Denham was born in Perth Amboy, NJ, in 1745 and died in Pulaski Co., KY in 1820. He donated land for the Fishing Creek Baptist Church and Cemetery in Kentucky. During the construction of Cumberland Lake, the Church was moved and reconstructed and still exists. Denham's body was moved by the U.S. Corps of Engineers to an unmarked grave in a cemetery in

Ringold, KY. William Denham donated necessary supplies for the Revolutionary War.

HILL, RONALD GUY SR. – Ron was born in Andrews, Cherokee County, NC. He received his formal education at; the University of Nebraska in Omaha and the Industrial College of the Armed Forces in Washington, D.C.

Ron enlisted in the United States Army in 1952 and is a veteran of three wars; the Korean War, Vietnam War and Desert Storm. He retired Dec. 31,1973 from the Office of the Deputy Chief of Staff for Military Operations, Headquarters, Department of the United States Army, the Pentagon, Washington, D.C.

Ronald G. Hill, Sr.

On Jan. 3, 1974 he was employed as Human Resources Director at Alston, Miller and Gaines, the oldest and most prestigious law firm in the southeast in Atlanta, GA. From November 1974 to 1981, he was County Manager, Cherokee County.

Ron was recruited in 1981 and served until 1985 as Site Manager of a U.S. corporation providing some 300 staff and faculty to the largest senior Kingdom of Saudi Arabia military school, teaching English, advanced courses in electronics, computer science and military management at Taif, Saudi Arabia.

In 1985, Ron became the first native born to become the Director of the John C. Campbell Folk School located in Cherokee County.

In February 1991, By order of the Secretary of the United States Army. Ron was ordered to active military duty from retired status, for service in support of operation Desert Storm until August 1991.

In September 1991, he was recruited by officials of the State of Mississippi for a five year development contract. Ron was the Founding Director of the Allison Wells School of Arts and developed a small business incubator center for Artists. Concurrently; he served as project coordinator for the total restoration of many historical buildings on the square in downtown Canton, MI.

In 1996, after a remarkable career of 44 years of progressive military, local, regional, national and international executive management experience, he retired. They sold their 140 acre farm and home in Cherokee County and built their present home on their farm in Sautee Nacoochee, GA. Since 1999. he has devoted daily research work to his family genealogy and history. As of 2007 more than 22,000 kin are in his family listings. He coordinated the first Charles Hill (born 1776) family reunion, held on Sept. 11, 2004 in Highlands, NC. Numerous descendants came from all across the United States.

On Nov. 15, 1955 in Blue Ridge, GA, Ronald married Shirley Hendrix, born in Ballground, Cherokee County, GA. Their children are Ronald, Jr., Rebecca and William.

Pvt. Adam Cooper, was born in Chester County, Oxford township, PA, February 1760. Adam Cooper, the younger, moved to Western North Carolina sometime in the late 1770's. Adam was one of the "Overmountain Men" who fought in the American Revolution. He enlisted in a unit under Colonel Isaac Shelby in Sullivan County, NC (now Tennessee).

A letter from Colonel Isaac Shelby states: "Adam Cooper was a soldier in the Regiment which I commanded, from Sullivan County, in the state of North Carolina, against the British and Tories in the War of the Revolution, and that the said Adam Cooper was severely wounded, inhumanly cut to pieces and taken prisoner by the British Dragoons in an action fought at a place called Cedar Springs, twenty five or thirty miles south of the Cherokee ford of Broad River, in the state of South Carolina, in the beginning of August 1780. That I saw Cooper near two years after the said action, when he appeared to me to be greatly maimed and debilitated from the wounds he had received and rendered unable to procure a livelihood by his labor. I have always believed him justly entitled to a liberal support from his Country." Dated February 12, 1825 and signed Isaac Shelby.

After the Revolution, Adam Cooper moved to Fairview, (now Buncombe County, NC) by at least 1783. He was one of the first settler's of Buncombe County.

Despite being handicapped, Adam Cooper was among the first citizens of the newly formed Buncombe County, NC to serve in a number of official capacities. He also served as tax collector for Buncombe County and carried money to Morganton, NC accompanied by a pet bear and two big dogs. On Oct. 1, 1795 he married Elizabeth Forgay and they raised a family of six children.

Adam Cooper; headstone "Adam Cooper a Revolutioner departed this fife April 27, 1830 whose memory shall be held sacred as long as honor or gratitude live amount men;" Cane Creek Cemetery, Buncombe County, NC.

HINKLEY, RAYMOND W. – Born Dec. 28, 1949 in Mount Kisco, NY, he is a central office technician for Verizon Communications. He is also a member of the Katonah Fire Dept. (Chief from 1980-82), and is a troop committee member for Boys Scouts of America Troop 1 in Katonah. He is married to Patricia M. Hinkley, with two children and five grandchildren.

Sands Raymond Sr. was born 1730 in Norwalk, CT. He was a 2nd Lt. in the Westchester County Militia, 2nd Regt. He is thought to have fought at the Battle of White Plains, NY. A farmer, he died Jul. 20, 1803 and died in South Salem, NY.

HINNANT, JOHN LESLIE – A 6th generation native of Texas, was born in Houston on Aug. 13, 1939, 19 days before Adolph Hitler started WWII with the invasion of Poland on Sept. 1, 1949.

The firstborn child of Reagan Cox Hinnant and Mary Louise Zimmerman, John's American Revolutionary War Patriot Ancestor is **William Hinnant**. William, the son of John Hinnant, was born and raised in the area that was formed into Edgecombe County, NC, 1729, and served as a Justice of Peace for Johnston County in the colony of North Carolina. He died in 1801 in Johnston, NC.

John Leslie Hinnant

Except for working in Mexico for two years, John has lived his entire life in Texas. A graduate of North Texas State University, 1963, he was the first member of his generation of Texas Hinnants to receive a college education. The Bachelor of Science degree enabled him to work in various industrial jobs, as well as teaching high school level manufacturing procedures and CAD-developed Engineering Graphics. He retired from the active work force in June 2005.

In addition to John's membership in the SAR, he is also a member of the Sons of the Republic of Texas. His great interest in American history was inspired by his grandfather, John Henry Hinnant, a Texas Ranger, 1903-06, and great-grandmother Mary Anne Adams Hinnant, who passed in 1964 at age 108.

Since retiring, John spends much of his time researching the details of the life of his ancestors. He is married to Sharon Anne Lothringer DeMasters Hinnant.

HINZMAN, JOEL PATRICK – Born Aug. 9, 1970 at Silver Spring, MD, presently living in Arlington, VA.

Joel is the Director of Federal and Legislative Affairs at Oracle. He has served as Professional Staff Member in the US House of Representatives Committee on Veterans' Affairs, and Committee on House Administration. He has also served as a schedule-C presidential political appointee at the US General Services Administration. He is engaged to Miss Jennifer Anne Cetta.

Joel is a member of Sons of the Revolution, Sons of Union Veterans, Sons of Confederate Veterans, St. Andrew's Society of Washington, DC, the Royal Society of St. George, Sovereign Military Order of the Temple of Jerusalem.

Henry Hinzman originally came to the colonies as a member of the Hesse Cassel regiments employed by the British, specifically as a member of the von Losberg regiment, Hessian-Oldendorf Grenadier in the 34d Grenadier Company of the regiment. He was captured in Washington's attack on Trenton, NJ and while in interment, converted to the American cause.

Henry served as a Private in Captain William Gray's Company of Fourth Pennsylvania Regiment; Colonel Daniel Heister Jr.'s Battalion of Philadelphia County Militia and Seventh Company of Philadelphia Militia Artillery. He was in the Battles of Brandywine, Germantown and Monmouth and the Sullivan Expedition. He was wounded three times.

Henry was a farmer in civilian life. He died Dec. 26, 1827 and is buried at Hinzman Hill Cemetery near Berlin, WV.

HISERMAN, RONALD W. – Born July 25, 1944 at Waynesboro, VA. Joined SAR in August 2007 (No. 169752). He has served as Historian, General Daniel Morgan Chapter.

Ronald served in the US Navy/PN3 and is a Vietnam Veteran. He has received the Vietnam Veteran Service Medal.

Ronald W. Hiserman

Ronald retired in July 2005 and is married to Sharon B. Hiserman.

He is a member of the Waynesboro, VA Disability Service Board, Shenandoah Valley Art Center, Active Member of Main Street UMC, Sons of the Confederate Veterans, and Eagle Scout.

Brightberry Brown was born Feb. 13, 1762. His parents were Benjamin Brown, Sr. and Sarah Thompson Brown. He was the youngest son of twelve or thirteen children.

Although Brightberry was very young at the time of the Revolutionary War, he came up though the ranks starting as a Private and then on to Sgt. Major and then Captain. He was a volunteer in the cavalry (*Histories and Genealogies,* W. H. Miller, 1907). It is reported that he became a captain under Henry (Lighthorse) Harry Lee's command. He served with Ninth Virginia Regiment and served to periods in the conflict with England.

Soon after he was married on Jan. 10, 1788 to Susan Thompson and became parents of eight children.

He was an engineer and inventor of the highest order for that time. He built "Headquarters" in Brown's Cove, which is still standing and beautifully restored. Another of his engineering feats was the surveying and construction of the road from Brown's Cove to the top of the Blue Ridge Mountains and into the Shenandoah Valley. For a century this was the main route to Charlottesville. He died in 1846 at the age of 84 and is buried in his family plot near "Headquarters."

HOGAN, CLEO G. – Born 1946 at Clarksville, TN, younger son of Byron Gordon Hogan (1905-1989), a tobacco farmer and Latha Haynes Hogan (1907-1991), housewife. Cleo studied by kerosene lamp and graduated from Clarksville High School in 1964, and Austin Peay State University in 1968, with double majors in Mathematics and Physics. He then enlisted in the US Air Force and completed a year's graduate study in Meteorology at the University of Michigan, and was commissioned a weather officer, serving from 1968-1978. He was the chief organizer of the Greater Omaha Genealogical Society in Nebraska in 1976 and the Old Buncombe County Genealogical Society in Asheville, NC in 1979.

Cleo G. Hogan

In Omaha in 1976, Cleo married at First Unitarian Church, Donna Bankey Cesta, a US Navy veteran, who was born in Syracuse, NY but grew up in southern California. From 1977 to 1984, Cleo was a Meteorologist in Asheville, NC, where his only child, Melissa was born in 1982. Moving to Memphis, TN in 1984, Cleo graduated from law school at the University of Memphis in 1987, and took a position at a law firm in his hometown of Clarksville, TN where he became a partner in 1994 in the law firm presently known as Harvill, Ross, Hogan and Ragland.

Cleo joined the Andrew Jackson Chapter, SAR, Nashville, TN in 1969. He served as Secretary-Treasurer of the Blue Ridge Chapter, Asheville, NC while living there, and received the Bronze Membership plaque for enlisting new members in that chapter. A veteran of the Vietnam War Era, he was awarded the SAR War Service Medal. He was among those members chartering the Valentine Sevier Chapter, Clarksville, TN and the Christopher Strong Chapter, Charlotte, TN. He is a member of the Colonial and Antebellum Bench and Bar, and the Sons of Confederate Veterans.

Since 1987, Cleo has resided at his birthplace, Hogan Century Farm, Clarksville, TN.

Colonel John Hogan (ca 1745-ca 1810) was probably born in Virginia, and probably died in Montgomery Co., TN or Orange Co., NC. He is first found as a witness to a deed in Orange Co., NC in 1762, and is spoken of as "deceased" in an 1810 deed in Montgomery Co., TN.

He ran a store in Hillsborough, NC before the War of Independence. He married about 1770 Mary Lloyd, daughter of Colonial Major Thomas Lloyd of Hillsborough, NC. Hogan was elected Colonel of the Minute Men of Orange Co., NC in 1775, and was paid for 32 days' service as a Partisan Ranger, under Col. Richard Caswell, and is in the list of participants at the Battle of Moore's Creek Bridge, NC, in 1776. He was Chairman in 1776 of the Orange County Safety Committee, a Justice of the Peace in 1777, Orange County Trustee in 1778, and State Senator in 1779.

Col. Hogan owned ten slaves by the 1790 census, and was among the first donors of 200 acres of land to establish the University of North Carolina at New Hope Chapel Hill in 1792. He contracted to make the bricks that his son-in-law, John Kimble, used to build the "Old East" building that is the oldest standing State University building in the United States.

In 1795, Col. Hogan moved to Brush Creek, Tennessee County, Territory South of the River Ohio, where he settled with several of his married children on a 1,047 acre plantation he had purchased in two tracts from Abraham Allen of Orange County. In 1796, this land became Montgomery County, TN. No stone marks his burial site in the Hogan cemetery that remains on that land. Family tradition suggests he may have returned to Orange County before his death.

HOLDER, PAUL B., CDR. USN (RET) – Born Mar. 24, 1947 in Seattle, WA and has served as his SAR chapter vice president. He served in the U.S. Navy for 24 years, attaining the rank of Commander (retired in 1993), and taught in the Corpus Christi Independent School District, retiring in 2007. He is a member of the Military Officers Assoc. of America, the Military Order of World Wars, and the Navy League.

He is married to Theresa Ann Holder, with three children and three grandchildren.

Peter Youngblood was born 1732 in SC. He was a Captain in the Colleton Co. SC Militia, and fought in the Reduction of Charleston. A farmer, he died in 1786 and is buried in Abbeville, SC.

HOLLOWAY, DR. E.W. JR. – Born Nov. 6, 1932 in Americus, GA, he joined the GA Society SAR on Jun. 18, 2008. He served in the U.S. Navy, Korean War, HM2, and later worked as an MD (Radiologist), retiring in Aug. 2007. He is married to Virginia, with four children and two grandchildren.

James Prather was born 1729 in Prince Georges Co., MD. A farmer, he died on Jul. 22, 1791 in Prince Georges County, MD.

HOOS, E. LOU – Lou and his wife, Marty, reside in Grand Rapids, MI. They have three children, i.e. Jennifer Hoos Rubenstein, Stephanie K. Hoos and M. Bradley Hoos. Their children are members of the DAR and SAR respectfully. Lou is an Attorney and Counselor at Law in Grand Rapids, MI and a retired Navy Captain, and Marty is an elementary school teacher. Hoos became a member of the SAR on August 14, 1997 through Lieutenant Colonel Joab Houghton and two Supplementals through Aaron Houghton and William Golden. Compatriot Hoos has been Chapter President of West; MISSAR Chancellor, and President; NSSAR Trustee, and Vice President General. He has served as MISSAR Chairman of the following Committees: JROTC-ROTC; Nominating; Resolutions; Veteran's; Medals and Awards; Revolutionary War Patriot's Memorial and a Committee member of: Law Enforcement; Membership, Emeritus; Resolutions, Board of Managers; Boy Scouts; Fundraising; and JROTC/ROTC. Lou is member of NSSAR Committees: Veterans; ROTC/JROTC; Partners in Patriotism; Americanism; Council of State Presidents; and Council of Vice President's General. Lou is a member of American Legion; VFW; Vietnam Veteran's; Naval Order of US; Military Order of Foreign Wars; Sovereign Military Order of the Temple of Jerusalem; Mason; Shriner; Sojourners; War of 1812; SOUVCW; and MOLLUS. He was awarded: Bronze Good Citizenship Medal; Silver Good Citizenship Medal; Meritorious Service Medal; Liberty Medal; Distinguished Service Medal; Council of State President's Medal; Patriot Medal; and War Service Medal.; (2) Certificates of Distinguished Service; (6) Certificates of Appreciation; (2) Certificates of Distinguished Leadership and VPG Appreciation Award.

Lieutenant Colonel Joab Houghton, was born July 10, 1725, in Hopewell, New Jersey, and died October 17, 1798 in Hopewell, New Jersey. He is buried at the Old Baptist Church Cemetery in Hopewell, New Jersey.

Houghton was among the first appointments of Field Officers made by New Jersey for the Continental Army, raised for the Army of the United Colonies. Houghton received his commission as a Captain in the First New Jersey Regiment, October 19, 1776.

Lt. Col. Houghton commanded the first New Jersey Regiment in the Brigade of General Nathaniel Green. Lt. Col. Joab Houghton was with General George Washington at the Battles of Long Island, Harlem Heights, and Hoyt Plains, New York, Trenton and Princeton, German Town, and Monmouth Courthouse in New Jersey. In December 1776, Captain Joab Houghton crossed the Delaware River with General George Washington to surprise the British Brigade.

"He was a brave officer, greatly loved by his men, and served with distinction all through the War" ... as stated by Revolutionary Historian Ralph Ege.

Aaron Houghton was born April 15, 1761 in Hopewell, New Jersey and died October 8, 1835 in Menard County, IL. He was a private, 1st Regiment, Hunterdon County Militia, under Captain Joab Houghton (his father) and Lieutenant William Parke. He participated in The Battle of Long Island, New York, Harlem Heights, White Plains, New York and Monmouth Courthouse. He served in the Revolutionary War four years.

William Golden was born Oct. 7, 1743, in Hopewell, NJ. He was a Revolutionary War Soldier and enlisted as a Private in Captain William Tucker's Company, 1st Regiment NJ Continental Army and served for the duration of the War. After the War, he became a Captain in the New Jersey Militia. Captain William Golden died on Feb. 10, 1816 and is buried in the old Golden Cemetery at Hillside Farm now owned by Johnson and Johnson (Hart Ave and State Route 518). William Golden's three brothers were also soldiers in the Revolutionary War.

HOOS, M. BRADLEY – Born on May 25, 1978, in Grand Rapids, MI. Graduated from Michigan State University with a Bachelor of Science Degree in Environmental Engineering. He obtained his Master's Degree in Environmental Engineering from the University of Iowa. Presently he is in the MBA program at the University of Chicago and will graduate in June 2008. Brad joined the SAR on Feb. 18, 1998 and is a member of the Michigan Society and the West Michigan Chapter, (NSSAR No. 149804 and MISSAR No. 3034).

Lieutenant Colonel Joab Houghton, was born July 10, 1725, in Hopewell, New Jersey, and died October 17, 1798 in Hopewell, New Jersey. He is buried at the Old Baptist Church Cemetery in Hopewell, New Jersey.

Houghton was among the first appointments of Field Officers made by New Jersey for the Continental Army, raised for the Army of the United Colonies. Houghton received his commission as a Captain in the First New Jersey Regiment, October 19, 1776.

Lt. Col. Houghton commanded the first New Jersey Regiment in the Brigade of General Nathaniel Green. Lt. Col. Joab Houghton was with General George Washington at the Battles of Long Island, Harlem Heights, and Hoyt Plains, New York, Trenton and Princeton, German Town, and Monmouth Courthouse in New Jersey. In December 1776, Captain Joab Houghton crossed the Delaware River with General George Washington to surprise the British Brigade.

"He was a brave officer, greatly loved by his men, and served with distinction all through the War" ... as stated by Revolutionary Historian Ralph Ege.

Aaron Houghton was born April 15, 1761 in Hopewell, New Jersey and died October 8, 1835 in Menard County, IL. He was a private, 1st Regiment, Hunterdon County Militia, under Captain Joab Houghton (his father) and Lieutenant William Parke. He participated in The Battle of Long Island, New York, Harlem Heights, White Plains, New York and Monmouth Courthouse. He served in the Revolutionary War four years.

William Golden was born Oct. 7, 1743, in Hopewell, NJ. He was a Revolutionary War Soldier and enlisted as a Private in Captain William Tucker's Company, 1st Regiment NJ Continental Army and served for the duration of the War. After the War, he became a Captain in the New Jersey Militia. Captain William Golden died on Feb. 10, 1816 and is buried in the old Golden Cemetery at Hillside Farm now owned by Johnson and Johnson (Hart Ave and State Route 518). William Golden's three brothers were also soldiers in the Revolutionary War.

HORTON, FRANKLIN NELSON – Born Sept. 24, 1937, Hope, Hempstead, AR. He joined SAR May 17, 1993. He has been NC State Sr. VP 2007-Present, NC State Sec. 2003-2007, Past President, Le Marquis de Lafayette Chapter, Fayetteville, NC.

Franklin has received Bronze Good Citizenship, State Meritorious Service Medal, Patriot Medal, Liberty Medal (2 awards), Bronze Color Guard Medal, and Certificate of Appreciation.

He served as LTC, USA, Ret. Infantry/Adjutant General Corps.; Awarded: BSM (4th OLC), ARCOM (2 OLC), US Army MSM, Defense MSM, Air Medal, RVN Cross of Gallantry with Palm and Star, Combat Infantryman's Badge, Master Parachutist Badge, Ranger Tab.

Franklin and wife Joan (Dodd) have three children and two grandsons, both Jr. Members. He is a Driving School Owner/Instructor. Franklin retired from the Military Dec. 1, 1981.

He also belongs to NC Society of Mayflower Descendants (Deputy Governor), Sons of the Revolution (Past President), Society of the War of 1812, Military Order of the Stars and Bars, Sons of Union Veterans of the Civil War, Sons of the confederate Veterans. He has 20 proven Revolutionary ancestors. Some are:

James Bushnell, born Nov. 21, 1762, Saybrook, CT; died Dec. 3, 1858.

LTC Johann Peter Wagner, born Jan. 8, 1722, probably Stone Arabia, NY. Served as Lieutenant colonel in Klock's German Militia Regiment from the Mohawk Valley. Was at the battle at Oriskany Creek.

Joseph Barber, served in Herrick's Regiment.

Sergeant Timothy Munson, 8th Company, 5th Continental Regiment and 6th Regiment Connecticut Line.

William Horton, VA Militia and Continental Line, and was at Valley Forge.

Patrick Kendrick, VA Militia.

Mathew Bishop, Virginian at the Battle of Kings Mountain.

William S. Kelly, NC Line at Valley Forge.

John George Hohenschild, Oriskany Creek.

Simeon and Phillip Harvey, brothers who are buried in Bennington, VT Cemetery. Phillip served under his Uncle Moses Harvey. Simeon was a member of the Committee of Safety in VT.

HOUSLEY, JAN EDWARD – Born in Steubenville (Jefferson City), OH on Jan. 14, 1939. President & Secretary, Mt. Evans Chapter, COS-SAR, and also Chairman, Education, Census Committee. Housley served in the military form Jul. 25, 1960 through June 30, 1981, in Vietnam, Thailand and Germany. He later worked for Lockheed Corp., Sunnyvale, CA, retiring in 2005. He is a member of Rocky Mountain Honor Flight.

He was married to Blanche (Rankin) Housley (Dec.) with three children and one grandchild.

James A. Watts was born 1750 in Anson City, NC, and was a private during the Revolutionary War. He died in 1823 and is buried in Covington County, MS.

HOWELL, CHESTER ARCH – Chester Arch Howell was born Jan. 16, 1921 in Anna, Collin County, TX, the only son of Archer Cleveland "Arch" Howell and Frances Elizabeth Powell Howell. He has a sister two years older and one two years younger than he. When he was 5 years old, the family moved to West Texas and lived in Hall, Hockley and Lubbock Counties from 1926 to 1929. When his father died in Lubbock in 1929, Chester's mother moved with her three children back to Anna, TX. This became his home until after his graduation from Anna High School in May 1938. In January 1939, he enrolled in Texas A and M University, from which he graduated in May 1942. His majors were economics and accounting. After graduation, he entered the U.S. Army Air Corps, serving from August 1942 to February 1946. He served in several stateside bases before serving in the 20th Air Force on Tinian, Guam and Saipan. It was the airbase on Tinian, called Conley Field, from which B-29's were flown to drop the atomic bombs on Hiroshima and Nagasaki.

In McKinney, TX, the county seat of Collin County and ten miles from the town of Anna, Ashburn Army General Hospital was being converted to a Veterans Administration Hospital. Beginning work in April 1946, Chester was one of the first employees employed there and was assigned to the Finance Service as Chief Accountant. In January of the following year, Chester's future wife, Lettie Geraldine Willbanks from West Monroe, LA, came to work at the hospital as a nurse. She previously had been a nurse in the Navy. They were married on May 15, 1948 in West Monroe. On March 21, 1951, their first child, Katherine Elizabeth, was born. Four months later, Chester was promoted to the position of Chief of Finance at the VA Hospital in Fayetteville, AR. While there, on Nov. 28, 1952, their second daughter, Susan Abigail, was born. After three years there, Chester was promoted to the position of Chief of Finance at the VA Hospital in Topeka, KS and remained there 18 years. On April 25, 1958, a son, John Robert, was born.

In 1972, given an opportunity to return to his native Texas after 21 years, Chester eagerly accepted a transfer to the position of Chief of Finance at the VA Hospital in Waco, from which he retired in January 1980.

Chester is a member of the Austin Avenue United Methodist Church and the Friendship Class. He is also a member of Waco Masonic Lodge 92. He is 32nd Degree Scottish Rite Mason, member of Karem Shrine, Sons of the Republic of Texas, Sons of Confederate Veterans, Waco Kiwanis Club, Art Guild of Waco and Waco Rose Society.

Chester and Lettie's three children have provided them with five grandchildren. One is deceased. They have one great-great grandchild.

Chester Howell's father was born April 17, 1892 in Anna, TX. His mother was born July 18, 1893 also in Anna. They married in 1916.

John Bomar, Patriot Ancestor of Chester Arch Howell, was not a soldier, but made generous contributions to the cause of the Colonists. He was the son of Edward Bomar and Isabell Fielding. He was born in 1725 in England, died April 22, 1799 in Halifax County, VA. He married Barbara Bush in 1745 in Essex County, VA, daughter of Bibby Bush and Susannah Spencer. Barbara was born in 1720 in Essex County, VA and died after January 17, 1799 in Halifax County, VA.

HUNSINGER, HARRY THOMAS – Born May 16, 1942 in Berwick, Columbia County, PA, the first son of Harry Leroy Hunsinger and Dorothy June (Bankes) Hunsinger. He has two younger siblings, Jeffery Hunsinger and Cynda (Hunsinger) Prohidney.

He graduated from the public schools in Berwick where he was very active in the Boy Scouts of America. He attained the rank of Eagle Scout and was an assistant scoutmaster. At age 18, he joined the United States Air Force where he attended technical schools for two years becoming proficient as an aircraft communication / navigation technician. He served eight years in the USAF. He was stationed in the continental US repairing electronics on Interceptor aircraft for the Air Defense Command. His last 4 years were spent in the Far East, Viet Nam and the Philippines working for the Tactical Air Command. Harry and his wife Elaine (Romania) Hunsinger had two children, Angela Marie (Hunsinger) Livengood and Stuart Scott Hunsinger.

Harry T. Hunsinger

In 1969 he and his family moved to Bethlehem, PA where Harry joined the Bethlehem Steel Corporation working at the Homer Research Laboratory on the grounds of Lehigh University, where he was involved in the development, construction and installation of instrumentation and measurement systems for the steel industry. His last several years were dedicated to the installation and service of two large nuclear CAT scanning gauges for the steel industry in Bethlehem, PA and Sparrows Point, MD. He chose retirement in June 2000.

Harry was a founding member and the first President of the Huntzinger/Hunsinger Family Association dedicated in 1995 to the continuation of the family reunions and the collection and sharing of the family genealogy.

Harry was accepted by the SAR as a member of the Governor Joseph Hiester Chapter in Reading, PA in June 2007. His Revolutionary War Patriot is Bernhard Huntzinger/Hunsinger b. May 6, 1753 in Brunswick Twp., Berks County PA. Bernhard served with the Brunswick Township Militia in Berks County, PA in 1780. Harry is now an active member of the Columbia County Historical and Genealogical Society in Bloomsburg, PA.

Bernard (Bernhard) (Hunsinger/Huntsinger) Huntzinger, born May 6, 1753 in Berks County, PA served as a private. He was 8th Class of Capt. Christoff Baldi's Company of Brunswick Township, Berks County, PA commanded by Colonel Lindemuth in the 3rd Battalion, listed on April 25, 1780 and certified by Capt. Baldi on May 2, 1780, where Bernard is listed as "Lernhart" Huntzinger. (Further research did not find a Lernhart Huntzinger in that area. Bernard's brother George was also in the 5th Class of Capt. Baldi's Company so it has been assumed this was Bernard.)

Bernard "Handsinger," private, received Depreciation Pay in Caption Weston's Company, Berks County Militia Continental Line.

Bernhard Huntzinger appears on Captain Conrad Minich's Muster Roll of Berks County, PA.

He died Feb. 6, 1832 and is buried at Trinity Church Cemetery, Mt. Grove, Black Creek Township, Luzerne County, PA.

HURLEY, LAWRENCE E. – Born in Saginaw, MI, joined SAR in November of 2007. He served in the US Navy Reserve ET3, 1943-1946 and 1947-1952.

Lawrence and Dorothy L. Hurley have two children and five grandchildren.

He was employed at General Dynamics Corp. as Chief Data Management until retirement in December of 1990.

Lawrence E. Hurley

Lawrence served on Groton, CT Town Council 10 years, 2 as Mayor; Groton Board of Education five years; Chairman Groton Town Committee four years; Charlotte County, Genealogical Soc., FL, President, January, 2007 to present.

John Branner, born Aug. 12, 1752, at Indianfield, PA and was a farmer in civilian life.

John was a private in the 8th Regiment of Foot, Dunmore County Militia. He was at Fort Moultrie against Clinton and Cornwallis, and later saw action at Brandywine.

John died April 30, 1837 and is buried at Solomon's Lutherans Cemetery, Forestville, VA.

HURLEY, WILLIAM J. – Born on Dec. 23, 1942, he joined the California SAR on Mar. 11, 2008. He serves on the chapter Law Enforcement Committee and received the Law Enforcement Commendation Award from the George S. Patton Chapter, CSSAR. William was a captain in the U.S. Army, 173rd Abn. Bde., and later was a special agent, FBI, U.S. Dept. of Justice, retiring on Dec. 31, 1999. He is married to Mary Ritter Hurley, with three children and six grandchildren.

Thomas Winn was born about 1750 in Lunenburg Co., VA. He worked in civil justice, and died about 1799 in Virginia.

IRISH, ERNEST LEOPOLD – Born on May 8, 1929 in Standish, ME.

Graduated from Standish High School in 1945 and later obtained a degree in Electrical Engineering at the University of Colorado.

Joined the U. S. Army Air Force in May of 1947. Was selected for Officer Candidate School six years later and retired from the U. S. Air Force in 1975 as a Lieutenant Colonel. All assignments were in communications-electronics functions which included tours with Alaskan Air Command, NATO, the North American Air Defense Command, Vietnam and the Pentagon.

Ernest Leopold Irish

After retiring from the Air Force spent 15 years working for several government defense contractors mostly in naval communications functions. Retired again in 1991 and has lived in Maryland since.

Since retirement he has been active in the genealogical societies and the historical societies of St. Mary's and Charles counties.

Life member of the Solomons Island Yacht Club having served for several years on the Board and as Commodore in 1984.

From 1997 through 2000 served on the Board of Directors of the St. Mary's County Chapter of the American Red Cross.

Became a member of the Thomas Stone Chapter, Maryland Society, Sons of the American Revolution in May 1997. He has served as Registrar of the Chapter since 1999 and as President for three years. He has served as Chairman of the MDSSAR ROTC/Outstanding Citizenship Committee since April 2003, is a member of the MDSSAR Color Guard and served as MDSSAR President from March 2007 to April 2008.

Thomas Thomes Irish, was born on Jan. 29, 1737 at Falmouth (now Portland), ME. The family moved to Gorham, ME between 1738 and

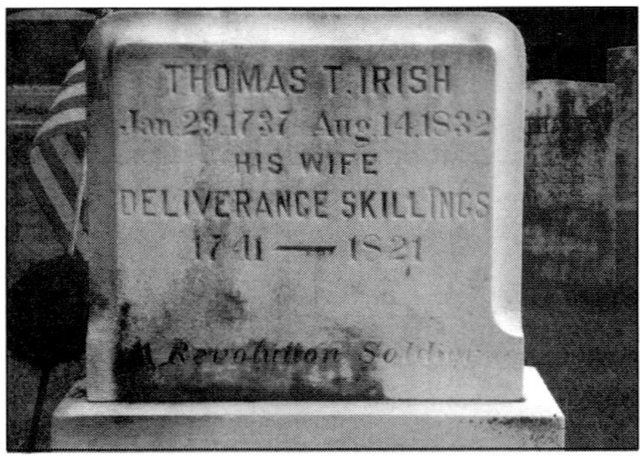

Gravestone of Thomas T. Irish.

1740. On July 7, 1759 he married Deliverance Skillings in Gorham, ME, where they lived and had 10 children. Enlisted in Captain William's Company, Colonel Phinney's Regiment, Massachusetts Troops, in 1775 and served eight months in response to the Lexington Alarm. Served again, for two months, in Captain McLellan's Company, Colonel Mitchell's Regiment, Massachusetts Troops, in 1779 as a Sergeant and participated in the "Penobscot Expedition" (an unsuccessful attempt to capture the British installation near the mouth of the Penobscot River). For these services, he was awarded a pension to commence on the 4th day of March 1831. Thomas Thomes Irish died in Gorham, ME on Aug. 14, 1832. He is buried there in the North Street Cemetery.

IVES, JAMES H. – Born Nov. 14, 1934 in Santa Maria, CA. SAR offices held include: State President, State Treasurer and Registrar, Chapter President, Treasurer and Registrar, and State Webmaster. He has received the Meritorious Service Medal, Good Citizenship Medal, Patriot Medal, and Membership Recruiting Medal.

James was a 2nd Lt. in the Oregon State Defense Force, ROTC, University of California, Santa Barbara. He has worked as owner/operator of a tractor business, design engineer, production manager, and pastor, and retired in Oct. 1988.

He is a member of the Mobile Missionary Assistant Program (MMAP) and the Lower Umpqua Ministerial Association (LUMA). He is married to Roberta Sawyer (3rd Wife), with five children and 14 grandchildren.

Lt. Lazarus Ives was born Nov. 7, 1734 in Meriden, CT. He served in the CT Militia under Gen. McDougall, and participated in the battle of Rips' Bay, Sept. 15, 1776. A lumberman and stock farmer, he died Sept. 17, 1812 and is buried in Wallingford, CT.

IVORY, HARRY G. SR. – Born April 26, 1928 in Camden, NJ. He served in the US Coast Guard (Seaman 1st Class) Nov. 1951 to May 1954, and worked for the US Dept. of Defense as Chief, Industrial Operations in Fort Monmouth, NJ. retiring on Jan. 4, 1994. He is a member of Disabled Veterans of America, Knights of Columbus (Grand Knight 3rd Degree, Navigator), and President, Board of Trustee Holiday Via. He is a veteran of the Korean War, 1950-53 (injured).

Harry G. Ivory Sr.

He is married to Catherine (De Fino) Ivory with two children, five grandchildren and three great-grandchildren.

Jacob Wright was born Jan. 12, 1747 in Long Island, NY. He was a private in the First New Jersey Regt., John Polhemis' Co., and fought at the Battle of Monmouth. He died in Oct. 1807.

JACKSON, RALPH – Lt. Col. Jackson (Ret.) was born Feb. 6, 1920. He joined the SAR State Society in Arizona in 1980.

Ralph served in the US Air Force and became a Lt. Col.

He and R. Jeane Rowles Jackson have four children and five grandchildren. Ralph also was Asst. Comptroller, Valley National Bank. He retired Dec. 1, 1969.

Ralph also belongs to MOAA, MOWW, F and AM, BOOE.

Julius Augustus Jackson, born 1732 in Maryland, was a doctor with the 8th Delaware Regiment. In civilian life, he was a doctor of physics. Julius died 1800 and is buried at Seaford, DE.

JACOBS, TIMOTHY – Born March 24, 1968 in New Haven, CT. He presently lives in Fort Myers, FL.

Timothy is the Editor of Patriots of the American Revolution magazine.

He also belongs to the Connecticut Society of Genealogists, Southwest Florida Historical Society, and Gulf Coast Writers Association.

Ezekiel Jacobs was born June 20, 1755 at North Haven, CT. Ezekiel was a private in Connecticut State Troops Regiment in Col. Andrew Ward's Company.

He was a volunteer with the Connecticut Militia under Captain Joshua Barnes and Col. Thompson; Retreat of Long Island, New York. He marched to Fort Independence; marched to Fishkill along the Hudson River; saw the burning of Esopus; and Battle of New Haven.

Ezekiel was a farmer and earned $500 for building the steeple for the North Haven Meeting House in 1799. He died March 6, 1834 and is buried at Montowese Cemetery, North Haven, CT.

JAMES, CHARLES MILTON – Born Jun. 2, 1925 a few minutes before his twin sister, Doris Maxine, at Rantoul, IL, he was admitted to SAR on Sept. 16, 2008.

Charles enlisted in the Army Air Corps Aviation Cadet Program in 1943, received his pilot wings in late 1944 and retired as a Regular Air Force Lt. Colonel in 1974. His various assignments included troop carrier and cargo glider operations, training command, special activities, special air missions, medical air evacuation, flight test and special operations. Ten years of active duty was served in overseas locations of Japan, Eritrea (Ethiopia), Libya, Germany and Vietnam. Awards included the Distinguished Flying Cross, nine Air Medals, Meritorious Service Medal and Commendation Medal.

Following retirement from the U.S. Air Force, Charles worked for 17 years with hearing instruments. His son, Charles Milton Jr., succeeded him in 1991, at which time he fully retired. He has been involved with several organizations, including: ruling elder for finance in a Presbyterian church, president of a Rotary Club, secretary of a Masonic Lodge, and secretary/treasurer of lesser organizations. He was elected as the first president of the AC-119 Gunship Assoc., a member of the National WWII Glider Pilots Assoc., WWII Pilots Assoc., AC-119 Gunship Assoc., and VFW.

Charles married Marilyn Grace Bridge on Aug. 2, 1946. Their four children are: Deborah James Arata, one grandchild; Cheryl James Richardson, two grandchildren; Charles Milton Jr., three grandchildren; and Dennis Keith. Charles and Marilyn settled in Idaho following full retirement.

Charles Milton and Marilyn Bridge James.

He is descended from John Williams, a farmer, born in Ohio in 1867, of German ancestry and his patriot maternal great, great, great grandfather **Benjamin Allison**. Benjamin, born about 1756, in Haverstraw, Orange County, New York, served as private with the Orange County Militia and The Line – Additional Corps. He died before 1807 and is buried "on a high hill between Centenary Cemetery and Fairfield, Green Township, Gallia County, Ohio."

JAMES, JOHN E. JR. – Born June 15, 1920 in Johnstown, PA; member of PASAR since Feb. 9, 2007. He is the Chairman of the Philadelphia Continental Chapter, Knight Essay Contest.

John served in HQ Detachment, 242nd Quartermaster Battalion, TEC 5, and later worked with the U.S. Postal Service, retiring in Oct. 1976. He is a member of the Society of Descendants of Washington's Army at Valley Forge, and Friends of Valley Forge Park. Military decorations include the Good Conduct Medal, American Defense Service Medal, American Campaign Medal, European-African-Middle Eastern Campaign Medal w/ 5 Bronze Stars, and World War II Victory Medal.

John E. James Jr.

Issac Brown was born about 1759 in Charles City County, VA. He served in the 7th, 11th and 15th VA Regts. under Capt. Charles Porterfield and Capt. William Smith, attaining the rank of Sergeant. Hi participated in the battles of Guilford Courthouse, the Siege of Fort Ninety Six, and Eutow Springs. He was a farmer. Issac died Aug. 19, 1830 and is buried at Old Elam Cemetery in Charles City County, VA.

Abraham Brown was born about 1745 in Charles City County, VA. He furnished supplies during the American Revolution. A farmer, he died June 17, 1790 and is buried at Old Elam Cemetery in Charles City Co., VA.

JANIK, CONRAD J. JR. – Born on Oct. 4, 1981 in Buffalo, NY to Conrad and Marlene Janik. A life long resident of Niagara County, NY, Conrad received his Baccalaureate Degree in Secondary Social Studies Education from Niagara University along with a Masters Degree in Special Education. Currently Mr. Janik is a special education teacher in the Western New York area. On Aug. 21, 2007 Conrad's membership application for the Sons of the American Revolution was approved and on Nov. 15, 2007 Mr. Janik was inducted into the Buffalo Chapter of the SAR at its monthly meeting.

Conrad Janik, Jr.

Daniel Roberts, Conrad Janik's patriot ancestor, was born on Dec. 29, 1754 in Killingly, Connecticut and served in the Connecticut Militia as a Private during the American Revolution. During the Revolution Private Roberts defended and saw action on the Connecticut frontier in addition to skirmishes along the New York border. Being of tall stature, 6 feet 6 inches tall, Private Roberts engaged in such sporting activities as wrestling and boxing. In one such match, Mr. Roberts demonstrated his boxing talents in the ring for General George Washington and his fellow soldiers. At the conclusion of the American Revolution Daniel Roberts moved with his wife Asenath Tucker to the rich and fertile forests of western New York where he tilled and farmed the land with his nine children. With the American Republic firmly established through his efforts and the efforts of millions like him, Private Roberts entered eternal rest on March 4, 1827 and was buried in Darien, NY as a true patriot.

JEFFRIES, ARTHUR JR. – Born in London, Laurel Co., KY, the son of Arthur and Easter Jones Jeffries. He graduated from Williamsburg H.S., attended Cumberland College, and graduated from Eastern Kentucky University.

Arthur worked as an Industrial Electrician, educator, Regional Vocational Education Administrator, and a building contractor.

He has been a member of the 1st. Bapt. Church since 1951, and served as Deacon. Arthur was S.S. Class Pres. for 20 yrs. He served in the Army Natl. Guard for 21 yrs. He is a 50 yr. Mason, a Shriner, and Organizing President Whitley Co. Optimist Club.

Arthur is a member of the Capt. Charles Gatliff Chapter NSSAR. He continues to work to increase membership in the SAR. He and wife, Wanda, have two children, John and Laurel; five grandchildren, John, Melissa, Aaron, Steven Jeffries, and Whitley West.

Arthur Jeffries, Jr.

His genealogy research led to Revolutionary Patriot, Pvt. and Corp. **Stephen/Stephen L. Jones**, born 1750 in St. Mary's Co., MD. He volunteered in 1779 while residing in Granville Co., NC. Stephen is buried on his Jones Creek property at Verda, Harlan Co., KY. His grave marked by the SAR. Another patriot is **Wm. McFadden**.

JEWELL, RALPH – Born Aug. 17, 1930 in Columbus, IN. He joined the Indiana SAR on Oct. 17, 2008 (member no. 172707). Ralph served in the U.S. Air Force, attaining the rank of Colonel, and later was a partner in a law firm, retiring on Jul. 1, 1988. He is a member of the Reserve Officers Assoc. and Military Officers Assoc. of America. He is married to Maureen T. Jewell, with three children and three grandchildren.

John (Hizer) Hiser was born ca. 1760 in Bucks Co., PA. He was a private in the 5th Pennsylvania Regt. commanded by Capt. Doyle, and fought on Long Island. A farmer, he died on May 5, 1839 and is buried in Barren Co., KY.

JOHN, WALTER WEINHAGEN – Born June 16, 1939, Milwaukee WI. Walter received an Honorable Discharge from the US Army. He became a member of SAR March 1, 1991 under Patriot Nathaniel Head. He belonged to PA Chapter No. 9875 and now State Society is Alaska No. 150

Walter received his BA-Michigan State University and MBA-Columbia University. He is Vice President and General Manager of Alaska Distributors Co. Walter and wife Sharon Richards John have three children and two grandchildren.

Walter W. John

He also belongs to the Society of the Cincinnati in the State of New Hampshire; Ancient and Honorable Artillery Company of Massachusetts. He is a member of Society Descendants of Washington's Army at Valley Forge 1777-78; Order-Crown of Charlemagne; Order-Merovingian Dynasty.

Nathaniel Farmer, 5th Great-Grandfather. Born Jan. 29, 1725, Billerica, MA. Married Hannah Fessenden in 1755. Died Sept. 3, 1778, Lexington, MA. Served as a Minute Man in Captain John Parker's Company at Lexington where he was wounded during the Battle of April 19, 1775 on or near the Lexington Common. He died three years later from this wound. Nathaniel's daughter was Ruth Farmer who married Jonas Parker. Jonas' father was Edmund Parker.

Nathaniel Head, 4th Great-Grandfather. Born Oct. 9, 1742, Bradford, MA. Married Abigail Stickney, Dec. 1, 1768. Died - NA. Lieutenant, Captain, Colonel and Brigadier General of the New Hampshire Militia. In August 1778, as Ensign, Nathaniel marched from New Hampshire to Rhode Island under the command of Colonel Moses Nichols' Regiment to join the Continental Army under the command of General John Sullivan. August 28th was the Battle of Rhode Island in Newport.

Jonathan Lawrence Sr., 6th Great-Grandfather. Born Oct. 4, 1703, Groton, MA. Married Tryphena Powers, about 1726/27. Died Dec. 8, 1789 Littleton, MA. Private- Massachusetts. Served in April 1777 and again in August-November 1777 including Saratoga. Furnished money and clothing to carry on the war.

Timothy Lawrence, 5th Great-Grandfather and son of Jonathan Lawrence Sr. Born March 31, 1748, Littleton, MS. Married Sarah Reed Nov. 30, 1769 Littleton. Sarah Reed is the daughter of Jonathan Reed and Sarah Lawrence. Died Nov. 3, 1815 Hollis, New Hampshire. Private - Lexington and Concord Alarm April 19, 1775 and September-October 1777 in Saratoga in Colonel Jonathan Reed's Regiment. Sarah Reed's father is Jonathan Reed.

Josiah Oakes, 5th Great-Grandfather. Born April 14, 1751, Hingham, MA. Married Silence Willcutt whose father is Joseph Willcutt. Died Jan. 20, 1798, Cohasset, MA. Served as Ensign and Lieutenant of Heath's Massachusetts Regiment May-December 1775.

Edmund Parker, 5th Great-Grandfather. Born Feb. 7, 1730/31, Reading, MA. Married Elizabeth Sheple, July 10, 1751. Died Aug. 13, 1813, Pepperell, MA. Served several enlistments as a Private under different commands including command under Colonel Jonathan Reed's 6th Middlesex Company Regiment.

Jonathan Reed, 6th Great-Grandfather. Born March 8, 1729 Lexington, MA. Married Sarah Lawrence Jan. 30, 1752. Their daughter is Sarah Reed who married Timothy Lawrence. Died Oct. 8, 1803, Littleton, MA. Served as Colonel of the 6th Middlesex Company Regiment of the Massachusetts Militia April 1775-1779. Timothy Lawrence and Edmund Parker served under his command.

William Thom, 4th Great-Grandfather. Born about 1741, Windham, NH. Married Margaret Park. Died about 1835, Salem, NH. Served as a Private in the New Hampshire Militia. William and Margaret's daughter was Sarah Thom who married Asa Woodbury. Asa's father was Israel Woodbury Jr.

Joseph Willcutt, 6th Great-Grandfather. Born March 2, 1717. Married Rachel Phillips, July 17, 1745. Died Aug. 7, 1782. Served as a Private in the Massachusetts Militia. Joseph is the father of Silence Willcutt who married Josiah Oakes.

Israel Woodbury Jr., 4th Great-Grandfather. Born Dec. 10, 1759, Salem, NY. Married Mehitabel Hall, June 30, 1784, Salem, NH. Died Oct. 16, 1859 (almost 100 years old), Salem, NH. Served as a Private in the NH Militia. He was captured by the Indians and held as a prisoner in Canada.

Luke Woodbury, 3rd Great-Grandfather. Baptized June 23, 1751, Salem, NH. Married Elizabeth Kemp, March 11, 1782, Salem, NH. Died March 6, 1827, Salem, NH. Served as a Corporal, Ensign, 2nd Lieutenant and 1st Lieutenant initially in the New Hampshire Militia and then the Continental Army under the Command of General George Washington.

Gravestone of Luke Woodbury.

1775 - 23 April - enlisted in the New Hampshire Militia at the age of 24; 17 June: the Battle of Bunker Hill- stationed at the Rail Fence in John Stark's Regiment;

1776 - Went with General John Sullivan to the Relief of the Army before Quebec; then in end-December was with General George Washington at The Battle of Trenton;

1777 - With General George Washington at the Battle of Princeton in January and during the winter at Morristown (January 1777); then the Battle of Hubbarton in July; Battle of Bennington with John Stark in August; 1st and 2nd Battles at Saratoga in September & October;

1778 - With General George Washington during the winter at Valley Forge (End 1778/79) and then at the Battle of Monmouth in June;

1779 - Battle of Newton/Chemung "Six Nations" under General John Sullivan; Winter 1779/80 at Morristown with General Washington;

1780 - "On Command" near West Point when General Benedict Arnold turned Traitor in September;

1827 - Died March 6 and buried in the Old Cemetery, Salem Center, NH.

JOHNSON, PETER W. – Born Aug. 1, 1951 in Toronto, Ontario, Canada. He joined the Empire State Society, NYSAR in 2008. As a Canadian and Past President of the United Empire Loyalists' Assoc. of Canada, he is perhaps not a typical SAR member. He has about ten Loyalist ancestors, but also at least three Patriot ancestors: Jacob DeLong, **Abraham Devins** and **Nathan Richardson**.

Peter Johnson

A retired teacher from Toronto, he now lives in the Bay of Quinte area of Ontario with his wife, Angela (who also has Loyalist and Patriot ancestors), and they have four children. He has been a keen Loyalist reenactor, and genealogist for over 30 years with a strong interest in his ancestors on both sides of the Revolution.

Jacob DeLong was from Pittstown, NY. He was born in the 1740s and served in the 14th Albany Co. Militia during the Rev. War. He and his extended family moved to Canada in 1801. His pro-American sympathies during the War of 1812 led to a quick departure from Canada in 1815 to Geauga Co., OH, where he died in 1816. There are many descendants in Canada today.

JOHNSON, ESQ. SCOTT E. – Born Dec. 3, 1968 in North Charleroi, PA, he served in the U.S. Army Reserve from 1990-2002, active duty Kosovo/Kosova 2001. He is currently employed as a lawyer, assistant attorney general, and is a member of the American Legion, Veterans of Foreign Wars, Sons of Union Veterans of the Civil War, and Sons and Daughters of the Colonial and Antebellum Bench and Bar. He is married to Amie Louise with two children.

Simeon Everly, Sr. was born Oct. 15, 1763 in Cumberland (MD/PA?). He was an Indian Spy with the Virginia Militia, and skirmished with Indians on the Western Virginia Frontier. A farmer and justice of the peace, he died on Mar. 17, 1843 and is buried at Everly Cemetery, Monongalia County, WV.

KAUFFMAN, CARL F. – Served in the U.S. Navy from Oct. 11, 1943 to April 18, 1946 (Aviation Electronic Technician's Mate 2/C) and when discharged was the first generation in his family to leave Lancaster County, PA. Carl is married to Beverly Bissett has three daughters, five grandchildren with one in the Navy, and two great-granchildren.

Carl Franklin Kauffman, USN, Appr. Seaman.

Johannes Georg Lutz arrived at Philadelphia on the ship Windsor in 1753 from Wurtemburg, Germany. Having lived through the Reformation, of Lutheran persuasion, yearning for liberty, settled in Manor Township, Lancaster County, PA. They were farmers and Bible teachers, talented in vocal and instrumental music, and active in church and civic affairs.

Tombstone of George Lutz who married Elisabet Werwel. Their marriage date is given on the tombstone. George Mann Cemetery, Manor Twp, Lancaster County, PA.

When the American Revolution became evident, Caspar and son **Georg Lutz**, 2nd and 3rd generations in America, enlisted as soldiers and *"did duly attened muster in the years 1777, 1778, 1779..."* (Pennsylvania Archives). Note: patriot listed erroneously in Ancestor Section, p. 572 as <u>John Mann Lutz</u> but should be <u>GEORG(E) LUTZ</u>.

KELLEY, WILLIAM – Born Dec. 23, 1941; retired as a manager with Midas in Dec. 2006. He is married to Carolyn Kelley, with two children and four grandchildren.

His patriot ancestor is **John Kelley**, who was born 1755 in NC. He served in the 11th VA Regt. under Charles Porterfield, a private. He was wounded at the battle of Brandywine. A farmer, he died June 11, 1853 and is buried in Rix Mills, Muskingum County, OH.

KELLOGG, CASEY – Born Jul. 11, 1981, he joined the Dakota SAR on Sept. 5, 2008. He is a Seabee in the U.S. Navy, assigned to Naval Mobil Construction Battalion One. He is married to Kelly, and they have two children, Kaitlyn and Taylor.

Seth Kellogg was born Feb. 8, 1739 in Norwalk/Fairfield, CT. He was a private in the 1st Connecticut Regiment, 4th and 6th Company (serving from Apr. 22, 1777 to Jan. 5, 1788), under Gen. Waterbury's State Brigade, Capt. Samuel Granger's Company; Col. Samuel B. Webb's Regiment, Capt. Thomas Wooster; and Col. John Durkee, Liet. Col. Thomas Grosvenor, Col. Zebulon Butler. A farmer in civilian life, he died on Jun. 26, 1819 and is buried at Old Baptist Cemetery, Centerville, Montgomery, OH.

Casey Kellogg

KELLOGG, CHRIS – Born Mar. 2, 1979, he joined the Dakota SAR on Sept. 5, 2008. He served in the U.S. Army as a specialist, is a welder and heavy machine operator, and worked for the Edgemont Fire Dept.

Seth Kellogg was born Feb. 8, 1739 in Norwalk/Fairfield, CT. He was a private in the 1st Connecticut Regiment, 4th and 6th Company (serving from Apr. 22, 1777 to Jan. 5, 1788), under Gen. Waterbury's State Brigade, Capt. Samuel Grang-

Chriss Kellogg

er's Company; Col. Samuel B. Webb's Regiment, Capt. Thomas Wooster; and Col. John Durkee, Liet. Col. Thomas Grosvenor, Col. Zebulon Butler. A farmer in civilian life, he died on Jun. 26, 1819 and is buried at Old Baptist Cemetery, Centerville, Montgomery, OH.

KELLOGG, DON – Born Apr. 6, 1955, he joined the Dakota SAR on Sept. 5, 2008. He is a locomotive engineer with the BNSF Railway. He is also a member of Boys Scouts of America - Cubmaster, Scoutmaster, served at district level, 2nd Scoutmaster Jamboree, Wood Badge NC-178-01; was an assistant little league coach for three years; Edgemont Ambulance EMT for ten years; fire department five years; and served two years and eight months for the Edgemont City Council.

Don Kellogg

Seth Kellogg was born Feb. 8, 1739 in Norwalk/Fairfield, CT. He was a private in the 1st Connecticut Regiment, 4th and 6th Company (serving from Apr. 22, 1777 to Jan. 5, 1788), under Gen. Waterbury's State Brigade, Capt. Samuel Granger's Company; Col. Samuel B. Webb's Regiment, Capt. Thomas Wooster; and Col. John Durkee, Liet. Col. Thomas Grosvenor, Col. Zebulon Butler. A farmer in civilian life, he died on Jun. 26, 1819 and is buried at Old Baptist Cemetery, Centerville, Montgomery, OH.

KELLY, KEVIN T. – Born April, 1953 at Richmond Heights, MO. Kevin joined SAR In November of 2004, Missouri.

Kevin also belongs to St. Luke the Evangelist, Richmond Heights, MO. He is a Past President of the St. Louis Genealogical Society.

William Bizzell was born ca 1730 in Nansemond County (now Suffolk), VA. Family tradition states that he was a grandson of Thomas Bizel, an English-born man of Huguenot background. This family is probably from Albiez Le Vieux, Savoie, France.

All that is known about William Bizzell's wife is that her name was Hannah (most of the Nansemond County, VA records were burned in several courthouse fires). In 1763, William purchased 400 acres in Edgecombe County, NC. In a 1771 land sale there is a mention of Bizzell's Mill Branch, so William could have operated a grist mill in Edgecombe County, NC. A few months later, he sold that property and moved to Duplin County, NC, where he purchased 470 acres. This land was situated on North Goshen Swamp and the East side of White Oak Branch, near the present day Sampson County, NC.

William and two of his sons (James Bizzell and Arthur Bizzell) served in the North Carolina State Militia, Bladen County, from 1781 to 1783. It is possible that they saw action in the Battle of Tory Hole, Elizabethtown, NC.

William was a farmer and died ca. 1800. He is buried at Duplin County, NC.

KELSOE, JOHN ALAN – Joined SAR November, 2005 in Alabama. He has served as Wiregrass Chapter Treasurer, on Patriot Graves Committee, and as Web Master.

He has received the Bronze Good Citizenship Bronze Color Guard and Meritorious Service awards.

John and Lynn Bowden Kelsoe have one child. John works in Banking.

Charles Spann Sr. was born in the year 1753 at Mount Royal in Northampton County, NC. Charles first volunteered 1775 in Halifax County, NC in Captain Samuel Welding's Company of Colonel Loring's regiment. In 1776 he volunteered to serve in Captain Robert Peebles Company of Colonel Thomas Eaton's regiment. His pension application states they marched to Norfolk, VA "in a company of volunteers called Minute Men."

Moving to Sumter District South Carolina, Charles Spann Sr. volunteered in 1778 in Captain Nathaniel Moore's company. Taken prisoner by the British and Tories in 1780 and sent to Camden where he developed smallpox and released. After recovering from smallpox he volunteered in Captain Josiah Furman's company, served under the "Swamp Fox" General Francis Marion and was at the taking of Fort Watson and Fort Motte. Charles Spann Sr. died June 7, 1844 in Sumter County, SC.

Robert Weston Sr., born in England Aug. 29, 1763; he served as a private and sergeant in North Carolina and South Carolina Militia under Generals Marion and Sumpter. Was captured and sentenced to death, but was able to make his escape. Moved to Sumpter County, AL were he died July 21, 1845 and is buried in the Panola Methodist Church Cemetery in Panola, AL.

Benjamin Haile Sr., born near Fredericksburg, VA, 1768; he relocated to Lynches Creek, Lancaster Count, SC. During the Revolution he served as Lieutenant and Captain in the South Carolina Militia under Colonels Marshall, Taylor, Bratton, Washington and Generals Sumpter, Marion and Green. Benjamin Haile Sr. also served in the South Carolina Legislature representing Lancaster County and died 1842.

KENNEDY, EARL E. – Born Jul. 11, 1947 in Fairmont, WV, he joined the Florida SAR on May 15, 2008 and is in the color guard of his chapter. He is a retired major in the USAR and a Vietnam veteran. In civilian life, he worked as a safety engineer-mining, retiring in 1997. He is a member of the American Legion, VFW, DAV, Combat Infantry Assoc., 32nd Degree Mason, and the 506th Infantry Assoc.

Earl is married to Vicky, with three children and six grandchildren.

Joshua Jones was born in Aug. 1760 in Bucks Co., PA. A member of the 4th Pennsylvania Regt., he guarded prisoners of war. He owned a mill at Mill Fall Run, WV. Joshua died on Jun. 20, 1845 and is buried at Mill Fall, Marion Co., WV (exact location unknown).

KENT, LAWRENCE – Dr. Lawrence Kent, a Dayton, OH native, has also lived in Florida, California, and Arizona. He is a real "winter soldier" who served as a Regular Army enlistee for 467 days over two bitterly cold winters in a war-torn and devastated Korea from Nov. 11, 1956 to Feb. 20, 1958. Border incursions had continued beyond the so-called "cease fire," a time when more than 1,200 additional American GIs died. His Honorable Discharge Sept. 30, 1962, after service of 4 months and 2 days beyond his 6-year obligation, the added time due to a stop-loss order in the beginning of the Vietnam era. He resided in Beverly Hills, CA at that time and had the rank of Specialist 5th Class (E-5).

Lawrence attended 13 post-secondary institutions attaining the AA, BA, MA, and PhD degrees. Professionally, he was an officer/director/instructor/counselor/writer in the fields of banking, government, education, mental health, social services, and consulting. Formerly licensed by the state of Ohio (LSW No S.0018086), Dr. Kent became semi-retired in 1993, though he continued in civic and volunteer positions, and as a published writer.

His 436 affiliations since the 1940s reflect his broad interests and concerns in many fields. These include Phi Delta Kappa, Pi Lambda Beta, Phi Alpha Beta, Mensa, Poetic Genius Society, Intertel, Top One Percent Society, 18 veterans groups; and 30 hereditary societies. Sharing blood-ancestry with 24 Presidents and 14 First Ladies of the United states, he is The Founder and 1st President, Presidential Families of America and Founder/Group Administrator, Ohio Veterans for Obama. Barack Obama is his 8th cousin-by-blood. Lawrence joined SAR in Tucson AZ (Life member No. 100221) and he has five qualifying Revolutionary War ancestors, I.e., **Captain Zechariah Clevenger Sr., Private Caleb Witt, Constable Matthias Hollo von Peter, Patriot William Homer Sr.,** and **Patriot John Allred.** His membership dates to Dec. 2, 1970.

Dr. Kent is referenced on some 40 websites and in over 400 publications. These include social directories in Los Angeles and Palm Beach, *WHO'S WHO IN AMERICA,* (2008), *WHO'S WHO IN THE WORLD* (2009), and multiple publications in America, Britain, and Australia.

He recommended Barack Hussein Obama Jr. for NSSAR membership.

KENTSMITH, DAVID K., COL (RET) – SAR #169168 has five patriots who have been approved by the SAR. They are:

Josiah Frost, b. Jul. 6, 1745, CT, d. Mar. 30, 1813, Alegany Co., MD; served as a private in the VA Militia. He was married to Elizabeth Parcell (b. 1745 NJ, d. Mar. 1813, Frostburg, MD); married Mar. 1, 1768, New Providence, NJ.

Samuel Dorris Sr., b. 1738, Baltimore, MD, d. 1818 Sumner Co., TN; Oath of Allegiance, MD, petitioned VA Legislature, wife Marth Hughes (b. 1738, Baltimore, MD, d. ?); married 1758, Baltimore, MD.

John Cole (Maryland), b. 1731, MD, d. 1781, Richmond Co., NC; Constable, Overseer of the Road, served on Jury Richmond/Anson Co., NC, 1774-81; married to Rachel Perkins.

Joseph Underwood, b. 1745, Middlesex, VA, d. Dec. 1822, Elbert Co., GA; Oath of Allegiance VA, wife Winifred Henderson (b. 1760, Culpepper Co., VA, d. 1828, Elbert Co., GA); married 1782, Culpepper Co., VA.

William Hailey/Haley, b. Jul. 27, 1748, Culpepper, VA, d. Nov. 24, 1830, Elbert Co., GA; Private of the Line, Continental Army (for the duration); married to Mary Turman (b. Oct. 15, 1744, Lunenberg, VA, d. Aug. 19, 1838, Elbert Co., GA); married Oct. 10, 1779, Elbert Co., GA.

KEPHART, WILBER J. – Born Feb. 20, 1998 at Johnson County, MO. Joined SAR February 1998. He was of President Martin Warren Chapter MOSSAR, four years. Sergeant-at-Arms Martin Warren Chapter, two years. MOSSAR Color Guard.

Wilber J. Kephart

Wilber was in USMC, 1951-1953. In civilian life, he was owner-operator of a dairy farm of Purebred Jerseys. He retired in May 1991. Wilber is married to Laurabelle Martin Kephart.

He also is a life member NASSAR, Life Member, MOSSAR, American Legion paid up for life, Life member of the American Friends of Lafayette, Military Order of Foreign Wars of the United States, Order of the Honorable Artillery Company, Life Member Johnson County (MO) Historical Society, West Central Genealogical Society.

Thomas Anderson Swift Jr. was born in Hanover County, VA, July 4, 1760. His father was Thomas Swift Sr., his mother was Almediah Duke. Thomas Swift, age 18, enlisted Feb. 14, 1778 in Captain John Winston's Company, Colonel Davies' 14th VA Regiment of the VA Continental Line. He saw action in the battle of Monmouth. He was discharged March 17, 1779. He re-enlisted and served in Captain Price's Company of Colonel Holt Richardson's 10th Regiment of the VA Continental Line. He saw action in the battle of Camden, Aug. 16, 1780. On Dec. 27, 1781 he married Frances. This union produced nine children. He applied for his Revolutionary War Pension on Aug. 15 1818; his age at that time was 58. In his pension application, he called himself a school master and farmer. His last documentation was in the 1830 census of Shelby County, KY.

Thomas Swift Sr., born in Bermuda, ca. 1725, was an Anglican minister. His father was William Swift, born in England in 1696, a minister in the Church of England. Thomas Swift was listed a patriot because he furnished supplies to the troops.

John Dourdan Reeves, born 1759 in Halifax County, NC. He enlisted in the Continental Army as a private and served for 16 months with Captain DeCourtes under Cols. Lane, Hill and Mebane. He saw action at Guilford Courthouse and Eutaw Springs. At the time of his discharge, he held the rank of Commissioned Lieutenant in the North Carolina Line. In 1787 he married Sally Locke Elwell, daughter of Richard Elwell. In 1804 they purchased land in Surry County, NC and remained there until their deaths. John Dourdan Reeves was awarded his Revolutionary War Pension on Feb. 12, 1833. He died 1840 and was buried on his farm in Surry County.

KERN, JOHN E. "JACK" – Born July 1934 at Westfield, MD. He currently resided in McMurray, PA. Jack served in the US Marine Corps.

Jack worked at DuPont Co. Coppeng and retired in August 1993. He and Darlene L. (deceased) had three children; Deborah Dillon, Brenda Divincenzo and Katherine Campbell; and six grandchildren, Jeffery R. Dillon, Jordan A. Dillon, Claudia M. Divincenzo, Christopher A. Divincenzo, Ashley L. Campbell and Maygan K. Campbell.

Jack also belongs to the Berks County Genealogy Society and Western Pennsylvania Genealogy Society.

Michael Kern was born May 4, 1757 at Germantown, PA. He served as a private in the Militia. He was in battles at Brandywine and Germantown. When they crossed the Delaware River, the group he was with didn't make it across the river and had to return to the Pennsylvania side.

Michael married Mary Boone, born Jan. 26, 1767 in Berks County, PA. In civilian life, Michael was a farmer. He died Feb. 11, 1850 and is buried in Berks, County, PA.

KINNER, THE RT. REV. KENNETH HARRISON – Born Oct. 25, 1927 in Danbury, CT, he joined the Wyoming SAR on Nov. 18, 2008. Military service includes: AG 2, USN (1945-48), USS PCE 884, USS Bairoko, CVE-115. He served as a Bishop, Missionary to the American Indian people (Wind River Indian Reservation, Wyoming, and people in Lander and Casper), and is still active in the Anglican Rite, Holy Catholic Church. He is married to Priscilla Elizabeth Sturges, with four children and grandchildren.

Kenneth H. Kinner and Priscilla S. Kinner with grandson, Sgt. Ryan C. Kinner, U.S.M.C.

Jonathan Kinner, born in Scotland, Jun. 21, 1744, grew up in Suffolk Co., eastern Long Island, NY. Enlisted as a private on May 31, 1776, Capt. Griffing's Co. 2nd New York Regiment. Battles of Harlem Heights and White Plains. Garrison of Fort Montgomery. Enlisted Lien of 1777, 4th New York Regiment, Capt. Sacket's Co. Battles of Freeman's Farm, Bemis Heights and Saratoga. Wintered at Valley Forge 1777-78, sick two months. By order of Gen. Washington, detached in Aug. of 1778 to the whaleboat service under Capt. Brewster out of Norwalk, CT. Five years attacking British shipping on Long Island Sound, capturing officers, destroying supplies, reporting enemy movements to the Commander in Chief. Discharged, a private, on Town Green, Fairfield, CT, June 1783. Badge of Merit for six years of faithful service signed by Gen. Washington. Served eight years over all. Married 1782, Eunice Treadwell, daughter of Thomas Treadwell, a private in the Connecticut Militia. Seven sons, one died War of 1812. Buried Gilbertown Cemetery, Black Rock Turnpike, Easton, CT.

KINTER, LARRY JOSEPH – Born Sept. 23, 1938 in Grafton, WV, he joined the Boerne #64 Chapter, TXSSAR on Sept. 5, 2008 and serves as a member of the chapter color guard.

Larry is a U.S. Air Force veteran, where he served as a Communications Specialist at Hahn Air Force Base, Germany. Following that service, he became an Information Systems Consultant serving various employers and retired in March 2002.

Larry J. Kinter

Larry's wife, Catherine Theresa Koch, is deceased. He is the father of Susan, David, Stephen and Wesley; and grandfather to twins, Kim and Stephanie, and grandsons Lukas, Jared and Lachlan, the latter two of Australia.

He is the sixth grandson of Revolution War Patriot:

Peter Kinter, born in 1757 in what is now Dauphin County, PA. Peter served in 1779 and 1781 in Col. Robert Elder's 10th Battalion; Capt. James Murray's 1st Company of Upper Paxton Township, PA.

In civilian life, he was married first in 1782 to Mary Todd Findley (1st cousin of Mary Todd Lincoln) and second to Elizabeth Jackson in 1811. He had six sons and six daughters. He was a farmer and blacksmith and died Mar. 8, 1816 in Rayne Township, Indiana County, PA.

KIRKUP, PETER ELLERY – Born Jan. 20, 1959 in Bay Shore, NY, he joined the NY SAR in 2008. He is the historian for Grumman Aerospace and a teacher, and Curator, Kirkup Veteran's Tribute, a private military museum. He married to Debra with two children.

David Leeke was born Mar. 11, 1740 in East Hampton, NY, died in 1802 and is buried at North Cemetery East in Hampton, NY.

KIRTLEY, JIM – Born Oct. 15, 1947 in Charleston, WV. He joined the SAR May 7, 2008 in Ohio.

Jim's military service was in the US Army, as Specialist 5th Class.

Jim retired April 1, 2005, serving as an Executive with GM. He is married to Gorgann, and they have four children and eight grandchildren.

His memberships include Sons of the Union Veterands of the Civil War, Sons of Confederate Veterans of the Civil War and the Mahoning Valley Civil War Roundtable.

Samuel Beaumont, fifth generation New

Englander, whose ancestors had arrived in Boston before 1640, clearly knew his allegiance as a Patriot in April 1776. At the age of eighteen, he enlisted at Saybrook, Middlesex Co., CT, his home town, as a private in Colonel Selden's regiment. He fought under Gen. Washington at Harlem Heights, September 1776, and at White Plains, October 1776. He also fought at Flat Bush, Turtle Bay and Elizabethtown Point. In February 1778, Samuel Beaumont was appointed corporal, Third Connecticut, in Colonel Samuel B. Webb's regiment. And, in August 1778, he fought under General John Sullivan at Newport. In June 1780, Samuel was appointed sergeant, again Third Connecticut, in Colonel Samuel B. Webb's regiment. He was discharged from the Continental forces in February 1781 at the age of twenty-three.

Following the marriage of Samuel Beaumont to Thankful Towner, at Middlesex County, CT, five children were born there, of whom Virginia Frances (Fannie), Anna and Sophia survived.

Samuel Beaumont died on Nov. 27, 1837 in his home near Charleston, Kanawha County, (W) V. He, his wife, his mother, his son and his son-in-law were all interred in the family cemetery on his property, alongside the banks of the great Kanawha. Sadly, the cemetery faded from history, undoubtedly in 1873, with the advent of the railroad across West Virginia. Currently standing at this site is the Chesapeake & Ohio Depot.

KNIGHT, GERALD PATRICK – Born Jul. 3, 1938 in Cincinnati, Hamilton County, Ohio. He served in the U.S. Navy and was a letter carrier for the U.S. Post Office, retiring Oct. 2, 1992. He is a member of the Indiana Pioneers, Mayflower Society, Citizens of Patrol, and Delhi Citizen Police.

He is married to Mary Louise (Wolfer) Knight, and they have six children and 16 grandchildren.

William Langston was born Apr. 15, 1762 in Granville, NC, the son of Capt. James B. Langston. He was a private serving with the 6th North Carolina Regt., 7th Company (the same company as his father). William Langston was a farmer, and his father was a Justice of the Peace He died Dec. 7, 1853 and is buried in Mason County, IL.

KOHLER, JOHN – Born July 7, 1960 in Cambridge, MA to Christopher Kohler and Janice Bingham.

John is married to Mary and they have five children and ten grandchildren. John is employed in the Logistics Dept. at Apria Healthcare as a Dispatcher. John and Mary reside in Shawnee, Kansas.

On April 19, 2007, John was inducted as a member of the Monticello Chapter of the SAR. On that date 232 years before John's patriot ancestor led his troops to fight the war for freedom.

Captain Joshua Partridge Sr., was born July 27, 1713 in Medfield, MA. He married Elizabeth Kingsbury on Dec. 23, 1742 and they had six children. During the war, Joshua Partridge Sr. was a Selectman from the town of Medway, MA. On April 19, 1775 he commanded The First Military Company of Medway. He and 37 patriots marched 20 miles to Roxbury, an area of Boston. Once they arrived, their orders were to secure the area from British troops. From April 19, 1775 to December 1777, the soldiers of the First Company were given 24 marching orders within southern New England and New York. After the war, Captain Partridge returned to Medway, MA. He died on Jan. 19, 1795. He is buried at the Old Church Yard Cemetery in Millis, MA.

KRAMER, LESLIE MYRON – Les was born on May 2, 1956 in Berea, OH. He was accepted into the SAR on Jan. 14, 2008. Les is a police officer in Cleveland, OH. He has an Associate's Degree in Law Enforcement from Cuyahoga Community College, Parma, OH.

Les Kramer (on left) being inducted into the Western Reserve Chapter of the SAR on Oct. 10, 2008.

Organizational memberships include the Mayflower Society; Lorain County, Ohio First Families & Settlers lineage societies; the Pilgrim John Howland Society; the Elder William Brewster Society.

Les is married to Heidi Kramer (Gerlach). They have two children: Jessica Weber and Sgt. Alexander Kramer, 82nd Airborne. They have one grandchild: Eden Weber.

John McRoberts was born on July 29, 1758 in Kirkinner, Scotland, immigrated to American in 1773 and settled in Springfield, Vermont. John first enlisted in 1775, serving in Col. Warner's Vermont Regiment and was in the Canadian Expedition of 1775-76. In 1777 he served three months fighting in the battles of Bennington, VT; Bemis Heights, NY; an the battle of Saratoga, NY, witnessing the capture of General Burgoyne and his army. John re-enlisted on Jan. 1, 1778. He served for two years as a Sergeant under Captain Lee in the Independent Company of Rangers annexed to Col. Warner's Vermont Regiment. In 1780 he again re-enlisted and served three months as a private under Capt. Blakesley in Col. Malcolm's Regiment. John married Lucy Bradford in 1782 in Springfield, Vermont and resumed his occupation as a farmer. John died on April 4, 1813 in Sudbury, Vermont and is buried there in Wallace Cemetery.

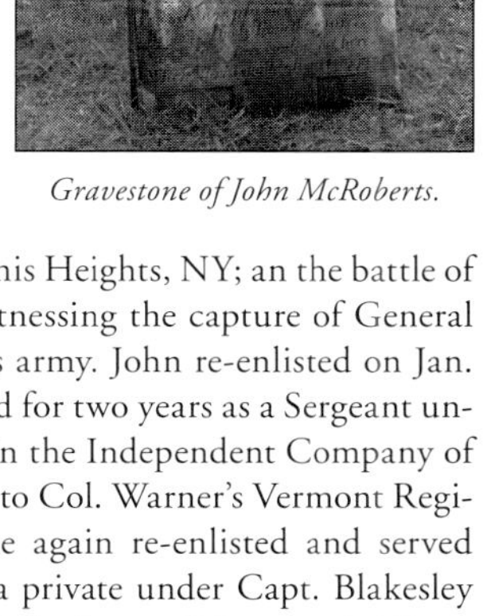
Gravestone of John McRoberts.

LAIR, ROBERT E. JR. – Dr. Lair was born May 2, 1939 in Collin County, TX. He joined SAR in March 1994 in North Carolina.

He served in USMC and US Army. He was a Chaplain (Colonel) AUS (Ret.) Robert served as a military officer, pastor and university teacher. He retired in May, 2001.

Robert E. Lair, Jr.

Robert married Judith Anne Trevvett and they have three children and six grandchildren.

In addition to the SAR, he is also a life member of V.F.W., R.O.A., Military Officers Ass'n., N.R.A.; member of Rotary Club, American Legion, Military Order of Foreign Wars.

Andrew Lair (Andreas Lehrer) was born Feb. 18, 1750 at Philadelphia, PA. He was a Lieutenant in the Virginia Frontier Militia. Local commanders mustered troops under orders from George Rogers Clark to retaliate against Indian attacks on Ruddle's Fort and Martin's Fort. He was in battles at Old Chillicothe and Piqua.

Andrew was a farmer of 400 acres. He died April 26, 1826 and is buried in Lincoln County, KY.

LAND, RICHARD D. – Served in the Army, 47th Infantry, 9th Division as Staff Sgt.

Richard married Stella Mae Brown and they have three children and six grandchildren.

He was employed as city engineer, Sidney, NE; city manager, Valentine, NE; construction engineer at various locations including the Boeing Company for 25 years. Richard retired in July 1988.

At times, he held leadership roles with Boy Scouts and DeMolay organizations. He is a former member of a Lions Club and several Rotary Clubs. He served nearly 10 years on the Kent (WA) Planning Commission and was a member of the King County (WA) Citizens Water Advisory Committee during the planning for the third wastewater treatment plant. He is a life member of the newly formed Kent Meridian VFW Post and Kent Verity Masonic lodge. He is a member of Alexander Hamilton Chapter of SAR.

Richard and Stella Land, 2008 Old Timers King and Queen.

Robert Dickson, born Feb. 10, 1763 at Cherry Valley, NY acted in the capacity of Pvt. Capt. Thomas Whitaker's company, Col Samuel Campbell's regiment, svc. 5 months and Capt. Robert McKean's company, Col John Harper's regiment, svc. 9 months. He served about 3 months in Capt. Stephen White's Co. of Col. Marinus Willet's Reg.

Robert died at Ripley, NY, Aug. 20, 1832. He was a farmer and innkeeper at Middlefield Center, NY.

LANGWORTHY, JOHN ALAN – National No. 132023, D.C. No. 3848 (11 Nov. 1988), born Aug. 20, 1947 in San Antonio, Bexar County, TX. Songwriter/Singer/Entertainer/Founder and Leader, THE LEGENDARY BAND. Sole Proprietor, Maxern Records. Host, THE T.V. JOHN SHOW on Baltimore City and Washington, D.C. Metropolitan Area Cable Television. Professional Affiliations and Honors: Songwriters Hall of Fame, Professional Member; Broadcast Music, Inc. (BMI); Who's Who in Poetry; International Poetry Hall of Fame; *lyrics published by* International Library of Poetry. Education: Bachelor of Arts in European History - University of Massachusetts; Acting School (full scholarship) - American Conservatory Congress.

John Alan Langworthy

6th-generation Great Grandfather **James Stone,** born Oct. 21, 1747, Haverhill, Essex County, MA. Married Lydia Abbott. Minuteman on Breed's Hill at Battle of Bunker Hill, Charlestown, MA, June 17, 1775. Thereafter, served as private 1) nine months in Capt. J. Bowman's Company; 2) in Capt. Gordon Hutchin's Company; 3) in Col. Stark's Regiment; and then 4) on April 15, 1778, reenlisted for a year in Capt. Robinson's Company, in the Northern Army. Participated in the Battle of Bennington, VT, and served out his full term. Died May 15, 1790, Henniker, Merrimack County, NH. Four children: John, Jane, James, Rebecca.

James Stone, Minuteman, Battle of Bunker Hill

5th-generation Uncle **Joseph Langworthy**, born 1761, Stonington, New London County, CT. Unmarried without issue, enlisted as a private in the Continental Army when 16 years old, served seven years, killed in action against Miami Indians. Aug. 29, 1781, Ezra Hoyt, Muster Master for Berkshire County, MA, certified that he had mustered said Joseph Langworthy to serve in the Continental Army for the term of three years. Receipt dated Jan. 22, 1782 for bounty paid Joseph Langworthy by Capt. William Douglas to serve in the Continental Army for the term of three years to the credit of the town of Hancock.

Joseph Langworthy, Continental Army Soldier

LEA, WALKER JR. – Born at Port Arthur, TX on July 31, 1924. Wife, Beverly Hayes was born in Port Arthur on Oct. 2, 1925. Both attended school in Port Arthur and graduated from Thomas Jefferson High School in Port Arthur, Texas. (He in 1943 and she in 1945.)

Dr. Lea married Beverly Hayes at Port Arthur, TX in 1947. They have three children, Scott, M.D. at St. Luke's Hospital, Houston, TX; Walker Lea, III, banker; and daughter, Kristen, living in New Orleans, LA.

Walker was in the Ninth General Dispensary of the US Army from 1942 to 1945. When he got out he went to medical school at Baylor Medical Center, Houston.

Walker is a Master Mason, Cosmopolitan Lodge in Port Arthur, TX, holding a Knight's Templer position. He also belongs to the Scottish Rite Bodies and American Legion at Port Arthur. He joined the American Legion right after he received his discharge from the US Army.

Walker, Bob Knight and Lee Lockwood, who worked for Waco Savings and Loan, formed the Waco Chapter of the Sons of the American Revolution several years ago. They utilized one of their homes as a meeting place.

Father, Walker Lea Sr., was born at Alford, LA in 1893. He married Alice Townsend in 1919 at Port Arthur, TX. Alice was born at Kenan, TX in 1895.

James Lea was born and raised in North Carolina, Caswell County. He was in the Kings Mountain Battle of the Revolutionary War in North Carolina. He married Ann Herndon in North Carolina. They are buried in the Lea Family Cemetery in North Carolina in an unmarked grave.

LEE, MACK DALE – Born Feb. 12, 1942 in Gatesville, Coryell County, TX, to Verner Ray (V.R.) Lee and Myrtle Emma (Hill) Lee. He had two sisters - Rae Juan and Rita Joy. In June 1954, at age 12, Mack sustained a spinal cord injury in a gun accident and was afterward confined to a wheelchair. He graduated from Gatesville High School in 1960 as Vice President of his senior class.

Mack worked for a short time for Powell Supply Company. In 1966, he bought a music and electronics shop, The Gallery. He was active in the local Jaycees, serving twice as secretary, once as Vice President and once as President in 1970-71. He received the "Distinguished Service Award" for 1969-70. In 1980, he added a Radio Shack franchise to his business and in 1984-1985 worked as a disc jockey for the local radio station. He retired in 1985.

In 1970, Mack met Marsha Leigh Whitlow, a first-year English teacher at Gatesville High School. be They were married on June 8, 1972 in Gatesville. Marsha is a member of the DAR.

Mack and Marsha sponsored a little girl from the Cherokee Children's Home from 1976-1982. They hosted a Swedish exchange student, in their home in 1981-1982. They worked as area representatives for the ASSE (American Scandinavian Student Exchange) from 1983-1988, placing students in central Texas homes. Mack is a deacon for the Cedar Ridge Church of Christ. They have a small business on the side, M and M Specialty Merchandise and attend craft shows and gun and knife shows on weekends.

"Long" David Lee Sr. was born Jan. 17, 1746 in Isle of Wight County, VA to William Lee Jr. (ca 1715 in Prince George County, VA-August 1794/7 in North Carolina) and Elizabeth Ann Westbrook. David married Martha Blackman. He owned considerable land in Johnston County and Sampson County, NC. He died on Aug. 27, 1812, in Johnston County, NC. All that is known about David's military records is that he is cited with "Revolutionary Service, North Carolina." David and Martha's gravesite has reportedly been found by Clel Lee at David Lee Cemetery near Bentonville Battleground, near Newton Grove, NC.

LEE, MATTHEW STEPHEN – A native of Tyler, TX, he is a partner with LPH Productions, a marketing and video-production company founded by his father, SAR Chapter President, Stephen Lee. Matthew is a 2007 honor graduate of The University of Alabama where he was a member of Phi Delta Theta Fraternity. He is an Eagle Scout and a member of Green Acres Baptist Church. Matthew is a member of the Captain William Barron Chapter, Texas Society, Sons of the American Revolution Color Guard and currently serves as Sergeant-at-Arms. He participates in flag retirement and naturalization ceremonies, re-enactments and scouting activities. He also is a member of The Society of the Descendants of Washington's Army at Valley Forge, The Sons of the Republic of Texas and The Sons of Confederate Veterans.

So far, he has been able to prove thirteen Revolutionary

Matthew Stephen Lee

War ancestors, three of which served under General George Washington at Valley Forge: **Captain James Harris, Lieutenant Robert Mann and Private George Carpenter, Sr.**

Other patriot ancestors of which he is so proud include: **George Carpenter Jr., John Carpenter, Jacob Fry, John Fry, Thomas Jopling, Andrew McClure, Josiah McClure, Jesse Nichols, Edmund Powell** and **George Spears**.

LEE, STEPHEN – Resides in Tyler, TX where he serves as President and Color Guard member of the Captain William Barron Chapter, Sons of the American Revolution. Steve is also a member of The Descendants of Washington's Army at Valley Forge and Sons of the Republic of Texas. A graduate of the University of Texas at Austin, Lee is a founding partner in LPH Productions, a marketing and video-production company in Tyler. He enjoys genealogical research and has discovered six Revolutionary War ancestors. His wife, Anna, is the Regent of the Mary Tyler Chapter, DAR and sons Matthew and Britton, are both Eagle Scouts and active members in SAR.

Stephen Lee

Lee's original patriot ancestor is **James Harris**. Harris served as a 1st Lieutenant in the 15th Virginia Regiment at Valley Forge under the leadership of General George Washington. Following the long winter, Harris was promoted to Captain and subsequently served as Colonel of the Virginia Militia.

His wife, Anna, has two ancestors who also served at Valley Forge and they sometimes contemplate how their patriots may have become friends and know that they would be proud that their sacrifices for this country would still be so appreciated by their descendants, after 230 years.

LEGER, JOHN PAUL – John is of Littleton, MA joined the SAR in September 1997.

John is an architectural/auto glass agent. He and wife, Kathleen, have three children and three grandchildren.

In 1776, **Lt. Peter Casy (Pierre Caissie), Corp. Michael Bourg (Bourque)** and **Pvt. Joseph Leger** served in the Massachusetts Militia under the command of Jonathan Eddy.

In March of 1776, Jonathan Eddy and an Acadian met with General George Washington in Cambridge, MA to discuss plans from inhabitants of Nova Scotia to join the United Colonies in the struggle for Independence.

General Washington thought the plan had merit and should be presented before the Continental Congress in Philadelphia. Once in Philadelphia the idea was well received. Commitments were eventually made to recruit 3,000 men to carry out plan.

In the ensuing months, recruitment and financial support for Jonathan Eddy's efforts faded. Undaunted, Eddy and his small band of men, persevered and were determined to bring Nova Scotia into the fold of the United Colonies fighting for freedom.

Finally in the autumn of 1776, Jonathan Eddy and his men traveled from Massachusetts to Nova Scotia, recruiting men. Once in Nova Scotia, he recruited a contingent of Acadians led by 1st Lt. Caissie, Corp. Bourque and Pvt. Joseph Leger.

Jonathan Eddy and his new group managed to have several successful guerilla raids on the British. They captured several British soldiers in the process. A plan was then devised to capture Fort Cumberland, a key British fort in the area.

In November of 1776, the plan to capture Fort Cumberland was carried out. It was decided that the Acadian contingent would be the first unit to attack the fort. 1st Lt. Caissie, Corp. Bourque and Pvt. Joseph Leger led the attack. Eventually the assault became a stalemate and evolved into a siege. The arrival of British reinforcements proved to make the critical difference. The "patriots" reinforcements never arrived, forcing a retreat to Maine where Jonathan Eddy and his men continued their "guerilla warfare" against the British. The British had to divert troops to try to contain Eddy and his men, troops that otherwise would have been sent to fight the patriots elsewhere in the colonies.

LEGLER, THEODORE R. II – Sixth generation Hoosier from Evansville, IN, commissioned Regular Army 2LT through DMG ROTC Indiana University June 10, 1986, retired Colonel, USA on Aug. 31, 1995. Graduate degree programs completed at Webster University, USA Academy of Health Sciences, and USA Command and General Staff College. Faculty at LU. School of Optometry, Pennsylvania College of Optometry, Southern College of Optometry, USA Academy of Health Sciences. Stationed in Germany for 12 years. Military Awards LOM, MSM(5), ARCOM, AAM, WWIIOM(Berlin), NDSM(2), OVSM, EFMB, ABN, AASL T, NCOPDR, OVSR(2), ASR.

Theodore Rex Legler II

Currently Director, Eye Disease and Primary Care, Martinsville Vision Clinic, PC, Indiana. Fellow American Academy of Optometry; member American Optometric Association, Indiana Optometric Association.

Entered SAR 1989, National Life Member, Indiana Society Primary Member, South Carolina Society Life Member.

SAR Offices: Chapter President, State President Indiana, National Trustee Indiana, National Committees: Co-Chair National Eagle Scout, Youth Awards, Master of Ceremonies, Medals and Awards, Medical Advisory.

SAR AWARDS: War Service Medal(3), Patriot Medal, Meritorious Service Medal(2), Silver Good Citizen Medal, Robert E. Burt Medal, Liberty Medal(4), Silver and Bronze CG Medals, Silver Council of State Presidents Medal, GWEF, Arthur M. King Medal, CAAH Medal.

BSA 50 yr. Vet, Eagle Scout, Silver Beaver, OA Vigil; Lions Club - Lion of the Year; GS of USA Life Member - Outstanding Volunteer Award; Life Member VFW; American Legion PUFL member.

Wife - April C. Arington DAR, two daughters DAR, one son SAR, three grandsons SAR.

Primary Patriot: **John Turney**, Pvt. Northhampton County militia, PA. Supplemental: **Andrew Mann,** Captain Bedford County militia, PA.

LEWIS, DR. RICHARD MEAD – Born 1946, New York; joined SAR Oct. 30, 2007, TN Society membership no. 170456. Lewis served both active duty and reserve in the US Army, and served in the Republic of Vietnam. He is a life member of Veterans of Foreign Wars (VFW), member of Disabled American Veterans (DAV), and the American Assoc. of University Professors (AAUP). Military awards include the Army Commendation Medal, Good Conduct Medal, Vietnam Service Campaign Medal, and National Defense Medal.

Lewis is married to Theresa Ellen Conrad with three children and six grandchildren. He worked as a college/university professor, retiring in 2006.

Abraham Slover was born about 1753 at New River, August District, VA. In 1764 at age 11, he survived an Indian raid on his family's farm near New River, and as a result he became an orphan. During the Revolution, he served in Capt. Charles Reed's Company, PA Volunteer Militia, Washington County, 4th Battalion. Family tradition holds that he served under Col. John Sevier at the Battle of Kings Mountain; Rendezvous March 1 and July 24, 1782.

He was a mill operator, farmer and nine-year member of Jefferson County, Tennessee Grand Jury, and a lieutenant in militia of George Daughtery's regiment, Jefferson County Infantry, Hamilton District.

He was married to Martha Anderson, with five sons. He died about Sept. 1834 and is buried in Jefferson County, TN.

LIPPHARDT, GEORGE ABBOTT – Born Nov. 30, 1946. Served aboard the *USS Hornet* (CVS-12) between 1964-66. He is descended from Andrew (see below) from his mother's side of the family. He joined SAR in 2007.

Andrew Cunningham was born Feb. 16, 1760 in Boston, MA. In 1777 he was a private in Capt. Mayo's Company, Col.

George A. Lipphardt

Brooks' Regt., Massachusetts Militia, and was on duty with the American troops at the Cambridge Arsenal.

Andrew Cunningham

In early life he was a merchant in Boston and became Secretary of the Massachusetts Mutual Fire Insurance Company in 1799. He joined the Ancient & Honorable Artillery Company on Aug. 4, 1786. He was third sergeant of the Artillery Company in 1788, first sergeant in 1795, lieutenant in 1789 and commander in 1793.

There is a large black and white reproduction of a painting of him in the Ancient & Honorable Artillery Company Museum, on the 4th floor of Faneuil Hall. He is shown as Major Andrew Cunningham, 1793.

He was a proven SAR Patriot in 1981.

Tomb of Andrew Cunningham.

He died in Roxbury, MA on May 20, 1829. He is buried in the historic Old Granary Burying Ground, Boston, about 50 feet from the tomb of Paul Revere. He is in Tomb No. 128 (No. 8).

LITTLE, THE REV. C. K. – Born Dec. 30, 1934, Trenton, NJ, he serves as chaplain for the John Sevier Chapter in Tennessee. Rev. Little served as a pastor in the Presbyterian Church, retiring on Dec. 31, 1999, and is the author of "Fabrics of Freedom," based upon the life of Patriot Robert Liddle. He is married to June McCusker Little, with four children and three grandchildren.

Robert Liddle was born 1754 in Pennsylvania. He was a sergeant in A. Ogden's Company, 1st New Jersey Regt., and found at Short Hills, Springfield, Brandywine, and Monmouth. A tailor, he died in 1853 and is buried at Lamington, NJ.

LITTLE, MORRIS L. – Born Oct. 13, 1939, he is a member of the Continental Society SAR, joining on Feb. 28, 2008 (#171145). Morris served in the USAF from Aug. 1957 to Aug. 1961, 2nd AF S.A.C., 19th Air Div., 7th Heavy Bombardment Squadron, 7th FMS, A/2c, an aircraft and missile electrical repairman. He had classified and secret security clearance. He later worked for Daimler Chrysler Corp., retiring on Jan. 31, 2006.

He is married to Carol Kay Snyder, with three children and three grandchildren.

Peter Bowyer was born Oct. 10, 1760 in Germany. He served in Capt. Turnbull's Company, 2nd Regt. of Artillery, Pennsylvania, commanded by Col. Proctor, rank of Matross (PA Archives Series 5, pp. 1013-1014). He died in Cass Co., Tipton Township, IN, on Oct. 10, 1850, and is buried in the Mays Cemetery, Miami Co., Pipe Creek Township, accessible only through Cass Co. from Road 10.75 east at approximately 4.00 south (back of a long driveway).

LIVINGSTON, GEORGE E. – Born Dec. 16, 1934, Moundsville, Marshall County, WV. George and wife Beverly were married May 9, 1959 at the First Christian Church, Weirton, WV, where they still maintain active membership. They have one son, two daughters and five grandchildren.

George and Beverly Livingston

During most of his working life he was a Production Supervisor, Department Manager and Graphic Arts Manager for Continental Can Co./U. S. Can Co., and later was a Production Manager for Heekin Can Co./ Ball Corp. Retired June 1, 1995 at age 60.

SAR membership application approved Aug. 11, 1998. Charter and founding member, Ebenezer Zane Chapter, Ohio Society. Chapter Genealogist since 1998 and Historian since 1999. Both offices that he currently holds. Chapter President, 2003 and 2004. He serves on the Ebenezer Zane Chapter book committee and also on the grave marking committee. Member of the Chapter Color Guard and Executive Committee.

SAR medals: Bronze Good Citizenship medal; Meritorious Service Medal with Oak Leaf Cluster; Liberty Medal.

Military service from June 1954 to June 1957. U. S. Army Security Agency with the rank of SP/5. Served overseas with the 10th USASA Field Station, (8610 AAU) Kyoto, Japan from May 1955 to May 1957.

John Supler, born Oct. 20, 1756 in Philadelphia, PA. Son of John Supler and Susannah Gray. In 1784, John Supler married Rachel Kirk, born 1767, the daughter of Isaac Kirk. John and Rachel were the parents of at least eight children; three sons and five daughters. Early in the Rev. War, c1775/76, John Supler was drafted and served two months under Capt. Jacob Randolph, Chester County, PA Militia. In the spring of 1777 he served as a 'Seaman' aboard the Brig *Andrea Doria*, known as the "Black Brig," under command of Captain Kolinnson. Late in 1777 he served a two month tour of duty under Captain John Lindsay and later under Captain William Brady in the Chester County, PA Militia. In 1778/79, he served as a 'Seaman' aboard the *Walker Privateer* under Captain Matthew Roller. John next enlisted as a 'Private' in the 8th Company, 6th Battalion, Chester County, PA Militia under Captain William Kirk from 1780 to c1783. John Supler died in Washington County, PA, June 14, 1835. Rachel died in 1850. Both are buried in the Old Presbyterian Church cemetery in West Alexander, Washington County, PA.

(Military information from the PA Archives, 5th Series, Vol. 5, pages 711 to 758 and from pension records, NARA file #W4521.)

LOOMIS, JO GILBERT JR. – Born in Evanston, IL on Dec. 7, 1927. He attended Senn High School until his senior year, and at age 17 he left to join the U.S. Navy on Feb. 24, 1945. He served in the Pacific, and was on board the *USS Missouri* to witness the Japanese surrender to Gen. McArthur. He was discharged at Great Lakes in July 1946. He was awarded the medals and ribbons of Asiatic Pacific, Japanese Occupation, Philippines Occupation, Chinese Theater, American Theater, and the Victory Medal.

After finishing high school, he joined the U.S. Army in 1947 and transferred to the USAF and was discharged in June 1950, three days before the start of the Korean War. Jo joined the Berry Bearing Co. in 1956, and worked for the company for 35 years before retiring in Dec. 1989.

He is married to Marilyn F. Loomis (May 7, 1949), and they have six children, four grandchildren and one great-grandson.

Ensign **Nathaniel Loomis II** was born at Coventry, CT on Aug. 28, 1747. H married 1st Lavinia Clark of Lebanon, CT. After her death he married a Sims of Simsbury, CT. His 3rd wife was Rachel White. Nathaniel Loomis moved in 1794 to Westmoreland, Oneida Co., NY. His son, Erastus, was taken hostage by Indians on their arrival in Oneida Co., but was returned after three days. Nathaniel is said to be the first white settler in Westmoreland, and it is said that Whitestown was named for him. He served as an Ensign in the Coventry troops in the Revolution. He died on Dec. 16, 1825.

LUDWIG, JOHN ALBERT – Born Mar. 5, 1949 in Cincinnati, OH, John joined the SAR along with his son, Nicholas G. Ludwig, on Dec. 9, 2008.

Having no formal military service, John worked 23 years for the prime contractor of the Feed Material Processing Center at the Fernald

John A. Ludwig with his son, Captain Nicholas G. Ludwig, USMC viewing the USS (Mighty Mo) Missouri.

Plant, northeast of Cincinnati. During the Cold War, this Atomic Energy facility manufactured uranium products that were used in bombs for airplanes and munitions for tanks.

John lives with his wife, Elizabeth Ann Hadler Ludwig, who is married to Heidi Marie Cooper Ludwig with a daughter, Aubrey Klara-Lane Ludwig.

John is descended from his patriot ancestor on his mother's side, Marjorie Branch Ludwig.

John Branch was born Oct. 7, 1729 in the city of Preston, New London Co., CT. John served as a private in the Massachusetts Militia under Capt. John Strong's Co. and Col. John Brown's Regt. Although 47 years of age, he marched from Pittsfield, MA to Fort Ann in the defense of Fort Ticonderoga, which was threatened by the advancement of Gen. Burgoyne up Lake Champlain.

His civilian occupation was a farmer. He was the father of ten children. John died Mar. 5, 1812 and was buried in Whiting Cemetery, Whiting, VT.

LUNA, CHARLES E. – Born Dec. 27, 1937 in Jackson, TN. Joined the Texas SAR May 26, 2004. His SAR offices and committees include TXSSAR Chairman of CCP, Chairman of Patriot Fund Endowment, Chairman of 2009 TXSSAR Convention, Chapter President, Chapter Vice President, Chapter Chairman Eagle Scout Scholarship, JROTC and Grant Committees.

Charles retired in 2005, serving as the Regional VP for Fortune 500 Company and owner of Video Promotion Co. He and wife Betty D. Mitchell have a daughter, Rhonda, and a son, Charles. The have four grandchildren.

Charles has received the Patriot Medal, Meritorious Service Medal, Bronze Congressional Medal, State Service Medal, and Chapter Service Medal.

He also has memberships in Society of Colonial Wars, Society of War of 1812, The Sons of the Republic of Texas, and Sons of Confederate Veterans.

James Maitland Lauderdale was born 1709 in Ireland and died 1796 in Tennessee.

Peter Luna (Looney) was born Oct. 1, 1759 in Augusta, VA. He served as a private and sergeant in the Virginia Militia. He was in the Battle of Holston Flatts, served as an Indian spy and a border guard.

As a civilian, Peter was a farmer and a Militia Captain in Tennessee. He died Feb. 16, 1851 and is buried in Marshall, TN, on Fishing Ford Rd.

LUNA, CHARLES E. JR. – Born Sept. 15, 1964 in Memphis, TN. Joined the Texas SAR Nov. 4, 2004.

Charles is an architect, currently residing in Switzerland. He is married to Shelia Louise Morris and they have two daughters, Alexandria and Juliet.

Charles is also a member of The Sons of the Republic of Texas.

Peter Luna (Looney) was born Oct. 1, 1759 in Augusta, VA. He served as a private and sergeant in the Virginia Militia. He was in the Battle of Holston Flatts, served as an Indian spy and a border guard.

As a civilian, Peter was a farmer and a Militia Captain in Tennessee. He died Feb. 16, 1851 and is buried in Marshall, TN, on Fishing Ford Rd.

LUTTRELL, ALLEN W. – Born Dec. 8, 1949 at Springfield, IL. He joined SAR (Life Member) in 1970, Illinois Society. He has served as President of the Springfield Chapter, and was the State Chairman of the Veterans Committee. He has received the SAR Silver Good Citizenship Medal.

Luttrell served in the Regular Army/MAC/V and Sup Com./Thai/SFC E-7. He received the Vietnam Service & Campaing Medals, Nat. Defense, Good Conduct, ARCOM, AARCOM, and Meritorious Service Medals. He later was the Executive Director and Lobbyist for the ISEA.

He is married to Judith I. Luttrell, and they have two sons.

LYNCH, KENNETH HOWARD – Born Jan. 5, 1939 in Vallejo, CA. He joined the California SAR on Jul. 11, 2008. A registered professional engineer, he worked for over 33 years in the space rocket industry (Rocketdyne), retiring on Apr. 28, 1995 as engineering design manager.

Kenneth H. Lynch

He is married to DAR member Lois Loraine Green Lynch, with three children and five grandchildren.

William Gatton was born in Maryland abt. 1756. He married Sarah Murphy in Montgomery Co., MD, on May 6, 1781. He served as a Private in the Montgomery Co., Lower Battalion Militia, with the 6th Company in 1777 and the 3rd Company in 1780. He also rendered aid by providing wheat for use in the military in 1781. In 1814, William purchased land in Richland Co., OH near an area that later became known as Gatton Rocks. He died in Belmont Co., OH, on Jan. 6, 1816.

LYNN, ROBERT JAY II – Born Mar. 21, 1989 in Placerville, CA. He joined the Redlands Chapter, California SAR on Nov. 10, 2008. He is a member of Boy Scouts of America, becoming an Eagle Scout on Nov. 23, 2002 at the age of 13. He is currently a college student and living historian for the Revolutionary War.

Robert J. Lynn II

Barnabas B. Haley, at the age of 17, enlisted in the US Continental Line Army, at the Charlotte Court House Va., serving under the Company commanded by Capt. John Brunt, 11th Regt. This was commanded by Col. David Morgan, Morgan's Rifle Regt. Within weeks Barnabas was marched directly to NY, on

Gravestone of Barnabas Haley.

to Jersey and then very near Brandywine. Shortly afterwards he was transferred to Gen. George Washington's unit at Valley Forge, PA now served under Col. Lamb. He received a written discharge in full of his term of enlistment from his Capt and signed by Col. Lamb. Barnabas received a Revolutionary War Pension for his military service.

LYONS, MSG JOHN W. SR. – Born June 23, 1952 at Ft. Benning, GA. Served in the US Army June 24, 1969 through Aug. 31, 1994. He is a member of the Tucson Chapter SAR and is Eagle Scout Chairman. Other memberships include the Kentucky Colonels, and Disabled American Veterans (Life Member), and the Bellevue Vets, Bellevue, KY.

MSG John W. Lyons, Sr.

He owned D&H Air Conditioning and Heating Company, retiring in Nov. 1999. He has two children and three grandchildren.

Sgt. Beverly Daniel was born Feb. 11, 1762 in Spotsylvania, VA He was a Citizen Soldier under Gen. Meeden and Cpt. Upshire in the Culpepper Militia, attaining the rank of Sgt. He fought in the battles of Jamestown and Fredericksburgh, VA. Daniel was a teacher, justice of the peace, and operator of the Red River Foundry in Clark County, KY. He died Sept. 18, 1851 and is buried in Montgomery County Cemetery, Montgomery County, KY.

MABEE, DOUGLASS M. – Born Sept. 7, 1949 in Portchester, Westchester Co., NY and joined SAR in 1986, Vermont and Empire Societies. He was the Vice President, Marketing and Facilities for The Adirondack Trust Company, retiring Jun. 1, 2007.

Douglass is Chair, Wesley Foundation of Saratoga Springs and Chair, Saratoga Springs Downtown Special Assessment District. He is also a member of the General Society of Mayflower Descendants, Society of Colonial Wars, Holland Society of New York, Sons of the Republic of Texas, Welles Family Assoc., St. Nicholas Society, Military Order of Loyal Legion, and Dutch Settlers of Albany.

He and his wife, Heather, have two children.

David McNair, born Dec. 18, 1736 in Mifflin Co., PA, was a private in Thomas Bales Co., Pennsylvania Regt. under Col. Thomas Torbett. He died Feb. 19, 1777 in Trenton, NJ.

Hugh McManus was baptized Jun. 14, 1747 in Albany, NY, and was a lieutenant in the NY 6th Regt., Albany Co. Militia under Col. Stephen J. Schuyler. He died Sept. 2, 1832.

William Brattle was born Aug. 29, 1745 in Wethersfield, Hartford, CT, and was a lieutenant in the MA 3rd Berkshire Regt., Capt. William Well's Co. He died Nov. 6, 1826 and is buried at Pittsfield Cemetery, Berkshire, MA.

Johannes Mebie was born Jan. 10, 1728 in Rotterdam, Schenectady, NY. He was a private in the Albany Co. Militia under Col. Abraham Wemple. He died Nov. 24, 1796 in Schnectady, NY.

MAGRUDER, JOHN DANIEL (J.D.) – Born Jun. 30, 1966 in Meadville, PA. J.D. joined the SAR on Jan. 30, 2008 at age 41. J.D. serves as the Chapter Secretary and Publicity Chairman for the Henry Laurens Chapter of the SCSSAR and has also held an interim post as Chapter Genealogist.

J.D. served in the US Navy from 1985-1993 in the Navy's Nuclear Power Program. He served on the fast attack submarine, USS Cincinnati (SSN 693), during the Persian Gulf War, and later served as an Instructor at the Navy's Nuclear Field 'A' School in Orlando, FL. J.D. now works as an independent consultant for clients such as Nabisco, Hewlett Packard, AT&T, and others.

J.D. Magruder

J.D. is descended of patriots Haswell Magruder on his father's side and Daniel Pardee on his mother's father's line.

Haswell Magruder, born 1736 in Prince Georges County, MD. Haswell served the American Revolution as a civilian, serving as a Constable for the New Scotland Hundred, May-Nov. 1777, and as Overseer of Highways in 1779, both in Prince Georges Co., MD.

Daniel Pardee, born Oct. 19, 1762 in Southington, CT. Daniel enlisted in Jul. 1779 in Capt. Asa Bray's Co., Col. Phelps' Regt., serving six weeks. He served in Capt. Ten Eyck's Co., Light Infantry, Connecticut Line, from Jul. 1 to Dec. 13, 1780. He reenlisted in Mar. 1781 as Corporal in Capt. Matthew Smith's Co., and again in Apr. 1782, serving until the end of the war under Capt. Nathaniel Jones. He was engaged in two battles at Frog's Point, NY, and under Capt. Jones was in service on Long Island Sound, aiding in the capture of 20 vessels. He was present at the surrender of Cornwallis.

MANN, DAVID L. – Born Jan. 31, 1955. David joined SAR in Jul. 2008 and is the current Secretary/Treasurer le Marquis de LaFayette Society NCSSAR, and Fayetteville NC Color Guard member. He is a certified public accountant, member AICPA, NC Associations of CPA's.

Jacob Mann arrived in Philadelphia in 1730 with his father, George Bernhardt Mann. His father received a patent from Thomas and John Penn in 1740, but left for the Shenandoah Valley of Virginia on land surveyed by Thomas Lewis. Jacob Mann would, like his father, travel as a pioneer, this time in the Greenbrier Valley of Virginia. Jacob Mann settled along the banks of Indian Creek, a watershed providing a source of power along the mill built there.

Jacob Mann assisted in the building of Cook's Fort and Mann's Fort during the French and Indian War and along with sons Jacob II and Adam would serve as private scouts in Virginia during the Revolutionary War. The family of Jacob Mann, being from the industrial section of Germany that was the center of gun powder manufacture in Europe, would also aid the Revolutionary cause by supplying mined salt peter to regions of Virginia and North Carolina.

The picture is of Cook's Mill in Greenville, WV which was built along Indian Creek near the site of Cook's Fort and still stands.

The community that sprang up along the banks of Indian Creek in this section of Virginia was known in early records as Springfield, but is now known as Greenville, WV and is near the Revolutionary War Muster Grounds of Union, WV. The community today contains descendents of many of the same families that were early settlers here, and still retains the character and beauty of one of the Greenbriar Valley's earliest settlements.

MANNON, DANA J. – Born July 12, 1927 in Dewanee, IL. He joined the Illinois SAR Dec. 9, 2008.

His military service was with the Army as Bayreuth Military Com Sgt.

Dana retired Jan. 1, 1995 as a self employed farmer. He and his wife, Leah E., have three children and six grandchildren.

Elijah Dana, was born Sept 4, 1740 in Pomfret, CT. He served as corporal in the 11th Regiment. His death was Nov. 30, 1784 and he is buried in Pomfret, CT.

MARSH, DAVID ANTHONY – Born July 4, 1940 Albany, NY. Joined NSSAR, Saratoga Battle Chapter and Empire State SSAR, 2003. BS and MS SUNY at Albany, MPH Grad. School of Public Health, Univ. Pittsburgh. 1966-1995 Professor of Biological Sciences and Chairman of Natural Sciences Dept. SUNY Coll. of Agriculture and Technology at Cobleskill. NEHA registered Public Health Sanitarian/Environmental Health Specialist. Member NEHGS and NYGBS. Former library volunteer in genealogy and local history New York State Library. Former President and Vice President Capital District (Albany, NY) Genealogical Society. Trustee Lansingburgh (Troy, NY) Historical Society. Descendant of three documented Revolutionary War patriots-Capt. David Dalrymple, farmer of Petersham and Colrain, MA and Walworth, NY; Solomon Southwick II editor and publisher of Newport, RI; and Nathan Hinckley farmer of Stonington, CT and Walworth, NY.

David Anthony Marsh

Capt. David Dalrymple, b. Feb. 3, 1766, Petersham, MA. m. 1789 Mary Donelson, Colrain, MA; eight children. Death date and place unknown at present. Burial place unknown. Enlisted June 8, 1780. Regiment Massachusetts Line. Served six months as Private under Gen. Patterson, Col. Michael Jackson, Maj. Trott, Capt. Taylor, Lt Wilder, Ensign Chalender. Enlisted again March 1781 in 8th Regiment Massachusetts Line under same officers, serving until war's end. Discharged at West Point November, 1783. Militia Captain Colrain, MA early 1800's. Settled and farmed Walworth, Wayne Co., NY. Revolutionary War Pension file No. S12719.

Nathan Hinckley, b. Feb. 23, 1748, Stonington, CT. m. Sept. 8, 1776 Mary Babcock, Stonington, CT; nine children. d. Feb. 21, 1814, Walworth, Wayne Co., NY. Buried Walworth Village Cemetery, Walworth, NY. Farmer in Stonington during Revolution. Signatory to a petition addressing Governor and Council demanding assistance in protecting farms farm operations, produce, intracoastal transit of commodities and other interference by British coastal patrols who were commandeering goods to resupply their vessels. Participation in this protection effort constituted patriotic service to the livelihood, farms and economy of Connecticut. Nathan and Mary later migrated to Walworth, Wayne Co. NY where they farmed.

Gravestone of Nathan Hinckley.

Solomon Southwick II, b. 1731, Salem, MA. M. 1769 Ann Gardner Carpenter, Newport, RI. d. 1797, Newport, RI. Buried Old Burying Ground, Newport, RI. Employed by James Franklin family publishing the *Newport Mercury*. At death of Mrs. Franklin, Solomon acquired the newspaper where he published articles and commentary on the Continental Congress, Thomas Paine's Common Sense writings and other political philosophy. When British warships entered Newport Harbor he buried the "Franklin printing press" and fled to Rehobeth, MA where he lived out the occupation. When British troops evacuated, he returned to continue publication of the *Mercury* and was Asst. Commissary General of Stores.

Gravestone of Solomon Southwick II.

MARSHALL, JOHN CLELLAN – The Honorable John Marshall was born in 1943 in Dallas, TX. He joined the SAR in 1968.

He has been Past President, Brevard (FL) Chapter, 1973; Dallas (TX) Chapter, 1979; District 6 VP, TXSSAR, 1980; NSSAR Law Enforcement (Committee 1976-80). He has received the Silver Good Citizenship Medal (1980) and Law Enforcement Medal.

John served in the Texas State Guard, Inspector General, Col. He married Jamie Lynn Hamner and they have two children.

He has served as State of Texas – Judiciary for 20+ plus, and is a Senior District Judge.

John belongs to Society of the Cincinnati (VA); International Academy of Astronautics; Fellow of the College of the State Bar (TX).

He is also a Honorary Professor of the University, UMCS, Lublin, Poland, title conferred in 2004.

John Marshall, born Sept. 25, 1755 at Fauquier County, VA, was a Captain with the 3rd VA Continental Line. He was in battles at Great Bridge, Valley Forge, Yorktown and Brandywine.

John was a Chief Justice of the Supreme Court from 1801 – 1835. He died July 6, 1835 and is buried in Hollywood Cemetery, Richmond, VA.

MARTIN, JAMES A. – Born in Jacinto City, TX; joined SAR, Dallas Chapter, March 8, 1999.

James is married to Patricia Martin. He is Vice President, Martin Media, Richardson, TX.

He is an Amateur Radio Operator and is President, Texas Lighthouse Radio Society.

James A. Martin

Lt. Joseph Allison, born c. 1750 in Orange County, NC was a Lieutenant. He died in 1826 and is buried at Gordonsville, Smith County, TX.

MAYCUMBER, GORDON W. – Born Apr. 19, 1928 in Syracuse, NY. He joined the Empire State Society SAR (#172693) on Oct. 17, 2008. Gordon served in the U.S. Navy, WWII, Seaman; NY Air National Guard, Private; US Coast Guard Auxiliary, Div. II, Captain, National Staff Historian. He served no the Syracuse, NY Fire Dept. for 35 years, retiring as Deputy Chief on Feb. 3, 1984, and later was Safety Director for Cornell University, Ithaca, NY, retiring on May 27, 1990.

Gordon W. Maycumber

He is a member of the National Eagle Scout Assoc., American Legion, NY North Coast, Coast Guard Assoc., NY State Fire Chief's Assoc., and NY State Retired Fifefighters Assoc.

He is married to Donna E. (Mothorpe) Maycumber, and they have one child and one grandchild.

George Jackson McCumber was born 1756 in Argyle, NY. He was a crewman on the Privateer, *The Lady Washington*, commissioned by the Governor of Rhode Island. The sloop was from Newport, Rhode Island, 73 tons, eight guns, 10 swivels, 70 men; Capt. James Godfrey, 1st Lt. Henry Weeden, 2nd Lt. Daniel Sewat, Master Thomas Cottrel. *Lady Washington* may have served on the Hudson River near West Point, and was one of four ships protecting "The Great Chain" spanning the Hudson River. A farmer, he died Feb. 17, 1851 (85 years) and is buried at Elmwood Cemetery, Preble, NY, Cortland County.

MAZZEO, MICHAEL J. JR. – Born July 12, 1959 in Buffalo, NY. He joined the Maryland Society of SAR on Oct. 17, 1986.

He has held the following offices: Registrar, John Hanson Chapter 1987-1988; Charter Member, Thomas Stone Chapter (3-30-91); Registrar, Thomas Stone Chapter 1991-1993; Secretary, Thomas Stone Chapter 1999-2000; Vice-President, Thomas Stone Chapter 2004-2005; President, Thomas Stone Chapter 2005-2008; and Historian, Thomas Stone Chapter 2007–present.

Other civic organizations include: President, The Historical Society of Charles County 1986-1992; Chairman, Charles County Tourism Advisory Board 1989-1990; President, Charles County Heritage Commission 1995-1997; Board of Directors, The Smallwood Foundation 1996-2000; and Chair, The Friendship House Foundation 2006-present.

Michael is the author of *The Simmons and Welch Family of Charles County, Maryland, 1979.* Received Maryland History Day Teacher of the Year from Charles County, 2007. Illustrations Editor, *Pathways to History, Charles County Maryland 1658-2008.*

Aaron Simmons served as a Private in Regiment of Colonel William Grayson's 16th Additional Troops, Captain Heaberd Smallwood's Company. His military experience was at Camp Paramus, PA; Camp White Plains, NY; North River, Robinson Plains, NY; and Camp Middle Brock, NJ.

In civilian life, Aaron was a farmer. He died March 1, 1832 and is buried in Charles County, MD.

MCCORKLE, LOUIS – Louis is a descendant of Archibald McCorkle through the eighth child, Archibald, Jr. Born in 1921, Louis is a Catholic priest, artist, retired teacher, and life member of the American Artists Professional League. He was named a monsignor by John Paul II. SAR Natl. No. 169503.

Archibald McCorkle was born Oct. 27, 1754 at Waxhaw Settlement, SC. He was the son of Robert and Margaret McCorkle. He married Joanna White, daughter of Joseph White and Elizabeth Russell, in 1776.

During the Revolutionary War, Archibald served both as a drafted militia soldier and a volunteer in the regiment commanded by Col. Joseph Kershaw in South Carolina. He was also a member of the Waxhaw Volunteers militia.

Gravestone of Archibald McCorkle.

He took part personally in the battles of Reedy River, Coosawhatchie Bridge, Rocky Mount, Hanging Rock, Sumter's defeat, and Greene's battle at Camden.

His miliary service began in October 1775 when he was first drafted as a militia soldier for a three months tour and served in the battle at Reedy River. After some light skirmishing and taking of prisoners, the army disbanded without any formalities.

His second tour commenced in late October 1778, when he was again drafted. This expedition was to oppose the British who had appeared in Georgia. Since he was at Charleston the time of the draft, he met his comrades near a point on the Savannah River. He was discharged verbally in January of 1779.

Soon after returning home, he volunteered for three months more in early February 1779. During this tour he was in the very unequal contest at Coosawhatchie Bridge, and had to retreat before an overwhelming force. When the army reached Dorchester, since Archibald's time had expired, he was discharged in early May 1779.

He spent 42 days with his wagon, team, and driver under the command of Major Robert Crawford, from Dec. 27, 1779 to Feb. 7, 1780.

When Charleston was taken in 1780, Sumter called for volunteers. Archibald responded without concern for any specific time of service or anything other than, as he said, "the end of the momentous struggle or end of life in the conflict." He spent 50 days as a horseman under the command of Captain Hugh White in General Sumter's brigade and Major Marian's cavalry, beginning on June 30, 1780 and ending Aug. 18, 1780 with Sumter's defeat. He lost a horse and saddle in this attempt to regain Charleston.

He was in the attempt on Orangeburg 17 days, from July 27 to Aug. 13, 1781, under Col. Frederick Kimble in General Marion's Cavalry. When the British reenforced Orangeburg it became prudent to desist. So the army fell back to the High Hills of Santee. Being a volunteer not committed to any specified time, he was discharged.

He served 43 days as a private foot soldier in guard duty at Waxhaw jail from Nov. 25, 1781, to Jan. 6, 1782, under the command of Major Thomas Thompson. Thus ended his military service.

On Aug. 3, 1803 Archibald's wife Joanna died at Waxhaw Settlement. They had raised ten children. Two of their sons and three grandsons became ministers. After her death, Archibald moved in 1806 from the place where he was born to Montgomery County, TN, and settled near Clarksville. Sometime before 1833 he moved to near Dover in Stewart County.

Archibald was a devout Christian, a pious and upright father, supportive of the religious revival of the early 1800's in the Carolinas, and in his new home in Tennessee. His son Arch Jr., recalled that the McCorkle family went to the first religious "camp-meeting" held in the area after their arrival in Tennessee.

In December 1811 Archibald's daughter Margaret died, leaving three children. In April 1816 Archibald signed a guarding bond placing the children in the care of his son-in-law, Jesse Watkins, husband of his daughter Mary White McCorkle.

Mary and Jesse later moved to Texas. Jesse was killed in 1837 by Indians. Sam Houston had asked Jesse to attempt to make a treaty with several tribes. Jesse was directed to meet with tribal leaders in what is now the Dallas area. Louis Sanchez, his interpreter, returned alone and reported how the Cherokees made a porcupine of Watkins with pine needles and burned him.

A deed of gift dated Feb. 23, 1821 shows that Archibald, "now of Cooper County," was in Missouri about the time his daughter Jane Wear, "lately Jane McCorkle," married.

In about 1838, crippled by a fall from his horse and unable to care for himself, Archibald moved to Henderson County to be with family.

In April 1843 his grandson Joseph McCorkle died in Missouri. Joseph was the child of Archibald's son, Rev. Archibald Jr. Joseph's brother Hugh wrote to Archibald's grandson, Arch H. Wear: "Dear Cousin,.. Brother Joseph is dead... Brother Jo died on Thursday morning in April 20th. Signed, Cousin H. McCorkle."

Archibald McCorkle Sr. died June 6, 1844 and is buried in the City Cemetery at Henderson, TN. His grave has a marker placed by the D.A.R. Courageous and devout, may he rest in peace, and may we and future generations God and Country.

MCDONALD, CAPERS W. – Born in Georgetown, SC in Nov. 1951, the sole son of WalBern and Cecilia McDonald. Since 2004, he has been an Executive in Residence and faculty member of Johns Hopkins University in Maryland. For the previous 12 years, Capers led BioReliance Corp. as its President and CEO. Headquartered in Maryland, BioReliance provides testing, development and manufacturing services to biotechnology and pharmaceutical companies worldwide. Capers was named the 2002 Greater Washington Entrepreneur of the Year in the Life Sciences by Ernst & Young. During 2003, BioReliance was ranked #1 nationally by *Forbes* in earnings per share growth among "200 Entrepreneurial Hot Shots" and ranked #11 by *Fortune Small Business* among "The FSB 100, America's Fastest-Growing Small Companies." Capers served three terms as chair of the Technology Council of Maryland and is a founder and past chair of the Maryland Bioscience Alliance. He and his wife, Marion, have endowed annual awards for "Excellence in Mentoring and Advising" both nationally and internationally. He was named the Duke University School of Engineering's Distinguished Alumnus for 2005 and has been included among *Who's Who in Science and Engineering* and *Who's Who in the World*. Capers married Marion in 1975, and they have one child, Adam.

Capers W. McDonald

Maj. Adam McDonald was born in Craven (now Williamsburg) County, SC in about 1743, the second or third son of Daniel and Mary McDonald. He represented Prince Frederick's Parish as a member of the "committee of ninety-nine" in 1774.

When the first two Continental regiments of foot were raised in SC in 1775, officers were chosen by ballot, with the highest rank going to those who received the most votes in the First Provincial Congress. Adam McDonald received only five votes fewer than Francis Marion, and became the seventh ranking captain of the First Regiment of Infantry on Jun. 17, 1775. He was appointed a major of the First Regiment of Infantry, SC on Sept. 16, 1776.

A veteran of the Indian Wars, and described by Gen. William Moultrie as "a very bold, adventurous man," Capt. McDonald soon became one of America's first spies. He first posed as a Tory sergeant from the SC backcountry and called upon British Governor William Campbell on Sept. 13, 1775. The Governor revealed his plan for supporting the Tories, which he had steadfastly denied, and the information was promptly reported back to the General Committee's Council of Safety.

Capt. McDonald later was sent on a secret mission to East Florida to ascertain the strength of that British garrison. He posed this time as an out-of-work manager of an indigo plantation, and was interviewed by the Royal Lieutenant Governor, John Moultrie, brother of then Col. William Moultrie. Capt. McDonald and John Moultrie had been tent mates during the Cherokee Expedition, and after he was recognized, Capt. McDonald barely escaped. He was captured and imprisoned at least once during 1777.

Adam McDonald had married Izabellah Fitch on Oct. 15, 1762 in Prince Frederick's Parish, SC. They had four children including one son, also Adam, and Maj. McDonald died at his home in St. Stephen's Parish in Dec. 1778.

John Durdan Reeves was born in Halifax, NC on May 20, 1759, the eldest child of Malachi and Fortune Durdan Reeves. He first volunteered for Revolutionary War service in Halifax at the age of 20 as a private with the 3rd Regiment, NC, in Jan. 1780. He reenlisted four times during 1780-81, and was commissioned a lieutenant in the 3rd Regt. of the Maryland Continental Line under Maj. Gen. William Smallwood in May 1781.

John D. Reeves served during several significant battles of 1780-81. These included the battles of Camden and Monk's Corner, SC (both Apr. 1780), during which time he may have first encountered the Maryland forces. He later joined the Maryland troops while they encamped near Charlotte, NC during Oct.-Dec. 1780. He was wounded just prior to the battle of Guilford Courthouse in NC (Mar. 1781), during the opening advance in which Lt. Col. Henry "Lighthorse Harry" Lee was taken prisoner.

As a lieutenant in the 3rd Regiment, Maryland, he fought in the battle of Eutaw Springs, SC (Sept. 1781), and later was working on the approaches to Yorktown, VA when British Gen. Cornwallis surrendered there on Oct. 19, 1781. Lt. John D. Reeves and other officers were deranged (rendered supernumerary) by a Resolution of Congress recorded in the Journals of the Continental Congress on Dec. 31, 1781.

After the war, Lt. Reeves returned to NC and married Sally Lock Elwell in about 1787, settling in Surry County, where they farmed and raised seven children until her death in 1810. In Jun. 1811, he married Eleanor Howard in Surry County. He held land in Madison County, MO from 1812-1834, but applied for his Revolutionary War pension in Feb. 1832 in Surry County, NC, and died there in Aug. 1840.

MCGLONE, ROBERT E. – Born Dec. 27, 1940 in Stoneham, MA, but grew up in Melrose, MA. He served in the US Army from 1963-65, and worked in Parks & Recreation Administration for 40 years, retiring in June 2004. He married first Margaret (deceased) and second Alice, and has five children and three grandchildren.

Nathan Putnam was born Sept. 8, 1749 in Danvers, MA. He was a member of Capt. Hutchinson's company of minutemen, which responded to the alarm of Apr. 19, 1775 by joining forces with minutemen from surrounding towns in the attack of British forces under the command of Lord Percy at Menotomy as they retreated back to Boston from Concord and Lexington. In "... the bloodiest half-mile of all the Battle Road," Nathan was wounded near the right shoulder by a musket ball. His brother Perley was killed.

According to Eban Putnam's "History of the Putnam Family," the following advertisement appeared in the "New England Chronicle or Essex Gazette" of May 25, 1775: "Lost in the battle of Menotomy, by Nathan Putnam, of Capt. Hutchinson's Company, who was badly wounded, A French Firelock, marked D., No. 6, with a marking iron on the Breech. Said Putnam carried it to a cross Road near a mill. Whoever has said Gun in Possession, is desired to return it to Col. Mansfield of Lynn, or to the Selectman of Danvers, and they shall be well rewarded for their trouble."

Nathan re-enlisted in Capt. Putnam's Company, 19th Regiment, Oct. 6, 1775. He later served as a constable in Danvers in 1785 and in 1787 he served on a committee to regulate the schools.

Nathan Putnam died on Apr. 10, 1823 in Danvers. He is buried there in the High Street Cemetery. He was a descendant of John Putnam, who was baptized at Aston Abbots, Bucks, England on Jan. 17, 1579 and migrated to Salem, MA around 1640-41.

MCKENZIE, RALPH A. – Mr. Ralph A. McKenzie was born Aug. 16, 1933 in Columbia, MS. His military service was in the Air Force. He joined the SAR Nov. 7, 2002 in Louisiana.

He worked for the Louisiana Department of Health and Human Resources, as Adm. Law Judge (hearing officer). He retired on Sept. 12, 1986.

Ralph A. McKenzie

He served as a LASSAR board member, Sgt. At Arms, Program Chair, Vice-president, and President in 2007 of the Gen. Philemon Thomas Chapter. He was awarded a Meritorious Service Medal by the Gen. Philemon Thomas Chapter. He is also a member of the Society of War of 1812; E.R. Civil War Round Table; St. Andrew Society; and Friends of French – LSU.

He is married to Gwenda D. McKenzie, who is a member of Baton Rouge Chapter of DAR, and they reside in Baton Rouge, LA.

Edward Ball was born in Feb. 1745 in Prince Frederick Winyaw, GA. He served as 2nd Lt. in Capt. John Bacon's Company of Riflemen. He was a member of Provincial Congress in 1775 of St. John's Parish, GA. He was killed in battle in 1779 and is buried in Liberty County, GA.

MCMICHAEL, WESLEY D. – Born Aug. 4, 1935 at Burt Lake, Cheboygan County, MI.

Wesley has served as Michigan State Historian and Vice President, West Michigan. He has been on the Patriot and Information Technology committees. Wesley received the Bronze Good Citizenship Medal.

Wesley has four children, He has been the Personnel Director-DMH Hospital, Coldwater, Central Off and Traverse City, MI. He retired in 1989.

Christopher McMichael, was born about 1757 in Ireland. He served as a Private in Col. Samuel Miles Company, the Pennsylvania Line. He was involved in the Battle of Long Island and others.

Christopher was a farmer and died Sept. 7, 1812. He is buried in Butler County, PA in a graveyard under a shopping center; no graves moved.

MCNEIL, JOHN – Born Sept. 28, 1923. He has held the office of President and Treasurer. John was the Illinois Medal awards committee chairman. He has been presented the Past Pres. and WWII Veteran awards.

John was in the U.S. Navy, 1943-46 Radioman Third Class. He married Janice Armstrong and they have two children and five grandchildren.

John has been a principal, college teacher, and high school teacher. He retired in May, 1991.

John is also a member of Golden K Kiwanis Club and the Wesley Methodist Church. He is interested in history and enjoys travel.

McNeil Station at Barbarsville, KY is his ancestor's homestead.

Johnathan McNeil, or McNaill was born in 1700 in Scotland. Johnathan was a soldier in the Militia of Capt. Simon Kenton's Company under the Command of George Rogers Clark, 1782. He served against enemy Indians under command of Ger.

In civilian life, Johnathan was a farmer, blacksmith and hunter. He is buried at the Family cemetery near Mack.

MCNEIL, NORMAN LEON – Served in the Republic of Vietnam with the 101st Airborne Division. Upon completion of his military service, attended Arkansas Tech. University at Ozark, AR. He then continued government service and will retire with over 30 years of service. He is married with three children and four grandchildren.

Reverend George McNeil sailed to America between 1745 and 1750, arriving in Virginia. He was ordained as a Baptist minister about 1775. He was also a member of the Regulator Movement, and after the battle of Alamance, was forced to flee for his safety.

During the Revolutionary War, he served as a Chaplain in the Regiment of Col. Benjamin Cleveland at the time of the battle for King's Mountain. He was associated with many churches in and around Wilkes County, as well as Register of Deeds for Wilke County from 1787 until his death in 1805. He is buried in the family cemetery.

Reverend John Cleveland is a 4th generation American and was ordained at Prince William County, VA in 1772. He was one of the first preachers in backwoods and was associated with several churches in Virginia, Georgia and the Carolinas.

During the Revolutionary War, he served as a Chaplain in his brother, Col. Benjamin Cleveland's regiment.

Pvt. John Stovall Sr. was the son of Bartholomew Stovall (b. 1665), who arrived in America in 1684 as an indentured servant. John served as a private solder in the County Militia of North Carolina from 1775 to 1778. After 1778, he became a supplier to the Army.

Bartholomew Stovall, was the son of John Stovall Sr. and a patriot of North Carolina, who took the Oath of Allegiance in 1778. He also supplied the Army for the duration of the war.

MEESE, RAYMOND L. – Born Dec. 1, 1945 at Canton, Stark County, OH. He joined SAR Ohio Society in July, 2004.

Raymond served as 1st Lt. in the US Army, Field Artillery Unit from 1968 to 1970. He graduated Officer Candidate School at Fort Sill, OK. He was Airborne qualified at Fort Benning, GA and served in Republic of Vietnam during 1969. After military service, he was an FBI Special Agent from November 1970 until his retirement in January 2001.

Raymond also is a member of Army Historical Foundation, America/Division National Association, 1/1 Armored Calvary Association, Save Ft. Laurens Association, Ohio Historical Association and the American Legion.

Raymond and Marjorie have two children.

Baltzer Meese was born March 20, 1756 in Lancaster County, PA. He was a Private with the 2nd Pennsylvania Regiment. He served five years (1776-1781). Baltzer participated in the battles of Brandywine, Germantown, Block House at the North River, Monmouth Meeting, plus others.

Baltzer was a miller, who died May 15, 1838. He is buried in Somerset County, PA.

MEISER, PROF. CHARLES WILLIAM – Born Jan. 29, 1940 in Muncie, IN. He joined the Alabama Society of the SAR on Dec. 9, 2008 (NSSAR #172951). Charles married Gretchen Antje Liste on Oct. 24, 1964 in Lafayette, IN. They have a son, a daughter, and four granddaughters. A graduate of Purdue University with degrees in Electrical Engineering and Economics, he was a Walton Free Enterprise Fellow. He retired his professorship in 2000 and his fellowship in 2002. Charles is a member of numerous genealogical organizations.

Charles W. Meiser standing at the marker for The Overmyer Fort, Northumberland County, PA, named in honor of Captain John George Overmeyer.

Captain John George Overmeyer was born Oct. 27, 1727 in Blankenloch, Baden-Wurttemberg and arrived in Pennsylvania in 1751. His service included: Capt., 6th Company, 4th Battalion, Northumberland County Militia under Col. Cole, Oct. 8, 1776; attached to Col. Potter's 2nd Battalion at Reading, Jan. 1777; joined Gen. Washington at Morristown, Jan. 8, 1777; returned to Pennsylvania, ca. Feb. 1777; Committee of Public Safety, Buffalo Township, Northumberland County, 1777-78; raised a company of Frontier Rangers, serving as Captain, 1779-80.

He died Sept. 22, 1805 in Northumberland County and buried on the bank of Penns Creek.

MEISER, MICHAEL KEVIN – Born May 13, 1966 in Lafayette, IN, and joined the Alabama Society of the SAR on Dec. 9, 2008 (NSSAR #172952). He was enrolled in Junior ROTC for two years. Michael married April Dawn Anderson on Aug. 12, 2000 in Shelbyville. A graduate of Johnson & Wales University, with degrees in Culinary Arts and Food Service Education, he has worked in numerous chef and management positions. Michael is a life member of the Meisser Genealogical Association and is very active in his church.

Captain John George Overmeyer was born Oct. 27, 1727 in Blankenloch, Baden-Wurttemberg and arrived in Pennsylvania in 1751. His service included: Capt., 6th Company, 4th Battalion, Northumberland County Militia under Col. Cole, Oct. 8, 1776; attached to Col. Potter's 2nd Battalion at Reading, Jan. 1777; joined Gen. Washington at Morristown, Jan. 8, 1777; returned to Pennsylvania, ca. Feb. 1777; Committee of Public Safety, Buffalo Township, Northumberland County, 1777-78; raised a company of Frontier Rangers, serving as Captain, 1779-80.

He died Sept. 22, 1805 in Northumberland County and buried on the bank of Penns Creek.

MELLEN, CHRISTOPHER E. – President of the Boston Chapter of MASSAR, born in Boston, MA married to Elaine; three children, Chris Jr., Amanda and Chad. BBA, Temple University, major in Real Estate, a Certified Property Manager, Graduate Certificate in Project Management and a Master of Science Degree in Management from Boston University. Vice President of the Simon Companies and an Instructor at Boston University. With the Institute of Real Estate Management, a Faculty Member, on the National Executive Committee, 2004 President, Boston Chapter, and 2006-2007 Regional VP. He has twice been named Real Estate Executive of the Month by the *New England Real Estate Journal.*

James Griffin, born in North Carolina in 1753, took part in the battles of Brandywine, Germantown, Monmouth and Guilford Court House. Married Sarah Lodge and lived in Irwin County, GA.

Thomas Bradford, best friend of James Griffin, married to Elizabeth Marshall. He served as a lieutenant from Halifax district.

Both Patriots settled on their respective plantations near the old Columbus Stage Road in Irwin County, GA. Their children, William Bradford and Elizabeth Griffin, married. Both Patriots were buried on their plantations, where the James Jackson Chapter of D.A.R. Valdosta placed markers.

MELNICK, LOUIS D. – Mr. Louis D. Melnick was born Aug. 2, 1934 in Chicago, IL.

He worked at Bankers Life and Casualty in Life Insurance Management 1963-1986. He is a live member of the National Genealogical Society and Society of Genealogists, London.

He attended Downers Grove (IL) High School and graduated from North Central College, Naperville, IL in 1960. He resides in Evanston, IL.

Isaac Baldwin was born Dec. 12, 1738 in Sudbury, MA. At the news of the Battle of Lexington, Isaac Baldwin gathered a group of volunteers at Hillsborough, NH, and marched to the headquarters of the American Army at Cambridge, MA.

He was given command of a company of men from the vicinity of Hillsborough, which was assigned to Col. John Stark's New Hampshire Regiment.

Rubbing of Eunice Baldwin Stone, wife of Capt. Isaac Baldwin, Hillsborough Center Cemetery, Hillsborough, NH. Inscription on monument reads: "Eunice. relict of Capt. Isaac Baldwin, who fell at Bunkerhill, June 17, 1775, died Jan. 8, 1813. Et. 74."

Capt. Baldwin was wounded June 17, 1775 at the Battle of Bunker Hill, and died that evening in Medford, opposite Col. Royall's mansion-house, Stark's headquarters.

We know that his widow, Eunice Baldwin, on Aug. 20, 1783 received out of the administration of Capt. Baldwin's estate 27 pounds and 11 shillings for the support of their four children who were under seven years of age.

Recent research in manuscript records at the New Hampshire Historical Society, Concord, reveals Eunice Baldwin petitioned the State of New Hampshire June 3, 1801, for relief due to Capt. Baldwin's death.

On June 16, 1801, the New Hampshire House of Representatives approved a $200 payment to Eunice Baldwin, which was made on June 17, 1801, the twenty-sixth anniversary of her husband's death.

MELTON, WILLIAM RAY – LtCol William Ray Melton was born September 9, 1937 in Marysville, CA to Raymond Lee Melton and Alice Ruth Hieter Melton Olsen, and was raised in Rio Oso, CA. He now makes his home in Oklahoma City, OK.

LtCol William R. Melton

He is a 37-year veteran of the U.S. Marine Cops and served in combat in Vietnam as an infantry sergeant in 1965 and 2nd and 1st lieutenant in 1968-69. As a captain he commanded an infantry company during the evacuations of Phnom Penh, Cambodia and Saigon, Vietnam in 1975. For service in Vietnam he was awarded the Silver Star Medal. Bronze Star Medal with V, Purple Heart, Navy Commendation Medal with V, Navy Achievement Medal, two Combat Action Ribbons, and received a combat commission to second lieutenant. He was inducted into the Oklahoma Military Hall of Fame in 2007. The Moore, Oklahoma Malcolm Hunter DAR Chapter awarded him the NSDAR Medal of Honor in 2008, and the Oklahoma City SAR Chapter awarded him the NSSAR War Service Medal with Vietnam Bar and Certificate in 2008.

He is a past President of the Central Oklahoma Chapter, Military Officers Association of America, a past Vice Chairman of the Oklahoma Veterans Council and a two-term past Chairman of his Church Parish Council.

Gravestone of Bennett Wellman.

He is a life member of the National Society of the Sons of the American Revolution, the 2nd Vice President/Awards Chair of the Oklahoma City SAR Chapter and a George Washington Fellow.

Bennett Wellman was born Feb. 9, 1754 in St. Mary's County, MD. He served as private in the 3rd Company of Middle & Upper Battalions of Montgomery County, Maryland Militia.

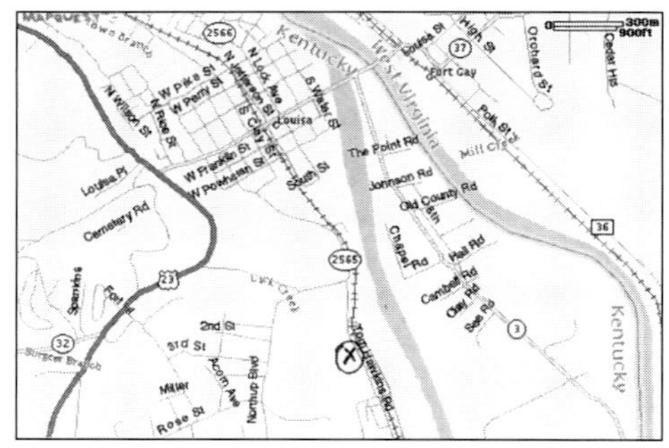

Map to Bennett Wellman's grave site, marked by X.

Bennett was a great huntsman as well as a shoemaker. He died Sept. 15, 1830 and is buried in what was originally called "The Northrup Farm" but has been incorporated into a cemetery, name unknown, located south of Louisa, KY.

MERITT, ELDON RAY – Son of Alice Combs and Elmer Meritt, Ray was born Nov. 10, 1938 in Jefferson, OK. Ray has been a teacher, consultant for a mining company, and administrator, retiring as Assistant Superintendent of Operations at Gordon Cooper Technology Center in Shawnee, Oklahoma, in 2002.

Ray and his wife, Mary Louise Badgwell, have three children Stephannie, Shannon and Robert, and five grandchildren, Carly, Gabriel, Isabella, Macy, and Dylan.

Ray volunteers weekly at the Church of the Servant United Methodist Church and served as Payne County Democratic Party Chairman. Other organizations Ray belongs to are: American Heart Association and the American Diabetes Association.

Captain Stephen Merritt (b. 1750 VA/d. ca. 1830 KY) led colonial troops during the entire revolutionary struggle for independence. He distinguished himself at the battles of Kings Mountain, Charleston, Monks Corner, Georgetown, and was wounded in a charge by Tarleton's cavalry at Cowpens, and in a hard contested battle at Guilford Court House. He never drew a pension.

Stephen was married (Jul. 1, 1771, Granville, NC) to Winnefred Rose (b. 1756).

Stephen's son was Ephraim Merritt (b. 1776, Granville, NC/d. Aug. 1844, IL), who was married Mar. 27, 1798 in NC to Elizabeth Mickeljohn (b. 1780). Her father, Rev. Micklejohn, minister of the Established Church of England, was ordained by the Bishop of London.

Stephen's grandson, George Merritt (b. Jan. 30, 1799 in SC) was married to Elizabeth Files (b. Feb. 18, 1795 SC/d. Sept. 9, 1864, Wayne Co., IL), and was a teacher whose long life allowed him record stories of distinguished service rendered in the Revolutionary War and the bravery Stephen demonstrated as the Merritts moved west. George reported that the paternal ancestor of the branch of the Merritt family was from Wales and emigrated during the time of colonization by Sir Walter Raleigh.

MILLER, HAROLD (HAL) F. JR. – Hal Miller, a member of SAR for fifty-four years, currently serves as Vice-Chairman of the Finance Committee, having previously served for two years as NSSAR Chairman of the Investment Committee and a member of the Finance Committee. He was recently appointed Vice-Chairman of the Partners in Patriotism Committee. NSSAR Committee memberships: George Washington Endowment Fund-Distribution, ROTC/JROTC; and Hospitality/Music.

He was formerly the Florida National Alternate Trustee 2006-07; National Trustee 2005-06; State President of the FLSSAR 2004-05; FLSSAR Senior Vice-President 2003-04; FLSSAR Chaplain 2002-03; and FLSSAR Chapter Challenge Committee Chair 1999-2002. He currently serves as one of the three Trustees of the Florida SAR Endowment & Operating Budget Trust Funds, and Chairman of the FLSSAR Patriotic Activities Committee. FLSSAR Committee memberships: Chapter Challenge, DAR Liaison, Education, NSSAR Constitution & Bylaws Review, JROTC, & Trust Fund Development.

Locally: President of the Saramana Chapter SAR (Sarasota & Manatee County), 2000-01; V.P. & Treasurer, 1999; Color Guard Commander for 3 years; Co-Chairman of History Fairs and Publicity Committees, 2002-05.

He is a life member of NSSAR, a George Washington Fellow, and is a recipient of the Patriot Medal, the Meritorious Service Medal, and the Bronze Color Guard Medal. In addition, he is a life member of The Society of the Descendents of Washington's Army at Valley Forge.

Hal retired in 1997 after 13 years in banking and 16 years in investment banking and brokerage. He graduated from Amherst College in 1950, and received a certification from College of Financial Planning in 1991. He and his wife, Pru-Ann, have two children and four grandchildren.

Col. John Harris was born April 1, 1753 to Thomas Harris and Elizabeth Bailey. He was married to Mary Bowen in 1776 and they resided in Willistown, Chester County, PA. He died Dec. 25, 1838 and is buried at his church, the Great Valley Presbyterian Church located on Swedesford Road, Malvern, PA.

MILLER, NEVIN COOLEDGE – Born July 11, 1925 in Schuylkill Haven, Schuylkill County, PA. Joined Gov. Joseph Hiester Chapter in August 1998.

Nevin has served as Pennsylvania State Society Eagle Scout Chairman; Past President Gov. Joseph Hiester Chapter; Secretary Gov. Joseph Hiester Chapter and Sgt. Gov. Joseph Hiester Color Guard.

Nevin C. Miller

He has been awarded the Meritorious Service Medal Dec. 9, 2004; Founder of the Gov. Joseph Hiester Color Guard June 2005; Meritorious Service Oak Leaf Cluster by PASSAR May 6, 2006; War Service Meda, March 8, 2007; and Robert E. Burt Boy Scout Volunteer Award by the National Society SAR July 9, 2007.

Nevin served in WWII as a Cpl., US Marine Corp Pacific Theatre. His spouse is decreased. Nevin has three children, five grandchildren, 12 step-grandchildren and five step-great-grandchildren.

Nevin was employed as District Manager Snap on Tools Corp.; Automotive Service Manager; and Treasurer Retired State Employees of Pennsylvania. He retired September, 1987.

He is a 33rd Degree Mason and member of Rajah Shrine; East Penn Chapter PA Order of Eastern Star; Past president of the Rajah Shrine Chanters; Ray Master Post 217 American Legion and Berks County Genealogical Society.

Nevin says: "I have been proud to serve SAR through my local chapter and the state society. Service is the glue that binds us all together. As chairman of the SARIBSA Scholarship Award Program I attended Eagle Scout Courts of Honor in order to personally award the certificates of achievement and the SAR scholarship applications. While serving as state chairman I mailed hundreds of certificates and scholarship forms to Eagle Scouts all over the State of Pennsylvania. The Robert E. Burd Boy Scout Volunteer Award represents one of my proudest achievements. I still attend Eagle Scout Courts of Honor. Establishing a Color Guard for the Gov. Joseph Hiester Chapter has been a most satisfying experience for me and the chapter has gained recognition through this unit.

Currently, I am working to establish a Youth Awards Fund for our SAR chapter. This fund will provide monetary awards to local Eagle Scouts, ROTC and Essay winners as well as awards to outstanding American History students of 20 local high schools. I approach this with the same determination as our Patriot Ancestors knowing "If it's to be, it's up to me!"

Conrad Roeder was born in Germany, migrated to America at 20 years old in 1772 on a "Sail now- pay later" journey. He was "sold" to pay his debt of 17 Pounds, 3 Shillings and was obligated to work for a period of three years. He enlisted as a Private in the Army of the United States in 1776 under Captain Hettering in Windsor Twp., Chester Co., PA.

He was at Fort Lee, Amboy and Fort Washington. He was taken prisoner and held for eight weeks at Bridewell Prison. After being released, he reenlisted and was at Trenton, Amboy, White Plains Valley Forge, Brandywine, Germantown and Monmouth Meeting House. He was a farmer. He died on the 6th of August 1834 and is buried at St. Paul's Cemetery, South Manheim Twp., Schuylkill Co., PA.

MINTON, TYREE (TY) GOODWIN – Born Nov 7, 1938 in Roswell, NM. He joined SAR Apr. 4, 2008.

Ty has a doctorate in environmental studies. In 1972, he founded a graduate program in environmental studies at Antioch University, New England. He retired as director of that program in 2001. In 1990 he received the New England regional award for outstanding environmental educator.

Ty lives in Taos, NM with his wife, Gael Rockwell Minton. They have two children, Bronwyn Ariana Minton and Nathaniel Teal Minton (SAR member).

Ty is descended from **Obadiah Badger**, born Apr. 19, 1727 in Newberry, MA. Obadiah lived in Amesbury, MA, where he was a gunsmith. He served as a private in Capt. Timothy Banard's company at Lexington, which marched on the alarm of Apr. 19, 1775 from Amesbury. In 1776 he served for one year as Armorer with the Massachusetts troops under Capt. Eli Gale and Col. Jonathan Brewer. He served as a private under Capt. Jonathan Evan in Col. Sam Johnson's regiment in 1777. He served as a private under Capt. Richard Titcomb's company under Col. Nathaniel Wade's regiment in 1780. The Company was raised to reinforce the Continental Army.

MITCHELL, JAMES E. – Born Jan. 11, 1946 in Monroe, LA; presently residing in Kingwood, TX. Joined the Texas Society in June 2005.

James was Chapter President, 2006-08; Freedom No. 38; Region 6 Oration Chairman and Rumbaugh Oration Contest, 2007. He has received the Past Chapter Presidents Medal 2007, TXSSAR; Cold War Medal Recipient as Special Agent – Federal Bureau of Investigation (Retired); National Intelligence Community – Exceptional Human Intelligence Collector Award and numerous letters of accommodation for exemplary service to the United States Government.

James was a Special Agent of the Federal Bureau of Investigation and retired July 2001 after 32 years of service. He married Anne T. Sullivan,

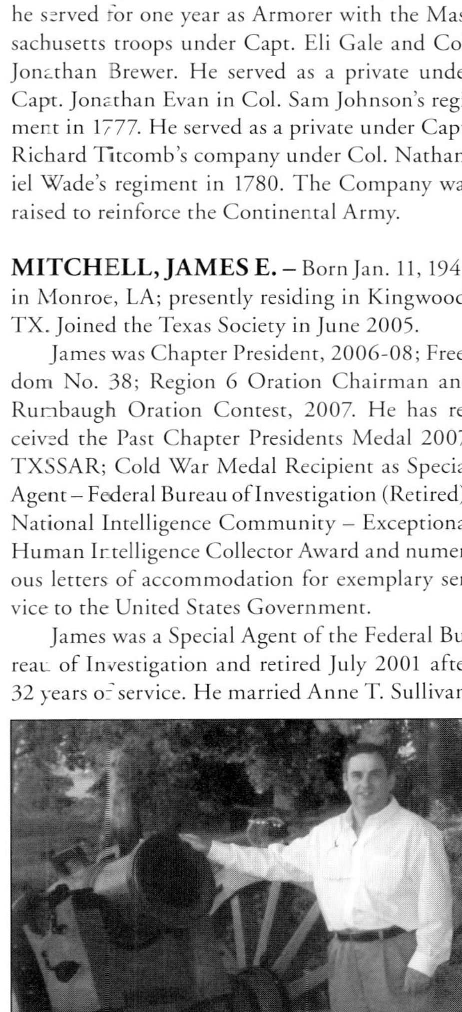
James Edward Mitchell

and they have two children.

James also belongs to the Society of Former Special Agents of the Federal Bureau of Investigation.

Benjamin Gaar

James shares identical male Y-DNA markers with Benjamin Gaar, Michael's great-nephew and their common ancestor is Andreas Gaar, born June 14, 1685 in Illenschwang, Bavaria.

John Adam Gaar was born Dec. 24, 1711 in Illenschwang, Bavaria. Son **Michael Gaar** was born c. 1740, Gaar Mountain, Brumfield Parish, Orange County, VA. He was County Lieut. with Culpepper Minute Men, VA Militia. Served 75 days, June and October, 1781, under order of VA Militia Cmdr. Thomas Nelson Jr.

He was a farmer and owner and operator of Gaar Grist Mill and wheelwright. Michael died January 1797 and is buried in Elbert County, Ruckersville, GA at Van(n)s Creek.

MIX, RICHARD LAWRENCE – He has a BA, Lycoming College 1951, an MA, Bucknell University 1956 and additional Graduate Studies from PA State University, Ohio University and Cortland State College, NY.

He is the 12th generation to live in America with no name change–only spelling (Thomas Meeks New Haven Colony 1643). With wife Miriam, we co-authored *A BICENTENNIAL POSTCARD HISTORY OF WILLIAMSPORT.* We have FIVE books on Genealogy in the Library of Congress. I was the Chairman for the Northumberland Presbytery History Committee in 1986 and created a slide program on its history. For the 50th celebration of the Council of Churches of Lycoming County, created a slide program of their history. We have 12 slide programs on local history which we show to the public. Miriam and he give four awards–two to the local high school and two to Lycoming College.

Richard L. Mix

Civil Organizations he belongs to: Mayflower Society (John Billington), Sons of Colonial NE, Sons and Daughters of Pilgrims, First Families of CT, Registry of Infamous and Famous Relatives.

He is a Member of Bicentennial Committees NAT 1976, Lycoming County 1995, City of Williamsport 2006, Life Member Lycoming County Historical Society and Muncy Historical Society, Life Member Lycoming County Genealogical Society, Roger Williams Family Association (Direct Descendant).

Richard's patriots: **Ezra Spaulding**, **Joseph Beach Sr.**, **Joseph Brown**, **Herman Carter**, **Israel Carter**, **Isaac Chaapel**, **Joseph Eaton**, **Thomas Gates**, **Henry Hotchkiss Sr.**, **Henry Hotchkiss Jr.**, **Eldad Mix**, **Deliverance Parmenter**, **Joshua Parmenter**, **Armach Randall**, **Timothy Scott**, **Joseph Slater**, **Ebenezer Wilcox**, and **Philemon Wilcox**.

MOBLEY, BENNY GENE – Born in Newhall, Los Angeles County, CA, he joined the Texas SAR on Jun. 11, 2008 (Nat. #171851/ TXSSAR #10226). He is a ranch foreman for Wayward Wind Ranch. He holds a Certificate of Arkansas Ancestry for the Territorial Period to Benny Mobley for David Mobley Sr., son-in-law of Morgan Cryer Sr. who resided in Clark Co., AR, Jul. 8, 1817. David Mobley Sr. served in the War of 1812.

Benny Gene Mobley

BennyGene is married to Symthia Irene, with two children and two grandchildren.

Morgan Cryer Sr. was born Feb. 22, 1756 in South Carolina, married to Barbara Morris of SC. He was a private in the 6th South Carolina Regiment, joining on Aug. 27, 1776. Around 1778 he served one year under Capt. Samuel Taylor and Col. Sumter. He went on an expedition and was shot and wounded in the leg. He recovered and served just over three years.

A farmer, Morgan died on Nov. 27, 1833 in Clark Co., AR, near Arkadelphia.

MONIGHETTI, RICHARD O. – Born September 1949 in Santa Maria, CA. Joined the CA State Society in 2007.

Richard served in the Army – 82nd Airborne Division, HHC 1st Brigade. He is now self employed as a rancher/farmer. Richard and wife Donna (decreased) have two children and two grandchildren.

He belongs to the American Legion "Boots N Chutes" All Airborne Assn.; Life member – 82nd Airborne Assn.

Richard's sons, Richard A. and Brian, are also members of the Sons of the American Revolution.

James Green was born November, 1761 at Rhode Island. He was a Private in various companies with the Rhode Island Line. James was at the battle of Saratoga.

In civilian life, James was a shoemaker. He died June 1, 1842 and is buried at Youngsville Brokenstraw, Warren County, PA.

Cornelius Nieuwkerk/Newkirk was baptized May 1, 1715 at Kingston, Ulster County, NY. He was a Private with the Ulster County Militia, Rochester/Wawarsing Regiment. Cornelius died Dec. 15, 1781 and is buried at Laurenkill Cemetery, Wawarsing, Ulster County, NY.

Gerret C. Newkirk was baptized Sept. 23, 1739 at Kingston, Ulster County, NY. He served as a Private with the 3rd Ulster County Regiment of the Militia. Gerret died Dec. 26, 1813 and is also buried at Laurenkill Cemetery, Wawarsing, Ulster County, NY.

Jonas Harrison was born about 1852 in New Jersey. He served as a Private with the Essex County "Minute Men." Jonas died Nov. 6, 1798 and is buried in Newark, Essex County, NJ.

Rev. David Bolles was born Jan. 14, 1743 in New London County, CT. He was a Capt. with the 9th Train Band, under the 5th Regiment.

In civilian life, David was a farmer, tanner, currier, and Baptist minister. He died Feb. 14, 1807 at Ashford, CT and is buried at "Old Cemetery," Eastford, Windham County, CT.

Stephen Olney was born Dec. 22, 1752 at Smithfield, Providence County, RI. He served as a Captain with the Continental Army and Rhode Island Militia. Stephen was a farmer who died Dec. 12, 1841 at Youngsville, PA. He is buried at Oakland Cemetery, Warren, Warren County, PA.

Joshua Abell was born July 16, 1731 at Rehoboth, Bristel Co., MA. He was private in Cols. David Wells and Elisha Porter Regiment. He was at Ticonderoga and Bennington battles. His civilian occupation was Goshen, MA Town Treasurer. Joshua died Aug. 20, 1774 and is buried near Goshen Village, Goshen, Hampshire Co., MA.

John Abell was born May 3, 1763 at Rehoboth, Bristol Co., MA. He enlisted as a private, served as in Capt. Bartlett's Company with Col. Wesson's Regiment and in Capt. Elisha Cranston's Company with the 5th Hampshire Co. John was a farmer who died March 5, 1842 and is buried at Herrick Cemetery, Fairfield, Franklin Co., VA.

Andries A. DeWitt was born April 23, 1732 in Kingston, Ulster County, NY. He was a private and served in Capt. John Hasbrock's company, Ulster Co. Militia and with Cols. Levin Pauling's Company, 3rd Regiment and Col. John Cantine's Company, Cantine Regiment.

Andries was a Reformed Dutch Church deacon and died in 1803. He is buried at Wawarsing, Ulster County, NY. Andries was a signer of "Articles of Association" and member of "Safety Committee."

Silas Rice was born in 1747 in Sudbury, VT. He served as a private with Capt. John Boynton's Company, in the regiments of Col. Nathan Sparhawk, the Massachusetts Regiment and Col. Jacob Cushing's Regiment. Silas was in the Bennington Expedition and at the battle of Bennington, VT. He was a farmer who died Jan. 4, 1821 and is buried at Endsburg Cemetery, Endsburg, VT.

George Gaby was born about 1747 in Trowbridge, England. He was a private and served in Col. R. Putnam, Mass. and Hampshire Regiments under Capt. Israel A. Richardson; in Col. Wright's Regt., Mass, in Capt. Jonathan Ballard's Company; in Col. Joshua Benson's Regiment under Capt. D. Shay; and at the Battle of Bennington, VT under Capt. Gates. George was a barber in civilian life, and died April 23, 1828, buried at Bennington, VT.

Asa Grant was born Oct. 23, 1732 at Wrentham, Norfolk, MA. He was a private in Capt. Christopher Bannister's Company in Col. John Dickinson's Regiment. Asa was at the Battle of Bennington, VT and also served in Connecticut. He died Dec. 6, 1816 and is buried at Herrick Cemetery, Fairfield, VT.

MONROE, GREGORY GRANT – Born Sept. 12, 1989 in Nashville, TN, Grant joined the SAR on Jan. 25, 2008 at the age of 18.

Grant first became involved with genealogy in high school. His American History teacher assigned him a family heritage project, involving the study of genealogy and how their family had an affect on American history. Grant researched his ancestors and discovered William Horner, Sr., a Revolutionary Warpatriotfrom Pennsylvania.

G. Grant Monroe

Grant submitted a 400-page ancestry book for his class and also to the History Channel's "Save Our History" contest. He was selected as one of 25 National winners.

Grant is currently a Freshman at the University of Tennessee at Martin, and is double majoring in History and Political Science. He hopes to become a Constitutional Lawyer.

William Horner, Sr., born Oct. 30, 1746 in York Co., PA, rendered Patriotic services during the war by hauling a four-horse load of beef to Gen. George Washington and his troops at Valley Forge in 1777.

William's civilian occupation was a surveyor. He was the father of 14 children. William died Oct. 12, 1824 in Hamblen Co., TN and is buried in Bent Creek Cemetery in Whitesburg, TN.

MONTAGUE, THOMAS DRU – Born April 10, 1958 at Lexington, KY; lives at Yorktown, VA.

Thomas was in the USAF as a TSgt. and is retired. He presently works as a Field Engineer III at the SOUTHCOM DISA Field Office in Miami, FL.

Thomas married Victoria Lee Gough and they have two children. Thomas is a lifetime member of Jamestowne Society and a member of the Williamsburg Chapter of VASSAR.

John M. Oldham was born Nov. 10, 1757 in Prince William County, VA. He attained the rank of Captain. John was an Ensign of North Carolina Troops in Colonel Moore's Regiment at battle of Camden under Gen. Gates. He was a Captain and Company Commander at battles of Cowpens and Guilford under Gen. Green and saw the defeat of Lord Cornwallis. In civilian life, he was a Judge, landowner (Madison and Estill Counties), ferry owner (Kentucky River near the mouth of Falling Branch), and hog drover. John died Nov. 17, 1831 and is buried in Estill County, KY.

MONTEITH, JOEL D. – Born May 8, 1942 in Pinewald, NJ. He presently lives in Preston, MO.

Joel and Carolann G. have seven children and 10 grandchildren. He is presently employed at Tan-Tar-A Resort as Golf Club, Marina and Waterpark--Loss Prevention Supervisor.

Joel D. Montieth

Joel is a Past Master, Urbana, MO Lodge No. 421 A.F. and A.M. His hobbies include genealogy, gun collecting and restoration, and a small farm operation.

Jacob Tilton was born in 1752 in Goshen, NJ. He was a Captain in First Regiment – Cols. Cook, Holmes and Breese with Monmouth County, NJ Militia.

From 1775 through 1780, he was in defense of vital salt works at Shelter Cove, Monmouth County NJ. March 24, 1782, defense and loss of fort at Port of Toms River, Monmouth County, NJ.

In civilian life, Jacob was the father of eight children; a farmer and Bayman. He died in 1833 and is buried at Kettle Creek, Monmouth County, NJ.

MOORE, JERRY J. – Jerry joined the society in 1999 and is a member of the Illinois Chapter, American Bicentennial Chapter. He is a former archaeologist and is the author or co-author to many archaeological reports and an illustrator for several journal articles on archaeology and cultural history.

Jerry J. Moore

Private Jesse Edwards is Moore's Revolutionary War ancestor. Edwards was born March 4, 1756 in Bucks County, PA, to William Edwards and Polly (Cramer) Edwards. Jesse was apprenticed to Thomas Buckman, a farmer, at the age of 4 and taken to Hunterdon County, NJ, until the age of 19, when he returned to Bucks County.

On May 1, 1776, Private Edwards was drafted into Captain William McCalla's Pennsylvania Company, marching to Amboy, NJ, for two months service " ... in the fortifying of Amboy's outer trenches and standing guard along the river." Edwards then reenlisted at Amboy as a Private in Captain Thomas Craig's company in Colonel Baxter's Pennsylvania Regiment of the Flying Camp.

Edwards volunteered for an expedition to Staten Island, NY. After a short march they surprised the Hessian Guards, taking 19 prisoners after a short skirmish. The Flying Camp was sent to Ft. Lee, NJ, and then across the Hudson River to Ft. Washington, NY.

Jesse Edwards, with his signature.

After a fierce battle on Nov. 16, 1776, the fort capitulated to English and Hessian troops at about 4 p.m. Private Edwards was taken prisoner and marched to New York City. On Feb. 1, 1777 he was released on " ... parole of honour ... but on pain of death not to serve against the King of England." He returned to Bucks County later moving to Loudoun County, VA. There, he was drafted again for two months service in 1781 as a Private in Captain Beaver's Virginia Company serving at Fredericksburg, VA.

In 1777, Edwards married Catherine (Beekman) Skillman, born in Virginia in 1744.

They had five children: Susannah (1779), Elizabeth (no date), Nancy (12 April 1784), Jesse Jr. (1786), and Samuel (1791). The Edwards's moved to Bourbon County, KY and in 1791 to Adams County, OH. Daughter Nancy married John S. Moore in 1803 in Ohio.

Edwards moved to Indiana in 1822 and back to Adams County in 1824. He was granted a pension (No. S 17401) in 1832. His wife died in 1840 and Jesse died on Nov. 2, 1856, being buried in Newman Cemetery near Rarden, Scioto County, OH.

MORIARTY, DONALD PETER II – Donald Peter Moriarty II was born in Alexandria, LA, Jan 26, 1935 to Donald Peter and Catherine Graham (Stafford) Moriarty. Universities: Colorado; Louisiana State (BS, Economics, 1957); Florida Atlantic (MA, History, 1973).

Donald Peter Moriarty II

U.S. Army officer, 1957-1980, with service in Germany, Belgium, Vietnam; retired as Lieutenant Colonel of artillery. Awarded Legion of Merit, Bronze Star Medal (with oak leaf cluster); Meritorious Service Medal (with oak leaf cluster); Air Medal (with oak leaf cluster); Vietnamese Cross of Gallantry (with palm).

Engineering Program Manager with Hughes Aircraft Company, Fullerton, CA, 1980-1995.

President, The Episcopal Synod of America, 1993-1998. Elected to the Republican State Central Committee in Louisiana, 2004-2012, and as an alternate delegate to the Republican National Convention, 2008. Who's Who in the West, 1987-1998. Who's Who in California, 1990-1998.

Seth Stafford was born in New Hanover County, NC, about 1750. Subsequently relocated to Beaufort District, SC where he settled permanently in St. Peter's Parish. Served in Colonel Horey's Corps of Horse, South Carolina Milita, from 20 August 1779 to 1 January 1782. With his brother, William, Seth Stafford was a delegate from St. Peter's Parish to the constitutional convention called in 1787 to ratify the proposed United States Constitution. Died in 1803.

MOTES, DAVID LANGSTON – Born Mar. 13, 1940 in Laurens, SC. Joined the Gen. James Williams Chapter, South Carolina SAR on Nov. 7, 2008. He served in the South Carolina National Guard and the U.S. Army Reserve, and also worked as a real estate broker and appraiser, retiring in Mar. 2002. He is a member of Sons of Confederate Veterans, and is a member of Laurens School District 55 Athletic Hall of Fame.

He is married to Mary E. Motes, and they have two children and two grandchildren.

Jonathan Motes was born 1731 in England and was a member of the 3rd South Carolina Regiment. He died Oct. 20, 1815 in South Carolina.

MOUNTS, WILLARD – Born March 30, 1915 at Cedar, Mingo County, WV. Joined SAR in 1998; National No. 156303; State Society No. 1827.

Willard was at Citizens Military Training Camp at Fort Knox, KY, 1931-2-3, promoted to Corporal, two years. Given a citation for the Manual of Arms. Was in the Crack Squad Rifle Team.

Willard's wife is deceased. He has three daughters, seven grandchildren and eight great-grandchildren. Willard was employed at Luhy Chev. Co. as Comptroller/Business Manager for 21 years; Jack Kent Cadillac as Comptroller/Business Manager for 12 years.

He was the President Denver People-to-People, Sister Cily Organization, 1974-75 - achieved at winning with Nairobi, Kenya. Put on a two weeks celebration – won first place National from the Readers Digest Contest. Joined the Boy Scouts in 1927 – was a Scoutmaster for 32 years. Joined the Masons, 1952 – Scottish Rite – Shrine – Eastern Star, 1996.

During the Civil War, Williard Mount's mother's side of the family was for the South and his father's side was for the North. He is wearing a shirt made with the Confederate flag on the gray and a US flag on the blue.

James Marcum, 13th generation grandfather was the Business Manager for John Rolfe, who was in the tobacco business, in Jamestown, VA.

Josiah Marcum, a great-great-grandson of James, and 7th generation grandfather was born May 2, 1759, in Chesterfield County, VA.

At age 21, Josiah volunteered for an "18 month" enlistment in the Virginia Militia as a wagoner/blacksmith/bugler/drummer. He was in the last four battles of the American Revolution before Lord Cornwallis' Army surrendered to General George Washington at Yorktown, Oct. 19, 1781. Those battles were (1) Gates Defeat, (2) Kings Mountain, (3) Cowpens, (4) Guilford Court House.

When Josiah was discharged at the Hillsborough Courthouse in Virginia, the Government gave him a parcel of land in present Wayne County, WV, where he became a successful land holder/blacksmith and gunsmith.

Josiah died in March, 1846, and was buried at Jennies Creek near US Route 52 northwest of Kermit, WV.

My mother, Margaret Nancy Marcum, was born April 30, 1894, in Webb, Wayne County, WV. She married Kimble Anderson Mounts, Jan. 10, 1910, in Mingo County, WV. I was born March 30, 1915, in Cedar, Mingo County, WV.

MYERS, ALBERT E. – NSSAR No. 73197, resides in Fort Myers, FL. Albert is a Genealogist, Miami and Caloosa Chapters, FLSSAR 2007-8 President, Caloosa Chapter, FLSSAR.

Albert has received the Silver Citizenship Medal.

George Michael Breiner of Lynn Twp., Lehigh Co., PA - served in Battle of Stony Point.

Joshua Williams of Great Pond, Hancock Co., ME; Col. Ward's Regiment of the Massachusetts Militia.

Andrew Morr of Snyder Co., PA - Private, PA Pennsylvania Line.

David Dunbar Jr. of Scituate, MA; Minuteman, 1775; Continental Army at battles of Frogs Point and White Plains.

William Tupper of Machias, ME - militia at Machias.

John Archer of Cherryfield, ME - Sgt. in Artillery Co.

Andrew Cobb of Gorham, ME - Second Lt. in Capt. Jonah Washburn's Co., Col. Eben White's Regt.

Samuel Colson of Cherryfield, ME - Private, MA Militia.

MYERS, NORMAN LEWIS – Norman Lewis Myers was born Oct. 21, 1932 and 20 years later in 1952 be began his 24 years service with the U.S. Navy – Naval Reserve from which he retired in 1974 as a CWO3. Fifty years after joining the Navy he became a member of the Central Florida Chapter SAR in November 2002 and is its current President. His civilian employment included the Ohio Supreme Court; United Way and 25 years as Senior Assoc. Dir. of the Nationwide Children's Hospital Foundation, Columbus, OH.

Norman L. Myers

Norman is a retired Fellow of the National Association for Hospital Development (AHP) and a member of the First Baptist Church of Winter Park, FL. He has three sons, six grandchildren and six great grandchildren. Son Jeffrey and grandson Brent are members of the SAR.

Norman L. Myers, President, Central Florida Chapter SAR.

He is a descendant of **Henry Myers** who served in the Pennsylvania Militia as a Private. Henry's pension application recited that his duty stations included Old Redstone, Fort Pitt, Middle Island, Fishing Creek and Jarets Fort with battles at Sandusky Plains, Yellow Creek Station and Picketts Fort. He further stated that he was a friend of George Washington. His brothers Adam and Frederick were also veterans of the Revolutionary War.

MYERS, STORRES FREDERICK – Born in Lock Haven, PA, he served in the US Army from 1966-1970. A Vietnam veteran, he served in the 509th Radio Research Group, 313th Battalion. He is Former Asst. Facilities Engineer, AT&T Bell Laboratories, SSTC, Breinigsville, PA, retiring on Sept. 11, 2008. He is a member of the Muncy Historical Society and Clinton County Genealogical Society. He is a Clemson University supporter and IPTAY member since 1992.

He is married to Jane Rebecca Cruse.

Heinrich Gernhardt was born ca. 1740-45 in Germany. He served in the Northampton Co., PA Militia, 7th Company, 3rd Battalion, Private 4th Class. He served from 1780-82 under Capt. John Deter. A farmer in Northampton, Berks and Northumberland Counties, PA, he died in 1820 and is buried at St. John's Delaware Run Church Cemetery, Northumberland Co., PA.

NASH, REV. WILLIAM – Born March 18, 1955 in Ogden, UT, joined SAR Michigan State Society, December 2002.

William served as Specialist 4 in US Army, 101st Airborne Division.

He and Donna Jean Nash have four children and one grandchild. William is a psychologist at Development Centers, Inc. He is an ordained Minister and Chaplain with a Master of Arts degree from the University of Detroit/Mercy.

William Nash

William belongs to General Society of the War of 1813, Order of Indian Wars of the United States, Sons of Union Veterans of the Civil War.

His two supplemental ancestors are Rowland Judd Sr. and John Judd.

Andrew Swallows was born April 17, 1760

at Berks County, PA. He was a private with Capt. Ward's Company, with Pennsylvania and North Carolina Troops.

1777: Spring. Served two months as a substitute in Pennsylvania. Participated in the Battle of Brandywine, as a Rifleman. His unit was placed on the right wing of the Army on a hill. After the battle marched towards Philadelphia- stopped at Bunker's Hill until his term expired. During that time Philadelphia was taken by the British.

1778: Second term of Service. Hired for two months as a substitute. Marched down near Philadelphia under Captain Washington's Army. The British still held Philadelphia.

1779: Third term of Service. Was a Wagoner for one year. Participated in activities in Connecticut and in White Plains, NY. Engaged in hauling ammunition from Redding, PA to the United States Army at White Plains. He saw General Washington frequently. The Officer was Captain Archibald.

1780: Andrew had moved to Virginia in the Spring and volunteered in the Fall. He was in Wythe County. For this fourth term of Service, he went with 76 men into the State of North Carolina under Captain Buchannen. His unit was to join General Green but this did not take place. There was an engagement with some Tories in which 17 or 18 Tories were killed and one man was killed from Andrew's unit. The engagement took place near the Yadkin River. Term of Service lasted nine months. He was Wagoner. Andrew also served under Captain Ward during this enlistment. He says he marched with his unit against Indians and guarded the fort on the Clinch River.

1781: Andrew volunteered in February for his fifth term of Service. Went with Col. Preston with 150 men to Guilford County, NC and joined General Green. Andrew went on a mission with other soldiers to pursue some Tories-and participated in an engagement at Hawes River. Andrew and the other men were afterward pursued by the British.

Andrew died Sept. 30, 1843 and is buried at Roaring River Cemetery, Overton County, TN.

NEAL, WILLIAM BENJAMIN – Bill a native of Wilmington, DE, taught history for 33 eventful years. These years saw such challenges as the race riot, desegregation, busing and two major teacher strikes. He was Chairman of the History Department of the Bellamy Award Winning Pierre S. duPont High School for 17 years and coached for 10 years it's tennis team during which it won two Conference Championships and the Delaware State Championship.

William B. Neal

He graduated first in his class from Grove City College (Magna Cum Laude).

With a Harvard University Scholarship, he earned a Master of Arts in Teaching Degree. He served in the U.S. Air Force as Senior Personnel Specialist during the Korean War.

He is a member of over 40 organizations, many of which he served in various capacities: First President of the Delaware Genealogical Society; three term Governor of the national Swedish Colonial Society, receiving it's Distinguished Service Medal; Commanded the Richard C. du Pont Post and Delaware's District 2 of the American Legion; Board member of the Federation of Genealogical Societies, Descendants of Founders of New Jersey and the Scotch Irish Society of the U.S.; Grand High Priest of Royal Arch Masons of Delaware; the York Rite College; Senior President and Registrar of the Delaware Society of the Children of the American Revolution; four term Commander of Appomattox Camp, Department Commander, and National Historian of the Sons of Union Veterans of the Civil War; Founding Governor General of the National Society of First Families of Delmarva. Bill designed for four organizations medals produced by J. E. Caldwell Jewelers. Also, his memberships include The National Gavel Society, The Baronial Order of Magna Charta, and the Order of the Crown of Charlemagne in the U.S.A. He was proud and honored to be selected as the 1998 Grand Marshall of the Wilmington Memorial Day Parade.

Since 1981, he has been a member of the SAR and has served as Chapter and State President, National Trustee, National Committee Chairman, NSSAR Swedish Ambassador, a member of the National Nominating Committee, and three terms as Genealogist General. He has been awarded most of the Society's medals, including the Patriot, the Silver Good Citizenship, the Minuteman, 28 Liberty and five Florence Kendall Medals. He is in the Recruiting Hall of Fame having sponsored 292 members. He is the founding President of the Major Peter Jaquett Chapter, a Sen. Thomas F. Bayard Fellow and a George Washington Fellow.

Bill has 14 approved Revolutionary patriots from the states of Delaware, Maryland, New Jersey and Pennsylvania. His initial patriot was **Bartholomew Adams** of Sussex County, DE. He enlisted June 1, 1777 as a Private in Captain Peter Jaquett's Company. He was just in time to participate in the Battle of Monmouth, the longest Battle of the War and the last important engagement in the North. Apparently, he enlisted again on March 18, 1778, age 20, height 5' 7", black hair. He was at the Battle of Camden and still in the service in 1782. He applied for a pension (S35781) on April 20, 1818, aged 64. Interestingly, Bill was unaware, when he named the SAR Chapter that he founded, The Peter Jaquett Chapter that 200 years ago his ancestor Bartholomew served in Jaquett's Company.

Another of his patriots was at Valley Forge with General Washington. Bill's ancestor **John Neal** died in 1764 and his son Arthur, from whom he descends, was probably too young to participate. However, John's wife Margaret White Neal, who bore him six daughters and four sons, paid the Federal Supply Tax qualifying as a patriot herself. Her oldest son William Neal, my 4th Great Granduncle, was" warranted for substitute money." The next oldest brother was John, a Private in Captain Isaac Lewis' Militia Company.

NELSON, THOMAS ALVIN – Born Feb. 1, 1945 in Lennox, CA, he joined the Arizona SAR on May 9, 2006. Thomas served in the U.S. Army/Infantry/11th Air Assault Division/Pfc. He later was a Systems Analyst in Madera Co., CA, retiring on Jan. 31, 1996.

He is married to Janet (Bruce) Nelson, and they have four children and three grandchildren.

Benjamin Perry was born Nov. 1952 in Spotsylvania, VA. He enlisted in the Continental Army at Spotsylvania on Apr. 17, 1781. He served under Generals Washington and Lafayette. On his pension application, he mentions participating in the Battle of York, taking part in the capture of General Cornwallis, being at the farmhouse and witnessing the surrender.

He next went into Tennessee and Kentucky, listed as an Indian Spy on his service record. He served out of Bryan's Station and participated in Indian battles. His eldest son and his grandson married daughters of Morgan Bryan. As Benjamin was a Baptist, and persecuted in Virginia for refusal to join the State Anglican Church, he took his family with him.

Acting as a surveyor and spy, he chose the land he built his plantation on, founded the town and the Cane Run Baptist Church at Port Royal, Henry County, Kentucky. Family members still live on the original plantation.

Benjamin and Mary (Head) Perry had 14 children. At his death on May 11, 1839, 11 of the children were living. He and Mary are buried in the Port Royal Cemetery, behind the church the founded and where he served as Deacon.

NEWTON, BYRON L. – Born April 5, 1927 in Emanuel County, GA joined Georgia State Society in January, 2007. National Society number 168445; Georgia Society number 4476.

Byron was Private with the US Army. In civilian life he was a rural letter carrier with the US Postal Service. He retired in January, 1993.

Byron and Bernice H. Newton have two children and five grandchildren.

He also belongs to the American Legion and United Sons of the Confederacy.

Philip Dorsett Newton was born Jan. 17, 1760 in Halifax, NC; died 1850-Emanual County, GA. Enlisted 2nd S.C. Regiment –Sept. 11, 1777. Reenlisted Nov. 1, 1779 under Captain Richard Mason. Son of Reverend John Newton, Revolutionary Soldier b. Aug. 7, 1732 in Kent county, PA [now Delaware.] d. Nov. 20, 1790, and Keziah Dorsett, b. 1735. Rev. John enlisted as a Sgt.

Philip Newton's Siblings: Sgt. John Newton Jr., b July 5, 1755, died as Revolutionary Soldier aboard British Prison Ship. Newton County, GA named in his honor. Jemima, b. July 5, 1757, married William Smith. James Newton b. Jan. 23, 1763. Moses Newton, b. Aug. 14, 1766. d. 1826-Revolutionary Soldier, served as a Fifer 2nd S.C. Regiment from July 26, 1777 to Nov. 15, 1783 under Captain Mason. Phoebe b. April 24, 1771. Mary {Polly} b. Nov. 16, 1773.

Philip Newton's 1st wife-Lucy Lanier, daughter of Benjamin Lanier/Susanna Green. Issue-Bird Lanier Newton, b. 1805.

2nd wife-Annie Lane, b. June 5, 1809, daughter of Abraham Lane/Martha Wood.

Philip/Annie's children: John Lane Newton;

Benjamin L. Newton; Marath Ann Newton; Frances Ann Newton; Elizabeth Newton; Dicy Newton; Philip Dorsett Newton Jr.; Frances M. Newton.

NICHOLS, CHRIS – Born March 29, 1969 at Waterbury, CT. Joined Connecticut State Society in August, 2007.

Chris served in the US Navy as Electrician's Mate Petty Officer 3rd Class. He is married to Pamela Ruggio and they have two children.

Chris is business manager at UnitedHealthcare. He also belongs to Mayflower Society and Sons of Union Veterans of the Civil War.

Christian Stauffer's grandfather, Hans Stauffer, Anabaptist from Switzerland, began his journey to America on Nov. 5, 1709 with his wife Kinget and their three sons, including Christian's father Jacob. Following a perilous journey, they landed probably near Philadelphia in the spring of 1710 and settled near Valley Forge. Han's sons bought large tracts of land in the vicinity of Colebrookdale, which at that time was almost a wilderness.

Christian was born to Jacob and Barbara Stauffer on Dec. 18, 1728 and was a Mennonite. He married Susanna Buckwalter on Aug. 23, 1756 and had five children, including John, who also served in the Revolutionary War.

At the outbreak of the war, Christian's neighbor, Anthony Wayne, recruited a regiment of volunteers. Christian joined the Sons of Liberty, enlisted in General Anthony Wayne's regiment and accompanied him throughout the conflict. He took part in the battles of Three Rivers, Ticonderoga, Brandywine, Monmouth, Stony Point, Green Springs, VA, and the decisive battle of Yorktown. After the close of the war he settled down to farming in New Hanover Township. He died on May 14, 1797 at the age of 68 at his home, and is buried in the Hereford Mennonite Cemetery in Bally.

NOEGEL, RICHARD A. – (170418) Born May 1, 1955, Augusta, GA; son of Frederick W. Noegel and Nellie V. Swann; grad. Univ. of Georgia, 1977; veteran US Army; mar. Ruth Redfern Brannen, Aug. 23, 1980, Holy Trinity Lutheran Church, North Augusta, SC; daughter: Eleanor Page Noegel, b. July 27, 1982, Monterey, CA (mar. Dennis M. Smolen, Aug. 20, 2004, Our Redeemer Lutheran Church, Augusta, GA); son: Richard Alexander Lanier Noegel, b. Aug. 23, 1986, Harlaching (Munich) Germany; grandson: Christian Brannen Michael Smolen, b. May 15, 2005, Augusta, GA; member William Few Chapter GASSAR, Augusta, GA.

Richard A. Nogel, GASSAR, William Few Chapter, August, GA, with grandson Christian Smolen.

Lineal descendant of **Nathaniel Boddie**, b. Feb. 22, 1732 (N.S.), Isle of Wight County, VA; son of William Boddie and Mary Bennett; elected 1774 to Edgecombe County, NC, Committee of Safety; represented Edgecombe County in NC Provincial Congress at Halifax, April 1776; elected 1777 to first General Assembly of North Carolina; member, NC Senate for Nash County, 1778--81; member of commission that chose Raleigh the capital city of NC; died Dec. 7, 1797; bur. Boddie family cem. at Rose Hill Plantation, Nash County, NC; called "the father of Nash County."

Nathaniel (Nathan) Boddie, 1732-1797.

NORVILLE, ZACHARY S. – Mr. Zachary S. Norville was born Oct. 5, 1928 in Arcadia, FL. His served the military in the USAF, Far East HDQR, as a 1st lieutenant. He was employed with Norville Industries for 52 years, and served as chair.

He joined the SAR Jan. 25, 1996 in Georgia. The Dalton, Georgia Chapter is very small, so each member has served all offices.

Zachary S. Norville on the steps of the DAR Administration Building.

He earned his BS in Tex. Eng. from Georgia Tech, and has his single/multi, inst. & comm. licenses. He was awarded the Wright Bros. Master Pilot Award.

He is involved with Kiwanis, Ancient Planters, Sons of Indian Wars, Loyalists and Patriots, Mayflower Soc., American Colonists, and Sons of Pilgrims. He has proven to be descended from sixteen Rev. patriots/soldiers.

He and his wife, Rita Weaver, have four children and ten grandchildren.

William Addington was born Sept. 7, 1759 in Pennsylvania. His father was Henry Addington, born in S. London, England. He served as 1st lieutenant in the Pickins Regiment, Maj. Jolly Batt Company. He served the Continental Line, Cowpens, SC. He was a farmer by trade. He died Sept. 8, 1845 and is buried in the Methodist Church Cemetery, Murphy, NC.

NOSTRAND, PETER F. – Mr. Peter F. Nostrand was born in Cleveland, OH. He retired in 2006 from Sun Trust Bank, and is Chairman Emeritus.

He joined the SAR in the District of Columbia in 2006. He is also a member of the Founders and Patriots of America, and Sons of the Revolution.

He and his wife, Nancy R. Nostrand, have six children and four grandchildren.

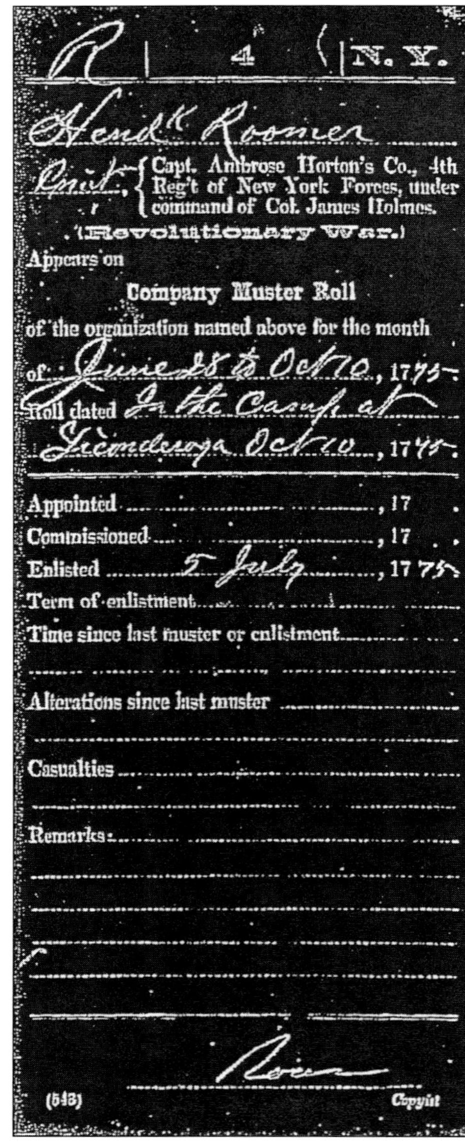

R | 4 | N.Y.

Hend'k Roomer

Pvt. Capt. Ambrose Horton's Co., 4th Reg't of New York Forces, under command of Col. James Holmes.

(Revolutionary War.)

Appears on
Company Muster Roll
of the organization named above for the month
of June 28 to Oct 10, 1775.
Roll dated In the Camp at Ticonderoga Oct 10, 1775.

Appointed ...., 17
Commissioned ...., 17
Enlisted 5 July, 1775
Term of enlistment ....
Time since last muster or enlistment ....
Alterations since last muster ....
Casualties ....
Remarks: ....

Roer

(543) Copyist

Pay stub for Henry Romer (Hendrick Roomer), stationed at Ft. Ticonderoga June 28-Oct. 10, 1775 before advancing north to invade Canada.

Henry Romer was born Jan. 1754 in Westchester Co., NY. He was at Ft. Ticonderoga from June 28-Oct. 10, 1775, awaiting orders to invade Canada. He enlisted July 5, 1775 as Private in Col. James Holmes' NY 4th Regiment, Capt. Ambrose Horton Company. He participated in the invasion of Canada under Gen. Montgomery. He was discharged April 1, 1776, and reenlisted in 1776 in Westchester Co. Militia under Col. Joseph Drake, 1st Reg. He died Nov. 5, 1830 and is buried at St. Peters Cemetery (formerly Van Cortlandt Cemetery), Cortlandt, Westchester County, NY. An additional ancestor was Pvt. **James Spock**, Westchester County, NY, who died in 1804.

NUTT, DONALD DUANE – Donald Duane Nutt was born Oct. 12, 1952 in Ann Arbor, MI. He served the military for six years in the Michigan Army National Guard, Specialist E-5, Company Clerk HQ. Co. 156th Signal Battalion.

SAR Offices: MISSAR – State President

(2007/08), treasurer (3 yrs); River Raisin Chapter – President (2004/06), secretary (7 yrs). SAR Committees: Membership, Finance & Audit, Emeritus/Ethics, Nominating, Bylaws & Resolutions. SAR Awards: State Medal of Distinguished Service, Meritorious Service Medal, Silver & Bronze Good Citizenship Medals, Military Service Medal.

He is also a member of Lenawee County Civil War Round Table and Cornerstone Baptist Church. He retired June 30, 2007 from Chrysler Corporation as Durability Engineer. His hobbies include history, genealogy, shooting sports and woodworking. He and his wife Peggy Ann have four children and two grandchildren.

Samuel Nutt was born December 1728 in Londonderry, NH. He was briefly an enlisted soldier in the filed early in the war; afterward was a member of NH Committee of Correspondence and NH Committee of Safety. He was the first town clerk of Francestown, NH. He was a carpenter, and was said to have built half of all homes in Francestown. He was of Scotch race. He died July 5, 1808, burial place unknown.

OAKES, FREDERICKE JOSEPH – Born on Sept. 9, 1937 in Newark, NJ, and joined the South Carolina SAR on Nov. 10, 2008. He served in the U.S. Navy from 1954-58 as a 3rd Class Petty Officer, USS *Lake Champlain* (CVA-39), N.S. Coco Solo, C.Z., and USS *Saratoga* (CVA-60). He later was an operating engineer in Essex County, NJ, retiring on Jan. 31, 1999. He is a member of Sons of Union Veterans of the Civil War, USS Saratoga Reunion Assoc., Knights of Columbus, and a former member of the American Legion.

Fredericke Joseph Oakes

He served for 26 years as a volunteer fireman, from lieutenant, captain, assistant chief to chief, and served as a part-time fire marshal in Hopatcong, NJ. He has three children and five grandchildren.

Fredericke Joseph Oakes, circa 1995.

Roswell Graves was born 1740 in East Haddam, CT. He was a sergeant in Col. Huntington's 17th Regt., Capt. Jewett's Company, Connecticut Continentals. He was at the Lexington Alarm, in Apr. 1775, with the army at Roxbury, MA on Mar. 25, 1776, and the Battle of Long Island on Aug. 27, 1776. He was officially reported as missing after that battle. He was taken prisoner and was confined in the "Old Sugar House Prison" where the City Hall building now stands in New York City, and died there of starvation. Tradition has it he was found with a piece of brick in his mouth.

O'BRIEN, EUGENE FRANCIS – Eugene Francis O'Brien was born Sept. 22, 1957 in the Bronx, NY. Eugene joined the Heart of Texas Chapter of the Texas Society of the Sons of the American Revolution in 2005. He is also a member of the Ancient Order of Hibernians and the American Association of Retired Persons. Eugene works as a Product Specialist at Heidelberg USA, Inc. He holds a Cisco Certified Network Associate (CCNA) and Microsoft Certified Professional (MCP) certifications.

Eugene Francis O'Brien

Eugene married Mary Alice Atkins on Oct. 17, 1981 in West, Texas where they now make their home. They have three daughters: Erin Florence Dodd, Lauren Mary Vorderkunz and Megan Colleen O'Brien, and one granddaughter, Chloe Florence Dodd. Eugene is a descendant of Laurence Landt, his Great-Great-Great-Great-Great-Great-Grandfather.

Laurence Landt was born in 1743 in Claverack, Columbia County, NY; the son of Johannis Valentin Landt and Elizabetha Philip. Laurence passed away in May of 1798 in New York. Laurence Landt and four of his brothers and three of their sons enlisted and served in the NY Militia, 8th Regiment of Albany County, NY, commanded by Colonel Robert Van Rensselaer.

O'DONNELL, LELAND LAMOINE – Born Oct. 2, 1952 to Lester O'Donnell and Vivian Lauretta Pearson in Pendleton, OR. Leland attended Ventura College and the University of California at Santa Barbara.

Leland enlisted as an Intelligence Specialist in the Selected Naval Air Reserve stationed at Pt. Mugu Naval Air Station and assigned to the Anti-Submarine Warfare VP-65 "Tridents" Naval Reserve Patrol Flight Squadron flying Lockheed P-3C Orion aircraft on submarine reconnaissance patrols.

During the time he served he was awarded the National Defense Service Medal, the Vietnam Service Medal (1974), the Noel Davis "Battle 'E'" Trophy for Excellence (1972), Cold War Commemorative Medal, Navy Commemorative Service Medal, the Reserve Commemorative Medal, the Honorable Service Commemorative Medal, and the American Defense Service Commemorative Medal. He was Honorably Discharged on Dec. 1, 1977.

Leland married Debra West on Nov. 15, 1989 and had two children, a girl Shannon Nicole O'Donnell (1989) and a boy Colin Patrick O'Donnell (1991).

Leland Lamoine O'Donnell family

Leland L. O'Donnell became a proud member of the National Society of the Son's of the American Revolution on Dec. 9, 2008, by decent from Bennett Wellman.

Bennett Wellman was born Feb. 9, 1754 in Saint Mary's, St. Andrews Parish, MD. He served in the American Revolution as a private (PVT PS MD). Having taken the oath of allegiance in Montgomery County, MD sometime in March 1778, he served in the American Revolution from Montgomery County, MD in the Upper Battalion, 3rd Company, under Zadock Magruder, First Colonel and Frans. Deakins, Lieutenant Colonel.

Gravestone of Bennett Wellman.

He was married to Mary Milligan on Feb. 11, 1777 in Baltimore, Baltimore County, MD. Bennett was a shoemaker and farmer. He ranked as one of the great "huntsmen" of his day. Wellman's always like the woods and the liking caused them to procure large boundaries of land.

He died at the age of 76 on Sept. 15, 1830. He was buried in Wellman Cemetery, Louisa, Lawrence County, KY.

O'LEARY, JAMES R. – Born Oct. 9, 1940 in North East, Erie County, PA. He joined the Michigan SAR on Sept. 24, 2007. He worked as a teacher, retiring in 1993. James is married to Marilyn Montgomery, and they have two children and three grandchildren.

Alexander Lowry was born Dec. 1725 in Ireland. He was a colonel in the Lancaster Militia, Third Battalion at Brandywine and Germantown. An Indian trader, merchant and farmer, he died on Jan. 31, 1805 in Donegal, Lancaster Co., PA.

OLSEN, LESTER PAUL – Dr. Olsen was born in Valentine, NE on Aug. 10, 1945. He joined the SAR in 2006. His wife is Alva. He has seven children and eight grandchildren. He is a retired Science and Math Teacher, retiring in 2007. His grandmother was Laura Seger, whose great, great, great grandfather was Cpt. Andrew Englis, Patriot. He has degrees from U of Sioux Falls B.S., Augustana College M.A., and U of

Biblical Studies. D.M. He is also an advanced instructor in pilot ground school.

He has been active in the Berean Church for 35 years as board member, camp board member and secretary. He is a Major in the Civil Air Patrol. He has been a member for 20 years and has been pilot, cadet commander, supply officer and personnel officer. He graduated from the National Staff College at Maxwell AFB in Montgomery, AL in 2007.

Dr. Lester Paul Olsen

He has been a "Fellow" at Johns Hopkins University doing research projects in the summer of 2003-4. His focus was on diabetes in a specific Native American Population. He has also attended Harvard Graduate School with interest in "Making Learning Visible" and "Brain Research as it applies to education.

He has written one book, *Cybernetics – Come of Age* and completed one doctoral dissertation titled *The Great Commission.*

Capt. Andrew English was born in Palmer, MA, Feb. 2, 1752. He was educated in Massachusetts. He became a Math teacher at an early age in Connecticut and later in Schenectady, NY. After the Battle of Lexington, he enlisted at Roxbury, MA near Boston. Washington organized his troops in Cambridge. He enlisted as private. In the winter he went to Valley Forge as the Continental Army was being trained. He supplied his own horse, saddle and clothing. On June 14, 1775 he became a sergeant in Bailey's regiment. On Feb. 20,1776 was appointed an orderly sergeant. Then on Sept. 1, 1776, he was commissioned a second lieutenant in the 12th MA regiment.

On June 28, 1778 he participated with the main Army in the Battle of Monmouth. There were 6,000 troops to start. Gen. Washington brought another 6,000 troops and the American forces stood their ground with the British Troops. This battle proved the Patriots could fight the British and win if given a chance. During the battle, Lt. English was shot. The bullet entered one side of the jaw and came out of the other side of the jaw. When he recovered from his wounds, he returned to service and was commissioned as Captain-lieutenant. He served as adjutant in Col. Sprout's 2nd MA regiment. On. Nov. 14, 1782, he was promoted to Captain in the 1st MA regiment. He was then honorably discharged at West Point in November of 1783.

He then married Rachel Moore in 1786 and moved to Tully, NY. He served as a justice of the Onandago County of New York beginning in 1794. He later passed away and was buried in the Tully Cemetery in 1832.

OLSON, ELLIS NORMAN – I was born Nov. 8, 1938 in Rochester, Minnesota and moved to Cheboygan Michigan in 1944.

My first wife, Mary C. Hilborn (deceased) and I have five daughters: Cynthia, Margaret, Susan, Christine, and Melanie. Presently, I am married to Sandra Jean (Kwapis) and have one daughter, Diedra.

I received a B.S. Degree and Lifetime Teaching Certificate from Central Michigan University. Having begun teaching at age 18 in 1957, I retired in 1997 after 40 years.

Ellis N. Olson

Besides teaching, my working career includes: 16 years as a professional chef, 12 years as a builder and contractor, 16 years on the Cheboygan City Council (10 years as Mayor), and 12 years as cemetery sexton.

Pursuing historical and archeological interests gave me the opportunity to erect and build Cheboygan County's first Historical Museum in 1969 and organize the county's first Historical Society. In 1972, I discovered Historic Old MILL CREEK, now Michigan's 84th state park.

I have authored two books and received the GOVERNOR JOHN B. SWAINSON AWARD in 1999.

I joined the SAR (MI 3069, National 152390) August 1999. My Patriot Ancestors are: Abijah Lee, Andrew Finley, John Jack, Christopher Earnest, Philip Wagerman, and George Geller. I am presently the MISSAR President.

Abijah Lee was born Aug. 20, 1764 at Middletown, CT, the son of Abijah Lee and Abigail Smith. His father was a veteran of the French and Indian War.

Abijah Lee

Abijah enlisted from Sandisfield, Berkshire County, MA into Captain Robbin's Reg't. about Dec. 2, 1780 and was a private from July 1, 1781 in Col. Tupper's (10th) Regiment serving in New York.

Abijah married Anna Fellows March 27, 1785. They had nine children. Their sons , Harvey and Asabel, built the second Vandalia, IL after the Capitol moved from Kaskaskia.

Andrew Finley, Jr.

Andrew Finley was born in 1750, the son of John and Martha (Barclay) Finley. He married Jenny Jack.

Lieutenant Andrew belonged to the Eighth Pennsylvania Regiment of the Continental Mercantile Rangers).

The Eighth was at Bound Brook, Brunswick, New Jersey, Brandywine, Paoli, Germantown, and White Marsh, PA. They wintered at Valley Forge.

His death was reported in *THE INDEPENDENT CHRONICLES* and *BOSTON PATRIOT.* Andrew Finley, 72, died in South Hampton, PA. He was one of the remaining few who had a commission under George Washington in the regular service during the Revolutionary War.

John Jack was born March 11, 1726 at Ardstraw County, Armagh, North Ireland, the son of James Jack and Elizabeth McNulty.

John married Eleanor Stevenson and together they came to Westmoreland County, PA from Frankland County about 1772.

John Jack was an active participant in promoting the HANNA'S TOWN RESOLVES adopted by Westmoreland County on May 16, 1775. It was a condemnation of the alarming situation occasioned by the dispute with Great Britain.

John Jack was a Lieutenant in John Turner's 8th Company of Col. Stockley's Battalion of Associates Westmoreland County, PA.

Christopher (Stophel) Ernst was born Aug. 23, 1748 in Lancaster County, PA to Johann Wilhelm and Eva Catarina (Bach) Ernst, married Anna Margaret Sichele, 1768.

He enlisted as a private in the Company of Captain Jacob Fridley on May 27, 1776. The Company served in the Trenton and Princeton Campaigns.

He marched to Bedford County in 1779 with Captain Rutherford for the protection of the inhabitants.

Christopher Ernst is buried near Circleville, Pickaway County, OH according to the D.A.R.

Philip Wagerman (Wagaman) was born Aug. 5, 1744 at Bucks County, PA and died at his farm at Hyndman, Londonderry Township, Bedford County, Oakford Lane, near Hyndman.

The Wagamans came from the German Palatinate, Rhineland, Switzerland and settled first in Northampton Co., PA on Nov. 1, 1736.

Philip was a private in Capt. Roger's Co. 8th Battalion, Pennsylvania Militia.

Philip married Mary Greisher in 1787. Their son, John, married Christina Geller in 1789, Christina was the daughter of George Geller (Keller) another Revolutionary Soldier.

George Geller (whose ancestral name could be Keller) was born about 1755, whether in Germany or Pennsylvania is not certain. He died about April 1, 1822 at Bedford Co., PA.

George was a private in private in Jacob Ladich's Co. of militia and was a private in Daniel Will's Co. as well as belonging to Jacob Rothermels Co.

George married Mary Kramer in 1781. Their daughter Christina married John Wagaman in 1819. John and Christina Wagaman had a daughter, Mary in 1811.

OLSON, RAYMOND HAROLD – (State 3065 / National 151979). Born June 16, 1937 to Harold and Viola (Finley) Olson at Rochester, MN. Married to Priscilla Jean Percy. Three Children: Thomas (deceased), Norman, and Paula. A graduate from University of Michigan (1964) and

Central Michigan University (1970, 1977) Retired from Cheboygan Area Schools in 1998 with 37 years as a special education teacher and from Michigan Army National Guard in 1977 achieving the rank of First Sergeant. Served 4 years in the US Air Force and is currently the Command Sergeant Major of the 6th Battalion of the Michigan Volunteer Defense Force.

Raymond Harold Olson

Patriots are the same as Ellis Olson: **Abijah Lee, Andrew Finley, John Jack, Christopher Earnest, Philip Wagerman** and **George Geller.**

O'NEILL, MARK A. – Mark A. O'Neill was born June 1, 1976 in Williamsport, PA. His military service includes serving as Lieutenant Commander in the Medical Service Corps, U.S. Navy, 2001-2008. He was awarded the Military Service Medal.

He is the Executive Director of Lancaster Gastroenterology, Inc. He is a Fellow of the American College of Healthcare Executives (ACHE) and a Certified Medical Practice Executive by the Medical Group Management Association.

He is also a member of Rotary Club, Naval Reserve Association, Ancient Order of Hibernians, American Legion, National Rifle Association, University of Pittsburgh Alumni Association, Johns Hopkins University Alumni Association.

He and his wife Kelly Ann (Hynes) O'Neill have two children and reside in Lancaster, PA.

Peter Kaylor was born Nov. 12, 1753 in Germany. He served in New Jersey Militia in the Wagonmaster General's Dept. as Wagonmaster. He was involved in the Battle of Brandywine, and helped Lafayette from the field after he was wounded. He was also at Valley Forge and Jersey Campaign. His is listed as Peter Kohler in the Official Register of the Officers and Men of New Jersey in the Revolutionary War. His civilian occupation was a farmer. He died Sept. 19, 1840 and is buried in St. Michael's Cemetery, Loretta, Cambria County, PA.

OUGH, DR. LEE DUDLEY (deceased) – Born May 30, 1903, Clinton, IA, he graduated from Clinton High School in 1922. He received a B.A. degree, State University of Iowa, 1929, and M.S., State University of Iowa, 1930, and a Ph.D., State University of Iowa, 1932, and during these years worked for Miles Savings Bank. He later was a Research Chemist for Clinton Corn Processing Co./Standard Brands, Inc., retiring about May 1, 1968.

Professor Donald J. Pietrzyk (left), Dept. of Chemistry, University of Iowa, presenting the Iowa Award to Dr. Lee Dudley Ough, Oct. 29, 1965.

He was married to Elinor T. (Stephens) Ough, with two children and four grandchildren.

Peter A. Vrooman was baptized on Oct. 16, 1743 in Schoharie, NY. He served in the 15th Regt., New York, Co. 2, Albany County Militia.

OUGH, STEVEN EDWARD – Born Jan. 30, 1945 in Clinton, IA, at age 17 he legally changed his name for 50¢ at the Clinton Co. Courthouse, from his birth name, Edward Stephens Ough. He was named for Edward H. Stephens (family lore), supposedly a direct descendant of an uncle of Alexander H. Stephens, Vice-President of the Confederate State of America, and twice Governor of the State of Georgia. Edward H. Stephens's dad, Hiram W. Stephens, served in the Union Army.

Steven joined the Iowa SAR on Sept. 5, 2008. He served in the U.S. Army: 5th Army Band (PFC, SP4, SP5), 266th Army Band (SP5), 24th AG Co. Band (SP4, SP5); U.S. Army Reserves, Reinforcement (SP6); GA Army National Guard, 116th Army Band (SP5); GA Air National Guard, 530th Air Force Band (SSGT); IA Army National Guard, Co. D, 235th Sig Bn (SGT); U.S. Army Reserves, 85th Div. Band (TPU) (SGT); and IA Army National Guard, 34th Div Band (SGT) and HQ, 334th FSB (SGT).

After retirement on Jan. 1, 1998, he worked as a municipal transit bus driver for the city of Dubuque, IA. He is married to Jean Arlene (Godde) Ough, with two children and two grandchildren.

Peter A. Vrooman was baptized on Oct. 16, 1743 in Schoharie, NY. He served in the 15th Regt., New York, Co. 2, Albany County Militia.

PAGE, RAYMOND WALDO – Served in the US Army as Sergeant First Class.

Raymond married Susan S. and they have three children and nine grandchildren.

He was employed as Central Schools Superintendent of Schools, Greece, NY and Assistant Professor – State University of New York, Oneonta, NY, retiring in 1998.

Raymond also belongs to American Legion Post No. 206, Greece, NY and American Legion Post No. 31, Westminster, MD.

Raymond W. Page

He has received the New York State Congress of Parents and Teachers-Distinguished Service Award for Educational Leadership-Brockport State University College-Rose Rock award for outstanding educational leadership and US Army War Service Medal.

Gershom Page was born Aug. 22, 1743 in Sandwich, MA. He was a Captain in the 4th Light horse Conn. Regiment. Gershom was in agriculture in civilian life. He died March 22, 1810 in Burlington, NY.

Raymond W. Page's Patriot gravesite in New York with DAR marker.

PATTON, PERKINS L. – Rev. Perkins L. Patton was born Sept. 11, 1938 in Washington, DC. His military service was with the U.S. Army serving in Alaska as a Specialist-4. He is a Presbyterian Pastor, and has served Parishes in South Dakota, Maryland, Iowa and Texas. He retired June 2003.

He joined the SAR November 1995 in Iowa. He is now a member of the New Mexico Society with dual membership with Iowa & Texas Societies. SAR offices and committees include: 1998-2004 – President, Central Iowa Chapter, IASSAR; 2002-2004 – President, Panhandle-Plains Chapter 10, TXSSAR; 2003-2004 – Vice-President, District 2, TXSSAR; 2006-2008 – President, Las Cruces Chapter, NMSSAR; 2006-2008 – President NMSSAR; 2002- – Member, Chaplain Committee, NSSAR; 2003- – Member, History Committee, NSSAR; 2006-2007 – Vice-Chair. Task Force to Review Elimination of Annual Dues, NSSAR; 2007-2009 – National Trustee from NMSSAR; 2008- – Chaplain, NMSSAR.

Rev. Perkins L. Patton

Honors include War Service Medal, 2003; Silver Color Guard Medal, TXSSAR, 2004; and Meritorious Service Medal, TXSSAR, 2004.

He is also a member of Knight Templar; Life Member of Disabled America Veterans, Chapter 38, Department of New Mexico (Past Commander, Chapter 33 and State Chaplain, Department of Iowa); National Association of Presbyterian Scouters; and Baden Powell Society.

He and his wife, Patricia Ann (Strack) Fleming, have one child and 3 grandchildren. Rev. Patton is the grandson of Harry L. Patton, who was President of NMSSAR when he died June 1941.

Robert Patton was born in 1750 in Pennsylvania. He served as Captain in the 10th Pennsylvania Continental Line. He died in 1815 and is buried in Knox County, TN.

John Pyeatt was born in 1735. He served as a soldier in the North Carolina Continental Line. He died in service, burial place unknown.

Jacob Pyeatt was born in 1760 in North Carolina. He served as Captain in Pyeatt's Marines Company, Ill. Regt. VA Militia. He died in 1844 and is buried at Cane Hill, AR.

Morris Mitchell was born in 1762 in Montgomery County, MD. He served as Pvt. in Capt. Rose's Company, 5th Battalion, Washington Co. PA Militia. He was a Methodist preacher. He died in 1848 and is buried in Polk County, MO.

James Cunnyngham was born in Ireland. His patriotic service was to rent wagons to the Revolutionary Army in Shenandoah County, VA. He died in 1786 and in buried in Shenandoah County, VA.

PEAK, ROGER WORLEY – Born June 2, 1950 in Columbus, Franklin County, OH. Peak joined the National and Virginia State Societies of SAR in 1984. Military service consisted of two years active duty in the US Coast Guard Reserve, and advancement to Petty Officer Third Class (Yeoman). Civilian service includes nearly 35 years working for the US Government, and most recently the Administrative Office of the US Courts in Washington, DC.

Roger Worley Peak

He is a member of several other lineage societies including Jamestowne Society, Order of the First Families of Maine, Order of the First Families of Rhode Island and Providence Plantations, Society of Mayflower Descendants, Society of the War of 1812, and Sons and Daughters of the Colonial and Antebellum Bench and Bar 1565-1861.

Peak achieved Eagle Scout in 1967, and Distinguished Toastmaster, Toastmasters International, in 1985. He is active as a Freemason, and he has served as presiding officer of several bodies, including Charter Worshipful Master of Kemper-Macon Ware Lodge No. 64. He is a member of St. George's Episcopal Church, Arlington, VA.

Peak is married to the former Leandra Mae Bruhl. They have one daughter, Susan.

Peak is descended from **Josiah Cleaveland** on his mother's side. Cleaveland was born December 1758 at Salisbury. CT, He served as Private in the 3rd Massachusetts Line. He died Dec. 26, 1831 in Western, Oneida County, NY.

PEEBLES, JOSEPH WOODROW – Joseph Woodrow Peebles was born Sept. 16, 1948 in Swainsboro, Emanuel County, GA. Admitted to Mill Creek Chapter GA Society, SAR on June 1, 2006. Military service was in the U.S. Army as a sergeant 1967-70. Entrepreneur retired, founder and CEO, Peebles Enterprises, Inc.

Organizational memberships include American Legion Post 103, La Societe Voiture 867, Zorn Chapter 70 Disabled American Veterans, McLeod-Moring Camp 1386 Sons of Confederate Veterans, Gordon Chapter 88 Military Order of the Stars & Bars, Jenkins Camp 164 Sons of Spanish American War Veterans, Swainsboro Lodge 244 F&AM, Ancient and Accepted Scottish Rite of Freemasonry, York Rite Freemasonry, Emanuel Genealogical Society.

Joseph W. Peebles

Awards received include the War Service Cross Medal, Knights Templar Medal, Master of Royal Secret 32° Medal, Service to Veterans Medal, Consistory Medal, Distinguished Service Award, Certificates of Commendation & Appreciation, Recruitment Citation, Leadership Award, Outstanding Volunteer Award, Advance the Colors Award.

Joseph is married to Vicki Ann Sedberry. They have one daughter, Katherine Anne Peebles Roady, and three grandchildren.

He is a direct descendant of Patriot **Ephraim Peebles** of Brunswick County, VA and Jefferson County, GA.

PELL, PAUL ROBERTS – Born Sept. 24, 1961, resides in Addison, NY. He is a Certified Braille Proofreader through the National Library of Congress; attended Florida State University and graduated from the school—Leader Dogs for the Blind. Paul is descended from John Woodside—Paul's great (x5) grandfather.

Paul Roberts Pell

John Woodside was born on March 9, 1760 in Lancaster-Dauphin County, PA. He married Margaret McMullen in 1779 and they had 11 children. He died on Sept. 11, 1835 in Upper Paxton Township, PA. John Woodside served during the Battles of Brandywine and Germantown.

John Woodside served in Captain Rutherford's company of the Fourth Battalion of Lancaster County Pennsylvania as indicated in the muster role dated Aug. 12, 1777 (refer to Pennsylvania Archives, 5th Series, Volume 7, pages 357-358).

John Woodside's grandson wrote the following in 1893: "And when General Howe invested Philadelphia, General Washington slipped around through the northern counties to recruit soldiers with which to oust General Howe, which afterward he did. My grandfather-John Woodside-hearing that he was recruiting at Harrisburg made ready to go and enlist." quoted from a letter by Dr. H. Benjamin Woodside (refer to NSDAR Record Copy #112381).

PENLAND, CARL WARREN – Born Jan. 13, 1931 in Vero Beach, FL, joined NSSAR Feb. 25, 2008, member Captain John Smoot Chapter MSSAR. Wife Lorraine is a member of Samuel Chase Chapter MSDAR. They have three children and three grandchildren.

L-R: MDSSAR President R. Duane Tackitt presenting Carl Warren Penland the Certificate of Membership into NSSAR. Witnessed by Ray Jackson, President, MDSAR Capt. John Smoot Chapter.

Carl served in the U.S. Navy as an Aerographer's Mate during the Korean War, stationed at Patuxent River NATC, MD for two years, and two years aboard the aircraft carrier, USS Wasp (CVA-18) in Korea, Japan, Pacific, and South China Sea.

He graduated as a landscape architect from the University of Florida in 1959 and was Chief, Site Planner/Landscape Architect for the Public Buildings Service of the U.S. General Services Administration (GSA) until he was named Director, Office of Environmental Affairs for GSA, the position he held until he retired in 1981.

George Penland Sr. was born in Newcastle County, PA (now Delaware) in 1753. Prior to 1770, he traveled to Morganton, NC through the Shenandoah Valley. He was a Captain in the Morgan District 3 Militia of NC, and fought in the Revolutionary War in battles of Ramsour's Mill, King's Mountain, Cowpens in SC, and against the Cherokee Indians from 1776-82.

George and his wife Ann Alexander had 11 children. He died in 1829. They are buried in the Zebulon Vance Cemetery, Buncombe Co., NC.

PEREZ, RUEBEN M. – Reuben M. Perez was born March 3, 1944 in San Antonio, TX. His military service was in the U.S. Army. He retired on Jan. 1, 2006. He and his wife, Carrie S. Perez, reside in San Antonio, TX. They have one child.

He is currently the Vice-President of the SAR Chapter San Antonio, TX and a member of the R.O.T.C. Committee. He is also a member of the Sons of the Republic of Texas.

Jose Antonio Curbelo was born January 1746 in San Antonio, TX. For his patriotic service, he provided and donated 1069 head of cattle to Bernardo de Galvez. He was Lt. Governor of the Province of Texas, served as mayor of San Antonio, and a rancher and cattleman. He died Sept. 6, 1789 and is buried in San Antonio, TX.

PERKINS, DAVID L. – David Perkins was born in a small, two-room farmhouse in northeastern South Dakota. He suffered through the Depression and Dust Bowl days of the early 1930's while attending a one-room country school. David enlisted as a Naval Aircrewman immediately after his 17th birthday and spent the next eight years on active duty.

After discharge from the Navy, his career included working at Cape Canaveral, with the Air Force on supersonic interceptors and the Navy on their Polaris, Poseidon and Trident intercontinental missile systems.

During this time period he pursued a degree at San Jose State University and graduated with a BA in Art (painting) minoring in writing.

On July 8, 1961 he married Isabel Ramos, a California native. He retired in 1992 and currently lives in Lincoln, CA.

AEC David L. Perkins, June 6, 1953.

Daniel Buck Perkins, b. May 13, 1760 Norwich, CT, d. September 1806 Manlius, NY.

Daniel enlisted May 20, 1777 as a private for a term of three years in Capt. John Shumway's Co., 1st Battalion of Connecticut as a private from Mansfield.

On guard duty, detachment to Norwalk, guard at various places in New York including West Point (November 1779).

Upon completion of the war, the family lived for a brief period at Deerfield, Orange County, NY. Then Daniel purchased a piece of property at Manlius, Onondaga County which is close to Syracuse.

According to family tradition, he was riding his horse through the forest or some trees in early September, 1806 when he was struck by lightening. He apparently survived long enough to write a will disposing of his estate. He was 46 years of age when he died.

His widow then married another Revolutionary War survivor by the name of Shepard.

PETERMAN, TIMOTHY EDWARD – Born 1959 in Kansas City, MO and still resides there. Timothy joined SAR Kansas State Society Nov. 2, 1982.

Timothy E. Peterman, #121096

He has served as Delaware Crossing Chapter President, 2007-08; Kansas Society Membership Secretary and Registrar, 1995-; and Genealogist, 2007- .

Timothy has received the Patriot Medal, Distinguished Service Medal, Meritorious Service Medal, Silver Good Citizenship Medal, Liberty Medal and Bronze Good Citizenship Medal.

Timothy has worked at UMB Bank as an analyst since 1984.

Isaac Ellis was born in 1752 in Frederick County, MD. He was a Captain in the Pennsylvania Militia. In 1782 he was at the Siege of Fort Henry, Wheeling, VA. Isaac died in 1833 and is buried in Owen County, KY.

David Eagleton was born in 1748, possibly Scotland. He was a Private in Washington Co., NC Militia. David died in 1828 and is buried in Blount County, TN.

John Montgomery was born in 1764. John served as a Private in Capt. Dasey's Company, 7th Virginia Regiment. He was at Whitsall's Mills and Guilford Court House. John died in 1845 and is buried in Peoria County, IL.

Patrick Porter was born in 1737. He served as a Sergeant for Washington Co., VA. Patrick died after 1795.

Jonathan Hoar was born in 1747 in Sudbury, MA. He was a Lieutenant in Maynard's 4th Company, Col. Howe's Regiment, Massachusetts Militia. On April 19, 1775 he was at the Lexington Alarm. Jonathan died in 1813 and is buried in Dublin, NH.

Josiah Hoar was born in 1747, also at Sudbury, MA. He served as a Captain with the Massachusetts Militia. Josiah died about 1779 and is buried in Sudbury, MA.

Richard Heard was born in 1720 at Sudbury, MA. He served as a Captain with the Massachusetts Militia. As a civilian, Richard was a member of Massachusetts 1st Provincial Congress in 1774. He died in 1792 and is buried in E. Sudbury, MA.

Francis Powers was born in 1742 in Hollis, NH. He was a Private with Dow's Company, Prescott's Regiment, with New Hampshire Militia. Francis was wounded at the Battle of Bunker Hill. He died I n1796 and is buried in Hollis, NH.

Asa Eggleson Jr. was born in 1763 in Voluntown, CT. Asa served as a Private in Capt. Burdeck's Company, Col. Dyer's Regiment with Rhode Island Militia. In civilian life, Asa was a stone mason. He died in 1840 and is buried at Antwerp, Jefferson County, NY.

Asa Eggleson Sr. was born about 1735 in Stonington, CT. Asa was drafted into Rhode Island's Militia and sent his son Asa Jr. as a substitute. He died about 1816 and is buried at Greenwich, Washington County, NY.

John Roley was born about 1749. He served as a Private with McClelland's Company, Westmoreland Co. Regiment, Pennsylvania Militia. John died in 1822 and is buried in Westmoreland County, PA.

Joseph Robinson was born about 1735 in Henrico County, VA. Joseph was in public service in Cumberland County, VA. He died in 1812 and is buried in Halifax County, VA.

Henry Kivett was born about 1753 in Randolph County, NC. He served as a Private in the North Carolina Militia. Henry died in 1806 and is buried in Randolph County, NC.

Peter Kivett (or Kuwit) was born in 1726 in Germany. He provided Patriotic Service in North Carolina. Peter died in 1794 and is buried in Randolph County, NC.

William Aldridge was born about 1729 in Anne Arundel County, MD. William also provided Patriotic Service in North Carolina. He died in 1789 and is buried in Randolph County, NC.

John Aten was born in 1732 in Hunterdon County, NJ. John was a Private in Capt. Foreman's Company, York County, PA Militia. He died about 1809 and is buried at Brooke County, VA.

Matthew Hillis was born about 1742 in Delaware. Matthew was a Private with the Pennsylvania Militia. He died in 1803 and is buried in Washington County, PA.

Nathan Coffey was born about 1760. He served as a private with the North Carolina Militia. Nathan was at the Battle of King's Mountain. Nathan died after 1827 and is buried in Jackson County, AL.

Francis Burch Vermillion was born about 1758 in Prince Georges County, MD. He provided Patriotic Service for Maryland. Francis died in 1842 and is buried in Pike County, MO.

Robert Vermillion was born about 1725 in Prince Georges County, MD. He also provided Patriotic Service for Maryland. Robert died in 1779 and is buried in Prince Georges County, MD.

Matthew McGlasson was born in 1756 in Buckingham County, VA. Matthew was a Sergeant in the Virginia Militia. He died in 1834 and is buried in Adair County, KY.

Jesse Barbre was born before 1749 in Tyrell County, NC. Jesse was a soldier with the North Carolina Militia. He died in 1802 and is buried in Warren County, KY.

James Weeks was born in 1749 in Westmoreland County, VA. He served as a Sergeant with the Virginia Militia. James died in 1834 and is buried in Spencer County, KY.

Joseph Hampton was born before 1755 in Fairfax County, VA. He provided Patriotic Service for Virginia. Joseph died in 1803 and is buried in Fauquier County, VA.

John Hampton III was born in 1727 in New Kent County, VA. He was a Private with Col. Baylor's Dragoons. John died in 1794 and is buried in Fairfax County, VA.

John Hathaway was born in 1733 in Lancaster County, VA. John was a Captain with Fauquier County, VA militia. He died in 1786 and is buried in Fauquier County, VA.

Samuel McCampbell was born about 1743 in County Autrim, Ireland. Samuel was an Ensign with Rockbridge County, VA Militia. He died in 1804 and is buried in Shelby County, KY.

George Wilson was born about 1762 in Augusta County, VA. He was a Private with the Virginia Militia. George was at the Battle of Blue Licks. He died in 1813 and is buried in Bourbon County, KY.

Henry Wilson Sr. was born about 1727 in Northern Ireland. Henry provided Patriotic Service. He operated Wilson Station near Harrodsburg, KY after 1779. Henry died after 1817 and is buried in Bourbon County, KY.

Quinton Moore was born before 1765 in Rockbridge County, VA. He was a Private with the Virginia Militia. Quinton received an Invalid Pension in 1809. He died in 1821 and is buried in Lincoln County, MO.

Thomas Fletcher was born about 1753. Thomas was a Lieutenant with Westmoreland Company, Pennsylvania Militia. He died in 1799 and is buried in Montgomery County, KY.

Edward Lovell was born about 1757. He was a Captain with the North Carolina Militia. Edward was a delegate to Fayetteville, NC Convention (1789) that ratified the US Constitution. He died in 1816 and is buried in Surry County, NC.

James Badgett was born after 1750 in Granville County, NC. James provided Patriotic Service for Surry County, NC. He died in 1835 and is buried in Knox County, TN.

Samuel Freeman was born about 1715 in North Carolina. He also provided Patriotic Service for North Carolina. Samuel died in 1796 and is buried in Surry County, NC.

Giles Hudspeth was born about 1730 in Henrico County, VA. Giles provided Patriotic Service for Surry County, NC. He died in 1796 and is buried in Surry County, NC.

Mordecai Hord was born about 1730 in Caroline County, VA. He provided Patriotic Service for Virginia. Mordecai died in 1789 and is buried in Henry County, VA.

PETERS, HOWARD M. – Born in 1940 in Beech Creek (Clinton/Centre Co), PA. He left the farm to become an honors chemistry graduate of Geneva College ('62) and earned a Ph.D. in organic chemistry from Stanford ('67). He was research chemist with Dow in Midland, MI and SRI-INT. in Menlo Park, CA. In 1978 he received the Juris Doctor degree from Santa Clara U. Law School. After many years in private patent law practice in Palo Alto, CA, he retired in 2007.

He has served in many volunteer capacities with the national American Chemical Society (ACS), including on its Board of Directors (2005-7), was an invited judge for chemistry for many years with the INTEL International Science and Engineering Fair, serves on Santa Clara U. Law School's Board of Visitors and "Lawyers who Lead," and is an elected Fellow of the Royal Society of Chemistry (London).

Sally and Howard Peters.

Howard is married to the former Sally Brown, also a chemist-type, and has two scientistdaughters, Theresa and Liz and two grand girls. Howard and Sally share a passion for chocolate and have given fun talks "Chocolate-Food of the Gods"" in many ACS and Cafe Scientifique venues. In 2008 they were invited scientist/author lecturers on Cunard's Queen Mary 2. He joined the SAR in 2002 and now has confirmed six SAR patriot families. See http://www.howard-peters.com.

Nicholas Paul was born on July 8, 1748. He married Anna Barbara Vass around 1775 in Northampton County, PA.

Nicholas was a veteran of the Revolutionary War. He was a second lieutenant in the 3rd company, 5th Battalion of the Northampton Co. Militia as early as 1777. He was also enlisted in the Northampton Co. militia in 1784 and 1785.

After the Revolutionary War, Nicholas and Barbara resided in Bethlehem Township, Northampton County, where Nicholas was listed as a farmer with 150 acres in the 1786 and 1788 tax rolls.

Nicholas and Barbara Paul headstones, Riverview Cemetery, Northumberland, PA.

While in Northampton Co., they became parents of: John, Susanna, Anna Margaret, Anna Maria, Joseph, Catherine, Nancy Ann, Sarah, Elizabeth, and Christina. These children were christened at the Dryland Church, Northampton Co. About 1799, the Paul family moved to Northumberland County and purchased a farm in Point Township. Nicholas Paul died on April 16, 1820. Barbara died on Nov. 17, 1823. They are buried in Riverview Cemetery, Northumberland, PA - 30 paces from controversial minister, inventor and radical British exile, Joseph Priestley - The Father of American Chemistry. Daughter Elizabeth Paul married John Orner and moved to Centre Co, PA. Her father-in-law, Johann Orner, and family squatted on land still owned by the William Penn descendants. After failed ejectment proceedings, in 1796 the Penn family finally sold the land in Northampton County to the Orners. See www.howard-peters.com.

PHILLIPS, H. EDWARD III – Born Apr. 28, 1968 at Brookhaven, Suffolk Co., NY. He is a member of the Raleigh, NC Chapter Color Guard. Phillips is an attorney and a member of Sons of Union Veterans of the Civil War (John A. Logan Camp No. 4) and The Knights of Columbus, Council 11234, Wake Forest.

He is married to Janna Nicole Phillips and they have one child.

Clemmons Phillips was born Feb. 18, 1763 in Anson Co., NC. He joined the Anson Co., NC Militia in late 1779, about four months before his 17th birthday, a member of Col. Thomas Wade's Company with the rank of private (a ranger). He participated in several skirmishes and he and his unit also participated in activity near Wilmington, NC.

Clemmons was a land owner and farmer. He died Jul. 20, 1847 and is buried in Morgan Co., TN.

PIERCEALL, LTC BOBBY A. – Born Oct. 5, 1931 in Monroe Co., MO, he joined SAR on Oct. 1, 2008. LTC Pierceall served in the U.S. Army, 142 Trans. Bn., Aviator, fixed wing and rotary wing qualified, Master Army Aviator, retiring on Oct. 31, 1986. He is a member of Lions Club (President), AARP, and NARFE (President). He is married to Ola Mae (Heizer) Pierceall and they have three children and seven grandchildren.

Richard Pierceall was born Mar. 25, 1744 in St. Mary's Co., MD. He was a private in Col. Richard Barns' Regt., 5th Independent Co. under Capt. John A. Thomas. He guarded Leonard Town and Pautuxet Landing. A farmer and county road overseer, he died on Aug. 9, 1840 at is buried at Calvary Cemetery, Holy Name of Mary Church, Lebanon, KY.

John Aaron Spalding was born in 1752. His Revolutionary War service began Jan. 1776 in Capt. John Allen Thomas' Company, Col. William Smallwood's Regt. as a private, and served until Jul. 1783 when he was honorably discharged a sergeant at James Island, SC. He was in the following battles: Long Island, White Plains, Brandywine, Staten Island, German Town, Camden, Cowpens, Guilford Court House, Eutaw Springs, and Monmouth.

PIKE, ROGER A. – Roger was born July 27, 1940 in Hagerstown, MD. He resides in San Dinas, CA. In November, 2007 he joined the CT and CA State Societies.

Roger A. Pike

Roger and wife, Rebecca A., have two children and four grandchildren. He worked in the newspaper industry in sales and marketing. Roger retired in December, 2004.

He also belongs to The Order of Descendants of Pirates and Privateers; International Pike Family Association; Walter Palmer Family Association; Stonington, CT Historical Society; Mercer County, MO Historical Society; LaSalle County, IL Genealogy Society; and Greenwood County, KS Historical Society.

James Palmer was born Aug. 2, 1754 to the family of Walter Palmer of Stonington, CT. He enlisted in August, 1775 in the local militia for the defense of Stonington, CT and served one month. After the month expired, he enlisted as a Sergeant in Capt. Oliver Smith's company of Colonel Webb's regiment and served until Dec. 7, 1775, when he enlisted as a sailor on the US ship *Alfred* under Capt. Dudley Saltonstall, Lieut. John Paul Jones and Commodore Esek Hopkins, they sailed for the island of New Providence, landed and took the South Ford and the City, and as much of the military stores as they could carry away and made Governor Brown a prisoner. Also took a ship belonging to the Governor, which was afterwards ransomed. On their return, they captured a Bomb Brig and the Schooner *Polly* off Montauk Point, and afterwards were in an engagement with His Majesty's Ship *Glasgow*, he was in this service seven and one half months. In 1776 he was Sergeant in Nathan Palmer's company, Colonel John Ely's regiment and served until Jan. 1, 1777, when he reenlisted in the same company and regiment and served seven or nine months more. In 1778 he was in Sulivans Expedition to Rhode Island and in 1778 and 1779 was on the Privateer *Revenge* under Captain Nathan Post, while on board of her they captured a British ship laden with clothing and provisions bound for New York and several smaller prizes. Served about 18 months. In 1781, he volunteered under Captain Sands Miles and went to New London, served five days.

He married at Stonington, CT, Feb. 23, 1780, Pamela Miner and died at Sparta, NY, Sept. 15, 1840. Their children were Rufus and James.

POWELL, DELMER H. SR. – Delmer H. Powell Sr. serves in the U.S. Marines during the Korean War. His civilian employment was 37 years in nursing at the Veterans Administration Hospital, Danville, IL.

Delmer H. Powell, Sr.

His organization memberships include: Trinity Lutheran Church, Danville IL; life member of National & Illinois Field Archery Association; Society of the Descendents of Washington's Army at Valley Forge; and a member of National and Illinois Chapter Sons of the American Revolution since 2001.

Delmer married Margaret Ella Reik in April 1952 in Danville, IL. They have a son, Delmer Jr., also a member of SAR; and a daughter, Lt. Commander Lisa Lewis RN, U.S. Navy, a member of DAR.

Revolutionary grandfathers: **Thomas Morrow**, patriot server in Virginia, born 1791 in Virginia, died 1809 in Wayne County, KY. **John Small**, patriot service in Virginia, born 1710 in Ireland, died 1791 in Patrick, Virginia. **Jeremiah Burnett**, Franklin's Company of Foot 10th Virginia Regiment, born 1740 in Talbot, VA, died 1816 in Turkey Creek, KY. **Jacob Sowder**, Virginia Brigade Company, Stitbs 3rd Division, born 1734 in Montgomery, VA. Jacob was an orderly for Washington's Army at Valley Forge. He died 1785 at Montgomery, VA, and is buried on his farm.

PRANG, HON. JEFFREY – Born on June 15, 1962 in Detroit, MI, Jeffrey graduated from Michigan State University with a B.A. in International Relations in 1984. He attended the John F. Kennedy School of Government at Harvard University, State and Local Government Program in 2004.

Jeffrey Prang

He was elected to the West Hollywood City Council (California) in 1997. He served as Mayor from 2000-01, 2003-04, and 2008-09.

Prang currently serves as Assistant City Manager for the City of Pico Rivera, CA. He previously served as a senior aide to the Los Angeles County Sheriff and for a member of the L.A. City Council. He also served as a member of the California Council on Criminal Justice, as President of the California Contract Cities Association, and as a Member of the Platform Committee at the 1996 Democratic National Convention.

He is descendant of **Richard Wooldridge**, born in Chesterfield County, VA in 1738, died in Russell County, KY on March 17, 1828. Wooldridge served in the Lincoln County Militia; Captain John Snoddy's company against the Shawnee Indians in 1782. He later served as a Constable in Washington County, NC and owned a grist mill in Green County, KY. He is presumed buried in Russell County, KY.

PRICE, COL. PAUL V. III – Born April 4, 1960 in Jenkins, KY, resides in Williamson, WV. He joined the WV State Society in May, 2007.

Thomas Price the Revolutionary War Soldier, Cherokee trader, and Linguist was born in 1738 Culpeper, VA to Kalem and Mary Price. Thomas joined the Fincastle Militia before the Revolution. One of his duties included being assigned to Capt. Daniel Smith at the Elk Garden Fort on the Clinch River. Thomas Price probably believed it was his duty to defend his community as did all the Price men. His uncle, Richard Price even owned the land the fort stood on. Thomas, along with many other men from the Fincastle Militia fought in the Battle of Point Pleasant where he took an Indian arrow in the left arm. He recovered from his wound and continued to visit what are now Kentucky, Tennessee, and North Carolina on many hunting trips trading with the Cherokees. It is documented on more than one occasion he was with Daniel Boone among others on these trips. He was a Cherokee linguist who assisted in the translation of the Cherokee language for treaties. One of the treaties Thomas Price signed as the Cherokee Linguist was the Treaty of Sycamore Shoals. Archibald Henderson's book *The conquest of the old Southwest; the romantic story of the early pioneers into Virginia, the Carolinas, Tennessee, and Kentucky* describes the scene as "Gathered about him (Judge Henderson), picturesque in garb and striking in appearance, were many of the buckskin-clad leaders of the border--James Robertson, John Sevier, Isaac Shelby, William Bailey Smith, and their compeers--as well as his Carolina friends John Williams, Thomas and Nathaniel Hart, Nathaniel Henderson, Jesse Benton, and Valentine Searcy." This treaty was a significant event toward settlement west of the Appalachian Mountains because it transferred the land, about seventeen million acres between the Ohio River and the headwaters of the streams flowing into the Kentucky and Cumberland Rivers, to the Transylvania Land Company.

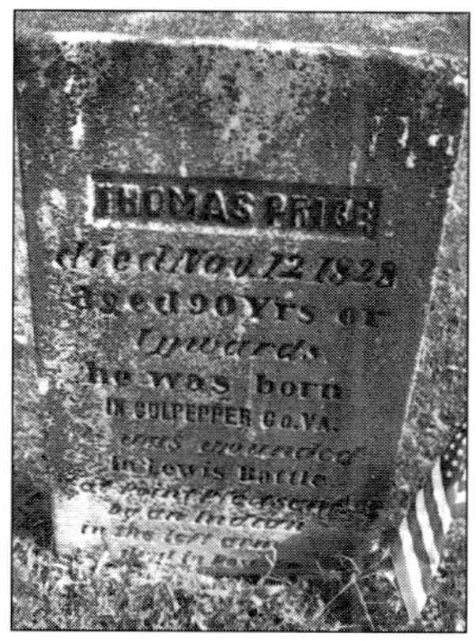

Gravestone of Thomas Price.

During the Revolutionary War, Thomas served in the 3rd Virginia Battalion, The Virginia Continental Line. He fought in several battles including the battle of Kings Mountain. After the war, he relocated with most of his family to what is now Johnson County, KY, then still part of Virginia, called the Virginia Military District. Thomas Price settled in this land he found on his adventures with Daniel Boone, Isaac Shelby, Colonel William Preston, and Judge Henderson of the Transylvania Land Company. Thomas knew the land well, and had taken several trips not only as a long hunter, but as a guide for others at times. Colonel Hart and Judge Henderson described Thomas Price on one of these trips while guiding them as being "guided by the experienced Indian trader, Thomas Price." Several years after his move to Kentucky, he became one of the first settlers into what is now Posey County, IN. Thomas lived out the rest of his life in Indiana. He died Nov. 12, 1828 at 90 years old, and is buried at Bethsaida Christian Church Cemetery Stewartsville, Posey Co, IN.

PULFREY, ROBERT EARL – Born Aug. 16, 1916 Brown Co., SD; BS Physics-Math 1937 Jamestown College, ND; Juris Doctor 1953 George Washington University, DC; Col US Army Air Force WW-2; 2nd Lt. November, 1940; CO 64th Basic Combat Training Sqdn, Kelly Army Air Field, TX 1941; CO 498th Twin Engine Training Sqdn; CO 615t Bomb Sqdn (B-26); Director of Flying Training (B-26) Dodge City, KS; CO 2617th Air Force Reserve Center, Wash, DC; CO 8375th Reserve Recovery Group; War Plans, Hq, 2nd US Air Force, Andrews Air Force Base, MD; total US Army and US Air Force service, 36 + yrs; Professor: Physics-Math, Jamestown College, ND; DC bar 1953; airplane pilot 52 yrs; Director: Mechanical and Plant Patent Examining, US Patent Office, retired GS 16, Dec. 7, 1974; US Registered Patent Attorney; m1 Alta Mae Davidson, m2 Ruth Anna (Caldwell) Brilhart, m3 Flora Elizabeth (Heater) Maynard.

Robert Pulfrey

Ch by m1: (1) Robert, b. 1942, m. Regina Maria Dieter; ch: Brian E., b. 1969; Julian C., b 1973, m. Annie Marie Fernandez, dau. Lila Regina, b. 2005; (2) Ellen Jean, b. 1945, m. Harold Hershey: ch: Owen D., b. 1973; Nicholas A., b. 1975; (3) James A., b. 1947, m. Charlotte Brooks: ch: J Alan, 1978, m Jill Baker; Stephanie E., b. 1980.

Gilbert Drew, b. April 11, 1732, Carmel, Dutchess Co., NY, m. July 5, 1753, Sarah Hunt (1732-1835); Sgt., Capt. Hezekiah Mead's Company, Col. Henry Luddington's (Luddenton's) 7th Rgmt. Vol. Militia, Dutchess Co, NY; d. March 26, 1812, bur. Drews-Clift Cem., Dutchess (now Putnam) Co., NY.

David Longwell, b. Feb. 3, 1736/7, Stamford, CT; Pvt., Capt. Nathaniel Webb's Co. 4th Rgmt. CT Militia, Aug. 12-Sept. 12, 1776; Pvt.; Capt. Jonathan Whitney's Co., Gen. Wooster's 4th Rgmt. CT Militia, Nov. 7, 1776-Jan. 11, 1777; Sgt. 4th Rgmt. Westchester Co., NY Militia (Thomas Hunt, Adjutant); certified for land bounty rights by Thomas Hunt, Adjutant of 4th Rgmt. for Rev War service; m. Sarah Tyler, July 28, 1771, Church of Christ, South Salem, Westchester Co., NY; Sarah b. May 27, 1753; David d. Jan. 10, 1815, Vernon twp. Sussex Co., NJ.

Amos Miner, b. April 8, 1755, New London, CT; Pvt.; Capt. James Clark's 6th Co., Brig. Gen. Israel Putnam's 3rd Rgmt., CT Militia, May 8-Dec. 18, 1775; 1776, Sgt.; Capt. Benjamin Throop's Co, Col. Charles Burrell's 10th CT Rgmt. Gen. Washington's Continental Line; in battle at Breed's (now Bunker) Hill, June 1776; in battle of Long Island, August 1776; crippled by gunshot in left elbow whereby he was honorably medically discharged Nov. 9, 1776 from Stamford, CT hospital. Granted disabled soldier's pension Sept. 4, 1793, $30.00 per year; farmer; m. Dec. 14, 1780, Mary Rowley (1760-1840); he d. Nov. 11, 1836, Palmyra, NY.

Eber Townsend, b. 1760 Dutchess Co., NY; enlisted June, 1778 Pvt.; Capt. Hezekiah Mead's Company, Col. Henry Luddington's (Luddenton's) 7th Rgmt., Dutchess Co. Vol. Militia, NY; m. Elizabeth Drew, 1765-Dec. 14, 1841. Eber d. July 17, 1822, age 62 yrs., Urbana twp., Steuben Co., NY; bur. Old Drew (private) Cemetery.

RAILLING, EDWARD B. – Born Dec. 14, 1951 in Saginaw, MI; joined Michigan State Society in March, 2005. He has received the Certificate of Distinguished Service.

Edward and wife Sarah have four children and two grandchildren. He is employed at General Motors Skilled Trades as a tinsmith.

Edward also is past president of Chesaning High School Sports Boosters and past Little League Coach.

Yost Railing was born in 1752 in Pennsylvania. He was a private with the Pennsylvania Militia, serving with Bucks County Associators, Lower Millford Township, Capt. Henrich (Henry) Huber, 1775-1776. He was a Private, Class 6th, Northampton County, PA Militia, 3rd Company, 2nd Battalion, Capt. Peter Schuller, 1778. In 1780, Class 5, 6, 7, 8, Bucks County, PA Militia, 2nd Battalion, Capt. Cuters.

Yost lived in the northern most part of Bucks County, very near the then Northampton County line. Yost and his wife Catharina had 10 children. The first two were both boys; Henry, born in 1773, and George, born in 1775; both died very young during the hardships of our war for independence.

Yost was the son of German immigrants. He could not read or write, so his last name and even his first name appears in many different spellings. (Yost is German for Joseph.)

In civilian life, Yost was a farmer and weaver. He died Nov. 5, 1822 and is buried at Mifflin Twp., Cumberland Co., PA (homestead).

RAMSEY, ROGER DALE – Born Aug. 14, 1946 in Parma, Stoddard County, MO. He joined the Spirit of St. Louis Chapter Missouri SAR on Jul. 21, 2008. He served in the US Army (SP4) from Jan. 10, 1966 - Jan. 9 1968, and later worked in maintenance for Chrysler Corporation for 43 years, retiring on Jun. 1, 2007. He is married to Linda Joyce (Henry) Ramsey, and has two daughters, Rhonda Leach and Renee Goessler, and five grandchildren, Kayla Zumwalt, Megan Ramsey, Joshua Leach, Kyle Goessler, and Sarah Leach.

John Houis was born 1765 in Lincoln Co., NC. He was in the Lincoln County, North Carolina Militia, a private under Capt. James Houston, and fought at the Battle of Ramsour's Mill, Lincolnton, NC, Jun. 20, 1780. John was a farmer and had nine children. He died Dec. 1834 and is buried at Houis Cemetery at Hardin, Lincoln Co., NC.

RAY, STEPHEN KERMIT – Born Aug. 25, 1967 in Corinth, MS. Steve joined the Benjamin Tennille Chapter of the Louisiana State Society of the SAR on Sept. 1, 2008 at the age of 41.

A graduate of the University of West Alabama (formerly Livingston University), Steve holds a B.S. degree in Biology. Steve has been employed with the Louisiana Office of Public Health in Monroe, LA as a licensed Sanitarian for 15 years and currently holds the position of the Safe Drinking Water Program Coordinator for Region 8, which is comprised of 12 parishes in northeast Louisiana.

Steve has been a member of the Louisiana Public Health Assoc. and was elected to the Offices of Environmental Health Section Treasurer, Environmental Health Section Vice Chair, Environmental Health Section Chair, LPHA 2nd VP, LPHA 1st VP, LPHA Secretary President Elect and LPHA President. However, Steve resigned the Office of LPHA President 2007-08, since he refused to hold a required membership in the American Public Health Assoc., as the organization publicly opposed the war in Iraq. Steve has also served for the last 10 years as the elected Treasurer for the West Monroe Chapter of the Sons of Confederate Veterans, Major Thomas McGuire Camp 1714 and has received the honor of a SCV Meritorious Service Medal in 2008 for his decade of work. Some of Steve's favorite pastimes are genealogy, history and helping coach his son's ball teams.

Steve lives in West Monroe, LA with his wife, Leigh Ann Bailey Ray, and their son, Alexander Davidson Ray, where they are members of the Cedar Crest Baptist Church.

Steve is a descendant of **Arthur Brown**, through his father William Kermit Ray, who is a veteran of the Persian Gulf War. Arthur Brown, who was the son of James Brown, was born on Dec. 18, 1761 in Pitt County, NC. Arthur served as a Private in Captain Anthony Sharp's Company in Major Reading Blount's Battalion of the 2nd North Carolina Infantry Regiment. Arthur saw action under the command of General Nathanael Green in the battle of Eutaw Springs and while assisting a fellow wounded soldier, was wounded himself by having a British bayonet run completely through his chest and missing his heart by only inches. Left for dead on the field, miraculously Arthur survived this ordeal and went on to raise a family of six children.

Arthur moved from Pitt County, NC, first to Caldwell County, KY, but later settled in Carroll County, TN between the towns of McLemoresville and Huntingdon, where he was a farmer. One of Arthur's grandsons, Samuel Arthur Brown, was a Union Soldier and served in Company F of the 52nd Indiana Infantry during the War Between the States, and went on to serve many years as the Registrar for Carroll County, TN. Samuel was himself instrumental in the collection and preservation of his family's history, and to whom much is owed and recognition rightfully bestowed. Arthur lived in Carroll County, TN until his death on Apr. 23, 1849 and is buried in the city cemetery in McLemoresville.

REDMON, KEITH – Born Aug. 29, 1957 at Winston-Salem, NC, he joined the Bethabara SAR in Nov. 2008. He works for the City of Winston-Salem (Sergeant), and is also a member of Sons of Confederate Veterans. Keith has two children and two grandchildren.

John Tuttle was born Mar. 22, 1761 in Fairfax Co., VA and was a private in Capt. Peter O'Neal's Co., NC Militia. He fought at the Battle of 12 Mile Creek near Catawba River. John died on Sept. 30, 1840 and is buried at Stokes Co., NC.

REEB, JOHN VINCENT – Born Feb. 10, Sequoyah County, OK; presently resides in Alameda, CA.

John V. Reeb and son.

John was in the United States Air Force, 20 years service (Aug. 11, 1955-Oct. 1, 1975). John and wife, Misako Takagi (formerly) have one child and two grandchildren.

He was employed as retail stock room and warehousing supervisor, Host Marriott, retiring May 7, 1994.

John also belongs to Veterans of Foreign Wars, Post 1205, San Francisco, CA.

Peter Reeb was born May 21, 1759 in Philadelphia, PA. He was a Private in the North Carolina Militia. In civilian life, his occupation was a farmer. Peter died Jan. 16, 1825 and is buried at Wesley Chapel Cemetery, Union County, NC.

REED, HARRY DAN – Born April 15, 1940 in Fort Worth, TX, presently resides in St. Paul, TX.

Harry has served as Plano Chapter 37 Registrar. He received the Good Citizenship Medal in 2007.

He and wife Carolyn have three children and one grandchildren. Harry was employed by Union Pacific Corp., retiring Jan. 1 2003.

Harry is in the North Texas SAR Color Guard – Rank Lt.

Thomas Tucker was born Feb. 11, 1757 in Edgecomb, NC. He served as a Private in Col. Whitaker's Militia North Carolina Regiment in the companies of Capt. Kidd NC and Capt. Griffin NC. Thomas served from 1779 to 1782. Thomas was a farmer and died May 1, 1840. He is buried in Putnam, IN Cemetery.

REED, JERRY W. SR. – Born Jul. 1, 1947 in Tulsa, OK. He is a member of the River Raisin Chapter, Genealogist/Registrar, and was nominated for the Michigan State Secretary in 2009.

He was in the U.S. Navy Submarine Service from 1969-80, Chief Warrant Officer Medical Corps, and works for the University of Michigan Hospital, Ann Arbor, as a Physician Assistant Surgical Oncology.

Jerry is a member of the Society of the War of 1812, Scottish American Military Society, St. Andrews Society of Detroit, Sons of Union Veterans of the Civil War, and Families of U.S. Presidents. He is descended from Abraham Lincoln through Mordicai Lincoln and Mary Millard (Robinson?).

He is married to Barbara Ann (Powers) Reed, and they have five children and 13 grandchildren.

William Langston was born Apr. 15, 1762 in Granville, NC, the son of Capt. James B. Langston. He was a private serving with the 6th North Carolina Regt., 7th Company (the same company as his father). William Langston was a farmer, and his father was a Justice of the Peace. William died Dec. 7, 1853 and is buried in Mason County, IL.

REES, LANE CHARLES – Born Longview, TX. He joined the SAR in 1987 (129860 Nat. no.), Alaska Society, now in Florida. He was the Alaska State President and National Trustee from Alaska. Lane has received the Silver Good Citizenship Medal and Society Centennial Medal.

Lane C. Rees

He and wife Brenda (Anderson) Rees have two children, Brian A. and Lauren C, and one grandchild, Leighton C.

Lane was President, Human Resource Solutions, Inc., for 10 years and formerly Sr. Human Resources Director/Advisor for Atlantic Richfield Company for over 20 years.

He was elected Walton County Commissioner 2000-2004 (Chair), appointed by Florida Governor Jeb Bush to the Medical Examiners Commission, Foundation for Evangelism of UMC (Chair), Alaska Missionary Conference Lay Leader, United Methodist Communications Commission, Texas A and M University International Board, Former Students Association of Texas A and M Board, Florida Association of Counties Trust (Vice Chair), Republican Party of Alaska (Chair) and Life Member Republican National Committee, Municipality of Anchorage Utility Regulatory Commission (Chair) and numerous other involvement.

Additional remarks: Part of Republican Delegation for President George Bush (Alaska) in 1992 and for President George W. Bush (Florida) in 2000.

John Sutton Jr. was born May 25, 1759 in Virginia. He achieved the rank of Sergeant and served from 1777 to 1779 with the Virginia Militia. John died April 22, 1826 and is buried at Sutton Graveyard overlooking Cane Run in Scott County, KY.

RENNIE, CHRIS – Chris is an Eagle Scout. He is a Collegiate All-American and a National Champion Marksman. He is a National Record Holder in Small-bore International Shooting and was invited to try-out for the US Olympic Team in 1972 and 1976. Chris also set State Records in High School Track and Cross-Country.

Chris earned a Bachelor of Science degree with Honors in Industrial Engineering Technology, Technology Education, and Military Science. He earned a Master of Science degree with Honors in Occupational Education and Instructional Design.

Chris served a total of ten years in the United States Army and was promoted to the rank of Major.

Chris is a teacher. He has taught courses in Computer Aided Design and Engineering in both secondary and post-secondary education. Chris conceived, developed and implemented a degree program for an Accredited College where he served as Academic Dean Pro-Temp.

Chris manages software development teams that produce Computer Aided Design software applications. His teams are located in the United States, Europe, and Asia.

Chris served two terms as President of the Major Robert Kirkwood Chapter, Delaware Society, Sons of the American Revolution. Chris has one child.

Michael Schock was born Nov. 24, 1757 in Germany. He was a Private in Capt. Shradel's Company of the 3rd Pennsylvania Regiment. Michael died December, 1814 and is buried at St. Michael's, Berks County, PA.

Samuel Slocomb was born July 25, 1756 at Kingston, RI. He was a Private with the Continental Army of Rhode Island and was at the Battle of Bennington. Samuel died Dec. 22, 1827 and is buried at Shaftsbury, Bennington County, VT.

Michael Rentchler was born Oct. 18, 1722 in Germany. He was a Private with Pennsylvania Militia of Berks County. Michael died before March 20, 1797 and is buried at Bern, Berks County, PA.

William Deibert was born Nov. 3, 1751 at Wittenburg, Germany. William was a Patriot in Col. Lindemuth's 3rd Battalion, Pennsylvania Militia of Berks County. He died April 20, 1832 and is buried at Manheim, Schuylkill County, PA.

REYNOLDS, WILLIAM R. JR. – Retired in 2005 from Civil Service employment with the USAF where Bill worked at the civilian grade GM-13 as Chief ICBM Facilities Engineer for USAF Space Command in Colorado Springs, CO.

William R. Reynolds, Jr. with first great granddaughter, Sylvia Deaver, April 2008.

Bill is a member of SAR Oregon Society Republic Chapter in Salem, OR. He is married to Diane Robinson and they live outside of Hebo, OR. They have nine children, 17 grandchildren and one great-grandchild.

Joseph William Pickens was born Feb. 1, 1737, Paxton, Lancaster, PA. He served as Captain leading a company in the Upper Ninety-Six Regiment of the South Carolina Militia under his brother Colonel (future General) Andrew Pickens. Their father, Andrew Pickens, previously served as Captain of the state militia company in which the brothers served in the mid 1750's during the Cherokee wars.

Captain Pickens saw service at the Battle of Kettle Creek, GA; the Battle of Cowpens, SC; and was mortally wounded early in the Siege of Ninety-Six, SC and died about three weeks later (June 17, 1781) just two days prior to the patriots' withdrawal from the siege.

He was married Sept. 1, 1760 to his cousin Eleanor Baskin Pickens.

RICHARDS, ROBERT THOMAS – Robert Thomas Richards is a retired U.S. Marine Captain. His education includes AB French, AB Economics and Master of Public Administration. Robert's civilian employment consists of work as a High School Spanish teacher and as a Federal Investigator for the U.S. Equal Opportunity Commission.

Robert Thomas Richards

Present and past organizational memberships included the Sons of Confederate Veterans, the Brotherhood of Saint Andrew, the Chi Phi Fraternity, The Modern Language Association and the American Association of Teachers of Portuguese and Spanish. Robert was awarded a federal stipend for the study of Spanish under the National Defense Education Act.

Robert is married to Barbara Baldwin Richards. They have two children, Dawn Richards Rush and John Grayson Richards. Dawn is a Community College teacher and John is a Civil Engineer with the U.S. Army Corps of Engineers. There are two grandchildren, Pili Robert Richards and Ai Mary Richards.

Johannes Peter Moll/Mull was the son of Christophel and Ana Catharina Moll. Peter was born in 1736 in Montgomery County, PA and died in 1805 in Burke County, NC. Peter was married to Barbara Cline/Kline. The Moll family was active in the Goshen German Reformed Church which stands today about one mile west of East Greenville, Montgomery County, PA.

Various records and documents show that Captain Peter Moll/Mull served on the Committee of Safety from Rowan County from 1774-1776, served in the Battle of King's Mountain, led a scouting party in search of Indians who had broken in on area inhabitants and served as High Sheriff of Burke County, NC in 1779, 1790 and 1791.

RIDGEWAY, JONATHAN WOLK – Born July 29, 1947 in Compton, Los Angeles County,

CA; raised in Northern Virginia, 1949 to 1965. During the 1960s and 1970s, hitchhiked over half a million miles through 38 States. In 1974 he met Lynne Rosemary (Volpe) in New York's Central Park and 10 months later they were married, Feb. 20, 1975. Began working for the NYC Department of Public Works as an engineering technician trainee in 1968, progressed through competitive civil service examinations to titles of staff analyst, associate staff analyst, project coordinator and senior project coordinator. Retired from NYC Department of Environmental Protection as a senior level capital projects manager, Aug. 2, 2002, after more than 33 years of progressively responsible administrative career public service experience in operations and financial management, project and multi-project program management.

Jonathan W. Ridgeway

In March 1988, Jonathan Ridgeway was appointed Associate Project Manager in Charge of Drainage Plans and Records Management, responsible for every phase of operation and improvement that followed. The drainage plans are an immeasurably valuable hundred year old collection of original hand drawn, hand signed public documents that legally adopt vital engineering factors about the city's storm water and sanitary drainage. Being the only existing source of these critical data; information establish by these records is essential to every sewer works project in the city, public or private, except Federal and State projects, due to superior sovereignty. Ridgeway identified every goal, formulated every plan and standard, produced and processed every document to achieve every success. He provided leadership, management and stewardship to transform the archaic nineteenth century methods into a model of twenty-first century technology. Electronic scanning of the drainage plans, was substantially complete in October 1998 and fulfilled his 10 year old proposal. Nearly 8,000 images of records in 200 map file drawers, 1,500 square feet of file room storage, were completely self contained in a desktop computer. Ridgeway was also responsible for scanning nearly 80,000 other water and sewer drawings by 2002. Redundancy realized by production of the images eliminated for all time the risk that the only existing inventory of the vital public records could ever be destroyed. Suspending the practice of handling original records as part of the every day operation helped assure that the documents would be preserved for posterity.

In his private life, as well as in his career, Jonathan Ridgeway dedicated his life to public service. He served as Captain of the Color Guard for Sons of the Revolution in the State of New York from 2003 to beyond the date of this publication. SR-NY is the owner and operator of the Fraunces Tavern Museum where General Washington bade farewell to his officers Dec. 4, 1783, shortly after the British occupation forces evacuated NYC and America's War for Independence was over. Jonathan Ridgeway was admitted as a Life Member of the Virginia Society of the Sons of the American Revolution, June 8, 2005, National Number 165110 and later became a member of the Empire State Society as well. Since 1981, he has been an organizer and participant of the Little Neck / Douglaston Memorial Day Parade, the largest and one of the oldest Memorial Day parades in the nation and never missed a year. As an active environmentalist, he is President of the North American Bluebird Society, a Board Member and Area Coordinator for the New York State Bluebird Society and an Executive Committee Member of the Sierra Club Mid-Hudson Group. In the areas of civic evolvement, he serves as the Town of Plattekill Historical Society Treasurer, was a Member of Plattekill Zoning Board of Appeals in 2005, a Member of Queens Community Planning Board No. 11, NYC from 1993 to 2002, a Member of Queens Council on the Arts and Friend of Queens Theater in the Park from 1995 to 1998, a Member of a Congressional Screening Committee for Candidates to the United States Military Academies from 1995 to 2002, President of the Westmoreland (homeowners) Association of Little Neck, Queens from 1986 to 2002, President of the Little Neck Community Association from 1991 to 2002, a Founding Member and Trustee of the Douglaston / Little Neck Historical Society from 1990 to 2002 and Vice President of the CERC - Community Education Resource Center of Little Neck from 1993 to 2001. He graduated from the NYPD Citizen's Police Academy in 1997.

Jonathan Ridgeway was a recipient of proclamations from the Congress of the United States and the NYC Council, a plaque from the Westmoreland Association and was elected Man of the Year by the LN/DMDP Committee in 2002. He was elected LN/DMDP Fourth Marshal in 2000 and first recipient of the LN/DMDP Community Service Award in 1992. He was recipient of a plaque from the VFW, American Legion and JWV in 1991 and certificates from the NYC Council in 2001, the NYS Assembly in 1997 and 1992, the VFW in 1993 and the NYS Senate in 1978. He was profiled by Queens Publishing in the Little Neck Ledger in 1993 and Newsday in 1994.

Jonathan Wolk Ridgeway, was a son of Lindsay Dewey Ridgeway (born Jan. 30, 1904 in St. Louis, MO, died March 19, 1989 in Paducah, McCracken County, KY) and Charlotte Wolk (born July 12, 1918 in Brooklyn, NY, died Oct. 5, 1986 in Kew Gardens, Queens, NY), a daughter of Max Wolk (March 15, 1888 in Minsk, Belarus, died Sept. 4, 1970 in Monticello, NY) and Frieda Scharf (born Nov. 1, 1894 in Suchostaw, Galicia, died Jan. 1, 1972 in Brooklyn, NY). Lindsay, was a son of Sanford David Ridgeway (born April 1, 1878 in Alabama, died Sept. 18, 1938 in Blauntsville, Blaunt County, AL) and Martha Anne Ingram (born Dec. 23, 1881 in Columbia, SC, died Oct. 2, 1926 in Gadsden Falls, Etowah County, AL). Sanford, (born April 1, 1878 in Alabama; died Sept. 18, 1938 in Blauntsville, Blaunt County, AL), was a son of CSA Private David Albert Ridgeway (born 1847 in Alabama, died before Nov. 3, 1936) and Martha Ann Coker (born Sept. 28, 1853 in Greenville, SC, died Nov. 3, 1936 in Guntersville, Marshal County, AL). David was a son of Elijah Baker Ridgeway (born about 1807 in Alabama, died between 1870 and 1880) and Clarissa H. Tranham (born 1812 in South Carolina). Elijah was a son of Private John Ridgeway and Fannie Ragsdale.

On Sept. 9, 1862, in Limestone County, AL, **David A. Ridgeway** enlisted for three years, as a Private in Company "G" of Lt-Colonel Malone's 9th Alabama Cavalry Regiment which was organized under Captain Thomas J. McDonald on Sept. 9, 1862 at New Garden, AL. Although absent from duty for the Oct. 31 to Dec. 31, 1863 muster roll, it is known that he received his pay from Captain Sharpe on July 1, 1863 and that he was seen at the hospital. He also received pay for "risk of horse from Oct. 3, 1863 to Jan. 27, 1864" on Oct. 31, 1863. On March 1, 1863, Private Ridgeway was taken as a Prisoner of War at Bradyville, TN and taken, presumably via Louisville, KY, to Camp Butler, IL on March 11, 1863 where it seems he arrived on March 14, 1863 and sometime thereafter, he was granted a parole upon condition that he pledge upon his honor not to take up arms against the United States. At the time he was captured he was serving in Company C of the 14th Alabama Cavalry Regiment and it appears that he was captured by the 4th Ohio Cavalry. Private Ridgeway "appears on a register of 1st Mississippi CSA Hospital, Jackson, MS," that he was admitted on July 22, 1864 for gonorrhea and returned to duty Aug 18, 1864. Private Ridgeway also "appears on muster roll of a detachment commanded by Lieutenant John Rutledge, guarding Baker Creek Bridge on Muscogee RR, near Columbus, GA, for Nov. 30, 1864" dated Dec. 5, 1864.

John Ridgeway was born 1741 in Virginia, son of Samuel Ridgeway, born 1709 in St. James Parish, Clerkenwell, London, England and his wife Elizabeth Woodson married, Nov. 2, 1739, in Goochland County, VA. By 1775 their land had been spoiled by the tobacco so John Ridgeway and the families of the other farmers from his area moved to the back country of South Carolina. John became a Captain under Colonel Levi Casey in Lt-Colonel Joseph Hayes' Little River Regiment of the South Carolina Militia. He served in engagements at Augusta, in Ninety Six at the battle of Young's Store and at Cowpens. He commanded Ridgeway's Fort, a small structure located in the Lebanon area comprised of two blockhouses with outbuildings and usually garrisoned by thirty patriots. Sept. 3, 1781, the fort was attacked by a band of Tories led by the infamous, William "Bloody Bill" Cunningham. Some battle ensued before the patriots surrendered. After being taken prisoner, Captain Ridgeway, another officer and eight privates were killed. The exact location of the fort is not known but it was close to the present day town of Honea Path, near the site of Sullivan's Grove where he and a dozen other Revolutionary Patriots were buried. The graves are marked with river rocks and the Captain's is the one next to the crypt. About a mile and a quarter to the east, there are markers in the Lebanon United Methodist Church yard, for him, Private John Ridgeway, and other founders of the original Grove Church, established prior to 1790 as one of the earliest Methodist "preaching stands" in upper Carolina.

Samuel Ridgeway, Captain John's father, lived between Lebanon and Raburn Churches on what was known as the Francis Monroe place during the War for Independence. He built himself a place of safety in a huge hollow sycamore tree which stood at the mouth of a cave above his house on Reedy River and forked about six feet above the ground. It was hollow inside; big enough to hold a bedstead and necessary camping utensils. When word came down that "Bloody Bill" or other Tory raiding parties were headed his way, he would flee to this sanctuary until the danger was past. Sometimes he eluded his pursuers by diving into the river, coming up into the cave and thence into the hollow tree. It was an important place of historical curiosity up until the middle of the nineteenth century.

John Ridgeway was born Jan. 27, 1760, in Buckingham County, VA, a son of Captain John Ridgeway and Charity Hendrix who had married about 1757. In the fall of 1777, at age 17 he volunteered for three months as a private in the South Carolina Militia under Captain John Rodgers and assisted in building a block house on the Indian line to protect the white citizens from the Indians. In January 1778, he volunteered for a three month tour at the blockhouse under Captain James Mulwee in Colonel Joseph Hayes' Regiment; William Mulwee was his major. In the fall of 1779, Private Ridgeway was drafted for about two months into Captain John Stephens' Company when Stephens was cashiered for improper conduct, in consequence of the approach of the Tories under Colonel Boyd being dispersed.

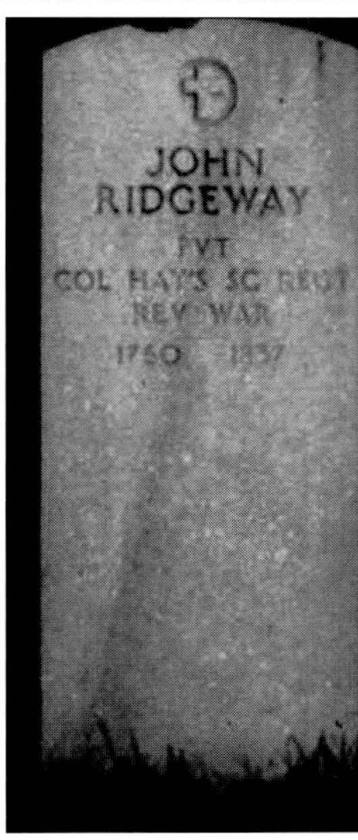

Gravestone of John Ridgeway

In March 1780, Private Ridgeway was drafted for another three month tour under Captain John Richie in the SC Militia Regiment commanded by Colonel Robert McCreary (McCrary). His unit was marched to Covut (Covert?) Hill near Augusta, GA. From there they started toward Charleston and heard about the fall of Charleston along the way so they were marched to the opposite side of the Santee River for safety. Later they were marched to Granby, where they were discharged a few days before the term of their service expired. Generals Williamson and Pickens were their commanders during this expedition.

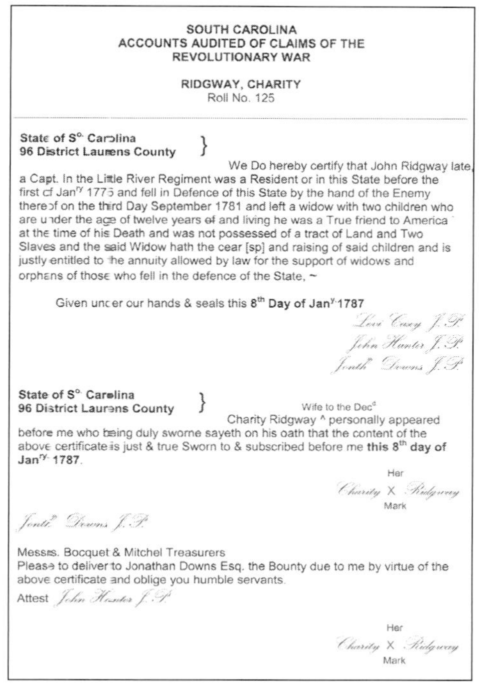
SOUTH CAROLINA
ACCOUNTS AUDITED OF CLAIMS OF THE
REVOLUTIONARY WAR

RIDGWAY, CHARITY
Roll No. 125

State of S^o. Carolina
96 District Laurens County }

We Do hereby certify that John Ridgway late a Capt. In the Little River Regiment was a Resident or in this State before the first of Jan^ry 1775 and fell in Defence of this State by the hand of the Enemy thereof on the third Day September 1781 and left a widow with two children who are under the age of twelve years of and living he was a True friend to America at the time of his Death and was not possessed of a tract of Land and Two Slaves and the said Widow hath the cear [sp] and raising of said children and is justly entitled to the annuity allowed by law for the support of widows and orphans of those who fell in the defence of the State, ~

Given under our hands & seals this **8th Day of Jany. 1787**

Levi Casey J.P.
John Hunter J.P.
Jonth^n Downs J.P.

State of S^o. Carolina
96 District Laurens County }

Wife to the Dec^d
Charity Ridgway ^ personally appeared before me who being duly sworne sayeth on his oath that the content of the above certificate is just & true Sworn to & subscribed before me **this 8th day of Jan^ry. 1787**.

Her
Charity X Ridgway
Mark

Jonth^n Downs J.P.

Messrs. Bocquet & Mitchel Treasurers
Please to deliver to Jonathan Downs Esq. the Bounty due to me by virtue of the above certificate and oblige you humble servants.
Attest John Hunter J.P.

Her
Charity X Ridgway
Mark

Original (and typewritten) Pension for Charity Ridgeway, widow of Capt. John Ridgeway.

In November 1780, Private Ridgeway enlisted under the command of his father, Captain John Ridgeway, marched to Georgia to join Colonel Clark and on to Augusta where they met an engagement with the Tories. Then they returned to Colonel Clark's station and back to South Carolina. December 1780, Private Ridgeway volunteered for another tour in his father's company in Lt-Colonel Joseph Hayes' Little River Regiment, during which he fought in the engagement at Young's Store in the Ninety Six District where the Tories were defeated. Jan. 4, 1781, they were marched to Grindal Shoals on Pacolet River where they joined General Morgan. Jan. 17, 1781, at the outset of the battle of Cowpens, Lt-Colonel Hayes' Regiment, including Private Ridgeway, were on the road, left of center in the front militia line.

After Cowpens, Private Ridgeway's unit was marched to Virginia where he was discharged. On about March 1, 1781, while residing in Bedford County, VA, he enlisted as substitute for his cousin Thomas Ridgeway of Bedford County and served a three month tour in Captain William Jones' Company in a Virginia Militia Regiment commanded by Colonel Lynch and Lt-Colonel Callaway. At the time a refugee from South Carolina to Bedford County, Private Ridgeway joined the Army of the United States under the command of General Greene at Carter's Ferry on Dan River. From there he was marched to North Carolina and fought in the battle of Guilford Courthouse on March 15, 1781, in which his commander was killed. Then he was transferred to serve as Rifleman in Captain James Dillard's Company under the command of Lt-Colonel William Washington and continued with the Army until it reached Deep River, his tour expired and he was regularly discharged. When he returned to Virginia he was drafted for a three month tour under Captain John Nickels in a Virginia Militia Regiment commanded by Colonel Nickles, during which he was marched to battle in the siege of Yorktown. Then he joined the American Army under General Washington and remained until the fall of Yorktown when he was discharged before the expiration of his term of service. He served more than 18 months, all together.

At age 30, Private John Ridgeway married Fannie Ragsdale, (daughter of Peter Ragsdale and Sarah Carlton) on Dec. 25, 1790 in Greenville, SC. John and Fannie lived on Peachland Creek near "viscuit Baldwin" and had five children, Elizabeth (born c. 1798), William (born 1800 in South Carolina), John (born 1805, died 1824), Richard (born c. 1806, died May 19, 1865) and Elijah Baker Ridgeway (born c. 1807 in South Carolina, died in Alabama c. 1880). After Fannie's father died in 1805, Fannie's mother lived most of the time with John and Fannie. She was there during the War of 1812 when cost of homespun and such necessities became exorbitant. She tried to get relatives in the State Legislature to pass a law to control prices on these items. Even in that faraway day, the women of South Carolina were fighting profiteering and other such evils of war.

At aged 73, while residing in Laurens District, SC, Private Ridgeway was granted pension on his application, sworn to, subscribed and executed in open Court, with his mark "J", on Oct. 23, 1833, where he appeared personally before his Honor John S. Richardson, Judge of the Court of Common Pleas and John Garlington, Clerk of Laurens District Court. Reverends John Potter and Richard Simpson were present to testify as to his character for veracity and good behavior and Robert Long to testify as to his Revolutionary Service. John Ridgeway was issued Pension Certificate No. 23023 dated Nov. 29, 1833, rate $60.00 per annum., pursuant to a June 7, 1832 Act of Congress, SC Agency.

While visiting his brother William in Georgia, Private Ridgeway died about Nov. 21, 1839 and was buried in Hall County, GA. There are commemorative markers in the present day Lebanon United Methodist Church yard in Honea Path, SC for Private John Ridgeway, his father, Captain John Ridgeway, his in-laws, Sargent Peter and Sarah Ragsdale and other founders of the original Grove Church.

Sargent Peter Ragsdale was born 1730 in Bristol Parish, Prince Georges County, VA and died Sept. 16, 1799 in Greenville County, SC. He married Sarah Charlton before 1765 in Goochland County, VA and they emigrated to South Carolina in 1775. Sargent Ragsdale served the cause of patriotism as Overseer of the Roads in the Virginia Militia. Sarah was born 1730 in Mecklenberg County, VA (formerly Lunenburg) and died Feb. 5, 1830 in Laurens County, SC, at age 100. They were both buried in Sullivan's Grove cemetery. Their daughter, Fannie Ragsdale, who married Private John Ridgeway was born about 1767 in Mecklenberg and died 1837 in Laurens County.

RIEGER, MICHAEL DAVID – Born Mar. 9, 1959 in Middletown, OH. Michael was admitted to the Ohio Society of the SAR May 7, 2008. He is the son of a WWII Army veteran who was well decorated for his part in the Pacific theater. Michael has owned and operated Valley Painting Co. for 32 years, is an active member of the Germantown Lions Club as Vice President, and is on the board of The Historical Society of Germantown. He also belongs to the historical societies of Ohio and Berks County, PA, along with The Colonial Williamsburg Foundation.

Michael enjoys traveling with his wife, Deborah, to historical sites.

His patriot ancestor is his five greats grandfather, **Michael Emrich**, born Feb. 10, 1756 in Bethel Twp., Berks Co. PA. He served with the Berks Co. Militia from 1777-80 as a lieutenant in Capt. Folmer's Company, and then from 1781-83 as a lieutenant 8th class in Capt. Shepler's Company. Michael married Christina Kantner on Sept. 22, 1778 in Stouchsburg, PA. They had six children and moved to German Twp. in 1806. Michael was part of one of the founding families of Germantown and his civilian occupation was farming. He died Oct. 14, 1820 and is buried at Sunbury Cemetery in German Twp., Montgomery Co., OH.

RIEGLE, CHARLES W. – Born June 25, 1935 in Buffalo, Erie County, NY. Joined NSSAR in 1995 and Life Member since then. Life Member CTSSAR and Captain Matthew Mead Branch, CTSSAR since 1995; Life Member FLSSAR and Saramana Chapter, FLSSAR since 2001. Charles is currently Vice President of Saramana Chapter, FLSSAR. He was President, Captain Matthew Mead Branch, CTSSAR (1999-2001), Vice President CTSSAR (two years), Asst. Trustee CTSSAR (two years), National Committeeman (W3R committee) – five years).

Charles has received the Silver Good Citizenship Medal and Meritorious Service Medal; Gen. George Washington Military Service Award, Founders and Patriots Certificate of Appreciation, CAAH certificates (three times).

Charles served in the 3rd U.S. Army 2nd Battalion, 10th Regiment, Company D. He was a Private to Airman 3rd Class. Also served 335th Troop Carrier Wing, US Air Force Reserve. Charles was an Army Corpsman and Air Force Pharmacist.

Charles William Riegle

Charles and wife Ausra Vedeckas Riegle have three children. Charles W. Riegle Jr. (NSSAR No. 146125); Christopher V. Riegle (NSSAR No. 146126); and Kristina Anne Riegle. Grandchildren are: Phoebe Anne Riegle; Coleman William Riegle (NSSAR Youth Member No. 9105); Evan Charles Riegle (NSSAR Youth Member No. 9107); AND Oliver Charles Riegle (NSSAR Youth Member No. 9106); and Genevieve Elizabeth Riegle.

In civilian life, Charles was a partner in Rolf Werner Rosenthal, Inc. Advertising (1969-1983) with title of Executive VP/COO and President of World Health Communications Division. He served on the Management Committee and was Vice Chairman of Healthcare division of Ogilvy and Mather Advertising Company, New York City (1983-85). Charles retired June 24, 1985.

Charles has also served on Board of Directors Boys and Girls Club of Greenwich, CT (five years); Board member of the Diabetes Association of New York City (four years); Board member and Vice President of the Greenwich Symphony Orchestra (15 years); Boy Scout Council Greenwich, CT (two years), Board member of the Innis Arden Golf Club (10 years); Vice President of the Riegel Reunion (eight years), Life Member of Berks County Historical Society, Millersburg Historical Society and Gratz Historical Society.

Father: Warren Coleman Riegle, Memorial Membership NSSAR 2008.

John Daniel Riegel was born ca. 1713, Gumbsweiler, Rhineland-Pfalz, son of Johann Cornelius and Anna Gertruitha Riegel. John arrived in America on the Briganteen *Pennsylvania Merchant*, landing on Sept. 18, 1733. John Daniel married Maria Dorothea Beitler in Berks County, PA in 1744 and they had four sons and three daughters. John Daniel was a farmer and miller.

John Daniel was 63 years old when the Revolution started, but he took the Test Oath of Allegiance and Fidelity to the State of Pennsylvania on May 26, 1778. He also paid Supply Taxes during the war.

John Daniel died May 25, 1786 and is buried in Row 20, Grave 5 in Host Church Cemetery, Tulpehocken Township, Berks County, PA.

Andreas (Andrew) Riegel, born ca. 1750 (baptized July 7, 1751), Tulpehocken Township, Berks County, PA, was the son of John Daniel and Maria Dorothea Riegel. Andreas married Anna Catharina Hoffman in 1770, and had four of his 10 children at the time of his service. Andreas was a Private in Captain Sherman's Company and Captain Henry Shepler's 3rd Company, 6th Battalion, Berks County Militia from 1777-1779. In civilian life, Andreas was also a farmer and miller. He died May 14, 1815 and is buried in Hoffman family plot, Loyalton Road, Lykens Township, Dauphin County, PA.

John Coleman was born ca. 1745, Tulpehocken Township, Berks County, PA. John served as a Private 7th Class in Captain Isaac Adams Company, Col. Peter Grubb's 3rd Battalion of Pennsylvania Militia (Associators) from Lancaster County, PA. In military experience, he served in "The Jerseys." John was also farmer and miller in civilian life. He died Sept. 29, 1793 and is most likely buried in St. Matthew's (Coleman's) Evangelical Church Cemetery, Lykens Township, Dauphin County, PA.

George Klinger was born in Berks County, PA. He was a Private 2nd Class with Captain Martin Weaver's Company, Pennsylvania Militia (Associators) from Lancaster County, PA, listed in 1781. In civilian life, he was a farmer. George is buried at Klingerstown, Lykens Township, Dauphin County, PA.

Gravesite of John Peter Hoffman.

John Peter Hoffman was born 1709 in Riegenroth, Rhineland-Pfalz. Although too old to serve, John paid the Effective Supply Tax to Wiconisco District, Lancaster County, PA on 100 acres in 1779. (Noted in Pennsylvania Archives, 3rd Series, Vol. 17, page 582). He also paid the Continental Tax for Upper Paxton Township, Wiconisco District in 1777. John Peter did serve in the French and Indian Wars of 1756. In civilian life, he was a farmer. He is buried in Hoffman family plot, Lykens Township, Dauphin County, PA.

John Nicholas Hoffman was born March 21, 1749 in Tulpehocken Township, Berks County, PA. John Nicholas was a Private and served with companies of Captain Martin Weaver (4th Battalion), Albright Deibler's Company (Pennsylvania Associators) and with Col. Burd at Long Island, in the regiments of Col. James Burd (at Long Island), the 4th Battalion, Pennsylvania Militia (Associators) from Lancaster County, PA and 10th Pennsylvania Regiment. John was in the Battle of Long Island (captured), then with Col. Rodger's Regiment at Brandywine and Germantown.

In civilian life he was a farmer. He died April 28, 1814 and is buried at St. Peter's (Hoffman's) Church Cemetery, Lykens Township, Dauphin County, PA.

John Harman was born ca. 1750 at Lykens Township, Lancaster County, PA. He was a Private 5th and 6th Class and by 1781 had attained the rank of Sergeant. He was with Captain Martin

Weaver's 7th Company, 10th Battalion, Pennsylvania Militia (Associators) from Lancaster County, PA. John was with Col. Rodger's Regiment at Brandywine and Germantown. In civilian life he was a farmer. He died after 1815 and is buried in St. Peter's (Hoffman's) Church Cemetery, Lykens Township, Dauphin County, PA.

John Phillip Klinger Sr. was born July 11, 1723 at Pfaffen-Beerfurth, Rhineland-Pfalz. He was a Private with Captain Albright Deibler's Company, Col. James Burd's 4th Battalion, Pennsylvania Militia (Associators) from Lancaster County, PA. He was at the Battle of Long Island, Aug. 27, 1776. John Philip was a farmer in civilian life. He died Sept. 30, 1811 and is buried at Zion Lutheran (Klinger's) Church Cemetery, Erdman, Dauphin County, PA.

RIGG, COLBY CHARLES – Colby Charles Rigg was born Aug. 13, 1982 in Mt. Carmel, IL. He is currently the 911 Emergency Services Directory for Wabash County, IL. He is Mayor of the Village of Bellmont (2004-), and a lieutenant with the Bellmont Fire Department. He is married to Marci Tupper Rigg and they have one child.

Charles Rigg was born June 8, 1756 in Charles County, MD. He served as corporal with the 1st Maryland Regiment, Captain Starret's Company. He was involved with the Battle of Brandywine and the Battle of Monmouth. His civilian occupation was a farmer. He died Feb. 24, 1839 and is buried at Sand Hill Cemetery in Mt. Carmel, IL.

ROBERTS, GEORGE HARRISON III – Born Jan. 4, 1942, George joined SAR Jan. 22, 2001, No. 155053; Washington Crossing, PA No. 11072.

He married Dorothy M. Campbell and they have two children and one grandchild. George worked as Vice President – Operations, Bell Atlantic (now Verizon) and retired March 31, 1997.

In addition to SAR, George also is a board member of Fox Chase Cancer Center, Walnut Street Theatre, and a member of Sons of Union Veterans of Civil War.

John Roberts, 1710-1776, is my family's Patriot who served in the Revolution War. He was the grandson of John Roberts, 1648-1724, who came to America from Wales to Merion Township, Philadelphia County, PA in 1683. He, along with many other Quakers, built the Merion Meeting House and his family farm house, which he called "Pencoyd." He left behind in Wales an illustrious family with a history dating back to 0990 A.D. when his relative was Collwyn ap Tango, the Lord of Llyn.

John Roberts grew up on the "Pencoyd" farm and was very active in Colonial times and held the commission of "Justice" from 1757 until his death. He married Rebecca Jones on May 4, 1733 at the Merion Friends Meeting House his grandfather had helped to build. They had 12 children. Two of the children, Algernon and Robert, served in the Revolutionary War with their father. Robert was a member of the First City Troop of Philadelphia while Algernon attained the rank of Lt. Colonial of the Seventh Battalion, Philadelphia Militia. This Battalion took an active role in the operations for the defense of Philadelphia.

The interesting aspect of these men who served in the American Revolution is that they were all Quakers with a long family history of following the Quaker doctrines. However, their belief in their country and their desire for freedom was so strong that they made the decision to serve, even knowing it would draw strong criticism from their Quaker brethren. The Roberts family was very well off financially but decided to risk it all to follow their belief in the individual's right to freedom, the very reason their forefather had come to America in the first place.

John Roberts was my great, great, great, great, great grandfather and I cannot begin to tell how proud I am that he had a hand in our nation's birth. I am both proud and grateful that my family played a role in making our country the great nation we are today. I am a member of the National Society, No. 155053, and the Pennsylvania Society, Washington Crossing Chapter, No. 11072.

ROBERTS, HAROLD K. JR. – Born Oct. 24, 1950 in Salisbury, Rowan County, NC; joined SAR North Carolina Society June 21, 2007.

Harold K. Roberts

Harold married Susan Annette Bell and they have one child. He is President of Statewide Title Inc.

Harold also belongs to Andrew Jackson Masonic Lodge No. 576, York Rite Mason, Oasis Shrine Temple, American Institute of CPAs and NC Association of CPAs.

Gravestone of William McScwain.

William McSwain was born July 22, 1762 in North Carolina. He was a Private with Captain Brewer in Brevard's Company, 10th North Carolina Infantry. He was in the Battle of King Mountain. William died Dec. 9, 1838 and is buried at the Old McSwain Family Cemetery in Cleveland County, NC.

ROCKWELL, WILLIAM D. – SAR Compatriot William D. Rockwell was born in Troy, NY on Aug. 6, 1943. Retired since 2001 from a career in the food service industry, where he attained the position of Vice President of Marketing, Bill is enjoying retirement with his wife of 43 years, Mary Beth. Bill, his four brothers and a cousin joined The Empire State (NY) Society chapter of the SAR on June 15, 2006. He and his brother James give presentations about the life and times of their patriot ancestor to local genealogy societies.

William Rockwell

Revolutionary War Patriot **Robert Ayers** was born on April 12, 1765 in Stillwater, NY. On April 1, 1782, he ran away from his apprenticeship at a Stillwater tannery and joined Captain Job Wright's Company of Colonel Marinus Willett's Regiment of The New York State Troops. In February 1783 he went on an expedition against Fort Ontario.

Robert Ayers gravesite.

Discharged on January 8, 1784 as a non commissioned officer, he was awarded 500 acres of land for his service. He became a successful farmer in Ballston Spa, NY.

Robert Ayers received a soldier's pension of $70.88 per year just before his death on April 30, 1833 at the age of 68. His grave is in the Ballston Spa Village Cemetery.

ROE, RAYMOND E. SR. – Born at Manchester CH, raised in Texas, Korean Veteran serving the US Army, 25th Recon Armored Tank Div., achieving the rank of Corporal. Ray was the driver of a personnel carrier, received several combat pays for crossing the 38th parallel to rescue wounded soldiers. At the close of the war, he and his carrier were stationed in a mountain side undercover, just above Freedom Bridge, where he had a spectacular view and he witnessed the exchange of prisoners. He served inactive reserved from 1954-1957 and honorably discharged as Sergeant. His civilian employment was in the retail grocery business, starting as bag boy at Piggly Wiggly. Raymond

Ray and Vanita Roe, 1952.

moved to Upstate New York where he became a produce and store manager for P & C Foods and the Weedsport Big M where he retired.

Organization memberships include life memberships at Thurston-Schram-Reynolds Post #8137, Montezuma, NY, American Veterans-Robert F. Stryker Memorial Post #513, Montezuma, NY and American Legion Post #568, Weedsport, NY. Awards received include medals for Good Conduct, Sharp Shooting, National Defense, Korea United Nation, Korea Service with 3 Bronze Stars as well as the Korea Service Medal issued by both the US and Korean Governments.

Raymond married Vanita A. Wilson, who is a member of the Owasco Chapter NSDAR. With his wife of 57 years they have 9 children and 15 grandchildren.

Grave of John Leap. Monument erected by Boone County, IN.

John Leap, born April 15, 1745 near the River Rhein, Manheim, Germany, died Sept. 16, 1845 in Boone Co., IN. Served as Pvt Buck Co. Militia and Capt. John Jameson' Co., Col. Arch McIlroy's 4th PA Rgt. He was in the battles of Staten Island, Trenton, and Princeton. John was one of the soldiers that crossed the Delaware with General Washington. He was discharged at Battle Hill in Morristown, NJ. After the war, he moved to Switzerland Co., IN and later Boone Co., where he was a farmer. John married Margaret Emily Crow and had 5 children. He married second Sarah Barbara and was blessed with another 6 children. John is buried at Mount Tabor Cemetery in Fayette, Boone Co., IN.

ROHRBOUGH, COL. FRANK G. – Born July, 1939 in Harrisburg, PA., presently residing in Boerne, TX. He served with the US Air Force for 30 years, attaining the rank of Colonel. Frank retired from the Air Force May 31, 1991.

He joined the Texas Society in June 1996. He has served as President, San Antonio Chapter; Color Guard Commander, San Antonio Chapter; Chairman Grave Marking Committee. G W Chapter, Mount Vernon, VA. Frank has received the Meritorious Service Medal w/Oak Leaf Cluster; Bronze Good Conduct Medal; Color Guard Service Award; TXSSAR Chapter Service Medal; War Service Medal (S.W. Asia).

Col. Frank G. Rohrbough

Frank and Diane (Ross) Rohrbough have four children, 11 grandchildren and two grandchildren on the way. Frank also worked for the Military Officers Assn. of America, Dep. Dir. Gov't Relations and retired from MOAA October 31, 2004.

He also belongs to the USAF Medical Svc. Corps Assn. and Knights of Columbus. Frank conducted four grave marking ceremonies for Revolutionary Patriots' graves with SAR grave markers that had never been marked before.

Gravestone of John Rorabaugh.

John Rorabaugh was born July 1740 in Hochstadt, Germany. John provided pasturage and feed to the militia as he was a farmer. He died Oct. 30, 1821 and is buried at Milam, Hardy County, WV on the homestead farm.

ROHRBOUGH, STEPHEN W. – LtCol Stephen W. Rohrbough was born July 10, 1939 in Harrisburg, PA. His military service was with the U.S. Air Force. He retired Sept. 1, 1989 from Lincoln Financial Group as a Registered Rep.

He joined the SAR June 5, 1996 in Texas. He currently serves as Vice-President of the TXSSAR Americanism Program, and Chairman of the TXSSAR CAR Liaison Committee. He has received the Patriot Medal, Meritorious Medal (2OLC), Silver Good Citizenship Medal, Bronze Good Citizenship Medal, and TXSSAR Service Medal (2OLC). He helped initiate the TXSSAR CAR Essay Contest. He is a member of the Knights of Columbus and the National Defense Transportation Association.

LtCol Steven W. Rorbough

Gravesite of John Conrad Rohrbough.

He is married to Marie McGuire Rohrbough and they reside in San Antonio, TX. They have two children.

John Conrad Rohrbough was born July 31, 1740 in Hochstadt, Germany. His civilian occupation was a farmer. He died Oct 31, 1821 and is buried on a farm in Milam, WV.

ROLPH, DANIEL EDWARD – Daniel Edward Rolph was born Sept. 19, 1970 in Baltimore, MD. His military service was 1993-2000 as a sergeant in the U.S. Army, in Military Intelligence and a Russian/German/Serbian linguist.

He currently holds the office of Treasurer for the Fairfax Resolves Chapter, Virginia Society, and is a VASSAR Color Guard Member.

He is employed as a Senior Software Engineer with BIT Systems. He is married to Christine Marie Wile and they have two children.

Thomas Rolph was a private in the 20th Battalion, Maryland Militia, Flying Camp with Captain John Dean's Company. His company fought in the Battle of Harlem Heights. He was a blacksmith. His death was in 1797 and his burial place is unknown.

ROUNDS, MICHAEL S. – Born June 29, 1947 at Laconia, NH, joined New Hampshire Society June 9, 2005. Michael has been Publicity Chairman and an Official NHSSAR photographer.

Michael's military service was as SP5-E5 with US Army Security Agency.

He and Violet Mae have two children. Michael was also owner of Mike Rounds Photography Services, retiring Dec. 14, 2007.

Michael also belongs to the American Legion, Scottish-American Society, Asa Chitose Association, and National Army Security Agency Association.

Michael S. Rounds

His sons Derek and Zachary Rounds are both members of NHSSAR.

Eliphalet Kilburn was born Dec. 13, 1752 at Rowley, MA.

He entered service at Battle of Lexington. He enlisted in the 12th Continental Regiment and fought in the Battle of Bunker Hill. Reenlisted December, 1775. Transferred to

Elisha Marston, original Son of the American Revolution. He was the oldest living SAR member in 1902. Photo was taken on his 100th Birthday.

13th Massachusetts. Stationed at Fort Ticonderoga in fall of 1776. Crossed Delaware River Dec. 25, 1776 with Colonel Cadwalader. Fought in second Battle of Trenton. Served under Col. Daniel Hitchcock at Battle of Princeton. Lead into battle by General Washington.

In July 1777 enlisted in the 4th Essex County, MA Militia and marched to Bennington, arriving too late for battle. Proceeded to Mt. Independence in failed attempt to dislodge British and Hessians. Marched south to join Gen. Gates at Stillwater. Was at surrender of Gen. Burgoyne.

In 1778 he enlisted at Rowley, MA for six months in the Massachusetts Militia to serve under General Sullivan at Rhode Island.

In 1779 he enlisted at Newbury, MA for four months in Col. Jacob Gerrish Massachusetts Militia. He marched directly to Greenbush, NY spending the entire time there in support of the Continental army.

RUBY, HERMAN EDGAR – Born Dec. 31, 1926 in Pittsburgh, PA. Joined the South Carolina Society Dec. 19, 2008.

Herman's military service was as Aviation Radioman 3rd Class, U.S. Navy/VPB 114.

He retired from the U.S. Government as a Planner/Estimator on July 1, 1982. He is a former member of The Southernaires Big Band. He and Betty Louise Sanders have two children and two grandchildren.

John Hughes was born Aug 9, 1747 in Ireland.

He served with Col. Thomas Clark's 4th Reg., Capt. John Summer's Co. as Orderly Sergeant with the N.C. Militia, Rowan Co. N.C. He was involved in the Battle of Monmouth, NJ.

John died Sept. 19, 1830 and is buried in Henderson Co., KY.

RUCH, GEORGE R. – Born Oct. 24, 1937 in Pleasant City, OH. Served as Eastern District Chrmn. OHSSAR, Chapter President (two terms), V-Pres., Sec., Registrar, Newsletter Editor for Chapter Newsletter, (Zanes Trace) for six years. Also served as Chairman JRROTC committee (eight years).

George R. Ruch

George has received the OHSSASR Distinguished Serv., Meritorious Serv./Oak Leaf cluster, Bronze Good Citizenship, Bronze Color Guard Medal, Certificate of Commendation (George S. and Stella M. Knight Essay Contest). He served with the USAF from 1956 to 1959.

George and Darlene J. Ruch have two children and seven grandchildren. He was an Asst. Controller and Auditor, and retired in 1996.

George also belongs to the Cumberland Trail Genealogical Society.

Elijah Foote was born Oct. 29, 1740 in Newtown, CT and died October 15, 1813 at West Liberty, Ohio Co., VA. (now, WV). His wife was

Gravestone of Elijah Foote.

Eunice Peck, b. abt. 1742 and died Feb. 23, 1776. They had seven children.

Elijah Foote served and saw military action in the Eighth Regiment of the Connecticut Line of the Continental Army. He enlisted Sept. 3, 1777 for three years and was in Captain Comstock's Company. Elijah fought under General McDougall at Germantown, Oct. 4, 1777. They wintered at Valley Forge, 1777-1778, and on June 28th following were present at the battle of Monmouth. He was discharged Sept. 3, 1780. His Militia group was called up by General George Washington in the late summer of 1776. Foote served in this capacity as part of the Sixteenth Regiment of Connecticut Militia (Captain John Botsford's Company), which comprised trainbands (local militia groups) from Danbury, Ridgefield, New Fairfield, and Newtown. Elijah enlisted in the Continental Line from service in the 16th. The regiments that served that brief time under Washington were heavily recruited for extended Continental service.

A bronze memorial marker in his honor was placed in the Old West Liberty Cemetery, West Liberty, Ohio Co., WV on June 18, 2005.

RUYLE, DONNIE MAX – Born March 19, 1935 near Canute, Washita County, OK, resides in Burlington, WA. He joined Cascade Centennial State Society in March 2004.

Donnie and Sandra Jayne (Savage) Ruyle have two children and three grandchildren.

Donnie and Sandra Ruyle

He worked at a sawmill as head sawyer, retiring June 30, 1994.

Henry Field was born Feb. 3, 1755 at Culpepper County, VA. He enlisted in the fall of 1775, John Green's Company, First Regiment of the Virginia Line of the Continental Establishment. Served in First Regiment until fall of 1776. He then re-enlisted in the same First Regiment Company of Capt. John Green for a period of three years. After serving for about three months, he was taken from the ranks by General Finney, who was stationed at Williamsburg, VA, for the purpose of riding and carrying express. He served to the end of the three year term for which he enlisted, and was discharged at Williamsburg, VA, fall of 1779. Henry served with the rank of Private. This was recorded in Fifth Judicial District Bullitt County, KY, May 20,1818. Henry Field applied for a Revolutionary Pension. Witnesses, Colonel Richard Taylor, Colonel Patrick Henry and Abraham Field under oath that Henry Field did serve as stated. Pension was granted under Pension No. W8811.

After service, Henry was a farmer, died May 27, 1823 and is buried at Bullitt County, KY.

RYAN, THOMAS F. – Born April 12, 1943 at Lockport, NY. He belongs to the Continental Congress Chapter, York, PA.

He has served as Awards Chairman-ROTC/Jr. ROTC, Eagle Scouts for Adams, York and Lancaster Counties, PA.

Thomas served in the USAF as a Sergeant, MAC Command, 1964-1968. He later worked for Goodyear Tire & Rubber Co., York Penn. Mach'y Co. for 32 years, retiring in Aug. 2005.

He married Nancy C. Anglin. They have two children, Dave and Matt, and two grandchildren, Dave and Alicia. Other relatives include brother Jack, sister Constance, father Henry, mother Lucille (Perry), and Oliver Hazard Perry.

Thomas is a member of SAR (I.D. 168576, Feb. 2007), American Legion Post 403, and the Lions Club. He owns Tom Ryan Mach Tools and O'Ryan's Shillelagh's - walking sticks. His hobbies include golf, genealogy-ancestors tipperary, Ire. woodworking, and gardening.

Abner Crandall was born July 3, 1762 in Tiverton, RI. He served as a Private in the companies of Capt. I. Cook, Howe and Col. N. Miller in Elliott's RI Artillery and RI Militia. Abner took part in RI battles, 1778-1779 (pension file W.F. 18.972, N.Y.)

Abner's civilian occupation was as a farmer/blacksmith. He married Mary Wilcox and they had 12 children. Abner is descendant of Elder John Crandall of Rhode Island. He died Dec. 12, 1840 and is buried at Tibbetts Farm-Hoosick Falls Rural Cemetery, Hoosick Falls, NY.

SATTERFIELD, CHARLES M. – Born on Aug. 19, 1933, he was admitted to the South Carolina SAR on Nov. 18, 2008. Charles was a captain in the USAR, Artillery branch, and later was a senior staff engineer for Jacobs Engineering, retiring on Aug. 31, 1998. He is married to Elizabeth M. (Graney) Satterfield, with seven children and five grandchildren.

Joseph Purinton (Purington) was born Jul. 20, 1746 in Middleboro, MA. A hard working farmer, he was well educated and had the Bible at his tounge's end. He was famous among his neighbors for his ready and apt quotations. Joseph married Lucy Allen in 1772. They had nine children.

Joseph enlisted in 1775, as a private, in Capt. Isaac Wood's Company, Col. Theophilus Cotton's Regt. The Company's return was dated Oct. 6, 1775. He enlisted again in 1776 and 1778 in Capt. Abram Washburn's Company. Joseph's good friend and fellow patriot, Stoddard Totman, testified at his pension application hearing. Joseph was awarded a yearly pension of $63.33. Joseph's grandson, Dr. Orpheus Purinton later married Stoddard Totman's granddaughter, Mary Elizabeth Call.

Both Joseph and Lucy are buried at the Branch Cemetery, Colrain, MA.

SCATES, GEORGE F. – Born May 13, 1935 in Cleveland, OH, he joined the Ohio SAR on Feb. 25, 2008. George served in the U.S. Navy, MM3, Brunswick NAS, Quonset Point NAS, and USS Ticonderoga (CVA-14). He was an over the road teamster driver for 43 years, retiring on May 29, 1999. He married Ruth Ellen Ruggles Scates, and they have four children and eight grandchildren.

George F. Scatess

John Scates was born 1724 in Berwick, ME. He was a corporal in John Shapleigh's Company, was stationed at Kittery, ME, Hodsdon's Company and was in the Penobscot Expedition. A farmer, he died in 1822 and is buried in Berwick, ME.

SCHERCINGER, JOHN MARSHALL – (National Number 159245). Born Washington, DC. Married to Mary "Anne" Narcissis Reamy in Washington, DC; two children and four grandchildren. Reside Hootingtown, Calvert Co., MD. Member other Societies: Order of Charlemagne in the U.S.A.; The Baronial Order of the Magna Charta (14 ancestors); Jamestowne Society (six ancestors); The National Society of the Washington Family Descendants; Hereditary Order of the Families of the Presidents and First Ladies of America (through Augustine Washington, Father of George); Nicholas Martiau Descendants Association; descendant of William the Conqueror and Merovech, King of the Salic Franks, 448-457; and a JCI Senator. Retired Director Highway-Railroad Grade Crossing Programs, Association of American Railroads.

John Marshall Schercinger

Col. Fielding Lewis Sr., the SAR member's 4th Great Grandfather and Brother In-Law of George Washington was born at "Warner Hall," Gloucester Co., VA, July 7, 1725.[1] At the outbreak of the Rev. War, he held his former rank in the French and Indian War of Brigadier General in the VA Militia,[2] During the Rev. War, Fielding was Commissioner of Safety, Spotsylvania Co., VA, as well as, Chief Commissioner of the Gun Factory (Arsenal) at Fredericksburg, VA. Col. Lewis, along with "Maj. Charles Dick, were appointed by the Virginia Convention in 1775 as commissioners to 'form, establish and conduct a manufactory of small arms at Fredericksburg."[3] Much of the funds expended for the operation of the factory was that of Col. Lewis' for which he was never reimbursed (in excess of $1M in 1998)[4]. Col. Lewis was a man of extensive influence in Virginia prior to and during the War. Ill health compelled him to resign his position at the Gun Factory sometime in 1781. Various accounts have been written about when he died and where buried, BUT he was NOT laid to rest under the steps of St. George's Episcopal Church, Fredericksburg[5] but more likely near his son Fielding Jr.'s "western" estate in Frederick Co., VA.[6] His death was "between Dec. 10, 1781, when he added a codicil to his will, and 17 days later when on December 27 his name was recorded in Frederick County as deceased ...."[7]

Portrait of Col. Fielding Lewis, Sr., John Wollaston, c. 1755.

Capt. George Lewis, son of Fielding Sr., nephew of General Washington and 3rd Great Grandfather of the above SAR member, was born at "Kenmore," Fredericksburg, VA, March 14, 1757[8] and died at "Marmion," King George Co., VA, Nov. 15, 1821.[9] Commissioned a 1st Lt. in the Commander-in-Chiefs Guard March 12, 1776; battle of White Plains, NY, Oct. 28, 1776; detached to Newtown, PA, Dec. 14, 1776 to recruit a troop of cavalry. His success resulted in promotion to Captain, Light Dragoons, 3rd VA Regiment. Captain Lewis was subsequently detached to the Commander-in-Chiefs Guard, May 1, 1777, fought at the battles of Brandywine, PA, Sept. 11, 1777; Germantown, PA, Oct. 4, 1777 and Monmouth, NJ, June 28, 1778. Capt. Lewis rejoined the 3rd VA Regiment Sept. 26, 1778 and was at the skirmish of Tappan, NY, Sept. 28, 1778.[10]

Capt. George Lewis, by unknown artist.

References:

1. Sorley, Merrow Egerton, *Lewis of Warner Hall: The History of a Family*, p. 131, Key Letters "AC", (1935).

2. Heitman, Francis B., *Historical Register of Officers of the Continental Army During the War of the Revolution April, 1775, to December, 1873*, p. 348, Reprint of the New, Revised and Enlarged Edition of 1914 with Addenda by Robert H. Kelby, 1932.

3. Sorley, op. cit, p. 139.

4. *Inflation: the Value of the Pound 1750-1998*, Research Paper 99/20, Robert Twigger, Economic Policy and Statistics Section, House of Commons Library, 23 February 1999.

5. Undated (aft. 1994) pamphlet, *A Brief History of St. George's Episcopal Church*, Fredericksburg, VA, "The Cemetery," paragraph 2, p. 7. (Commentary on Fielding's burial location).

6. Felder, Paula S., *Fielding Lewis and The Washington Family – A Chronicle of 18th Century Fredericksburg*, p. 300 (1998). (Commentary with Footnote 10 about Fielding's burial location).

7. Duke, Jane Taylor, *Kenmore and the Lewises*, Chapter XIII, p. 144 and Footnote 27, p. 251 (1949). (Commentary on the approximate date of Fielding's death).

8. *The Lewis Family Bible of Col. Fielding Lewis, Sr.* with Transcription from the Kenmore Manuscript Collection, George Washington's Fredericksburg Foundation, Fredericksburg, VA.

9. Sorley, op. cit, p. 153, Key Letters "ACG."

10. Numerous Resources covering the War Service of Capt. George Lewis including:

A. Commemoration Ceremony and Biography by the Col. Fielding Lewis Chapter, Virginia Society SAR, 10 June 2006, Willis Cemetery.

B. Sanchez-Saavedra, E.M., *A Guide to Virginia Military Organizations in the American Revolution*, 1774-1787, Richmond: Virginia State Library, pp. 80, 104-106, (1978).

C. Godfrey, Carlos E., M.D., *The Commander-In-Chief's Guard, Revolutionary War*, pp. 205-6, originally published Washington, DC, 1904; reprinted Genealogical Publishing Co., Inc., Baltimore (1972, 1995, 2000 and 2001).

D. Scott, Craig R. CGRS and President/CEO Heritage Books, Westminster, MD *E-Mail* 13 April 2006 to John Marshall Schercinger pertaining to *Captain George Lewis and the Virginia 3rd Light Dragoons, Continental Line.*

SCHIEMAN, CHARLES TOMPKINS III – Born Mar. 24, 1940 in Wichita, KS, he joined the Ohio SAR on Oct. 8, 2008. Charles worked for DuPont, retiring as a senior project engineer in 1998. He is married to Karen Tefft Schieman, and they have three children and five grandchildren.

Stiles Judson was born Nov. 18, 1752 in Stratford, CT. He was a captain in the 4th Connecticut Regt., 5th Company, and served during the New Haven Alarm, 1775. He died on Mar. 10, 1834 and is buried in the Congregational Church Burial Ground, Stratford, CT.

SCHOOLEY, JOHN HEILMAN – Born Feb. 8, 1943, resides at Fairmont, WV.

John and Anne (Weaver) Schooley have two children. John was Professor of Music, Fairmont State University, Fairmont, WV.

Remarks: A complete updated biographical sketch including photograph is available on line by typing in John Heilman Schooley on your google search entry space.

Samuel Schooley was born in 1742 at Hunterdon Co., NJ. He served as 1st Lieutenant in 1st Regiment Sussex County Militia, NJ in Captain Andrew Malick's Company. Samuel was at the Battles of Long Island, NY (Aug. 27, 1776) and White Plains, NY (Oct. 28, 1776). Samuel was probably a farmer. He died in 1807 and is buried in Northampton Co., PA.

SCHRADER, DR. DAVID E. – Born Oct. 1, 1947 at Northfield, MN. Joined Delaware and Pennsylvania Societies on Nov. 12, 1985.

SAR offices: Edmund Terrel Chapter (TX), Secretary, President; George Washington Chapter (PA0, Secretary, Vice-President, President; Maj. Robert Kirkwood Chapter (DE), V.P., President; PA Society, Chaplain, Chair of Americanism Committee, Chair of Knight Essay Contest Committee. Dr. David has earned the Patriot's Medal (PA Society), Silver Good Citizenship Medal, and Meritorious Service Medal.

David and Sandra Thompson Schrader have two children and three grandchildren. He is Executive Director, American Philosophical Association.

David also belongs to St. Paul's Lutheran Church, National Humanities Alliance Board of Directors, International Society for Valve Inquiry – President. Also Delaware Department of Health and Social Services Human Subjects Review Board.

Eldad Spafford was born Jan. 2, 1745 in Rowley, MA. He was a farmer who died Jan. 6, 1809 and is buried at (Old) Temple, NH, Cemetery.

SCOFIELD-MACDOWELL, ROY – Residing in Waltham, MA; was born Jan. 20, 1926.

Roy served with the United States Marine Corps from Jan. 29, 1943 through Dec. 18, 1945. He participated in action against the enemy – Bougainville 1943; Okinawa 1945.

Roy and Josephine Marie have five sons: Roy Jr.; Lance; Bruce; Brian and Scott and nine grandchildren.

Roy worked for Artisan Industries Inc. Vice President of Manufacturing for 41 years, retiring Jan. 1, 1991.

Roy is a Life Member DAV, VFW, American Legion America's First Families, Sons of Colonial New England.

Thomas Scofield was born about 1746 in England. Thomas was a Private in Bristol Co., MA Militia, 1777 Col. Thomas Carpenter's Regmt., Capt. Peleg (Sherman's Company). Thomas was a farmer in civilian life. He died before 1820, burial place unknown.

SEACHORD, STEPHEN CLEO SIMONEAU SR. – Stephen Cleo Simoneau Seachord Sr. was born Feb. 10, 1945 in Hastings, Adams County, NE. He married Harriet Charlene Morgan on Sept. 30, 1967 at Beale Air Force Base, Maryville, Sutter County, CA. Steve and Charlene have three children (Melissa Francine, Donna Marie, Stephen Cleo Jr.) and three grandchildren (Thomas Dale, Savanna Marie, Phillip Christopher).

Steve is an active member of the Plano Chapter #37 and a Perpetual Member of the Texas Society SAR. National number: 154582; Texas State number: 8702. He has held the office of Historian, Treasurer and President of the Plano Chapter when the Chapter was awarded Honorable Mention in the President General's Cup. Steve received the Chapter Service Award, War Service Medal and the rank of Captain of the Texas Color Guard.

Stephen Cleo and Carlene Seachord.

Steve was a member of the U.S. Air Force during the Vietnam War. His service was from April 5, 1966 through April 4, 1969 with a grade of E-5 as an Air Operations Specialist. Steve is a Code Enforcement Officer licensed by the State of Texas. He retired from the City of Dallas in 1999. He was ordained as a Deacon in the Church of God. His grandfather, John Phineas Winslow, was an active member of the SAR.

Samuel Winslow was born in Epping, Rockingham County, NH on July 28, 1775. He married Anna Ladd on May 4, 1778. They had ten children: Elisha, Jane, Anna, Eisha, Abigail, Sarah, Samuel, Betsey, Mary and Martha.

Gravesite of Samuel Winslow at South Ridge Cemetery, Caledonia County, VT.

Samuel volunteered as a private for six months in July 1775 with Col John Stark. He was ordered to Winter Hill and remained there until the enlistment expired in January 1776. In February 1776 he enlisted again for two months with Stark Militia as a corporal. He was ordered in May to Charlestown, NH and stationed there when his service expired May 1776.

Samuel volunteered again in July 1776 as a private in the New Hampshire Militia for five months. He was ordered to Ticonderoga and marched directly to Charleston. He crossed the Connecticut River at Charleston and marched to Greensboro, where he took a boat to Ticonderoga. He was at Mount Independence until his discharge in December 1776.

Samuel enlisted in July 1777 for two months as the orderly sergeant with General John Stark. He marched to Charleston for rations and then directed their march to Bennington. He stayed at the barn of Lt. Floyd until he fought in the Battle of Bennington. He returned to the barn and stayed there until he was discharged in September 1777.

Samuel died March 12, 1850 at Sutton, Caledonia County, VT and is buried at South Ridge Cemetery, Caledonia County, VT.

SEALES, BOBBY JOE – Born Feb. 4, 1945 in Shelby County, AL; joined Alabama State Society Feb. 5, 1999. He was the Founding President, Cahaba-Coosa Chapter; Historian, Alabama Society; and Sergeant-At-Arms, Birmingham Chapter.

Bobby Joe Seales

Bobby has received the Meritorious Service Medal (August 2003 and November 2003); George Washington Fellow (2004); Distinguished Service as President (2004 and 2005); Certificate of Distinguished Service (2005, 2006 and 2007); and Certificate of Appreciation (2005).

Bobby married Diane Bradenberg and they have two children and two grandchildren.

Bobby was an Internal Auditor and Corporate Credit Manager for ITT, retiring in July 1992.

He also belongs to Shelby County Historical Society, President 2000 to Current; 2004 Leadership Shelby County Graduate; Shelby County Hospitality Association, President 2007; and Alabama Cemetery Preservation Alliance, Shelby County Representative.

David Lindsay was born c. 1750, place of birth unknown. David was in the 2nd, 3rd, 4th, and 6th Regiments, Virginia Continental. In civilian life, David was a farmer. He died c. 1835 and is buried at Lindsay Historic Site, Hwy. 17, Shelby County, AL.

John Horton was born c. 1746, Surry County, VA. John served in the Militia under Ltc. Eli Kershaw; Col. Joseph Kershaw; and Francis Marion. John was a farmer and died Aug. 16, 1813. He is buried at Kershaw District, SC.

Charles Seale was born Feb. 10, 1729 in King George County, VA. He was a soldier with the North Carolina Militia. Charles was at the Battle of Camden, SC and Battle of Eutaw Springs, SCS. He was a farmer in civilian life, and died c. 1798. He is buried in Fairfield County, SC.

SEALES, DAVID MICHAEL – Born Jan. 24, 1973 in Jefferson County, AL, resides in Pelham, AL. David was a Charter Member, 2003, Cahaba-Coosa Chapter, Alabama Society.

David and Joy Michelle Greer Seales have two children. David is the Regional Manager/Paramedic, RPS Ambulance Service and Deputy Coroner, Shelby County, AL.

David is a 2005 Graduate, Leadership Shelby County.

David Lindsay was born c. 1750, place of birth unknown. David was in the 2nd, 3rd, 4th, and 6th Regiments, Virginia Continental. In civilian life, David was a farmer. He died c. 1835 and is buried at Lindsay Historic Site, Hwy. 17, Shelby County, AL.

SEALES, JOSHUA CALEB – Born May 1, 1982 in Jefferson County, AL, resides in Alabaster, AL. Joshua was also a Charter Member, 2003, Cahaba-Coosa Chapter, Alabama Society.

Joshua was a 2004 Graduate, University of Alabama. Electrical Engineering major, double minor in Physics and Mathematics. He is the Project Manager, Southern Nuclear Operating Co.

David Lindsay was born c. 1750, place of birth unknown. David was in the 2nd, 3rd, 4th, and 6th Regiments, Virginia Continental. In civilian life, David was a farmer. He died c. 1835 and is buried at Lindsay Historic Site, Hwy. 17, Shelby County, AL.

SEIDULE, ARNOLD J. JR. – Born Oct. 29, 1926 in Biloxi, MS. Joined the Texas State Society in 1997. Arnold has been the Chapter V. P. and President, State District V. P., State Chairman Projects Committee Patriot Fund.

He has received the following awards: Outstanding Dist. V. P., Meritorious Ser., Bronze and Silver Serv., and Silver Good Citizenship.

Arnold J. Seidule, Jr.

Arnold served as FT/3C in the USNR during WWII and Korean Conflict.

Arnold married Janice E. Chapin and they have six children and four grandchildren. Arnold was employed as production manager for Dow Chemical Co. He retired in November 1992.

He also belongs to the American Legion, Amer. Chem. Soc., and V. P. of Exploring in B.S.A. He served as Chrm. Lake Jackson Parks Board, Secretary Dow Employees Credit Union, and V. P. and President of Dow Retirees Club.

William Goff Sr. was born May 1, 1761 in Duplin Ct., NC. He served as Lt. in the 19th Regiment under Gen. Marion in South Carolina. William died Oct. 22, 1847 and is buried in Florida.

SEITZ, GEORGE S. – George S. Seitz and his wife, June Kirkman Seitz, reside in Brighton, MI.

George Banfill, Sergeant, enlisted in 1778 and served 18 months under Capt. Simeon Stevens, Col. Bedel's Regt. from Vermont. He served as a Minuteman, guarded against the invasion from Canada via Hagen Road in Newberry to the Canadian Line. He also was engaged in guarding Tories held as prisoners. He was a farmer and boat builder.

SELLERS, MELVIN L. – Lt. Melvin Lonnie Sellers was born Dec. 22, 1934 at Supply, Brunswick County, NC to Walter Robert and Thelma Marie Singletary Sellers. He married Norma Yvonne Sue Bailey on Dec. 22, 1962 at Willow Oak, Polk County, FL. They have two sons, Jeffery Wayne and Robert Marvin, and three grandchildren. Both sons and one grandson, Raphael Alexander Sellers-Bibbs, are members of the SAR. His wife was the recipient of the SAR Martha Washington Medal.

Melvin L. Sellers

Melvin served in the U.S. Coast Guard form April 1, 1952 to June 30, 1974, retiring at Charleston, SC as a lieutenant. He then worked as a County Veterans Officer for Polk County, retiring in February 1997.

In Charleston, he served as Master of the Franklin Lodge, Ancient Free Masons; Commander, General E.M. Law SCV Camp; President, Lakeland Chapter SAR; Commander, South Florida Bulldogs Camp, CSA Florida; and President, Polk County Historical Association. He is a member of Imperial Polk Genealogical Society; Military Order of the Stars & Bars; Coast Guard Combat Veterans Association; National Genealogical Society; Florida Genealogical Society; Coast Guard Sea Veterans of America; American Legion; Military Officers Association of America Life Member; and Tin Can Sailor, The National Association of Destroyer Veterans.

Melvin has received awards from several organizations. SAR: War Service Medal; Meritorious Service Medal; Bronze Good Citizenship Medal; Certificate of Appreciation (4 awards). Military: U.S. Coast Guard Good Conduct Medal (4 awards); Navy Expeditionary Service Medal (Cuban Missile Crises); National Defense Service Medal (2 awards); U.S. Coast Guard Rifle Marksman Service Ribbon; U.S. Coast Guard Pistol Marksman Service Ribbon. United Daughters of the Confederacy: Jefferson Davis Historical Gold Medal; Armed Forces Expeditionary Service Medal; National Defense Medal; Certificate of Appreciation (3 awards). Sons of Confederate Veterans: Superior Achievement Award. Military Order of the Stars & Bars: Major General Patrick R. Cleburne Meritorious Service Award; Certificate of Appreciation. Polk County Historical Association: Certificate of Appreciation.

John Cason was born 1752 in North Carolina. He served as private in the North Carolina Militia, Taylor and Rutledge Company. His pension application states that as a civilian he was captured at the Battle of Moore's Creek Bridge while delivering cattle to the Army. He was a farmer. He died about 1840, his burial place unknown.

SHAAK, A. ROBERT "BOB" – A. Robert "Bob" Shaak was born Aug. 17, 1933 in Annville, Lebanon County, PA. He served in the U.S. Army Aviation, 3rd Inf. Div. Helicopter Co. from 1953-1956. He joined the SAR May 16, 1996 in Illinois. He has served as FMB Chapter Registrar for four years. He was awarded the Good Citizenship Medal w/4 Bronze OLC, and the War Service Medal (Korea). He is a member of the National/Local Army Aviation Association of America; Army Helicopters Association; and National/Local Antique Clock Association.

As a Department of Army (DAC) civilian employee, he was sent on a one-year assignment to Vietnam as a technical representative in support of the gas turbine engine in the UH-1D (hudy helicopter) in April 1967-May 1968. He was then sent to Germany (with his family) on a three-year assignment in support of the CH-47 cargo helicopter power plant, to provide technical assistance to the Army Aviation groups in Germany. After returning to the U.S., Ft. Bragg, NC, I was again sent to Vietnam on a six-month tour in support of the army's policy to return serviceable helicopters and equipment to inspect, repair and return the items to the U.S. or other locations. I retired from the U.W. Army Aviation Command as chief logistian, located in St. Louis, MO in October 1988 with 34 years of Federal Civil Service.

Gravesite of John Adam Heilman, Hill Church Cemetery, No. Annville Twp., Lebanon County, PA.

He and his wife Joan M. (Leclar) have four sons, Dale Robert, Curtis Allen, Todd Eugene and Douglas Reuben, and three grandchildren.

There are few families that do not have one or more among their members who stand out above the rest, who may attract the attention of the community. Such a person was Lt. **John Adam Heilman Jr.**, born Aug. 2, 1745, a patriot during the American Revolution War (Apr. 19, 1775-Sept. 3, 1783).

His father, John Adam Heilman, at the age of 23 years old, left his native town of Zuzenhausen, Baden, Germany April 20, 1738 and immigrated to America. Arriving at Philadephia Sept. 9, 1738, aboard the ship *Snow Two Sisters*, sailed from Rotterdam, last from Cowes, England, and settling in Lebanon Township, Lancaster County, PA. Here he secured 366 acres of land consisting partly of rich meadows, and partly of fertile uplands, for which he paid the sum of 66 shillings.

Patriot John Adam Heilman Jr. served in the War of Independence, and on Aug. 28, 1775 he was commissioned a second lieutenant. He served as a company Lt., of a foot (infantry) unit, assigned to the 2nd Company, 2nd Battalion of the Lancaster County Militia, organized for the protection of the Province of Pennsylvania.

On Aug. 26, 1776, Lt. Heilman took part and fought in the Battle of Long Island, and also the battle and capture of Fort Washington. In addition to these battles, he fought around New York in the autumn of 1776 and early part of 1777. Of these services, General George Washington spoke in terms of highest praise, saying, "These battles have been one of the most important and desperately fought battles of the entire war."

Upon returning home and settling down as a husband, father and farmer, he and his wife, Catharine (Schmidt), eventually had a total of ten children – five boys and five girls. In 1793 he built and operated a sawmill and also a paper mill. Later on, one of his sons, John Adam III took over the operations. The Heilman paper mill produced a good quality of paper, and supplied the State Departments at Harrisburg with its products and also many newspapers and other publishers.

Patriot John Adam Heilman Jr. died Oct. 4, 1827 in Heilman Dale, Lebanon County, PA at the age of 82, and was buried in the Hill Lutheran/Reformed Church Cemetery. On Nov. 21, 1865, A. Robert Shaak's great grandfather, Reuben Andrew Shaak, married Christanna A. Heilman, and through her direct ancestors, he became a Sons of the American Revolution. They too are buried at the Hill Lutheran/Reformed Church (founded in 1745).

On May 19, 1910. The Lebanon Chapter of the Daughters of the American Revolution placed a bronze burial marker to his memory, with suitable ceremonies in the presence of a large assemblage of people.

SHAFFER, ROBERT N. – I was born an identical twin in Buchanan, MI in 1938; served two years in the Army National Guard and four years in the US Air Force as a flight engineer, serving two years in the Far East, including Vietnam. I graduated from Lake Michigan College and retired from Sears after 31 years in management. I am presently the president of The Old Rugged Cross Foundation, helping to restore the church in Pokagon, Michigan, where "The Old Rugged Cross" was first sung in 1913, and am in my twelfth year as an elected Pokagon Township board member.

Robert N. Shaffer

In the SAR, I have 22 proven patriots and seven pending. In addition to the SAR, I belong to the Society of Descendants of Washington's Army at Valley Forge, the Mayflower Society, Barons of the Magna Carta, American Legion, Shrine, Scottish Rite, and am a life member of the Masons and the VFW.

My primary patriot, **Cpl. Joseph Walker**, served in the 4th Connecticut Continental Line for six years, in the battles of Brandywine, German Town, White Plains, Ft. Mifflin, Valley Forge, Trenton and Monmouth. He assisted in carrying General Lafayette off the battlefield after Lafayette was shot in the leg at Brandywine.

SHALIS, ELIJAH JACOB – Born Jan. 24, 1980 in Bangor Twp., Bay County, MI, and received a B.A. in History and Political Science from Albion College in 2002.

Nathan Durkee was born May 1, 1760 in Woodbury, Litchfield, CT and was a private in the Washington County Militia. He served as a scout leader in the Washington County region and in Saratoga, Ticonderoga, and escaped as a POW in 1781 from Canada. He retired in 1810 at the rank of Vice Major in the Washington County Militia. A farmer, trustee and signer of the charter for a library in Washington County, he died Dec. 25, 1841 and is buried on the family farm in Pembroke Twp., Genesee, NY.

SHIPE, MARTIN ALLAN JR. – Born January 1967 in Camden, NJ. He joined the NJSSAR in July of 2007; NJSSAR Vice-President March 28, 2009-present; Chapter Chair of the Eagle Scoult Committee; and received Meritorious Service Award.

Martin Allan Shipe, Jr.

Martin married Kimberly Marie Bailey and they have three children. He is employed as an electrician, I.B.E.W. Local 351.

Peter Shipe/Shive was born Nov. 2, 1743 in Bedminster, PA. He was a Private with Capt. William McHenry's Company, 3rd Battalion Burks Co. Militia.

In civilian life, Peter was farmer. He died March 6, 1821 and is buried at Tohickon Union Cemetery, Section A-18, Bedminster, PA.

SHIRAH, CLARENCE EUGENE – Clarence Eugene Shirah of Midland City, AL is U.S. Army retired and U.S. Civil Service retired. He served on Midland City Council for eight years, was the Midland City Man of the Year in 2002, on the Town Planning Commission and Zoning Board. He is a member of the Midland City Historical Society and a Master Mason. He aided in the purchase of city hall, installation of town traffic lights and helped organize the little league ball club. He is a member and a deacon of Midland City Baptist Church.

Clarence Shirah

Captain **Richard Byrd** of the North Carolina Militia is a hero of the Battle of Moore's Creek Bridge in 1776. The militia knew the British were coming. They removed the planks from Moore's Creek Bridge, leaving only two logs across the creek. They greased the logs with bees wax and bacon drippings. They dug a trench on the other side, got in and watched the British slip off the log into the creek. They captured the British and won the battle. Eventually the patriots won the war.

SHOENFELT, HENRY ELVIN II – I am related to Captain Hugh Wardlaw through my mother. Her mother's maiden name was Flora Caroline Wardlaw. On Oct. 2, 1948 I was born in Dallas, TX.

By age 10, I had lived in Virginia, California, Texas, Japan, and the Canal Zone since my father was an Army Officer.

Henry Elvin Shoenfelt II

I graduated from Alamo Heights High School in San Antonio, TX in 1967. I attended the University of Texas at Austin, and participated in the Two-Year Army ROTC Program. I graduated with a Bachelor of Arts Degree in History. I was Honorably Discharged from the U. S. Army in 1973.

I have been married for 31 years. Our son and daughter are grown and married. We have one granddaughter.

Patriot Hugh Wardlaw was born in Augusta Co., VA, circa 1740. He married Miss Elizabeth Coalter on Sept. 22, 1763. They moved to Ninety-Six District, subsequently Abbeville District, SC.

Hugh Wardlaw was a Captain and Quartermaster in the South Carolina Militia.

He died at four A.M. on Sunday, Nov. 14, 1802. Captain Wardlaw is buried in the Greenville Presbyterian Church cemetery, just northeast of Abbeville, SC.

SIDDENS, MAJ. GEN. (RET) PAUL JACKSON JR. – Born Jan. 9, 1931 in Holland, Allen County, KY. Paul was in the US Army 1953-1955, Army Reserve 1955-1961, Indiana Guard Reserve 1964-1989, and retired a Major General.

Paul and wife Marjorie Joan Thacker Siddens have one child, Paul Jackson Siddens, III, PhD.

MG Paul J. Siddens, Jr.

Paul was Manager of Distribution Operations for United Technologies Corporation, and retired in February 1996.

He also belongs to the American Legion, First Cavalry Division Assn., Third Armored Division Assoc. 8th Cavalry Regiment Association, 38th Infantry Division Assoc., Indiana Guard Reserve Association.

James Campbell was born Dec. 25, 1754 in Lancaster, PA. He was a Private in the North Carolina Line at Kings Mountain under General Campbell. James was a farmer in civilian life and died about 1820 and is buried in Barren County, KY.

SILER, FREDERICK G. – Born Oct. 11, 1946 at Trenton, NJ. He joined Delaware State Society in December of 2003.

Frederick served as Petty Officer 3rd Class in the US Navy. He and Lynn Bergstresser Siler have one children and two grandchildren.

Frederick was employed as Education Program Specialist for the State of New Jersey and retired January of 2001.

He also belongs to the American Legion, *USS Betelgeuse* AK 260 Assoc.; *USS Little Rock* CLG4 Assoc.; Past Post and County Commander American Legion. Avid genealogist, website at http://freepages.genealogy.rootsweb.com/~typeeiffer/.

Samuel Scott Scruggs Sr. was born March 28, 1757 most likely in that part of Albemarle County, VA that later became Amherst County. He married Jane Childress and to this union seven children were born. Samuel lived most of his adult life in Nelson County, VA where he died in 1830.

Samuel enlisted, Aug. 22, 1777, into James Franklin's Company of Foot under the alias of Scott Martin. This unit was re-designated as Company 3 of the 10th Virginia Regiment. On Oct. 4, 1777, the 10th VA Regiment fought in the Battle of Germantown as part of Colonel Weedon's 3rd Brigade. Following this event Samuel spent the winter with the Continental Army at Valley Forge, PA. Samuel participated in the, June 28, 1778, battle at Monmouth, NJ. He may have been wounded in this engagement because his service records show him in the North River Hospital in August. After Monmouth, the 10th VA Regiment became part of the 6th VA Regiment. From December 1778 to March 1779 Samuel was at Camp Middle Brook, NJ, and in November 1779 at Camp Haverstraw, NY. Samuel spent the winter of 1779-80 with the Continental Army at Morristown, NJ.

SMALLEY, JACK VINCENT – Born March 15, 1949 in Stuttgart, AR, joined the SAR July 11, 2008. He spent 24 years with the U.S. Air Force with service from the Vietnam War through the Gulf War. Assignments included South American, the South Pacific, Asia, Europe and the Middle East. He worked on communications sites, the west coast missile test range, as an inspector in the Titan and Minute Man missile systems and the SR-71 program overseas. He became a Special Agent with the Air Force Office of Special Investigations (OSI), and while involved in many investigative aspects specialized in intelligence collection and executive protection. He spent five years 110 miles behind the Iron Curtain in West Berlin. In 1986 he was on the Glienecky Bridge ("Freedom Bridge") maintaining custody of prisoners being traded back by the United States and West Germany as part of the "largest prisoner exchange since WWII." Of the 23 traded back to the West, the first to cross the bridge was Anatoly Sharanski (later Deputy Prime Minister of Israel). During the 750th Anniversary of Berlin he was responsible for gathering intelligence that precluded an attack on Queen Elizabeth and when President Reagan came to Berlin to give his "Tear Down This Wall" speech his assignment made him the only non-US Secret Service official in close proximity to the President. After Berlin he provided full time executive protection to an "at risk" individual in Southern Germany and during the Gulf War was the Personal Security Advisor to the Secretary of the Air Force. He worked protective missions in Europe, the Middle East and elsewhere. After OSI he entered into the private sector and became part of an investigative agency working as a private investigator/detective in the District of Columbia, the Commonwealth of Virginia, Maryland and elsewhere. He was a member of the Air Force Pistol Team and while in OSI provided specialized firearms training to other agents; upon leaving he became a NRA Law Enforcement Certified firearms instructor (handgun, shotgun and select fire weapons); Chief Range Safety Officer; NRA Training Counselor/instructor for handguns and shotguns; received certifications as a firearms instructor from the District of Columbia, the Commonwealth of Virginia and the State of Maryland. In addition to working as an investigator he is the assistant training director for a training school in Virginia that is recognized by the Virginia Department of Criminal Justice Services, the DC Metropolitan Police Department and Maryland State Police. When not providing investigative service for corporate clients he provides firearms training to Retired and active law enforcement officers, private sector security, individuals deploying to "overseas" locations and private citizens. He is a member of both the VFW and the American Legion.

Jack is descended from **David Smalley** who is descended from John Smalley who left London, England on the *William & Francis* arriving in Plymouth, MA in 1632. John was part of the original Plymouth Colony. John and his wife Ann had four children, one, a daughter; Mary married the grandson of *Mayflower* voyager Stephen Hopkins. John and his family were among the first settlers of Piscataway, NJ. David was born Dec. 20, 1755 in Hunterdon, NJ, he lived in Loudon Co. VA at the time of enlistment in the Virginia Militia where he served as a private. He also served in the New Jersey Militia as a private under Capt. Ratican, Maj. Rucker and Col. West. He had a cousin that also served in the New Jersey Militia, James Smalley and two cousins that served with the New Jersey State Troops, Capt. Davis Smalley and Sgt. Jacob Smalley. Three of his cousins signed the Declaration of Independence, William Whipple as the Representative of New Hampshire, Roger Sherman, Representative from Connecticut, also a signer of the Constitution and Caesar Rodney, Representative from Delaware who also was a member of the Continental Congress. After the war David resided in Loudon County until 1806 when he moved to Wood Co., VA and after four years there moved to Highland Co. OH. David was 83 years old when he died Oct. 20, 1838 in Madison Township, Highland Co., OH.

SMARKER, BRIAN V. – Born Nov. 14, 1961 in North Kansas City, MO and lives in Excelsior Springs, MO.

Brian is married to Scarlet A. Smarker and they have two children. He is a Computer Support Instructor for Excelsior Springs School District.

Brian also belongs to the Sons of Union Veterans of the Civil War, Department of Missouri, Westport Camp No. 64.

George Gordon was born July 9, 1755 at Cumberland County, PA. He served as a Corporal in Capt. William Rippey's Company with Col. William Irvine's Regiment. On June 8, 1776, George was at the Battle of Three Rivers and probably at Ticonderoga. He died Nov. 24, 1826 and is buried at Springboro, Warren County, OH.

SMITH, DONALD JAY – Born Sept. 26, 1970 in Columbus, OH, he joined the Ohio SAR in Sept. 2008. He served in the US Marine Corps, HQ Bn, Corporal, and currently serves in the US Army Reserve, Training Support Bn, Sergeant. A payment coordinator for Big Lots, he is a member of the Society of the War of 1812, Sons of Union Veterans of the Civil War (life member), and American Legion. He is married to Jenene N. Smith.

William Hall was born 1760 in Middleborough, Plymouth, MA. A private in Col. Sprout's Regt., he served under the command of Brig. Gen. John Glover at Ft. Arnold at West Point, NY. A farmer, he died in the 1840s (?) and is buried in Yates County, NY (?).

SMITH, FREELAND KNIGHT – Born Mar. 21, 1925 at the Trull Hospital in Biddeford, York County, ME. His father, John G. Smith, and a half brother, John, were both members of SAR, and two of his sons are also members. Freeland became a journeyman shipfitter at Portsmouth Naval Shipyard in Kittery, Maine in 1963, and in 1964 was transferred to the Planning Dept. as a Marine/Mechanical Draftsman in the Design Division. In 1969 he transferred to PERA(SS), helping to develop a Submarine Overhaul Work Package. He retired in May 1986.

Freeland is a Past Master of Arundel Lodge #76, AF&AM, Past High Priest of Murray Royal Arch Chapter #33, and a Saint Armand Knight Templar. He married Irene Bois and they were blessed with five sons. Irene passed away Sept. 3, 2002.

Lt. John Gilpatrick, Jr. was born Oct. 20, 1728 in Wells, York, Maine. A farmer, he died Jun. 28, 1818 and is buried in a private cemetery off Holland Road, Kennebunk, Maine.

SMITH, HUBERT ORMAN – Born June 1, 1912 in Marine City, MI. He joined the Michigan Society in January 2008. He is probably the oldest member (age 95-1/2 years) and newest member.

Hubert worked at Chris Craft Corp, Algonac, MI during the war years, receiving "E" award for service building PT boats and landing craft. He worked 17-1/2 years as foreman and mill assembly. He later worked for General Mo-

Hubert Orman Smith, about 1930.

tors in styling, retiring in February of 1980 as a model maker.

Hubert was married to Loretta Doris (Widdas) Smith (deceased) and they had one daughter, Sharon Smith Staiger. They had two grandchildren, John L. and Julie A. Staiger; and two great-grandchildren, Erika and John IV Staiger.

Hubert O. Smith giving Gary Grant a check for his application to the SAR, Nov. 20, 2007.

Hubert was honored by Michigan Historical Society for work in Woodlawn Cemetery, raising money to build a seawall to keep older graves from falling into Belle River, across from his home. He presently is working to save the old historic "Marine City Hall" in Marine City, MI. Hubert is descended through both parents from Reuben, as his parents were second cousins.

Reuben Smith was born July 15, 1755 in Brookfield, West Parish, Worcester County, MA. He was a private serving as a Green Mountain Boy with the Connecticut Cont. Line. He was stationed in Boston, MA from 1775 to 1776. Descendants have a letter telling about his experience.

Reuben was a farmer and father of seven children. He died Feb. 2, 1840 and is buried at Smith's Cemetery, Cottrellville Twp., St. Clair County, MI.

SMITH, JOHN THOMAS – John Thomas Smith was born Nov. 13, 1952 in Jacksonville, FL. His military service consisted of service at Naval Air Station Patuxent River, MD in Operations from September 1971 to June 1975. His service ended with an Honorable Discharge. His second military service was from April 1976 to July 1978 stationed with VS-30 at Jacksonville, FL, and also ended with an Honorable Discharge. John retired in February 1986 on Disability Social Security and in 1987 at a 100% service connected from the VA.

He joined the SAR on Sept. 23, 2003. He belongs to the Daniel Morgan Chapter and has held office as Chapter Registrar, Chapter Genealogist, and South Carolina State Registrar. He has proven his first line of descent from his ancestor, Zophar Smith, and as of this date has proved eleven more, some being from both sides of his family.

Zophar Smith was born Nov. 26, 1756 at Bucks County, PA and served as a Sergeant in the light dragoons under Captain William Smith, his brother. He was the son of Ralph Smith, who was also a Patriot of the Revolutionary War.

SMITH, LEON L. – Born Nov. 25, 1949, Kansas City, MO; resides in Mission Viejo, CA. He was the Chapter Registrar.

Leon has received the Law Enforcement Medal, Bronze Good Citizenship Medal, Silver and Bronze Color Guard Medals.

He served in the US Army Reserves from 1971-1977. Leon was a Detective 3 (Detective Supervisor) with the Los Angeles Police Department, retiring July 5, 1997.

Leon and Bunita Camden Smith have three children and four grandchildren. He also belongs to the South Orange County, CA Genealogical Society.

Thomas Guthrie Moore was born Jan. 24, 1760 in Buckingham County, VA. Thomas was a Private with the Virginia Militia. He substituted two times for three months each time. In civilian life, Thomas was a farmer. He died Nov. 2, 1843 and is buried at the Moore Cemetery, Carlinville, Macoupin County, IL.

SMITH, TROY ANTHONY – Born May 25, 1965 in Jackson, AL, he joined the U.S. Air Force in 1938, retiring on May 24, 2008. He is currently a Traffic Safety Coordinator for the Baldwin County Highway Dept., and is a member of the Air Force SergeantsAssoc. He is married to Christina, and they have four children.

Troy A. Smith

Benjamin Mills was born 1757 in North Carolina. He was a Leutenant in the 8th North Carolina and Corps of North Carolina Light Dragoons, and fought at the Battles of Brandywine and Germantown, and the Defense of Philadelphia. Benjamin was Magistrate for Brunswick County, NC from 1792-1810. He died in 1810 and is buried in Brunswick Co., NC.

Lt. Benjamin Mills, ca 1777.

SNYDER, EDWARD COURTLAND JR. – Edward Courtland Snyder Jr. was born 1931 in Oklahoma City, OK. He goes by the name of Court or Courtland. Commissioned from the U.S. Naval Academy in 1954 and served as a surface warfare officer until his retirement in 1975. Awards include the Meritorious Service, Joint Services, China Service, Defense Service (2), and Expeditionary Service Medals.

Following retirement, Courtland earned an MBA at the College of William and Mary. He then worked for Brown & Root, Inc. until 1994. Courtland married Patricia Ellen Funk of Virginia in 1963. They have two children, Tracy Ellen and Edward III, two granddaughters and two grandsons. Courtland became a member of SAR in 2003 and his son in 2005.

Edward Courtland Snyder, Jr.

Henry (Hal) Dixon Jr. was born 1740 in Caswell County, NC. On Feb. 27, 1775, Dixon was among a force of 1,000 patriots that intercepted and destroyed an 800-man loyalist force at the Battle of Moore's Creek Bridge. He was appointed Captain, 1st North Carolina Continental Line Sept. 1, 1775. This unit fought at Brandywine, Germantown and Monmouth. He was promoted to Major Oct. 4, 1777 and assigned to the 3rd North Carolina Regiment. He was at Valley Forge during the winter of 1777-1778. Dixon was promoted to Lt. Col. in 1778. In 1779 Lt. Col. Dixon was severely wounded at the Battle of Stono Ferry. In 1870 Dixon commanded the North Militia at the Battle of Camben where he and his "raw" militia held their ground against veteran British infantry. He was also at the Battle of Whitsell's Mill and Guilford Courthouse in 1781. On Feb. 6, 1782 Lt. Col. Dixon was transferred to the 2nd North Carolina Regiment and sent to besiege the British the British at Charleston, SC. It was here that Dixon died in service of battlefield wounds on July 17, 1782 in camp at Round O. The location if his burial is not known.

SPARKS, JAKE LAWRENCE II – Jake was born Oct. 24, 1953 in Corpus Christi, TX. He served in the U.S.M.C., Dec. 22, 1975 – Oct. 31, 1987 as a Captain.

Jake also has served as Korea Region Lodging Program Manager for the Department of the Army.

He is a member of the "Sons of the Republic of Texas" and the "Order of the First Families of Maryland."

Matthew Sparks Sr. was born about 1730 in Frederick, MD. Matthew performed civil service, Sept. 7, 1778. Wilkes County, NC - Appointed Overseer of the new marked road from the top of the blue ridge to the ford on the south fork of the New River. Matthew died in November of 1793. He is buried in an unmarked Grave in the then Franklin County, GA near Sparks Fort on Shoal Creek.

STANLEY, EARL R. – Earl R. Stanley was born in 1921 in Windham, OH, graduated from Kent State University in 1943 and from George Washington University Law School in 1949 with honors. He was admitted to practice in the District of Columbia in 1949 and the Supreme Court in 1955. He served as an attorney at the FCC and therefore was in private practice until retirement in December, 1994.

He enlisted in the U.S. Navy m 1942 as an intern in midshipman, was commissioned and served until mid-1946 with 15 months in the pacific theater.

Earl is a past President of the Federal Communication Bar Association, a Broadcast Pioneer, and a past National Chancellor of the Delta Theta Phi Law Fraternity. He was a member of the Sons of the American Revolution since March 6, 1960; the First Families of Ohio, and The Order of the Crown of Charlemagne in the United States.

Earl Stanley

Earl and his wife, Alberta, lived in Washington, D.C. from 1946 to 2000 when they moved to Brentwood, TN. He's also proud of two daughters and three grandchildren. His ancestors arrived in this county on the *Mayflower* in 1620. Others came on the *Ann* in 1623 and on the *Mary-John* in 1630.

Stephen Pardee served as a Captain in the 6th Alarm _____ Co. in New Fairfield, 16th Regiment of Conn. Militia during the Revolutionary War (and of some 15 other patriots who served in the Revolution).

STAPLETON, EDWARD PATRICK – Edward Patrick Stapleton was born Jan. 12, 1966 in Washington, DC. He joined the SAR March 25, 2008 (National #171354). Edward is currently in his 20th year with the Horry County (South Carolina) Sheriff's Office. Edward is the proud parent of two wonderful children (Edward Markham Stapleton, 5/06/1988 and Jacklyn Michelle Stapleton, 7/25/1991). Edward is in his second marriage to Sherry and has a fantastic step-son Jade. Edward is civically minded and has been the president of the Avalon at Carolina Forest HOA for the last five years.

Edward P. Stapleton family

Zachariah Callaway was born 1757 in Delaware and married Ellender Boyd in 1775 in Monroe County, VA (now WV). Zachariah served as a soldier in Valentine White's Second Battalion of Augusta County, VA. He was under Colonel William Meade on June 18, 1777 when loyalist John Hook was tarred and feathered. An order exists for his pay as Armourer in the Virginia Militia 1777 with the Cherokee Expedition and an order to pay him for two gun locks. Zachariah Callaway died (and is buried) on his farm on Trigger Run near Peterstown, WV in 1816.

Zachariah and Ellender had ten children: Andrew, Margaret, Nancy, Polly, Sarah, Joshua, James, Pricilla, Elizabeth and Charles.

Edward Patrick Stapleton is a descendent from Zachariah through Joshua Moses Callaway (1783-1879), Garner Callaway (1810-1891), Joshua Moses Callaway (1850-1934), Macie (Macy) Callaway (1883-1907), Sylvia Irene Quesenberry (1901-1978), Mary Louise Karr (1920-1991), and Evelyn Irene Brown (1947-).

STARR, BRIAN – Born Aug. 8, 1960 at Painesville, OH; presently resides in Hendersonville, TN.

Brian is Treasurer Local Council Sumner County, TN.

He served in USMC Communications. Brian and spouse Julieta Lopez Starr have one child, Gabriella Maria Starr. Brian is employed as Controls Engineer Automation Nth.

Brian also belongs to General Society of Mayflower Descendents, Knights of Columbus, The International Society of the Descendants of Charlemange.

Alexander McNish was born in 1748 at Ayr, Scotland. He served as a Sergeant in Capt. John Armstrong's Company and Capt. Joseph McCracken's Company of Col. John Williams' Regiment. Alexander was at the battle at Fort Ticonderoga. His civilian occupation was a Wool Merchant. Alexander died March 24, 1827 and is buried at Washington County, Salem, NY.

STARR, DAVID POWELL – Born July 15, 1980 in Baltimore City, MD, resides in Linthicum, Anne Arundel County, MD. Joined Maryland 3603 John Paul Chapter in May 2002.

David works at Kop-Flex, Inc. Division of Emerson Power Transmission, Product Development Intern.

David Powell Starr

David is a senior at University of Maryland Baltimore County Campus-Mechanical Engineering, received Associate Degrees in Applied Sciences in Electronic Engineering and Electronic Engineering Telecommunication from Anne Arundel Community College, Eagle Scout Troop 550, Linthicum Elementary School.

Timothy Matlack, a merchant, brewer, soldier and statesman, was born in Haddonfield, Camden County, NJ on March 28, 1736. He is the descendant of one of the first families of New Jersey. William Matlack who arrived on the ship *Ken*" at Racoon Creek, West New Jersey in 1677 and Mary Hancock his future wife arrived on the ship *Paradise* in 1682. Timothy attended Quaker schools in Haddonfield and Philadelphia. Matlack was employed by Charles Thomson as clerk of the Continental Congress on May 15, 1775. He prepared the commission for George Washington as Commander in Chief on May 20, 1775; member of the Pennsylvania Constitutional Convention of July 15th through Sept. 28th 1776; penned the Declaration of Independence on parchment and he was on the Declaration of Rights with Judge George Bryan and James Cannon during the July 25th session; Colonel Timothy Matlack and James Cannon were appointed to the committee responsible for writing an essay for the frame of government; Timothy Matlack served in the Fifth Rifle Battalion, known as the "Shirt Battalion" of Philadelphia Associate's. As Colonel he commanded the battalion that destroyed the bridges across Rancocas and Pensauken Creeks near Dunk's Ferry near Trenton in December 1776 and served throughout the campaign that ended at the battle of Princeton in January 1777; a member of the Pennsylvania's Council of Safety on July 24, 1776; chosen Secretary of the Supreme Executive Council of Pennsylvania on March 6, 1777 and served until the end of the war; he was keeper of the Great Seal of Pennsylvania; he was made storekeeper of military stores on Feb. 20, 1778; presided at the court martial of Benedict Arnold in Morristown, NJ on Dec. 3, 1779; Matlack help found the Society of Free Quakers in 1781 and designed the Free Quaker Meeting House at Fifth and Arch Streets in Philadelphia; member of the board of trustees of the University of the State of Pennsylvania 1779-1785; elected to the Second Continental Congress in 1780-1781; Matlack was a Director of the Bank of North America from 1781-1785; elected to the American Philosophical Society, serving as secretary from 1781-1783. He became Master of the Rolls of Pennsylvania 1800-1809. In Philadelphia, he was appointed Prothonotary of the United States District Court at Philadelphia, March 14, 1817 and a member of the Board of Aldermen from 1813-1818. He died on April 14, 1829 at Holmesburg, PA; interment was in the Free Quaker Burial Ground, Philadelphia, PA and re-interment was in 1905, Bakewell Cemetery, Montgomery County in Audubon (Fatlands) on the Schuylkill River near Valley Forge, PA.

Colonel Timothy Matlack, Jr., born 26 Mar 1736, died 14 Apr 1829. Painted by Charles Willson Peale about 1790.

STARR, GERALD POWELL – Born April 14, 1941, Altoona, Blair County, PA; resides in Linthicum, Anne Arundel County, MD. Gerald joined Maryland No. 3602, John Paul Jones Chapter in May 2002.

Gerald and wife Harriet Louise (Kelley) Starr have six children and seven grandchildren. He retired Dec. 31, 1991 from Westinghouse Electric, Corp. Comptroller's Administration. He currently is a realtor with Coldwell Banker, Severna Park, MD.

Gerald P. Starr

Gerald also belongs to Society of the Sons and Daughters of the Pilgrims, MD No. 89, Graduate University of Baltimore-1972-Business Management, appointed to Anne Arundel County Electrical Board-1995, 1999, 2003 and 2007, appointed Liquor Board 1995-1999, appointed to Anne Arundel Co. State Central Committee-1991, elected 1994, 98, 2002 and 2006, President District 32 Republican Club, Life Member National Eagle Scout Assoc. and received Four Rivers District Award of Merit in Scouting-2004, Charter Member of Boy Scout Troop 550-Linthicum Elementary School-1964, President of Linthicum-Shipley Improvement Assoc. 1992-1996 and 1998-1999, currently member, attend Emmaus Anglican Church, Catonsville, MD.

Timothy Matlack, a merchant, brewer, soldier and statesman, was born in Haddonfield, Camden County, NJ on March 28, 1736. He is the descendant of one of the first families of New Jersey. William Matlack who arrived on the ship *Ken*" at Racoon Creek, West New Jersey in 1677 and Mary Hancock his future wife arrived on the ship *Paradise* in 1682. Timothy attended Quaker schools in Haddonfield and Philadelphia. Matlack was employed by Charles Thomson as clerk of the Continental Congress on May 15, 1775. He prepared the commission for George Washington as Commander in Chief on May 20, 1775; member of the Pennsylvania Constitutional Convention of July 15th through Sept. 28th 1776; penned the Declaration of Independence on parchment and he was on the Declaration of Rights with Judge George Bryan and James Cannon during the July 25th session; Colonel Timothy Matlack and James Cannon were appointed to the committee responsible for writing an essay for the frame of government; Timothy Matlack served in the Fifth Rifle Battalion, known as the "Shirt Battalion" of Philadelphia Associate's. As Colonel he commanded the battalion that destroyed the bridges across Rancocas and Pensauken Creeks near Dunk's Ferry near Trenton in December 1776 and served throughout the campaign that ended at the battle of Princeton in January 1777; a member of the Pennsylvania's Council of Safety on July 24, 1776; chosen Secretary of the Supreme Executive Council of Pennsylvania on March 6, 1777 and served until the end of the war; he was keeper of the Great Seal of Pennsylvania; he was made storekeeper of military stores on Feb. 20, 1778; presided at the court martial of Benedict Arnold in Morristown, NJ on Dec. 3, 1779; Matlack help found the Society of Free Quakers in 1781 and designed the Free Quaker Meeting House at Fifth and Arch Streets in Philadelphia; member of the board of trustees of the University of the State of Pennsylvania 1779-1785; elected to the Second Continental Congress in 1780-1781; Matlack was a Director of the Bank of North America from 1781-1785; elected to the American Philosophical Society, serving as secretary from 1781-1783. He became Master of the Rolls of Pennsylvania 1800-1809. In Philadelphia, he was appointed Prothonotary of the United States District Court at Philadelphia, March 14, 1817 and a member of the Board of Aldermen from 1813-1818. He died on April 14, 1829 at Holmesburg, PA; interment was in the Free Quaker Burial Ground, Philadelphia, PA and re-interment was in 1905, Bakewell Cemetery, Montgomery County in Audubon (Fatlands) on the Schuylkill River near Valley Forge, PA.

Colonel Timothy Matlack, Jr., born 26 Mar 1736, died 14 Apr 1829. Painted by Charles Willson Peale about 1790.

STARR, LOGAN ERLE HALL SR. – Born July 13, 1942, Altoona, Blair County, PA; resides in Millersville, Anne Arundel County, MD. Logan served in the United States Army, 949 Transportation Corps., Sergeant E5. Logan joined Maryland No. 3633, John Paul Jones Chapter in October 2002.

Logan and Sandra Josphine (Malecki) Starr have three children and seven grandchildren. He was a Fire Fighter V, National Registered Emergency Medical Technician Paramedic, retiring in July 1993.

Logan E.H. Starr, Sr.

Logan also is a graduate Anne Arundel Community College-1986; Associate Arts Emergency Medical Services, American Legion Lodge 007 – Annapolis, MD International Association of Fire Fighters, Anne Arundel County Retired Fire Fighters Association, Anne Arundel Alarmers Association-Director, Maryland Mobileers Ham Radio Operator-N3WZK, Glen Burnie B.P.O. Elks-Past Exalted Ruler, Past Exalted Rulers Association, Odenton Lodge 209-AF and AM-Senior Warden (Master Mason), Bonnie Blink Day Light Lodge 011AF and AM Cockeyville, MD (Senior Deacon), Scottish Rite, Baltimore, MD 32 Degree, KCCH-Life Member, Knights of Pythias-Laurel Lodge-155.

Timothy Matlack, a merchant, brewer, soldier and statesman, was born in Haddonfield, Camden County, NJ on March 28, 1736. He is the descendant of one of the first families of New Jersey. William Matlack who arrived on the ship *Ken*" at Racoon Creek, West New Jersey in 1677 and Mary Hancock his future wife arrived on the ship *Paradise* in 1682. Timothy attended Quaker schools in Haddonfield and Philadelphia. Matlack was employed by Charles Thomson as clerk of the Continental Congress on May 15, 1775. He prepared the commission for George Washington as Commander in Chief on May 20, 1775; member of the Pennsylvania Constitutional Convention of July 15th through Sept. 28th 1776; penned the Declaration of Independence on parchment and he was on the Declaration of Rights with Judge George Bryan and James Cannon during the July 25th session; Colonel Timothy Matlack and James Cannon were appointed to the committee responsible for writing an essay for the frame of government; Timothy Matlack served in the Fifth Rifle Battalion, known as the "Shirt Battalion" of Philadelphia Associate's. As Colonel he commanded the battalion that destroyed the bridges across Rancocas and Pensauken Creeks near Dunk's Ferry near Trenton in December 1776 and served throughout the campaign that ended at the battle of Princeton in January 1777; a member of the Pennsylvania's Council of Safety on July 24, 1776; chosen Secretary of the Supreme Executive Council of Pennsylvania on March 6, 1777 and served until the end of the war; he was keeper of the Great Seal of Pennsylvania; he was made storekeeper of military stores on Feb. 20, 1778; presided at the court martial of Benedict Arnold in Morristown, NJ on Dec. 3, 1779; Matlack help found the Society of Free Quakers in 1781 and designed the Free Quaker Meeting House at Fifth and Arch Streets in Philadelphia; member of the board of trustees of the University of the State of Pennsylvania 1779-1785; elected to the Second Continental Congress in 1780-1781; Matlack was a Director of the Bank of North America from 1781-1785; elected to the American Philosophical Society, serving as secretary from 1781-1783. He became Master of the Rolls of Pennsylvania 1800-1809. In Philadelphia, he was appointed Prothonotary of the United States District Court at Philadelphia, March 14, 1817 and a member of the Board of Aldermen from 1813-1818. He died on April 14, 1829 at Holmesburg, PA; interment was in the Free Quaker Burial Ground, Philadelphia, PA and re-interment was in 1905, Bakewell Cemetery, Montgomery County in Audubon (Fatlands) on the Schuylkill River near Valley Forge, PA.

Colonel Timothy Matlack, Jr., born 26 Mar 1736, died 14 Apr 1829. Painted by Charles Wilslon Peale about 1790.

STEED, JAMES M. – Born May 1, 1937 at Lexington, KY. Joined Lafayette State Society in February 1971. James served as former Registrar.

James was a Boy Scout in Troop 2 and earned the rank of Life Scout. He and his brother Virgil attended Camp Pet-O-Se-Ga in Michigan.

James served in the Army, 101st Abn. Div., Spec 4. He was awarded the Senior Para. Badge. James graduated with a BS from Eastern KY University. He was in the Ag. Honor Society.

James and Sharon B. Steed (DAR) have two

children. James is a retired farmer of cattle and tobacco.

James M. Steed

He also belongs to Society of the D of W R at Valley Forge.

Captain Charles West of Loudoun County, VA raised a company of soldiers (recruits, volunteers) to fight in the Revolutionary War for the Americans. They served in the federal Army known as The Continental Line. At the age of 21, Charles Lander was among them. He was born Dec. 9, 1754 in Louisa County, VA. Boys were fired with the spirit of patriotism. When the war broke out there was a prompt enlistment.

Charles Lander did serve in the Army but his military record has been embellished and exaggerated. I think one of his grandsons, Willis Spencer, was responsible for this. These "tales" have been entered into the records of the DAR and have been a curse to descendants attempting to research his military record. He did not cause this and in no way should be blamed for it.

He gave his war record on oath when applying for a pension before the Bourbon Circuit Court at Paris, KY, Aug. 14, 1832.

He enlisted from Loudoun County, VA in October 1775 and served in Company 6 of the Third Virginia Regiment of The Continental Line commanded by Lt. Col. William Heath. He also served under Capt. Charles West and Col. Wilden.

This was a 6-month enlistment. He was discharged. Then he reenlisted in the spring of 1776 for two years with the same unit.

He was later given a medical furlough due to illness. He rejoined his command in August 1777. That winter they went to Valley Forge. By now he had worked his way up to the rank of Sergeant.

He spoke of a hard battle at "Brandywine." He fought at "Valley Forge," "Fort Washington," "White Plains," "Warren Tavern," and "Germantown."

I do not think he crossed the Delaware River barefooted, but he might have crossed the Delaware River in 1777-78.

He served for 2-1/2 years. One winter he was down with illness in the home of a Skinner relative.

He farmed in Hampshire County, VA. He later moved to Bourbon County, KY and settled near North Middletown. He was elected to the state legislature. He was active in the Methodist Church. He lived to almost 79 years and led an exemplary life.

He met and married Catherine Forman. His father, Henry Lander, was married to Hannah Skinner.

He died Aug. 8, 1833, Bourbon County, KY and was buried on John J. Redmon's farm with his father, Henry Lander.

STEIN, MELVIN JAMES – Born Nov. 15, 1928 in Chicago Heights, IL. Presently resides in Bakersfield, CA. Joined CA State Society 5904 in 1991.

Melvin was in the National Guard, 40th Division Artillery. He and wife Shirley (DAR) have two children, four grandchildren and two great-grandchildren.

He retired in April 1989 as a Missile Guidance Engineer.

John Henry Winkleblack was born Sept. 25, 1756 and was alive March 3, 1834. He was the third child born to Peter and Maria Margaretha Schaeffer Winckelblech of Jonestown, PA. He was baptized Oct. 17, 1756 in the Trinity Reformed (Tulpehocken) Church in Lancaster, PA. He migrated to Greenbrier, VA before the American Revolution where he changed the spelling of his name to Winkleblack.

John Henry entered the Continental Army of Virginia as a substitute as Henry Squires. He served nine months at Fort St. Lawrence under Capt. Uriah Springer, served nine months at Fort Pitt, served at Fort Henry under Capt. Beck and again at Fort Pitt under Capt. Clark and then at Fort McIntosh.

After his discharge, he returned to Greenbrier VA. John Henry married a Christian lady named Elizabeth. They lived in what is known as "The Sinks" area. Records show at least five children born to this couple. Records show he received a grant of 52 acres of land probably for his service. In 1832 he received a pension for his service. His grave has not been located. I am descended through his son Samuel.

STEINER, ROGER JACOB – Born Mar. 27, 1924 in South Byron, Fond du Lac County, WI, Roger joined the SAR on Mar. 3, 2008 at almost age 84.

Roger's military service was three years in Naval training for the invasion of Japan. His civilian position as a Methodist minister started after achieving a Master of Divinity degree, and 15 years later with a Ph.D. he started 33 years of teaching at the University of Delaware. Not really retired, he writes and revises dictionaries, all of them published.

Roger J. Steiner standing in front of Legislative Hall, Dove, DE, after receiving his membership certificate and rosette at his induction into DESSAR.

Graduating from college, Roger received a medal for scholarship, leadership and character, given to only one senior, and was elected to the honorary fraternity Phi Beta Kappa. He was a Scoutmaster (BSA) for 25 years.

Roger's wife, Ida Kathryn Posey Steiner, is deceased. They had two sons, and now he also has two granddaughters.

Asa Cowles, Roger's great-great-great-grandfather, was born May 31 (or June 11), 1747, in Belchertown, MA. Asa served as a sergeant with the John Cowles' Co. of minutemen, Col. Woodbridge's Regt., Massachusetts Militia. He was stationed in Boston, MA for eight months and participated in the Battle of Bunker Hill.

Asa's civilian occupation was a farmer. He was the father of 13 children. Asa died Jul. 20, 1837 in New Lebanon, NY, where he is buried.

STEVES, MYRON F. – Myron F. Steves was bourn July 11, 1912 in Atlanta, GA. In 1939 and 1940, he was a trooper in the last of the National Guard Horse Calvary units in New Orleans, LA. Injured in an automobile accident on Nov. 10, 1940, he was in Touro Infirmary in New Orleans when his unit went into the Federal Service in January 1941. Thereafter, his draft classification was 47. All of the military services declined his applications. He is the founder of Myron F. Steves & Company (Insurance General Agency) in 1955 and worked until his retirement in 1989.

He joined the SAR Dec. 4, 1995 in Texas. He was President of the Paul Carrington Chapter #5 in 2006 and was Chapter Genealogist 2002-2005. He has received SAR Certifications of Appreciation (2002 and 2004), Liberty Award SAR New Member Recruitment (2003, 2004, 2005).

He is a member of some 12 genealogical and historical societies, particularly: Houston Genealogical Forum, New York Genealogical and Biographical Society, Clayton Library Friends (Houston), New England Historical Genealogical Society, and Federation of Genealogical Societies.

He and his wife, Maria Luisa Benteen Steves (now deceased), have three children and six grandchildren.

Jeremiah Steves was born Jan. 23, 1762 in Westchester County, NY. He was 14 in 1776. He served as a corporal in the Westchester and Peeksville Militias. The Colonel of his Westchester Militia was his uncle, Samuel Drake. When the British pushed north past the Croton River area where he lived (where this river flows into the Hudson), he crossed over to Peeksville and joined the Militia there. Under the 1832 law, he had to prove at least two years service, but from 1776 to 1783 he was something of a "minuteman." Jeremiah was a farmer. He died Oct. 1840 and is buried at Rome, Oneida County, NY.

Lt. Aaron Holbrook was born Aug. 31, 1930 in Bellingham, Norfolk County, MA. He served as a lieutenant in the Massachusetts Militia. He and his family were successful farmers. Until 1832, a soldier had to prove need to be awarded a pension. Aaron died April 15, 1818. He never applied for a pension. Aaron is buried in the Bellingham town cemetery, Norfolk County, MA.

STEWART, HAROLD "SKIP" – Lives in Waynesboro, GA. John Tiller Sr. was his ggggg grandfather. He is a member of the Patrick Carr Rangers Chapter.

John Tiller was born in Amherst County, VA and was married to Nancy Hooper. John's father, William Tiller, was born in Chesterfield County, VA ca. 1730 and was in the Patriotic Service that provided supplies to the militia. He died in June 1792.

John Tiller served under Capt. John Stewart (later Brigadier General of the 2d Brigade) in the Virginia Militia. In 1784 John Tiller was granted 300 acres along the Broad River Valley in Oglethorpe County, GA. His land was in the Goose Pond Militia District near Millstone Baptist Church, est. 1788.

Skip and Sandy Stewart

Marker at the site of the Millstone Creek Community Militia District.

Others that came and settled in the area were Col. George Matthews (later governor of Georgia), Elijah Clarke and Meriwether Lewis (the explorers), and other Virginians. They came through North Carolina and brought cows, household furniture, peach seeds, and other seeds. John built a large, five-room log house, hand-hewn near a large spring, and cleared enough land for wheat, rice and flax for linen. John Tiller had 13 children, six daughters and seven sons. From these children came 20 Tiller's that served and died in the Civil War. One serving was Capt. John H. Tiller (Tiller's Artillery) that had nine Tiller family members serving in his unit.

John Tiller's grave.

John Sr. died ca. Oct. 1829 and is buried on his land not far from his original home site.

STONE, DONALD LESLIE, JR. – Born Nov. 26, 1933 in Minneapolis, MN. Degrees include: BA.(Hamline University), M. Th. (Perkins School of Theology) and M.B.A. (University of Houston). He has served as both a minister and a chief financial officer. After the death of his first wife Kay Doris Peck, he married Kaye Berkey Ellis.

Rev. Stone was approved for membership in the Sons of the American Revolution June 12, 2002. He is past president of the Freedom Chapter and served as TXSSAR Historian (2005-2008). As Historian, he republished of Volume 1(1896-1980) of TXSSAR History and the published Volume II (1980-2005). Awards include the Patriot Medal, the Meritorious Service Medal (state and local), the Bronze Good Citizenship Medal (state), the Bronze Color Guard Medal, the Service to Veterans Medal, and the TXSSAR Silver Service Medal (four times).

Rev. Stone is a direct descendant of **William Stone Jr.** who was born in Norton, MA on Dec. 15, 1761. Two weeks after his 14th birthday on Jan. 1, 1776, he joined George Washington's main army and served over five years.

STONE, JAMES K. – Born April 20, 1961 in Liberty County, GA. Joined the Col. Benjamin Cleveland State Society, serving on the Americanism Award Committee and as Chapter Treasurer. He has received the SAR Medal and Military Service Medal.

James served as Chief Master Sergeant, U.S.A.F. and in the 118th Tennessee Air National Guard. He and wife Rebecca have two children.

James is Fire Captain with Chattanooga Fire Department. He retired from the Tennessee Air National Guard on Dec. 31, 2001.

Where does one start talking about a person who was part of their new beginning? Long after Columbus arrived and the Jamestown disaster, and long after thousands arrived in the new world, our American heritage began. Some time after the 1600's, and from a place unknown, William Stone's father arrived by ship, desiring to start anew.

William Stone is my 5th great grandfather and he states that he fought in the war against England that was called the War of the Revolution. It is my relation to him that has enabled me to join the Sons of the American Revolution.

All that is known about William Stone is entailed in the sworn statements that he gave to Chief Justice John C. Miller in Rusk County, TX on April 9, 1855, and June 7, 1856. He states that he was in the war against England and that he, at the age of 16, was a private in the company commanded by Captain Parish in Colonel Haynes regiment. He reported that he went into the service in Guilford County, NC, about the year 1780 or 1781, and was honorable discharged in Greenville, NC.

In his April 1855 statement, William Stone stated that he would be 92 years of age on Sept. 20, 1855, and that he was born in Halifax County on the Roanoke River on Sept. 20, 1763, and that he moved from there to Franklin County on the Tar River, 55 miles from his residents on the Roanoke He lived nearly 50 years in Franklin County, and 20 years in Hancock, Putnam and Greene Counties of Georgia. His last seven years were spent on the county line of Smith and Rusk Counties in Texas.

William Stone stated that he was first drafted in Franklin County, NC about a mile from his residence. His first captain was Benjamin Eaves, and his first lieutenant was Joe Parish. He was attached to the infantry service commanded by Colonel Haynes, and Rene Eaton was his mayor who belonged to the regular army. They came to lead the men together at High Rock Ford on the Tar River and from there marched to Guilford County. Before joining with General Green, their company was engaged in a battle with some British troops.

Some time after he was discharged from this tour of service, he found a cart and horse belonging to the regular army that he delivered to the officer in charge, and then stayed through another skirmish before being released several months later.

William Stone was again drafted in Louisburg, where General Newton was located. He marched to Willington to prevent British retaliation. He served on this tour for two months under Captain Turner, and another officer named either Scarborough or Yarborough.

William Stone said that he was always invited to join and march on the 4th of July in this country. He was also invited to march in Georgia. He also remembered that General Butler took charge of them on his first tour when he was first drafted in Franklin County.

STOUT, ALLEN LEWIS – Born June 7, 1939. Joined the Indiana SAR August 2008.

Allen is a dairy, hog and grain farmer. He is married to K. Cynthia Thompson Stout and they have three children and 8 grandchildren.

He is a Deacon of First Brethren Church, and is a member of the Masons, Gideons and Indiana Pioneers.

Benjamin Kirkpatrick was born 1755 in Hampfield, PA. He served as private in the 4th Battalion Reg., Cestmoreland PA Co. His civilian occupation was a farmer.

Benjamin died Aug. 5, 1826 and is buried in the Congruity Presbyterian Church Cemetery, Salem Twp, Westmoreland Co., PA.

STOVER, RICHARD C. – Born Feb. 9, 1932 at Pittsburgh, PA. Richard retired Sept. 1, 1975 from U. S. Navy (Air) Ldr.

Richard enlisted in the Naval Reserves in high school. After graduating from Penn State with a degree in Industrial Engineering, was commissioned in 1955. Served aboard the aircraft carrier *USS Hancock*

Richard C. Stover

CUA-19 and *USS Range CUA-58* as member of Carrier Airborne Early Warning Squadron Eleven (UAN-11) and as Combat Information Center Officer aboard *USS Enterprise CUA(N)-65* IN THE Gulf of Tonkin. Then served on staff of Commander Second Fleet board the cruiser *Newport News 09-148*, flew with Navy Hurricane Hunters and retired as Operations Officer of Commander Tactical Support Wing One.

For 21 years, Richard has futilely endeavored to sway the Postal Service's Citizens' Stamp Advisory Committee's approval of a stamp commemorating the loss of the five Sullivan brothers, "The Fighting Sullivans" who perished at sea in the battle for Guadalcanal in 1942.

Richard and wife Norma Jean have three children and three grandchildren.

Richard is a United Presbyterian Church Elder, belongs to Penn State Alumni Association, Military Officers Association of America, is a benefactor to Girls and Boys Town, St. Labre and St. Joseph's Native American Schools for Youth.

Valentine Stover was born 1757 in Pennsylvania. **Conrad Brumbaugh** was born 1735 in Germany. They served as Privates in the militia. They were probably farmers. Valentine Stover died Feb. 25, 1834 and is buried at Stover, Aaronsburg, PA.

STRIPE, ROBERT GENE – Born Oct. 14, 1927 in Van Wert, Wan Wert County, OH, he joined the Ohio SAR on Apr. 11, 2008. He served in the U.S. Navy as a Seaman, Second Class, and later was an Appraisal Supervisor for the Dept. of Transportation, retiring in 1992. He was a member of the American Legion, Ohio Genealogical Society, Van Wert County, OGS, and Van Wert Historical Society. He was married to Marilyn Joan Mohr and had three children and seven grandchildren. Robert Gene Stripe died on July 25, 2008.

Christian Straley was born Sept. 21, 1742 in Germany. A fifer in the militia at Ft. Hinkle, 5th Batt., he died on Aug. 14, 1818 and is buried at the Jane Lew Cemetery, Lewis County, WV.

STROZIER, MAX – Born in San Antonio, TX. Joined the Texas Society in March of 2007. Has served on Executive Committee and is the Webmaster for San Antonio Chapter. Max works as a chemist for Standard Aero.

Peter Strozier was born 1740 in Westphalia, Germany. He was a Private in Paddy Carr's Company in the Georgia Militia. He was in the battle of Kettle Creek and battle of Kings Mountain. In civilian life, he was a planter. He died Jan. 18, 1807 and is buried at Sardis Baptist Church in an unmarked grave.

SUTTON, ERNEST LORAN – Born in Charleston, SC and presently residing in Greensburg, PA.

Ernest has served as Chapter Secretary and Chair, Eagle Scout Committee. He has received the War Service Medal, Silver Good Citizenship Medal, is a Life Member, and George Washington Fellow.

Ernest is a retired Colonel from U. S. Army Medical Corps. He is a Professor Medicine, University of Pittsburgh Medical Center.

Ernest also received the U. S. Army Legion of Merit and DOD Distinguished Service Medal.

Ernest Sutton

He is an Eagle Scout and Silver Air Scout; Wood Badge Scouter; Roundtable and Unit Scout Commissioner.

Lemual Foster was born April 30, 1764 at Dudley, MA. He served as a Sergeant in the Massachusetts Militia. Lemuel died Aug. 17, 1827 and is buried at Elba, NY.

Timothy Foster was born in 1715 at Walpole, MA. He served as Captain in 2nd Lincoln Company of the Massachusetts Regiment. He died April 5, 1795 and is buried at Oxford, MA.

William Ridgway was born June 21, 1746 at Goochland County, VA. He was a Private with the South Carolina Militia. He was at the battle at Waxhaw's Church. William died Feb. 9, 1816 and is buried at Manning, SC.

SWEENEY, JOHN E. – John Eldredge Sweeney, son of John Joseph Sweeney and Ella Margaret Hathaway, was born in 1942 and raised on Long Island, NY. At 17 years of age he joined the New York Army National Guard; served six months of active duty; and completed his obligated service while also attending Kent State University, Kent, OH. Graduating with an Army infantry ROTC commission, he served in Vietnam with the 4th and 25th Infantry Divisions and Military Assistance Command-Vietnam. During over 28 years of active duty, he had many assignments overseas and in the U.S. and retired as a Colonel in October 1992. He then became a Department of Defense civilian and retired again in April 2006.

Col. John E. Sweeney at joint VA & MA SAR grave marking ceremony on 11 Nov 2007, marking the grave of Robert Hathaway, Pine Grove Cemetery, Warren, MA.

John met his wife, Carol Lee Jenkins, at Kent State. She is a retired public school educator. They have been married for over 40 years and have two sons, John Scott and Brett Matthew, and a daughter, Janelle Maxine Marie Hall. Both sons have served in the Army. John is a Naval Criminal Investigative Service Agent and Major, USAR and Brett is a Dept. of Defense Civilian, a former Army Sergeant and now Virginia Army National Guard 1st Lieutenant who since September 2007 has been in Iraq as an infantry platoon leader. Janelle is a Regional Sales Manager for Ryan Homes. John and Carol have two Grandsons, John William and Luke Ambrose Sweeney and three Granddaughters, Caroline Maxine and Annabelle Shay Hall and Olivia Christine Sweeney.

Robert Hathaway was born c. 1762 at Freetown, MA. He married Susanna Hill, born c. 1762 at Brookfield, MA.

Robert served as a Private in various companies with 1st Rhode Island Regiment of the Rhode Island Continental Line, 1776-1778 with two years of service in Capt. Jacob Haskin's Co., Massachusetts Militia, 1778-80. He was possibly at the Battle of Quaker Hill or Rhode Island, 1778, RI Rev. War Pension No. S-8692.

Robert was a farmer and possibly a stone mason. He died Feb. 28, 1852 and is buried at gravesite no. 45, Pine Grove Cemetery, Warren, MA.

SYMPSON, J. DAVID – Historian General of National Society of the Sons of the American Revolution, residing in Louisville, KY.

J. David Sympson

William Sympson, born in Pennsylvania and moved to Sullivan County, NC, presently Kingsport, TN. In 1780, at 14 years of age he entered the militia service of the United States serving under Colonel Arthur Campbell against the Cherokee Nation. Campbell joined Colonel John Sevier on the French Broad River and engaged Indians daily, and for several weeks occupied the Cherokee town of Telico while conducting raids against additional towns.

In 1781, Sympson served under Colonel Isaac Shelby. The command passed into South Carolina joining General Francis Marion. Under Marion's command they planned to attack the heavily garrisoned British outpost Fair Lawn Plantation. The plantation was bypassed so as not to give time for a pursuing British Calvary to attack from the rear. In a couple of miles they attacked a Way Station taking 96 prisoners before burning the fortification. During this enlistment Sympson's brother-in-law Mess Sergeant Thomas White served the sweet potato dinner between Marion and Lt. Colonel Banister Tarleton that prompted the famous 1836 painting by John Blake White.

In 1783, Sympson served as an Indian spy under Colonel Thomas Hutchens.

Sympson reentered the Militia in 1788 under Major George Vincent and was involved in the last attempt to dislodge Chickamaugan Chief Dragging Canoe from Lookout Mountain. During the attempt all officers over Sympson were killed except Vincent who was wounded.

In 1795, Sympson settled in Kentucky and became Sheriff of Green County.

TATUM, ROBERT S. – Born Jan. 13, 1953 in San Diego, CA, he is a member of the Gen. Joseph Martin, TN SAR. Robert worked as a building inspector at Colonial Heights, VA, retiring on Jun. 1, 2006 due to disability. He is a member of

Sons of Confederate Veterans and Military Order of the Stars and Bars, and is currently making application into the Jamestowne Society while continuing to research other ancestors for supplemental SAR acceptance. He is married to Susan D. Hudson-Tatum, with two children and three grandchildren.

His primary patriot ancestor is **Edward Tatum**, who was the subject of a biography written in 1968 by Dr. Edward S. Smith titled "Edward Tatum, The Forgotten Revolutionary Soldier of Jefferson County, Alabama," where he died in 1835. It covers his long life from his birth about 1745 in Brunswick County, VA as a merchant, planter, gentleman justice and soldier. He served in the Henry County, VA Militia as 1st Lt., and fought in the battles of Eutaw Springs, SC, and Guilford Courthouse, NC and witnessed the surrender of Lord Cornwallis at Yorktown, VA. His ten children were 7th generation Virginians whose family came from London, England and settled in Jamestown in 1619.

Robert's supplemental patriot ancestors include: **Hamon Critz**, **Hamon Critz Sr.**, **Samuel Dalton Sr.**, **Ebenezer Frost**, **Archelaus Hughes**, **James Hunter**, **James Hylton**, **John King**, **Joseph Martin**, **John McFarland**, **Abram Penn**, **Samuel Staples**, **George Stovall Jr.**, **George Stovall Sr.**, **Edward Tatum**, **John White**, and **John Wilson**, with **William Dalton** pending.

TAUSEND, STEPHEN A. – Born Dec. 14, 1984 in Houston, TX. Joined the Texas SAR Oct. 11, 2005.

Stephen is a law student at the University of Texas – Austin. He is also a member of the Sons of the Republic of Texas.

Peter Luna (Looney) was born Oct. 1, 1759 in Augusta, VA. He served as a private and sergeant in the Virginia Militia. He was in the Battle of Holston Flatts, served as an Indian spy and a border guard.

As a civilian, Peter was a farmer and a Militia Captain in Tennessee. He died Feb. 16, 1851 and is buried in Marshall, TN, on Fishing Ford Rd.

TAUSEND, WILIAM E. – Born Sept. 2, 1988 in Houston, TX. Joined the Texas SAR May 31, 2007.

William is a student at Texas A&M University – College Station. He is also a member of the Sons of the Republic of Texas.

Peter Luna (Looney) was born Oct. 1, 1759 in Augusta, VA. He served as a private and sergeant in the Virginal Militia. He was the Battle of Holston Flatts, served as an Indian spy and a border guard.

As a civilian, Peter was a farmer and a Militia Captain in Tennessee. He died Feb. 16, 1851 and is buried in Marshall, TN, on Fishing Ford Rd.

TAYLOR, GLENN JENKINS – Glenn Jenkins Taylor was born April 21, 1945. He grew up on a farm and lived in a house that was in the family for 105 years. He was educated in the local school system and also Middle Tennessee State University. He is married to Carolyn A. Taylor.

Organizations memberships include: Past President of the Exchange club of Murfreesboro, TN; Incorporating Secretary and Board Member of Crime Stoppers of Rutherford County; Scottish Society of Middle Tennessee; Rutherford County Historical Society; Bedford County Tennessee Historical Society; Board Member of Friends of the Rutherford County Archives; Heritage Society of Rutherford County; Main Street Organization of Murfreesboro; First Families of Tennessee; Stones River Chapter SAR; Sons of the Confederate Veterans Camp #33; past President and Board Member of Historical Jenkins Lutheran Chapel; Board Member of the Historical Shofner Lutheran Chapel and past Committee Chairman of the bicentennial Celebration in 2008; Financial Manager of the Middle Tennessee Trivent Chapter; and Church Council Member of Advent Lutheran Church.

Glenn J. Taylor

Samuel Knox is Glenn's sixth great grandfather, born in Ballymoney, Ireland about 1753 of Scottish decent. He married Catherine Jones in Chester County, SC. Samuel entered the service of the U.S. in Captain Brown's Company in Sumpter's Regiment. He served in the Continental Line, which rallied to the defense of the Port. He was in Fort Moultrie when the British attacked. When his term of service expired, he joined a volunteer company commanded by Captain McClure. He saw action at Rock Mount July 30, 1780, and Hanging Rock a week later. He also was in action at Black Stocks and King's Mountain.

TAYLOR, DR. JAMES C. – Born in Washington, D.C. and currently resides in San Antonio, TX. James joined the Texas State Society in 2000. He has served as Chaplain and as Genealogist for San Antonio Chapter No. 4. James has received the Outstanding Citizenship Award, Bronze Good Citizenship medal; War Service Medal (Vietnam) and Liberty Medal.

James served as Chaplain (LTC) USA actively for 28 years. He served as a Pastor for Evangelical Lutheran Church in America. James retired in December of 2007.

Dr. James C. Taylor

James and Patricia Ruth Taylor have four children and seven grandchildren.

James also belongs to the American Legion, AUSA, Retired Chaplain Association, and National Association of Interim Pastors.

I am a direct male descendent of Patriot **Joel Taylor**, born March 4, 1764 in Merrimack, Dunstable, NH. (MA) He was the third son of Timothy and Rachael Taylor who was a tavern and stage coach stop owner on the road between Concord, MA and Philadelphia, PA in Merrimack, NH. He was one of the six men who were enlisted from Dunsiable, MA to the Second Massachusetts Regiment of the Continental Army by Commissioner, Brig. General John Glover at Springfield, MA, July 7, 1780. Joel Taylor was discharged Jan. 7, 1781. His service to his city, state and the United States was 6 months, 13 days, including travel (220 miles) home.

After the Revolutionary War was over he left Merrimack and went to Rupert, Vermont. It was here that his 50 acres plot of land for service in the Revolutionary War was located. He married Hannah Farrar in 1784, the daughter of Jonathan and Mary Farrar another Revolutionary soldier, Jonathan had been at the Battle of Concord. On the land that he cleared he planted Apple Trees and Sugar Maples.

Joel Taylor died Jan. 19, 1846 at the age of 82. He and his family were members of the Church of Christ in Rupert and he is buried with his wife, Hannah Farrar Taylor in The Old Cemetery, Rupert, Bennington County, VT.

I am a descendant of **Lt. Johanthan Farrar**, born July 27, 1731, the son of Jonathan Farrar and Rebekah Rigby of Concord, MA. His daughter Hannah Farrar married Joel Taylor in 1784.

On the morning of April 19, 1775, Lt. Jonathan Farrar was the Commander of the Guard guarding North and South Bridges where the minute men and militia from Concord were gathered. Following the historic battle at Concord he was asked to give a disposition of the action of the British on April 19 to the Continental Congress.

After the Revolutionary War was over he moved to Rupert, VT where he had been given 50 acres of prime farm land for his part in the Battle of Concord and subsequent battles before the British were driven out of the Colonies. He lived as a farmer with his wife Mary and is buried in Old Cemetery, Rupert, VT.

TAYLOR, LARRY A. – Born in 1943 in Phenix City, AL and still resides there.

Larry served three years in the U.S. Army, two years in the Army Reserve, and eight years in the Georgia National Guard. While in the Army he was in security in Korea for 13 months, Infantry School Support at Fort Benning, GA. In the National Guard he was in field water purification.

Larry Arnold Taylor

Larry and his wife Patricia Leatherwood Taylor have two children and three grandchildren. Larry also worked as a Security Guard at Columbus Regional Senior Living, Columbus, GA.

John West, was born about 1745 in Craven County, NC. He was a Privateer on the ship *General Nash.* They captured three British ships, *Brigg Agie, Brigg Prince of Wales,* and the *Brigg Kitty.* These ships and many valuables were sold for the nation.

John was a farm in civilian life. He died Oct. 6, 1800 and is buried in Craven County, NC.

THARP, RAYMOND ROY – Born July 12, 1930 in Rogers, Bell County, TX. He joined the SAR Sept. 16, 2008.

Raymond graduated from Howard Payne University, Brownwood, TX in 1954 with a Bachelor of Arts degree. He received his Master of Religious Education degree from Southwestern Baptist Theological Seminary, Fort Worth, TX in 1965 and a Master of Science in Education degree with Counseling Certification from Baylor University, Waco, TX in 1970.

During his career, Raymond taught school in Alderpoint, CA and in Troy, TX. He served as a counselor for the Bell County Schools Co-op Program and the Temple Independent School District, Temple, TX. For seven years, Raymond was Director of Guidance and Placement at Central Texas College, Killeen, TX. Also, he pastured several churches during his career. He retired in 1992 after 37 years in the education field.

He is a member of the following organizations: Sons of the Republic of Texas, Texas Association of Retired Teachers, a charter member of the Baylor Phi Delta Kappa in Waco, and the East Bell County Genealogical Society.

Raymond's wife, Dixie DeAnn Stoneman Tharp is a retired school teacher and a member of DAR. They have two children: a daughter, Carla Jean Tharp Cleveland and a son, Gregory Scott Tharp. They have four granddaughters: Diana Marie Cleveland, Emily Grace Cleveland, Lydia Rae Cleveland, and Andrea Elizabeth Tharp.

He is descended from **Henry Wax (Wachs)**, born ca. 1743. He married Margaret Geschwind May 11, 1767 in Berks Co., PA. Henry served as a Sergeant in a company commanded by Michael Lindemute, Berks Co., PA and as a Sergeant in Captain DeTruck's Company from Berks Co. in 1776. He died Nov. 6, 1796 in Botetourt Co., VA. He is buried in the Fincastle Presbyterian Cemetery (formerly Church of England Cemetery) located in Fincastle, VA.

THOMAS, DON RAY JR. – Don Ray Thomas Jr. was born Dec. 20, 1975 at Baton Rouge, LA. He is employed at AB Beverage as Warehouse Manager. He is a member of Willam Few Chapter, Georgia State Society. He played minor league baseball for Houston Astros. He has two children.

Lazarus Reeves was born 1756 in Dinwiddie County, VA. A sergeant and one of 2,500 men, he fought as Guerilla under the command of Lt. Col. Francis Marion. He served as soldier in the South Carolina Militia as minuteman under Capt. R. Goodwin and fought in the Battle of Sullivan's Island for defense of Charleston, SC. His final rank was sergeant. He died after Dec. 11, 1827 and is buried in Lazarus Reeves Cemetery at Pike County, MS.

THOMAS, DON RAY SR. – Don Ray Thomas Sr. was born Oct. 30, 1946 in McComb, MS. He is married to Patricia Dianne Freeman, and they have four children and two grandchildren. He worked for IBEW Local 995 as an electrician. He retired in 1995. He is a member of William Few Chapter, Georgia State Society.

Lazarus Reeves was born 1756 in Dinwiddie County, VA. A sergeant and one of 2,500 men, he fought as Guerilla under the command of Lt. Col. Francis Marion. He served as soldier in the South Carolina Militia as minuteman under Capt. R. Goodwin and fought in the Battle of Sullivan's Island for defense of Charleston, SC. He died after Dec. 11, 1827 and is buried in Lazarus Reeves Cemetery at Pike County, MS.

THOMAS, JAMES ROBERT "BOB" – Born Jan. 22, 1947 in Birmingham, Jefferson Co., AL, he joined the Alabama SAR in 2008. He served in the U.S. Marine Corps, 1st Div., Lance Corporal, and later worked as a finance director, retiring in 2003. He is a member of Sons of Confederate Veterans and Vietnam Veterans of America. He has five SAR patriots.

Bob Thomas

Bob received a Meritorious Service Medal from the General Richard Montgomery Chapter SAR for his work from Apr. 12, 2008 to Feb. 22, 2009 to establish a SAR chapter in Lamar Co., AL.

Bob has two children and three grandchildren. Son Ronald J. Thomas is an SAR member and grandsons Chase and John are youth members. His granddaughter, Shaelyn and grandson, Chase, are CAR and CofC members.

Captain Robert Cleveland was one of the heroes of King's Mountain, born Jan. 8, 1744 at Blue Run, Orange, VA. He lived in Fauquier County, VA (Records of Prince William County, Brentsville, AA, Book T, 1775. Lease Holtz to Robert Cleveland of Fauquier Co., VA; Robert Cleveland to Holtz for rent of farm in Prince William County, VA.) He accompanied his brother, Col. Benjamin Cleveland, to NC. Removed from Prince William Co., VA in 1778 and settled in Wilkes Co., NC on the Yadkin River, and owned land there. He spent the rest of his life on the Yadkin River. He was prominent in the community and was one of five Clevelands who served in the Electoral College, and was the first one chosen to that office. He was elected for the 6th Presidential election for 1809 North Carolina electors. He and his first wife, Aley Matthis, are buried side by side within 150 yards of the old homestead dwelling now owned and occupied by Jesse Yates.

Gravestone of Capt. Robert Cleveland. Metal grave marker reads: "Revolutionary Soldier, Capt. Robert Cleveland, 1744 - 1812, Placed by Lady Washington Chapter, NSDAR, Houston, Texas." Picture was taken in Sept. 2007.

Captain Robert Cleveland was a Captain in Colonel Benjamin Cleveland's regiment at the battle of King's Mountain, Oct. 1, 1780, and bore a most important part. A soldier of his corps, Dan White, used to say that to this brave Captain was due to the success of the battle, for in the middle of the conflict, when all were giving way before Ferguson's bayonets, Capt. Cleveland alone stood firm and unmoved, sustained the charge until Col. Benjamin Cleveland could rally the fleeing troops and come to his assistance. He was accessory to many daring deeds. On Apr. 15, 1781, he gathered some 30 good men and the next morning rescued Col. Cleveland, a prisoner of the Tories, with whom they had a skirmish.

He died on Apr. 10, 1812 and is buried in Wilkes County, NC.

THOMAS, JOHN CHRISTOPHER – Born Feb. 20, 1984 in Terre Houte, IN, he joined the Indiana SAR on Jan. 15, 2008. He is a student at Indiana State University in Terre Houte. His grandfather, John Joel Thomas, father, John Brian Thomas, and brother, Matthew James Thomas, are all SAR members.

Abraham Thomas was born 1755 in Montgomery, IN. A private, he fought at Dunsmore's War. He died in 1843 in Troy, OH.

THOMAS, JOHN E. JR. – Born in July of 1928 in Philadelphia, PA. He joined the Penna. Society in August of 2006.

John and Marian G. Thomas have no children. John retired in June of 1985 from Westinghouse Elect. – Non Destructive Testing Tech.

John E. Thomas, Jr. and wife, Marian Thomas.

Asa Thomas was born Feb. 2, 1758 in Hilltown, PA. From pension application: during 1775-1776 he was an Associator in Hilltown Township, Bucks Co. Associators. May of 1777, was a volunteer private in battalion commanded by Capt. Nicholas Patterson, Major Long commanded the battalion and Fenton was the adjutant and served two months. August of 1777 was drafted as a private in a company commanded by

Capt. Robert Thorn, Major Folwell and Adjutant Hughes commanded the battalion in General Potter's brigade. Took part in the battle of Brandywine. Again, served two months. December of 1778, was drafted and served as a private in company commanded by Capt. Stinger. Their duty was to guard a regiment of Hessians that had been captured. Was discharged after serving two months.

Gravestone of Asa Thomas.

In civilian life, Asa was a stone mason. He died May 10, 1839 and is buried at Hilltown Baptist Cemetery at Fricks, where first church was built in 1737.

THOMAS, MATTHEW JAMES – Born Oct. 2, 1987 in Terre Haute, IN, he joined the Indiana SAR on Jan. 15, 2008. He is a student at Indiana University in Bloomington. His grandfather, John Joel Thomas, father, John Brian Thomas, and brother, John Christopher Thomas, are all SAR members.

Abraham Thomas was born 1755 in Montgomery, IN. A private, he fought at Dunsmore's War. He died in 1843 in Troy, OH.

THOMAS, RICHARD RYAN – Born Aug. 25, 1988 in Little Rock, AR. He transferred from CAR to SAR December 2008. He is also a member of the Arkansas State Society of the Sons of the American Revolution.

His military service was as a member of the U.S. Navy Sea Cadets from 2002 to 2006 attaining rank of Petty Officer 3rd Class.

Robert Rankin was born May 29, 1759 in Guilford Co. NC. He married Mary (Polly) Cusick, born 1759 at Dauphin, PA.

Robert Rankin entered the militia in service of his country on June 16, 1776 at Martinsville, NC. His first tour was for four months as a draftsman under Captains Bell and Caval and General Rutherford. During his second tour from March 3 or 4 to June 3 or 4, 1780 under Captain Reden Moore, Colonel Pasley, and Generals Caval and Rutherford, he fought in the battle at Monk's Corner, SC. July 1780 to March 16, 1781 he served under Captain Forbis and General Green while fighting in the Battle of Guilford Courthouse. Robert's last tour was for three months as a minute horseman under Captain McAdoo and Colonel Pasley. He died on Dec. 21, 1840 in McNairy Co., TN.

THOMPSON, RICHARD – Belongs to Waco Chapter 32. Richard was the Gggggrandson of William Hill Jr.

William Hill Jr. was the son of William and Suzanna Singleton Hill. He was born in 1737 in Virginia and died in North Carolina. William was listed in his father's will drawn in 1777. (Vol. 2 pg. 73 Surry Co., NC)

William was a Baptist minister and was a chaplain in the American army at the Battle of Guilford Courthouse. He was a member of the Hillsboro Convention that met Aug. 2, 1775 to improvise a system of government for the state of North Carolina.

He married Hannah Elizabeth Halbert in about 1758. Their children were: Thomas m. Catherine Shropshire; James m. Nancy Royalty; Mary m. Osborn Childers; John m. Obedience Cullum; Green m. Nancy Mitchell; William m. Sarah Geddy; Joab m. Elizabeth Millican; Elizabeth m. James Moore; Frances m. Mark Hardin; Caleb m. Mary Flint and Joel m. Mildred Golding.

His son, John Hill, was at the Battle of the Horse Shoe under General Jackson and was called "Captain Big John Hill" by the Indians. John's and Obedience's children were: Elizabeth, William, Nancy, James, Gresham, Frances, Cynthia, Naomi, John, Mary and Thomas.

John Hill's daughters, Cynthia and Naomi, and their families, moved to the Texas frontier to Van Zandt County in the 1840s. Naomi married John George Washington Bivins on March 21, 1824 in Tennessee. After they migrated to Texas they operated the first hotel in Canton, TX. He was commissioned to build the first courthouse in Canton. Thus, William Hill's legacy lives on in many descendants in Texas.

THOMPSON, SAMMIE WRAY – SAR National 158723; State 3115.

Sammie Wray Thompson

Richard Thompson was born in Ireland in 1742, the son of John and Mary Thompson. John Thompson's will was dated Jan. 22, 1760 in North Carolina. It is believed Richard and two brothers migrated to Virginia in the early 1770's, settling in Russell Co., VA. He died in Lawrence Co., KY after Sept. 16, 1822-30. He was married to Margaret Barr in 1770.

Gravestone of Richard Thompson.

Richard resided in Halifax Co., NC during the American Revolution as a patriot and soldier. He appears on the roster of North Carolina soldiers, NC Revolutionary Army Account. He was listed as a corporal on the list of Captain Woods in Malmedy's Regiment as a wagon maker, Aug. 23, 1781. He also furnished supplies, Augusta Co., VA, April 29, 1872. He appears on pension 535 of Edward Burgess. There is an affidavit Richard Thompson, Lawrence Co., KY Order Book 1, page 38-39. Also Augusta Co., VA Court of Claims, page 100. Fathergills Virginia Taxpayers of 1782, page 126.

Richard and Margaret had 11 children: Samuel; Andrew; James; Richard; George; William; John; Nancy; Rebecca; and Margaret.

THOMPSON, REV. WILLIAM ARTHUR – Born in Terre Haute, IN, he has been a member of the Indiana SAR (#3381) since 2008, and serves as Vice President and Chaplain. Rev. Thompson served in the USAF from 1963-68, and has worked as an Indiana State Welfare Consultant (10 yrs) and a Minister (11 yrs), retiring in 1991. He is a member of Grace Point Church, Disabled American Veterans, Sons of Confederate Veterans, and Sons of Union Veterans.

He is married to Jayne Ann Messmer-Thompson, with six children, 13 grandchildren, and four great-grandchildren.

Thomas Thompson was born 1760 in Virginia, and married Nancy Anne Kinchelo-Thompson (b. 1780) of Virginia. He served on the Virginia Line, a private, and fought at Guilford House, the Siege of Ninety Six, and Eutaw Springs. A farmer, he died in 1828 and is buried in Marshall, IL.

TIMMAN, HENRY R. – Henry Reinier Timman, a charter member of Firelands Bicentennial Chapter of SAR in Ohio, bears Ohio Number 6257 and National Number 110672, I was born Jan. 30, 1943 in the Blue Fly neighborhood of Norwalk Township in Huron County, OH.

After being graduated from Norwalk High School in 1961, I served two years in the U. S. Army and eventually was employed 25 years as the Chief Deputy of Huron County Probate Court. My retirement was effective June 29, 2001. I'm a member of Norwalk High School's Hall of Fame as a distinguished citizen and have received the same awards from the Norwalk Area Chamber of Commerce.

For 50 years I have been interested in and engaged in genealogical and local history research, and have assisted with several record preservation projects. Other memberships include The Firelands Historical Society of Norwalk; the Ohio Genealogical Society; the American Legion; and the Vietnam Veterans of America.

I married Marty Wise on Sept. 2, 1972, and we reside at 3985 Medusa Road, Norwalk, OH 44857.

Jonah Bartow, a patriot of the American Revolution, was born Dec. 15, 1760 at Hempstead, Suffolk Co., Long Island, NY, a son of Francis Bartoo (sic) and Mary Ketchum.

He enlisted in April of 1779 at Albany and served under Capt. Bevier in the 5th New York Regiment, which consolidated with others into the 2nd Regiment. He was discharged at Newburgh, NY, on June 8, 1783. At that point he was awarded a Badge of Merit. His original discharge paper is on file with his pension file at the National Archives.

After marriage (spouse's name unknown) he lived at Greenfield in Saratoga County and at Scipio in Cayuga County in New York. About 1815 he moved to Vermillion in Huron County, OH, with his four children: John, Jonah, Jr., Alvin T., and Mary. He was pensioned there in 1818.

Jonah Bartow died Dec. 2, 1827 in Lyme Township, Huron County, OH, and probably is buried in the Raymond Cemetery west of Monroeville, OH. A cenotaph stone in his memory can be seen in the cemetery at Milan, OH.

TIMOSCHUK, BASIL ERIC – Basil works at Nissan Motor Corporation as a manager. He is an Eagle Scout from BSA.

Thomas Crawley was born April 25, 1755 in Amherst, VA. His wife was Margaret, born 1761 in Virginia. Thomas was a resident of White and Van Buren County, TN. He served five tours. His civilian occupation was as a farmer and a blacksmith.

First, he entered into the service of volunteer corps who were known by the title of Minute men. He enlisted in Pittsylvania County, VA January 1776 under Capt. Abraham Penn, in the Regiment of Col. Edward Carrington. He was discharged after eight months. Battles: Jamestown, Williamsburg, Gwynns Island. He fired on Lord Dunsmore Troops in Williamsburg. He was in Williamsburg when the Declaration of Independence was signed July 4, 1776.

His second tour of service was an enlistment for one year. He enlisted in Pittsylvania Co., VA under Capt. Samuel Scott, in the Regiment of Col. Habersham and in Gen. McIntosh's Brigade; this service was intended for and rendered in the State of Georgia. Spectator of the duel fought between Gen. McIntosh and Button Gwinnett. Battles: Hillsborough, Camden, Savannah River, Galphins Fort, Cowpens, Phillips Fort.

His third tour was a voluntary enlistment for six months in the Company of Capt. John Davis, Regiment of Col Charles McDowell in the Brigade of General Butler. Battles: Guilford Courthouse, Salisbury, Charlotte, Briar Creek, Bacon's Bridge, Stono Fort.

His fourth tour of service was a substitute for William Astill in Guilford County for three months. Captain was Archibald Campbell, Regiment of Col. Smoky Camps, Charleston, SC.

His fifth tour of service was voluntary enlistment in Charleston under Capt. George Lemmon in the Regiment of Col. William Lytle.

Gen. Lincoln surrendered Charleston on May 12, 1780, and himself and his army prisoners of war were never being exchanged for until after the capture of Lord Cornwallis at Yorktown, VA. He performed no further actual service during the war.

Thomas died July 7, 1843 and is buried at Big Fork Cemetery, Van Buren Co., TN.

Richard Shockley was born Jan 1, 1726 in Kent County, MD. He took the Oath of Allegiance to the USA in the Sate of Virginia. He was a planter, primary crops being tobacco and Indian corn, and ran a grist mill. His wife, Elizabeth Adkins, was born 1740 in Henrico Co., VA. She died in 1784 in Grayson Co., VA. Richard died in 1800 in Grayson Co., VA.

Robert Moffitt served in the war from North Carolina.

TIMOSCHUK, JEFFORY ALAN – Jeffory Alan Timoschuk resides in Smyrna, TN.

Thomas Crawley was born April 25, 1755 in Amherst, VA. His wife was Margaret, born 1761 in Virginia. Thomas was a resident of White and Van Buren County, TN. He served five tours. His civilian occupation was as a farmer and a blacksmith.

First, he entered into the service of volunteer corps who were known by the title of Minute men. He enlisted in Pittsylvania County, VA January 1776 under Capt. Abraham Penn, in the Regiment of Col. Edward Carrington. He was discharged after eight months. Battles: Jamestown, Williamsburg, Gwynns Island. He fired on Lord Dunsmore Troops in Williamsburg. He was in Williamsburg when the Declaration of Independence was signed July 4, 1776.

His second tour of service was an enlistment for one year. He enlisted in Pittsylvania Co., VA under Capt. Samuel Scott, in the Regiment of Col. Habersham and in Gen. McIntosh's Brigade; this service was intended for and rendered in the State of Georgia. Spectator of the duel fought between Gen. McIntosh and Button Gwinnett. Battles: Hillsborough, Camden, Savannah River, Galphins Fort, Cowpens, Phillips Fort.

His third tour was a voluntary enlistment for six months in the Company of Capt. John Davis, Regiment of Col Charles McDowell in the Brigade of General Butler. Battles: Guilford Courthouse, Salisbury, Charlotte, Briar Creek, Bacon's Bridge, Stono Fort.

His fourth tour of service was a substitute for William Astill in Guilford County for three months. Captain was Archibald Campbell, Regiment of Col. Smoky Camps, Charleston, SC.

His fifth tour of service was voluntary enlistment in Charleston under Capt. George Lemmon in the Regiment of Col. William Lytle.

Gen. Lincoln surrendered Charleston on May 12, 1780, and himself and his army prisoners of war were never being exchanged for until after the capture of Lord Cornwallis at Yorktown, VA. He performed no further actual service during the war.

Thomas died July 7, 1843 and is buried at Big Fork Cemetery, Van Buren Co., TN.

Richard Shockley was born Jan 1, 1726 in Kent County, MD. He took the Oath of Allegiance to the USA in the Sate of Virginia. He was a planter, primary crops being tobacco and Indian corn, and ran a grist mill. His wife, Elizabeth Adkins, was born 1740 in Henrico Co., VA. She died in 1784 in Grayson Co., VA. Richard died in 1800 in Grayson Co., VA.

Robert Moffitt served in the war from North Carolina.

TIMOSCHUK, PHILLIP STEPHEN – SSgt. Phillip is serving in USAF Jet Engine Mechanic and Quality Inspector at Seymour Johnson AFB in Goldsboro, NC. Phillip and Nicole Getts have a son, Phillip Jr.

Thomas Crawley was born April 25, 1755 in Amherst, VA. His wife was Margaret, born 1761 in Virginia. Thomas was a resident of White and Van Buren County, TN. He served five tours. His civilian occupation was as a farmer and a blacksmith.

First, he entered into the service of volunteer corps who were known by the title of Minute men. He enlisted in Pittsylvania County, VA January 1776 under Capt. Abraham Penn, in the Regiment of Col. Edward Carrington. He was discharged after eight months. Battles: Jamestown, Williamsburg, Gwynns Island. He fired on Lord Dunsmore Troops in Williamsburg. He was in Williamsburg when the Declaration of Independence was signed July 4, 1776.

His second tour of service was an enlistment for one year. He enlisted in Pittsylvania Co., VA under Capt. Samuel Scott, in the Regiment of Col. Habersham and in Gen. McIntosh's Brigade; this service was intended for and rendered in the State of Georgia. Spectator of the duel fought between Gen. McIntosh and Button Gwinnett. Battles: Hillsborough, Camden, Savannah River, Galphins Fort, Cowpens, Phillips Fort.

His third tour was a voluntary enlistment for six months in the Company of Capt. John Davis, Regiment of Col Charles McDowell in the Brigade of General Butler. Battles: Guilford Courthouse, Salisbury, Charlotte, Briar Creek, Bacon's Bridge, Stono Fort.

His fourth tour of service was a substitute for William Astill in Guilford County for three months. Captain was Archibald Campbell, Regiment of Col. Smoky Camps, Charleston, SC.

His fifth tour of service was voluntary enlistment in Charleston under Capt. George Lemmon in the Regiment of Col. William Lytle.

Gen. Lincoln surrendered Charleston on May 12, 1780, and himself and his army prisoners of war were never being exchanged for until after the capture of Lord Cornwallis at Yorktown, VA. He performed no further actual service during the war.

Thomas died July 7, 1843 and is buried at Big Fork Cemetery, Van Buren Co., TN.

Richard Shockley was born Jan 1, 1726 in Kent County, MD. He took the Oath of Allegiance to the USA in the Sate of Virginia. He was a planter, primary crops being tobacco and Indian corn, and ran a grist mill. His wife, Elizabeth Adkins, was born 1740 in Henrico Co., VA. She died in 1784 in Grayson Co., VA. Richard died in 1800 in Grayson Co., VA.

Robert Moffitt served in the war from North Carolina.

George Banfill, Sergeant, enlisted in 1778 and served 18 months under Capt. Simeon Stevens, Col. Bedel's Regt. from Vermont. He served as a Minuteman, guarded against the invasion from Canada via Hagen Road in Newberry to the Canadian Line. He also was engaged in guarding Tories held as prisoners. He was a farmer and boat builder.

TIMOSCHUK, WALTER JOSEPH III – Major Walter Joseph Timoschuk III was born June 27, 1959 in Spencer, TN. He joined the Michigan SAR in 2006. His military service was as a major with the U.S. Air Force and Civil Air Patrol.

He serves as the MISSAR State Registrar, is on the National DAR-SAR Committee and a Huron Valley Trustee. He is employed with Ford Motor Company as a manager.

Walter and Cyndi have three children and one grandchild.

He is a member of the Explorer Scouts BSA, Masons, Van Buren Historical Soiciety, Sons of Confederate Veterans, and Military Order and Stars and Bars.

Thomas Crawley was born April 25, 1755 in

Amherst, VA. His wife was Margaret, born 1761 in Virginia. Thomas was a resident of White and Van Buren County, TN. He served five tours. His civilian occupation was as a farmer and a blacksmith.

First, he entered into the service of volunteer corps who were known by the title of Minute men. He enlisted in Pittsylvania County, VA January 1776 under Capt. Abraham Penn, in the Regiment of Col. Edward Carrington. He was discharged after eight months. Battles: Jamestown, Williamsburg, Gwynns Island. He fired on Lord Dunsmore Troops in Williamsburg. He was in Williamsburg when the Declaration of Independence was signed July 4, 1776.

His second tour of service was an enlistment for one year. He enlisted in Pittsylvania Co., VA under Capt. Samuel Scott, in the Regiment of Col. Habersham and in Gen. McIntosh's Brigade; this service was intended for and rendered in the State of Georgia. Spectator of the duel fought between Gen. McIntosh and Button Gwinnett. Battles: Hillsborough, Camden, Savannah River, Galphins Fort, Cowpens, Phillips Fort.

His third tour was a voluntary enlistment for six months in the Company of Capt. John Davis, Regiment of Col Charles McDowell in the Brigade of General Butler. Battles: Guilford Courthouse, Salisbury, Charlotte, Briar Creek, Bacon's Bridge, Stono Fort.

His fourth tour of service was a substitute for William Astill in Guilford County for three months. Captain was Archibald Campbell, Regiment of Col. Smoky Camps, Charleston, SC.

His fifth tour of service was voluntary enlistment in Charleston under Capt. George Lemmon in the Regiment of Col. William Lytle.

Gen. Lincoln surrendered Charleston on May 12, 1780, and himself and his army prisoners of war were never being exchanged for until after the capture of Lord Cornwallis at Yorktown, VA. He performed no further actual service during the war.

Thomas died July 7, 1843 and is buried at Big Fork Cemetery, Van Buren Co., TN.

Richard Shockley was born Jan 1, 1726 in Kent County, MD. He took the Oath of Allegiance to the USA in the Sate of Virginia. He was a planter, primary crops being tobacco and Indian corn, and ran a grist mill. His wife, Elizabeth Adkins, was born 1740 in Henrico Co., VA. She died in 1784 in Grayson Co., VA. Richard died in 1800 in Grayson Co., VA.

Robert Moffitt served in the war from North Carolina.

TIMOSCHUK, WALTER JOSEPH IV – Walter Joseph Timoschuk IV works at Discount Tire and is going to college. He was Tire Tech of the Year and Safety Officer of the Year with the Civil Air Patrol, Michigan Wing, 2008. He is an Eagle Scout from BSA.

Thomas Crawley was born April 25, 1755 in Amherst, VA. His wife was Margaret, born 1761 in Virginia. Thomas was a resident of White and Van Buren County, TN. He served five tours. His civilian occupation was as a farmer and a blacksmith.

First, he entered into the service of volunteer corps who were known by the title of Minute men. He enlisted in Pittsylvania County, VA January 1776 under Capt. Abraham Penn, in the Regiment of Col. Edward Carrington. He was discharged after eight months. Battles: Jamestown, Williamsburg, Gwynns Island. He fired on Lord Dunsmore Troops in Williamsburg. He was in Williamsburg when the Declaration of Independence was signed July 4, 1776.

His second tour of service was an enlistment for one year. He enlisted in Pittsylvania Co., VA under Capt. Samuel Scott, in the Regiment of Col. Habersham and in Gen. McIntosh's Brigade; this service was intended for and rendered in the State of Georgia. Spectator of the duel fought between Gen. McIntosh and Button Gwinnett. Battles: Hillsborough, Camden, Savannah River, Galphins Fort, Cowpens, Phillips Fort.

His third tour was a voluntary enlistment for six months in the Company of Capt. John Davis, Regiment of Col Charles McDowell in the Brigade of General Butler. Battles: Guilford Courthouse, Salisbury, Charlotte, Briar Creek, Bacon's Bridge, Stono Fort.

His fourth tour of service was a substitute for William Astill in Guilford County for three months. Captain was Archibald Campbell, Regiment of Col. Smoky Camps, Charleston, SC.

His fifth tour of service was voluntary enlistment in Charleston under Capt. George Lemmon in the Regiment of Col. William Lytle.

Gen. Lincoln surrendered Charleston on May 12, 1780, and himself and his army prisoners of war were never being exchanged for until after the capture of Lord Cornwallis at Yorktown, VA. He performed no further actual service during the war.

Thomas died July 7, 1843 and is buried at Big Fork Cemetery, Van Buren Co., TN.

Richard Shockley was born Jan 1, 1726 in Kent County, MD. He took the Oath of Allegiance to the USA in the Sate of Virginia. He was a planter, primary crops being tobacco and Indian corn, and ran a grist mill. His wife, Elizabeth Adkins, was born 1740 in Henrico Co., VA. She died in 1784 in Grayson Co., VA. Richard died in 1800 in Grayson Co., VA.

Robert Moffitt served in the war from North Carolina.

George Banfill, Sergeant, enlisted in 1778 and served 18 months under Capt. Simeon Stevens, Col. Bedel's Regt. from Vermont. He served as a Minuteman, guarded against the invasion from Canada via Hagen Road in Newberry to the Canadian Line. He also was engaged in guarding Tories held as prisoners. He was a farmer and boat builder.

TREVINO, DR. GILBERTO S. – Born Jan. 11, 1925 at Laredo, TX. He is on the SAR ROTC Committee, and has received Outstanding Citizen and Military Service awards. His military service includes the U.S. Marine Corps (1944-46), U.S. Army (1952-54 during the Korean War, and 1958-76). In civilian life, he had a private veterinary practice in Hollywood, CA; retired as Full Professor, Texas A&M University, 1982. He currently operates a cattle ranch in Webb County, TX.

PFC Gilberto S. Trevino, USMC, Guan, 1945 after the Battle for Iwo Jima.

Col. Gilberto S. Treviono

Dr. Trevino served as President, Lions Club, Laredo, TX; served as Commandant, Marine Corps League, Laredo; and founded and directed two different community organizations, the Prazos County Residents Against Drug Abuse, College State, Dryan, TX, and the Laredo Organized Volunteers for Elderly and Disadvantaged, Laredo.

He is married to Christine V. Trevino and they have two children and six grandchildren.

James White was born 1747 in Iredell County, NC. He was a captain in the North Carolina Militia, serving in the American Revolutionary War (1779-81) and the War of 1812. James was a private developer; public servant; member of the legislature, NC; member, convention ratification committee of the Constitution of the U.S.; founder of Knoxville, TN; and donated land where the First Presbyterian Church and the University of Tennessee (Knoxville) are located.

He died Aug. 14, 1821 in Knoxville, and is buried at the First Presbyterian Church Cemetery.

TROUTMAN, STEVE E. – Steve E. Troutman was born May 4, 1952 in Danville, PA. He is employed with Troutman Brother, Inc. He is married to Joan E. Troutman and they have two children. He is a graduate of Franklin and Marshall College, Lancaster, PA.

He joined the SAR in Pennsylvania (#11249) on March 26, 2002. He is involved with the Bicentennial Committees and marking of Patriot's graves. He has assisted with the dedication of eight Revolutionary War soldier gravestones at Zion Lutheran (Klinger's) Church in Erdman PA, and Jacobs (Hewerter's) Cemetery in Leck Kill, PA.

He is a member of Gratz Historical Society; Northumberland County Historical Society; Masonic Lodge Number 702 of Herndon, PA; and Klingerstown Fire Company.

Steve E. Troutman, Klingerstown Bicentennial, 1807-2007.

Irvin L. Trautman of San Bernardino, CA and Schuyler Brossman of Rehrersburg, PA assisted many Troutman-Trautman researchers to connect to patriot ancestors. These men, now both deceased, assisted Steve in compiling *The Trautman/Troutman Family History, Vol. I* published in 1988 and *The Trautman/Troutman Family History, Vol. II* published in 1997. Irvin L. Trautman introduced Steve to the SAR.

Peter Trautman was born about 1738-1740 in Reichelsheim, Germany. He was a pioneer settler in the wilderness of Mahantongo Valley, PA. He was a private in the Northumberland County Militia in Captain Weaver's Company. He assisted in the defense of Northumberland County from the British soldiers and Indian incursions as recorded in April and May of 1779. He died 1809 and is buried in Mahantongo Valley, PA.

TUCK, JOSHUA A. – Dr. Tuck was born in 1977 in Dover, NH. He resides in Brunswick, ME. He joined New Hampshire State Society in September of 2006.

Dr. Joshua A. Tuck

Joshua's military service was USN/VP-8-"Fighting Tigers"-LT/0-3. He is a U. S. Navy physician/flight surgeon. Joshua and wife Frances Yvonne have no children.

Joshua also belongs to the Sons of Union Veterans of the Civil War, Veterans of Foreign Wars, Knights of Columbus, is a Veteran of Operation Iraqi Freedom – Orthopedic Surgeon.

Jonathan Tuck Jr. was born Oct. 10, 1736 in Hampton, NH. He signed test papers on June 4, 1776 at Hampton, NH, Committee of Safety Meeting. Jonathan was a farmer and miller in civilian life. He died July 20, 1780, burial place unknown.

TUNGET, GARY W. – Born Jan. 20, 1956. He is President, Gary's Fleur De Lis Inc., a florist, and is both the owner and floral designer. He is a member of the West Central Kentucky Family Research Assoc., and Sons of Confederate Veterans, and is very active in cemetery and headstone restoration, and marking historic sites. He is married to Mary Lisa Gore.

Joseph Benton Sr. was born ca. 1724-30 in Prince George County, MD. He took the patriot oath and provided supplies for the cause. His son, Joseph Benton Jr., was a solider, private, 2nd Co., Lower Batt., Militia, 1777. A farmer by trade, Joseph Sr. owned several acres of land in Montgomery County, MD. He died Mar. 6, 1807 and is buried in the Benton Family Cemetery in Frederick County, MD.

ULRICH, DAWSON – No. 746

Reverend John Cleveland is a 4th generation American and was ordained at Prince William County, VA in 1772. He was one of the first preachers in backwoods and was associated with several churches in Virginia, Georgia and the Carolinas.

During the Revolutionary War, he served as a Chaplain in his brother, Col. Benjamin Cleveland's regiment.

ULRICH, HUNTER – No. 873

Reverend George McNeil sailed to America between 1745 and 1750, arriving in Virginia. He was ordained as a Baptist minister about 1775. He was also a member of the Regulator Movement, and after the battle of Alamance, was forced to flee for his safety.

During the Revolutionary War, he served as a Chaplain in the Regiment of Col. Benjamin Cleveland at the time of the battle for King's Mountain. He was associated with many churches in and around Wilkes County, as well as Register of Deeds for Wilke County from 1787 until his death in 1805. He is buried in the family cemetery.

ULRICH, MONTANA – No. 747

Bartholomew Stovall, was the son of John Stovall Sr. and a patriot of North Carolina, who took the Oath of Allegiance in 1778. He also supplied the Army for the duration of the war.

VANCE, JOHN CHARLES – John was born July 21, 1943 in Chicago, IL. He is married to Mary Ellen Krauth Kweller Vance.

John worked in the Motion Picture Exhibition industry for forty-two years, retiring March 30. 2005. He worked for Kohlberg Theatres, Inc.; General Cinema Corp.; National Cinema Service, Inc.; and was owner of Vance Technical Services, Inc.

John has four children and two step-children, and seven grandchildren and four step-grandchildren.

William Blackburn was born in 1748 in Washington County, VA. He was a farmer.

William served in Col. William Campbell's Regiment, Captain Robert Craig's Co. in the Virginia Militia as Lieutenant. He was killed Oct. 7, 1780 in the Battle of King's Mountain, NC. He is buried south of King's Mountain in York County, SC.

VARNEY, THOMAS K. – Born in Waukegan, IL and presently resides in Windsor, CT. He joined the Connecticut State Society in 1999 and is Treasurer.

Thomas K. Varney

Thomas and wife Marisa have three children. He is the director of The Hartford Fire Insurance Co.

Thomas also belongs to Presidents and First Ladies, Society of Descendants of the Founders of Hartford, National Society of the Sons and Daughters of the Pilgrims, Founders and Patriots of America, First Families of Connecticut.

Timothy Bliss was born March 22, 1745 at Lebanon, CT. He was the Quartermaster in Capt. Thomas Bull's Company in Col. Ira Allen's Regiment. In civilian life he was a Justice of the Peace and a Vermont legislator. Timothy died May 3, 1817 and is buried at Essex, VT.

VERSTREATE, DARYL JR. – Born July 3, 1974 Clifton Springs, NY, resides in Marion, NY. Daryl joined SAR, March 17, 2003, Empire State Society, CT State Society.

He has served on the National Graves Committee, Graves Chair Rochester, ESSSAR Graves Committee, Webmaster Rochester SAR. He has received SAR Awards Bronze Good Citizenship, Silver Good Citizenship, and Mildred Taylor Award.

Daryl's military service was with the USN and New York Guard.

He and Amanda Verstreate have 3 children. Daryl is a Master Trainer State of New York, OMRDD.

Daryl also has served as Service Officer Marion American Legion, SAL Commander, 3VC Wayne Co., SAL.

Patriots: **Pvt. Thomas Beadle, Jr.**, NY; **Pvt. Josiah Barton**, MA – Submitted; **CS Reuben Barton**, MA – Submitted; **Pvt. Thomas Beadle, Sr.**, NY; **Pvt. David Carter**, RI; **Lt. Holthom Dunham**, NY; **Capt. Samuel Dunham**, CT; **Pvt. Oliver Force**, NY; **Pvt. Benjamin Hammond**, NY; **BSN Christopher Latham**, CT; **CS Benjamin Peckham**, RI; **Patriot Josephus Peckham**, RI; **Pvt. James Pettys**, RI; **Cpl. John Selfridge**, NY; **Patriot Oliver Selfridge**, NY; **CDR Cyrus Sholes**, CT; **Patriot Hutchinson Sholes**, CT; and **Pvt. Jonathan Reynolds**, RI.

VESCELUS, STEPHEN JOHN – Earned a Humanities degree, 1973; also studied at Chicago Art Institute and American Academy of Art, Chicago, IL; sculpture at Northern Illinois University under professor instructed by a pupil of Picasso, Botany at Morton Arboretum, Lisle, IL; Ass't. Instructor at Junior College in Field Geology; Marine Biology; Photographic processes/Lecturer of Paleontology. Assisted research in several Illinois field Archaeology sites and Geology dig of Mammoth remains.

Stephen John Vescelus

Stephen served with the USN and is a Vietnam Veteran. He is the owner of Courier Service for Attorneys in Greater Chicago Area and owns a locksmith shop in Winfield, IL. He has two sons: Daniel John and Brian William Vescelus and their families.

Stephen also has memberships in Audobon, Moose, American Legion, Earth Science Club of Northern Illinois, Tejas Trail Riders Assoc., German Bohemian Heritage Society, Luxembourg Society, Minnesota. Avid collector of Minerals and Fossils, the latter exhibited at Field Museum of Natural History, Chicago and Lizzadro Museum of Lapidary Art, Elmhurst, IL.

Samuel Strode, Sergeant, Virginia, Joseph Bowmans' Company, under Col. George Rogers Clark Illinois Expedition, 1778., ref. Collins *History of Kentucky,* Vol. II, Curtwells' *History of Frederick County, Virginia,* page 104, Wm. H. English, *Conquest of the Northwest,* Vol. II, pages 842-1119.

William Roe, Sergeant, Flushing, L. I., Stamford, Conn., Col. Smiths' Regt. of James Brown crew, captured as spy by Hessians, Dec. 11, 1782, Prisoner of War.

VETS, TONY LEE – Born July 21, 1959 in Danville, IL, residing in Colfax, LA. Tony joined the LA State Society in November of 2002. He has been Chapter Secretary, Registrar and Treasurer.

Tony served as a MSG in the Army, retiring in June of 2006. He and wife Karen have three children.

Tony also belongs to the American Legion and Veterans of Foreign Wars.

Marsham Brashear was born in 1752 in Prince George's, MD. He was a Trustee appointed by Thomas Jefferson to Louisville, KY. Marsham died in November of 1807 and is buried in Bullitt, KY.

VETS, TONY LEE II – Tony was born Dec. 28,1979 at Fort Polk, LA and presently resides in Colfax, LA.

Tony joined the LA State Society in November of 2001. He has been Chapter Vice President.

Tony and wife Patricia have no children. He is Director of the Autism Center at St. Mary's Training School.

Tony also belongs to the Sons of Confederate Veterans.

Barthelemy Rachal was born November of 1755 in Natchitoches, LA. He was a Rifleman and in the Cavalry with the Galvez Expedition. Barthelemy died after October of 1818 and is buried at Natchitoches, LA.

VETTE, WILLIAM GEORGE – Born Apr. 17, 1949, Flint, MI. William joined the SAR Aug. 14, 2008 at age 59, currently a member of the River Raisin Chapter, MI, SAR.

William's military service was with the US Army 5th mechanized infantry division, Delta Company 1/11, where he served during the Vietnam War. He was honorably discharged as a noncommissioned officer.

He earned his master's degree in education, was a former Eagle Scout, pilot, Airframe and power plant technician, college professor, later college administrator. Currently he is a senior analyst, state of Michigan.

William and wife Kristin live on Lake LeAnn, south of Jackson, MI. He has a son, Steve, daughter, Angela, stepsons, Nathan and Adam, and four grandchildren, Jordan, Troy, Loren and Noah.

William is descended from Patriot Moses Hutchins.

Moses Hutchins, born 1760 Charlton City, Worcester, MA. Moses served with the Massachusetts Line in 1776-78, where he fought in the following battles: Siege of Boston, Nantucket Shoals, Fort Stanwix (Fort Schuyler), Oriskany, and Saratoga. His father was Edward Hutchins, and mother was Sarah Smith. Children: Nancy, Sarah, Diana, Jacob, Caleb. Moses died in 1837, Burton, OH. He is buried in Memorial Cemetery in Geauga County, OH.

VILLARREAL, JESSE O. SR. – Jesse was born in San Antonio, TX on Feb. 4, 1945. His parents were Santos C. Villarreal and Juanita Solis Villarreal. His siblings are Santos S. Villarreal, Paul S. Villarreal, Janie Villarreal Mora, and Teresa Villarreal Rodriguez. His mother died when Jesse was 2 years old and he was reared by his maternal grandmother and uncle. He grew up on San Antonio's West Side and as a child would hear his family's oral history about his ancestors. Later, through extensive research, they were able to document his mother's lineage to the first Spanish soldiers and settlers (1718) and builders of present day San Antonio, TX.

Jesse joined the Patrick Henry Chapter of the SAR Dec. 20, 2008. He also has memberships in Tejanos in Action Veteran's Organization, Austin TX; TCARA (Texas Connection to the American Revolution Association); and Tejano Genealogy Society.

Remark: On Dec. 20, 2008, eight Villarreal members were inducted into the SAR at the same time: Santos S. Villarreal, Jesse O. Villarreal Sr., Rene Villarreal, Orlando Villarreal Mora, Leonard Villarreal Rodriguez, Santos H. Villarreal, Jesse O. Villarreal Jr., and Dr. Ruben Villarreal Mora.

Jesse graduated from Sidney Lanier High School in San Antonio, TX and the served in the U.S. Army from Sept. 1965-Sept. 1967. After his military service, Jesse worked at Kelly AFB. He married Guadalupe C. (Connie) Perez Villarreal on June 17, 1972. He received a Bachelor of Social Work Degree from Our Lady of the Lake University in 1975. Jesse later worked with the Department of Labor Statistics and The Occupational Safety and Health Administration. He retired in 2002 with 35 years of service and is currently a part-time bailiff with the Travis County Courthouse in Austin, TX. Jesse and his wife have two children, Jesse Jr. and Criselda Villarreal Villanueva. Their two grandchildren are Cristian A. Villanueva and Olivia Grace Villanueva.

Cayetano Hernandes was born on Feb. 10 1753. As his father and grandfather before him, he was a Spanish soldier stationed at the Presidio of San Antonio De Bexar. His duties included: protecting settlers, roads, ranches, and cattle from Indian raids. These cattle were sent on cattle drives to Gov. Bernardo de Galvez in Louisiana. Cayetano Hernandez and his family provided cattle, monetary assistance and protection for these cattle drives.

On Feb. 6, 1871, while picking fodder at El Fuerte del Cibolo, six Spanish soldiers were attacked by about 100 Comanche. They were eventually overcome and the aftermath is documented by a surviving soldier. Cayetano was scalped and died at this battle. During this period, the British were known to have traded guns to the Indians for horses. This was an intentional attempt at sabotaging any assistance provided to the Patriots by the Spanish in Texas.

VINT, ROBERT JAMES – Robert James Vint was born Jan. 30, 1934 in Washington, D.C. He served as a sergeant (E-5) in the U.S. Army at Fort Huachuca, AZ from 1957-1959. He retired in 1995 from Sundt Corp. in Tuscon, AZ as Vice President, Management Information Systems. He is married to Katherine Lois (Brown) Vint and they have five children and eight grandchildren.

James Orcutt was born Jan. 17, 1754 in Taconic, Albany County, NY. He served as a private in Col. John Fellow Regiment, Capt. William Bacon's Company. He was involved in the Battle at Bunker Hill. He died Sept 4, 1804 and is buried at Aurelius, Cayuga County, NY.

VOGEL, DAVID – Born Mar. 6, 1972, he served in the US Marine Corps, Sergeant, 2000-05, Operation Enduring Freedom, Fallujah. A member of the American Legion, Deerfield, OH, he is a consultant and commercial pilot.

Patrick Sinnett was born Mar. 17, 1752 in WV. He was a private in the war, and fought at the battles of Jamestown, Hotwater, and Yorktown. A farmer, he died Dec. 19, 1850 and is buried in West Virginia.

WAGNER, WILLIAM M. JR. – William is a direct descendent of Major General John Peter Gabriel Muhlenberg, as documented by the SAR, on his father's mother's side. He earned a Bachelor of Science Degree in Organizational Behavior/ Applied Psychology from Albright College, 2000. He is a U.S. Navy Veteran from the Vietnam-era (1969-1972), where he was a Communications Yeoman on the *USS Forrestall*, a large attack aircraft carrier, and served overseas. He is currently employed by the County of Berks and has been since 1990.

He is on the board and a life member of the Conrad Weiser Family Association, life member of the Trappe Historical Society, Trappe, PA, member of the Berks County Genealogical Society, and a member of the Historical Society of Berks County. William is also Vice President of the Sons of the American Revolution, (Governor Hiester Chapter) Berks County, PA. William is on the Advisory Board of the Speaker's House, the home of Frederick A. Muhlenberg, who was General Muhlenberg's brother. It is where Frederick moved in 1782 and is currently being restored to that time period. A Pennsylvania Historical and Museum plaque is to be dedicated April 12. William is a member of the Veterans of Foreign Wars and the American Legion.

He has been on TV several times presenting a program about the Muhlenberg family. He also has done presentations at various historical societies. He and his cousin, the late Dr. J. Peter G. Muhlenberg, have been pictured with a story about the Muhlenberg family in publications such as *The Reading Eagle* and *Antique Week* magazine. He learned much from his grandmother, Augusta (Muhlenberg) Wagner.

Subsequently, he likes to preserve the history of the Muhlenberg family and Conrad Weiser, like the Trappe Historical Society, Berks County Genealogical Society, The Conrad Weiser Family Association, Muhlenberg College, Friends of Conrad Weiser Homestead, and many other organizations and individuals. Bill Wagner resides in Berks County, PA.

John Peter Gabriel Muhlenberg (1746-1807) was a Lutheran Minister in Woodstock, VA

John Peter Gabriel Muhlenberg

who raised and commanded the Eighth Virginia Regimen for the continental army in 1775, at the urging of George Washington and Patrick Henry. Prior to this he served in the Virginia House of Burgesses in 1774. He was also the chairman of the Virginia committee of safety for Dunmore County, VA. At the beginning of the Revolutionary War in January 1776 he threw off his clerical robe, after preaching to the congregation, "The Bible tells us there is a time for all things and there is a time to fight, and that time has now come," (*The Epic Story of the Heroic Muhlenberg Family, Muhlenberg College Bicentennial Celebration*, Inc. p. 7, Gordon Fister, Editor, 1942) to reveal a colonels uniform. He had read from the first eight verses of the third chapter of Ecclesiastes. Later he states "I am a member of the clergy and my heart is in it" Muhlenberg started, "but I am also a member of our society just like the poorest layman. My liberty is as dear to me as it is to any man who hears my voice." "Should I sit and enjoy myself at home when the blood of our best men is spilling on the ground? If America should be conquered ..., if America is lost ... do you think that I would be safe? I think not!" "I'll tell each and every one of you that would much rather fight like a man than die like a dog. And I choose to fight." And fight he did. This is quoted in many other sources. This was his final sermon in Woodstock, VA. He recruited 300 men that day as he was a Colonel in the Colonial guards. Quickly promoted to Brigadier General in 1777, Muhlenberg and his men in the Eighth Virginia regiment, fought in many battles, including Brandywine, Germantown, Monmouth, Stony Point, for example. He commanded the first brigade on the assault on Cornwallis at the battle of Yorktown in 1781, and was in command of 1000 Continental Light infantry under General Lafayette. He also saved Mad Anthony Wayne's brigade who found themselves in a trap and were badly mauled. Muhlenberg heard a large volume of gunfire. Without waiting for orders he and his brigade rushed to the rescue. Even "Mad Anthony" was uneasy at Muhlenberg's daring (Wallace, pp. 224-234). This battle at Yorktown was considered to be the final major battle to end the war. Paul Wallace's book describes many of these battles.

At the beginning of the war, Muhlenberg and his men spent the winter at Valley Forge in 1777-1778 with George Washington and Baron Von Steuben. The huts of the Muhlenberg Brigade are currently restored at Valley Forge National Park. He was promoted to Major General in 1783, at the end of the war. Returning a hero, second only to Washington in Philadelphia, he was elected to the Supreme Executive Council in 1784 and was Pennsylvania Vice President under Benjamin Franklin from 1785 to 1788. He was elected to the first Congress in 1788 and served in several successive Congresses. He was elected to the Senate in 1801, but shortly resigned to become Supervisor of Revenue for the port of Philadelphia, PA.

There is a good book about the General, and I own two copies. It is entitled *The Life of Major-General John Peter Gabriel Muhlenberg*, Henry A. Muhlenberg, Carey and Hart, Philadelphia, PA. 1849. It tells of the beginning of Peter's life, how he liked to hunt and fish and was an excellent shot. He even went hunting with George Washington early in life, and they became good friends.

In his youth, he was sent to Halle Institute in Germany in 1763-1766, along with his brothers to receive a formal European education. However, it did not work out and Peter was sent as an apprentice to work with a druggist. He was taken advantage of by the druggist, and he later escaped and joined a German regiment of Dragoons who were leaving for America. Later, upon his release from their service his father wondered what Peter should do. He eventually was ordained a minister and received a call to Woodstock, VA. In Virginia, a Minister still had to be ordained by the Church of England, so Peter traveled to England and was ordained a priest in the Anglican Church in 1772.

There are also many interesting stories in Paul Wallace's book and Henry A. Muhlenberg's book. One tells of a British officer taking a pot shot at Muhlenberg when he is asleep on his horse, after two nights and a day in the saddle, at the battle of Germantown. The General immediately pulls out one of his pistols and shoots the officer dead (Henry A. Muhlenberg, pp. 113-114). This is one of the reasons he did not want to return to the clergy after the war.

Another story tells about the inauguration of George Washington on April 30, 1789. Before the inauguration there was much talk about what the President should be called, "your Highness," "your Excellency" or what. Peter Muhlenberg was invited by Washington to dinner and was seated next the tall Henry Wynkoop and opposite short and tubby John Adams. As the story goes, Washington felt the title "High Mightiness" was fitting for him and asked Peter Muhlenberg what he thought. Peter stated "that if a man as large as Washington or Mr. Wynkoop held the position, it would be appropriate, but if someone as short as John Adams were elected, it would be ridiculous." (Wallace, p. 279). Washington was not amused. There is even part of a letter Peter wrote to Benjamin Rush about it on that page. Peter Muhlenberg had no time for such frivolities.

These books tell of his whole life from beginning to end. There is an interesting story of Peter's journey to the Ohio Valley to survey 11,662 acres granted him for his war service. After the war with hunting the likes of Sir William Howe, Sir Harry Clinton, Benedict Arnold, and Lord Cornwallis, Peter could not sit home too long. He was restless and decided to go visit the lands given him in the Ohio valley. Peter is described as "looking like Robinson Crusoe with two brace of pistols, a sword and a rifle slung, and large tobacco pouch and pipe" (Wallace, p. 254). When he arrived at Louisville, the Indians had wondered why the government had not attempted to contact them. They were tired of waiting and the Indians felt it was their land. Peter was also asked by General Von Steuben to survey his land. Besides Von Steuben's, he was also to survey Governor Benjamin Harrison's, Patrick Henry's, and others. Peter later explained he did what could be done, that they were not Virginia's lands to survey without negotiating with the Indians. The Indians would not allow it, and two years earlier Abraham Lincoln the later president's grandfather was killed near there by Indians (Wallace, p. 256). So Peter would not claim it without purchasing it from. He felt like his grandfather Conrad Weiser before him, that we had to maintain peace with the Indians. The Indians were starting to distrust the white man and were tired of being cheated and moving farther west. Some white men considered them savages. So Peter returned to the Philadelphia area and became elected to positions in the early U. S. Government.

Paul Wallace's Book includes many copies of letters to and from General Muhlenberg and from many of the officers of the Continental Army such as George Washington, Baron Von Stueben, Nathaniel Greene, and Edward Hand, for example, that my grandmother Augusta Muhlenberg Wagner had possession of. She is the first name mentioned in the acknowledgments for sources. She had many of these letters, and I recently found out she donated them to The American Philosophical Society in Philadelphia in 1952. Also, General Muhlenberg's journal of his trips to the Ohio in 1784 and 1797 are listed. She also had certificates of civil and military commissions signed by Presidents Jefferson, Madison, and Jackson among 100 items she and her grandfather Frederick A. Muhlenberg III presented to the Society. Examples are listed on their website, www.amphilsoc.org/library/mole/m.htm., pps. 31-34, with her name listed as presenting them, among other Muhlenberg descendants. I remember when working on her farm in Sinking Spring, she talked about her helping Wallace with his book.

There is a statue of him in the Rotunda of the U. S. Capital building for being the most distinguished soldier in the Revolutionary War from Pennsylvania. He died Oct. 1, 1807 from a recurrent liver infection he contracted during the war and is buried behind Augustus Lutheran church, along side his wife Anna Barbara Meyer and his parents. Four sons and two daughters survived him.

Frederick Augustus Conrad Muhlenberg (1750-1801) was the brother of General Muhlenberg. He was a Lutheran Minister who preached in Stouchsburg, Lebanon, and Lancaster areas from 1770-1774 and New York City from 1774-1776. He married Catherine Schaeffer on Oct. 15, 1771, and they had three sons and four daughters. He was a member of the Continental Congress in 1779-1780 and served in the State House of Representatives 1780-1783, and elected speaker Nov. 3, 1780. He was a delegate and President of the State constitutional convention and was called to ratify the federal Constitution in 1787. He was elected to the first and three following U. S. Congresses from March 4, 1789-March 3, 1797. He was the Speaker of the First and Third U. S. House of Representatives. His signature is the first one on the U. S. Bill of Rights, followed by John Adams Vice President of the United States. He was called upon to cast the deciding vote on passing the Jay Treaty, which benefited the country, but was not considered favorable by many opponents. At this time there was conflict between the Federalists and the anti-Federalists. The Federalists wanted this passed to settle unresolved issues with England after the war. This cost him his re-election to a fifth term in Congress. He is buried in Lancaster, PA.

Today, we hear many debates about the Bill of Rights, in particular the 1st and 2nd amendments. Since both Frederick and his brother Peter were in the first Congress, and I have many sources written about how they and others felt at that time. Peter was largely instrumental in the freedom of religion clause in the first amendment. (See the *Good News Newsletter*, November, 2000, Volume 26, Issue 11, p. 2.) It is available on the Internet at http//www.gslclasvegas.org/newsletter/. As for Amendment I which states, "Congress shall make no law respecting an establishment of religion, or prohibiting the free exercise there of, or abridging the freedom of speech, or of the press, or of the people to peaceably assemble, and to petition the government for a redress of grievances." The colonists had just fought a war with England, and as you may recall under colonial rule, as in Virginia, the Church of England was the required religion. The founding fathers wanted freedom of religion, not freedom from religion. They did not want the government to establish a state religion. However, most of the founding fathers were Christians, and there were a vast number of various religious faiths, especially in Pennsylvania. There were Lutherans, Episcopalians, Moravians, Amish, Mennonite, Methodist, Quakers, Schwenkfelders, Anglicans, Catholics, and Jews, just to name some off the top of my head. The writers of the Bill of Rights primarily George Mason, who wrote the Virginia declaration of Rights in 1776, and James Madison relied heavily on the 10 Commandments, other religious principles, and The Articles of Confederation of 1781. They even went as far back as the Magna Carta of 1215 in England.

As far as the 2nd Amendment, "a well regulated Militia, being necessary to the security of a free state, the right of the people to keep and bear arms shall not be infringed." The delegates who just fought a war with England felt too much of a powerful government could be dangerous, and they wanted personal weapons just in case. Besides they needed them for hunting and self defense.

During the debates on the adoption of the Constitution, opponents repeatedly charged the Constitution as it was, would open the way to tyranny by the central government. They just got over the British violation of their civil rights and they demanded a "bill of rights" that would spell out the immunities of individual citizens. See the U. S. Bill of Rights presented by The National Archives and Records Administration available on the Internet and many other sources.

WAGONER, PAUL DONALD – Born in Rochester, IN. He joined the United States Air Force in 1954, became a fighter pilot, commanded five high level organizations, and retired after 30 years of service. A few career highlights include: flying off the aircraft carrier USS Enterprise as an Air Force exchange pilot making 173 carrier landings; performing 101 combat missions in Vietnam in the F-4 Phantom; and during the Cold War, while Commander of Air Forces Iceland, he and his pilots made a total of 276 intercepts, without incident, of Soviet bomber and reconnaissance aircraft flying within Icelandic airspace. He retired in 1984 at the rank of Brigadier General. His 16 military decorations include the Defense Superior Service Medal, Legion of Merit, Bronze Star with Valor, and six Air Medals. He and his wife, the former Peggy Lichtenwalter of Rochester, IN, have three children and five grandchildren in Mt. Vernon, VA.

Paul Donald Wagoner

John Waggoner, Sr., born 1758, Wasselonne, Alsace, France, enlisted in Reading, PA as private in Capt. Von Heer's Light Dragoons and served in Gen. Washington's Life-Guard. His civilian occupation was farmer. He was the father of ten children. He died Dec. 15, 1842 and was buried in Four-Mile Cemetery, Fremont, OH.

WALLS, RAY E. – Born July 18, 1943 in San Antonio, Bexar, TX; presently resides in Sisterdale, TX.

Ray has been Chapter President, Vice-President, Registrar and served on Texas Awards Committee. Ray was a B-52 Radar Navigator and is a Vietnam Veteran.

Ray and spouse Mary Ellen (Potts) Walls have two children. He retired in July of 2005.

Ray also belongs to Sons of Confederate Veterans, Society of the War of 1812 (State Secretary/Treasurer), Society of Colonial Wars (State Secretary), Baronial Order of the Magna Charta.

John Wall Sr. was born ca. in Virginia. He was a Private in the Virginia Militia. John died ca. 1827 and is buried in Montgomery County, VA.

WALTERS, FLETCHER DENNIS – Fletcher Dennis Walters was born Nov. 8, 1938 in Reidsville, NC. He was a member of the North Carolina National Guard. He retired in 1993 as a supervisor from American Brands. He is married to Linda Dixon Walters and they have two children and two grandchildren.

He is a member of North Carolina Civil War Round Table; Rockingham County Historical Society; and Sons of Confederate Veterans.

Charles Colley was born Jan. 25, 1756 in Stafford County, VA. He served in Col. Lewis' Virginia Regiment, Captain Peter Perkins' Company as a private. Charles was a farmer. He died Sept 21, 1846 and in buried in Pittyslvania County, VA.

WALTON, TERENCE MICHAEL – Born in 1938 in Norwalk, CT; presently resides in Fort Myers, FL. He has been VP/Treasurer/Editor, Caloosa Chapter, FLSSAR, and Recording Secretary, FLSSAR. He has served on the FLSSAR/NSSAR Library Committee.

Terence has received the War Service Medal. He was in the U. S. Army from 1953-1954. Terence is married to Ruth Rachel Walton.

Terence Michael Walton

Terence retired in 2000 after serving as a Library Administrator, Academic/Public, Associate Dean, Old Dominion University, Norfolk, VA.

He belongs to the Sons of the Revolution, Society of Colonial Wars, First Families of Maryland, Descendants of Loyalists and Patriots of the American Revolution, United Empire Loyalist Association of Canada, American Legion, Sanibel FL Post 123, University of California Alumni Association, Arizona State University Alumni Association and University of Hawaii Alumni Association.

George Croghan was born 1720 in Dublin, Ireland. He was a Colonel with the Pennsylvania Militia. He was in the French and Indian War, Chairman, Committee of Correspondence, Fort Pitt, PA. See Journal of George Washington Commanding A Detachment of Virginia Troops.

In civilian life, George was an indian trader, frontiersman, land speculator/investor, Deputy Supt. of Indian Affairs in North American under Sir Wm. Johnson. See George Croghan and the Westward Movement 1741-1782 by Albert T. Volwiler.

George Croghan's headstone at St. Peter's Episcopal Churchyard in Philadelphia.

George died Aug. 31, 1782 and is buried at St. Peter's Episcopal Churchyard, Philadelphia, PA.

Other patriots are **Henry Griffith Sr.** (MD); **George Shipley** (MD); **Talbot Shipley** (MD); **Seth Warfield Sr.** (MD); **Azel Warfield** (MD); **Joshua Owings** (MD); **John Welsh Sr.** (MD); and **Samuel Welsh** (MD).

WARE, COL. JOSEPH M. – Presently residing in San Antonio, TX, was born June 19, 1930, Ft Monroe, VA. He has held the office of Chapter Pres. and District VP.

Joseph has received the following medals: Patriot, War Service, Meritorious Service, Silver Cit., Bronze Cit., and Chap Srv.

Joseph served in the USAF. He and wife Nita have two children and two grandchildren.

Joseph also belongs to Dep. Gov. Gen., Colonial Wars; 1812 State Pres.; Valley Forge, TX Brigade Cmdr., Huguenot Mannikin; Magna Carta.

Lt. Col. Ambrose Rucker was born c. 1725, Spotsylvania Cty., VA, d. 1807, Amherst Cty. VA.

He was a Planter and Member, VA House of Delegates; Member Committee of Safety; Justice of the Peace. Although he was 6' 6" and weighted 303 pounds, he outrode Tarleton's cavalrymen during the latter's Charlottesville raid. Ambrose's oldest son, Reuben was KIA in the last year of the Revolution.

WATSON, MARSTON – Mr. Watson was born 14 Nov. 1935 in Cambridge, Massachusetts, is a genealogist and author of three books on *Royal Families: Americans of Royal and Noble Ancestry*. He graduated from Burlingame High School (California) and received his BS degree in business administration from the University of California at Berkeley. He performed his military service with the California National Guard. His early career was in corporate finance and management before he became a management consultant.

Marston Watson

Marston was president of CASSAR (1970-71) at age 34, the youngest in its 132-year history. He received the Patriot Medal in 1971 and, later, was Trustee and Vice President General. Marston has chaired the Genealogy Committee, Handbook Committee and is Chairman of the Task Force for Wreaths Across America. He is a member of the Society of Mayflower Descendants and Editor-in-Chief with the Military Order of the Loyal Legion. He was knighted in the Sovereign Military Order of the Temple of Jerusalem and holds the rank of Grand Officier. He serves as its Grand Editeur and is Prior of the Priory of St. David of Wales in New England.

Marston has a daughter Karen and son Erik, as well as grandchildren Michael Amador, Sophia Amador, Haley Watson and Alexia Watson. Marston and Kathleen Todd Watson have been married fifteen years. Marston has proved seventeen patriot ancestors with the National Society of the Sons of the American Revolution.

Colonel Marston Watson, Esq. (1756-1800) served as 2nd Lieutenant, 3rd Company, 14th Continental Regiment, of Captain John Glover, Esq. in the Revolutionary War. Col. Marston crossed the Delaware with Colonel John Glover and General George Washington on 25 Dec. 1776, and fought with them in the battles of Trenton, Princeton and Monmouth. Marston was a Boston merchant after the war and became an early member (1800) of the Massachusetts Historical Society (a few months before his death).

As noted in his obituary, "Col. Watson was born in Plymouth, and received there his early education…Upon leaving School he was placed with Colonel Jeremiah Lee [uncle of Marston's wife Lucy], then an eminent merchant at Marblehead. In the early part of the revolutionary war, when the mercantile pursuits of the country were suspended, He [Marston] engaged in the military service as an officer in the regiment of Colonel Raymond R. Lee [Lucy's brother], and had the honor of participating in the brilliant affair at Trenton, under the banner of Washington…He was afterwards engaged for a short time in the sea service in one of the privateers from Marblehead. In that town he afterwards settled as a merchant… In the year 1797, he removed to *Boston*, where he greatly extended his business and connections…" [*Massachusetts Mercury*, Aug. 18, 1800, 2]

William Bowen, M.D. (1747-1832) graduated in 1766 from Yale College and is mentioned frequently in various family papers as being the physician who treated departed family members. Dr. Bowen was a Revolutionary War Surgeon in April 1777, in the 2nd Battalion of the Rhode Island Continental Troops. He served in the same Battalion with his brother Captain Ephraim Bowen, Jr. (later Colonel). Dr. Bowen's Revolutionary Pension number is S45605 (of Connecticut & Rhode Island) or S21654 (Rhode Island). He was co-founder of the First Congregational Church Society in Providence. Dr. Bowen was very active during the yellow fever epidemic of 1797, which he contracted but survived.

Edmund Bridge (1739-1826), son of Samuel Bridge, was a patriot of the American Revolution, in which he was appointed to the Committee of Safety and Correspondence. He was chosen on 22 June 1775 to a committee of five persons, "to purchase on Behalf and on the credit of the town [of Pownalborough] such corn and Bread as may be thought Best and Least Expensive." He was one of several men who refused to supply firewood and lumber to General Gage in June, 1774. Edmund became a Magistrate in the Revolutionary times, "an office involving consideration and distinction."

Samuel Bridge (1705-1791) was a private in Capt. Edmond Monroe's Detachment in the Lexington Alarm Company from 16 May to 20 May 1775, five days at Cambridge, by order of the Committee of Safety. The records of Lexington show that Samuel Bridge, with others, furnished a man for the campaign to Bennington." Specifically, he served "in the 8th campaign of the Revolutionary War to the Jerseys for three months, the 11th campaign to Bennington, 1777, and the 13th campaign in December, 1777 to guard the lines near Cambridge." According to the scant records, "Samuel was one of the most influential men of the town, in those trying days prior to the Revolution."

Captain George Corlis (1719-1790) is recorded in the *Proceedings of the People of Providence, in Town Meeting*, reported in Providence on 17 Dec. 1774, as having been appointed (along with 17 others) to the Committee of Inspection. They were "to see that the association entered into by the general Continental Congress, be strictly adhered to..." The Proceedings of 24 Dec. 1774 recorded the following: Captain Corlis procured gold and silver coin, for the operations in Canada. Also, he furnished 35 oars for service in the Revolutionary War. He was a merchant and mariner.

Captain Josiah Crocker (1743-1808) served his apprenticeship with Captain Moore, a merchant of Newport, Rhode Island. He opened his shop in Taunton, Massachusetts, which he operated for many years. Afterwards, he opened a reputable public house in Taunton, which was located on the northwest corner of the Green in Taunton. Captain Crocker served in the Revolutionary War in which he commanded a company of Taunton patriots, but his military career was uneventful. He marched from Taunton to Rhode Island in July 1778.

David Devens (1747-1792), son of Richard Devens, acquired a part of the wharf property given by his grandfather. He acquired all of it later and continued its management for many years. David was Town Treasurer for almost a quarter of a century and for thirty years was one of the board of directors of the Bunker Hill Bank, twenty of which years he was its president. During his business career, David was one of the first vice presidents of the Warren Institution of Savings and a Director in the Charlestown Mutual Fire Insurance Company. His name appears on a list of Massachusetts citizens who loaned money to the government during the Revolutionary War. [*DAR Third Report*, 3:23]

Richard Devens, Esq. (1721-1807) was a cooper and a merchant and a prominent citizen of Charlestown. He served as Commissary General in the Revolutionary War from 1776-1782 and was a member of the Committee of Safety with John Hancock and other patriots. Earlier on, he fought in the French and Indian Wars in 1757, as a member of Thomas Brigden's Company. Richard's residence was opposite the head of his wharf, near the spot where he furnished Paul Revere with a horse from Deacon Larkin's barn just before Revere made his famous ride to Lexington and Concord on 18 April 1775. Richard's name appears on a list of Massachusetts citizens who loaned money to the government during the Revolution. [*DAR Third Report*, 3:323]

Colonel John Lee, Esq. (1716-1789) was one of seven men who was voted on 27 Dec. 1774 to choose a Committee of Inspection "to see that the Resolves of the Continental Congress be carried into Execution." Col. Lee was made a member of the Committee of Correspondence in July 1775 and was a Revolutionary War colonel in the 6th Essex Regiment (2nd Company), to which position he was elected on 7 July 1775. He defended the attack on Beverly in 1775 by the British sloop of war *Falcon*, in which "Colonel Lee immediately mustered his battalion and made a rapid march to the relief of that town."

Colonel Arthur Lithgow (1751-1835), son of Col. William Lithgow, early engaged in trade in Winslow, Maine. He became High Sheriff in 1799 of Kennebec County, Maine and removed to Augusta, Maine, holding that office until 1809. He was a colonel in the Maine Militia and was a popular Sheriff, portly in person, hospitable and generous. He moved to Boston and was appointed to the office of Weightier and Measurer in the Custom House, which office he held until 1829. Col. Lithgow served in the Revolutionary War in General Joseph Lovell's Brigade from 4 July to 26 Sep. 1779. His Revolutionary War Pension number is W15341.

Colonel William Lithgow, Esq. (1715-1798) arrived at Merrymaking Bay on 6 Nov. 1722 and was a gunsmith and trader. He was one of three people who were appointed to receive applications for the settlement of the "Kennebunk Purchase" in May 1763. He was appointed Chief Judge of the Inferior Court for Lincoln County, Maine. Col. Lithgow served in the Revolutionary War in

1775, when he "collected a company which went to Portland [Maine], at the Lexington Alarm, under orders from Colonel Mitchell." He was commissioned Judge of the Court of Common Pleas in Lincoln County, Maine, in 1775 under the Revolutionary government.

Captain Charles Morris (1763-1838), son of Lt. Lemuel Morris, fought at the age of 16 and 17 with the Continental Army in the Revolutionary War, serving under General Marquis de La Fayette in Rhode Island. Captain Morris was taken prisoner and held on a prison ship in New York Harbor. He became half-owner of a vessel engaged in the West Indies trade after the war. Captain Morris served as Purser on the USS *Baltimore* under Captain Samuel Barron in the United States Navy in 1799 and was later assigned to the USS *Congress* until his discharge in 1801. His Revolutionary War Pension number is W9207 [BLWT. 26054-160-55].

Lieutenant Lemuel Morris (1737-1813) served in the Revolutionary War with the 2nd Company of the Militia, in the 5th Regiment of Connecticut under Captain Joseph Kimball, Jr., 1st Lt. Gideon Cornell and Ensign Jonathan Smith. Lemuel was appointed ensign on 14 May 1789 and lieutenant on 10 May 1792. He sold his farm on 17 Dec. 1798 to his brother-in-law, Ebenezer Lille, and relocated to the State of New York after the death of his wife. He made his home with his son Samuel, who had settled at Fly Creek, about six miles west of Coopertown, in Otsego county.

Captain Jonathan Nichols (1727-1814) was among the men responding to the Lexington Alarm. He served as a captain and assisted Lt. Colonel Storrs in exercising and training their regiment. Captain Nichols was appointed in April, 1777 to a committee to encourage enlistments, and to a committee in September to provide clothing for soldiers in the Continental Army. He joined the First Church of Christ in 1771 where his pew was number 27. His home was on the road from Mansfield to Ashford near the Mount Hope River. Captain Nichols resided with his son-in-law Billy Manning in Vermont until his death in 1814, at age eighty-seven.

Captain Elkanah Watson, Esq. (1732-1804) was a Revolutionary War patriot as described in the *Memoirs* of his son Elkanah: "My father and all my relatives, with a few exceptions, were zealous and active Whigs, aiding with their hands and purses the glorious struggle for Independence." He was chosen to serve on the Grand Jury on 24 Apr. 1780 and as Moderator *Pro Tem* for the Plymouth Town meeting of 3 July 1780. His name was included on 26 Nov. 1781 as one of the Classes of Inhabitants [of Plymouth] for the procurement of Revolutionary War soldiers.

David West (1737-1799) was bred a merchant in Boston under Melatiah Bourne Esq. He participated in the Revolution War as a private clerk or secretary to Brigadier General John Nixon. David continued in this capacity until the year 1778 when he entered the naval service on board the ship *Mifflin*, a privateer of 12 guns and died at sea aboard the *Mifflin* on 13 Jan. 1779.

Captain Benjamin Wilkinson (1713-1803) served in the Revolutionary War as noted in the *Records of Rhode Island*: "This Assembly taking into consideration a resolution of the Honorable the Continental Congress, of the 20th January last [i.e. 1776], for the procuring gold and silver coin, for the operations in Canada, -- Do vote and resolve, and it is voted and resolved, that the committee of safety, the commissary, Messrs. Benjamin Wilkinson (along with 49 others), be a committee, to procure as much gold and silver coin, as they can, for the use aforesaid." This resolution empowered the Committee of Safety to receive this money and pay it into the general treasury.

WEBB, WILLIAM STEPHEN JR. – Born in 1940 in Wheeling, WV. He presently resides in Bennington, NE.

Stephen was an Airman 1st Class with the Air Force, Air Defense. In civilian life he was the Administrator with Nebraska Department of Health and Human Services. He retired Jan. 1, 2008.

Stephen and wife Georgia have four children and 13 grandchildren.

Cornelius Atkinson, born about 1732 in Ireland, settled in Pennsylvania about 1750 among others of Scotch Irish decent. Cornelius and two sons, Charles and James, enlisted in the PA Militia, Northumberland County Associators, Jan. 14, 1776 and served until the end of the War. They served with several units as the enlistments were short in duration. First, they were members of the Pennsylvania Militia, 1st Company, 2nd Battalion of the Northumberland County Associators commanded by Colonel James Potter. Cornelius' rank was First Lieutenant. Cornelius, Charles and James served in the Sullivan's Campaign. They were engaged in guarding provisions going up the Susquehannah River with supplies for General Sullivan's army, engaged in destroying an Indian Company which was boating green corn up the Susquehanna from the Indian cornfields to their stockade at Tioga Point and in the expedition up the West branch of the Susquehanna River. Legend has Cornelius being wounded during this campaign. Later in the war his youngest son, William, joined Robinson Rangers, Pennsylvania Militia.

Gravestone of James Atkinson.

Cornelius lived his final days with his wife in Dauphin County, PA. Cornelius died April 1815. Both are buried in Halifax Township, Dauphin County, PA.

After the Revolution, Charles, James, William and two other brothers, Mitchell and Isaac immigrated to the North West Territory, Monroe County, OH to settle and make their home. Charles (1760-1834), James (1762-1845) and William (1764-1840) are buried in the Hartline Cemetery, Cameron, OH.

Gravestone of William Atkinson.

Gravestone of Charles Atkinson.

John Webb was born July 3, 1739 in Doulting, Somerset, England. He first settled in Cumberland, PA then moved to Hardy County, VA (now West Virginia). He immigrated to this country shortly before the Revolution. He assisted with this conflict by furnishing supplies to the Continental Army.

John died Nov. 25, 1807. He is buried in an unmarked grave near the house where he lived, located East of Moorefield, WV.

Charles Atkinson, born 1760 in Northumberland, PA. He enlisted in the PA Militia, Jan. 14, 1776 and served until the end of the conflict. His rank was Private. Charles served in the Sullivan campaign and was engaged in guarding provisions going up the Susquehannah River for General Sullivan's Army, engaged in destroying an Indian company which was boating green corn up the Susquehanna from their corn fields to their stockade at Tioga Point, and he was involved in an expedition up the West branch of the Susquehanna.

Gravestones of Charles and Elizabeth Atkinson

After the War, Charles continued serving with the military at Waynesburg, PA and Fort Henry, Wheeling, WV. About 1797 he and four brothers settled in the newly opened North West Territory at Monroe County, OH.

Charles lived his final days in Monroe County, OH. He died April 23, 1834, buried with his brothers James and William in the Hartline Cemetery at Cameron, OH.

WEE, JAMES JOHN – James John Wee was born Dec. 31, 1970 in Fontana, CA. He joined the SAR Redlands Chapter, CA in December 2007. He has one child.

Barnabas B. Haley, at the age of 17, enlisted in the US Continental Line Army, at the Charlotte Court House Va., serving under the Company commanded by Capt. John Brunt, 11th Regt. This was commanded by Col. David Morgan, Morgan's Rifle Regt. Within weeks Barnabas was marched directly to NY, on to Jersey and then very near Brandywine. Shortly afterwards he was transferred to Gen. George Washington's unit at Valley Forge, PA now served under Col. Lamb. He

James John Wee

Gravestone of Barnabas Haley.

received a written discharge in full of his term of enlistment from his Capt and signed by Col. Lamb. Barnabas received a Revolutionary War Pension for his military service.

WEE, STEVEN MICHAEL – Steven Michael Wee was born Dec. 25, 1971 in Fontana, CA. He joined the SAR Redlands Chapter, CA in December 2007.

Steven's military service was as a navy machinist, Mate 2nd Class aboard the USS *California* CGN-36. He has one child.

Steven Michael Wee

Barnabas B. Haley, at the age of 17, enlisted in the US Continental Line Army, at the Charlotte Court House Va., serving under the Company commanded by Capt. John Brunt, 11th Regt. This was commanded by Col. David Morgan, Morgan's Rifle Regt. Within weeks Barnabas was marched directly to NY, on to Jersey and then very near Brandywine. Shortly afterwards he was transferred to Gen. George Washington's unit at Valley Forge, PA now served under Col. Lamb. He received a written discharge in full of his term of enlistment from his Capt and signed by Col. Lamb. Barnabas received a Revolutionary War Pension for his military service.

Gravestone of Barnabas Haley.

WEED, JOHN L. "JACK" – John L. "Jack" Weed was born Nov. 6, 1959 in Middletown NY.

His military service was with the U.S. Navy 1979-1983, serving as Petty Officer 2nd Class. He is married to Jull Murtlow and they have two children. He works for the U.S. Postal Service as a Retail Window Clerk.

He is also involved with Little League Baseball, and is a member of Walker Valley Sportsman Association. In 2007, he co-authored a book with his cousin, James H. Wiseman, "From Northamptonshire to Walker Valley – A History and Genealogy of the Weed Family."

Nathan Bullard was born Jan 15, 1754 in Medfield, MA. He was a private in the 3rd Massachusetts Regiment. He was discharged from military service at New Windsor, NY by General George Washington. He was a farmer. He died Dec. 25, 1836 and is buried in Monticello, NY.

WEIDEMEYER, CARLETON LLOYD – Carleton Lloyd Weidemeyer was born June 12, 1933 in Maryland. He is an attorney and a musician. He has been admitted to the Bar in Florida and Washington, D.C. He served with Hurricane Tracking Squadrons in the U.S. Navy during the Korean War. He gives lectures on Genealogy and History. His memberships include Fleet Reserve, American Legion, VAV, Sertoma, Scottish Rite, Shrine, American Federation of Musicians and Sons of Union Veterans of the Civil War. He is a board member of several charities.

Carleton Lloyd Weidemeyer

Carleton resides in Clearwater, FL with his wife, Diane Draper Weidemeyer. They have four children and eleven grandchildren.

Henry Greninger Sr. was born October 1757 in Germany. He immigrated to Pennsylvania as a child and married Anna Maria Zartman of Warwick, PA. He served during the Revolution with his father-in-law, Jacob Zartman. Henry had three enlistments, the first of which was under Captain Benjamin Weiser for two months in Germantown and Philadelphia in the winter of 1777. The second was with Captain Adam Shaefer protecting settlers from the Indians on the Susquehanna River for six months in 1778. His last enlistment in July 1779 was also for six months on the "Western Frontier" near Sunbury.

Henry and Anna Marie had nine children and the descendants now number in the hundreds. Henry died Sept. 11, 1833 and is buried in Tylersville, PA.

WENZEL, ALLAN – Born Dec. 28, 1946 in Seattle, WA. Allan retired Jan. 25, 2002 from The Boeing Company; Factory Manufacturing Engineer.

Allen also belongs to the Sons of the Union Veterans of the Civil War, Order of the First Families of Maryland, Orders and Medals Society of America. He has compiled and written 13 genealogy books, four being published, chapters of several history books, and numerous magazine articles.

John Van Cleave was born in 1739 in Middlesex County, NJ. John served as a Private with Captain Chenoweth in the Jefferson County Kentucky Territory of Virginia Militia. He was at the Siege of Fort Booneboro, Long Run Massacre.

John was a farmer in Kentucky and Indiana, 1775-1812. He died May 12, 1812 and is buried at the Ryker Family Cemetery, Ryker's Ridge, Madison, Jefferson County, IN.

WESTLAKE, JAMES ROGER – Born Feb. 11, 1928 in Kansas City, MO; died in Covington, GA on March 25, 2008 was a member of GA State Society of SAR. James and wife Joyce C. had four children, nine grandchildren and 11 great-grandchildren.

James R. Westlake, 1989, President General National Society SAR

James served in the US Navy, WWII, Pacific Theater, 1945-46. He was Deputy Administrator of US Environmental Protection Agency, 1971-1975; Deputy Secretary of US Department of Commerce, 1976-1981; Deputy Administrator of US Economic Development Administration, 1981-1995; retiring in 1995.

James was a member of the Georgia State House of Representative, 1965-1971; an Elder, Trinity Presbyterian Church, PCA of Covington, GA; President of National Society of Washington Family Descendants; Commandant of Old Guard of the Gate City Guard of Atlanta; Chairman of the Board of Atlanta University of Biblical Studies; President of Georgia State University Alumni Association, 1961-62; Member of Georgia Historical Trust; Sons of the Confederacy; and Sigma Chi, University of Missouri Chapter.

James held the President General National Society, 1989-90; President Georgia Society and President Atlanta Chapter. He received the following awards: 1975 – War Service Medal WWII; 1975 – Bronze Good Citizenship Medal; 1976 – Silver Good Citizenship Medal; 1976 – Law Enforcement Medal; 1983 – Patriot Medal; 1986 – Britain Special Congress Medal; 1989 – Minuteman Medal; 1989 – SAR Centennial Medal; 1990 – France Special Congress Medal; 1990 – Former President General Medal; 1992 – Meritorious Service Medal; 1993 – Liberty Medal; 1993 – Commendable Service Medal; 1993 – Stephen Taylor Aware; 2000 – Bronze Color

Guard Award; and 2006 – Silver Color Guard Award.

Joseph Dameron Jr. was born Feb. 2, 1763 in Northumberland County, VA. He was the manager of his father's plantation in Amelia County, VA.

Joseph was drafted September 1780 in the Amelia Co., VA Militia, Capt. Rbt. Mumford's Company, Col. Wm. Downman's Regiment, General Nathaniel Greene's Army; served three months from Cabin Point to Petersburg, VA.

In January 1781, he volunteered with Capt. Rbt. Bolling's Company, VA Militia, answering the general alarm for defense of Petersburg, VA; served three weeks.

In February 1781, he volunteered with the Brunswick Co., VA Militia, Capt. Wm. Harrison's Company, Col. Rbt. Mumford's Regiment, General Nathaniel Greene's Army; was at the battle of Guildford County Courthouse on March 15, 1781 and served three months. He was discharged May 1781.

Joseph died about 1837 and is buried in Caswell County, NC.

WESTON, BRIAN A. – Born in 1960 in Evanston, IL; resides in Grand Rapids, MI. Brian joined Michigan State Society in February of 2007. Brian is married to Julie Ann (Barnes) Weston. He is a bookseller and writer.

Brian A. Weston

Joseph Weston (1760-1840) is my 4th great grandfather. He was a soldier in the Revolutionary War. Joseph was born March 27, 1760 in Gorham, ME. He was the second of five children born to Joseph and Catherine (Mosher) Weston, likewise of Gorham, ME.

On Feb. 14, 1777, Joseph formerly enlisted as a private under the command of Capt. George Smith of Falmouth, ME. His company eventually became part of the 2nd MA Brigade, 1st MA Regiment commanded by Col. Joseph Vose, Gen. Glover's Brigade. According to an affidavit for assistance submitted in 1818 he was at the taking of Burgoyne, wintered at Valley Forge, saw action at Monmouth and was present at the siege of Rhode Island. He was discharged in January 1780 near West Pointe, NY.

He also served a three month enlistment in Lieutenant William Bird's Co., Col. Thayer's Regiment, July 19, 1780, dis. Oct. 10, 1780. It is also stated that he was a prisoner of the British from which he later escaped.

I am proud to have been the first to have claimed him for the SAR Register. Joseph Weston passed away on Jan. 29, 1840 and is buried at Bell Hill Cemetery in Otisfield, ME.

WHITE, DR. JOHN O. – (PhD from Arizona State University, 1971) is Professor of English at California State University, Fullerton. He is married to Hilary, and has one son, Thomas, age 16.

Dr. John O. White

John served as a Sergeant in the USMC Reserve from 1961 – 1967. He also belongs to the Sons of the Revolution, Sons of Confederate Veterans and Military Order of Stars and Bars.

His great-great grandfather, **John White** (1764-1849) was born in Caroline County, VA, where his father was a tobacco farmer. John White served as a young private in the Virginia Cavalry during the Revolutionary War. His uncle Francis White helped supply provisions for the army. John White entered service in about 1880 with Colonel George Baylor's Regiment. That regiment was later commanded by William Washington and saw considerable action in the South. He was discharged on July 7, 1783, with a stipend of 39 pounds, eleven shillings, and eight pence.

Gravestone of John White.

After the war, John married a Ms. Tompkins, and had one son. In 1799 he married Elizabeth Estes, the daughter of a prominent family in Caroline County. They had nine children, including my great-grandfather Robert White, born Feb. 22, 1805. John and Elizabeth and family moved to Kentucky in 1806, and on to Obion County, TN in the 1820's where they had a large plantation. John White died in 1849 and is buried in Union City, TN.

WHITE, WILLIAM G. – Born May 7, 1964, Camden, NJ. Joined the US Army in January 1982 as a high school senior and attended basic training at Fort Leonard Wood, MO in July 1982. Following AIT he was stationed from October 1982-December 1983 at Fort Riley, KS, with the 509th Engr. Co.

William G. White

From January 1983-October 1989 he was assign to the 814th Engr. Co. in Hanau West Germany. Before ending his tour in Germany, he enlisted in the PA National Guard. He was assign to the 103rd Engr. Bn. In 2002, Bill was activated and sent to Bosnia with SFOR-12 and Joint Military Affairs. He assisted in de-mining efforts from August 2002 - April 2003.

After returning from Bosnia, Sgt. White retired in October 2003 with more than 21 years of military service. Medals he received were: Army Commendation, Army Achievement, Good Conduct, Expeditionary, National Defense, Army Reserve Achievement, Overseas, Armed Forces Reserve, NCO, and NATO medals.

He now resides in Deptford, NJ and works growing a family owned commercial building maintenance company. Bill married MaryBeth Pilarchik, his high school sweetheart, on Jan. 29, 1983 and has three sons: William Jr., Wesleigh and Zackerie. Bill was admitted into the National SAR (No. 168346) and the NJ State SAR Society on Jan. 22, 2007.

Ichabod Tilson was born April 25, 1750, Plymouth, MA. Enlisted as a drummer in Captain John Bridgham's Co. on May 3, 1775. They marched on the alarm of April 19, 1775 to Marshfield and returned by order of Col. Theophilus Cotton's Regt.; muster roll dated Aug. 1, 1775. Served 3 month, 6 days; Rank Pvt. Re-enlisted for one year in Col. Bailey's Reg in 1776. He married Azuba Thomas on Dec. 24, 1778. Ichabod died in 1822.

WHITFIELD, DAVID LEWIS – Born March 1937 in Vincennes, IN, resides in Chesterfield, MO. David Joined SAR in 1999 - Spirit of St. Louis Chapter – MOSSAR.

David has held the office of Awards Chairman and has earned the Bronze Good Citizenship Medal with cluster and Certificate of Distinguished Service.

David served in the United States Army Reserve, 1960 to 1966. He and spouse Rosalie Ann Whitfield have four children, Mark, Scott, Kathleen, Patrick; and six grandchildren, Savannah, Melissa, Jeff, Cody, Jake, Makenzie. David has been a Retired Architect since 2003.

Other organizations David belongs to are: American Institute of Architects; Architectural Review Board, City of Chesterfield, MO; American Red Cross, First Families of Tennessee; Memory and Aging Project, Washington University School of Medicine.

William Whitfield II, born May 20, 1715, Chowan County, NC; married Nov. 6, 1741 to Rachel Bryan. William joined the North Carolina Militia in 1755 as Captain, and served during the Revolutionary War on Governor's Council. William III, Needman and Bryan, Whitfield II's sons, also served in the Revolutionary War as did his oldest grandson, William Whitfield IV.

In civilian life, he was a mason, businessman and civic leader. William died March 31, 1795 and is buried at the family cemetery, Seven Springs, Wayne County, NC.

WHITTEN, SAMUEL JACKSON JR. – Sam was born Jan. 11, 1940 in Troup, TX. Received his B.B.A. from North Texas State University. Served six years in the USAF Reserves. Married to Karen (Kesler) Whitten since 1962. They have three children and three grandchildren. Retired from AXA Advisors LLC in 2004 after

35 years service. Admitted to the company Hall of Fame in 1985.

Samuel Jackson Whitten, Jr.

Member of the Texas Society Athens Chapter since 1995. Served as Chapter President twice. Currently serves as Secretary/Treasurer. Served as Texas Society Poster and Essay Chairman, Reports Coordinator for NSSAR Competition, and District 10 Vice-President. Received the Meritorious Service, Patriot and Silver Good Citizenship Medals.

Serves as Membership Director/Secretary of the East Texas Arboretum & Botanical Society and President of the Lake Athens Property Owners Association. Served on the First United Methodist Church Athens Finance Committee. Currently serves on the Usher, Greeting and Communion Committees. Member of the Sons of the Republic of Texas and the Dallas Genealogical Society.

Of his 14 patriot ancestors, Sam is descended from Lieutenant **Reece Bowen**, Continental Army Virginia, who fought at Point Pleasant and was killed at the Battle of King's Mountain.

WILCOX, BRUCE A. – Bruce Wilcox graduated from the U.S. Naval Academy in 1958 and was commissioned a Naval Aviator. After his retirement from the Navy in 1978 he served as a Defense Consultant from which he retired in April 2006.

Bruce A. Wilcox

He has been a member of the Sons of the American Revolution since 1982. At the National level he has served at Trustee, Librarian General (three terms), Historian General (two terms), Registrar General, Treasurer General, Secretary General, and as President General. His awards include the Gold Good Citizen, Minuteman Award, Distinguished Service Medal, War Service Medal, Patriot Medal, Meritorious Service Medal (three awards), Silver Good Citizenship Medal (two awards), Virginia Medal (three awards), and Bronze Good Citizenship Medal.

He and his wife of 50 years, Theresa, live in Alexandria, VA. They have three children and eight grandchildren.

Robert Hedges was born June 4, 1760 in Prince William County, VA. His father was Capt. John Hedges, a Revolutionary War Patriot. He enlisted in 1776 in the Virginia Militia and served first as a clerk to the commissaries and paymaster. His unit, under the command of Generals Burr Harrison, Joseph Newell, and John Newell marched and traveled by boat in October 1776 from Dumfries, VA to Point Pleasant where they engaged in several Indian skirmishes. In mid-1777, he reenlisted and served five months as a cadet in his father's company in Colonel Jesse Ewell's regiment. From the spring of 1778 to 1781, he was a guard at strategic Potomac River points. In 1781 he enlisted again as a sergeant and quartermaster in Capt. Robert Bowling's Company of Colonel D. Coll's Cavalry Regiment. During this six-month period he saw action at the Battle of Petersburg and the Siege of Yorktown. Robert Hedges died in 1848 and is buried near Shelbyville, KY. Capt. John Hedges died in 1804 and is buried at the family farm near Quantico, VA.

Daniel Fitzgerald was born 1757 in Orange County, VA and died in 1834 in Franklin County, KY. He first enlisted in June 1779 as wagon driver and guard. Reenlisted twice. Served in campaigns in Philadelphia, New Jersey, Stony Point, New York, New England, Richmond and Yorktown. Served under Captain James Finley, Colonel Mathews' Regiment of the Virginia Line, Captain Quailly, and Major Well's battalion in Colonel Cole's Regiment.

WILLIAMS, DR. BENJAMIN BUFORD – Born on April 28, 1923. He graduated from Murphy High School in Mobile, AL in 1942. He served on active duty in the U.S. Army from Feb. 1, 1943 to Feb. 11, 1946, with 16 months in the European Theater with the 78th Infantry Division, including the Battle of the Bulge, the Remagen Bridgehead, and the Ruhr Pocket. He joined the Army reserve in 1946, and was commissioned in the Air Force Reserve in 1948. With 35 years active and reserve service, he retired as a Colonel in 1978.

Dr. Benjamin Burford Williams at the re-marking of grave of Simeon Buford.

He graduated from the University of Alabama, BA (1948) and MA (1950), and received the Ph.D. from Vanderbilt University. Over 40 years he served on the faculties of Martin College, TN, the University of Alabama, and Auburn University Montgomery. Among his publications is *A Literary History of Alabama*. He is a member of the General Richard Montgomery Chapter, SAR, and has served as president. He is Professor Emeritus from Auburn University, and a member of several honor societies and veterans organizations.

He is married to the former Marilyn Simpson of Nashville, TN. They are the parents of Julianne Moores Sinclair, Benjamin Buford Williams III, Randall Simpson Williams, and Marilyn MacCallum Best.

The graves of Simeon Buford and his wife Margaret Kirtley Buford in the family plot outside of Glasgow, KY on the land he once owned. Marked with SAR Ceremony in 2000.

Simeon Buford was born in Culpeper County, VA, Dec. 19, 1756 and died in July 1835 in Barren County, KY. In 1775 he enlisted as a minuteman in the company of his older brother, Captain (later Colonel) Abraham Buford, and joined other Virginia troops in driving governor Lord Dunmore out of the colony at the Battle of Great Bridge. In 1776 he served again under Captain McClanahan, and in 1777 under Captain Chapman. In 1781 he became an Ensign in Captain Elijah Kirtley's Continental company under General Lafayette. He served for two months as Lafayette's quartermaster, and in July replaced Kirtley as company commander when he became ill. In his pension letter in 1833, Simeon wrote: "that he was with Lafayette the whole time he was combatting Cornwallis." He remained in service through the Yorktown campaign. In his pension letter he said that he had served eleven months as a Virginia minuteman and eight months as an Ensign and Captain as a Continental. He married Margaret Kirtley in 1777, and moved from Virginia to Kentucky in 1789 with his wife and four children. He bought 255 acres in Woodford County about 12 miles west of Lexington. In July 1798 he traded his horse farm "Fairview" for 1200 acres on Beaver Creek in Barren County, KY, where he lived until his death in 1835. He became a large landholder and represented Barren County in the Kentucky legislature.

WILLIS, JAMES E. – James was born Feb. 25, 1936 in San Angel, TX. He joined the SAR in Texas Sept. 5, 2008. He serves as the Sec.-Treas. of the Daniel Wood Chapter.

His military service was with the U.S. Air Force, Strategic Air Command as 1st Lieutenant.

James retired from the Texas Railroad Commission on Sept. 30, 1993, serving as a rate analyst, auditor and district supervisor.

He is also a member of American Legion; General Society of the War of 1812; Society of the Descendants of Washington's Army at Valley Forge; and Sons of Union Veterans of the Civil War.

James was married to Diana Moritz Willis, who is now deceased. They had no children. He is the twin brother of Rev. Lewis E. Willis of Duncanville, TX, also a member of SAR.

Robert Willis was born about 1750 in Scotland. He served in the Westmoreland County Pennslyvania Militia as a private. Robert was a farmer and a tavern keeper. He died March 13, 1830 and is buried in Crab Orchard Cemetery, Belmont County, OH.

WILLIS, REV. LEWIS EUGENE – Rev. Lewis was born Feb. 25, 1936 in San Angel, TX in Tom Green County. He joined the SAR in Texas Sept. 18, 2006.

His active military duty was with the U.S. Army, Ameds Co. BGH/ Sp 4. His Reserves duty is the U.S. Army 4161st ARSU Austin USAR School as 1st Lieutenant.

Rev. Lewis was ordained a Presbyterian Minister on Jan. 3, 2001.

He is also a member of Society of the Descendants of Washington's Army at Valley Forge; The General Society of the War of 1812; The Sons of Union Veterans of the Civil War; and the First Families of Ohio.

Rev. Lewis is married to Nina Joan Young, and they have two children and three grandchildren.

Robert Willis was born about 1750 in Scotland. He served in the Westmoreland County Pennslyvania Militia as a private. Robert was a farmer and a tavern keeper. He died March 13, 1830 and is buried in Crab Orchard Cemetery, Belmont County, OH.

John Stanclift was born Sept. 26, 1754 in East Middletown, CT. He was a farmer.

His military service was as a private with the 4th Conn. Regt., Capt Shubael Griswoldin's Co. in 1775; as a private in Col. Charles Burrall's Continental Regt., 3rd Co. (Capt. Aaron Austin) in 1776; and as a private in 5th Conn. Regt., Capt. Joseph Allen Wright's Co. in 1776.

John's military experience included the capture of Ft. St. John in Lower Canada in 1775; and the Battle of Georgetown as part of Washington's Army and its retreat and establishment of winter quarters at Valley Forge in 1777 and 1778.

John died Dec. 20, 1847 in North Collins, Erie Co., NY. He is buried at the Congregational Church Cemetery in North Collins, NY. The exact location of his grave has been lost.

WILLS, THOMAS STANLEY – Born March 1950 in Grand Prairie, TX; resides in Sprague, WA. Thomas joined the Washington State Society on Mar. 1, 2006 and was President, Spokane, WA Chapter No. 1. He has received the Military Service Award.

Thomas served in the USN – Submarines (20 years) as Senior Chief (E-8). He retired in August 1988. He married Beverly Jane Cookson and they have one child and one grandchild. Thomas is presently a farmer/rancher.

Thomas also belongs to F.T.R.A. (Former Texas Ranger Association) and S.R.T. (Sons of the Republic of Texas).

Enoch Furr was born 1752 in Faquier County, VA. He was the son of William Furr and Charity Bates. He married Sarah Clawson, March 5, 1787 in Loudoun County, VA and had nine children from this union. A daughter, Charity, marries Benjamin E. Wills, my descendant. This Furr line is of French descent. Per Enoch's pension file no. w11030 he enlisted in November 1775 as a private in the "Minute Men Company" raised by Captain George Johnson. On Dec. 9, 1775, he was in the Battle of Great Bridge attached to Colonel Spotswood's regiment He was later at the burning of Norfolk by Lord Dunmore. He continued in scouting parties for 12 months. In September, 1777 he served for three months as a substitute for his brother Moses Furr. In June 1781 he was appointed as Lieutenant of the Loudoun County, VA Militia. Enoch died April 3, 1845 at the age of 93. Despite having never learned to read or write, he became a large Virginia landowner with an estate valued at $25,000 when he died.

Thomas Crandall Wills was born Sept. 22, 1765 in Anne Arundel, MD. He was the son of Benjamin Willis, a blacksmith, and Sarah Crandall. He served in the Revolutionary War at Annapolis, MD. He was summoned to the militia at Fort Washington, MD in 1780. At this time the British had a blockade on Annapolis. He was there during the burning of the Stephen Steward Shipyard in 1781. He remained at Fort Washington until the end of the war, obtaining a rank of sergeant. He was housed in the State House used as a barracks. He was at the State House when George Washington resigned his commission as Commanding General of the Army. His brother, John Wills, and step-brother, William Crandall, also served near Annapolis. He married Sarah Ann Wall in Prince George County, MD, on May 26, 1787. They were blessed with three children: Benjamin, b. 1787; Ann, b. 1799; and Elizabeth, b. 1801. Thomas and Sarah lived in Montgomery County, MD until they moved to Virginia in 1799. Thomas was a blacksmith in Loudon County, VA. They moved to Henry County, TN in 1826 along with their daughter, Ann, and her husband, Osborn Beaty. Thomas applied for and received his pension in 1832 (S3561). Thomas died 1834 and Sarah 1831 in Henry County, TN.

WINKLER, RALPH EUGENE – Born Feb. 3, 1927 in Elkville, IL, and is married to Margaret M. Novaria. He has a daughter, Esther M. Milligan, and a granddaughter, Michele M. Milligan.

He is a descendant of **Gasper Butcher**, a member of Col. George Rogers Clark's Illinois Regiment of Virginia.

Ralph Winkler graduated from the University of Illinois with a B.S. in Management in 1950. He retired as a regular Air Force major in 1970, after spending most of his service in the Office of Special Investigations (OSI), where he received the AF Meritorious Service Medal.

Maj. Ralph E. Winkler, USAF, Ret., and Margaret M. Winkler, July 22, 1994, at Hotel del Coronado, near San Diego, CA, on the occasion of the 100th anniversary banquet of the San Diego Chapter of the SAR.

Winkler was chairman of N.O.S.I. in 1977-79, an organization he founded to oppose the surrender of the Panama Canal. The name "N.O.S.I." was derived from the movement's slogan, "Not One Square Inch!"

He was an elected member of the Orange County, CA Republican Central Committee during 1977-83. Winkler was a candidate for California secretary of state in the 1986 primary election. He came in second among three candidates, with almost a half million votes, and out-polled his major opponent in 24 of the 58 counties of California.

He has been an apartment building investor since 1956, and acquired a California. real estate broker license in 1978.

Winkler is a member of 17 historical, genealogical, and veterans organizations including the Military Order of the Loyal Legion of the United States and Sons of Union Veterans of the Civil War. He became a member of the San Diego, CA Chapter of the S.A.R. in 1985.

WINSLOW, JOHN PHINEAS – John Phineas Winslow was born May 4, 1884 at Formoso, Jewell County, KS. He died April 5, 1973 at the Veterans Hospital, Grand Island, Hall County, NE. He married Margaretta Cecelind Shenberger on Dec. 30, 1919 at Enola, PA. John and Margaretta had four children: Leah, Clara, Edith and Glen.

John Phineas Winslow, b. May 04, 1884, d. Apr 05, 1973.

John was an active member of the Nebraska State SAR Society. State number: 812; National number: 82811. He joined the U.W. Army because of World War I. He entered the U.S. Army at Beatrice, NE on July 15, 1917 and was discharged as a private at Raritan Arsenal, Metuchen, NJ on March 8, 1919. He was with the Infantry during the European War. John retired from the Naval Ammunition Depot, Hastings, NE on June 14, 1954.

Samuel Winslow was born in Epping, Rockingham County, NH on July 28, 1775. He married Anna Ladd on May 4, 1778. They had ten children: Elisha, Jane, Anna, Eisha, Abigail, Sarah, Samuel, Betsey, Mary and Martha.

Samuel volunteered as a private for six months in July 1775 with Col John Stark. He was ordered to Winter Hill and remained there until the enlistment expired in January 1776. In February 1776 he enlisted again for two months with Stark Militia as a corporal. He was ordered in May to Charlestown, NH and stationed there when his service expired May 1776.

Samuel volunteered again in July 1776 as a

private in the New Hampshire Militia for five months. He was ordered to Ticonderoga and marched directly to Charleston. He crossed the Connecticut River at Charleston and marched to Greensboro, where he took a boat to Ticonderoga. He was at Mount Independence until his discharge in December 1776.

Samuel Winslow, b. Jul 28, 1755, d. Mar 12, 1850.

Samuel enlisted in July 1777 for two months as the orderly sergeant with General John Stark. He marched to Charleston for rations and then directed their march to Bennington. He stayed at the barn of Lt. Floyd until he fought in the Battle of Bennington. He returned to the barn and stayed there until he was discharged in September 1777.

Samuel Died March 12, 1850 at Sutton, Caledonia County, VT and is buried at South Ridge Cemetery, Caledonia County, VT.

Submitted by Stephen Seachord, grandson.

WOOD, JAMES H. – Born Dec. 19, 1944 in Memphis, TN; presently residing in Charlotte, NC.

James joined the SAR in 2006, Mecklenburg Chapter. North Carolina State Society He has held SAR offices of Mecklenburg Chapter Secretary and Color Guard.

James is a Retired Colonel of the US Army Reserves. He and spouse Shelia F. have two daughters.

James H. Wood

Jim Wood is the Chief Information and Administrative Officer at Forest2Market, Inc. in Charlotte, NC. He is an information systems expert who had spent more than 30 years using information and technology to solve business problems for several multinational companies. Wood was influential in developing the strategy for the F2M online pricing component which is offered on the F2M web site. The web site earned the prestigious IBM Beacon Award for Best E-Business Solutions of the Year in 2001. His accomplishments at a large consumer good company were featured in a 1998 Harvard Business School case study. He received his bachelor's degree, magna cum laude, in accounting from Midwestern State University and a MBA degree from the University of Arkansas. He is an Eagle Scout and holds the God and Country Award.

Rev. Henry Wood was born Dec. 16, 1756 in Butte (now Warren) County, NC; died June 12, 1843 in Spartanburg County, SC. He married Susan Elizabeth Mayfield in July 1777 and then married Nancy Burns.

Henry served in the North Carolina Militia under General Thomas Eaton and Captain Henry Sullivan Guinn and Colonel Herbert Haynes. He was called to serve on March 1, 1781 and with his unit marched to High Rock Ford on the Haw River. Here Henry requested permission to joint the Light Infantry commanded by Captain White, with whom he had served under in a previous tour. With this infantry unit, he marched to Guilford Courthouse and was in this engagement. Henry Wood was in the first line of defense at the Battle of Guilford Courthouse. Following the Revolutionary War, he moved to South Carolina where he started a Methodist Meeting House which today is known as Woods Chapel United Methodist Church. At his death in 1843, the Greenville Mountain Times noted in his obituary "Rev Henry Wood espoused the cause of liberty, was a local preacher of the Methodist Church for the last 50 years and left a large circle of relatives and friends." He is buried in the front lawn of the church that carried his name.

WOOD, TERRY J. – Terry J. Wood is a native of the Ozarks region of Southwest, Missouri. He is a veteran school teacher with the Marshfield R-I Schools. He is also a former professional musician, who played with both Nashville, TN and Branson, MO show bands. He still writes and records music with area singers and musical groups. Organizational memberships and awards include: The Missouri State Teachers Association, The Aspiring Missouri Elementary Principals Association, and The National Art Educators Association. Awards include being a three time recipient of The Who's Who of American Universities and Colleges, lifetime member of Alpha Lambda Sigma National Honors Society and graduating with Summa Cum Laude honors from Drury University. Terry has a Bachelor of Science Degree in both Studio Arts and Art History, a Masters in Education and a Masters Degree with emphasis in Elementary Administration. Terry is married to Lisa Ann Vo Wood. Their three children are Amy, Jackie and Zane. Terry actively participates in the church they attend as Sunday School Teacher and as the Youth Minister.

Terry J. Wood

Nathaniel Holman was born March 13, 1735 at St. James Parish, Goochland, VA. Nathaniel was commissioned a 1st Lieutenant with the with the Virginia militia and aided in the Colonist fight for independence. It has been documented that he also gave aid with vast amounts of food and supplies to aid the Continental Army. He participated with one of the three brigades of Virginia militia under General George Washington's command at the Battle of Yorktown, VA during the fall of 1781. He was present when Lieutenant General Lord Cornwallis surrendered to General Washington's command after the Battle of Yorktown. Nathaniel Holman and his wife Ann Winn lived out their lives in Virginia and they had eleven children. Her family had helped with the Continental independence too. Nathaniel died Feb. 7, 1804 and was buried on the plantation farm they owned near present day Richmond, VA. I am very proud of my 4th great grandparents, Nathaniel Holman and his wife Ann Winn Holman.

WOODEN, GARY STEVEN – Born July 1953 in Alton, IL, currently resides in Lennon, MI. Gary joined the MI State Society in 2006. He has served as State Treasurer Michigan Society, SAR and as a George Washington Fellow.

Gary is Vice President at Morgan Stanley. He and wife Sharon L. have three children and two grandchildren.

Gary is also a member of General Society of the War of 182 and member of the Sons of Union Veterans of the Civil War.

Frederick Sever was born December of 1734 in Fredericksburg, MD. He died in April of 1804 in Muhlenberg County, KY. He was married to Caterina Rhoads, the sister of Henry Rhoads Jr. who later became the founder of Muhlenberg County, KY. Frederick's occupation was a machinist and he worked on the wheels, axles and turning gears of wagons.

Frederick served as a private in Captain Tom Paxton's company of the Bedford County, PA militia. He participated in the fighting around Perth Amboy and was also in the ill-fated Canadian invasion attempt with Benedict Arnold where he was wounded in the thigh. He lost a couple fingers and toes to frostbite on the way back.

Frederick was also in the battle of Brandywine. In a family bible owned by his descendants there were pages torn out with a note written by Henry Rhoads Jr. which said, "Have arrived this day at Brandywine and a battle is to be fought. We have been issued bread and beer. General Washington gave us a cheer and as he rode by Frederick and Daniel (Rhoads) touched his boot. We have been issued shot and powder but no wadding and have turned to using your sacred book for same. We beseech you our Dear Lord to forgive us this sacrilege." The passage was signed by Henry Rhoads Jr., Peter Rhoads and marked with an X by the names of Frederick Sever, Daniel Rhoads and Conrad Meiner.

In 1797 Frederick and two of his sons, Michael and Jacob, went to Kentucky to claim land on the Green River he had been given for his military service in what would later become Muhlenberg County, KY.

WOODS, WELTON DEWAYNE – Welton was born in 1934 in Caroway, AR and presently lives in Jonesburg, MO.

Welton served in the USAF, Security as an E4. He worked for (McDonnell Douglas) Boeing and retired in 1993.

Welton and Ruth Ann (Moore) Woods have three children and eight grandchildren.

He also belongs to the American Legion Post 122, Warrenton, MO and is a member of Jonesburg Baptist Church, serving as Trustee.

Pvt. William Underwood, alias William

Wedgbare, was a Revolutionary War soldier, Service Number, 2292.

Welton Woods

William was born in 1759 in Virginia. He enlisted in the Virginia Continental Establishment for the war. On the 19th of March 1780 for the war in the county of Culpeper. He was inspected at the Cumberland Courthouse and received by, Baron Stueben. He continued to serve faithfully in the Continental Army, as a soldier on various skirmishes, under the command of Baron Stueben in the First Regiment of Virginia Regulars commanded by, Colonel Posey, Major Finley and Captain Shelton's Company. Always in service, he was at the siege of Yorktown, where Lord Cornwallis surrendered. Then fell under the command of General Wayne and was marched South. Was at the evacuation of Charleston and also at Savannah. He continued in service until discharged. He was married three times and had 12 children by first wife, Mary Eastridge. I am descendent of their first son, Jesse Underwood. He had four children by each of his last two wives, for a total of 20 children. His descendents have served during every war since.

WOOTEN, TRAVIS AARON – Was born in Logan County, WV on Aug. 1, 1986 to Danice Lilly Bragg and George Fred Wooten Sr. His full siblings are George Fred Wooten Jr. and Daniel Elizabeth Justice. He spent his childhood in Clearfork, WV in Wyoming County. In High School, he was the President of the Wyoming County Youth Council and the STOP board, an anti-drug coalition. In his senior year he became a chairman for the Gold Senate Committee at Youth In Government.

Travis A. Wooten

He attended WVU in Morgantown for a year as a major in Education with a specialty in History. His second year of college has been spent at WVU Tech in Montgomery, WV as a major in History and Government.

He joined the Sons of the American Revolution in order to become closer to, and honor, both my family history as well as American History. His personal interests include collecting both rare and classical books, and reading and studying Theology as well as studying ancient cultures.

He feels to understand where we are we must firstly know the road we have traveled. Currently he works as a Residential Assistant for West Virginia University.

Mitchell Clay was married to Phoebe Belcher in Bedford County, VA in 1760.

Mitchell drew the land in then, Fincastle County, VA, for services rendered as a soldier in the French and Indian war, which began in 1754. Mitchell Clay had 1000 acres, both sides Bluestone Creek.

"Torment In Stone", Mitchell and Phoebe Clay

Mitchell Clay, April 1774, obtained a crown grant from Lord Dunmore, Royal Governor of Virginia, for 803 acres also both sides of Bluestone Creek, a branch of New River, and called Clover Bottom.

At Point Pleasant, Mitchell Clay was a soldier in the army of General Andrew Lewis, at the Battle of Point Pleasant, Oct. 10, 1774.

He was the first white settler in Monroe County. A statue representing Mitchell and Phoebe (Belcher) Clay stands on the lawn of the courthouse at Princeton, Mercer County, WV. The statue is named "Torment in Stone." It represents Mitchell Clay and his wife in a time of agony for the death of their children in 1783.

In August of 1785 there occurred the famous Shawnee Massacre, in which two of his children, Bartley and Tabitha, were killed, and a third, Ezekiel, carried captive to Chillicothe, and burned at the stake.

YATES, CHARLES C. – Lt. Col. USAF (Ret.), was born in Rutherford, TN and now resides in Benton, LA. He has a BA degree from Louisiana and MEd from LSU at Monroe.

Charles has held the office of President of Shelby Chapter and President of Memphis Chapter (not Isaac Shelby) Vice president of Tennessee Society. He has received the Patriot Medal.

Charles spent three years in the Army as a Cryptographer and 24 years in the Air Force as a Navigator, Radar Observer and Pilot.

He and wife Janice have six children and 10 grandchildren. Charles was a High School teacher, counselor and principal at Germantown High School, Germantown, TN. He retired: June 1, 1993.

Charles also belongs to the Sons of Union Veterans of the Civil War, Order of Indian Wars of the United States, and Order of Daedalians.

David Crockett was perhaps born in Frederick County, VA. As a civilian, David Crockett participated in the organization of the first free, independent, democratic form of self-government on the North American Continent by the Watauga Assoc., formed in the vicinity of what is now North Carolina, Virginia and Tennessee.

David was killed in the summer of 1777 by the Creek Indians under the leadership of one called "Dragging Canoe." He is buried at Rogersville, TN.

YORK, DARRELL L. SR. – Born at Valley Mills, Bosque County, TX; married to Ila Jo (Huffman); children (Carolyn Sue, Darrell L. Jr., Rhonda Kay and Clint Woodrow).

Darrell graduated from Valley Mills High School in 1950. Graduated from Radar Gun Fire Control School, US Navy Training Center, Bainbridge, MD (November 1953); Technical FAA training, Oklahoma City, OK.

He served with the US Navy (1951-1959) having served on destroyers *USS Wadleigh (DD689)* and *USS Hank (DD702)*; received the Good Conduct Medal.

Darrell was employed in Aircraft Installation and Repair, James Connally Air Force Base (1955-1957); Electronic Technician, FAA (1957-1985); Sears Electronic Technician (1986-1988); Assistant Engineer, Baylor University Telecommunications Department (1988-1996) all of Waco, TX.

Darrell has served as Youth Sunday School teacher at Meadowbrook Baptist Church in Robinson, TX for several years; is a member of the School Board, Robinson, TX (six years); VFW and American Legion; Secretary/treasurer of Waco Chapter No. 32 of TXSSAR (2006-2007).

His interests include American and Texas history, family genealogy, fishing, all sports involving young people having served as a Coach and Manager in Little League baseball and President, Teenage Baseball League.

Walter Slaughter was born around 1760 in Lunenburg County, VA; a private, Captain Thomas Wade's Light Horse Company, involved with the Battle of Cross Creek, Cumberland County, NC. Died circa 1828 Lawrence County, MS

YOUNG, PETER A. – Born June 4, 1937 in New York City, he joined the SC SAR on June 11, 2008. He served in the US Navy, HS9/LT; RIARNG/HQ/CAPT, and was a Captain for TWA, retiring on June 3, 1997. He is President of the RI Jaycees, and a member of the Military Officers Assoc. and Barbershop Harmony Assoc. He is married to Patricia Lee, with two children and two grandchildren.

Peter A. Young

Benjamin Durkee was born Oct. 18, 1744 in Hampton, CT. At 32 years of age he was commissioned an Ensign by John Hancock and served in the 20th Continental Line under Col. John Durkee for more than two years, where his unit participated in the Battle of Trenton in 1776 and accompanied Gen. Washington on his retreat through New Jersey.

On Nov. 23, 1781, he was commissioned 2d Lt. of an artillery company by Gov. John Trumbell of CT. On June 21, 1784, he was commissioned Captain of an Artillery and Mattrosas Company.

He finished his service as a Lt. of a 700-man regiment that defended the forts at Groton and New London, CT.

INDEX

The recipients of the Minuteman Award and the Gold Good Citizenship Award, presented in alphabetical order within their respective sections, are not included in the index.

PATRIOT INDEX

Only the Patriots listed in the biographies are included.

CONGRESSIONAL CHARTER

of the

NATIONAL SOCIETY OF THE SONS OF THE AMERICAN REVOLUTION

SIGNED JUNE 7, 1906

[Public—No. 214.]

H. R. 15332.

Fifty-ninth Congress of the United States of America;

At the First Session,

Begun and held at the City of Washington on Monday, the fourth day of December, one thousand nine hundred and five

---

AN ACT

To incorporate the National Society of the Sons of the American Revolution.

Be it enacted by the Senate and House of Representatives of the United States of America in Congress assembled, That Francis Henry Appleton, of Massachusetts; Lucius P. Deming, of Connecticut; William Seward Webb, of Vermont; Horace Porter, of New York; Joseph C. Breckinridge, of Washington, District of Columbia; Franklin Murphy, of New Jersey; Walter S. Logan, of New York; Edwin Warfield, of Mary-

the records of the individual services of the patriots of the war, as well as documents, relics, and landmarks; to mark the scenes of the Revolution by appropriate memorials; to celebrate the anniversaries of the prominent events of the war and of the Revolutionary period; to foster true patriotism; to maintain and extend the institutions of American freedom, and to carry out the purposes expressed in the preamble to the Constitution of our country and the injunctions of Washington in his farewell address to the American people.

Sec. 3. That said corporation shall have power to receive, purchase, hold, sell, and convey real and personal estate, so far only as may be necessary or convenient for its lawful purposes, to an amount not exceeding at any one time in the aggregate five hundred thousand dollars; to sue and be sued, complain and defend in any court; to adopt a common seal, and to alter the same at pleasure; to make and adopt a constitution, by-laws, rules, and regulations for admission, government, suspension, and expulsion of its members, and from time to time to alter and repeal such constitution, by-laws, rules, and regulations, and to adopt others in their places; to provide for the election of its officers and to define their duties; to provide for State societies or chapters with

rules for their conduct, and to regulate and provide for the management, safe-keeping, and protection of its property and funds: *Provided always*, That such constitution, by-laws, rules, and regulations be not inconsistent with the laws of the United States or any of the States thereof.

Sec. 4. That the property and affairs of said corporation shall be managed by not more than sixty nor less than forty trustees, who shall be elected annually at such time as shall be fixed in the by-laws, and at least one trustee shall be elected annually from a list of nominees to be made by each of the State societies and submitted to this society at least thirty days before the annual meeting, in accordance with general provisions regulating such nominations as may be adopted by this society.

Sec. 5. That the first meeting of this corporation shall be held on a call issued by any fifteen of the above-named corporators by a written notice signed by them, stating the time and place of meeting, addressed to each of the corporators personally named herein and deposited in the post-office at least five days before the day of meeting.

Sec. 6. That this charter shall take effect upon its being accepted by a majority vote of the corporators named herein who shall be present at said meeting, or at any other meeting specially called for that purpose; and